T0235382

Lecture Notes in Computer Science 11879

More information about this series at http://www.springer.com/series/7410

Swee-Huay Heng · Javier Lopez (Eds.)

Information Security Practice and Experience

15th International Conference, ISPEC 2019
Kuala Lumpur, Malaysia, November 26–28, 2019
Proceedings

 Springer

Editors
Swee-Huay Heng (iD)
Multimedia University
Malacca, Malaysia

Javier Lopez (iD)
University of Malaga
Malaga, Spain

ISSN 0302-9743   ISSN 1611-3349 (electronic)
Lecture Notes in Computer Science
ISBN 978-3-030-34338-5   ISBN 978-3-030-34339-2   (eBook)
https://doi.org/10.1007/978-3-030-34339-2

LNCS Sublibrary: SL4 – Security and Cryptology

This Springer imprint is published by the registered company Springer Nature Switzerland AG
The registered company address is: Gewerbestrasse 11, 6330 Cham, Switzerland

Preface

The 15th International Conference on Information Security Practice and Experience (ISPEC 2019) was held in Kuala Lumpur, Malaysia, November 26–28, 2019, and hosted by Universiti Tunku Abdul Rahman, Malaysia.

The ISPEC conference series is an established forum that brings together researchers and practitioners to provide a confluence of new information security technologies, including their applications and their integration with IT systems in various vertical sectors. In previous years, ISPEC has taken place in Singapore (2005), Hangzhou, China (2006), Hong Kong, China (2007), Sydney, Australia (2008), Xi'an, China (2009), Seoul, South Korea (2010), Guangzhou, China (2011), Hangzhou, China (2012), Lanzhou, China (2013), Fuzhou, China (2014), Beijing, China (2015), Zhangjiajie, China (2016), Melbourne, Australia (2017), and Tokyo, Japan (2018). All the ISPEC papers were published by Springer in the LNCS series.

Acceptance into the conference proceedings is very competitive. This year the conference received 68 anonymous submissions from 24 countries/regions. All the submissions were reviewed by experts in the relevant areas on the basis of their significance, novelty, technical quality, and practical impact. After careful reviews and intensive discussions by at least three reviewers for each submission, 21 full papers and 7 short papers were selected from 19 countries for presentation at the conference and inclusion in this Springer volume, with an acceptance rate of 31%. The accepted papers cover multiple topics in information security, from technologies to systems and applications. This state of affairs reflects the fact that the research areas covered by ISPEC are important to modern computing, where increased security, trust, safety, and reliability are required.

ISPEC 2019 was made possible by the joint effort of numerous people and organizations worldwide. There is a long list of people who volunteered their time and energy to put together the conference and who deserve special thanks. First and foremost, we are deeply grateful to all the PC members for their hard task of reading, commenting, debating, and finally selecting the papers. We are indebted to the PC's collective knowledge, wisdom, and effort, and we have learned a lot from the experience. The committee also used external reviewers to extend the expertise and ease the burden. We wish to thank all of them for assisting the PC in their particular areas of expertise. It was a truly nice experience to work with such talented and hard-working researchers. We also would like to express our appreciation to the keynote speakers: Prof. Chris Mitchell, Assoc. Prof. Hongjun Wu, and Dr. Tieyan Li.

We are also very grateful to all the people whose work ensured a smooth organization process: Honored Chair Bok-Min Goi, General Chair Wun-She Yap, Local Chair Denis C. K. Wong, Finance Chair Yee-Kai Tee, Sponsorship Chair Wai-Kong Lee, Web Chair Ji-Jian Chin, Publicity Co-Chairs Weizhi Meng, Shifeng Sun, and Donghong Qin. Also thanks to Anna Kramer for her help in the publication of the proceedings.

Last but certainly not least, our thanks go to all the authors, the attendees, and the sponsor Huawei International. The conference was also supported by the Malaysian Society for Cryptology Research (MSCR) and Guangxi University for Nationalities, China.

November 2019   Swee-Huay Heng
                                                                Javier Lopez

Organization

Honored Chair

Bok-Min Goi   Universiti Tunku Abdul Rahman, Malaysia

General Chair

Wun-She Yap   Universiti Tunku Abdul Rahman, Malaysia

Organization Committee

Local Chair

Denis C. K. Wong   Universiti Tunku Abdul Rahman, Malaysia

Finance Chair

Yee-Kai Tee   Universiti Tunku Abdul Rahman, Malaysia

Sponsorship Chair

Wai-Kong Lee   Universiti Tunku Abdul Rahman, Malaysia

Web Chair

Ji-Jian Chin   Multimedia University, Malaysia

Publicity Co-chairs

Weizhi Meng	Technical University of Denmark, Denmark
Shifeng Sun	Monash University, Australia
Donghong Qin	Guangxi University for Nationalities, China

Program Co-chairs

Swee-Huay Heng	Multimedia University, Malaysia
Javier Lopez	University of Malaga, Spain

Program Committee

Man Ho Au	The Hong Kong Polytechnic University, Hong Kong, China
Joonsang Baek	University of Wollongong, Australia
Aniello Castiglione	University of Salerno, Italy
David Chadwick	University of Kent, UK
Jiageng Chen	Central China Normal University, China

Xiaofeng Chen	Xidian University, China
Kim-Kwang Raymond Choo	The University of Texas at San Antonio, USA
Sherman S. M. Chow	The Chinese University of Hong Kong, Hong Kong, China
Jose Maria de Fuentes	Universidad Carlos III de Madrid, Spain
Josep Domingo-Ferrer	Universitat Rovira i Virgili, Spain
José M. Fernandez	Ecole Polytechnique de Montreal, Canada
Carmen Fernández-Gago	University of Malaga, Spain
Dieter Gollmann	Hamburg University of Technology, Germany, and National University of Singapore, Singapore
Dimitris Gritzalis	Athens University of Economics and Business, Greece
Stefanos Gritzalis	University of the Aegean, Greece
Gerhard Hancke	City University of Hong Kong, Hong Kong, China
Debiao He	Wuhan University, China
Swee-Huay Heng	Multimedia University, Malaysia
Shoichi Hirose	University of Fukui, Japan
Xinyi Huang	Fujian Normal University, China
Julian Jang-Jaccard	Massey University, New Zealand
Hiroaki Kikuchi	Meiji University, Japan
Kwangjo Kim	Korea Advanced Institute of Science and Technology, South Korea
Noboru Kunihiro	The University of Tokyo, Japan
Miroslaw Kutylowski	Wroclaw University of Science and Technology, Poland
Costas Lambrinoudakis	University of Piraeus, Greece
Albert Levi	Sabanci University, Turkey
Shujun Li	University of Kent, UK
Tieyan Li	Huawei International Pte Ltd, Singapore
Yingjiu Li	Singapore Management University, Singapore
Kaitai Liang	University of Surrey, UK
Joseph Liu	Monash University, Australia
Zhe Liu	Nanjing University of Aeronautics and Astronautics, China
Giovanni Livraga	University of Milan, Italy
Javier Lopez	University of Malaga, Spain
Jiqiang Lu	Beihang University, China
Rongxing Lu	University of New Brunswick, Canada
Tzu-Chuen Lu	Chaoyang University of Technology, Taiwan
Di Ma	University of Michigan, USA
Weizhi Meng	Technical University of Denmark, Denmark
Chris Mitchell	Royal Holloway, University of London, UK
David Naccache	École Normale Supérieure, France
Takeshi Okamoto	Tsukuba University of Technology, Japan
Kazumasa Omote	University of Tsukuba, Japan
Pedro Peris-Lopez	Carlos III University of Madrid, Spain
Günther Pernul	Universität Regensburg, Germany

Raphael C.-W. Phan	Monash University, Malaysia
Josef Pieprzyk	Queensland University of Technology, Australia
Geong Sen Poh	Singtel, Singapore
C. Pandu Rangan	Indian Institute of Technology, Madras, India
Indrajit Ray	Colorado State University, USA
Na Ruan	Shanghai Jiaotong University, China
Sushmita Ruj	Indian Statistical Institute, India
Pierangela Samarati	University of Milan, Italy
Jun Shao	Zhejiang Gongshang University, China
Miguel Soriano	Universitat Politècnica de Catalunya, Spain
Chunhua Su	University of Aizu, Japan
Willy Susilo	University of Wollongong, Australia
Syh-Yuan Tan	Newcastle University, UK
Qiang Tang	New Jersey Institute of Technology, USA
Jaideep Vaidya	Rutgers University, USA
Cong Wang	City University of Hong Kong, Hong Kong, China
Ding Wang	Peking University, China
Guilin Wang	Huawei International Pte Ltd, Singapore
Qianhong Wu	Beihang University, China
Shouhuai Xu	University of Texas at San Antonio, USA
Toshihiro Yamauchi	Okayama University, Japan
Wei-Chuen Yau	Xiamen University Malaysia, Malaysia
Kuo-Hui Yeh	National Dong Hwa University, Taiwan
Xun Yi	RMIT University, Australia
Yong Yu	Shaanxi Normal University, China
Tsz Hon Yuen	The University of Hong Kong, Hong Kong, China
Yuexin Zhang	Swinburne University of Technology, Australia
Jianying Zhou	Singapore University of Technology and Design, Singapore
Sencun Zhu	The Pennsylvania State University, USA

Additional Reviewers

Anglès-Tafalla, Carles	Feng, Hanwen
Bamiloshin, Michael	Georgiopoulou, Zafeiroula
Banerjee, Prabal	Hassan, Fadi
Bytes, Andrei	Iakovakis, George
Chen, Huashan	Kelarev, Andrei
Chen, Long	Kern, Sascha
Cheng, Yao	Kuchta, Veronika
Choi, Rakyong	Li, Deqiang
Chu, Cheng-Kang	Li, Wenjuan
Dai, Ting	Li, Zengpeng
Diamantopoulou, Vasiliki	Li, Zhidan
Du, Minxin	Lin, Chengjun

Liu, Jianghua
Liu, Ximing
Loh, Jia-Ch'Ng
Lyvas, Christos
Mitropoulos, Dimitris
Ng, Lucien K. L.
Ning, Jianting
Paulet, Russell
Pitropakis, Nikolaos
Salam, Iftekhar
Schlette, Daniel
Shen, Jun
Shirazi, Hossein
Simou, Stavros
Singh, Ram Govind
Sohrabi, Nasrin
Song, Yongcheng
Soupionis, Yannis
Su, Dan
Tanuwidjaja, Harry Chandra
Theocharidou, Marianthi
Tian, Yangguang

Vielberth, Manfred
Virvilis-Kollitiris, Nikolaos
Wang, Jiafan
Wang, Yunling
Wangli, Xiaoyang
Wen, Xuejun
Wu, Lei
Xu, Dongqing
Xu, Shengmin
Yang, Xiao
Yang, Xu
Yang, Yi
Yin, Wei
Zhang, Xiaoyu
Zhang, Yinghui
Zhang, Yudi
Zhang, Yunru
Zhao, Raymond
Zhao, Yongjun
Zhu, Yan
Ziaur, Rahman

Contents

Access Control and Authentication

Cryptography II

Data and User Privacy

Cryptography I

Plaintext-Checkable Encryption
with Unlink-CCA Security
in the Standard Model

Sha Ma and Qiong Huang[(✉)]

College of Mathematics and Informatics,
South China Agricultural University, Guangzhou, Guangdong, China
martin_deng@163.com, qhuang@scau.edu.cn

Abstract. Plaintext-Checkable Encryption (PCE) was first proposed by
Canard et al. to check whether a ciphertext encrypts a given plaintext
under the public key. This primitive is very useful in many applications,
e.g., search on encrypted database and group signature with verifier-local
revocation (GS-VLR). In the literature, existing PCE schemes only satisfies unlink notion that defines the adversary to get information about
whether two challenge ciphertexts share the same plaintext or not, without given the challenge plaintexts. Using the tool of pairing-friendly
smooth projective hash function (PF-SPHF), we propose the first PCE
construction with the most desirable unlink-cca notion, which is stronger
than unlink by additionally providing a decryption oracle. We prove it
in the standard model based on the hard subset membership problem.
Finally, by instantiating SPHF from DDH assumption, we obtain a PCE
instantiation from SXDH assumption and show that it achieves not only
the desired security but also efficient test computation complexity. Hence
it will be very useful in practical applications.

Keywords: Plaintext-checkable encryption · Unlink-CCA ·
Pairing-friendly smooth projective hash function

1 Introduction

In public-key setting, public key encryption with keyword search (PEKS) was
first introduced by Boneh et al. [6] to delegate the right of keyword search on
one's encrypted database to a proxy by sending a keyword-dependent trapdoor.
This proxy can check whether the encrypted message contains the keyword hidden in the trapdoor or not. Later, various forms of searchable encryption have
been studied intensively in different applications. Public key encryption with
equality test (PKEET), first proposed by Yang et al. [21], is a variant of searchable encryption to check whether two ciphertexts possibly from different users
have the same message. In this paper, we further explore a variant of searchable encryption, namely plaintext-checkable encryption (PCE), first introduced

© Springer Nature Switzerland AG 2019
S.-H. Heng and J. Lopez (Eds.): ISPEC 2019, LNCS 11879, pp. 3–19, 2019.
https://doi.org/10.1007/978-3-030-34339-2_1

by Canard et al. [7], to extend public-key encryption to achieve the following functionality: given a plaintext, a ciphertext and a public key, it is universally possible to check whether the ciphertext encrypts the plaintext under the public key. PCE is found to provide a direct way in the application of search on encrypted database using plain keyword (not using encrypted keyword in PEKS or PKEET). Another interesting PCE application is group signature with verifier-local revocation (GS-VLR), where the check procedure of revocation takes as input the revocation token (not encrypted revocation token by PEKS or PKEET). Below we list the differences between PCE and some variants of searchable encryptions for better understanding.

Difference Between PEKS and PCE. The differences between PEKS and PCE are shown in the following two aspects:

- *Private message-dependent trapdoor vs. public message.* In PEKS scheme, the search tool is a message-dependent trapdoor, which is generated by the secret key of the receiver and then transmitted privately to the tester. However, in PCE scheme, the search tool is plaintext without taking any secret information as input. Therefore, PCE is more suitable in searching on encrypted data without protecting the querying itself.
- *Without decryption vs. with decryption.* A traditional PEKS framework only provides search functionality without decryption. For adding the property of message recovery, some PEKS extensions combine PEKS and a conventional together, additionally being appended with a zero-knowledge protocol for assuring that the two parts share the same message. This combination possibly implies inefficiency in practice. However, a typical PCE framework provides both search functionality and message recovery, which is more expected in database encryption.

Difference Between PKEET and PCE. Both PKEET and PCE support to check whether a given ciphertext is an encryption of a guessing message. The difference between PCE and PKEET is shown as follows.

- *Ciphertext search vs. plaintext search.* PKEET and PCE have the difference in search token. Taking database encryption as an example, PKEET can be used for "join" on two encrypted attributes while PCE can be used for "selection" on the tuples of encrypted relation, where search condition is a certain plain message. It is not hard to see that PKEET could be trivially used for constructing PCE by first encrypting the plaintext and then calling PKEET test algorithm while PCE does not provide the privacy protection of querying intention, which might be an interesting property in some applications.

Motivation. As done in the case of deterministic encryption [1] and public key encryption with equality test [21], we assume that the plaintexts in PCE are drawn from a space of large min-entropy. (This is inherent in deterministic or efficiently searchable, not a weakness of our particular construction.) Due to PCE functionality, it is obvious that the traditional ind-cca security is not appropriate to define PCE security. Canard et al. [7] proposed unlink notion and gave the following relation:

$$\text{ind-cpa} \subsetneq \text{unlink} \subsetneq \text{priv1},$$

which shows that unlink is weaker than the well-known ind-cpa and stronger than priv1 (or ind-det in [7]) for deterministic encryption [1].

Another acceptable notion for PCE is s-priv1-cca security, which is originally proposed by [13] to define a stronger security of PKEET and is recently used by Ma et al. [16] to define for PCE security. They gave an in-depth discussion on the following security notions:

$$\text{ind-cca} \subsetneq \text{unlink-cca} \subsetneq \left\{ \begin{array}{c} \text{unlink} \\ \text{s-priv1-cca} \end{array} \right\} \subsetneq \text{s-priv1} \subsetneq \text{priv1},$$

which shows the key points that (1) s-priv1-cca is independent with unlink. Both s-priv1-cca and unlink are acceptable for attainable PCE schemes. (2) Being enhanced from unlink by additionally providing the adversary a decryption oracle, unlink-cca is considered to be the most desirable PCE security notion. However, to the best of our knowledge, we have not seen unlink-cca secure PCE scheme in the literature. This is the motivation of our work.

1.1 Our Contribution

Using the tool of pairing-friendly smooth projective hash function (PF-SPHF), we propose the first PCE construction with unlink-cca security, which is thought to be the most desirable PCE security notion. We prove its security in the standard model based on the hard subset membership problem. By instantiating SPHF from DDH assumption, we obtain a PCE instantiation from SXDH assumption, which has the advantages of both security and efficiency.

1.2 Related Work

The concept of plaintext-checkable encryption was first introduced by Canard et al. [7] to check whether a ciphertext contains certain plaintext or not without decrypting it. Later, Das et al. [9] proposed a plaintext checkable encryption with designated checker, where only the designated checker could execute the plaintext checkability on ciphertexts. Han et al. [11] presented an identity-based plaintext-checkable encryption and applied it in to an accountable mobile E-commerce scheme. Recently, Ma et al. [16] proposed a generic scheme of plaintext-checkable encryption for database applications, using smooth projective hash functions as building block. Next we introduce some related comparable encryptions since they have the similar functionality or similar security as plaintext-checkable encryption.

Public Key Encryption with Equality Test. Public key encryption with equality test (PKEET) was first introduced by Yang et al. [21] to check whether the ciphertexts possibly from two different users contain the same message or not. Its applications include privately join on encrypted database [14] and group signature with verifiable controllable linkability [5]. Later, many PKEET schemes [12,15,17–19] were proposed to enhance the original construction by adding various authorization policies.

Message-Locked Encryption. Message-locked encryption (MLE), first proposed by Bellare et al. [2], includes a tag-generation algorithm that maps the ciphertext, which may be randomized, to a tag. Identical plaintexts result in the equal tages. Naturally, MLE supports an equality-testing algorithm defined on ciphertexts, which is very useful to achieve secure deduplication on space-efficient secure outsourced storage [2], a goal currently targeted by numerous cloud-storage provides. We should note that MLE is constructed in symmetric-key setting while PCE is constructed in asymmetric-key setting.

Deterministic Encryption. Deterministic encryption (DE) was first proposed by [1], where the encryption algorithm is determined (not randomized). It is evident that DE supports checking whether a ciphertext is the encryption of a plaintext as any message would be only encrypted to an unique and determined ciphertext. Fast search on remote data storage in the form of outsourced database is its straightforward application [1]. Generally, DE provides a weaker protect on the plaintext as the ciphertext itself is a leakage of partial information about the plaintext.

1.3   Paper Organization

We introduce related preliminary and definitions in Sects. 2 and 3, respectively. We provide a PCE construction with unlink-cca security in Sect. 4. Then we give a SXDH-based PCE instantiation in Sect. 5 and draw a conclusion in Sect. 6.

2   Pairing-Friendly Smooth Projective Hash Function

Let PGGen be a probabilistic polynomial time (PPT) algorithm that on input k returns a description $\mathcal{PG} = (\mathbb{G}_1, \mathbb{G}_2, \mathbb{G}_T, e, g_1, g_2, p)$ of asymmetric pairing group, where $\mathbb{G}_1$, $\mathbb{G}_2$ and $\mathbb{G}_T$ are cyclic groups of order p for a k-bit prime p, g_1 and g_2 are generators of $\mathbb{G}_1$ and $\mathbb{G}_2$, respectively, and $e : \mathbb{G}_1 \times \mathbb{G}_2$ is a bilinear map between them. The map satisfies the following properties:

1. Bilinear: For any $U \in \mathbb{G}_1$, $V \in \mathbb{G}_2$ and $a, b \in \mathbb{Z}_p$, we have $e(U^a, V^b) = e(U, V)^{ab}$.
2. Non-degenerate: If g_1 is a generator of $\mathbb{G}_1$ and g_2 is a generator of $\mathbb{G}_2$, then $e(g_1, g_2)$ is a generator of $\mathbb{G}_T$.
3. Computable: There exists an efficient algorithm to compute $e(U, V)$ for any $U \in \mathbb{G}_1$ and $V \in \mathbb{G}_2$.

In the asymmetric setting $(\mathbb{G}_1, \mathbb{G}_2, \mathbb{G}_T)$, we consider SXDH assumption, which posits that DDH assumption holds in both $\mathbb{G}_1$ and $\mathbb{G}_2$(There are no computationally efficient homomorphic from $\mathbb{G}_2$ to $\mathbb{G}_1$ or $\mathbb{G}_1$ to $\mathbb{G}_2$).

Notations. We focus here on cyclic group $\mathbb{G}_s$ for $s \in \{1, 2, T\}$ of prime order p and define three operators on the group:

1. $\mathbb{G}_s \circledast \mathbb{G}_s \rightarrow \mathbb{G}_s$. For any $u \in \mathbb{G}_s$ and $v \in \mathbb{G}_s$, $u \circledast v \in \mathbb{G}_s$. Specifically, for any element $u \in \mathbb{G}_s$, we define $u \circledast u^{-1} = 1_{\mathbb{G}_s}$, which is the identity element of $\mathbb{G}_s$.
2. $\mathbb{Z}_p \bullet \mathbb{G}_s \rightarrow \mathbb{G}_s$ (or $\mathbb{G}_s \bullet \mathbb{Z}_p \rightarrow \mathbb{G}_s$). For any $r \in \mathbb{Z}_p$ and $u \in \mathbb{G}_s$, $r \bullet u = u \bullet r = u^r$.
3. $\mathbb{G}_1 \odot \mathbb{G}_2 \rightarrow \mathbb{G}_T$ (or $\mathbb{G}_2 \odot \mathbb{G}_1 \rightarrow \mathbb{G}_T$). For $u_1 \in \mathbb{G}_1$ and $u_2 \in \mathbb{G}_2$, $u_1 \odot u_2 = u_2 \odot u_1 = e(u_1, u_2)$.

For $s \in \{1, 2, T\}$ and $a \in \mathbb{Z}_p$ we let $[a] = g^a \in \mathbb{G}$ be an element in $\mathbb{G}$ or $[b]_s$ be an element in $\mathbb{G}_s$.

We recall that a smooth projective hash function (SPHF) based on an $\mathcal{NP}$ language $\mathcal{L} \subset \mathcal{X}$ onto a set $\mathcal{Y}$ is defined as follows [8].

- SPHFSetup(k): It takes as input a security parameter k and outputs $(\mathcal{L}, \mathsf{param})$ as the global parameters.
- HashKG($\mathcal{L}, \mathsf{param}$): It generates a hashing key hk.
- ProjKG(hk, ($\mathcal{L}, \mathsf{param}$), W): It derives the projection key hp from the hashing key hk, possibly depending on the word W.
- Hash(hk,($\mathcal{L}, \mathsf{param}$), W): It outputs the hash value hv $\in \mathcal{Y}$ from the hashing key on any word $W \in \mathcal{X}$.
- ProjHash(hp,($\mathcal{L}, \mathsf{param}$), W, w): It outputs the hash value hv$' \in \mathcal{Y}$ from the projection key hp and any word $W \in \mathcal{X}$ with the witness w. Note that we will omit $(\mathcal{L}, \mathsf{param})$ as input in SPHF system sometimes for brevity.

Note: we will omit $(\mathcal{L}, \mathsf{param})$ as input in SPHF system sometimes for brevity.

Correctness. The correctness of SPHF assures that if $W \in \mathcal{L}$ with a witness w, for all hashing key hk and associated projection key hp generated using ProjKG algorithm, we have Hash(hk, $(\mathcal{L}, \mathsf{param}), W$) = ProjHash(hp, $(\mathcal{L}, \mathsf{param}), W, w$).

Smoothness. The smoothness of SPHF assures that if $W \in \mathcal{X} \backslash \mathcal{L}$, the following two distributions are statistically indistinguishable:

$$\{((\mathcal{L}, \mathsf{param}), W, \mathsf{hp}, \mathsf{hv}) | \mathsf{hv} = \mathsf{Hash}(\mathsf{hk}, (\mathcal{L}, \mathsf{param}), W)\},$$

$$\{((\mathcal{L}, \mathsf{param}), W, \mathsf{hp}, \mathsf{hv}) | \mathsf{hv} \xleftarrow{\$} \mathcal{Y}\},$$

where $(\mathcal{L}, \mathsf{param}) = $ SPHFSetup(k), hk $= $ HashKG($\mathcal{L}, \mathsf{param}$) and hp $= $ ProjKG(hk, $(\mathcal{L}, \mathsf{param}), W$).

2-Smoothness. The 2-smoothness of SPHF assures that if $W_1, W_2 \in \mathcal{X} \backslash \mathcal{L} \wedge W_1 \neq W_2$, the following two distributions are statistically indistinguishable:

$$\{((\mathcal{L}, \mathsf{param}), W_1, W_2, \mathsf{hp}, \mathsf{hv}_1, \mathsf{hv}_2) | \mathsf{hv}_2 = \mathsf{Hash}(\mathsf{hk}, (\mathcal{L}, \mathsf{param}), W_2)\},$$

$$\{((\mathcal{L}, \mathsf{param}), W_1, W_2, \mathsf{hp}, \mathsf{hv}_1, \mathsf{hv}_2) | \mathsf{hv}_2 \xleftarrow{\$} \mathcal{Y}\},$$

where $(\mathcal{L}, \mathsf{param})$ = $\mathsf{SPHFSetup}(k)$, hk = $\mathsf{HashKG}(\mathcal{L}, \mathsf{param})$, hp = $\mathsf{ProjKG}(\mathsf{hk}, (\mathcal{L}, \mathsf{param}), W_2)$ and $\mathsf{hv}_1 = \mathsf{Hash}(\mathsf{hk}, (\mathcal{L}, \mathsf{param}), W_1)$.

Extended SPHF. We give the syntax of SPHF_{et} [8] as extended SPHF. It is defined by the five algorithms: ($\mathsf{SPHFSetup}_{et}$, HashKG_{et}, ProjKG_{et},, Hash_{et}, $\mathsf{ProjHash}_{et}$), where $\mathsf{SPHFSetup}_{et}$, HashKG_{et} and ProjKG_{et} are defined the same as $\mathsf{SPHFSetup}$, HashKG and ProjKG, and slightly modified Hash_{et} and $\mathsf{ProjHash}_{et}$ are described as follows.

- $\mathsf{Hash}_{et}(\mathsf{hk}, (\mathcal{L}, \mathsf{param}), W, aux)$: It outputs the hash value $\mathsf{hv} \in \mathcal{Y}$ from the hashing key hk on any word $W \in \mathcal{X}$ and the auxiliary input aux.
- $\mathsf{ProjHash}_{et}(\mathsf{hp}, (\mathcal{L}, \mathsf{param}), W, w, aux)$: It outputs the hash value $\mathsf{hv}' \in \mathcal{Y}$ from the projection key hp, the witness w for the word $W \in \mathcal{L}$ and the auxiliary input aux.

This extended SPHF is usually used for constructing encryption [8] to achieve chosen ciphertext security by its 2-smoothness property, as seen in this paper.

Language Representation. For a language $\mathcal{L}_{\mathsf{aux}}$, there exist two positive integers k and n, a function $\Gamma : \mathcal{S}et \mapsto \mathbb{G}^{k \times n}$ and a family of functions $\Theta_{\mathsf{aux}} : \mathcal{S}et \mapsto \mathbb{G}^{1 \times n}$, such that for any word $C \in \mathcal{S}et$, $(C \in \mathcal{L}_{\mathsf{aux}}) \Longleftrightarrow (\exists \boldsymbol{\lambda} \in \mathbb{Z}_p^{1 \times k})$ such that $\Theta_{\mathsf{aux}}(C) = \boldsymbol{\lambda} \odot \Gamma(C)$. In other words, we say that $C \in \mathcal{L}_{\mathsf{aux}}$ if and only if $\Theta_{\mathsf{aux}}(C)$ is a linear combination of (the exponents in) the rows of some matrix $\Gamma(C)$. It furthermore requires that a user, who knows a witness w of the membership $C \in \mathcal{L}_{\mathsf{aux}}$, can efficiently compute the above *linear* combination $\boldsymbol{\lambda}$.

Pairing-friendly SPHF (PF-SPHF) is a special type of the classical SPHF, which is in the context of pairing-based cryptography as the name suggests. Assume the existence of a (prime order) bilinear group $(\mathbb{G}_1, \mathbb{G}_2, \mathbb{G}_T, e, g_1, g_2, p)$. Compared with SPHF, PF-SPHF has the modified Hash (PF-Hash) algorithm and ProjHash algorithm (PF-ProjHash) described as follows.

- PF-Hash($\mathsf{hk}, (\mathcal{L}, \mathsf{param}), W, y$): It outputs a hash value $\mathsf{hv} \in \mathbb{G}_T$ from the hashing key hk on any word $W \in \mathbb{G}_1$ and an auxiliary element $y \in \mathbb{G}_2$.
- PF-ProjHash($\mathsf{hp}, (\mathcal{L}, \mathsf{param}), W, w, y$): It outputs a hash value $\mathsf{hv}' \in \mathbb{G}_T$ from the projection key hp, the witness w for the word $W \in \mathcal{L}$ and an element $y \in \mathbb{G}_2$.

Next, we introduce a general way to achieve PF-SPHF from every pairing-less SPHF. In fact, this way has been used to construct SPHFs with particular properties, for instance, structure-preserving SPHF [4] and trapdoor SPHF [3]. Using the language representation of SPHF, an approach to transform every pairing-less SPHF into PF-SPHF [4] in a bilinear setting is shown in the Table 1.

An interesting property is that PF-SPHF provides a new way to compute the same hash value by PF-ProjHash* algorithm, which is similar to PF-ProjHash algorithm but with the different intermediate process.

- PF-ProjHash*($\mathsf{hp}, (\mathcal{L}, \mathsf{param}), W, w, y$): It outputs a hash value $\mathsf{hv}^\star \in \mathbb{G}_T$ from the projection key hp, the witness w for the word $W \in \mathcal{L}$ and an element $y \in \mathbb{G}_2$.

Table 1. Transformation from SPHF to PF-SPHF

	SPHF	PF-SPHF
Word $C(\Theta(C))$	$[\boldsymbol{\lambda} \bullet \Gamma(C)]_1$	$[\boldsymbol{\lambda} \bullet \Gamma(C)]_1$
Witness w	$\boldsymbol{\lambda}$	$\boldsymbol{\lambda}$
hk	α	α
hp($\gamma(C)$)	$[\Gamma(C) \bullet \alpha]_1$	$[\Gamma(C) \bullet \alpha]_1$
Hash	$[\Theta(C) \bullet \alpha]_1$	$[(\Theta(C) \bullet \alpha) \odot g_2]_T$
ProjHash	$[\boldsymbol{\lambda} \bullet \gamma(C)]_1$	$[(\boldsymbol{\lambda} \bullet \gamma(C)) \odot g_2]_T$
ProjHash*	$[\boldsymbol{\lambda} \bullet \gamma(C)]_1$	$[\gamma(C) \odot (\boldsymbol{\lambda} \bullet g_2)]_T$

From the Table 1, we see that the difference between ProjHash algorithm and ProjHash* algorithm lies in that $\boldsymbol{\lambda}$ first operates on $\gamma(C)$ and then do pairing with g_2 in the former while $\boldsymbol{\lambda}$ first operates on g_2 and then do pairing with $\gamma(C)$ in the latter.

Correctness. It is inherited for word in $\mathcal{L}$ as this reduces to computing the same values but in $\mathbb{G}_T$. Especially, thanks to the property of bilinear mapping, we have

$$(\boldsymbol{\lambda} \bullet \gamma(C)) \odot g_2 = \gamma(C) \odot (\boldsymbol{\lambda} \bullet g_2).$$

Smoothness. For words outside the language, the projection keys, without being changed, do not reveal new information, so that the smoothness will remain preserved.

Remark. Under the case that this transformed version does not weaken the subgroup decision assumption linked to the original language, we can set $\mathbb{G}_1 = \mathbb{G}_2$. For a counter example, because DDH assumption is not hard in bilinear group, any PCE scheme based on SPHF from DDH assumption should not be allowed to defined over symmetric bilinear groups ($\mathbb{G}_1 = \mathbb{G}_2$).

An Instantiation of **SPHF** from DDH Assumption [8].

1. SPHFSetup(k): param=$(\mathbb{G}, p, g_1, g_2)$.
2. HashKG($\mathcal{L}_{\mathsf{DDH}}$, param) : hk = $(s_1, s_2) \xleftarrow{\$} \mathbb{Z}_p^2$.
3. ProjKG(hk, ($\mathcal{L}_{\mathsf{DDH}}$, param)) : hp = $g_1^{s_1} g_2^{s_2} \in \mathbb{G}$.
4. Hash(hk, ($\mathcal{L}_{\mathsf{DDH}}$, param), $W = (g_1^r, g_2^r)$) : hv = $g_1^{rs_1} g_2^{rs_2} \in \mathbb{G}$.
5. ProjHash(hp, ($\mathcal{L}_{\mathsf{DDH}}$, param), $W = (g_1^r, g_2^r)$, $w = r$) : hv$'$ = hp$^r \in \mathbb{G}$.

An Instantiation of **PF-SPHF** from **SXDH** Assumption [3,4] (transformed from DDH-based SPHF)

1. SPHFSetup(k): param=$(\mathbb{G}_1, \mathbb{G}_2, \mathbb{G}_T, e, p, g_{1,1}, g_{1,2}, g_2)$, where $g_{1,1}, g_{1,2} \in \mathbb{G}_1$ and $g_2 \in \mathbb{G}_2$.

2. HashKG($\mathcal{L}_{\mathsf{SXDH}}$, param) : hk $= (s_1, s_2) \xleftarrow{\$} \mathbb{Z}_p^2$.
3. ProjKG(hk, ($\mathcal{L}_{\mathsf{SXDH}}$, param)) : hp $= g_{1,1}^{s_1} g_{1,2}^{s_2} \in \mathbb{G}_1$.
4. Hash(hk, ($\mathcal{L}_{\mathsf{SXDH}}$, param), $W = (g_{1,1}^r, g_{1,2}^r)$) : hv $= e(g_{1,1}^{rs_1} g_{1,2}^{rs_2}, g_2) \in \mathbb{G}_T$.
5. ProjHash(hp, ($\mathcal{L}_{\mathsf{SXDH}}$, param), $W = (g_{1,1}^r, g_{1,2}^r), w = r$) : hv$' = $ hp$^r \in \mathbb{G}_T$.

An Instantiation of Extended PF-SPHF from SXDH Assumption

1. SPHFSetup(k): param $= (\mathbb{G}_1, \mathbb{G}_2, \mathbb{G}_T, e, p, g_{1,1}, g_{1,2}, g_2, H)$, where $g_{1,1}, g_{1,2} \in \mathbb{G}_1$, $g_2 \in \mathbb{G}_2$ and H is a collision-resistant hash function defined on: $\mathbb{G}_1^2 \times \{0,1\}^l \to \mathbb{Z}_p$. Assume that aux is a l-bit string.
2. HashKG($\mathcal{L}_{\mathsf{SXDH}}$, param) : hk $= ((s_1, s_2), (t_1, t_2)) \xleftarrow{\$} \mathbb{Z}_p^4$.
3. ProjKG(hk, ($\mathcal{L}_{\mathsf{SXDH}}$, param)) : hp $= (\mathsf{hp}_1, \mathsf{hp}_2) = (g_{1,1}^{s_1} g_{1,2}^{s_2}, g_{1,1}^{t_1} g_{1,2}^{t_2}) \in \mathbb{G}_1^2$.
4. Hash(hk, ($\mathcal{L}_{\mathsf{SXDH}}$, param), $W = (g_{1,1}^r, g_{1,2}^r), aux$) : hv $= e((g_{1,1}^{rs_1} g_{1,2}^{rs_2}) (g_{1,1}^{rt_1} g_{1,2}^{rt_2})^\theta, g_2) \in \mathbb{G}_T$, where $\theta = H(W, aux)$.
5. ProjHash(hp, ($\mathcal{L}_{\mathsf{SXDH}}$, param), $W = (g_{1,1}^r, g_{1,2}^r), aux, w = r$) : hv$' = e(\mathsf{hp}_1^r \mathsf{hp}_2^{\theta r}, g_2) \in \mathbb{G}_T$, where $\theta = H(W, aux)$.

3   Definitions

3.1   Plaintext-Checkable Encryption

We recall here the notion of plaintext-checkable encryption (PCE) [7], which is composed of the following five algorithms.

1. Setup is a probabilistic algorithm which takes as input a security parameter k and outputs a public system parameter pp.
2. KeyGen is a probabilistic algorithm which takes as input a public system parameter pp and outputs a key pair of (pk, sk) of public and secret key, respectively.
3. Enc is a probabilistic algorithm which takes as input pk and a plaintext M and outputs a ciphertext C.
4. Dec is a deterministic algorithm which takes as input sk and a ciphertext C and outputs a plaintext M or $\perp$.
5. Check is a deterministic algorithm which takes as input a plaintext M and a ciphertext C, and outputs 1 if C is an encryption of M, and 0 otherwise.

The correctness of PCE must verify the following two conditions:

1. Correctness of decryption. For any $k \in \mathbb{N}$ and $m \in \{0,1\}^*$,

$$\Pr[pp \xleftarrow{\$} \mathsf{Setup}(k), (pk, sk) \xleftarrow{\$} \mathsf{KeyGen}(pp), c \xleftarrow{\$} \mathsf{Enc}(pk, m) : \mathsf{Dec}(sk, C) = m] = 1.$$

2. Correctness of plaintext check. For any $k \in \mathbb{N}$ and $m \in \{0,1\}^*$,

$$\Pr[pp \xleftarrow{\$} \mathsf{Setup}(k), (pk, sk) \xleftarrow{\$} \mathsf{KeyGen}(pp), c \xleftarrow{\$} \mathsf{Enc}(pk, m) : \mathsf{Check}(M, C) = 1] = 1.$$

We assume that PCE plaintexts are drawn from a space of *high min-entropy* [7] since the adversary could win the game definitely when PCE plaintexts come from a space without enough entropy. This assumption is reasonable and has existed in many searchable encryptions.

Definition 1 (High min-entropy). *An adversary* $\mathcal{A} = (\mathcal{A}_f, \mathcal{A}_g)$ *is legitimate if there exists a function* $\ell(\cdot)$ *s.t. for all pk and* $m \in [\mathcal{A}_f(1^k, pk)]$ *we have* $|m| = \ell(k)$. *Moreover, we say that an adversary* $\mathcal{A} = (\mathcal{A}_f, \mathcal{A}_g)$ *has* min-entropy μ *if*

$$\forall k \in \mathbb{N} \; \forall pk \; \forall m : \Pr[m' \leftarrow \mathcal{A}_f(1^k, pk) : m' = m] \leq 2^{-\mu(k)}.$$

$\mathcal{A}$ *is said to have* high min-entropy *if it has min-entropy* μ *with* $\mu(k) \in \omega(\log k)$.

3.2 Unlink-cca Security

Informally, the unlink-cca security assures that the adversary $\mathcal{A} = (\mathcal{A}_1, \mathcal{A}_2)$ (assume that $\mathcal{A}_1$ and $\mathcal{A}_2$ share neither coins nor state) as a pair of polynomial time algorithms could not get any partial information about whether two ciphertexts share the same plaintext without given the challenge plaintexts even provided access to a decryption oracle. Note that $\mathcal{A}_2$ does not see M_0 and M_1 as the output of $\mathcal{A}_1$ and hence cannot trivially guess whether C^* is the encryption of M_0 or M_1. The following experiment $\mathbf{Exp}_{\mathcal{PCE}, \mathcal{A}}^{\mathsf{unlink\text{-}cca}}(k)$ is formally defined for the adversary $\mathcal{A}$ with high min-entropy against unlink-cca security of PCE.

$\mathbf{Exp}_{\mathcal{PCE}, \mathcal{A}}^{\mathsf{unlink\text{-}cca}}(k)$:

1. **Setup Phase.** The challenger runs the Setup(k) algorithm and then the KeyGen(pp) algorithm to generate (pk, sk). It sends (pp, pk) to the adversary $\mathcal{A} = (\mathcal{A}_1, \mathcal{A}_2)$, where $\mathcal{A}_1$ and $\mathcal{A}_2$ share neither coins nor state.
2. **Probing Phase I.** The adversary $\mathcal{A}$ submits a ciphertext C to the challenger. The challenger decrypts C using its secret key sk and returns the plaintext M back to $\mathcal{A}$.
3. **Challenge Phase.** The adversary $\mathcal{A}_1$ randomly selects two messages M_0 and M_1, and presents them to the challenger. The challenger selects a random bit $b \in \{0, 1\}$ and sends $(C_b^*, C_1^*) = (\mathsf{Enc}(pk, M_b), \mathsf{Enc}(pk, M_1))$ to $\mathcal{A}_2$.
4. **Probing Phase II.** For $\mathcal{A}$'s submitted ciphertext C, the challenger responses the same as in the probing phase I with the only constraint that C is equal to neither C_b^* nor C_1^*.
5. **Guessing Phase.** $\mathcal{A}_2$ outputs a bit b'. The adversary $\mathcal{A}$ is said to win the game if $b' = b$, inducing the output of experiment is 1, and 0 otherwise.

We say $\mathcal{PCE}$ has unlink-cca security if for any polynomial adversary $\mathcal{A}$,

$$\mathbf{Adv}_{\mathcal{PCE}, \mathcal{A}}^{\mathsf{unlink\text{-}cca}}(k) = \left| \Pr[b = b'] - \frac{1}{2} \right|,$$

which is negligible on the security parameter k.

4   PCE Construction with **Unlink-cca** security

In this section, we present a PCE construction with unlink-cca security and formally prove it in the standard model.

4.1   Construction

Let $\mathsf{SPHF} = (\mathsf{SPHFSetup}, \mathsf{HashKG}, \mathsf{ProjKG}, \mathsf{Hash}, \mathsf{ProjHash})$ and $\mathsf{PF\text{-}SPHF}_{et} = (\mathsf{PF\text{-}SPHFSetup}_{et}, \mathsf{PF\text{-}HashKG}_{et}, \mathsf{PF\text{-}ProjKG}_{et}, \mathsf{PF\text{-}Hash}_{et}, \mathsf{PF\text{-}ProjHash}_{et})$ be SPHF and extended PF-SPHF defined on the same language, respectively. We present a construction of $\mathcal{PCE} = (\mathsf{Setup}, \mathsf{KeyGen}, \mathsf{Enc}, \mathsf{Dec}, \mathsf{Check})$ as follows.

1. $\mathsf{Setup}(k)$: Let $\mathcal{PG} = (\mathbb{G}_1, \mathbb{G}_2, \mathbb{G}_T, e, g_1, g_2, p)$ be a bilinear group and the language $\mathcal{L}$ be hard-partitioned subset. Taking the security parameter k as input, it runs $\mathsf{SPHFSetup}(k)$ algorithm of SPHF and $\mathsf{PF\text{-}SPHFSetup}_{et}(k)$ algorithm of PF-SPHF to generate the public parameter $(\mathcal{L}, \mathsf{param})$ and $(\mathcal{L}, \mathsf{param}_{et})$ on group $\mathbb{G}_2$ of prime order p and group $\mathbb{G}_T$ of prime order p, respectively. Finally, it returns the public system parameter $pp = <\mathcal{PG}, \mathcal{L}, \mathsf{param}, \mathsf{param}_{et}>$.

2. $\mathsf{KeyGen}(pp)$: It outputs the public/private key pair (pk, sk) for the $\mathcal{PCE}$ scheme:

$$pk : (\mathsf{hp}, \mathsf{php}_{et}) = (\mathsf{ProjKG}(\mathsf{hk}, (\mathcal{L}, \mathsf{param})), \mathsf{PF\text{-}ProjKG}_{et}(\mathsf{hk}_{et}, (\mathcal{L}, \mathsf{param}_{et}))),$$

$$sk : (\mathsf{hk}, \mathsf{phk}_{et}) = (\mathsf{HashKG}(\mathcal{L}, \mathsf{param}), \mathsf{PF\text{-}HashKG}_{et}(\mathcal{L}, \mathsf{param}_{et})).$$

3. $\mathsf{Enc}(pk, M)$: It randomly picks a word $W \in \mathcal{L}$ with the witness w and computes for $M \in \mathbb{G}_2$:

$$X = \mathsf{ProjHash}(\mathsf{hp}, (\mathcal{L}, \mathsf{param}), W, w) \circledast M.$$

and then

$$Y = \mathsf{PF\text{-}ProjHash}_{et}(\mathsf{php}_{et}, (\mathcal{L}, \mathsf{param}_{et}), (W, X), w, \mathsf{hp}) \in \mathbb{G}_T.$$

Finally, it outputs a $\mathcal{PCE}$ ciphertext

$$C = (W, X, Y)$$

for the plaintext M under the public key pk.

4. $\mathsf{Dec}(sk, C)$: Upon parsing C as (W, X, Y), it verifies if

$$Y = \mathsf{PF\text{-}Hash}_{et}(\mathsf{phk}_{et}, (\mathcal{L}, \mathsf{param}_{et}), (W, X), \mathsf{hp})$$

holds. Through the validation, it computes

$$M \leftarrow X \circledast \mathsf{Hash}(\mathsf{hk}, (\mathcal{L}, \mathsf{param}), W)^{-1}$$

and returns the plaintext M for the ciphertext C, or $\perp$ otherwise.

5. Check(M, C): It checks if

$$Y = \mathsf{php}_{et}[W, X] \odot (X \circledast M^{-1})$$

holds, where $\mathsf{php}_{et}[W, X]$ is defined as $\gamma(C)$ with auxiliary input $[W, X]$ using language representation in Sect. 2. Through this validation, it returns 1 indicating that M is the plaintext of C, or 0 otherwise.

Remark 1. In fact, the above $\mathcal{PCE}$ ciphertext consists of an unlink-secure $\mathcal{PCE}$ ciphertext (W, X) combined with an extended SPHF value (a PF-SPHF value) Y for consistency check. This technology of extended SPHF with 2-smoothness property is usually used to guarantee the non-malleability of the ciphertext and hence could achieve CCA security, as seen in [8].

Remark 2. The advantage of using PF-SPHF instead of plain SPHF is to provide the third way to compute hash value besides through ProjHash and Hash algorithms. The essence is that the witness generally as an exponentiation can operate on both $\mathbb{G}_1$ and $\mathbb{G}_2$ thanks to the property of bilinear pairing.

Correctness. The correctness of decryption is easily to be verified using the property of SPHF. Here we only show the correct analysis of test algorithm by the following derivations.

$$\begin{aligned}
Y &= \mathsf{PF\text{-}ProjHash}(\mathsf{php}_{et}, (W, X), w, \mathsf{hp}) \\
&= \mathsf{ProjHash}(\mathsf{php}_{et}, (W, X), w) \odot \mathsf{hp} \\
&= \mathsf{php}_{et}[W, X] \odot (w \bullet \mathsf{hp}) \\
&= \mathsf{php}_{et}[W, X] \odot (X \circledast M^{-1})
\end{aligned}$$

4.2 Security Proof

Theorem 1. *$\mathcal{PCE}$ satisfies unlink-cca if it is computationally hard to distinguish any random element $W^* \in \mathcal{L}$ from any random element from $\mathcal{X} \backslash \mathcal{L}$.*

Proof We show that the existence of an adversary $\mathcal{A}$ against unlink-cca security with significant advantage implies the existence of an efficient algorithm $\mathcal{B}$ that decides a random element $W_{ch} \in \mathcal{L}$ or $W_{ch} \in \mathcal{X} \backslash \mathcal{L}$. We define the following game between a simulator (as a role of the distinguisher for the hard subset membership problem) and an adversary $\mathcal{A} = (\mathcal{A}_1, \mathcal{A}_2)$ that carries out an unlink-cca attack.

Game$_0$: Game$_0$ is the initial security game.

1. **Setup Phase.** This simulator emulates the initialization of the system as follows. It runs the Setup(k) algorithm by itself to generate the public parameter $pp = <\mathcal{PG}, \mathcal{L}, \mathsf{param}, \mathsf{param}_{et}>$. Then it runs the KeyGen(pp) algorithm to generate a public/secret key pair $(pk, sk) = ((\mathsf{hp}, \mathsf{php}_{et}), (\mathsf{hk}, \mathsf{phk}_{et}))$. It gives (pp, pk) to $\mathcal{A}$.

2. **Probing Phase I.** For $\mathcal{A}$'s submitted ciphertext C, the simulator returns the plaintext M via the Dec algorithm using its secret key sk.
3. **Challenge Phase.** $\mathcal{A}_1$ presents two random messages M_0 and M_1 to the simulator. The simulator computes the ciphertext $C_b^* = (W^*, X^*, Y^*)$ of M_b as follows and honestly computes C_1^* for M_1. Finally, it returns (C_b^*, C_1^*) to $\mathcal{A}_2$.
   - The simulator chooses a random word $W^* \in \mathcal{L}$, where W^* is the value input to the simulator, and computes $X^* = \mathsf{Hash}(\mathsf{hk}, W^*) \circledast M$ using the private evaluation algorithm Hash. Then it computes $Y^* = \mathsf{PF\text{-}Hash}_{et}(\mathsf{phk}_{et}, (W^*, X^*), \mathsf{hp})$ using the private evaluation algorithm $\mathsf{PF\text{-}Hash}_{et}$ and outputs $C_b^* = (W^*, X^*, Y^*)$.
4. **Probing Phase II.** For $\mathcal{A}$'s submitted query on the ciphertext C, the simulator responses the same as in the probing phase I with the only constraint that C is equal to neither C_b^* nor C_1^*.
5. **Guessing Phase.** $\mathcal{A}_2$ outputs its guess b'.

Let S_0 be the event that the simulator outputs 1 in Game 0. Due to the correctness of SPHF, we have

$$\left| \Pr[S_0] - \frac{1}{2} \right| = \mathbf{Adv}_{\mathcal{PCE},\mathcal{A}}^{\mathsf{unlink\text{-}cca}}(k) \tag{1}$$

Game$_1$: Game$_1$ is the same as Game$_0$ except that W^* is replaced by W_{ch}. We consider the behaviour of this simulator in two cases:

Case 1: The simulator is given a random element $W^* \in \mathcal{L}$. Let $\mathsf{Yes}^{(1)}$ be the event that the simulator outputs 1 in this case. Let $S_1^{(\mathsf{Yes})}$ be the event that the simulator outputs 1 in **Game$_1$**. The simulator is perfect and hence $\Pr[S_1^{(\mathsf{Yes})}] = \Pr[S_0]$. Therefore, we have

$$\left| \Pr[\mathsf{Yes}^{(1)}] - \frac{1}{2} \right| = \left| \Pr[S_1^{(\mathsf{Yes})}] - \frac{1}{2} \right|$$
$$= \left| \Pr[S_0] - \frac{1}{2} \right| \geq \mathbf{Adv}_{\mathcal{PCE},\mathcal{A}}^{\mathsf{unlink\text{-}cca}}(k). \tag{2}$$

Case 2: The simulator is given a random element $W^* \in \mathcal{X} \backslash \mathcal{L}$. Let $\mathsf{No}^{(1)}$ be the event that the simulator outputs 1 in this case. We will use the game-hopping technique for this case. Let $\Pr[S_{1.i}^{(\mathsf{No})}](i = 0, \ldots, 4)$ be the probability that the simulator outputs 1 in the game $\mathbf{Game}_{1,i}(i = 0, \ldots, 4)$ given a random element $W^* \in \mathcal{X} \backslash \mathcal{L}$.

$\widetilde{\mathbf{Game}_{1.0}}$: $\widetilde{\mathbf{Game}_{1.0}}$ is the same as $\widetilde{\mathbf{Game}_1}$ in the case of $W^* \in \mathcal{X}/\mathcal{L}$. We have $\Pr[S_{1.0}^{(\mathsf{No})}] = \Pr[S_1^{(\mathsf{No})}]$.

$\widetilde{\textbf{Game}}_{1.1}$: $\widetilde{\textbf{Game}}_{1.1}$ is the same as $\widetilde{\textbf{Game}}_{1.0}$, so that in addition to rejecting a ciphertext $C = (W, X, Y)$ but $Y = \mathsf{PF\text{-}Hash}_{et}(\mathsf{phk}_{et}, (W, X), \mathsf{hp})$. Let F be the event that $Y = \mathsf{PF\text{-}Hash}_{et}(\mathsf{phk}_{et}, (W, X), \mathsf{hp})$. We claim that

$$\left| \Pr[S_{1.1}^{(\mathsf{No})}] - \Pr[S_{1.0}^{(\mathsf{No})}] \right| \leq \Pr[F]. \tag{3}$$

Next, we analyze the probability that the event F happens. For all ciphertxts $C = (W, X, Y) \in \mathcal{X} \times \mathbb{G}_2 \times \mathbb{G}_T$ with $W \in \mathcal{X} \backslash \mathcal{L}$ submitted to a decryption oracle after the challenge phrase, we divide them into two cases:

1. $(W, X) = (W^*, X^*)$. Because Y is uniquely determined by (W, X), we have $Y = Y^*$. The simulator returns $\bot$ under the constraint that $(W, X, Y) \neq (W^*, X^*, Y^*)$.
2. $(W, X) \neq (W^*, X^*)$. Given (W, X, Y), phk_{et} is still uniformly distributed with the only constraint that $\mathsf{php}_{et} = \mathsf{ProjKG}_{et}(\mathsf{phk}_{et})$. Under this condition, due to the 2-smoothness property, $\mathsf{PF\text{-}Hash}_{et}(\mathsf{phk}_{et}, (W, X))$ is uniformly distributed over $\mathbb{G}_T$. We claim that the probability that the adversary outputs a valid ciphertext $(W, X, \cdot)$ submitted to the decryption oracle is negligible.

Assume that $Q(k)$ denotes the number of decryption queries. From the above analysis, we have

$$\Pr[F] \leq \epsilon_{\mathsf{2\text{-}smooth}}(k) \cdot Q(k), \tag{4}$$

where $\epsilon_{\mathsf{2\text{-}smooth}}(k)$ denotes the distinguishable probability in the definition of the 2-smoothness property of SPHF. We claim that

$$\left| \Pr[S_{1.1}^{(\mathsf{No})}] - \Pr[S_{1.0}^{\mathsf{No}}] \right| \leq \epsilon_{\mathsf{2\text{-}smooth}}(k) \cdot Q(k), \tag{5}$$

by combining the relations (3) and (4).

$\widetilde{\textbf{Game}}_{1.2}$: $\widetilde{\textbf{Game}}_{1.2}$ is the same as $\widetilde{\textbf{Game}}_{1.1}$ except that the simulator sets $X^* = y \circledast M_b$ in stead of computing $X^* = \mathsf{Hash}(\mathsf{hk}, W^*) \circledast M_b$, where $y \in \mathbb{G}_2$ is chosen at random. We claim that

$$\left| \Pr[S_{1.2}^{(\mathsf{No})}] - \Pr[S_{1.1}^{(\mathsf{No})}] \right| \leq \epsilon_{\mathsf{smooth}}(k), \tag{6}$$

where $\epsilon_{\mathsf{smooth}}(k)$ denotes the distinguishable probability in the definition of the smoothness property of SPHF.

$\widetilde{\textbf{Game}}_{1.3}$: $\widetilde{\textbf{Game}}_{1.3}$ is the same as $\widetilde{\textbf{Game}}_{1.2}$ except that the simulator sets $Y^* = y_T \xleftarrow{\$} \mathbb{G}_T$ in stead of computing $Y^* = \mathsf{PF\text{-}Hash}_{et}(\mathsf{phk}_{et}, (W^*, X^*), \mathsf{hp})$. We claim that

$$\left| \Pr[S_{1.3}^{(\mathsf{No})}] - \Pr[S_{1.2}^{(\mathsf{No})}] \right| \leq \epsilon_{\mathsf{smooth}}(k). \tag{7}$$

It is evident that the adversary's output b' in $\widetilde{\textbf{Game}}_{1.3}$ is independent of the hidden bit b. Therefore, we have

$$\Pr[S_{1.3}^{(\mathsf{No})}] = \frac{1}{2}. \tag{8}$$

Due to $\widetilde{\mathbf{Game}}_{1.0}$, $\widetilde{\mathbf{Game}}_{1.1}$, $\widetilde{\mathbf{Game}}_{1.2}$, $\widetilde{\mathbf{Game}}_{1.3}$, we have

$$\left| \Pr[\mathsf{No}] - \frac{1}{2} \right| = \left| \Pr[S_1^{(\mathsf{No})}] - \frac{1}{2} \right| \leq \epsilon_{\text{2-smooth}}(k) \cdot Q(k) + 2 \cdot \epsilon_{\text{smooth}}(k), \tag{9}$$

Combining relations (2) and (9), we have

$$\left| \Pr[\mathsf{Yes}] - \Pr[\mathsf{No}] \right| \geq \mathbf{Adv}_{\mathcal{PCE},\mathcal{A}}^{\text{unlink-cca}}(k) - (\epsilon_{\text{2-smooth}}(k) \cdot Q(k) + 2 \cdot \epsilon_{\text{smooth}}(k)), \tag{10}$$

Thanks to the hard subset membership problem, we have

$$\left| \Pr[\mathsf{Yes}^{(1)}] - \Pr[\mathsf{No}^{(1)}] \right| \leq \epsilon_{\text{dist}}(k), \tag{11}$$

where $\epsilon_{\text{dist}}(k)$ is the probability of solving hard subset membership problem. Therefore, combining relations (10) and (11), we have

$$\mathbf{Adv}_{\mathcal{PCE},\mathcal{A}}^{\text{unlink-cca}}(k) \leq \epsilon_{\text{dist}} + \epsilon_{\text{2-smooth}}(k) \cdot Q(k) + 2 \cdot \epsilon_{\text{smooth}}(k),$$

from which the theorem immediately follows.

5   PCE Instantiation from SXDH Assumption

In this section, we present a $\mathcal{PCE}$ instantiation on a bilinear group from SXDH assumption based on SPHF and extended PF-SPHF instantiations in Sect. 2.

1. $\mathsf{Setup}(k)$: Assume that $\mathcal{PG} = (\mathbb{G}_1, \mathbb{G}_2, \mathbb{G}_T, e, g_{1,1}, g_{1,2}, g_{2,1}, g_{2,2}, p)$, where $(g_{1,1}, g_{1,2})$ are random generators of $\mathbb{G}_1$ and $(g_{2,1}, g_{2,2})$ are random generators of $\mathbb{G}_2$. It runs $\mathsf{SPHFSetup}(k)$ algorithm of SPHF and $\mathsf{PF\text{-}SPHFSetup}_{et}(k)$ algorithm of PF-SPHF$_{et}$ to set the public parameter $pp = (\mathcal{PG}, \mathcal{L}_{\text{SXDH}}, H)$, where the collision-resistant hash function H is defined on $(\mathbb{G}_2)^3 \to \mathbb{Z}_p$.
2. $\mathsf{KeyGen}(pp)$: It outputs the following public/private key pair (pk, sk) for the $\mathcal{PCE}$ scheme: $pk = (\mathsf{hp}_1, \mathsf{hp}_2) = ((g_{1,1}^{s_1} g_{1,2}^{s_2}, g_{1,1}^{t_1} g_{1,2}^{t_2}), (g_{2,1}^{a_1} g_{2,2}^{a_2}))$ and $sk = (\mathsf{hk}_1, \mathsf{hk}_2) = (((s_1, s_2), (t_1, t_2)), (a_1, a_2))$.
3. $\mathsf{Enc}(pk, M)$: It chooses a random $r \in \mathbb{Z}_p$ and computes $W = (g_{2,1}^r, g_{2,2}^r)$ and $X = (g_{2,1}^{a_1} g_{2,2}^{a_2})^r M$ and $Y = e((g_{1,1}^{s_1} g_{1,2}^{s_2})^r (g_{1,1}^{t_1} g_{1,2}^{t_2})^{\theta r}, g_{2,1}^{a_1} g_{2,2}^{a_2})$, where $\theta = H(W, X)$. Finally, it outputs a $\mathcal{PCE}$ ciphertext $C = (W, X, Y)$ for the plaintext M.
4. $\mathsf{Dec}(sk, C)$: Upon parsing C as (W, X, Y), it verifies if $Y = e((g_{1,1}^{s_1} g_{1,2}^{s_2})(g_{1,1}^{t_1} g_{1,2}^{t_2})^{\theta}, (g_{2,1}^r)^{a_1}(g_{2,2}^r)^{a_2})$ holds, where $\theta = H(W, X)$. Through the validation, it computes $M \leftarrow X \cdot ((g_{2,1}^r)^{a_1}(g_{2,2}^r)^{a_2})^{-1}$ and returns plaintext M for the ciphertext C, or $\bot$ otherwise.
5. $\mathsf{Check}(M, C)$: Upon parsing C as (W, X, Y), it checks if $Y = e((g_{1,1}^{s_1} g_{1,2}^{s_2})(g_{1,1}^{t_1} g_{1,2}^{t_2})^{\theta}, X \cdot M^{-1})$, where $\theta = H(W, X)$. Through this validation, it returns 1 indicating that M is the plaintext of C under pk, or 0 otherwise.

Table 2. Comparison

	Model	Sec	Asmp	$\|C\|$	Encryption	Decryption	Test
[21]	ROM	OW-CCA	CDH	4ℓ	3E	3E	2P+3E
[7]	Standard	UNLINK	DLIN+SXDH	4ℓ	4E	2P+E	4P
[16]	Standard	S-PRIV1-CCA	DDH	6ℓ	7E	6E	4E
Ours	Standard	UNLINK-CCA	SXDH	4ℓ	P+4E	P+3E	P+E

Note:
[1] l: The length of group element in $\mathbb{G}_s (s = 1, 2, T)$.
[2] E: An exponentiation operation. P: A pairing operation.

5.1 Comparison

We choose existing PCE schemes [7,16] and PKEET scheme [21] (with similar functionality and security notion described in Sect. 1) for comparison in Table 2 with regards to proof model, security, assumption, ciphertext length and computation complexity of encryption, decryption and test algorithms. We see that our construction is the first PCE scheme with stronger unlink-cca security in the standard model. According to the experiment results in [10,20] that an optimized bilinear pairing costs nearly about two times than an exponentiation using Java-based PBC library, our scheme has the minimum ciphertext size, moderate encryption and decryption computation complexity, and the minimum computation complexity of test algorithm. In conclusion, our SXDH-based PCE instantiation achieves not only the desired security but also efficient test computation complexity, which will be very useful in practical applications.

6 Conclusion

By the tool of Pairing-Friendly Smooth Projective Hash Function (PF-SPHF), we proposed the first PCE construction that satisfies unlink-cca security in the standard model. We proved its security based on the hard subset membership problem. Finally, we instantiate the PCE construction from SXDH assumption and show its advantages on both security and efficiency by comparison with related work.

Acknowledgements. This work is supported by National Natural Science Foundation of China (No. 61872409, 61872152), Pearl River Nova Program of Guangzhou (No. 201610010037), Guangdong Natural Science Funds for Distinguished Young Scholar (No. 2014A030306021) and Guangdong Program for Special Support of Topnotch Young Professionals (No. 2015TQ01X796).

References

1. Bellare, M., Boldyreva, A., O'Neill, A.: Deterministic and efficiently searchable encryption. In: Menezes, A. (ed.) CRYPTO 2007. LNCS, vol. 4622, pp. 535–552. Springer, Heidelberg (2007). https://doi.org/10.1007/978-3-540-74143-5_30

2. Bellare, M., Keelveedhi, S., Ristenpart, T.: Message-locked encryption and secure deduplication. In: Johansson, T., Nguyen, P.Q. (eds.) EUROCRYPT 2013. LNCS, vol. 7881, pp. 296–312. Springer, Heidelberg (2013). https://doi.org/10.1007/978-3-642-38348-9_18

3. Benhamouda, F., Blazy, O., Chevalier, C., Pointcheval, D., Vergnaud, D.: New techniques for SPHFs and efficient one-round PAKE protocols. In: Canetti, R., Garay, J.A. (eds.) CRYPTO 2013. LNCS, vol. 8042, pp. 449–475. Springer, Heidelberg (2013). https://doi.org/10.1007/978-3-642-40041-4_25

4. Blazy, O., Chevalier, C.: Structure-preserving smooth projective hashing. In: Cheon, J.H., Takagi, T. (eds.) ASIACRYPT 2016. LNCS, vol. 10032, pp. 339–369. Springer, Heidelberg (2016). https://doi.org/10.1007/978-3-662-53890-6_12

5. Blazy, O., Derler, D., Slamanig, D., Spreitzer, R.: Non-interactive plaintext (in)equality proofs and group signatures with verifiable controllable linkability. In: Sako, K. (ed.) CT-RSA 2016. LNCS, vol. 9610, pp. 127–143. Springer, Cham (2016). https://doi.org/10.1007/978-3-319-29485-8_8

6. Boneh, D., Di Crescenzo, G., Ostrovsky, R., Persiano, G.: Public key encryption with keyword search. In: Cachin, C., Camenisch, J.L. (eds.) EUROCRYPT 2004. LNCS, vol. 3027, pp. 506–522. Springer, Heidelberg (2004). https://doi.org/10.1007/978-3-540-24676-3_30

7. Canard, S., Fuchsbauer, G., Gouget, A., Laguillaumie, F.: Plaintext-checkable encryption. In: Dunkelman, O. (ed.) CT-RSA 2012. LNCS, vol. 7178, pp. 332–348. Springer, Heidelberg (2012). https://doi.org/10.1007/978-3-642-27954-6_21

8. Cramer, R., Shoup, V.: Universal hash proofs and a paradigm for adaptive chosen ciphertext secure public-key encryption. In: Knudsen, L.R. (ed.) EUROCRYPT 2002. LNCS, vol. 2332, pp. 45–64. Springer, Heidelberg (2002). https://doi.org/10.1007/3-540-46035-7_4

9. Das, A., Adhikari, A., Sakurai, K.: Plaintext checkable encryption with designated checker. Adv. Math. Commun. 9(1), 37–53 (2015)

10. De Caro, A., Iovino, V.: JPBC: Java pairing based cryptography. In: IEEE Symposium on Computers and Communications (ISCC), vol. 2011, pp. 850–855 (2011)

11. Han, J., Yang, Y., Huang, X., Yuen, T., Li, J., Cao, J.: Accountable mobile E-commerce scheme via identity-based plaintext-checkable encryption. Inf. Sci. 345, 143–155 (2016)

12. Huang, K., Tso, R., Chen, Y., Rahman, S., Almogren, A., Alamri, A.: PKE-AET: public key encryption with authorized equality test. Comput. J. 58(10), 2686–2697 (2015)

13. Lu, Y., Zhang, R., Lin, D.: Stronger security model for public-key encryption with equality test. In: Abdalla, M., Lange, T. (eds.) Pairing 2012. LNCS, vol. 7708, pp. 65–82. Springer, Heidelberg (2013). https://doi.org/10.1007/978-3-642-36334-4_5

14. Ma, S.: Authorized equi-join for multiple data contributors in the PKC-based setting. Comput. J. 60(12), 1822–1838 (2017)

15. Ma, S., Huang, Q., Zhang, M., Yang, B.: Efficient public key encryption with equality test supporting flexible authorization. IEEE Trans. Inf. Forensics Secur. 10(3), 458–470 (2015)

16. Ma, S., Mu, Y., Susilo, W.: A generic scheme of plaintext-checkable database encryption. Inf. Sci. 429, 88–101 (2018)

17. Tang, Q.: Towards public key encryption scheme supporting equality test with fine-grained authorization. In: Parampalli, U., Hawkes, P. (eds.) ACISP 2011. LNCS, vol. 6812, pp. 389–406. Springer, Heidelberg (2011). https://doi.org/10.1007/978-3-642-22497-3_25

18. Tang, Q.: Public key encryption supporting plaintext equality test and user-specified authorization. Secur. Commun. Netw. **5**(12), 1351–1362 (2012)
19. Tang, Q.: Public key encryption schemes supporting equality test with authorization of different granularity. Int. J. Appl. Crypt. **2**(4), 304–321 (2012)
20. Wong, C.S., Tan, S., Ng, H.: An optimized pairing-based cryptography library for android. Int. J. Cryptol. Res. **6**, 16–30 (2016)
21. Yang, G., Tan, C.H., Huang, Q., Wong, D.S.: Probabilistic public key encryption with equality test. In: Pieprzyk, J. (ed.) CT-RSA 2010. LNCS, vol. 5985, pp. 119–131. Springer, Heidelberg (2010). https://doi.org/10.1007/978-3-642-11925-5_9

A Bitwise Logistic Regression Using Binary Approximation and Real Number Division in Homomorphic Encryption Scheme

Joon Soo Yoo, Jeong Hwan Hwang, Baek Kyung Song, and Ji Won Yoon[✉]

Korea University, Seoul, Republic of Korea
{sandiegojs,ju.su.splab,baekkyung777,jiwon_yoon}@korea.ac.kr

Abstract. Homomorphic Encryption (HE) is considered to be one of the most promising solutions to maintain secure data outsourcing because the user's query is processed under encrypted state. Accordingly, many of existing literature related to HE utilizes additive and multiplicative property of HE to facilitate logistic regression which requires high precision for prediction. In consequence, they inevitably transform or approximate nonlinear function of the logistic regression to adjust to their scheme using simple polynomial approximation algorithms such as Taylor expansion. However, such an approximation can be used only in limited applications because they cause unwanted error in results if the function is highly nonlinear. In response, we propose a different approximation approach to constructing the highly accurate logistic regression for HE using binary approximation. Our novel approach originates from bitwise operations on encrypted bits to designing (1) real number representation, (2) division and (3) exponential function. The result of our experiment shows that our approach can be more generally applied and accuracy-guaranteed than the current literature.

Keywords: Sigmoid · Homomorphic Encryption · Bitwise operation

1 Introduction

We are now living in a data-driven society where large amount of personal information is constantly collected and accumulated with or without knowing our privacy being compromised. Though not until recently has privacy issue become a priority demanding secured protocol or cryptosystems against this attack. In this response, many of the current research concentrates on data mining while preserving individuals' privacy. Among the famous known mechanisms, the Homomorphic Encryption (HE) is one of the solutions of providing secure data outsourcing between the users and the server in the aid of profound mathematical background. The feasibility of highly secured cryptosystem is due to the fact that HE allows any computation to run over encrypted data thereby preserving

© Springer Nature Switzerland AG 2019
S.-H. Heng and J. Lopez (Eds.): ISPEC 2019, LNCS 11879, pp. 20–40, 2019.
https://doi.org/10.1007/978-3-030-34339-2_2

user privacy. However, with the rigorous scheme that HE has, it had struggled with long execution time interfering deployment of HE for public usage. Worse, most algorithms in data mining and machine learning are designed with several complicated nonlinear operations such as 'inverse', 'exponential', 'log', and 'sigmoid' which cannot be easily designed with HE. Therefore, several researches related in HE have been conducted to develop practical data mining and machine learning algorithms which include various approximation [2,4,14].

Recently, HE based algorithms for logistic regression which is one of popularly used algorithms in data mining have been developed to successfully reduce their performance time with relatively high accuracy [6,10,11]. These algorithms followed the cryptosystem developed by Cheon et al. [5] to approximate real numbers by scaling with a factor of p to all elements z_i to support integer-based computation. This is due to MPC protocol which ensures non-leakage of private information of n users who participate in following the protocol to transmit scaled vector, $p \cdot z_i$ to the client. Although their work is advantageous in many ways, they missed some of the important nature of cloud computing model.

First of all, since they are following integer-based computation method, it requires for the server to perform rounding operation that is to multiply the scaling factor p. However, it is difficult to optimally decide p without deployment of MPC protocol among users and the client. Therefore, the clients are inevitably obliged to preprocess the data before sending it to the server. However, our system is effective in directly representing real number thereby troublesome processes such as rounding operation and extracting scaling factor are unnecessary.

Approximating the sigmoid function in the logistic regression is another issue from which many of existing literature suffers. They attempt to manipulate the sigmoid function with low-degree polynomials via the Taylor series polynomial approximation [3,14]. The Taylor series polynomial of degree 9 for sigmoid function $g(\cdot)$ can be derived as $g(z) = \frac{1}{1+e^{-z}} \approx \frac{1}{2} + \frac{1}{4}z - \frac{1}{48}z^3 + \frac{1}{480}z^5 - \frac{17}{80640}z^7 + \frac{31}{1451520}z^9$. Thus, the nonlinear logistic function can be feasibly but approximately calculated with HE addition and multiplication. However, the approach fails to approximate outside of the interval $(-2, 2)$ (See Fig. 1). The Taylor series polynomial approximation had been modified to broaden bounded domain of $(-2, 2)$ by adopting least square approximation [6,10,11]. This advanced approach is to find $g(x)$ that minimize mean squared error(MSE): $MSE(x) = \frac{1}{|I|} \int_I (g(x) - f(x))^2 dx$ where $|I|$ is the length of an interval. Although the method succeeded in providing larger interval than Taylor series, it still struggles to approximate logistic function outside of interval $(-8, 8)$ which can be explicitly checked in the Fig. 1.

In order to avoid calculating the scaling factor in integer-based HE scheme and reduce the unwanted error obtained by polynomial approximation, we found that HE scheme with bitwise operations is more robust scheme than traditional ones with integer operations in HE computation. In this paper, we propose a new HE logistic regression algorithm which includes approximated functions with bitwise operations. In addition, our approach is more ideal and rigorous than the integer-based HE logistic approaches in a broad sense of cloud computing

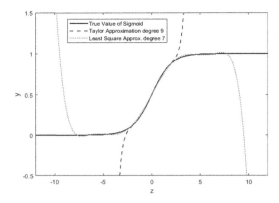

Fig. 1. Comparison of real sigmoid with Taylor and least square approximation

such that the user only submits his/her query and the computationally powerful server processes the given task and returns the result without compromisation of user privacy.

From this point of view, our key contributions of this paper are summarized below:

– We propose a novel approach of implementing basic Homomorphic operations with bitwise operation considering accuracy and speed.
– We also extend traditional number system based on lattice model from integer to real number.
– We provide more general logistic regression model that can be extensively used, compared to those of current literature.
– Our approach broadens horizon of feasibility in an application to diverse fields of studies that require secure cloud computing model.

Some Notation. Throughout this paper we denote $\mathbf{X}_j^{(i)}$ as ith row and jth column of the matrix $\mathbf{X}$ usually when we want to represent a dataset. In addition, most of the works constructing basic HE function treat with bits and arrays. Therefore, we represent a vector $\boldsymbol{a}$ as an array with elements (or bits) indexed by $[n]$ for $n \in \{0, 1, \cdots, l-1\}$ of length l. Moreover, we refer *bitwise* to apply operation element-wisely and sc to denote transformation of a vector to a scalar value. Lastly, boots is denoted by bootstrapping binary gates [7].

2   Preliminaries

2.1   Logistic Regression

Logistic regression is one of the basic statistical models that use a logistic function to predict a binary dependent variable from given input [16]. Given a d dimensional observed data $\mathbf{X}^{(i)} \in \mathbb{R}^d$ and its corresponding label $\mathbf{Y}^{(i)} \in \mathbb{Z}_2$

for $i = 1, 2, \cdots, n$, inference on parameters of logistic regression is within hypotheses, $h_\theta(\mathbf{X}^{(i)}) = g(\theta^T \mathbf{X}^{(i)})$, where the 'sigmoid' function is defined as $g(z) = \frac{1}{1+e^{-z}}$ where $\theta^T \mathbf{X}^{(i)} = \theta_0 + \theta_1 \mathbf{X}_1^{(i)} + \theta_2 \mathbf{X}_2^{(i)} + \cdots + \theta_d \mathbf{X}_d^{(i)}$ for $\mathbf{X}^{(i)} = [1, \mathbf{X}_1^{(i)}, \mathbf{X}_2^{(i)}, \cdots, \mathbf{X}_d^{(i)}]^T$, $\theta = [\theta_0, \theta_1, \theta_2, \cdots, \theta_d]^T$ and number of features, $d + 1$.

To make inference on parameter θ, logistic regression uses likelihood function. Simplifying the likelihood function for the whole data by log yields $L(\theta) = \sum_{i=1}^{n} \mathbf{Y}^{(i)} \log h_\theta(\mathbf{X}^{(i)}) + (1 - \mathbf{Y}^{(i)}) \log(1 - h_\theta(\mathbf{X}^{(i)}))$. Techniques to maximize or minimize $L(\theta)$ vary, however, in this paper, batch gradient descent algorithm will be introduced. Thus, defining cost, $J(\theta) = -L(\theta)$ facilitates gradient descent algorithm to be performed.

3   Proposed Strategy

Several challenges elaborated in introduction section can be handled by applying our technique starting from constructing HE functions based on encrypted bitwise operation scheme. First of all, we propose our definition of secure cloud computing model of which many current research fails to satisfy. Then, we introduce definition of our real number system to overcome quantization problem incorporated in the current literature [6,10,11]. Next, structures of two distinguished HE functions are discussed as they are utilized to approximate the logistic function. Finally, the performance of the proposed functions are articulated with respect to time and accuracy.

3.1   Secure Cloud Computing Model

The proposed model for secure computation on the cloud follows a simple and more secure protocol compared to the conventional methods. We initially assume that the server is *honest-but-curious* implying that it is curious of information received from the client, however, is honest to follow instruction correctly. We are excluding servers such that they do not follow instructions, collude, manipulate and etc. The Fig. 2(a) shows overall protocol of client-server communication model. The process initializes with client's encrypting data $\mathbf{X}$ with the generated secret key sk. Next, the client transmits the encrypted data $\mathsf{Enc}_{sk}(x)$ with a query f to the server. The server processes the client's query in HE scheme denoted by f_{HE} with its generated cloud key ck. Lastly, the server returns queried result to the client.

Based on the concept of our model, we claim that the proposed method is more powerful than the current literature. Most importantly, the proposed server does not interfere with the client requiring user-client interaction while the most renowned work among existing model [11] involves participation of users to encrypt the client's data. The method requires the intervention of many users and further creates new vulnerabilities in which colluded users can corrupt the original data or outsource the data to the third party. On the contrary, the server in our proposed model entirely holds responsibility to execute every instructions that are necessary for processing the query.

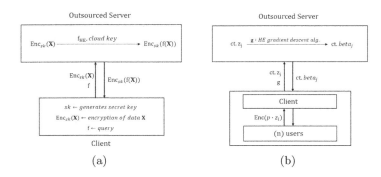

Fig. 2. Model comparison of (a) proposed model and (b) existing model [11]

3.2 Real Number Representation

The existing literature approximates real number data by a scaling factor from the user-client protocol phase since their number system only supports integer computation. However, such an approach entails users and clients to preprocess data by performing complex computations and protocols. On the contrary, we defined our real number systems based on number of bits designated for integer and fractional part.

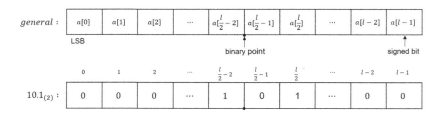

Fig. 3. Fixed point real number representation

Numbers in computer system are represented in two manners - floating point and fixed point. Although the prior system has a strength of expressing large range of numbers that contributes to high precision, we adopted fixed point number system due to its simplicity of processing fundamental arithmetic algorithm. The system facilitates complex real number arithmetic operations to simple integer arithmetic operations. This is crucial in FHE scheme because expensive time cost of bootstrapping on every encrypted bits are accumulated to delay the whole procedure. Figure 3 illustrates design of our proposed number system. Initially, the library adopts a way of representing arrays in an inverse direction, indexing from left to right. Next, we assign low $\frac{length}{2} - 1$ bits to indicate fractional part, $\frac{length}{2}$ for integer and lastly 1 bit for msb (most significant bit). Since some of

HE function such as HE logarithm and exponential function require more operations for deriving binary fractions, length of fractional word is less designated for faster computation.

3.3 Homomorphic Division

Most of the current research systems only allow HE addition and multiplication to perform a certain operation such as logistic regression. It is indeed feasible to construct any operation only containing the previous two HE functions, however manipulation of an equation requires cumbersome detour and often cannot be easily done. Consider for the case of logistic function $g(z) = \frac{1}{1+exp(-z)}$ where the equation holds division and nonlinear exponential function. As mentioned in the previous section, the current literature unavoidably performs inaccurate approximation technique into low-degree polynomials since their system cannot support division and exponential functions. In this light, our view approaches the problem more fundamentally than the existing ones.

Our encrypted division scheme originates from an approach that we perform when dividing a dividend q by a divisor m in plaintext. We adopted the process due to its simplicity which guarantees speed in time-consuming HE scheme. The procedure deduces quotient and remainder accurately within the boundary of designated length. Algorithm 1 explains the division process in plaintext to help understanding before articulating division in an encrypted domain.

Algorithm 1. Plain.Division$(\hat{q}, \hat{m}, l)$: plaintext division

---

```
 1: repeat
 2:     ŵ ← (q̂ || â)                                         ▷ Combine both vectors
 3:     ŵ ← RightShift(ŵ, 1)
 4:     â ← (ŵ[l], ŵ[l + 1], · · · , ŵ[2l − 1])
 5:     if sc(â) < sc(m̂) then
 6:         ŵ[0] ← 0
 7:     else
 8:         ŵ[0] ← 1
 9:         â ← â − m̂                                        ▷ Elementwise subtraction
10:     end if
11: until l + l/2 − 1 times until all fractional bits of q̂ are extracted
12: return q̂
```

The process begins with assigning $\hat{w}$ by combining array $\hat{q}$ quotient and $\hat{a}$ of zeroes with length l. Note that $\hat{a}$ will be the remainder after an iteration of l times. The process of comparing $\hat{a}$ and $\hat{m}$ and assigning the lowest bit of $\hat{w}$ refers to subtraction of remainder $\hat{a}$ by divisor $\hat{m}$. By repeating the process for more than l provides binary fractional part of quotient $\hat{q}$.

However, there are several limitations that follow in the case of division under the encrypted domain since the given input values are encrypted. First of all, it is infeasible to know the sign of input numbers which determine the sign of outcome. Next, comparison of encrypted values cannot be executed as in

---

Algorithm 2. HE.Division($\hat{q}$, $\hat{m}$) : division in encrypted state

---
1: $\hat{s}_1 \leftarrow$ boots.XOR($\hat{q}[l-1]$, $\hat{m}[l-1]$))
2: $\hat{q}_+ \leftarrow$ HE.AbsoluteValue($\hat{q}$)
3: $\hat{m} \leftarrow$ HE.AbsoluteValue($\hat{m}$)
4: **repeat**
5:     $\hat{c} \leftarrow (\hat{q} \parallel \hat{a})$
6:     $\hat{c} \leftarrow$ HE.RightShift($\hat{c}$, 1)
7:     $\hat{a} \leftarrow (\hat{c}[l], \hat{c}[l+1], \cdots, \hat{c}[2l-1])$
8:     $\hat{q} \leftarrow (\hat{c}[0], \hat{c}[1], \cdots, \hat{c}[l-1])$
9:     $d \leftarrow$ HE.CompareSmall($\hat{a}$, $\hat{m}$)
10:     $\hat{q}_+[0] \leftarrow$ boots.NOT(d)
11:     $\hat{a}_M \leftarrow$ HE.Subtract($\hat{a}$, $\hat{m}$)
12:     $\hat{a}_L \leftarrow$ *Bitwise* boots.AND($\hat{q}[0]$, $\hat{a}_M$)
13:     $\hat{a}_R \leftarrow$ *Bitwise* boots.AND($\hat{d}$, $\hat{a}$)
14:     $\hat{a} \leftarrow$ boots.AND($\hat{a}_L$, $\hat{a}_R$)
15: **until** $l + \frac{l}{2} - 1$ times until all fractional bits of $\hat{q}_+$ are extracted
16: $\hat{s}_2 \leftarrow$ boots.NOT($\hat{s}_1$)
17: $\hat{q}_- \leftarrow$ HE.TwosComplement($\hat{q}_+$)
18: $\hat{q}_L \leftarrow$ *Bitwise* boots.AND($\hat{s}_2$, $\hat{q}_+$)
19: $\hat{q}_R \leftarrow$ *Bitwise* boots.AND($\hat{s}_1$, $\hat{q}_-$)
20: $\hat{q} \leftarrow$ HE.Add($\hat{q}_L$, $\hat{q}_R$)
21: **return** $\hat{q}$

---

plaintext. Therefore, we concentrate on *encrypted bits* of the input values and apply *gate operations* to remove the limitations as stated in Algorithm 2.

To clear out the problem of sign, we initially perform absolute value operation on $\hat{q}$ and $\hat{m}$ to follow positive division algorithm, a loop in the Algorithm 2 in which the result will be denoted by $\hat{q}_+$. In addition, boots.XOR operation is performed on signs of given two input values where it is located in $l - 1$th position. boots.XOR operation is performed because the operation yields Enc(0) if $\hat{q}$ and $\hat{m}$ have the same sign and Enc(1) otherwise. Suppose both $\hat{q}$ and $\hat{m}$ have the same sign, then $\hat{s}_1$ is Enc(0). Since the result of division must be positive i.e. $\hat{q}_+$, we execute *bitwise* boots.AND of $\hat{s}_2$ and $\hat{q}_+$ to obtain positive result. Inversely, *bitwise* boots.AND of $\hat{s}_1$ and $\hat{q}_-$ is carried out in the same manner to yield negative outcome for different signs of input given. We add both of the results q_L and q_R to cover all of the possible cases of input signs.

The next problem of comparing values of ciphertext is solved with HE.Compare Small(a, b) function where the output is either Enc(1) if $a < b$ and otherwise Enc(0). If we set the input values of the function to be $\hat{a}$ and $\hat{m}$, then the function clearly determines the value of $\hat{w}[0]$(or $\hat{q}_+$ in Algorithm 2, equivalently) depending on the magnitude of $\hat{a}$ and $\hat{m}$. Therefore, we use the encrypted bit d as the result of the comparison function to extract the encrypted bits of $\hat{q}_+$ in the same manner of solving the first limitation. Suppose $\mathsf{sc}(\hat{a}) \geq \mathsf{sc}(\hat{m})$, then d is Enc(0) and by taking boots.NOT operation, the result of the encrypted bit is set to Enc(1) which is the intended result of $\hat{q}_+[0]$. In addition, *bitwise* boots.AND of $d(=\mathsf{Enc}(1))$ and $\hat{a}_m$ gives the result of subtracted outcome ($= \hat{a} - \hat{m}$). Inversely, we execute the same procedure for $\mathsf{sc}(\hat{a}) < \mathsf{sc}(\hat{m})$ to reach the same level of encrypted result. Lastly, addition of both results yields the solution to the second problem. We provide algorithmic detail of the HE.CompareSmall(a, b) function for verification in Appendix B.

3.4   Homomorphic Exponential Function

Exponential function has nonlinearity which an output of the function is either corresponded with look-up table or follows CORDIC (Coordinate Rotate Digital Computer) technique [9]. The former technique is based on matching an input value with huge range of number which on encrypted domain is not realistically computable. The latter technique has high potential of designing accurate exponential function, however it is expected to require considerable amount of time cost. Therefore, in this paper, we propose an alternative way to construct exponential function that is simple and highly accurate. We refer to our novel approach, **binary approximation** to coincide with exponential function with relatively small error. The approach consists of four steps: *preprocessing, binary positive exponential method, binary negative exponential method* and *selective integration*. We initially provide the methodology followed by its evaluation with accuracy; correctness is elaborated in Appendix A .

Preprocessing. The main step of *binary approximation* is to obtain 2^x, however, if base change process is performed in the first stage, a general exponential function value can be derived. Generally, base b of b^x can be exchanged by the formula $b^x = a^{log_a b^x} = a^{x log_a b}$. Therefore, for base 2, it can be converted by applying $b^x = 2^{x log_2 b}$. Thus, given the input value x, multiplication of $log_2 b$ and x should be delivered to the next step.

The problem is that $log_2 b$ has to be computed prior to multiplication of $log_2 b$ and x. However, since the current focus in this paper is to construct e^x for sigmoid function, we can simply multiply the input x by $log_2 e = 1.01110001\cdots_{(2)}$ to derive the new input. The mechanism of logarithm function in encrypted state is elaborated in [15].

Binary Positive Exponential Method. Algorithms to be performed in the case of the exponent part x being positive or negative follow different rules. In addition, since the input value x is encrypted for $2^{\mathsf{Enc}(x)}$, it is mandatory to execute both of the algorithms (positive or negative) to derive the result. However, the method entails simple processing rules and basic gate operations which guarantee effectiveness in time-performance. The whole idea of approximating $y = 2^x$ is basically combining line segments comprising of an initial point $(k, 2^k)$ and a terminal point $(k+1, 2^{k+1})$ for $k \in \mathbb{Z}$. Suppose in the case of unencrypted domain where $x = x_{int} + x_{frac}$ for x_{int} and x_{frac} are integer and fractional part of x, respectively. Then, the core technique is to add $\mathsf{RightShift}\,(\hat{x}_{frac},\, x_{int})$ from its initial point, $\mathsf{RightShift}\,(\hat{1},\, x_{int})$. To put it simply in a stepwise manner, the first step is to identify the integer value of x. Next, $\hat{1}$ is shifted to the right by x_{int}. In the same way, the fractional part of x is right-shifted by x_{int}. Lastly, addition of both of these results are desired outcome of 2^x for $x \geq 0$.

In the encrypted domain, the problem is that the value of x_{int} which determines the number of shift operations to be performed is unknown since x is given as an encrypted value. Therefore, we utilize $\mathsf{HE.CompareEqual}$ function to

Algorithm 3. HE.BinExpPositive($\hat{x}$) : $y = 2^x$ where $x \geq 0$

1: $\hat{x}_{int} \leftarrow (\hat{x}[\frac{l}{2} - 1], \hat{x}[\frac{l}{2}], \cdots, \hat{x}[l - 2])$ ▷ Integer bits of $\hat{x}$
2: $\hat{x}_{frac} \leftarrow (\hat{x}[0], \hat{x}[1], \cdots, \hat{x}[\frac{l}{2} - 2])$ ▷ Fractional bits of $\hat{x}$
3: $\hat{t}_1, \hat{t}_2 \leftarrow$ HE.EncryptNumber(0)
4: $\hat{k} \leftarrow$ HE.EncryptNumber(1)
5: **for** $i = 0$ to $\frac{l}{2} - 1$ **do**
6:     $\hat{e} \leftarrow$ HE.EncryptNumber(i)
7:     $\hat{o}[i] \leftarrow$ *Bitwise* HE.CompareEqual($\hat{e}$, $\hat{x}_{int}$)
8:     $\hat{s}_k \leftarrow$ HE.RightShift($\hat{k}$, i)
9:     $\hat{s}_1 \leftarrow$ *Bitwise* boots.AND($\hat{o}[i]$, $\hat{s}_k$)
10:     $\hat{t}_1 \leftarrow$ HE.Add($\hat{t}_1$, $\hat{s}_1$)
11:     $\hat{s}_f \leftarrow$ HE.RightShift($\hat{x}_{frac}$, i)
12:     $\hat{s}_2 \leftarrow$ *Bitwise* boots.AND($\hat{o}[i]$, $\hat{s}_f$)
13:     $\hat{t}_2 \leftarrow$ HE.Add($\hat{t}_2$, $\hat{s}_2$)
14: **end for**
15: $\hat{r} \leftarrow$ HE.Add($\hat{t}_1$, $\hat{t}_2$)
16: **return** $\hat{r}$

derive integer value of x_{int}. Specifically, the function takes two encrypted values and outputs Enc(1) if the two given encrypted values are equal and else Enc(0). For each iteration of i, we temporally create an encryption of i, Enc(i) and compare its value with x_{int} and at the same time we right-shift Enc(1) and $\boldsymbol{x}_{frac}$ by i times. At a certain point when the value of Enc(i) matches x_{int}, the HE.CompareEqual function will give Enc(1). In our last step, *bitwise* boots.AND computation of Enc(1) and right-shifted outcome yields the result of our exponentiation mechanism.

Binary Negative Exponential Method. Binary exponential method for $x < 0$ proceeds similar steps as to the positive case in unencrypted state. The absolute value operation of x is performed initially followed by obtaining integer value of $|x|$, $|x|_{int}$. Next, $\hat{1}$ is left-shifted by $|x|_{int}$ while fractional part of $|x|$ is shifted by $|x|_{int} + 1$ in the same direction. Finally, subtraction of the former outcome by the latter is conducted to produce the result. In short, the procedure is summarized as follows: LeftShift($\hat{1}$, $|x|_{int}$) + LeftShift($|\hat{x}|_{frac}$, $|x|_{int} + 1$). The binary negative exponential approach in encrypted frame is analogous to Algorithm 3. The differences are execution of absolute value operations in the first phase, direction and amount of shift operation and subtraction at the end. Since the method of deriving negative binary exponential function in encrypted state is much similar to the positive case, we state the algorithm in Appendix B for the sake of flow of the paper.

Selective Integration. In the last stage of exponential function, both encrypted results from stage 2 and 3 are integrated in the same manner as the procedure of determining sign in HE division. The main point is to extract the signed bit of $\hat{x}$ positioned at $l - 1$th bit and apply *bitwise* boots.AND operation. In short, the result of the whole procedure can can be summarized as the following equation.

$$\hat{r} = bitwise \text{ boots.AND}(\hat{x}[l - 1], \hat{r}_1) +_{HE} bitwise \text{ boots.AND}(\hat{x}_{not}[l - 1], \hat{r}_2)(1)$$

where $\hat{r}_1$, $\hat{r}_2$, $\hat{x}_{not}$ and $+_{HE}$ are the outcomes of stage 2, 3, boots.NOT($\hat{x}$) and HE.Add, respectively.

Algorithm 4. HE.Exponential(x) : $y = e^x$

1: $\hat{e}_{log}$ ← HE.EncryptNumber($log_2 e$)
2: $\hat{x}$ ← HE.Multiply($\hat{x}$, e_{log})
3: $\hat{r}_1$ ← HE.BinExpPositive($\hat{x}$)
4: $\hat{r}_2$ ← HE.BinExpNegative($\hat{x}$)
5: $\hat{x}_{not}$ ← boots.NOT$\hat{x}[l - 1]$
6: $\hat{r}_1$ ← $Bitwise$ boots.AND($\hat{r}_1$, $\hat{x}_{not}$)
7: $\hat{r}_2$ ← $Bitwise$ boots.AND($\hat{r}_2$, $\hat{x}[l - 1]$)
8: $\hat{r}$ ← HE.Add($\hat{r}_1$, $\hat{r}_2$)
9: **return** $\hat{r}$

Suppose, we consider the case of negative x to verify that the output of Eq. 1 is $\hat{r}_2$. Since the signed bit of x is Enc(1), the first term of Eq. 1 becomes Enc(0) whereas the second term yields $\hat{r}_2$. Therefore, the summation of both results is $\hat{r}_2$ which is the negative binary exponentiation of x. Likewise, we can easily verify that $\hat{r}_1$ is the result for positive x.

3.5   Performance of HE Functions

In this section, we provide execution time and the accuracy from basic operations to main HE functions that were utilized in the paper. The research was conducted in i7-7700 3.60 GHz, 16.0 GB RAM, Ubuntu 16.04.3 LTS, and the actual implementation was on TFHE version 1.0.

Time Performance of HE Functions. Major operations in the logistic regression algorithm are shift, compare, arithmetic and nonlinear functions. Each of the designed algorithms faced a challenge of maximizing usage of basic gate functions such as AND, OR, NOT and etc. while trying not to utilize arithmetic operations. Our experimentation Table 1 provides execution time for each of the operations in detail for optimizing the HE functions. The Table 1 shows that most of the HE functions except multiplication, division, logarithm and exponential functions operate approximately less than a second. It implies that the strategy for optimizing algorithms are minimization of these time-consuming functions. The delays for the lagging operations follow time complexity of $O(n^2)$ for the input length of n while other functions increase linearly by $O(n)$. This is due to the fact that the delaying operations include loops while others do not.

Accuracy of HE Functions. Every HE functions except the exponential function result accurate answers within the designated length l. Therefore, choosing the range of integer part and fractional bits is very important. Since we've assigned integer and decimal part to $\frac{l}{2}$ and $\frac{l}{2} - 1$ respectively, our number system, N is bounded by $-\sum_{i=1}^{l-1} 2^{i-\frac{l}{2}} \leq N \leq \sum_{i=1}^{l-1} 2^{i-\frac{l}{2}}$.

Table 1. Performance time for HE functions

No	Category	Operation	8-bit(s)	16-bit(s)	32-bit(s)
1	–	2's Comp	0.177	0.353	0.743
2	Shift	Left	4×10^{-6}	5×10^{-6}	8×10^{-6}
3		Right	7×10^{-6}	9×10^{-6}	12×10^{-6}
4	Min/Max	Min	0.444	0.892	1.797
5		Max	0.462	0.901	1.838
6	Compare	Equal	0.177	0.353	0.743
7		Larger	0.251	0.503	1.066
8		Less	0.247	0.507	1.031
9	Basic	Addition	0.408	0.866	1.768
10		Subtract	0.430	0.864	1.764
11		Multi.	5	22	99
12		Division	7	27	108
13	Nonlinear	Log	26	226	1767
14		Exp	14	56	227

We evaluated error of HE exponential function utilizing Absolute Percentage Error (APE), $|\frac{\hat{y}-y}{y}| \times 100$, where $\hat{y}$ and y are denoted by HE exponential function and the real exponential function, respectively. In addition, the mean of APE is 4.07 at the interval of $(-3, 6)$ and 4.00 in $(6, 10)$ which shows that our HE function is stable within the rate of error around 4.

4   Application to Logistic Regression

In this section, we elaborate the blueprint of HE logistic regression in terms of sigmoid function and batch gradient descent algorithm. First, we briefly propose our way of constructing HE logistic function. Then, HE batch gradient descent algorithm is explained slightly different to fit into our scheme to fortify efficiency. Finally, we articulate a way to scale data in an encrypted domain.

4.1   Sigmoid Function

We aim to deduce highly accurate HE logistic function from the basis of fundamental HE operations that we've built. This is because the core of logistic regression lies in the design of sigmoid function which critically affects precision of the parameters, θ. The sigmoid function is constructed under genuine HE operations that were presented in the previous sections. We first illustrate Algorithm 5 of sigmoid function and show graphical results compared with the original logistic function and traditional approaches, respectively.

Algorithm 5. HE.Sigmoid(z) : $y = g(z) = \frac{1}{1+e^{-z}}$

1: $z \leftarrow$ HE.TwosComplement(z)
2: $z \leftarrow$ HE.Exponential(z)
3: $e_1 \leftarrow$ HE.EncryptNumber(1)
4: $z \leftarrow$ HE.Add(z, e_1)
5: $r \leftarrow$ HE.Divide(e_1, z)
6: **return** r

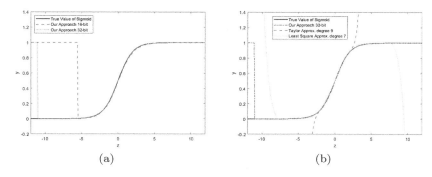

(a)   (b)

Fig. 4. Graphs of comparison between different approaches

The HE Sigmoid function of input 16 and 32 bits approximate the logistic function at the interval of $(-6, 6)$ and $(-11, 11)$, respectively which can be verified in Fig. 4(a).

Although, our number system supports integer value at the interval of $(-2^{\frac{l}{2}} + 1, 2^{\frac{l}{2}} - 1)$, exponential function's designed mechanism reduces the interval to the narrow depth which results from a few number of iteration loops in its algorithm. Nevertheless, our HE sigmoid function provides a wider range of precision interval than Taylor (degree 9) and the least square approximation (degree 7); Taylor approximation and the least square approach lose precision at the interval of around $(-2, 2)$ and $(-8, 8)$, respectively (see Fig. 4(b)).

4.2   HE Batch Gradient Descent Algorithm

We performed logistic regression by batch gradient descent algorithm. Recall from Sect. 2, the update rule for θ is as follows. $\theta_j := \theta_j - \frac{\alpha}{n} \sum_{i=1}^{n} \frac{\partial}{\partial \theta_j} J(\theta)$. Partial derivatives of $J(\theta)$ with respect to θ_j is $\frac{1}{n} \sum_{i=1}^{n} (h_\theta(\mathbf{X}^{(i)}) - \mathbf{Y}^{(i)})\mathbf{X}_j^{(i)}$. Thus, the update rule can be simplified as $\theta_j := \theta_j - \frac{\alpha}{n} \sum_{i=1}^{n} (h_\theta(\mathbf{X}^{(i)}) - \mathbf{Y}^{(i)})\mathbf{X}_j^{(i)}$. From this equation, our pseudocode for logistic regression is demonstrated in Algorithm 6.

We initialized parameters θ to 0 and updated our parameters using logistic function that we've implemented. Since logistic function requires HE division and exponential function that delay performance time, we cut down performance time not from logistic function but from a modification of the learning rate. From the analogy of client and server model, if the server performs regression upon receiving number of data n and if the server appoints α to 0.5, $\frac{\alpha}{n}$ can be

---

Algorithm 6. HE logistic regression by batch gradient descent

---
 - **Input:** Features $\mathbf{X}$, Target $\mathbf{Y}$
 - **Output:** Parameter $\theta = [\theta_0, \theta_1, \cdots, \theta_d]$

1: $\theta_0, \theta_1, \cdots, \theta_d \leftarrow$ HE.EncryptNumber(0)
2: $iter \leftarrow 25$
3: $\alpha \leftarrow$ Decide learning rate
4: $b \leftarrow$ Set b to an integer where $\frac{\alpha}{n} \approx 2^b$
5: **repeat**   ▷ Compute $\sum_{i=1}^{n}(h_\theta(\mathbf{X}^{(i)}) - \mathbf{Y}^{(i)})\mathbf{X}_j^{(i)}$
6:     **for** $j = 0$ to d **do**
7:         $\hat{grad}_j \leftarrow$ HE.EncryptNumber(0)
8:         **for** $i = 1$ to n **do**
9:             $\hat{s}_j \leftarrow$ HE.Sigmoid($\theta^T \mathbf{X}^{(i)}$)
10:             $\hat{s}_j \leftarrow$ HE.Subtract($\hat{s}_j$, $\mathbf{Y}^{(i)}$)
11:             $\hat{s}_j \leftarrow$ HE.Multiply($\hat{s}_j$, $\mathbf{X}_j^{(i)}$)
12:             $\hat{grad}_j \leftarrow$ HE.Add($\hat{grad}_j$, s_j)
13:         **end for**
14:         $\hat{grad}_j \leftarrow$ HE.RightShift($\hat{grad}_j$, b)
15:         $\theta_j \leftarrow$ HE.Subtract(θ_j, $\hat{grad}_j$)
16:     **end for**
17: **until** $iter$ times
18: **return** θ

---

calculated in an unencrypted state. Suppose, for example $\alpha = 0.5, n = 100$, then $\frac{\alpha}{n} = \frac{1}{200} \approx 2^{-8}$. The approximation leads to HE left shift operation instead of multiplication and division. For 32-bit input, left shift operation performs less than 1 s while multiplication and division show poor performance around 100 s.

4.3   Normalization of Data

Existing literature maintains a framework of scaling data by a client following complex protocols either in the encrypted or unencrypted domain. Conversely, we adhere to a strategy of imposing a burden on the cloud server to perform scaling with its own computational power. There are various ways to scale data, particularly normalization by standard deviation and min-max value. Among the two popular approaches, we adopted the latter method due to its less computational cost. Min-Max normalization is $\mathbf{Z}_j^{(i)} = \frac{\mathbf{X}_j^{(i)} - \min(\mathbf{X})}{\mathsf{Max}(\mathbf{X}) - \min(\mathbf{X})}$ where $\mathbf{X}_j^{(i)}$, $\mathbf{X}$, $\min(\mathbf{X})$ and $\mathsf{Max}(\mathbf{X})$ are denoted by normalized data, dataset, minimum value and maximum value in the dataset $\mathbf{X}$, respectively. Note that all internal operations of the normalization process are computed in the encrypted domain.

5   Performance Evaluation

We propose HE cloud computing model where not only a server delivers estimation of parameters, but also provides accuracy of the test data. The procedure requires the client to send encrypted training and test data. Then, the server carries out the scaling procedure to perform HE logistic algorithm for parameter estimation. Lastly, accuracy analysis is performed based on the encrypted test data. In the end, the client can evaluate the performance of the model upon receiving decrypted results of parameters and test accuracy.

We implemented HE testing step from the estimated parameters provided initially from Algorithm 6. First, the test dataset is min-max normalized for calculating predicted values using HE logistic function. Since the predicted values are encrypted, we conduct larger than comparison between the outcomes and Enc(0.5). If the predicted value is larger, then the function provides Enc(1) otherwise Enc(0). Next, boots.XNOR gate operation is performed between the previous bits and real values of the test dataset. The operation yields Enc(1) if the both bits are same and otherwise Enc(0). In last, we He.Add all the values of the compared results and divide it by number of data to produce accuracy.

5.1   Used Dataset

We implemented logistic gradient descent algorithm with two datasets. First data is a synthetic dataset and it is to show that our HE gradient algorithm works correctly with various HE functions incorporated inside. Also, we measured execution time of the algorithms to test time performance. Next, we expanded our scope to the real world dataset from the National Institute of Diabetes and Digestive and Kidney Diseases (NIDDK) [8]. We compared accuracy of our approach with the real logistic regression and the least square approximation method.

The syntheic dataset consists of a feature vector X and a target variable Y with 10 data created artificially. $X = [1, 1.1, \cdots, 1.9], Y = [0_{1 \times 5}, 1_{1 \times 5}]$. The iteration proceeded 25 steps to converge $\theta = (-1.980, 4.285)$ with threshold value, $\epsilon = 0.1$. We made a test dataset containing three elements to record performance time of an evaluation step. Thus, the execution times for normalization, batch gradient descent algorithm and evaluation are 17.6, 30 and 9.21 min with 32-bit input. We assume that the delay in gradient descent algorithm and evaluation step results from processing sigmoid function which includes exponential and division operations.

The Real world dataset from NIDDK is comprised of several medical predictor variables and a target variable. The purpose of this dataset is to predict whether or not patients will have diabetic symptom given their medical features. The features consist of age, BMI, glucose level, insulin level and etc. The number of data is 768×9 from which we sampled 15 data and evaluated values of estimated parameters with respect to each of the approaches. In our implementation of logistic regression, we only utilized one feature from the dataset and compared accuracy among three different approaches. The conditions such as an iteration number, learning rate, sampled data and gradient descent algorithm are fixed while only the sigmoid function differs. A measurement for the evaluation is computed on the basis of difference in values with respect to parameter θ, $ER(ErrorRate)$ (%) $= \sum_{params} |\frac{\hat{\theta}_{OLR} - \hat{\theta}_{TLR}}{\hat{\theta}_{OLR}}| \times 100$ where $\hat{\theta}_{OLR}$ and $\hat{\theta}_{TLR}$ are estimated parameters from original logistic regression and the two proposed approaches, respectively. The Table 2 is the result of accuracy based on the two datasets with learning rate α and iteration number to 0.25 and 25 respectively.

The result of the sample shows that the error rate differences between our approach and the least square approach are 4.7(%) and 4.577(%) for synthetic and NIDDK dataset, respectively. In last, we measured that the time performance for each step is 27.21, 5151 and 9.25 min. Likewise, we randomly selected three data from the dataset to measure evaluation time.

Table 2. Error rate comparison of synthetic and NIDDK data

Data set	Approach	θ_o	θ_1	Error (%)
Synthetic	Original sig	−2.016	4.276	0
	HE sig 32-bit	−1.980	4.285	2.029
	Least square	−2.083	4.421	6.729
NIDDK	Original Sig	−0.645	2.890	0
	HE sig 32-bit	−0.596	2.892	8.238
	Least square	−0.653	2.987	12.815

On the basis of the previous experimental results, we concluded that it would cost much time to execute every data of NIDDK in the encrypted domain. Since HE guarantees that the result of the ciphertexts match the results in plaintext, we conducted an experiment using the same dataset (NIDDK) and following the same procedure in plaintext situation to evaluate performance between the approaches.

We performed 4-fold cross-validation technique for estimating the validity of the three approaches: real logistic regression, our approach and least square method. The models are trained with learning rate $\alpha = 2.5$ and iteration number to 25. Next, we measured the performance of average accuracy and the AUC (Area Under the ROC Curve) for each method. The average accuracies ($threshold = 0.5$) for the three models are 69.401, 70.182 and 68.620 (%), respectively. In addition, the AUC scores (real/ours/least) are 0.800, 0.801 and 0.798 with the ROC curves.

6   Discussion

Traditional approaches mainly focus on implementing logistic regression with two basic HE operations: addition and multiplication. Although, their methods have high performance in time, they inevitably have to manipulate such function into the one that only requires computation of the two operations [2,4,6,10,11]. In addition, their approaches experience difficulty to design the logistic function with the two operations, unavoidably accepting low-degree polynomial approximation which in result causes error estimating parameters. In short, such an approach might only be suitable for the logistic regression. Using their scheme will eventually require longer time to design and optimize a new algorithm.

On the contrary, our novelty stems from the underlying basis of constructing fundamental HE operations to design one of the famous machine learning technique. We built subtraction, division and exponential function on the ground basis of encrypted bitwise operation with the FHE scheme. Our approach is not only suitable for implementing the logistic regression but also for developing new HE algorithms such as machine learning techniques and statistical modeling.

In addition, all of HE algorithms that we have implemented except the exponential function can accurately deliver outcome within designated length of an input. Although the exponential operation applies *binary approximation* to draw outcome, its error rate is stable upper bounded by less than 7 in 32-bit length input. The effectiveness had also been proven in approximating logistic function compared with up-to-date literature.

Our logistic regression has shown higher accuracy and AUC score from NIDDK data set albeit not enough data sets. However, most importantly, the power of our approach lies in the quantization of big data. If a big dataset, such as genomic information that contains at least more than a million cannot be scaled to the current literature's domain at most $(-8, 8)$ without data being undistorted. Even if some of less numbered big data is scaled, it would lose precision eventually due to the update phase in the gradient descent algorithm. Where the sigmoid function re-updates, its interval value would most probably fall outside of the boundary of $(-8, 8)$ and the precision will be lost.

On the contrary, it is possible to increase our length of input which contributes to enlargement of significant bits to ensure high precision of data even after scaling factor is multiplied. Moreover, as our length of input bits increase, so do accuracy of the logistic function and its compatible range. Data will not be distorted and the accuracy of prediction will be heightened as well.

Even though our strategy is highly proliferent both in a prospect of providing milestone to various developments of algorithms and high accuracy, delay in the execution time is the main critical reason that hinders practical usage of our scheme. However, it can be overcome through multiple improvements. In essence, an improvement in the current bootstrapping technique will have the greatest impact on processing speed since bootstrapping is involved in every bitwise operation. Suppose for example that an improvement of speed in the bootstrapping increases by 10 times, then the whole processing time will decrease by 90 handle a large number of processing bits simultaneously. Likewise, hardware-based accelerators such as GPU and FPGA can also boost operation speed in significant amounts [12].

7   Conclusion

In the world of data-driven society, secure data outsourcing in client-server model is crucial in protecting user's privacy from untrusted service provider. One of the most promising technique to settle the issue is applying Homomorphic Encryption scheme. However, many of current HE literature is obliged to adopt additive and/or multiplicative properties to design algorithms or functions that requires other than the two operations. Therefore, in this paper, we layed out a fundamental and unprecedented approach to implement HE logistic regression from the baseline of designing HE basic operations using gate operations.

Furthermore, our method is very proximate to an ideal cloud computing service model compared to other existing literature in a broad sense. According to NIST (National Institute of Standards and Technology) definition of an essential trait of cloud computing, on-demand self-service should be highlighted [13]. However, current approaches demand complex communication protocols such as multiparty computation (MPC) requiring user-client interactions [1]. As for our cloud computing model, the server can entirely process client's task such as normalization, parameter estimation and testing under encrypted state.

There still remains a variety of tasks that involve secure data outsourcing of cloud computing services. With the aid of our fundamental operations and the model in hold, numerous statistical inferences, machine learning techniques and etc. can feasibly be implemented under FHE scheme.

Appendix

A   Correctness of HE Exponential Function

We show that our method clearly approximates the exponential function with combination of line segments such that $(i, 2^i)$ and $(i+1, 2^{i+1})$ are the endpoints of ith line segment for $i \in \mathbb{Z}$. Since each mechanism in $x \geq 0$ and $x < 0$ is different, we provide a proof of the former interval followed by the latter.

A.1   (Case 1 : $x \geq 0$)

Suppose $x \in [k, k+1)$ for $k \in \mathbb{Z}^+ \cup \{0\}$. From the first step, 1 is right-shifted by $x_{int} = k$, that is 2^k. Likewise, right-shift operation of $x_{frac} = x - k$ by k times is $2^k \cdot (x - k)$. Lastly, addition of both results is the final outcome y i.e.

$$y = 2^k + 2^k \cdot (x - k) = 2^k \cdot x + 2^k(1 - k). \tag{2}$$

Therefore, Eq. 2 is the line segment of slope 2^k with the initial point $(k, 2^k)$ and the terminal point $(k + 1, 2^{k+1})$.

A.2   (Case 2 : $x < 0$)

For a negative integer x, we let $x \in [k, k+1)$ for $k \in \mathbb{Z}^-$. Then, absolute value of x is $|x| = -x \in (k-1, k]$. From the second step, 1 is left-shifted by $|x|_{int} = -k - 1$, that is 2^{k+1}. Similarly, $x_{frac} = -x - (-k - 1) = -x + k + 1$ is left-shifted by $|x|_{int} + 1$, that is $(-x + k + 1) \cdot 2^k$. Therefore, subtraction of the former outcome by the latter is y such that

$$y = 2^{k+1} - 2^k \cdot (-x + k + 1) = 2^k \cdot x + 2^k(1 - k) \tag{3}$$

which is the line segment of slope 2^k with the initial point $(k, 2^k)$ and the terminal point $(k + 1, 2^{k+1})$.

B   Additional HE Function

B.1   Addition and Subtraction

It is widely known that addition can be designed in full-adder scheme. Since the basic gate operations with bootstrapping are provided, HE addition operation can be easily implemented as in the Algorithm 7. Furthermore, HE subtraction(or HE.Subtract) is implemented by applying 2's complement operation. In short, HE.Subtract($\hat{a}$, $\hat{b}$) $= \hat{a} +_{HE} \hat{b}_{not}$ where $\hat{b}_{not}$ and $+_{HE}$ are 2's complement of $\hat{b}$ and addition in HE, respectively.

Algorithm 7. HE.Add($\hat{a}$, $\hat{b}$)

1: $\hat{c}[0] \leftarrow$ Enc(0)
2: **for** $i = 0$ to $l - 1$ **do**
3:     $t_1 \leftarrow$ boots.XOR($\hat{a}[i]$, $\hat{b}[i]$)
4:     $t_2 \leftarrow$ boots.AND(t_2, t_1, $\hat{b}[i]$)
5:     $\hat{r}[i] \leftarrow$ boots.XOR(t_1, $\hat{c}[i]$)
6:     $t_1 \leftarrow$ boots.AND(t_1, $\hat{c}[i]$)
7:     $\hat{c}[i + 1] \leftarrow$ boots.OR(t_1, t_2)
8: **end for**
9: $t_1 \leftarrow$ boots.XOR($\hat{a}[l - 1]$, $\hat{b}[l - 1]$)
10: $\hat{r}[l - 1] \leftarrow$ boots.XOR(t_1, $\hat{c}[l - 1]$)
11: **return** $\hat{r}$

B.2   2's Complement and Absolute Value Operation

In unencrypted domain, 2's complement operation is generally used to change sign of a number. Basically, the procedure is to take NOT gates for all bits of $\hat{a}$ and then add one. We apply this strategy to the encrypted domain where we replace addition operation by full adder. Therefore, we repeatedly apply bootstrapping gate operations to the encrypted bits by the following: $t_1 =$ boots.NOT($\hat{a}[i]$), $\hat{r}[i] =$ boots.XOR(t_1, $\hat{c}[i]$), $\hat{c}[i + 1] =$ boots.AND(t_1, $\hat{c}[i]$) where $\hat{r}$ is the result of HE.TwosComplement($\hat{a}$) and $\hat{c}$ plays as a carry.

Absolute value operation is an advanced algorithm with respect to 2's complement operation since it merely involves a change of sign if the value is negative. In this sense, we execute 2's complement operation on the given encrypted value, say Enc($\hat{a}$) judging by the sign bit of Enc($\hat{a}$). In the same manner as in HE exponential function, we perform the *selective integration* as the following: *bitwise* boots.AND(s_+, Enc($\hat{a}$)) $+_{HE}$ *bitwise* boots.AND(s_-, Enc($\hat{a}$)) where s_+ and s_- are Enc($\hat{a}[l - 1]$) and boots.NOT($\hat{a}$), respectively.

B.3   Shift Operation

Shift operation is basically moving the bits(or elements) of ciphertext to left or right direction, both of which are referred to HE.LeftShift and HE.RightShift, respectively. Either way, the moving bits simply occupy the new space(or position) with the same encrypted values whereas the rest of the bits are left with a choice of Enc(0) or Enc(1). In case of HE.RightShift($\hat{a}$, k), we fill the empty position with Enc(0), while Enc(1) is chosen for HE.LeftShift($\hat{a}$, k) where k is the amount of shift.

HE.EncryptedNumber(a) is used multiple times throughout the text for the purpose of encrypting real number to a binary vector by Shift and AND operation. Methodologically, we LeftShift a plaintext vector by one and execute AND operation of the first bit of $\hat{a}$ by 1. Also, the extracted bit is encrypted at the same time. Following the repetitive procedure for l times yields **Enc($\hat{a}$)**.

B.4   Comparison Operation

We implemented different types of comparison function where the output of the function yields Enc(0) or Enc(1) depending on the relationship between two encrypted input values. For instance, outcome of HE.CompareSmall($\hat{a}$, $\hat{b}$) is Enc(1) if sc($\hat{a}$) < sc($\hat{b}$) and otherwise Enc(0). The comparison operation takes boots.MUX(a, b, c) gate in which outcome of the operation depends on the value of a. Likewise, HE.CompareLarge is similarly designed as the Algorithm 8 with replacement of $\hat{a}$ in place of $\hat{b}$ in line 4.

Algorithm 8. HE.CompareSmall($\hat{a}$, $\hat{b}$)

1: $t_1 \leftarrow$ Enc(0)
2: **for** $i = 0$ to $l - 1$ **do**
3:     $t_2 \leftarrow$ boots.XNOR($\hat{a}[i]$, $\hat{b}[i]$)
4:     $t_1 \leftarrow$ boots.MUX(t_2, t_1, $\hat{b}[i]$)
5: **end for**
6: **return** t_1

B.5   Multiplication Operation

There are many ways to perform multiplication between binary arrays in plaintext. Among the existing multiplication methods, we adopted the simple and explicit way to process multiplication. If we assume that the multiplication is between l bits of vectors, then multiplication operation is transformed into l number of additions using only AND and Shift operations. In other words, suppose that we perform multiplication between $\hat{a}$ and $\hat{b}$ of length l. Then, $\hat{c}_j =$ AND($\hat{a}[i]$, $\hat{b}[j]$) for $i \in \{0, 1, \cdots, l-2\}$ is jth vector for addition. We right-shift $c_j[i]$ by j times and summation of all the vectors is the result of our approach. In short, the formula for multiplication in plaintext is the following: $\sum_{i=0}^{l-2}$ RightShift($\hat{c}_j$, j).

In the encrypted domain, we consider the problem of sign of the input values as in HE division and exponential function. Similarly, we perform absolute value operation for both of the given encrypted values at first. Next, we perform the same way of plaintext multiplication only in difference by HE gates and lastly *selective integration* is executed to provide the result of HE.Multiply function. Note that the outcome is double the length of input. Therefore, we restrict the boundary of the outcome by l to obtain the modified result in which the length of fractional and integer part to be equal to our setting.

B.6   Binary Negative Exponential Method

We provide binary negative exponential function that is similar to the positive case except execution of absolute value operation, direction and amount of shift and lastly subtraction instead of addition.

Algorithm 9. HE.BinExpNegative($\hat{x}$) : $y = 2^x$ where $x < 0$

1: $\hat{x} \leftarrow$ HE.AbsoluteValue($\hat{x}$)
2: $\hat{x}_{int} \leftarrow (\hat{x}[\frac{l}{2} - 1], \hat{x}[\frac{l}{2}], \cdots, \hat{x}[l - 2])$ ▷ Integer bits of $\hat{x}$
3: $\hat{x}_{frac} \leftarrow (\hat{x}[0], \hat{x}[1], \cdots, \hat{x}[\frac{l}{2} - 2])$ ▷ Fractional bits of $\hat{x}$
4: $\hat{t}_1, \hat{t}_2 \leftarrow$ HE.EncryptNumber(0)
5: $\hat{k} \leftarrow$ HE.EncryptNumber(1)
6: **for** $i = 0$ to $\frac{l}{2} - 1$ **do**
7:     $\hat{e} \leftarrow$ HE.EncryptNumber(i)
8:     $\hat{o}[i] \leftarrow Bitwise$ HE.CompareEqual($\hat{e}, \hat{x}_{int}$)
9:     $\hat{s}_k \leftarrow$ HE.LeftShift($\hat{k}, i$)
10:    $\hat{s}_1 \leftarrow Bitwise$ boots.AND($\hat{o}[i], \hat{s}_k$)
11:    $\hat{t}_1 \leftarrow$ HE.Add($\hat{t}_1, \hat{s}_1$)
12:    $\hat{s}_f \leftarrow$ HE.LeftShift($\hat{x}_{frac}, i + 1$)
13:    $\hat{s}_2 \leftarrow Bitwise$ boots.AND($\hat{o}[i], \hat{s}_f$)
14:    $\hat{t}_2 \leftarrow$ HE.Add($\hat{t}_2, \hat{s}_2$)
15: **end for**
16: $\hat{r} \leftarrow$ HE.Subtract($\hat{t}_1, \hat{t}_2$)
17: **return** $\hat{r}$

References

1. Acar, A., Aksu, H., Uluagac, A.S., Conti, M.: A survey on homomorphic encryption schemes: theory and implementation. ACM Comput. Surv. **51**(4), 79 (2018)
2. Aono, Y., Hayashi, T., Trieu Phong, L., Wang, L.: Scalable and secure logistic regression via homomorphic encryption. In: Proceedings of the 6th ACM Conference on Data and Application Security and Privacy, pp. 142–144. ACM (2016)
3. Bos, J.W., Lauter, K., Naehrig, M.: Private predictive analysis on encrypted medical data. J. Biomed. Inform. **50**, 234–243 (2014)
4. Chen, H., et al.: Logistic regression over encrypted data from fully homomorphic encryption. BMC Med. Genomics **11**(4), 81 (2018)
5. Cheon, J.H., Kim, A., Kim, M., Song, Y.: Homomorphic encryption for arithmetic of approximate numbers. In: Takagi, T., Peyrin, T. (eds.) ASIACRYPT 2017. LNCS, vol. 10624, pp. 409–437. Springer, Cham (2017). https://doi.org/10.1007/978-3-319-70694-8_15

6. Cheon, J.H., Kim, D., Kim, Y., Song, Y.: Ensemble method for privacy-preserving logistic regression based on homomorphic encryption. IEEE Access **6**, 46938–46948 (2018)
7. Chillotti, I., Gama, N., Georgieva, M., Izabachène, M.: Improving TFHE: faster packed homomorphic operations and efficient circuit bootstrapping. Technical report, Cryptology ePrint Archive, Report 2017/430 (2017)
8. Kaggle: Pima indians diabetes database (2016). https://www.kaggle.com/uciml/pima-indians-diabetes-database/home
9. Kantabutra, V.: On hardware for computing exponential and trigonometric functions. IEEE Trans. Comput. **45**(3), 328–339 (1996)
10. Kim, A., Song, Y., Kim, M., Lee, K., Cheon, J.H.: Logistic regression model training based on the approximate homomorphic encryption. Technical report, IACR Cryptology ePrint Archive (254) (2018)
11. Kim, M., Song, Y., Wang, S., Xia, Y., Jiang, X.: Secure logistic regression based on homomorphic encryption: design and evaluation. JMIR Med. Inform. **6**(2), e19 (2018)
12. Lee, M.S., Lee, Y., Cheon, J.H., Paek, Y.: Accelerating bootstrapping in PHEW using GPUs. In: 2015 IEEE 26th International Conference on Application-Specific Systems, Architectures and Processors (ASAP), pp. 128–135. IEEE (2015)
13. Mell, P., Grance, T., et al.: The NIST definition of cloud computing (2011)
14. Mohassel, P., Zhang, Y.: SecureML: a system for scalable privacy-preserving machine learning. In: 2017 38th IEEE Symposium on Security and Privacy (SP), pp. 19–38. IEEE (2017)
15. Yoo, J.S., Song, B.K., Yoon, J.W.: Logarithm design on encrypted data with bitwise operation. In: Kang, B.B.H., Jang, J.S. (eds.) WISA 2018. LNCS, vol. 11402, pp. 105–116. Springer, Cham (2019). https://doi.org/10.1007/978-3-030-17982-3_9
16. Zaki, M.J., Meira Jr., W., Meira, W.: Data Mining and Analysis: Fundamental Concepts and Algorithms. Cambridge University Press, Cambridge (2014)

Accelerating Number Theoretic Transform in GPU Platform for qTESLA Scheme

Wai-Kong Lee[1]([⊠]) [iD], Sedat Akleylek[2] [iD], Wun-She Yap[3] [iD],
and Bok-Min Goi[3] [iD]

[1] Universiti Tunku Abdul Rahman, Jalan Universiti, Bandar Baru Barat,
31900 Kampar, Malaysia
wklee@utar.edu.my

[2] Department of Computer Engineering, Ondokuz Mayıs University, Samsun, Turkey
sedat.akleylek@bil.omu.edu.tr

[3] Universiti Tunku Abdul Rahman, Jalan Sungai Long, Bandar Sungai Long,
43000 Kajang, Malaysia
{yapws,goibm}@utar.edu.my

Abstract. Post-quantum cryptography had attracted a lot of attentions in recent years, due to the potential threat emerged from quantum computer against traditional public key cryptography. Among all post-quantum candidates, lattice-based cryptography is considered the most promising and well studied one. The most time consuming operation in lattice-based cryptography schemes is polynomial multiplication. Through careful selection of the lattice parameters, the polynomial multiplication can be accelerated by Number Theoretic Transform (NTT) and massively parallel architecture like Graphics Processing Units (GPU). However, existing NTT implementation in GPU only focuses on parallelizing one of the three **for** loop, which eventually causes slow performance and warp divergence. In this paper, we proposed a strategy to mitigate this problem and avoid the warp divergence. To verify the effectiveness of the proposed strategy, the NTT was implemented following the lattice parameters in qTESLA, which is one of the round 2 candidates in NIST Post-Quantum Standardization competition. To the best of our knowledge, this is the first implementation of NTT in GPU with parameters from qTESLA. The proposed implementation can be used to accelerate qTESLA signature generation and verification in batch, which is very useful under server environment. On top of that, the proposed GPU implementation can also be generalized to other lattice-based schemes.

Keywords: Number Theoretic Transform · Lattice-based cryptography · Graphics Processing Units · Post-quantum cryptography

This work is supported by Fundamental Research Grant Scheme (FRGS), Malaysia with project number FRGS/1/2018/STG06/UTAR/03/1. Sedat Akleylek is partially supported by TUBITAK under grant no: EEEAG-117E636.

© Springer Nature Switzerland AG 2019
S.-H. Heng and J. Lopez (Eds.): ISPEC 2019, LNCS 11879, pp. 41–55, 2019.
https://doi.org/10.1007/978-3-030-34339-2_3

1 Introduction

1.1 Post-quantum Cryptography

Since the introduction of small scale quantum computers [1] in recent years, the cryptography community has focused a lot of attentions in investigating the potential threat from such machines. By using Shor's algorithm [2], conventional public key cryptography based on integer factorization (e.g. RSA) or discrete logarithm (e.g. ECDSA) hard problems can be broken easily by quantum computer. Since public key cryptography is used to protect many existing communication channels, the effect of such threat is devastating. In view of this potential threat that is becoming concrete very soon, National Institute of Standardization and Technology (NIST) had initiated a standardization process that call upon participations from all over the world. Submissions to this competition [3] include many schemes that build upon mathematically hard problems like lattice, multivariate polynomials, error correction code, hash function and isogeny, which are believed to be resistant to attack from quantum computer.

Among all the submissions to NIST [3], hard problems based on lattice are considered the most popular choice. Out of the 26 selected Round-2 candidates, 11 of them are designed based on lattice (three for digital signature and eight for public key encryption/key encapsulation mechanism). This motivates us to evaluate the speed performance of lattice based schemes, which is one of the criteria for standardization besides security.

Public key cryptography is widely used to establish secret key for encryption between two parties, or to authenticate the communicating parties through digital signature. In this regard, cloud servers that are communicating with many clients protected by security protocol (e.g. SSL/TLS) may need to handle huge amount of computation, mainly from the execution of public key cryptography. To mitigate this potential performance bottleneck, one can utilize hardware accelerator (e.g. FPGA and GPU) to speed up the execution of the most time consuming operations in public key cryptography. In this paper, we focus on offloading the polynomial multiplication, which is the most time consuming operation in lattice-based schemes, to a GPU with parallel architecture. While this paper only evaluates the lattice parameters from qTESLA, the proposed implementation techniques can be generalized to support other lattice-based schemes with a minimal effort.

1.2 Related Work

Accelerating polynomial multiplication on hardware platform is a hot research topic in the past decade. Du and Bai [4] showed that the FPGA can be utilized to accelerate polynomial multiplication in Ring-LWE based lattice-based cryptosystems. Dai et al. [5] presented a novel hardware architecture that is able to compute modular exponentiation for 1024-bit to 4224-bit operands. Their implementation in FPGA utilized NTT and Montgomery Multiplication [6] to achieve high speed performance. Although FPGA allows flexible configuration and potentially provide good speed performance, it is not widely adopted by cloud service providers as a hardware accelerator. This is because coding FPGA requires specialized hardware skills and relatively long design time. Compared to FPGA, GPU is more widely used as hardware accelerator in server environment, as it is cheap and easier to code.

The work from Maza et al. [7] is considered one of the earliest efforts in accelerating polynomial multiplication in GPU platform, which was implemented by mixing floating point and integer operations. They commented that Cooley-Tukey FFT is slower than Stockham FFT on GTX285 GPU. Later on, Emmart and Weem [8] proposed an implementation of Strassen multiplication algorithm, which shares many similarity with polynomial multiplication. Their implementation based on NTT and Cooley-Tukey FFT showed impressive speed performance for very large operand size up to 16320K-bit. Wang et al. [9] explored the feasibility to implement Fully Homomorphic Encryption on GPU, based on the NTT implementation from Emmart and Weem [8]. These prior work are not directly applicable to lattice-based cryptosystems due to the difference in NTT size, prime field and the supported operands.

Akleylek and Tok [10] presented the first polynomial multiplication implementation in GPU that aims an application for lattice-based cryptosystems. They concluded that iterative NTT is the fastest technique for polynomial degree up to 2000. Later on, Akleylek et al. [11] presented a thorough comparison of serial NTT, parallel NTT and cuFFT (NVIDIA library) based multiplication in GPU. Through experiments, they concluded that cuFFT based multiplication performed better when the degree of polynomial is larger than 2048. However, cuFFT library utilizes floating point arithmetic, which can potentially introduce small errors throughout the multiplication operations. Moreover, this work [11] only targets sparse polynomial multiplication, which may not be useful to other lattice-based cryptosystems.

1.3 Our Contributions

In this paper, we present the implementation of polynomial multiplication in the latest NVIDA Turing GPU (GTX2080) using NTT. The performance was evaluated based on parameters from qTESLA, a lattice based post-quantum signature scheme that enter Round 2 of NIST standardization process [3]. To the best of our knowledge, this is the first work that present the NTT implementation based on the parameters from qTESLA signature scheme. Our proposed technique can be easily adapted to other lattice-based cryptosystems with similar parameter sets.

2 Background

2.1 Overview of qTESLA

In this section we recall the main parts of the efficient and quantum secure lattice-based signature scheme named qTESLA (Quantum Tightly-secure, Efficient signature scheme from Standard LAttices) [3]. qTESLA is defined over the quotient ring $R_q = \mathbb{Z}/q\mathbb{Z}[x]/(x^n + 1) = \mathbb{Z}_q[x]/(x^n + 1)$, where q is a prime number and $n = 2^\ell$ with $\ell > 1$. Then, using a finite ring with nice properties yields efficient polynomial multiplication algorithm called Number Theoretic Transform (NTT). The properties of qTESLA can be grouped as simplicity, parameter flexibility, compactness, quantum resistant and achieves high speed performance. qTESLA is an updated version of ring-TESLA based on Bai-Galbraith signature scheme framework. The security of qTESLA uses the benefits of the hardness of the Ring-Learning with Error (R-LWE) problem. A lattice-based signature scheme has three main parts: key generation, signature generation and signature verification. For the sake of simplicity and focusing the importance of polynomial multiplication over the scheme, we only give the sketch/informal presentation of those algorithms. We refer the reader [12] for the detailed algorithms.

In Algorithm 1, key generation of qTESLA is described. Step 5 needs an input from Step 4. In Step 5, the polynomial multiplication operations $(a_i \cdot s)$ are independent. Thus, they can be performed in a parallel way.

Algorithm 1. Sketch of the key generation algorithm

Input: Size and dimension of the ring q, n.
Output: Private key set $(s, a_1, \ldots, a_k)$, error terms $(e_1, \ldots, e_k)$ and public key set
$\quad (a_1, \ldots, a_k, t_1, \ldots, t_k)$
1: Generate $(a_1, \ldots, a_k) \leftarrow (\mathbb{Z}/q\mathbb{Z})[x]/(x^n + 1)$
2: Generate $s \in (\mathbb{Z})[x]/(x^n + 1)$
3: **for** $j = 1$ to k **do**
4: $\quad$ Generate $e_i \in (\mathbb{Z}/q\mathbb{Z})[x]/(x^n + 1)$ with the desired conditions
5: $\quad$ Compute $t_i \leftarrow a_i \cdot s + e_i \in (\mathbb{Z}/q\mathbb{Z})[x]/(x^n + 1)$
6: **end for**
7: Return private key set $(s, a_1, \ldots, a_k)$, error terms $(e_1, \ldots, e_k)$ and public key set
$\quad (a_1, \ldots, a_k)$

In Algorithm 2, we roughly define the signature generation process of qTESLA by considering parallelization of the algorithm. Since the polynomial multiplications $(a_k \cdot y)$ are independent in Step 2, they can be achieved in parallel. The same observation is applicable to the polynomial multiplications $(a_i \cdot y)$ defined in Step 5.

Algorithm 3 shows a simplified description of the signature verification algorithm in qTESLA. Similar to our previous observation, the polynomial multiplication operations $(a_i \cdot z)$ in Step 2 can be executed in a parallel. From these observations, we conclude that there are many polynomial multiplications involved in qTESLA signature scheme, which can be accelerated through parallel implementation in suitable hardware platform (e.g. GPU). Besides the parallel implementation of polynomial multiplication, one can also process many signature generation/verification in parallel (batch processing), given sufficient hardware resources.

Algorithm 2. Sketch of the signature generation algorithm

Input: Private key set $(s, a_1, \ldots, a_k)$, error terms $(e_1, \ldots, e_k)$ and a message $m \in \{0,1\}^*$

Output: Signature of message m z, c.

1: Choose $y \in (\mathbb{Z}/q\mathbb{Z})[x]/(x^n + 1)$ with the desired properties
2: Compute $c \leftarrow H(a_1 \cdot y, \ldots, a_k \cdot y, m)$
3: Compute $z \leftarrow y + s \cdot c$ // Note that if z does not satisfy the desired properties, restart the procedure
4: **for** $j = 1$ to k **do**
5:    Compute $a_i \cdot y - e_i \cdot c$ // Note that if the result does not satisfy the desired properties, restart the procedure
6: **end for**
7: Return (z, c)

Algorithm 3. Sketch of the signature verification algorithm

Input: Public key set $(a_1, \ldots, a_k, t_1, \ldots, t_k)$, signature (z, c) and signed message $m \in \{0,1\}^*$

Output: valid or invalid

1: **for** $j = 1$ to k **do**
2:    Compute $w_i \leftarrow a_i \cdot z - t_i \cdot c \in (\mathbb{Z}/q\mathbb{Z})[x]/(x^n + 1)$
3: **end for**
4: **if** $c \neq H(w_1, \ldots, w_k, m)$ **then**
5:    Return "invalid"
6: **else**
7:    Return "valid"
8: **end if**

2.2 Number Theoretic Transform

NTT [13] and Discrete Fourier Transform (DFT) are computational techniques to transform a set of data between its time and frequency domain. DFT is widely used in signal processing applications, which is usually operating in complex domain involving floating point arithmetic. On the other hand, it performs transformation over a finite field $GF(p)$ where p is the modulus. In other words, NTT is analogous to DFT, but it operates on integers instead of floating point arithmetic. Computation in complex domain (DFT) involves floating point arithmetic, which is difficult in error analysis and might introduce round-off errors. Hence, NTT is more suitable for cryptographic applications because it only involves integer arithmetic, thus do not suffer from potential round-off errors.

Polynomial multiplication with NTT consists of three steps:

(i) Given polynomial **a** and **b** with degree of polynomial n, where their coefficients are written as $a_i, \ldots, a_n$ and $b_i, \ldots, b_n$ respectively. Convert polynomial **a** and polynomial **b** to NTT form. Assume p is a prime number and w is the primitive n-th root of unity (also referred as twiddle factors), NTT(**a**) transforms polynomial **a** into NTT form following the Eq. 1:

$$\mathbf{A} = NTT(\mathbf{a}) = \sum_{j=0;\ i=0}^{n-1} a_j w^{ij}(mod\ p) \tag{1}$$

The same operation is performed on polynomial $\mathbf{b}$ to transform it into NTT form, resulting the polynomial $\boldsymbol{B}$.

(ii) Perform point-wise multiplication between $\boldsymbol{A}$ and $\boldsymbol{B}$. Each coefficient in $\boldsymbol{A}(A_i)$ is multiplied with the corresponding coefficient in $\boldsymbol{B}(B_i)$, as shown in Eq. 2.

$$\mathbf{C} = A_i \times B_i, where\ i \in \{0, \ldots, n-1\} \tag{2}$$

(iii) Convert the resulting polynomial $\mathbf{C}$ back to ordinary form through Eq. 3.

$$INTT(\mathbf{C}) = \mathbf{c} = n^{-1} \sum_{j=0;\ i=0}^{n-1} C_j w^{-ij}(mod\ p) \tag{3}$$

Note that NTT was not efficient as the complexity is $O(n^2)$. Cooley-Tukey Fast Fourier Transform (CT-FFT) [14] is a more efficient way of computing DFT (as well as NTT). It allows large FFT to be decomposed and computed using multiple smaller-sized FFT in recursive manner. Consider the degree of polynomial n, applying CT-FFT one time yields smaller polynomials with degree $n_1 \times n_2$, where $n = n_1 \times n_2$. This decomposition process can continue further, where the level of recursion is determined based on the implementation requirement. Radix-2 CT-FFT is a common choice for efficient implementation, wherein the decomposition continues until the smallest possible FFT size ($n = 2$). Eventually, the complexity of NTT with CT-FFT becomes $O(n \log n)$. The same approach were also adopted by prior work [8,9].

Algorithm 4. In-place forward radix-2 Cooley-Tukey FFT

Input: polynomial $\mathbf{a}$ in time domain; pre-computed twiddle factors (w) polynomial $\mathbf{A}$ in frequency (NTT) domain
Output: polynomial $\mathbf{A}$ in frequency (NTT) domain
1: **for** $NP=n/2;\ NP>0\ NP=NP/2$ **do**
2:    $jf=0;\ \ j=0;\ \ jTwiddle=0;$
3:    **for** $jf=0;\ jf<n;\ jf=j+NP$ **do**
4:      **for** $j=jf;\ j<jf+NP;\ j=j+1$ **do**
5:        $temp = (w[jTwiddle] \times a[j+NP])\ mod\ p;$
6:        $a[j+NP] = (a[j]\text{-}temp)\ mod\ p;$
7:        $a[j] = (a[j]+temp)\ mod\ p;$
8:      **end for**
9:      $jTwiddle++;$
10:   **end for**
11: **end for**

Referring to Algorithm 4, the inputs to radix-2 forward CT-FFT are polynomial a and twiddle factors w. Note that the twiddle factors can be computed on

---

Algorithm 5. In-place inverse radix-2 Cooley-Tukey FFT

Input: polynomial **A** in frequency domain; pre-computed inverse twiddle factors (w^{-1})

Output: polynomial **a** in time domain

 1: **for** *NP=1; NP<n NP=NP*2* **do**

 2:    *jf=0; j=0; jTwiddle=0;*

 3:   **for** *jf=0; jf<n; jf=j+NP* **do**

 4:     **for** *j=jf; j<jf+NP; j=j+1* **do**

 5:       temp = a[*j*];

 6:       a[*j*] = temp + (a[*j+NP*]) mod *p*;

 7:       a[*j+NP*] = (w^{-1}[*jTwiddle*] × temp - a[*j+NP*]) mod *p*;

 8:     **end for**

 9:    *jTwiddle++*;

10:   **end for**

11: **end for**

---

the fly or pre-computed to reduce the computational effort. In this paper, we opt for pre-computing the twiddle factors as our aim is to improve the speed performance. The algorithm starts by decomposing the original polynomial of degree n into smaller degree with half the size (step 4). Then it follows by the butterfly operations (step 5–7) that computes the new coefficients in place, reusing the same memory space in polynomial **a** to conserve memory space. The output of Algorithm 4 is polynomial **A**, which is the transformation of **a** into its frequency domain. The inverse CT-FFT is similar to forward CT-FFT, except that the inverse twiddle factors w^{-1} are being used. The detail operations of inverse CT-FFT are described in Algorithm 5.

Note that in this paper, the NTT operation (through CT-FFT) accepts inputs in standard ordering and produces results in bit-reversed ordering. On the other hand, the INTT employs Gentleman-Sande butterfly; it absorbs inputs in bit-reverse ordering and computes the output in standard ordering. With such arrangement, we can avoid the use of bit-reversal operations, which can be time consuming in the implementation. This approach is proposed by the authors of qTESLA in the submission to NIST standardization [12].

2.3   Overview of Graphics Processing Units and CUDA

GPU is an emerging platform with massively parallel architecture, which is initially designed for graphics applications. Since the introduction of Compute Unified Device Architecture (CUDA) in 2007, GPU can be programmed for general purposed computing, which eventually opens up plethora of interesting applications. GPU is now widely used in Deep Learning [15], scientific computing [16], cryptography [17] and many other applications.

GPU comes with hundreds to thousands cores, enabling many tasks to be carried out parallely. Multiple cores (i.e. 64, 128 or 196 cores, depending on the generation of GPU) group together to form a Streaming Multiprocessor (SM). There are two types of memories in GPU: on-chip and off-chip memory. On-chip

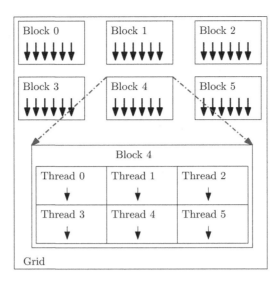

Fig. 1. Relationship between grid, block and thread.

memory includes register files and shared memory, which is very fast in speed but small in size (64K to 96K 32-bit word per SM). Shared memory is essentially the user-managed cache memory. On the other hand, global memory is the DRAM in GPU, which is also part of the off-chip memory. It is large in size (typically 2 GB–16 GB), but slow in speed (about 300× slower than registers). Constant memory is also part of DRAM, but it is read-only and being cached to offer higher access speed. Constant memory is part of DRAM and usually used to store pre-computed values and accessed as a look-up table.

Under CUDA programming terminology, multiple threads form a block; multiple blocks then form a grid (see Fig. 1). Each GPU card usually contains only one grid. It is the programmer's task to specify the number of blocks and threads to be used for computing a specific algorithm in parallel. The GPU also groups 32 threads in a unit called *warp*; all threads within the same warp will execute the same set of instructions. This is to facilitate the hardware scheduling as well as optimizing the memory throughput. In view of this, we need to specify the number of threads per block in multiple of 32 (warp size); otherwise some of the threads in a warp may be scheduled to perform tasks different with the other threads, resulting in poor performance (warp divergence).

3   Implementation Details

There are five versions of qTESLA submitted for NIST standardization; we have selected qTESLA-III for implementation in this paper as this variant can provide sufficient security level. The implementation details of NTT based on qTESLA-III parameters are presented in this section. Comparison was made between the qTESLA-III reference implementation (non-parallelised) against our proposed GPU implementation. Refer to Table 1 for the parameters of qTESLA-III and other versions.

Table 1. Parameters for qTESLA-III

Parameter	qTESLA-I	qTESLA-II	qTESLA-III	qTESLA-V	qTESLA-V-size
λ	95	128	160	225	256
n	512	768	1024	2048	1536
q	$4205569 \approx 2^{22}$	$8404993 \approx 2^{23}$	$8404993 \approx 2^{23}$	$16801793 \approx 2^{24}$	$33564673 \approx 2^{25}$

3.1   Optimizing NTT Parallellism

NTT offers rich parallelism which can be exploited by parallel architecture in GPU. Specifically, referring to Algorithm 4, the **for** loop jf (step 3) or j (step 4) can be executed in parallel by multiple threads. For example, one can parallelize the j loop by computing step 5–7 with multiple threads. The number of threads executing concurrently is depending on the index i, which varied according to the decomposition level in CT-FFT. Assuming $n = 1024$, the number of threads used to parallelize j loop ranges from 512–1; this implies that the parallelism is very low when decomposition level in CT-FFT proceeds. Moreover, when the number of parallel threads in a block is lesser than 32, warp divergence issue is going to happen, which seriously deteriorate the performance. On the other hand, parallelism in jf loop ranges from 1–512 following the decomposition level in CT-FFT, which is also undesirable for implementation in GPU. In view of that, we proposed a better strategy to improve the parallelism in computing NTT.

We have designed two kernels for computing NTT:

(a) Kernel 1 parallelizes j loop for decomposition level 0–level $log(n)/2 - 1$.
(b) Kernel 2 parallelizes jf loop for decomposition level $log(n)/2$–level n.

The snippets of main function, Kernel 1 and Kernel 2 are illustrated in Figs. 2, 3 and 4 respectively. The main function first initialized the memory required to store the polynomials for multiplication and other intermediate results, then it calls NTT Kernel 1 and Kernel 2 based on the decomposition level. Once the NTT completes, it proceeds to call the GPU codes to perform point-wise multiplication and INTT. Note that the variable BATCH defines the number of blocks, which should be large enough in order to fully harness the parallelism in GPU. In our implementation, each block computes one NTT in parallel. In other words, BATCH also defines the number of NTT that we want to perform in batch; it varies from 1K–256K in this paper.

Kernel 1 parallelized the j-loop with multiple threads in GPU, while Kernel 2 parallelized the jf-loop. Again, we assume $n = 1024$ for subsequent analysis. Since Kernel 1 is being used to compute decomposition level 0 to $log(n)/2-1$, the

```
void main()
{
    /* Initialization codes*/
    int NP = PARAM_N;
    for (int level = 0; level < log(n) / 2; level++)
    {
        NP = PARAM_N >> level + 1;
        ntt_kernel1 << <BATCH, NP >> >(a, level, NP);
        ntt_kernel1 << <BATCH, NP >> >(b, level, NP);
    }

    for (int level = log(n) / 2; level < log(n); level++)
    {
        NP = PARAM_N >> level + 1;
        ntt_kernel2 << <BATCH, NP >> >(a, level, NP);
        ntt_kernel2 << <BATCH, NP >> >(b, level, NP);
    }
    /* Point-wise multiplication*/

    /* Inverse NTT*/
}
```

Fig. 2. Relationship between grid, block and thread.

```
__global__ void ntt_kernel1(int32_t *a, uint32_t level, uint32_t NP)
{ // Forward NTT
    int jTwiddle = 1;
    int jFirst = 0, j = 0, level = 0, iter = 0;
    int tid = threadIdx.x;
    int bid = blockIdx.x;

    if (level == 0) iter = 1;
    else iter = level * 2;
    for (int i = 0; i < iter; i++)
    {
        sdigit_t W = zeta_constant[jTwiddle++];
        jFirst = i * NP;
        int32_t temp = reduce_gpu((int64_t)W *
            (int64_t)a[bid*PARAM_N + jFirst + tid + i]);
        a[bid*PARAM_N + jFirst + tid + i] =
            a[bid*PARAM_N + jFirst + tid] - temp;
        a[bid*PARAM_N + jFirst + tid] = temp +
            a[bid*PARAM_N + jFirst + tid];
    }
}
```

Fig. 3. Kernel 1: parallelizing the j-loop.

number of parallel threads ranges from 512 to 32. On the other hand, Kernel 2 is being called from level $log(n)/2$ to level n with parallel threads ranges from 32 to 512. This parallelism strategy ensures that there is always at least 32 threads

```
__global__ void ntt_kernel2(int32_t *a, uint32_t NP)
{ // Forward NTT
    int jTwiddle = 1;
    int jFirst = 0, j = 0, iter = 0;
    int tid = threadIdx.x;
    int bid = blockIdx.x;

    for (int i = 0; i < NP; i++)
    {
        jFirst = tid * NP * 2;
        int32_t temp = reduce_gpu((int64_t)W *
            (int64_t)a[bid*PARAM_N + jFirst + i + NP]);
        a[bid*PARAM_N + jFirst + i + NP] =
            a[bid*PARAM_N + jFirst + i] - temp;
        a[bid*PARAM_N + jFirst + i] = temp +
            a[bid*PARAM_N + jFirst + i];
    }
}
```

Fig. 4. Kernel 2: parallelizing the jf-loop.

(one warp) being used to compute the NTT in parallel, which effectively avoid the warp divergence issue.

Due to limitation of space, we do not describe the point-wise multiplication and INTT in details. Since the pattern of parallelism in INTT (Algorithm 5) is exactly the same as NTT, it can also adopt the parallelism strategy proposed in this paper in order to achieve good performance. Point-wise multiplication is straightforward to implement; n threads are launched, where each thread multiplies a coefficient between two polynomials.

3.2   Placement of Twiddle Factors

Referring to Algorithm 4, the twiddle factors are being accessed (step 5) to compute CT-FFT. These twiddle factors can be pre-computed to reduce the computational time. Since each twiddle factor is only being read once and being consumed immediately, there is no advantage to cache it at shared memory. Instead, we proposed to place these twiddle factors in constant memory (cached at L1-cache), which can enjoy lesser access delay compared to reading it directly from global memory. The twiddle factors and inverse twiddle factors used by qTESLA-III only consume 1K of 32-bit words each, which does not exceed the constant memory limit. They were only copied once into the constant memory in GPU at the beginning of the polynomial multiplication.

4   Experimental Results

The experiments were carried out in CPU and GPU platform with the specifications described in Table 2. All experiments carried out in this paper follows the parameters in qTESLA-III.

Table 2. Specifications of implementation platforms

Operating system	Windows 10
CPU	Intel Xeon(R) E5-2560 v3, 2.30 GHz, 16 GB RAM
GPU	GTX2080, 2944 cores, 8 GB RAM

Table 3. Timing performance (ms) of qTESLA-III in GPU

Number of batch	GPU (j-loop)	GPU (proposed)	Speed-up
1024 (1K)	2.72	2.61	1.03
2048 (2K)	6.22	5.51	1.13
4096 (4K)	10.92	8.84	1.23
8192 (8K)	24.81	19.93	1.24
16384 (16K)	45.13	32.52	1.39
32768 (32K)	90.54	65.22	1.39
65536 (64K)	171.34	126.61	1.35
131072 (128K)	350.93	245.14	1.43
262144 (256K)	685.41	542.14	1.26

To understand the effectiveness of our proposed parallelism optimization strategy, we had implemented the polynomial multiplication by parallelizing the j-loop in Algorithms 4 and 5. The results are compared against our proposed method, and the timing performance in GPU are presented in Table 3. It is noted that the proposed optimized parallelism is better than parallelizing only j-loop, wherein the performance is improved by 4%–43% across various batch sizes. This is because our proposed method ensures that there is always at least 32 threads (one warp) computing NTT in parallel, whereas parallelizing j-loop only results in poor parallelism and warp divergence. The implementation that parallelizes only jf-loop is not presented in this paper because the performance is similar to parallelizing only j-loop.

Table 4 shows the timing performance for implementation of qTESLA-III in CPU (serial) and GPU (parallel). The GPU implementation outperforms CPU version when the batch size is large enough (>16). The speed-up ratio increases proportionally when the batch size increases, eventually saturated at a fixed level (16K–128K). This is a common phenomena in GPU computing, which signifies that the GPU resources are fully utilized; increasing the workload further did not yield any improvement in performance.

Table 4. Timing performance (ms) of qTESLA-III in CPU and GPU

Batch size	CPU	GPU (proposed)	Speed-up
2	0.17	0.67	0.25
4	0.18	0.69	0.26
8	0.32	0.70	0.46
16	0.65	0.64	1.02
32	1.21	0.61	1.98
64	2.36	0.94	2.51
128	4.23	0.90	4.70
256	9.17	1.15	7.97
512	17.46	1.61	10.84
1024 (1K)	34.81	2.61	13.44
2048 (2K)	69.02	5.51	12.53
4096 (4K)	140.42	8.84	15.88
8192 (8K)	286.84	19.93	14.39
16384 (16K)	571.33	32.52	17.57
32768 (32K)	1113.41	65.22	17.07
65536 (64K)	2312.42	126.61	18.26
131072 (128K)	4726.41	245.14	19.28
262144 (256K)	8873.80	542.14	16.37

5   Discussions

From the results, we noticed that although our proposed strategy can optimize the parallelism in GPU, it may not work well for NTT with polynomial degree $n \leq 512$. This is because the minimum parallel threads would be lesser than 32 in such cases, so the warp divergence issue may happen. However, the proposed strategy is still better than parallelizing only j-loop or jf-loop when the polynomial degree $n \leq 512$, due to the higher parallelism. Besides that, all parameter sets in qTESLA are having $n > 512$ except qTESLA-I, so our approach is still considered as an optimized solution for most cases. On top of that, our proposed implementation can also be used to accelerate NTT in other lattice-based cryptosystems (e.g. CRYSTALS-DILITHIUM [18]).

The proposed technique can be applied to other GPU architecture except NVIDIA GPU (e.g. AMD). This is due to the fact that AMD GPU have warp size of 32, which is same as NVIDIA GPU. Even though some AMD GPUs from older generation are having larger warp size (i.e. 64), our parallelization strategy still can help in avoiding warp divergence.

In future, we aim to focus on the parallelization of entire qTESLA scheme into the GPU. Building on top of our efficient NTT implementation, the Gaussian sampler and other relevant operations will be offloaded to GPU as well.

With such implementation, the speed performance in signature generation and verification can be greatly improved, which is beneficial to the cloud servers that need to handle such computation in massive scale.

6 Conclusions

Post-quantum cryptography have received a lot of attention in the past decade, due to the emergence of small-scale practical quantum computer. In 2017, NIST initiated a standardization competition, wherein many submissions in this competition are designed based on lattice-based hard problems. In this paper, we present experimental results of parallel implementation of NTT, which is useful in accelerating polynomial multiplication used by qTESLA lattice-based cryptosystem. Our implementation in GPU shows impressive speed-up against CPU, with best speed-up ($17\times$–$19\times$) achieved when the batch size is large enough (16K–128K). The proposed implementation can be adopted by other similar lattice-based cryptosystems to accelerate the expensive NTT operation.

References

1. D-Wave Systems. https://www.dwavesys.com/quantum-computing. Accessed 24 May 2019
2. Shor, P.: Algorithms for quantum computation: discrete logarithm and factoring. In: IEEE Proceedings of the 35th Annual Symposium on Foundations of Computer Science, pp. 124–134. IEEE, Santa Fe (1994)
3. NIST Post-Quantum Cryptography Standardization: Round 2 Submissionn. https://csrc.nist.gov/Projects/Post-Quantum-Cryptography/Round-2-Submissions. Accessed 25 May 2019
4. Du, C., Bai, G.: Efficient Polynomial Multiplier Architecture for Ring-LWE Based Public Key Cryptosystems. In: IEEE International Symposium on Circuits and Systems (ISCAS), pp. 1162–1165. IEEE, Montreal (2016)
5. Dai, W., Chen, D., Cheung, R.C.C., Koc, C.K.: FFT-based McLaughlin's Montgomery exponentiation without conditional selections. IEEE Trans. Comput. **67**(9), 1301–1314 (2018)
6. Montgomery, P.: Modular multiplication without trial division. Math. Comput. **44**(170), 519–521 (1985)
7. Maza, M.M., Pan, W.: Fast polynomial multiplication on a GPU. J. Phys. **256**(1), 1–14 (2010). Conference Series
8. Emmart, N., Weems, C.C.: High precision integer multiplication witha GPU using Strassen's algorithm with multiple FFT sizes. Parallel Process. Lett. **21**(3), 359–375 (2011)
9. Wang, W., Hu, Y., Chen, L., Huang, X., Sunar, B.: Exploring the feasibility of fully homomorphic encryption. IEEE Trans. Comput. **64**(3), 698–706 (2013)
10. Akleylek S., Tok, Z.Y.: Efficient arithmetic for lattice-based cryptography on GPU using the CUDA platform. In: 22nd Signal Processing and Communications Applications Conference (SIU). IEEE, Trabzon (2014)

11. Akleylek, S., Dağdelen, Ö., Yüce Tok, Z.: On the efficiency of polynomial multiplication for lattice-based cryptography on GPUs using CUDA. In: Pasalic, E., Knudsen, L.R. (eds.) BalkanCryptSec 2015. LNCS, vol. 9540, pp. 155–168. Springer, Cham (2016). https://doi.org/10.1007/978-3-319-29172-7_10
12. Bindel, N., et al.: qTESLA. https://qtesla.org/wp-content/uploads/2019/04/qTESLA_round2_04.26.2019.pdf. Accessed 1 June 2019
13. Pollard, J.M.: The fast Fourier transform in a finite field. Math. Comput. **25**(114), 365–374 (1971)
14. Cooley, J.W., Tukey, J.W.: An algorithm for the machine calculation of complex fourier series. Math. Comput. **19**(90), 297–301 (1965)
15. Shone, N., Ngoc, T.N., Phai, V.D., Shi, Q.: A Deep Learning approach to network intrusion detection. IEEE Trans. Emerg. Top. Comput. Intell. **2**(1), 41–50 (2018)
16. Lee, W.K., Achar, R., Nakhla, M.S.: Dynamic GPU parallel sparse LU factorization for fast circuit simulation. IEEE Trans. Very Large Scale Integr. (VLSI) Syst. **26**(11), 2518–2529 (2018)
17. Emmart, N., Zheng, F., Weems, C.: Faster modular exponentiation using double precision floating point arithmetic on the GPU. In: Proceedings of the IEEE 25th Symposium on Computer Arithmetic, pp. 130–137. IEEE, Amherst Massachusetts (2018)
18. Lyubashevsky, V., et al.: CRYSTALS-DILITHIUM. https://pq-crystals.org/

Provably Secure Three-Party Password-Based Authenticated Key Exchange from RLWE

Chao Liu[1], Zhongxiang Zheng[2], Keting Jia[2(✉)], and Qidi You[3]

[1] Key Laboratory of Cryptologic Technology and Information Security,
Ministry of Education, Shandong University, Jinan, People's Republic of China
liu_chao@mail.sdu.edu.cn
[2] Department of Computer Science and Technology, Tsinghua University,
Beijing, People's Republic of China
ktjia@mail.tsinghua.edu.cn
[3] Space Star Technology Co., Ltd., Beijing, People's Republic of China

Abstract. Three-party key exchange, where two clients aim to agree a session key with the help of a trusted server, is prevalent in present-day systems. In this paper, we present a practical and secure three-party password-based authenticated key exchange protocol over ideal lattices. Aside from hash functions our protocol does not rely on external primitives in the construction and the security of our protocol is directly relied on the Ring Learning with Errors (RLWE) assumption. Our protocol attains provable security. A proof-of-concept implementation shows our protocol is indeed practical.

Keywords: Password authentication · Three-party key exchange · Provable security · RLWE · Post-quantum

1 Introduction

Key Exchange (KE), which is a fundamental cryptographic primitive, allows two or more parties to securely share a common secret key over insecure networks. KE is one of the most important cryptographic tools and is widely used in building secure communication protocols. Authenticated Key Exchange (AKE), which enables each party to authenticate the other party, can prevent the adversary from impersonating the honest party in the conversation. Password-based Authenticated Key Exchange (PAKE), which allows parties to share a low-entropy password that is easy for human memory, has become an important cryptographic primitive because it is easy to use and does not rely on special hardware to store high-entropy secrets.

The early solution to this problem was to achieve two-party password-based authenticated key exchange (2PAKE), in which both parties identified their communication partners with shared passwords. Many 2PAKE protocols have been

S.-H. Heng and J. Lopez (Eds.): ISPEC 2019, LNCS 11879, pp. 56–72, 2019.
https://doi.org/10.1007/978-3-030-34339-2_4

proposed [2, 6, 22]. However, in a communication environment where only 2PAKE protocols are available, each party must remember many passwords, for each entity with which he may wish to establish a session key corresponds to a password. In detail, assuming that a communication network has n users, in which any two users exchange a key, there will be $n(n-1)/2$ passwords to be shared, and all these passwords must be stored securely. This is unrealistic when the network is relatively large. To solve this problem, three-party PAKE (3PAKE) was proposed. In 3PAKE, each client shares a password with the trusted server, and then two clients will establish a common session key with the help of the server. This solution is very realistic in practical setup, because it provides each client user with the ability to exchange secure keys with all other client users, and each user only needs to remember one password. The 3PAKE protocol can be applied to various electronic applications, such as in the JobSearch International, trusted third parties can help employers and employees to hire on Jobsearch.

In 1995, Steiner et al. proposed the first 3PAKE protocol [26]. Then many works about 3PAKE protocols have been proposed [1, 7, 11, 16, 27]. For a security 3PAKE protocol, there are two types of attacks it should resist: *undetectable on-line password guessing attacks* [10] and *off-line password guessing attacks* [16]. In 1995, Ding and Horster [10] and Sun et al. [27] pointed out that Steiner et al.'s protocol [26] was vulnerable to undetectable on-line password guessing attacks. That is, an adversary can stay un-detected and log into the server during an on-line transaction. In 2000, Lin et al. [16] further pointed out Steiner et al.'s protocols [26] also suffer from off-line password guessing attacks. In this attack, an attacker can guess passwords off-line until getting the correct one. There is another attack: *detectable on-line password guessing attacks*, which requires the participation of the authentication server. In this attack, the server will detect a failed guess and record it. Since after a few unsuccessful guesses, the server can stop any further attempts, this attack is less harmful. In practice, password-based authenticated key exchanges are required to have a property, *forward secrecy*, that when the password is compromised, it does not reveal the earlier established session keys and the updating password.

However, the existed 3PAKE are based on the classic hard problems, such as factoring, the RSA problem, or the computational/decisional DH problem. It is well known that those problems are vulnerable to quantum computers [25]. Since the vigorous development of quantum computers, searching other counterparts based on problems which are believed to be resistant to quantum attacks is more and more urgent. Hence the motivation of this paper is that can we propose a proven security 3PAKE that can resist quantum attacks? Note that lattice-based cryptographic have many advantages such as quantum attacks resistance, asymptotic efficiency, conceptual simplicity and worst-case hardness assumption, and it is a perfect choice to build lattice-based 3PAKE.

Our Contributions. In this paper, we propose a 3PAKE protocol based on the Ring Learning with Errors (RLWE), which in turn is as hard as some lattice problems (SIVP) in the worst case on ideal lattices [20]. Our protocol is designed without extra primitives such as public-key encryption, signature or message authentication code, which usually lead to a high cost for certain applications. By having the 3PAKE as a self-contained system, we show that our protocol directly relys on the hardness of RLWE and Pairing with Errors problem (PWE), which can reduce to the RLWE problem, in the random oracle model. Our protocol RLWE-3PAK resists undetectable on-line passwords guessing attacks and off-line passwords guessing attacks, and enjoys forward secrecy and quantum attacks resistance. Furthermore, our protocol enjoys *mutual authentication*, which means that the users and the server can authenticate one another.

In terms of protocol design, benefitting from the growth of lattice-based key exchange protocols [8,23], we can utilize the key agreement technique to construct our protocol. We use Peikert's [23] reconciliation mechanism to achieve the key agreement in our protocol. At the same time, in order to make our protocol resist undetectable passwords guessing attacks and off-line passwords guessing attacks, we also use additional key reconciliation mechanism between server and clients to realize the mutual authentication. Our security model is modified from Bellare et al.'s model [2,3]. Since the interactions in three-party setting are more complex than that of two-party setting, proving the security of our 3PAKE protocol is a very tricky problem. We use a variant of the Pairing with errors problem [9] to simplify the proof and the proof strategy followed from [21]. Finally, we manage to establish a full proof of security for our protocol and show that our protocol enjoys forward security.

We select concrete choices of parameters and construct a proof-of-concept implementation. The performance results show that our protocol is efficient and practical.

Related Works. In the existed literatures, 3PAKE protocols are based on public/private key cryptography [10,16,26], which usually incur additional computation and communication overheads. Asymmetric key cryptography based protocols [11,15,17] usually require "the ideal cipher model", which is a strong assumption, to prove the security of the protocols. There are some other types of protocols [13,18] which are with no formal security proof.

Lattice-Based AKE or PAKE. Zhang et al. [32] proposed an authenticated RLWE-based key exchange which is similar to HMQV [14]. In 2009, Katz and Vaikuntanathan [12] proposed a CCA-secure lattice-based PAKE, which is proven secure in standard model security. In 2017, Ding et al. [9] proposed RLWE-based PAKE, whose proof is based on random oracle model (ROM), and its implementation is very efficient. Then in 2017, Zhang and Yu [31] proposed a two-round CCA-secure PAKE based on the LWE assumption.

Roadmap. In Sect. 2, we introduce our security model, notations and the Ring Learning with Errors background. Our protocol RLWE-3PAK is in Sect. 3. And in Sect. 4, we give the proof of the protocol's security. The parameter choices and proof-of-concept implementation of our protocol is presented in Sect. 5. Finally, we conclude and discuss some further works in Sect. 6.

2   Preliminaries

2.1   Security Models

The security model is modified from [2] and [3]. The 3PAKE protocol involves three parties, two clients A and B who wish to establish a shared secret session key and a trusted server S who try to help distribute a key to A and B. Let P be a 3PAKE protocol.

Security Game. Given a security parameter κ, an algorithmic game initialized is played between $\mathcal{CH}$ - a challenger, and a probability polynomial time adversary $\mathcal{A}$. For simulating network traffic for the adversary, $\mathcal{CH}$ will essentially run P.

Users and Passwords. There is a fixed set of *users*, which is partitioned into two non-empty sets of *clients* and *servers*. We also assume D is some fixed, non-empty dictionary with size of L. Then before the game starts, a password pw_U is drawn uniformly at random from D and assigned to each *clients* outside of the adversary's view. And for each server S, we set $pw_S := (f(pw_U))_U$, where U runs through all of *clients*. Usually, f is some efficiently computable one-way function (in our protocol we let f be a hash function).

User Instances. We denote some instance i of a *user* U as Π_U^i. The adversary $\mathcal{A}$ controls all the communications that exchange between a fixed number of parties by interacting with a set of Π_U^i oracles. At any point of in time, an client *user* instance Π_U^i may *accept*. When Π_U^i accepts, it holds a *partner-id (PID)* pid_U^i, a *session-id (SID)* sid_U^i, and a *session key (SK)* sk_U^i. The *PID* is the identity of the user that the instance believes talking to, and SK is what the instance aims to compute after the protocol completed. The SID is an identifier and is used to uniquely name the ensuing session. Note that the SID and PID are open to the adversary, and the SK certainly is secret for $\mathcal{A}$.

Oracle Queries. The adversary $\mathcal{A}$ has an endless supply of oracles and it models various queries to them with each query models a capability of $\mathcal{A}$. The oracle queries by the adversary $\mathcal{A}$ are described as follows:

- The **Send**(U, i, M) query allows the adversary to send some message M to oracle Π_U^i of her choice at will. The Π_U^i oracle, upon receiving such a query, will compute what the protocol P says, updates its state, and then returns to $\mathcal{A}$ the response message. If Π_U^i has accepted or terminated, this will be made known to the adversary $\mathcal{A}$. This query is for dealing with controlling the communications by the adversary.
- The **Execute**(A, i, B, j, S, t) query causes P to be executed to completion between two *clients* instances Π_A^i, Π_B^j and a *server* instance Π_S^t, and hands all the execution's transcripts to $\mathcal{A}$. This query is for dealing with off-line password guessing attacks.
- The **Reveal**(U, i) query allows $\mathcal{A}$ to expose session key SK that has been previously accepted. If Π_U^i has accepted and holds some SK, then Π_U^i, upon receiving such a query, will sends SK back to $\mathcal{A}$. This query is for dealing with known-key security, which means that when the session key is lost, it does not reveal the other session keys.

- The **Corrupt**(U) query allows $\mathcal{A}$ to corrupt the user U at will. If U is a *server*, returns $(f(pw_C))_C$ to $\mathcal{A}$, else returns pw_U to $\mathcal{A}$. This query is for dealing with forward secrecy.
- The **Test**(U, i) is a query that does not correspond to $\mathcal{A}$'s abilities. The oracle chooses a bit $b \in \{0, 1\}$ randomly. If Π_U^i has accepted with some SK and is being asked by such a query, then $\mathcal{A}$ is given the actual session key when $b = 1$; $\mathcal{A}$ is given a key chosen uniformly at random when $b = 0$. $\mathcal{A}$ is allowed to query this oracle once and only on a fresh Π_U^i (defined in the following). This query models the semantic security of the session key SK.

Ending the Game. Eventually, the adversary ends the game, and then outputs a single bit b'.

And next we define what constitutes the breaking of the 3PAKE protocol. Firstly we introduce the notions of instance *partnering* and instance *freshness with forward secrecy.*

Definition 1 (Partnering). *Let Π_A^i and Π_B^j be two instances. We shall say that Π_A^i and Π_B^j are partnered if both instances accept, holding $(sk_A^i, sid_A^i, pid_A^i)$ and $(sk_B^j, sid_B^j, pid_B^j)$ respectively, and the followings hold:*

- $sid_A^i = sid_B^j = sid$ *is not null and* $sk_A^i = sk_B^j$ *and* $pid_A^i = B$ *and* $pid_B^j = A$;
- *No instance besides Π_A^i and Π_B^j accepts with a SID of sid.*

Definition 2 (Freshness). *Instance Π_A^i is fs-fresh or it holds a fresh session key at the end of the execution if none of the following events occur:*

- **Reveal**(A, i) *was queried;*
- *a **Reveal**(B, j) was queried where Π_B^j is parted with Π_A^i, if it has one;*
- *before the **Test** query, a **Corrupt**(U) was queried for some user U and a **Send**(A, i, M) query occurs for some string M.*

Password Security. We say the adversary breaks the password security of 3PAKE if he learns the password of a user by either on-line or off-line password guessing attacks.

AKE security. We now define the advantage of the adversary $\mathcal{A}$ against protocol P for the authenticated key exchange (ake). Let $\mathrm{Succ}_P^{ake}(\mathcal{A})$ be the event that the adversary makes a single **Test**(A, i) query directed to some terminated fresh instances Π_A^i, and outputs a bit b' eventually, and $b' = b$ where b is the bit selected in the **Test**(A, i) query. Then $\mathcal{A}$'s advantage is defined as:

$$\mathrm{Adv}_P^{ake}(\mathcal{A}) \stackrel{\text{def}}{=} 2\mathrm{Pr}\left[\mathrm{Succ}_P^{ake}(\mathcal{A})\right] - 1$$

It is easy to verify that

$$\mathrm{Pr}(\mathrm{Succ}_P^{ake}(\mathcal{A})) = \mathrm{Pr}(\mathrm{Succ}_{P'}^{ake}(\mathcal{A})) + \epsilon \Longleftrightarrow \mathrm{Adv}_P^{ake}(\mathcal{A}) = \mathrm{Adv}_{P'}^{ake}(\mathcal{A}) + 2\epsilon.$$

The protocol 3PAKE is AKE-secured if $\mathrm{Adv}_P^{ake}(\mathcal{A})$ is negligible for all probabilistic polynomial time adversaries.

2.2   Notations

Let n be an integer, which is a power of 2. We define the ring of integer polynomials $R := \mathbb{Z}[x]/(x^n+1)$. For any positive integer q, we set $R_q := \mathbb{Z}_q[x]/(x^n+1)$ as the ring of integer polynomials modulo x^n+1, where every coefficient is reduced modulo q. For a polynomial y in R, identify y with its coefficient vector in $\mathbb{Z}$. Let the norm of a polynomial to be the norm of its coefficient vector. Assume χ is a probability distribution over R, then $x \xleftarrow{\$} \chi$ means the coefficients of x are sampled from χ.

For any positive real $\beta \in \mathbb{R}$, we set $\rho_\beta(x) = exp(-\pi\frac{||x||^2}{\beta^2})$ as the Gaussian function, which is scaled by a parameter β. Let $\rho_\beta(\mathbb{Z}^n) = \sum_{\mathbf{x}\in\mathbb{Z}^n} \rho_\beta(\mathbf{x})$. Then for a vector $\mathbf{x} \in \mathbb{Z}^n$, let $D_{\mathbb{Z}^n,\beta}(\mathbf{x}) = \frac{\rho_\beta(\mathbf{x})}{\rho_\beta(\mathbb{Z}^n)}$ to indicate the n-dimensional discrete Gaussian distribution. Usually we denote this distribution as χ_β.

2.3   Ring Learning with Errors

The Learning with Errors (LWE) problem was first introduced by Oded Regev in [24]. He showed that under a quantum reduction, solving LWE problem in the average cases was as hard as solving the worst cases of the certain lattice problems. However since with a large key sizes of $O(n^2)$, LWE based cryptosystems are not efficient for practical applications. In 2010, Lyubashevsky, Peikert, and Regev [20] introduced the version of LWE in the ring setting: the Ring Learning with Errors problem, which could drastically improve the efficiency.

For uniform random elements $a, s \xleftarrow{\$} R_q$ and an error distribution χ, let $A_{s,\chi}$ denote the distribution of the RLWE pair $(a, as+e)$ with the error $e \xleftarrow{\$} \chi$. Then given polynomial number of such samples, the search version of RLWE is to find the secret s, and the decision version of the RLWE problem ($\text{DRLWE}_{q,\chi}$) is to distinguish $A_{s,\chi}$ from an uniform distribution pair on $R_q \times R_q$. RLWE enjoys a worst case hardness guarantee, which we state here.

Theorem 1 ([20], Theorem 3.6). *Let $R = \mathbb{Z}[x]/(x^n+1)$ where n is a power of 2, $\alpha = \alpha(n) < \sqrt{logn/n}$, and $q \equiv 1 \mod 2n$ which is a ploy(n)-bounded prime such that $\alpha q \geq \omega(\sqrt{logn})$. Then there exists a ploy(n)-time quantum reduction from $\tilde{O}(\sqrt{n}/\alpha)$-SIVP (Short Independent Vectors Problem) on ideal lattices in the ring R to solving $\text{DRLWE}_{q,\chi}$ with $l-1$ samples, where $\chi = D_{\mathbb{Z}^n,\beta}$ is the discrete Gaussian distribution with parameter $\beta = \alpha q \cdot (nl/log(nl))^{1/4}$.*

We have the following useful fact.

Lemma 1 ([19], Lemma 4.4). *For any $k > 0$, $\Pr_{x \leftarrow \chi_\beta}(|x| > k\beta) \leq 2e^{-\pi k^2}$.*

Note that taking $k = 6$ gives tail probability approximating 2^{-162}.

Reconciliation Mechanism. We now recall the reconciliation mechanism defined in [23]. This technique is one of the foundations of our protocol.

For an integer p (e.g. $p = 2$) which divides q, define the modular rounding function $\lfloor \cdot \rceil_p : \mathbb{Z}_q \to \mathbb{Z}_p$ as $\lfloor x \rceil_p := \lfloor \frac{p}{q} \cdot x \rceil$ and $\lfloor \cdot \rfloor_p : \mathbb{Z}_q \to \mathbb{Z}_p$ as $\lfloor x \rfloor_p :=$

$\lfloor \frac{p}{q} \cdot x \rfloor$. Let the modulus $q \geq 2$ and be an even, define disjoint intervals $I_0 := \{0, 1, \ldots, \lfloor \frac{q}{4} \rceil - 1\}$, $I_1 := \{-\lfloor \frac{q}{4} \rceil, \ldots, -1\} \bmod q$. Note that when $v \in I_0 \cup I_1$, $\lfloor v \rceil_2 = 0$, and when $v \in (I_0 + \frac{q}{2}) \cup (I_1 + \frac{q}{2})$, $\lfloor v \rceil_2 = 1$. Define the cross-rounding function $\langle \cdot \rangle_2 : \mathbb{Z}_q \to \mathbb{Z}_2$ as $\langle v \rangle_2 := \lfloor \frac{4}{q} \cdot v \rfloor \bmod 2$. Note that $\langle v \rangle_2 = b \in \{0, 1\}$ such that $v \in I_b \cup (\frac{q}{2} + I_b)$;.

Define the set $E := [-\frac{q}{8}, \frac{q}{8}) \cap \mathbb{Z}$. Then suppose v, w are sufficiently close, and given w and $\langle v \rangle_2$, we can recover $\lfloor v \rceil_2$ using the reconciliation function rec: $\mathbb{Z}_q \times \mathbb{Z}_2 \to \mathbb{Z}_2$:

$$\mathrm{rec}(w, b) = \begin{cases} 0 & \text{if } w \in I_b + E (\bmod q), \\ 1 & \text{otherwise.} \end{cases}$$

When q is odd, to avoid the bias produced by the rounding function, Peikert introduced a randomized function dbl(): $\mathbb{Z}_q \to \mathbb{Z}_{2q}$. For $v \in \mathbb{Z}_q$, dbl$(v) := 2v - \bar{e} \in \mathbb{Z}_{2q}$ for some random $\bar{e} \in \mathbb{Z}$ which is independent of v and uniformly random moduloes two. Usually we denote v with an overline to means that $\bar{v} \leftarrow$ dbl(v).

For ease of presentation, we define function HelpRec(X): (1). $\overline{X} \leftarrow$ dbl(X); (2). $W \leftarrow \langle \overline{X} \rangle_2$; $K \leftarrow \lfloor \overline{X} \rceil_2$; (3). return (K, W).

Note that for $w, v \in \mathbb{Z}_q$, we need apply the appropriated rounding function from $\mathbb{Z}_{2q}$ to $\mathbb{Z}_2$, which means that $\lfloor x \rceil_p = \lfloor \frac{p}{2q} \cdot x \rceil$, $\langle x \rangle_2 = \lfloor \frac{4}{2q} \cdot x \rfloor$, and similar with rec function. Obviously, if $(K, W) \leftarrow$ HelpRec(X) and $Y = X + e$ with $||e||_\infty < \frac{q}{8}$, we have rec$(2 \cdot Y, W) = K$. These definitions also can be extended to R_q by applying coefficient-wise to the coefficients in $\mathbb{Z}_q$ of a ring elements. In other words, for a ring element $v = (v_0, \ldots, v_{n-1}) \in R_q$, set $\lfloor v \rceil_2 = (\lfloor v_0 \rceil_2, \ldots, \lfloor v_{n-1} \rceil_2)$; $\langle v \rangle_2 = (\langle v_0 \rangle_2, \ldots, \langle v_{n-1} \rangle_2)$; HelpRec$(v) = ($HelpRec$(v_0), \ldots,$ HelpRec$(v_{n-1}))$. And for a binary-vector $b = (b_0, \ldots, b_{n-1}) \in \{0, 1\}^n$, set rec$(v, b) = (rec(v_0, b_0), \ldots,$ rec$(v_{n-1}, b_{n-1}))$.

Lemma 2 ([23]). *For $q \geq 2$ is even, if v is uniformly random chosen from $\mathbb{Z}_q$, then $\lfloor v \rceil_2$ is uniformly random when given $\langle v \rangle_2$; if $w = v + e \bmod q$ for some $v \in \mathbb{Z}_q$ and $e \in E$, then rec$(w, \langle v \rangle_2) = \lfloor v \rceil_2$. For $q > 2$ is odd, if v is uniformly random chosen from $\mathbb{Z}_q$ and $\bar{v} \leftarrow$ dbl$(v) \in \mathbb{Z}_{2q}$, then $\lfloor \bar{v} \rceil_2$ is uniformly random given $\langle \bar{v} \rangle_2$.*

The PWE Assumption. To prove the security of our protocol, we introduce the Pairing with Errors (PWE) assumption. This assumption is following the work in [9], and we replace the reconciliation mechanism of them by Peikert's version. For any $(a, s) \in R_q^2$, we set $\tau(a, s) := \lfloor \overline{as} \rceil_2$ and if there is $(c, W) \leftarrow$ HelpRec(as), then $\tau(a, s) = c = $ rec$(\overline{as}, W)$. Assume that a PPT adversary $\mathcal{A}$ takes inputs of the form (a_1, a_2, b, W), where $(a_1, a_2, b) \in R_q^3$ and $W \in \{0, 1\}^n$, and outputs a list of values in $\{0, 1\}^n$. $\mathcal{A}$'s objective is to obtain the string $\tau(a_2, s)$ in its output, where s is randomly chosen from R_q, b is a "small additive perturbation" of $a_1 s$, W is $\langle \overline{a_2 s} \rangle_2$. Define

$$\mathrm{Adv}_{R_q}^{\mathrm{PWE}}(\mathcal{A}) \overset{\text{def}}{=} Pr\Big[a_1 \overset{\$}{\leftarrow} R_q; a_2 \overset{\$}{\leftarrow} R_q; s, e \overset{\$}{\leftarrow} \chi_\beta; b \leftarrow a_1 s + e;$$
$$W \leftarrow \langle \overline{a_2 s} \rangle_2 : \tau(a_2, s) \in \mathcal{A}(a_1, a_2, b, W) \Big].$$

Let $\mathrm{Adv}_{R_q}^{\mathrm{PWE}}(t, N) = max_{\mathcal{A}} \left\{ \mathrm{Adv}_{R_q}^{\mathrm{PWE}}(\mathcal{A}) \right\}$, where the maximum is taken over all adversaries times complexity which at most t that output a list containing at most N elements of $\{0, 1\}^n$. Then for t and N polynomial in κ, the PWE assumption states that $\mathrm{Adv}_{R_q}^{\mathrm{PWE}}(t, N)$ is negligible.

To states the hardness of PWE assumption, We define the decision version of PWE problem as follows. If DPWE is hard, so is PWE.

Definition 3 (DPWE). *Given* $(a_1, a_2, b, W, \sigma) \in R_q \times R_q \times R_q \times \{0, 1\}^n \times \{0, 1\}^n$ *where* $W = \langle \overline{K} \rangle_2$ *for some* $K \in R_q$, *where* $\overline{K} \leftarrow \mathrm{dbl}(K)$ *and* $\sigma = \mathrm{rec}(2 \cdot K, W)$. *The Decision Pairing with Errors problem* (DPWE) *is to decide whether* $K = a_2 s + e_1$, $b = a_1 s + e_2$ *for some* s, e_1, e_2 *is drawn from* χ_β, *or* (K, b) *is uniformly random in* $R_q \times R_q$.

In order to show the reduction of the DPWE problem to the RLWE problem, we would like to introduce a definition to what we called the RLWE-DH problem [9] which can reduce to RLWE problem.

Definition 4 (RLWE-DH). *Let* R_q *and* χ_β *be defined as above. Given an input ring element* (a_1, a_2, b, K), *where* (a, X) *is uniformly random in* R_q^2, *The DRLWE-DH problem is to tell if* K *is* $a_2 s + e_1$ *and* $b = a_1 s + e_2$ *for some* $s, e_1, e_2 \xleftarrow{\$} \chi_\beta$ *or* (K, b) *is uniformly random in* $R_q \times R_q$.

Theorem 2 ([9], Theorem 1). *Let* R_q *and* χ_β *be defined as above, then the* RLWE-DH *problem is hard to solve if* RLWE *problem is hard.*

Theorem 3. *Let* R_q *and* χ_β *be defined as above. The* DPWE *problem is hard if the* RLWE-DH *problem is hard.*

Proof. Suppose there exists an algorithm D which can solve the DPWE problem on input (a_1, a_2, b, W, σ) where for some $K \in R_q$, $W = \langle \overline{K} \rangle_2$ and $\sigma = \mathrm{rec}(2 \cdot K, W)$ with non-negligible probability ϵ. By using D as a subroutine, we can build a distinguisher D' on input (a_1', a_2', b', K'), solve the RLWE-DH problem :

- Compute $W = \langle \overline{K'} \rangle$ and $\sigma = \mathrm{rec}(2 \cdot K', W)$.
- Run D using the input $(a_1', a_2', b', W, \sigma)$.
  - If D outputs 1 then K' is $a_2' s + e_1$ for some $e_1 \xleftarrow{\$} \chi_\beta$ and $b' = a_1 s + e_2$ for some $s, e_1 \xleftarrow{\$} \chi_\beta$.
  - Else (K', b') is uniformly random element from $R_q \times R_q$.

Note that if $(a_1', b'), (a_2', K')$ is two RLWE pairs, with input $(a_1', a_2', b', W, \sigma)$ defined above, D outputs 1 with probability ϵ, hence RLWE-DH can be solved with probability ϵ using distinguisher D'. This means that RLWE-DH can be solved with non-negligible advantage, which contradicts RLWE-DH's hardness. $\qquad\square$

3 A New Three-Party Password Authenticated Key Exchange

In this section we introduce a new 3PAKE based on RLWE: RLWE-3PAK. The protocol RLWE-3PAK is given in Fig. 1.

3.1   Description of RLWE-3PAK

Let $q = 2^{\omega(logn)} + 1$ be an odd prime such that $q \equiv 1 \bmod 2n$. Let $a \in R_q$ be a fixed element chosen uniformly at random and given to all users. Let χ_β be a discrete Gaussian distribution with parameter β. Let $H_1 : \{0,1\}^* \mapsto R_q$ be hash function, $H_l : \{0,1\}^* \to \{0,1\}^\kappa$ for $l \in \{2,3,4\}$ be hash functions which is used for verification of communications, and $H_5 : \{0,1\}^* \to \{0,1\}^\kappa$ be a Key Derivation Function (KDF), where κ is the bit-length of the final shared key. We model the hash functions H_l for $l \in \{1,2,3,4,5\}$ as random oracles. We will make use of $\langle \cdot \rangle_2$, $\lfloor \cdot \rceil_2$, HelpRec() and rec() defined in Sect. 2.3.

The function f used to compute client passwords' verifiers for the server is instantiated as: $f(\cdot) = -H_1(\cdot)$. Our protocol which is illustrated in Fig. 1 consists of the following steps:

Client B initiation. Client B sends the identity of A, the one who he wants to communicate with, and his own to S as an initial request. (Note that, this step also can be executed by A.)

Server S first response. Server S receivers B's message, then S chooses $s_f, e_f, s_g, e_g \xleftarrow{\$} \chi_\beta$ to compute $b_A = as_f + e_f$ and $b_B = as_g + e_g$, and computes public elements $m_A = b_A + \gamma'$ and $m_B = b_B + \eta'$ where $\gamma' := -H_1(pw_1)$, $\eta' := -H_1(pw_2)$. Then S sends $\langle m_A, m_B \rangle$ to B.

Client B first response. After receiving S's message, client B checks if $m_A, m_B \in R_q$. If not, aborts; otherwise retrieves $b'_B = m_B + \eta$ where $\eta = H_1(pw_2)$ and chooses $s_B, e_B, e'_B \xleftarrow{\$} \chi_\beta$ to compute $p_B = as_B + e_B$ and $v_1 = b'_B s_B + e'_B$. Then B uses v_1 to compute $(\sigma_B, w_B) \leftarrow$ HelpRec(v_1), and computes $k_{BS} \leftarrow H_2(\langle A, B, S, b'_B, \sigma_B \rangle)$. B sends $\langle m_A, m_B, p_B, k_{BS}, w_B \rangle$ to A.

Client A first response. After receiving B's message, A checks if $m_A, p_B \in R_q$. If not, aborts; otherwise similarly with B, retrieves $b'_A = m_A + \gamma$ where $\gamma = H_1(pw_1)$ and chooses $s_A, e_A, e'_A \xleftarrow{\$} \chi_\beta$ to compute $p_A = as_A + e_A$ and $v_2 = b'_A s_A + e'_A$. Then A uses v_2 to compute $(\sigma_A, w_A) \leftarrow$ HelpRec(v_2), and computes $k_{AS} \leftarrow H_2(\langle A, B, S, b'_A, \sigma_A \rangle)$. Finally A sends $\langle p_A, p_B, k_{AS}, k_{BS}, w_A, w_B \rangle$ to S.

Server S second response. After receiving A's message, S checks if $p_A, p_B \in R_q$. If not, aborts; otherwise computes $\sigma'_A \leftarrow$ rec($2p_A s_f, w_A$) and checks if $k_{AS} = H_2(\langle A, B, S, b_A, \sigma'_A \rangle)$. If not, aborts; otherwise computes $\sigma'_B \leftarrow$ rec($2p_B s_g, w_B$) and checks if $k_{BS} = H_2(\langle A, B, S, b_B, \sigma'_A \rangle)$. If not, aborts; otherwise continues. Then, S samples $s_S, e_1, e_2 \xleftarrow{\$} \chi_\beta$, and computes $c_B = p_A s_S + e_1$ and $c_A = p_B s_S + e_2$ which will be used to retrieve the final messages by A and B. To give the authentication of S to B and A, S computes $k_{SA} \leftarrow H_2(\langle A, B, S, p_B, \sigma'_A \rangle)$ and $k_{SB} \leftarrow H_2(\langle A, B, S, p_A, \sigma'_B \rangle)$. Finally S sends $\langle p_A, c_A, c_B, k_{SA}, k_{SB} \rangle$ to B.

Client B second response. After receiving S's message, B checks if $p_A, c_A, c_B \in R_q$. If not, aborts; otherwise checks if $k_{SB} = H_2(\langle A, B, S, p_A, \sigma_B \rangle)$. If not, aborts; otherwise samples $e''_B \xleftarrow{\$} \chi_\beta$ and computes $v_B = c_B s_B + e''_B$, $(\sigma, w) \leftarrow$ HelpRec(v_B), $k = H_3(\langle A, B, S, m_A, m_B, p_A, p_B, \sigma \rangle)$, $k'' = H_4(\langle A, B, S, m_A, m_B, p_A, p_B, \sigma \rangle)$ and $sk_B = H_5(\langle A, B, S, m_A, m_B, p_A, p_B, \sigma \rangle)$. Finally B sends $\langle c_A, w, k, k_{SA} \rangle$ to A.

Fig. 1. Three-party password authenticated protocol: RLWE-3PAK, where $s_S, e_S, s_f, e_f, s_g, e_g, s_B, e_B, e'_B, e''_B, e_A, e'_A, e_1, e_2$ is sampled from χ_β. Shared session key is $sk = H_5(\langle A, B, S, m_A, m_B, p_A, p_B, \sigma \rangle)$.

Client A second response. After receiving B's message, A checks if $c_A \in R_q$. If not, aborts; otherwise checks if $k_{SA} = H_2(\langle A, B, S, p_B, \sigma_A \rangle)$. If not, aborts; otherwise computes $\sigma' \leftarrow \text{rec}(2c_A s_A, w)$. Then checks if $k = H_3(\langle A, B, S, m_A, m_B, p_A, p_B, \sigma' \rangle)$. If not, aborts; otherwise computes $k' = H_4(\langle A, B, S, m_A, m_B, p_A, p_B, \sigma' \rangle)$ and $sk_A = H_5(\langle A, B, S, m_A, m_B, p_A, p_B, \sigma' \rangle)$. Finally A sends k' to B.

Client B finish. After receiving k' from A, B checks if $k' = k''$. If not, aborts; otherwise terminates.

3.2 Design Rationale

In our protocol, the check for ring elements ensures that all ring operations are valid. The participants are split into clients and servers and servers are allowed to store a password file. By having the server store not pw_1, pw_2, but $\langle \gamma', \eta' \rangle$ allows us to improve the efficiency of the server.

Our 3PAKE may seem a bit complicated, but this is because of the need to provide authentication in the exchange sessions. When we remove all authentication functions, we will find that the main body of the protocol is very simple. In the absence of authentication, party A and party B send p_A and p_B to S, respectively. S computes c_A and c_B by using p_A, p_B and a random value s_S, and sends c_A (resp. c_B) to A (resp. B). Finally, A and B can calculate the same secret key by using the reconciliation mechanism with c_A, c_B and their own secret keys.

In the 3PAKE model, A and B can not authenticate each other, so they need the help of server S to provide the authentication. In our protocol, k_{AS} (k_{BS}) can be viewed as an authentication of A (resp. B) to S. Note that S and A share a password, so *only* A can calculate the corresponding b_A which is set by S, and *only* B can calculate b_B. Meanwhile, *only* A (resp. B) can calculate the same key value σ_A (resp. σ_B) with S through the reconciliation mechanism.

Note that the adversary can not guess the password in a limited number of times, so k_{AS} (or k_{BS}) can not be computed by adversary in a few tries, which makes our protocol resist undetectable on-line password guessing attacks [10]. Finally in order to resist off-line password guessing attacks [16], session values delivered by the server also need to provide authentication of S to A and B, that is why we add k_{SA} and k_{SB} in server's outputs. In the security proof, two types of password guessing attacks is discussed in detail. Note that the final **Client B finish** step may seems redundant, but it is indispensable for the property of forward security [2].

3.3 Correctness

Note that in protocol RLWE-3PAK, if $\text{rec}(2p_A s_f, w_A) = \lfloor \overline{v_2} \rceil_2$, the verification for k_{AS} would be correct. By the definition of the reconciliation mechanism and Lemma 2, we have $\|v_2 - p_A s_f\|_\infty < \frac{q}{8}$ should be satisfied with overwhelming probability. We have

$$v_2 = b_A s_A + e'_A = (as_f + e_f)s_A + e'_A$$
$$= as_f s_A + e_f s_A + e'_A$$

and

$$p_A s_f = as_A s_f + e_A s_f.$$

Hence we need $||v_2 - p_A s_f||_\infty = ||e_f s_A + e'_A - e_A s_f||_\infty < \frac{q}{8}$. Similarly for the verification of k_{BS}, we need $||v_1 - p_B s_g||_\infty = ||e_g s_B + e'_B - e_B s_g||_\infty < \frac{q}{8}$ with overwhelming probability. And to compute the correct key, it needs $\text{rec}(2c_A s_A, w) = \lfloor \overline{v_B} \rceil_2$, which means that $||v_B - c_A s_A||_\infty < \frac{q}{8}$. We have

$$v_B = c_B s_B + e''_B = (p_A s s + e_1)s_B + e''_B$$
$$= as_A s_S s_B + e_A s_S s_B + e_1 s_B + e''_B$$

and

$$c_A s_A = (p_B s_S + e_2)s_A$$
$$= as_A s_B s_S + e_B s_A s_S + e_2 s_A.$$

Therefore, it also needs $||v_B - c_A s_A||_\infty = ||e_A s_B s_S + e_1 s_B + e''_B - e_B s_A s_S - e_2 s_A||_\infty < \frac{q}{8}$ with overwhelming probability.

4 Security for RLWE-3PAK

Here we prove that the RLWE-3PAK protocol is secure, which means that an adversary $\mathcal{A}$ who attacks the system cannot determine the SK of fresh instances with greater advantage than that of an detectable on-line dictionary attack.

Theorem 4. *Let P:=RLWE-3PAK, described in Fig. 1, using ring R_q, and with a password dictionary of size L. Fix an adversary $\mathcal{A}$ that runs in time t, and makes $n_{se}, n_{ex}, n_{re}, n_{co}$ queries of type* **Send, Execute, Reveal, Corrupt,** *respectively. Then for $t' = O(t + (n_{ro} + n_{se} + n_{ex})t_{exp})$:*

$$\text{Adv}_P^{ake\text{-}fs}(\mathcal{A}) = C \cdot n_{se}^s + O\Big(n_{se}\text{Adv}_{R_q}^{\text{PWE}}(t', n_{ro}^2) + \text{Adv}_{R_q}^{\text{DRLWE}}(t', n_{ro})$$
$$+ \frac{(n_{se} + n_{ex})(n_{ro} + n_{se} + n_{ex})}{q^n} + \frac{n_{se}}{2^\kappa}\Big)$$

where $s \in [0.15, 0.30]$ and $C \in [0.001, 0.1]$ are constant CDF-Zipf regression parameters depending on the password space L [29].

The proof of above theorem will proceed by introducing a series of protocols $P_0, P_1, \ldots, P_7$ related to P, with $P_0 = P$. In P_7, the only possible attack for the adversary $\mathcal{A}$ is natural detectable on-line password guessing attacks. Eventually, there are

$$\mathrm{Adv}_{P_0}^{ake} \leq \mathrm{Adv}_{P_1}^{ake} + \epsilon_1 \leq \cdots \leq \mathrm{Adv}_{P_7}^{ake} + \epsilon_7$$

where $\epsilon_1, \ldots, \epsilon_7$ are negligible values in k. Together with above relations, our result is given by computing the success probability of detectable on-line attack in P_7 in the end of the proof. Due to the limitation of the space, we give a informal description of protocols $P_0, P_1, \ldots, P_7$ in Fig. 2, and given the proof sketches of negligible advantage gain from P_{i-1} to P_i in Fig. 3. The full proof of Theorem 4 is given in the full version of this paper in ePrint.

Let **correctpw** be the event that the adversary make a correct guess of password by detectable on-line passwords attacks. In most existing PAKE studies, passwords are assumed to follow a uniformly random distribution, and $\Pr(\mathbf{correctpw}) \leq \frac{n_{se}}{L} + negl(\kappa)$, where L is the size of the password dictionary, n_{se} is the max number of $\mathcal{A}$'s active on-line password guessing attempts before a **Corrupt** query and $negl()$ is a negligible function. Ding Wang and Ping Wang [29] introduced CDF-Zipf model and in this model $\Pr(\mathbf{correctpw}) \leq C \cdot n_{se}^s + negl(\kappa)$ for the Zipf parameters C and s which is depended on the password space L. CDF-Zipf model is more consistent with the real world attacks than traditional formulation. For example, when considering trawling guessing attacks, the actual advantage will be 6.84% when $n_{se} = 10^2$, and 12.45% when $n_{se} = 10^3$ [28], but the traditional formulation greatly underestimate Advantage to be 0.01% when $n_{se} = 10^2$, and 0.10% when $n_{se} = 10^3$. When further considering targeted guessing attacks (in which the adversary makes use of the target users personal information), advantage will be about 20% when $n_{se} = 10^2$, 25% when $n_{se} = 10^3$, and 50% when $n_{se} = 10^6$ [30]. So we prefer this model in our analysis.

5 Concrete Parameters and Implementation of RLWE-3PAK

In this section, we present our choices of parameters and outline the performance of our RLWE-3PAK.

Here we use the fact of the product of two Gaussian distributed random values that are stated in [32]. Let $x, y \in R$ be two polynomials with degree of n, and the coefficients of x and y are distributed according to discrete Gaussian distribution with parameter β_x, β_y, respectively. Then the individual coefficients of the polynomial xy are approximately normally distributed around zero with parameter $\beta_x \beta_y \sqrt{n}$. Hence for $||v_B - c_A s_A||_\infty = ||e_A s_B s_S + e_1 s_B + e''_B - e_B s_A s_S - e_2 s_A||_\infty < \frac{q}{8}$, by applying Lemma 1 we have that $||v_B - c_A s_A||_\infty > 6\sqrt{2n^2\beta^6 + 2n\beta^4 + \beta^2}$ with probability approximating 2^{-162}. Hence we set $6\sqrt{2n^2\beta^6 + 2n\beta^4 + \beta^2} < \frac{q}{8}$, then the two clients will end with the same key with overwhelming probability. And such choices of parameter also make $||v_2 - p_A s_f||_\infty < \frac{q}{8}$ and $||v_1 - p_B s_g||_\infty < \frac{q}{8}$ with overwhelming probability be satisfied.

P_0 The original protocol P.

P_1 The hash function H_1's outputs are no longer a randomly chosen element γ in R_q, but a ring element $\gamma = as + e \in R_q$, where s, e is sampled from χ_β.

P_2 The honest parties randomly choose m_A, m_B, p_A or p_B values which are seen previously in the execution, the protocol halts and the adversary fails.

P_3 The protocol answers **Send** and **Execute** queries without using any random oracle queries. Subsequent random oracle queries made by A are backpatched, as much as possible, to be consistent with the responses to the **Send** and **Execute** queries. (This is a standard technique for proofs involving random oracles.)

P_4 If an $H_l(\cdot)$ query is made, for $l \in \{3, 4, 5\}$, it is not checked for consistency against **Execute** queries. That means instead of backpatching to maintain consistency with an **Execute** query, the protocol responds with a random output.

P_5 If before a **Corrput** query, a correct shared secret key guess is made against client A or B (This can be determined by an $H_l(\cdot)$ query, for $l \in \{3, 4, 5\}$, using the correct inputs to compute k, k' or session key), the protocol halts and the adversary automatically succeeds.

P_6 If the adversary makes a shared secret key guess against two partnered clients, the protocol halts and the adversary fails.

P_7 The protocol uses an internal password oracle, which holds all passwords and be used to exam the correctness of a given password. Such an oracle aims at the password security. (It also accepts **Corrupt**(U) queries, which returns $(f(pw_C)))_C$ if U is an server and otherwise returns pw_U to A).

Fig. 2. Informal description of protocols $P_0, P_1, \ldots, P_7$

$P_0 \rightarrow P_1$ Unless the decision version of RLWE is solved with non-negligible advantage, theses two protocols are indistinguishable.

$P_1 \rightarrow P_2$ This is straightforward.

$P_2 \rightarrow P_3$ By inspection, the two protocols are indistinguishable unless the decision version of RLWE is solved with non-negligible advantage or the adversary makes an **Client A second response** (resp. **Client B finish.**) query with a k (resp. k') value that is not the output of an $H_3(\cdot)$ (resp. $H_4(\cdot)$) query that would be a correct shared secret key guess. However, the probability of these is negligible.

$P_3 \rightarrow P_4$ This can be shown using a standard reduction from PWE. On input $(a, X, Y = as_y + e_y, W)$, where s_y, e_y are unknown, we plug in Y added by random RLWE pair for client B' p_B values, and X added by random RLWE pair for server' c_B values. Then from a correct $H_l(\cdot)$ guess for $l \in \{3, 4, 5\}$, we can compute $\tau(X, s_y)$.

$P_4 \rightarrow P_5$ This is obvious.

$P_5 \rightarrow P_6$ This can be shown using a standard reduction from PWE, similar to the one for **Execute** queries. On input $(a, X, Y = as_y + e_y, W)$, where s_y, e_y are unknown, we plug in Y for client A' p_A values, and X added by random RLWE pair for server' c_A values. Then from a correct $H_l(\cdot)$ guess for $l \in \{3, 4, 5\}$, we can compute $\tau(X, s_y)$.

$P_6 \rightarrow P_7$ By inspection, there two protocols are indistinguishable. Finally, in P_7, the adversary success only if he breaks the password security or makes a correct shared secret key guess. We show these happens with negligible abilities by using a standard reduction from PWE.

Fig. 3. Proof sketches of negligible advantage gain from P_{i-1} to P_i

We take $n = 1024$, $\beta = 8$ and $q = 2^{32} - 1$. Our implementations are written in C without any parallel computations or multi-thread programming techniques. The program is run on a 3.5 GHz Intel(R) Core(IM) i7-4770K CPU and 4 GB RAM computer running on Ubuntu 16.04.1 64 bit system. The timings for server and clients actions of the authentication protocol are presented in Table 1.

Table 1. Timings of proof-of-concept implementations in ms

B initiation	S first response	B first response	A first response
<0.001 ms	0.165 ms	1.960 ms	1.779 ms
S second response	B second response	A second response	B finish
2.030 ms	2.195 ms	2.088 ms	<0.001 ms

Sampling and multiplication operations are the mainly time cost. The sampling technique used in our protocol is the same with [5], which use the Discrete Gaussian to approximate the continuous Gaussian. And to improve performance, we have used multiplication with FFT. Note that by the proof of concept implementation, our protocol can be very efficient.

6   Conclusion

In this paper, we propose a 3PAKE protocol based on RLWE: RLWE-3PAK. We provide a full proof of security of our protocol in the random oracle model. Finally, we construct a proof-of-concept implementation to examine the efficiency of our protocol. The performance results indicate that our protocol is very efficient and practical. Since some literature [4] show that it is delicate to prove quantum resistance with random oracle. It is meaningful to design an efficient 3PAKE protocol without random oracle heuristics in the future.

Acknowledgments. This article is supported by The National Key Research and Development Program of China (Grant No. 2017YFA0303903), National Cryptography Development Fund (No. MMJJ20170121), and Zhejiang Province Key R&D Project (No. 2017C01062). Authors thank Aijun Ge for discussions and the anonymous ISPEC'19 reviewers for helpful comments.

References

1. Abdalla, M., Fouque, P.-A., Pointcheval, D.: Password-based authenticated key exchange in the three-party setting. In: Vaudenay, S. (ed.) PKC 2005. LNCS, vol. 3386, pp. 65–84. Springer, Heidelberg (2005). https://doi.org/10.1007/978-3-540-30580-4_6
2. Bellare, M., Pointcheval, D., Rogaway, P.: Authenticated key exchange secure against dictionary attacks. In: Preneel, B. (ed.) EUROCRYPT 2000. LNCS, vol. 1807, pp. 139–155. Springer, Heidelberg (2000). https://doi.org/10.1007/3-540-45539-6_11

3. Bellare, M., Rogaway, P.: Provably secure session key distribution: the three party case. In: Proceedings of the Twenty-Seventh Annual ACM Symposium on Theory of Computing, Las Vegas, Nevada, USA, 29 May–1 June 1995, pp. 57–66 (1995)
4. Boneh, D., Dagdelen, Ö., Fischlin, M., Lehmann, A., Schaffner, C., Zhandry, M.: Random oracles in a quantum world. In: Lee, D.H., Wang, X. (eds.) ASIACRYPT 2011. LNCS, vol. 7073, pp. 41–69. Springer, Heidelberg (2011). https://doi.org/10.1007/978-3-642-25385-0_3
5. Bos, J.W., Costello, C., Naehrig, M., Stebila, D.: Post-quantum key exchange for the TLS protocol from the ring learning with errors problem. In: 2015 IEEE Symposium on Security and Privacy, SP 2015, San Jose, CA, USA, 17–21 May 2015, pp. 553–570 (2015)
6. Boyko, V., MacKenzie, P., Patel, S.: Provably secure password-authenticated key exchange using Diffie-Hellman. In: Preneel, B. (ed.) EUROCRYPT 2000. LNCS, vol. 1807, pp. 156–171. Springer, Heidelberg (2000). https://doi.org/10.1007/3-540-45539-6_12
7. Chang, T.Y., Hwang, M., Yang, W.: A communication-efficient three-party password authenticated key exchange protocol. Inf. Sci. **181**(1), 217–226 (2011)
8. Ding, J.: A simple provably secure key exchange scheme based on the learning with errors problem. IACR Cryptology ePrint Archive 2012, 688 (2012). http://eprint.iacr.org/2012/688
9. Ding, J., Alsayigh, S., Lancrenon, J., RV, S., Snook, M.: Provably secure password authenticated key exchange based on RLWE for the post-quantum world. In: Handschuh, H. (ed.) CT-RSA 2017. LNCS, vol. 10159, pp. 183–204. Springer, Cham (2017). https://doi.org/10.1007/978-3-319-52153-4_11
10. Ding, Y., Horster, P.: Undetectable on-line password guessing attacks. Oper. Syst. Rev. **29**(4), 77–86 (1995)
11. Dongna, E., Cheng, Q., Ma, C.: Password authenticated key exchange based on RSA in the three-party settings. In: Pieprzyk, J., Zhang, F. (eds.) ProvSec 2009. LNCS, vol. 5848, pp. 168–182. Springer, Heidelberg (2009). https://doi.org/10.1007/978-3-642-04642-1_15
12. Katz, J., Vaikuntanathan, V.: Smooth projective hashing and password-based authenticated key exchange from lattices. In: Matsui, M. (ed.) ASIACRYPT 2009. LNCS, vol. 5912, pp. 636–652. Springer, Heidelberg (2009). https://doi.org/10.1007/978-3-642-10366-7_37
13. Kim, H.S., Choi, J.: Enhanced password-based simple three-party key exchange protocol. Comput. Electr. Eng. **35**(1), 107–114 (2009)
14. Krawczyk, H.: HMQV: a high-performance secure Diffie-Hellman protocol. In: Shoup, V. (ed.) CRYPTO 2005. LNCS, vol. 3621, pp. 546–566. Springer, Heidelberg (2005). https://doi.org/10.1007/11535218_33
15. Lee, T., Hwang, T., Lin, C.: Enhanced three-party encrypted key exchange without server public keys. Comput. Secur. **23**(7), 571–577 (2004)
16. Lin, C., Sun, H., Hwang, T.: Three-party encrypted key exchange: attacks and a solution. Oper. Syst. Rev. **34**(4), 12–20 (2000)
17. Lin, C., Sun, H., Steiner, M., Hwang, T.: Three-party encrypted key exchange without server public-keys. IEEE Commun. Lett. **5**(12), 497–499 (2001)
18. Lu, R., Cao, Z.: Simple three-party key exchange protocol. Comput. Secur. **26**(1), 94–97 (2007)
19. Lyubashevsky, V.: Lattice signatures without trapdoors. IACR Cryptology ePrint Archive 2011, 537 (2011). http://eprint.iacr.org/2011/537

20. Lyubashevsky, V., Peikert, C., Regev, O.: On ideal lattices and learning with errors over rings. In: Gilbert, H. (ed.) EUROCRYPT 2010. LNCS, vol. 6110, pp. 1–23. Springer, Heidelberg (2010). https://doi.org/10.1007/978-3-642-13190-5_1
21. MacKenzie, P.: The PAK suite: protocols for password-authenticated key exchange. In: DIMACS Technical Report 2002–46, p. 7 (2002)
22. MacKenzie, P., Patel, S., Swaminathan, R.: Password-authenticated key exchange based on RSA. In: Okamoto, T. (ed.) ASIACRYPT 2000. LNCS, vol. 1976, pp. 599–613. Springer, Heidelberg (2000). https://doi.org/10.1007/3-540-44448-3_46
23. Peikert, C.: Lattice cryptography for the internet. In: Mosca, M. (ed.) PQCrypto 2014. LNCS, vol. 8772, pp. 197–219. Springer, Cham (2014). https://doi.org/10.1007/978-3-319-11659-4_12
24. Regev, O.: On lattices, learning with errors, random linear codes, and cryptography. J. ACM 56(6), 34:1–34:40 (2009)
25. Shor, P.W.: Polynomial-time algorithms for prime factorization and discrete logarithms on a quantum computer. SIAM J. Comput. 26(5), 1484–1509 (1997)
26. Steiner, M., Tsudik, G., Waidner, M.: Refinement and extension of encrypted key exchange. Oper. Syst. Rev. 29(3), 22–30 (1995)
27. Sun, H., Chen, B., Hwang, T.: Secure key agreement protocols for three-party against guessing attacks. J. Syst. Softw. 75(1–2), 63–68 (2005)
28. Wang, D., Jian, G., Wang, P.: Zipf's law in passwords. IACR Cryptology ePrint Archive 2014, 631 (2014). http://eprint.iacr.org/2014/631
29. Wang, D., Wang, P.: On the implications of Zipf's law in passwords. In: Askoxylakis, I., Ioannidis, S., Katsikas, S., Meadows, C. (eds.) ESORICS 2016. LNCS, vol. 9878, pp. 111–131. Springer, Cham (2016). https://doi.org/10.1007/978-3-319-45744-4_6
30. Wang, D., Zhang, Z., Wang, P., Yan, J., Huang, X.: Targeted online password guessing: an underestimated threat. In: Proceedings of the 2016 ACM SIGSAC Conference on Computer and Communications Security, Vienna, Austria, 24–28 October 2016, pp. 1242–1254 (2016)
31. Zhang, J., Yu, Y.: Two-round PAKE from approximate SPH and instantiations from lattices. In: Takagi, T., Peyrin, T. (eds.) ASIACRYPT 2017. LNCS, vol. 10626, pp. 37–67. Springer, Cham (2017). https://doi.org/10.1007/978-3-319-70700-6_2
32. Zhang, J., Zhang, Z., Ding, J., Snook, M., Dagdelen, Ö.: Authenticated key exchange from ideal lattices. In: Oswald, E., Fischlin, M. (eds.) EUROCRYPT 2015. LNCS, vol. 9057, pp. 719–751. Springer, Heidelberg (2015). https://doi.org/10.1007/978-3-662-46803-6_24

System and Network Security

KMO: Kernel Memory Observer to Identify Memory Corruption by Secret Inspection Mechanism

Hiroki Kuzuno[1,2]([⊠]) and Toshihiro Yamauchi[1]

[1] Graduate School of Natural Science and Technology, Okayama University, Okayama, Japan
kuzuno@s.okayama-u.ac.jp, yamauchi@cs.okayama-u.ac.jp
[2] Intelligent Systems Laboratory, SECOM CO., LTD., Tokyo, Japan

Abstract. Kernel vulnerability attacks may allow attackers to execute arbitrary program code and achieve privilege escalation through credential overwriting, thereby avoiding security features. Major Linux protection methods include Kernel Address Space Layout Randomization, Control Flow Integrity, and Kernel Page Table Isolation. All of these mitigate kernel vulnerability affects and actual attacks. In addition, the No eXecute bit, Supervisor Mode Access Prevention, and Supervisor Mode Execution Prevention are CPU features for managing access permission and data execution in virtual memory. Although combinations of these methods can reduce the attack availability of kernel vulnerability based on the interaction between the user and kernel modes, kernel virtual memory corruption is still possible (e.g., the eBPF vulnerability executes the attack code only in the kernel mode).

To monitor kernel virtual memory, we present the Kernel Memory Observer (KMO), which has a secret inspection mechanism and offers an alternative design for virtual memory. It allows the detection of illegal data manipulation/writing in the kernel virtual memory. KMO identifies the kernel virtual memory corruption, monitors system call arguments, and enables unmapping from the direct mapping area. An evaluation of our method indicates that it can detect the actual kernel vulnerabilities leading to kernel virtual memory corruption. In addition, the results show that the overhead is $0.038\,\mu s$ to $2.505\,\mu s$ in terms of system call latency, and the application benchmark is $371.0\,\mu s$ to $1,990.0\,\mu s$ for 100,000 HTTP accesses.

1 Introduction

Security studies have focused on kernel vulnerability, which is a significant security risk [1,2]. Countermeasures against such vulnerabilities must be developed to prevent adversaries from exploiting it in their attack scenarios.

Many kernel attacks aim to achieve privilege escalation. The adversary switches to the root account from a non-privileged user account by exploiting kernel vulnerabilities to override the credential information in the kernel virtual memory.

© Springer Nature Switzerland AG 2019
S.-H. Heng and J. Lopez (Eds.): ISPEC 2019, LNCS 11879, pp. 75–94, 2019.
https://doi.org/10.1007/978-3-030-34339-2_5

The operating system (OS) provides two features that act as countermeasures. One is a mandatory access control (MAC) mechanism (e.g., SELinux [3]), whereas the other is a capability [4]. Both features can prevent full control over OS features in case an adversary gains access to the root user account. Monitoring the return address on the stack is one method to detect kernel memory corruption [5]. Kernel Address Space Layout Randomization (KASLR) provides randomized kernel functions and data addresses in the kernel virtual memory to prevent the identification of the positions of vulnerable functions [6]. In addition, Control Flow Integrity (CFI) additionally imposes call and return relationships for kernel function validation to prevent the injection of malicious code [7].

Mechanisms for controlling access to virtual memory are already present in the CPU. The No eXecute bit (NX bit) manages the execution permission of a code in virtual memory. Supervisor Mode Access Prevention (SMAP) prevents access to user mode data, while Supervisor Mode Execution Prevention (SMEP) prevents the code execution of the user memory region in virtual memory at the supervisor mode [8]. Meltdown vulnerability exposes kernel functions and data virtual addresses to side channel attacks. Therefore, Kernel Page Table Isolation (KPTI) has been proposed as a means of isolating the virtual address space between the user mode and the kernel modes in Linux [9].

These countermeasures complicate the attack availability of kernel vulnerabilities based on the interaction between the user and kernel modes. Moreover, these methods restrict root privilege features to minimize damage to the OS environment in the event of a successful attack. However, these methods cannot prevent attacks that exploit kernel vulnerabilities in the kernel mode alone [10–13]. By executing a kernel exploit code in the kernel mode, the adversary can avoid various security countermeasures to override the security feature functions in the kernel virtual memory (e.g., some kernel exploits disable SELinux via memory corruption [14,15]).

In the present study, we designed a security mechanism, the Kernel Memory Observer (KMO) which can detect illegal data manipulation of the kernel virtual memory, and which could result in security features being defeated. KMO provides a secret inspection mechanism and creates an alternative kernel virtual memory as a secret virtual memory to protect the original kernel virtual memory. The kernel has one virtual memory at KPTI implementation. The design of KMO is such that the kernel virtual memory is completely separated; its secrecy can be maintained, and it is responsible for kernel monitoring code execution and valid data storing.

More specifically, KMO includes a switching function that changes the kernel virtual memory space to the secret virtual memory space at various timings during monitoring. The goal is to prevent two scenarios: (i) system call arguments containing invalid parameters that lead to suspicious code injection targeting kernel vulnerability, and (ii) overwriting of the kernel virtual memory by a kernel vulnerability attack that involves a modification of KMO monitoring code and valid data. Therefore, KMO achieves the identification of kernel virtual memory corruption.

In addition, the kernel virtual memory management adopts a direct mapping region that contains physical memory for effective allocation or collection. KMO forces the unmapping of the secret virtual memory and monitors valid data from direct mapping on the kernel virtual memory. It prevents the modification of this information through direct mapping.

The main contributions of this study are as follows:

- We design a novel security architecture, KMO, that provides a secret virtual memory that is used to monitor the kernel virtual memory. KMO supports three switching patterns between the secret virtual memory and the kernel virtual memory, while the unmapping method provides protection from direct mapping. Despite kernel protection being studied in multiple studies, there has been no study dealing with the monitoring of a kernel virtual memory at the kernel level. This approach offers the advantage of enhanced safety for kernel security features without virtualization. Moreover, we can apply it to the OS on a bare machine and to a guest OS on a virtual machine, thereby combining the features of existing security mechanisms.
- We implement KMO on the latest Linux kernel with KPTI. We also evaluate its detection capability with regard to eBPF kernel vulnerability [13] and the illegal kernel modules that corrupt the kernel virtual memory to bypass the security feature. An evaluation of KMO revealed that its overhead is $0.038\,\mu s$ to $2.505\,\mu s$ in terms of each system call round time, whereas the application overhead is $371.0\,\mu s$ $1,990.0\,\mu s$ for each switching pattern for 100,000 HyperText Transfer Protocol (HTTP) accesses.

2 Background

2.1 Separation of Virtual Memory

Kernel and user processes share virtual memory to enable high-speed management. Virtual memory access control relies on the protection of the privilege level in the kernel and the CPU. A meltdown attack overcomes this protection, and a user process can then easily access the kernel virtual memory through a combination of out-of-order, exception, and cache latency.

One countermeasure against a meltdown attack involves the separation of the virtual memory used for the kernel and user modes. The OS automatically changes the virtual memory at any privilege level transition from user mode to kernel mode. The user-mode virtual memory only has a small amount of kernel code that switches to the virtual memory to minimize the access range of any meltdown attack. The separation method in Linux is KPTI [9]; other OSs are equipped with similar mechanisms [16].

2.2 Kernel Vulnerability Attack

An adversary can exploit several types of kernel vulnerability [1] and exploitation techniques [17] to achieve privilege escalation. Malicious programs overwrite the credential variable in the kernel virtual memory to gain the root privilege.

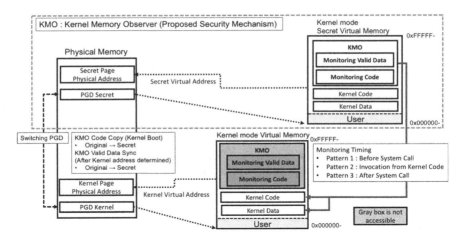

Fig. 1. Overview of monitoring on the secret virtual memory space.

The OS adopts privilege level management to protect the kernel code or data in the kernel virtual memory from the user mode, while KASLR/CFI reduces the success of kernel exploitation attacks, and SMAP/SMEP restricts the kernel mode execution of a malicious code in the user virtual memory. Nevertheless, some kernel vulnerabilities (e.g., the eBPF vulnerability [13]) are still available, whereby the directory allocates a malicious code to the kernel virtual memory through kernel vulnerability.

2.3   Threat Model

We postulate herein that a threat model (i.e., an adversary) exploits kernel vulnerability in only the kernel mode. It first attempts to avoid the security features to gain full administrator capability. Moreover, the adversary changes the Linux Security Modules (LSM) hook function pointer variable to disable MAC in Linux. After that, the adversary achieves privilege escalation in the OS. We ensure that overwriting of the kernel virtual memory space occurs only in the kernel vulnerability target memory region that includes the security feature functions pointer, kernel module management data, and a direct mapping region. In addition, we assume that the BIOS, MMU, TLB, and other hardware are safe.

3   KMO Design

We devised KMO (Fig. 1) to establish a secret virtual memory in the kernel mode. This is used to monitor the kernel virtual memory. It is established at a different location from the latest kernel (e.g., Linux with KPTI), and KMO's kernel has two kernel virtual memories (i.e., original and secret).

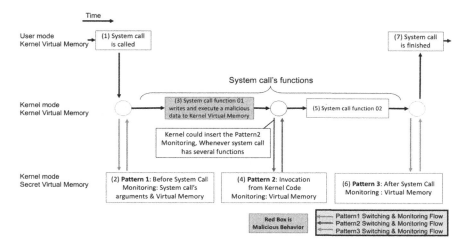

Fig. 2. Virtual memory switching patterns 1, 2, and 3

3.1 Design Goal

The goal of KMO is to monitor the kernel security feature code and data on the kernel virtual memory, then KMO detects the invalid overwriting of these memory regions.

The kernel virtual memory allows reading, writing, and execution in the kernel mode, but not in the user mode. The latest kernel (e.g., Linux with KPTI), that enables the isolation of virtual memories has the user and the kernel virtual memory. The kernel automatically switches both virtual memories during privilege transitions between the user mode and kernel modes. The kernel still provides one virtual memory space that is available for the various features at the kernel layer. Therefore, kernel memory corruption occurs only when the kernel code is running in kernel mode.

KMO creates a secret virtual memory space isolated from the original kernel virtual memory. The kernel virtual memory separation ensures that access violation is impossible as KMO places the valid monitoring valid data and the monitoring code on the secret virtual memory, which is not affected by corruption on the kernel virtual memory. KMO makes the valid monitoring data from an original kernel code and data that contain benign information at the kernel boot. KMO executes the monitoring code on the secret virtual memory. It checks the kernel code and data for modification by comparing them with the valid monitoring data.

3.2 Switching Patterns and Detection Capability

KMO adopts three virtual memory switching patterns depending on the kernel process transition between the user and kernel modes (Fig. 2).

Pattern 1: **Inspection point undertaken before the system call execution.** Pattern 1 involves inspecting suspicious data input at the system call argument before the adversary can execute a malicious code using the kernel vulnerability.

Pattern 2: **Inspection points during system call function or kernel code processing.** Pattern 2 inspects the kernel code and data in the kernel virtual memory. There may be inspection points having multiple functions during a system call having multiple functions. Pattern 2 involves the direct detection of memory corruption in the kernel virtual memory for any timing during the kernel function flow.

Pattern 3: **Inspection point undertaken after the system call execution.** Pattern 3 inspects the kernel code and data in the kernel virtual memory. It reliably detects memory corruption after an attack completes a system call execution.

Therefore, KMO automatically switches and combines multiple inspection points from every pattern for system call invocation. Although it is effective in detecting kernel memory corruption and attacks, the number of inspections results in a significant overhead. We examined the attacks on our mechanism to identify suitable inspection points in a running system.

Upon identifying the attack, the kernel handles the interruption of system calls by returning the error number to the user process. Additionally, we regard the kernel as being available to fix the modified memory region.

3.3   Design Approach

KMO overcomes three challenges facing the monitoring of kernel virtual memory in kernel mode.

Challenge 1: **Monitoring code has access permission for monitored data and will be executed in the secret virtual memory.** KMO has three virtual memory switching patterns with different inspection points on a running kernel. The timing at which memory corruption is detected is also different for each switching pattern. It efficiently monitors the already implemented kernel security feature and the module space in kernel virtual memory to detect memory corruption attacks.

For virtual memory switching, KMO writes the physical address of the multiple-page table of the secret virtual memory into a specific register (i.e., CR3 register points to the page table for x86_64). The monitoring code runs in the secret virtual memory space. After monitoring, the KMO writes the physical address of the original kernel virtual memory into a specific register (i.e., the CR3 register for x86_64), and then resumes the processing of the kernel code before the switching event occurs.

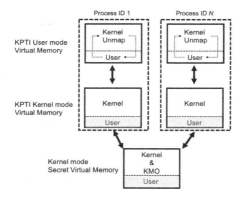

Fig. 3. Overview of secret virtual memory space for a Linux kernel

Challenge 2: **Kernel code cannot access the secret virtual memory space.**
KMO fully copies the secret memory space from the original one, such that both memory spaces have the same kernel code, kernel data, monitoring code, and monitoring data. The monitoring code and valid data that are not accessed through the page table flag management for the original kernel virtual memory. Therefore, in kernel mode, the virtual memory is completely isolated in KMO, ensuring that the kernel code acts on the original kernel virtual memory space using its virtual addresses. This ensures that the monitored kernel code cannot access the kernel mode secret virtual memory.

Challenge 3: **Monitoring code and valid data are not affected through a direct mapping space.** The kernel virtual memory management provides a direct mapping space containing the physical memory for effective page-based memory allocation and collection. KMO shares the physical memory between the kernel and the secret virtual memory, leading to the possibility of it being abused by allowing direct access to the monitoring code and valid data.
To exclude the monitoring code and valid data from the direct mapping of the kernel virtual memory, KMO forces the unmapping of these in kernel virtual memory.

4   KMO Implementation

We implemented KMO on Linux as the target OS and x86_64 as the CPU architecture.

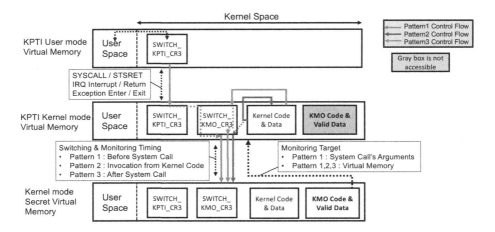

Fig. 4. Virtual memory space switching on a Linux kernel

4.1 Secret Virtual Memory Space Management

KMO can monitor the kernel virtual memory (Fig. 3). The latest Linux kernel has the KPTI feature, which already provides two virtual memory spaces for each process.

For the kernel, the **pgd** variable of **init_mm** in **mm_struct** points to the physical memory address of the kernel virtual memory. KMO creates an additional virtual memory space on the kernel whose physical address is a 4 page (16 KB on x86_64) logical conjunction from the **pgd** variable of the **init_mm**. Moreover, the kernel code and data are duplicated from the **pgd** variable. KMO uses the physical address of the created virtual memory to switch from the kernel virtual memory to the monitoring of each process in the kernel mode.

4.2 Switching of the Virtual Memory Space

We implemented KMO to provide a switching mechanism for the secret virtual memory space of the kernel mode (Fig. 4).

In user mode, Interrupt (SYSCALL, IRQ) and Exception are triggered for the transition to kernel mode. It calls the SWITCH_KPTI_CR3 function on the virtual memory of the user and then changes to the kernel virtual memory space.

In kernel mode, KMO fulfills **challenge 1**, that the kernel calls the SWITCH_KMO_CR3 function, which calculates a 4-page offset to the physical address of the secret virtual memory space from the **pgd** variable of **init_mm**. The kernel writes its value to the CR3 register, followed by automatically switching the virtual memory space for monitoring. After the monitoring process, the SWITCH_KMO_CR3 function writes the physical address of the **pgd** variable in the **active_mm** of the **current** (**task_struct**) variable to the CR3 register, which can change the virtual memory space for the currently running process in kernel mode. The kernel then calls SWITCH_KPTI_CR3 to change the virtual

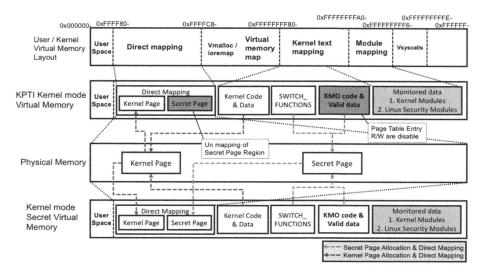

Fig. 5. Position and unmapped region for the virtual memory space on Linux x86_64.

memory space for the user, and the mode changes to user mode via an interrupt (SYSRET Interrupt return) or exception (Exception exit).

KMO currently uses TLB flush after the CR3 register writing. This clears the converting of caches between the virtual and physical addresses.

4.3 Monitoring of Virtual Memory Space

KMO has almost the same virtual memory space layout on Linux x86_64 (Fig. 5). KMO monitors the `security_hook_list` variable for LSM on the kernel text mapping and the module list variable `modules` in the kernel virtual memory. Additionally, KMO disables Copy on Write of the monitored data, whereas it supports targeted kernel space reading after virtual memory switching. KMO fulfills **challenge 2**, that both monitoring code and valid data have a designed flag setting that does not accept reading and writing at the supervisor level on the Page Table Entry.

KMO keeps the secret virtual memory space in the kernel boot sequence and then starts the monitoring feature according to the following sequence.

1. The `mm_init` function initializes the kernel virtual memory, whereas the `kaiser_init` function initializes the virtual memory for the user on the kernel boot sequence.
2. KMO initializes the secret virtual memory in physical memory.
3. The `security_init` function initializes the MAC mechanism.
4. The `load_default_modules` function executes the module reading process on the kernel.
5. KMO duplicates the valid monitoring data between the secret and kernel virtual memory spaces.
6. KMO starts the monitoring feature in the secret virtual memory space.

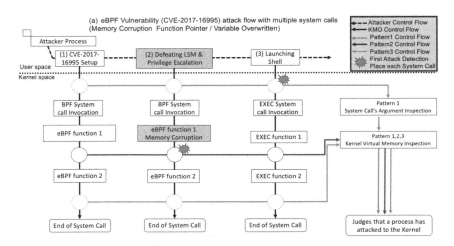

Fig. 6. Monitoring attacker process using the secret virtual memory space on Linux.

4.4   Direct Mapping Management

Linux 4.4 (x86_64) has a direct mapping space of 64 TB. Therefore, the machine physical memory is mapped to a space of less than 64 TB, and the kernel manages physical page allocation using direct mapping. Thus, it is possible to access the kernel code and the data virtual and direct mapping virtual addresses.

Linux uses the `init_mem_mapping` function to create the virtual memory direct mapping space. The `kernel_physical_mapping_init` function then maps the physical address to virtual memory. KMO covers **challenge 3**, that KMO uses the `remove_pagetable` function for unmapping secret pages of the monitoring code and data from the direct mapping space in the kernel virtual memory after establishing a secret virtual memory setup (Fig. 5). Any access to the unmapped pages occurs through a page fault. Subsequently, the kernel handles panic processing.

4.5   Kernel Vulnerability Attacking Case

In one of the kernel vulnerability cases, the adversary uses the eBPF vulnerability [13] to modify the targeted data on the kernel virtual memory. The attacker finally takes the shell as the root capability without any LSM limitation after memory corruption overrides the SELinux function pointer, as well as credential information. KMO monitors these modifications and detects the following sequences (Fig. 6):

1. The attacker executes the Proof-of-Concepts (PoC) code of the eBPF vulnerability with the user privilege. The PoC code inserts malicious BPF code into the kernel virtual memory via the `sys_bpf` system call. Although KMO traps the system calls, this does not lead to suspicious behavior at the time.

2. The adversary overwrites the LSM function pointer, and takes privilege escalation with memory corruption at the kernel mode. KMO also traps the issued system calls. The KMO's Pattern 2 monitoring identifies the LSM function pointer modification on the kernel control flow. It compares the `security_hook_list` variable with the monitoring data containing valid data and determines whether the monitored data is invalid.
3. The adversary launches the shell program from the PoC code. In KMO's Pattern 1, it traps the `sys_exec` system call and then determines whether it constitutes malicious behavior. System call arguments contain the shell program name, and memory corruption is already identified in `security_hook_list` variable modification.

5   Evaluation

5.1   Evaluation Purpose and Environment

We evaluated KMO effectiveness and overhead on a physical machine with an Intel(R) Core(TM) i7-7700HQ (2.80 GHz, x86_64) and 16 GB DDR4 memory. The implementation targeted Linux Kernel 4.4.114 on Debian 9.0. The evaluation items and objectives are described below:

E1: Monitoring system call argument experiment
   We evaluated switching Pattern 1 of KMO to inspect whether the target system call argument is valid before system call execution.
E2: Detection of overwriting of LSM function
   We assessed switching patterns 2 and 3 of KMO to check whether or not they correctly identify an eBPF vulnerability PoC that modifies the LSM function's virtual address. We then determined the timing at which the attacks on the kernel virtual memory are detected.
E3: Measurement of overhead of system call interaction with KMO
   We monitor the effect of kernel availability with KMO using switching virtual memory space. We then measure the overhead using benchmark software to calculate the system call latency.
E4: Measurement of the overhead of application with KMO
   We measure the performance overhead of a user process using benchmark software on KMO, which adopts several virtual memory switching patterns.

5.2   Monitoring System Call Argument

We assumed a rootkit installation. KMO monitors the module installation mechanism that uses the `init_module` and `finit_module` system calls. KMO inspects the kernel module binary image from the system call argument and then outputs whether the module is invalid as the detection result. In the log message, switching Pattern 1 shows the monitoring system call as "target system call" and the invalid module as "invalid module name".

```
// Switching to secret virtual memory and monitoring, pattern 1
1.  [58.690804] target system call
2.  [58.690821] system call number: 0000000000000139
3.  [58.721702] module name: malicious_module
4.  [58.721731] Invalid malicious_module
// Switching to secret virtual memory, pattern 1
5.  [58.727898] malicious_module: module license 'unspecified' taints kernel.
6.  [58.728542] Disabling lock debugging due to kernel taint
7.  [58.772438] Attack Module Init
```

(a) Monitoring of Linux System Call Arguments

Fig. 7. Monitoring result for Linux system call arguments

```
// Install LKM
1.  [78.654425] lkm_address_module: module license 'unspecified' taints kernel.
2.  [78.654853] Disabling lock debugging due to kernel taint
3.  [78.718498] dummy_hook_function Address Value ffffffffa0000000
4.  [78.718427] selinux_hooks[56].hook.file_permission Address ffffffff81e77c18
5.  [78.718444] selinux_hooks[56].hook.file_permission Address Value ffffffff812f3f20

// CVE-2017-16995 attack overrides LSM function address via sys_bpf()
6.  [*] attaching bpf backdoor to socket
7.  [*] UID from cred structure: 33, matches the current: 33
8.  [*] hammering cred structure at ffff88001c4399c0
9.  [*] replacing target function at ffffffff81e77c18
10. [*] credentials patched, launching shell...

// Switching to secret virtual memory and monitoring, pattern 2
11. [100.772834] Invalid lsm function is detected
12. [100.772854] Address ffffffff812f3f20    (Valid), ffffffffa0000000    (Invalid)
// Switching to kernel virtual memory, pattern 2

// Switching to secret virtual memory and monitoring, pattern 3
13. [204.010413] Invalid lsm function is detected
14. [204.010457] Address ffffffff812d5c70    (Valid), ffffffffa0000000    (Invalid)
// Switching to kernel virtual memory, pattern03

// LKM automatically outputs the target function virtual address
15. [108.769250] skpt_selinux_hooks[56].hook.file_permission Address ffffffff81e77c18
16. [108.769291] skpt_selinux_hooks[56].hook.file_permission Address Value ffffffffa0000000
```

(b) Monitoring of Linux Security Module's Function

Fig. 8. Monitoring result for Linux Security Modules (LSM) function

KMO correctly identifies the invalid kernel from the system call argument (Fig. 7). The monitoring function detects invalid module names via the module binary for only 0.05 ms before the kernel executes the system call and then invokes the module initial function.

We confirmed that switching Pattern 1 yields the correct evaluation results for the monitoring of the system call argument. Although the module executes its initialization function, the module installation process is not yet completed at the time of detection in Pattern 1. This indicates that KMO interrupts the running kernel code to determine if the validation is possible before system call processing.

5.3 Detection of Linux Security Module Overwrite

Our custom eBPF vulnerability PoC forces the exchange of one LSM hook function in the selinux_hooks variable to the module function on the kernel virtual memory. KMO stores the valid data at kernel boot. It then automatically identifies this memory corruption on switching patterns 2 and 3. These patterns

Table 1. Overhead of switching virtual memory space (μs)

System call	Vanilla kernel	KMO kernel	Overhead
fork+/bin/sh	933.515	946.758	13.243 (101.48%)
fork+execve	270.990	274.589	3.599 (101.32%)
fork+exit	250.266	255.276	5.010 (102.00%)
open/close	7.372	7.598	0.226 (103.06%)
read	0.318	0.358	0.040 (112.57%)
write	0.274	0.312	0.038 (113.86%)
stat	2.324	2.408	0.084 (103.61%)
fstat	0.341	0.384	0.043 (112.60%)

compare the target LSM hook function's virtual address with the valid data, and then outputs the result as a log message. An invalid case is "Invalid lsm function is detected" and "Virtual Address (Invalid)" in the detection.

KMO's detection result is successful on patterns 2 and 3 (Fig. 8). Patterns 2 and 3 determine whether the illegal memory is overwritten after the LSM function is modified for detection.

We also confirm that switching patterns 2 and 3 determine the illegal memory corruption at suitable detection timings. Therefore, KMO has an effective detection capability for kernel vulnerability against attacks that modify the LSM function's virtual address to prevent its existence in the kernel virtual memory.

5.4 Measurement System Call Interaction Overhead

We compare the Linux kernel, including KMO's mechanism, with a vanilla Linux kernel to measure the performance overhead. We use the benchmark software, lmbench. We execute it 10 times and calculate an average score to determine whether each system call has an overhead effect.

The overhead results are the measurement switching virtual memory features. The result is the switching of the virtual memory for each system call execution (Table 1). The lmbench shows different counts of system calls invoked for each benchmark. fork+/bin/sh has approximately 54; fork+execve has 4 invocations; fork+exit and open/close have two invocations; and the others have one invocation.

Table 1 shows that the system calls with the highest overhead are write (0.038 μs, 113.86%) and fstat (0.043 μs, 112.60%). The system calls with lowest overheads are fork+execve (3.599 μs, 101.32%) and fork+/bin/sh (13.243 μs, 101.48%). A kernel with KMO exhibits an overhead of 0.038 μs to 2.505 μs for each system call invocation.

5.5   Measurement Application Overhead

We compared the application overhead between the vanilla kernel and KMO kernel by switching patterns 1 and 3. We run an Apache 2.4.25 process. The benchmark software is ApacheBench 2.4. The environment includes a 100-Mbps network, one connection, and benchmark file sizes of 1 KB, 10 KB, and 100 KB. The ApacheBench calculates one download request average of 100,000 accesses to each file. The client machine is an Intel(R) Core(TM) i5 4200U (1.6 GHz, two cores), with 8 GB of memory and running Windows 8 as the OS.

The virtual memory switching patterns do not call the monitoring processing because the evaluation measures the performance effect of the kernel on each switching pattern. Pattern 1 calls the monitoring function before system call invocation, then executes the virtual memory switching with every 10 system call invocations. Pattern 3 calls the monitoring function for each system call and switches the virtual memory every 1,000 system call invocations (Table 2).

KMO has an overhead of 729.0 μs (107.27%) to 1,990.0 μs (282.73%) for Pattern 1 and 406.0 μs (137.28%) to 502.9 μs (150.16%) for Pattern 3 at 100,000 HTTP accesses.

The overhead of ApacheBench depends on the total count of system call invocations in the process. The ApacheBench result shows that Pattern 1 reduces the overhead factor for a large file, whereas Pattern 3 increases the overhead factor for a large file. When used on the benchmark, the overhead cost becomes relatively small at the application processing time. We consider that Pattern 1 requires a file transfer cost with a high impact. Pattern 3 incurs the same overhead cost, indicating that the switching of virtual memory has a constant load.

Table 2. ApacheBench overhead of virtual memory switching patterns 1 and 3 on the Linux kernel (μs).

File size (KB)	Vanilla kernel (T0)	KMO kernel		Overhead	
		Pattern 1 (T1)	Pattern 3 (T3)	(T1-T0)	(T3-T0)
1	1,089.0	3,079.0	1,495.0	1,990.0 (282.73%)	406.0 (137.28%)
10	1,895.0	2,266.0	2,413.0	371.0 (119.57%)	518.0 (127.33%)
100	1,002.4	1,075.3	1,505.3	729.0 (107.27%)	502.9 (150.16%)

6   Discussion

6.1   Performance Consideration

We consider the performance overhead, whereby KMO calls the TLB flush for every CR3 register update. We attempt to reduce the performance overhead for tag-based TLBs that provides an Address Space Identifier. The Process Context ID (PCID) on x86 is the cache for the virtual address to physical address conversion.

Moreover, the application process has no overhead in user mode. Nearly the entire performance effect involves the switching of the virtual memory, followed by the monitoring feature in kernel mode. The overhead cost in the system call latency evaluation is identical for all types of system calls. We estimate that the actual application performance is in proportional to switching virtual memory and the monitoring process in the kernel mode after system call invocation in user mode.

6.2   KMO Detection Capability

We consider that kernel vulnerabilities have two effect types in the kernel layer. One type indicates a memory corruption on the kernel virtual memory (e.g., eBPF vulnerability [13]), whereas the other does not create any kernel memory side effects (e.g., Dirty COW vulnerability [18]). KMO provides a combination of switching virtual memory patterns having different timings of inspection. Its feature detection capabilities compensate for the memory corruption of kernel vulnerability attacks for the kernel mode. During the evaluation the eBPF vulnerability attack overwrites the SELinux functions' virtual address of the LSM hook variable that was automatically detected on KMO.

Moreover, KMO identifies an attack code starting point from the user space and kernel space by using multiple system calls for the prevention of kernel vulnerability attacks leading to memory corruption. At an actual attack detection point, Pattern 1 determines the attack before system call execution on the kernel and prevents memory corruption. Although Pattern 2 identifies memory corruption, it interrupts the kernel execution flow of multiple functions having one system call. The user inserts a suitable detection point that reduces the effect of the kernel vulnerability attack. Preventing the execution of malicious code on one system call invocation for Pattern 3 is difficult because its checkpoint is just before switching back to the user mode. Therefore, Pattern 3 reliably detects memory corruption during kernel processing for multiple functions.

Additionally, we plan to support other security features that could run in the secret virtual memory space. This method could prevent attacks on a kernel vulnerability that could evade a monitoring mechanism of a security feature on the kernel.

6.3   KMO Limitation

KMO keeps the virtual memory switching functions in the kernel virtual memory space and then invokes them from the original kernel code. Although the adversary potentially targets that KMO's function, KASLR provides a random layout of the virtual memory space, and thus hinders the estimation of the KMO functions' virtual address.

The adversary identifies the valid data's virtual address of direct mapping to manually calculate the position from the physical page's virtual address. KMO unmaps secret pages of the direct mapping space in the kernel virtual memory to reduce the attack surface.

7   Related Work

Isolation models and mechanisms that control the separation unite in multiple layers from hardware to software [20,21].

Kernel and CPU Enhancement. Linux also has SELinux [3,22] and a capability [4] for restricting privileges. KASLR [6] for virtual memory randomization, CFI [7] for code flow integrity checking, and Code Pointer Integrity for the verification of a function's return address [23] have been presented. The CPU already has NX-bit [24] for execution management and SMAP/SMEP [8] for access and the execution of control between a supervisor and a user of the virtual memory space. These reduce the kernel vulnerability attack effects.

Kernel Attack. Several attack concepts target the kernel virtual memory [9,19, 25] to evade these security mechanisms. KPTI or another method that separates the virtual memory space between the user and the kernel can mitigate such attacks [9,26]. The kernel attack method uses both return oriented programming and anti-CFI [27], while the direct mapping space can execute the attack code only in the kernel mode [2,28]. The device driver has a directory threat surface [29]. We believe that kernel virtual memory monitoring is essential to mitigating these attacks in kernel mode.

Virtualization Protection. Kernel monitoring mechanisms have a hypervisor, and a secure mode is proposed [21,30–32]. Moreover, SecVisor [30] and TrustVisor [33] ensure that only the verified kernel code is running. GRIM also has a verified kernel code at the GPU layer [34], while the Trusted Computing Base [35] verifies the integrity of the kernel code at the boot sequence. These mechanisms are running under the kernel layer and are unaffected by kernel vulnerability. KMO's monitoring feature is in the kernel and could be embedded into the hypervisor and kernel of the secure mode as effective countermeasures against kernel vulnerabilities.

Virtual Memory Protection. Virtual memory protection methods adopt the separation of memory space using the domain and granularity of memory access control [36–39]. The CPU feature, MPK, supports virtual memory protection [40, 41], page-based separation instructions [42,43], and physical memory isolation for each process [44]. Moreover, the monitoring of the same layer as the OS or hypervisor has a low overhead when hardware assistance is available [45–47]. The separation between the module and the kernel virtual memory space on the hypervisor increases the system reliability [48].

Running Kernel Protection. The running kernel protection methods focus on invalid overwriting of kernel code and data, including the control flow or data flow tracing [7,49,50], and the monitoring of the stack status [5,51]. We regard these as being an effective reference to reduce or trigger kernel monitoring.

Kernel Protection. The kernel protection methods have randomized page table positions in physical memory [52], and $R^\wedge X$ restricts the permission of the kernel memory layout [53]. In addition, the separation of the device driver

Table 3. Kernel monitoring feature comparison ($\checkmark$ is supported; $\triangle$ is partially supported).

Feature	SecVisor [30]	SIM [45]	ED-Monitor [46]	KMO
Memory corruption detection	$\checkmark$		$\checkmark$	$\checkmark$
Memory corruption protection		$\triangle$		$\triangle$
System call argument inspection		$\checkmark$		$\checkmark$
In-kernel interception		$\checkmark$	$\triangle$	$\checkmark$
Kernel integrity	$\checkmark$		$\checkmark$	$\triangle$
Cloud environment deployment		$\triangle$	$\triangle$	$\checkmark$

code from the kernel provides granularity monitoring points [54, 55]. KMO has difference merits; that is, switching of the virtual memory space has no effect for attacks via kernel vulnerabilities and no interruption for running the kernel code.

7.1 Comparison with Related Work

We compared the security features of KMO and three research mechanisms (Table 3) [30, 45, 46]. KMO satisfies almost all the identified requirements for the running kernel and cloud environment.

Although the same privilege layer monitoring approach is similar to the KMO architectures, we provide finer inspection points for memory protection and detection through system calls or the insertion of a kernel function flow. Finally, despite KMO struggling to set a suitable inspection point on a kernel, users could manage effective kernel monitoring by considering a collaboration of existing methods. We believe that this would contribute to reducing the attack surface of the system for device drivers or other potentially vulnerable regions.

8   Conclusion

The OS kernel adopts MAC and capability restrict privileges. Although KASLR, CFI, KPTI, and SMAP/SMEP mitigate kernel vulnerability attacks for memory corruption leading to privilege escalation or the avoidance of security features, only kernel layer attacks can potentially succeed.

We propose a novel security mechanism, the Kernel Memory Observer (KMO), to provide a secret virtual memory to monitor the original kernel virtual memory. KMO has several inspection points to detect invalid kernel virtual memory overwriting, and prevents attacks via the direct mapping region. The evaluation of Linux with KMO could identify the memory corruption of security features. The system call overhead required 1% to 15% the invocation cost on our kernel, and the application overhead for KMO monitoring was 7% to 185% during the running process.

Acknowledgement. This work was partially supported by JSPS KAKENHI Grant Number JP19H04109.

References

1. Chen, H., et al.: Linux kernel vulnerabilities - state-of-the-art defenses and open problems. In: 2nd Asia-Pacific Workshop on Systems (APSys) (2011)
2. Kemerlis, P.V., et al.: Ret2dir - rethinking kernel isolation. In: 23rd USENIX Conference on Security Symposium, pp. 957–972 (2014)
3. Security-enhanced Linux. http://www.nsa.gov/research/selinux/. Accessed 10 Aug 2018
4. Linden, A.T.: Operating system structures to support security and reliable software. ACM Comput. Surv. (CSUR) **8**(4), 409–445 (1976)
5. Kemerlis, P.V., et al.: kGuard - lightweight kernel protection against return-to-user attacks. In: 21st USENIX Conference on Security Symposium (2012)
6. Shacham, H., et al.: On the effectiveness of address-space randomization. In: 11th ACM Conference on Computer and Communications Security (CCS), pp. 298–307 (2004)
7. Abadi, M., et al.: Control-flow integrity principles, implementations. In: 12th ACM Conference on Computer and Communications Security (CCS), pp. 340–353 (2005)
8. Mulnix, D.: Intel® Xeon® Processor D Product Family Technical Overview (2015). https://software.intel.com/en-us/articles/intel-xeon-processor-d-product-family-technical-overview. Accessed 10 Aug 2018
9. Gruss, D., Lipp, M., Schwarz, M., Fellner, R., Maurice, C., Mangard, S.: KASLR is dead: long live KASLR. In: Bodden, E., Payer, M., Athanasopoulos, E. (eds.) ESSoS 2017. LNCS, vol. 10379, pp. 161–176. Springer, Cham (2017). https://doi.org/10.1007/978-3-319-62105-0_11
10. CVE-2016-8655.   https://cve.mitre.org/cgi-bin/cvename.cgi?name=CVE-2016-8655
11. CVE-2017-6074.   https://cve.mitre.org/cgi-bin/cvename.cgi?name=CVE-2017-6074
12. CVE-2017-7308.   https://cve.mitre.org/cgi-bin/cvename.cgi?name=CVE-2017-7308
13. CVE-2017-16995.   https://cve.mitre.org/cgi-bin/cvename.cgi?name=CVE-2017-16995
14. Exploit Database, Nexus 5 Android 5.0 - Privilege Escalation. https://www.exploit-db.com/exploits/35711/
15. Grsecurity: super fun 2.6.30+/RHEL5 2.6.18 local kernel exploit. https://grsecurity.net/~spender/exploits/exploit2.txt
16. Lipp, M., et al.: Meltdown - reading kernel memory from user space. In: 27th USENIX Conference on Security Symposium (2018)
17. Linux Kernel Defence Map. https://github.com/a13xp0p0v/linux-kernel-defence-map

18. CVE-2016-5195. https://cve.mitre.org/cgi-bin/cvename.cgi?name=CVE-2016-5195

19. Hund, R., et al.: Practical timing side channel attacks against kernel space ASLR. In: 2013 IEEE Symposium on Security and Privacy, pp. 191–205 (2013)

20. Shu, R., et al.: A study of security isolation techniques. ACM Comput. Surv. (CSUR) **49**(3), 1–37 (2016)

21. Zhang, F., Zhang, H.: SoK a study of using hardware-assisted isolated execution environments for security. In: Hardware and Architectural Support for Security and Privacy 2016, pp. 1–8 (2016)

22. Spencer, R., et al.: The flask security architecture: system support for diverse security policies. In: 8th USENIX Conference on Security Symposium (1999)

23. Volodymyr, K., et al.: Code-pointer integrity. In: 10th USENIX Symposium on Operating Systems Design and Implementation (OSDI) (2014)

24. Ingo Molnar, [announce] [patch] NX (No eXecute) support for x86, 2.6.7-rc2-bk2 (2004). http://lkml.iu.edu/hypermail/linux/kernel/0406.0/0497.html. Accessed 10 Aug 2018

25. Jang, Y., et al.: Breaking kernel address space layout randomization with intel TSX. In: 2016 ACM Conference on Computer and Communications Security (CCS), pp. 380–392 (2016)

26. Hua, Z., et al.: EPTI - efficient defence against meltdown attack for unpatched VMs. In: 2018 USENIX Annual Technical Conference (ATC) (2018)

27. Carlini, N., et al.: Control-flow bending: on the effectiveness of control-flow integrity. In: 24th USENIX Conference on Security Symposium, pp. 161–176 (2015)

28. Shacham, H.: The geometry of innocent flesh on the bone: return-into-libc without function calls (on the x86). In: 14th ACM Conference on Computer and Communications Security (CCS), pp. 552–561 (2007)

29. Song, D., et al.: PeriScope: an effective probing and fuzzing framework for the hardware-OS boundary. In: 26th Annual Network and Distributed System Security Conference (NDSS) (2019)

30. Seshadri, A., et al.: SecVisor - a tiny hypervisor to provide lifetime kernel code integrity for commodity OSes. In: 21st ACM Symposium on Operating systems principles (SOSP), pp. 335–350 (2007)

31. Azab, A., et al.: SKEE: a lightweight secure kernel-level execution environment for ARM. In: 2011 Network and Distributed System Security Symposium (NDSS) (2016)

32. Cho, Y., et al.: Dynamic virtual address range adjustment for intra-level privilege separation on ARM. In: 2017 Network and Distributed System Security Symposium (NDSS) (2017)

33. McCune, M.J., et al.: TrustVisor - efficient TCB reduction and attestation. In: 2010 IEEE Symposium on Security and Privacy (2010)

34. Koromilas, L., et al.: GRIM - leveraging gpus for kernel integrity monitoring. In: 19th International Symposium on Research in Attacks, Intrusions and Defenses, pp. 3–23 (2016)

35. Trusted computing group. tpm main specification (2003). http://www.trustedcomputinggroup.org/resources/tpm_main_specification. Accessed 10 Aug 2018

36. Witchel, E., et al.: Mondrix: memory isolation for linux using mondriaan memory protection. In: 20th ACM Symposium on Operating systems principles (SOSP), pp. 31–44 (2005)

37. Castro, M., et al.: Fast byte-granularity software fault isolation. In: 22nd ACM Symposium on Operating systems principles (SOSP), pp. 45–58 (2009)

38. Hsu, C.T., et al.: Enforcing least privilege memory views for multithreaded applications. In: 2016 ACM Conference on Computer and Communications Security (CCS), pp. 393–405 (2016)
39. Litton, J., et al.: Light-weight contexts - an OS abstraction for safety and performance. In: 12th USENIX Symposium on Operating Systems Design and Implementation (OSDI) (2016)
40. Koning, K., et al.: No need to hide: protecting safe regions on commodity hardware. In: Twelfth European System Conference (EuroSys), pp. 437–452 (2017)
41. Vahldiek-Oberwagner, A., et al.: ERIM: secure and efficient in-process isolation with memory protection keys, CoRR abs/1801.06822 (2018)
42. Mogosanu, L., Rane, A., Dautenhahn, N.: MicroStache: a lightweight execution context for in-process safe region isolation. In: Bailey, M., Holz, T., Stamatogiannakis, M., Ioannidis, S. (eds.) RAID 2018. LNCS, vol. 11050, pp. 359–379. Springer, Cham (2018). https://doi.org/10.1007/978-3-030-00470-5_17
43. Frassetto, T., et al.: IMIX - in-process memory isolation extension. In: 28th USENIX Conference on Security Symposium (2018)
44. Kim, H.C., et al.: Securing real-time microcontroller systems through customized memory view switching. In: 25th Network and Distributed System Security Symposium (NDSS) (2018)
45. Sharif, I.M., et al.: Secure in-VM monitoring using hardware virtualization. In: 16th ACM Conference on Computer and Communications Security (CCS) (2009)
46. Deng, L., et al.: Dancing with wolves: towards practical event-driven VMM monitoring. In: 13th ACM SIGPLAN/SIGOPS International Conference (2017)
47. Zhang, Z., et al.: KASR: a reliable and practical approach to attack surface reduction of commodity OS kernels. In: 21st International Symposium on Research in Attacks, Intrusions and Defenses (RAID) (2018)
48. Srivastava, A., et al.: Efficient monitoring of untrusted kernel-mode execution. In: 18th Annual Network and Distributed System Security Conference (NDSS) (2011)
49. Song, C., et al.: Enforcing kernel security invariants with data flow integrity. In: 2016 Annual Network and Distributed System Security Symposium (NDSS) (2016)
50. Ge, X., et al.: GRIFFIN: guarding control flows using intel processor trace. In: 22nd ACM International Conference on Architectural Support for Programming Languages and Operating Systems (APLOS), pp. 585–598 (2017)
51. Huang, W., et al.: LMP: light-weighted memory protection with hardware assistance. In: 32nd Annual Conference on Computer Security Applications (ACSAC), pp. 460–470 (2016)
52. Davi, L., et al.: PT-rand: practical mitigation of data-only attacks against page tables. In: 23th Network and Distributed System Security Symposium (NDSS) (2016)
53. Pomonis, M., et al.: kR^X: comprehensive kernel protection against just-in-time code reuse. In: Twelfth European Conference on Computer Systems (EuroSys), pp. 420–436 (2017)
54. Boyd-Wickizer, S., et al.: Tolerating malicious device drivers in linux. In: USENIX Annual Technical Conference (ATC) (2010)
55. Tian, J.D., et al.: LBM: a security framework for peripherals within the linux kernel. In: 2019 IEEE Symposium on Security and Privacy (2019)

Peel the Onion: Recognition of Android Apps Behind the Tor Network

Emanuele Petagna, Giuseppe Laurenza(✉)(iD), Claudio Ciccotelli(iD),
and Leonardo Querzoni(iD)

Department of Computer, Control, and Management Engineering,
"Antonio Ruberti" (DIAG), Rome, Italy
petagna.795137@studenti.uniroma1.it,
{laurenza,ciccotelli,querzoni}@diag.uniroma1.it

Abstract. According to Freedom on the Net 2017 report [15] more than 60% of World's Internet users are not completely free from censorship. Solutions like Tor allow users to gain more freedom, bypassing these restrictions. For this reason they are continuously under deep observation to detect vulnerabilities that would compromise users anonymity. The aim of this work is showing that Tor is vulnerable to app deanonymization attacks on Android devices through network traffic analysis. While attacks against Tor anonymity have already gained considerable attention in the context of website fingerprinting in desktop environments, to the best of our knowledge this is the first work that addresses a similar problem on Android devices. For this purpose, we describe a general methodology for performing an attack that allows to deanonymize the apps running on a target smartphone using Tor. Then, we discuss a Proof-of-Concept, implementing the methodology, that shows how the attack can be performed in practice and allows to assess the deanonymization accuracy that it is possible to achieve. Moreover, we made the software of the Proof-of-Concept available, as well as the datasets used to evaluate it. In our extensive experimental evaluation, we achieved an accuracy of 97%.

Keywords: TOR · De-anonimization · Android · Traffic analysis

1 Introduction

Tor is a very popular anonymization network, currently counting more than two million daily users [24]. While Tor is mainly associated with preserving anonymity during Web navigation, its protection capabilities are not limited to such application. In general, Tor can be used to protect any TCP-based traffic, being it generated by a desktop or mobile application. Nowadays, smartphone apps are replacing web browsers for interacting with many online services, such as social networks, chat services and video/audio streaming. The usage of anonymization mechanisms, such as Tor, on mobile devices is gaining momentum and is motivated by the increasing interest of several actors in profiling

© Springer Nature Switzerland AG 2019
S.-H. Heng and J. Lopez (Eds.): ISPEC 2019, LNCS 11879, pp. 95–112, 2019.
https://doi.org/10.1007/978-3-030-34339-2_6

mobile users, e.g., for marketing purposes, government surveillance, detection and exploitation of vulnerabilities and other activities that may be harmful for users' privacy and security, or perceived as such by them. Several works in the past studied the privacy guarantees offered by Tor, focussing, in particular, on the Desktop PC scenario where a large fraction of the anonymized traffic is web data or file sharing services. Conversely, less attention has been devoted to the usage of Tor on mobile devices, and the level of anonymity it can provide. Given that mobile and desktop devices generate different traffic patterns, both due to the way they are used [16,25] and to the fact that the same application may behave differently in the two environments [14], we cannot assume that what was proved by past approaches still holds for mobile devices. The aim of this work is to show that Tor is vulnerable to app deanonymization attacks on Android devices through network traffic analysis. For this purpose, we describe a general methodology for performing an attack that allows to deanonymize the apps running on a target smartphone using Tor, which is the victim of the attack. Then, we discuss a Proof-of-Concept, implementing the methodology, that shows how the attack can be performed in practice and allows to assess the deanonymization accuracy that can be achieved.

Summarizing, this work provides the following contributions:

- a methodology for deanonymizing apps on Android-based smartphones that use Tor;
- a Proof-of-Concept that implements the deanonymization methodology, which can be used to verify Tor's vulnerability to app deanonymization and assess the level of accuracy that can be achieved;
- a dataset[1] of generated Android Tor traffic traces that can be used to check the validity of our Proof-of-Concept and compare alternative methodologies.

The remainder of the paper is organized as follows. Section 2 reports the related works. Section 3 presents the fundamental concepts related to Tor and the machine learning algorithms employed in this work. Section 4 introduces the threat model that we consider. Section 5 discusses the methodology for deanonymizing Android apps behind the Tor network. Section 6 describes the Proof-of-Concept. Section 7 reports the experiment performed to evaluate the accuracy of the methodology and discusses the obtained results. Finally, in Sect. 8 we draw some conclusions and discuss possible future directions for this work.

2   Related Works

Many works have been published in the broad area of traffic analysis both in the context of *desktop environments* and *smartphone environments* (mostly assuming the Android operating system). While, there are some works in the context

---

[1] Both the software necessary to reproduce the Proof-of-Concept and the dataset can be downloaded from the following repository: https://github.com/Immanuel84/peeltheonion.

of desktop environments that has focused on deanonymizing Tor traffic, to the best of our knowledge, there is no work assuming both a smartphone environment and that traffic is anonymized through Tor. Therefore, there is no work we can directly compare to.

In this section we report the most related works considering a desktop environment, with or without Tor anonymized traffic, and an Android environment without Tor.

Desktop Environment Without Tor: In the context of website fingerprinting, Hintz [18] proposes an attack against SafeWeb, an encrypting web proxy, that allows to determine the webpages visited by the users. The attack exploits the fact that, even if traffic is encrypted, many browser open separate TCP connection for downloading resources from visited pages, allowing an attacker to monitor their sizes. Such sizes can be used to fingerprinting webpages. The author proposes some protections based on the addition of noise or on multiplexing data on a single connection.

Bissias *et al.* [10] propose a statistical website fingerprinting attack. The attacker creates a profile of the target website by monitoring the distribution of packet sizes and inter-arrival times. These data are then compared to user traffic.

Liberatore *et al.* [20] describe a website fingerprinting attack against HTTPS connections. They use unique packet lengths to build profiles of HTTPS connections and compare them against a dataset of known profiles using a naive Bayes classifier.

Desktop Environment with Tor: In the context of Website fingerprinting, Wang *et al.* [31] propose an attack that uses a k–Nearest Neighbor Classifier to effectively fingerprint web pages behind Tor. They employ several types of features, including general statistics about total traffic, unique packet lengths, packet orderings, bursts and inter-packet times. They show that their attack has significantly higher accuracy than previous attacks in the same field.

AlSabah *et al.* [9] propose a machine learning based approach for Tor's traffic classification. The aim of the work is to recognize different classes of workloads that, in combination with QoS policies, can significantly improve the experience of Tor clients. However, since Tor's traffic is encrypted, it is not possible to rely on classical QoS to discriminate applications traffic. The proposed technique achieves an accuracy higher than 95%.

Juarez *et al.* [19] analyze the known website fingerprinting attacks on Tor. Known attacks claim to be effective under precise assumptions about threat model and user settings, which often do not hold in practical scenarios. The authors conduct a critical evaluation of these attacks and show their weaknesses when performed in real scenarios.

Chakravarty *et al.* [11] evaluate the feasibility and effectiveness of practical traffic analysis attacks on the Tor network using NetFlow data. It is not a passive attack as authors deliberately alter traffic characteristics at the server side and observe how this alteration affects client side through a statistical correlation.

They achieve 100% accuracy in laboratory tests, and 81.4% accuracy in real world tests.

Ling *et al.* [21] propose TorWard, a system that attempts to recognize malicious traffic over Tor. In their experiments they found that a considerable portion of the Tor traffic is malicious (around 10%) with 8.99% of the alerts generated due to malware and 78.03% of the alerts generated due to malicious P2P traffic.

Mittal *et al.* [22] exploit throughput information to gain information about the user. The attack can identify the Guard Node (entry point to Tor network) and identify if two concurrent TCP connections belong to the same user.

Habibi Lashkari *et al.* [17] focus on recognition of traffic types instead of websites. They consider 8 application traffic types: browsing, email, chat, audio streaming, video streaming, file transfer, VoIP and P2P. They perform network traffic analysis by splitting the traffic traces in flows of a given duration. For each flow they compute several features based on inter-arrival times, active and idle periods, packet rates and byte rates. They employ a supervised machine learning approach to classify the traffic type of each flow. In particular they explored k–Nearest Neighbor, Random Forest and C4.5 classifiers.

Android Environment Without Tor: A number of authors have proposed various approaches to identify smartphone apps through network traffic analysis. Some of these solutions focus on examining IP addresses and packet payloads. However, relying on IP addresses is less effective because a lot of applications exploit Content Delivery Networks (CDN) for scalability. AppScanner [30] targets mobile environments and uses traffic features to fingerprint mobile apps. They rely on a supervised machine learning approach using only features that do not require the inspection packet payloads, thus working also on encrypted traffic. They perform experiments with SVM and Random Forest classifiers achieving 99% of accuracy in their dataset with 110 of the most popular apps in the Google Play Store.

Dai *et al.* [13] propose a technique for app fingerprinting based on building network traffic profiles of apps. They run each app in an emulator, exercising different execution paths through a novel UI fuzzing technique, and collect the corresponding network traces. They compute a fingerprint of the app by identifying invariants in the generated network traces. Using the generated fingerprint they were able to detect the presence of apps in real-world network traffic logs from a cellular provider.

Conti *et al.* [12] describe a machine learning based network traffic analysis approach to identify user actions on specific apps (facebook, gmail and twitter). They achieve more than 95% of accuracy and precision for most of the considered actions.

Stöber *et al.* [29] focus on identifying smartphones from 3G/UMTS data capture. Even if 3G/UMTS data is encrypted an attacker could reliably identify a smartphone using only the information extracted from periodic traffic patterns leak side-channel information like timing and data volume. They show that they can identify smartphones with only 15 min of traffic monitoring and fingerprints computed on 6 h of sniffed background traffic, obtaining an accuracy of 90%.

Saltaformaggio *et al.* [27] develop a tool called NetScope which is able to detect user activities on both Android and iOS smartphones. They compute features by only inspecting the IP headers, and use a SVM multi-class classifier to detect activities. NetScope achieves a precision of 78.04% and a recall of 76.04% on average on a set of 35 widely used apps.

3 Background on Tor

In this section we briefly summarize the basic concepts about the Tor network. Tor [26] is a distributed overlay network that anonymizes TCP-based applications (web browsers, secure shells, mail clients) while trying to keep the latency low. The network consists of a set of interconnected entities called *Onion Routers* (ORs). Tor clients, also known as *Onion Proxies* (OPs), periodically connect to directory servers to download the list of available ORs. OPs use this information to establish *circuits* in the Tor network, to connect to a destination node (which is often outside the Tor network). A circuit is a path of ORs in which each OR knows only its predecessor and its successor ORs. A Tor circuit has three types of nodes:

- *Entry* or *Guard Node*: this represents the entry point to the Tor network for the Tor client.
- *Relay Nodes*: these are the intermediate ORs of the circuit.
- *Exit Node*: this is the last OR in the Tor circuit. That is, the one that connects to the destination.

Each Tor circuit must have one entry node, at least one relay node (but there may be multiple) and one exit node. The entry node is the only node in the circuit that knows the Tor client, while the exit node is the only one that knows the destination.

Messages exchanged between the Tor client and the destination are split into *cells* when they traverse the Tor network. Cells are the basic unit of communication among Tor nodes. Tor cells used to have a 512 bytes fixed size in earlier Tor versions. Though this choice provided some resistance against traffic analysis, it was inefficient and made Tor traffic easier to discover due to packet-size distribution [26]. Therefore, variable length cells have been introduced in newer Tor versions.

When establishing a circuit, the Tor client shares a symmetric key with each node of the circuit. When the Tor client sends a packet to the destination it encrypts the corresponding cells' payloads with all the shared keys, in reverse order from the exit node to the entry node. Each node along the path unwraps its layer using its key. Only the exit node can reconstruct the message to be sent to the destination in clear. The same happens in the opposite direction, with each node that instead encrypts with its own key.

Padding

Internet service providers and surveillance infrastructures are known to store metadata about connections. Collecting and analyzing such data is useful for characterizing traffic, but may also represent a threat to anonymity.

Per-flow records are emitted by routers on a periodic basis depending on two configurable timeouts: *active flow timeout* and the *inactive flow timeout*. The expiration of the active flow timeout causes routers to emit a new record for each active connection. The inactive flow timeout causes the emission of a new record when a connection is inactive for a certain amount of time. The value of such timeouts is configurable and the range depends on routers vendors, but active flow timeout is typically in the order of minutes, while the inactive flow timeout in the order of tens of seconds. Therefore, the aggregation level of records data (on a temporal basis) is at least the active flow timeout, but may be finer when there are inactive periods longer than the inactive flow timeout.

Thus, to reduce the granularity level of records' data (with the aim of hindering deanonymization techniques based on traffic analysis), long inactive periods should be avoided. For this reason, the Tor protocol introduced *connection padding*. With connection padding, special purpose cells (PADDING cells) are sent if the connection is inactive for a given amount of time, so as to reduce the duration of inactive periods.

Connection Padding. Connection padding cells are exchanged only between the Tor client and entry node. To determine when to send a connection padding cell, both the Tor client and the entry node maintain a timer. These timers are set up with a timeout value between 1.5 and 9.5 s. The exact value depends on a function that samples a distribution described in [23]. After the establishment of the Tor circuit the timers start on both sides, if any of the two timers expires, a padding cell is sent to the other endpoint. Exchanging any cell different from a padding cell resets the timers.

Reduced Connection Padding. Connection padding introduces an overhead in terms of exchanged data. Especially in mobile environments, this overhead may become excessive. Therefore, *reduced connection padding* has been introduced to lower the overhead due to connection padding. With reduced connection padding the timeout is sampled from a different range, between 9 s to 14 s.

4   Threat Model

In our threat model an *attacker* wants to deanonimize the apps on a *target smartphone* that uses Tor. That is, he/she wants to recognize which apps are being used by the target smartphone at any given time. We assume that the target is connected to the Internet through a wireless access point, either via a Wi-Fi LAN or via the cellular WAN, and that the attacker is able to passively capture the traffic between the target and the access point. We assume that the Tor client (i.e., an Onion Proxy) is installed in the smartphone itself and all apps' traffic passes through the Tor client.

5   Deanonymization Methodology

Figure 1 shows an overview of our methodology for deanonymizing Android apps behind Tor. The assumption at the basis of the methodology is that different apps produce different network traffic patterns, which are discernible, through proper network traffic analysis, even when the traffic is anonymized through Tor.

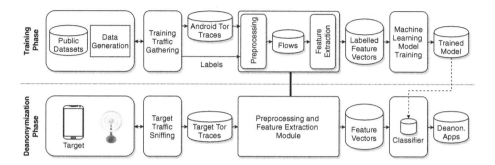

Fig. 1. Overview of the deanonymization methodology.

The methodology relies on a machine learning based network traffic analysis and consists of two distinct phases:

- *Training Phase*: during which we build a machine learning model of the distinctive characteristics of apps' Tor traffic. This is the preparation phase of the attack.
- *Deanonymization Phase*: during which we conduct the actual attack against the target, by monitoring the target's traffic and using the model built in the previous phase to recognize which apps the victim is using.

During the training phase we build a machine learning model of how different apps produce Tor traffic. We assume that the attacker is interested in recognizing a predefined set of apps $\mathcal{C} = \{app_1, \ldots, app_n\}$. If the target is using an app which is not included in $\mathcal{C}$, our methodology will not be able to recognize that app. Both the phases of our methodology include a *Traffic Gathering* and a *Preprocessing and Feature Exctraction* modules, followed by the building of the Machine Learning model for the Training Phase and Classifier module for the Deanonymization one. In the following sections we describe each logical block in details.

Traffic Gathering —Since we assume a supervised learning process, for the training phase, the first step is collecting a training dataset. In particular our methodology requires to gather, for each app in $\mathcal{C}$, raw Tor traffic traces. These traces can be picked from public datasets, if available (such as the one that we made available with this work), or can be generated synthetically, as described in Sect. 6.1. For the Deanonymization Phase instead, our methodology requires the attacker to passively capture the target's network traffic.

Preprocessing and Feature Extraction Module —This module processes the network traces gathered at the previous step and extracts the features that will be fed to the machine learning algorithm. For each network trace, we sort all TCP sessions (note that Tor only supports TCP) and we split sessions into flows. A *flow* is a portion of a TCP session of a predefined fixed duration T_F, the *flow timeout*. We split each TCP session into flows of T_F seconds. When, we find a TCP packet with the FIN flag set, we stop splitting. Thus, the last flow of each TCP connection may actually last less than T_F seconds. The flow timeout is a configurable parameter of our methodology that has an impact on the deanonymization accuracy. As detailed later, in Sect. 7, we performed experiments with $T_F = 10$ and $T_F = 15$. The experiments with $T_F = 10$ yielded slightly better results. For the Training Phase, once we have split all traces into flows, we label each flow with the app in C that has generated the corresponding traffic.

For each flow x_i we compute a vector of features $v_i = (f_1(x_i), \ldots, f_m(x_i))$. Section 6.2 reports the set of features that we considered in our Proof-of-Concept. The general methodology does not rely on a particular set of features. However, as always, the choice of such set strongly impacts accuracy. Our set of features has been derived from an experimental analysis involving various feature sets. Since many machine learning algorithms (e.g., SVM and k–NN) work best with standardized features, for each component $y_{i,k} = f_k(x_i)$ (of each feature vector) we compute its standard score.

Machine Learning Model Training —During this step we feed the machine learning training algorithm with the training set built by the other modules. Our methodology does not rely on a particular machine learning model, but assumes a generic multi-class classifier whose set of classes is the set of apps C. In our experiments we tested three different classifiers based on, respectively, Random Forest, k–Nearest Neighbors and SVM.

Classifier —In this step, each feature vector coming from the previous step is directly fed to the classifier that has been trained during the training stage. For each feature vector the classifier outputs a class, namely one of the apps in C. The output of the classifier is also the output of the methodology, i.e., the deanonymized apps. In our Proof-of-Concept we adopt an *offline* approach. That is, the two phases are not concurrent, they are performed subsequently. We first perform monitoring, collecting enough traces, and then we perform the classification. However, our methodology is general enough to allow for an *online* implementation, in which the two stages are actually executed simultaneously, and a new processing and classification step is performed as soon as the corresponding data is available.

6   Proof-of-Concept

This section presents details about our Proof-of-Concept implementing the methodology described in the previous section. We use a simple *architecture* made by a workstation, a wireless router connected to internet and two *target* smartphones connected to the router. On the targets we install *Orbot* [1], a proxy app that allows to use Tor on Android. The workstation is in charge of collecting the raw TCP traces, preprocessing them and extract feature vectors. We also use it to train the machine learning models and use them to deanonymize the network traffic.

6.1 Dataset

Since no public datasets collecting Android Tor's traces were available at the time of this writing, we generate our own datasets. To build them, we used AndroidViewClient [3], Culebra GUI and CulebraTester [4]. With these tools we developed different simulation scripts for each app, in order to reproduce a typical human user. We reported the details about simulated stimulation of the various apps in Appendix A. In this way we can create, for each app in $\mathcal{C}$, a synthetic, yet as realistic as possible, network trace. To sniff the traffic and perform basic network analysis, we execute *Tcpdump* [2] on the router and *Wireshark* [8] on the workstation. We collected two datasets of network traces: 11.24 GB of traces with default configuration, that we call *Reduced Connection Padding Dataset* and 9.84 GB with the (full) connection padding activated, that we call *Full Connection Padding Dataset*, see Sect. 3. In both datasets we collected about 4 h of network traffic for each of the following apps: Dailymotion, Facebook, Instagram, Replaio Radio, Skype, Spotify, TorBrowser Alpha, Twitch, uTorrent, YouTube.

6.2 Features

In our Proof-of-Concept we employed three types of features.

Time-based Features —Since Tor's relay cells (those that transport the actual payload) are fixed sized, initially we concentrated on time-based, rather than size-based features. In particular, we employed the following features, given that they led to good results in the context of recognition of traffic classes in desktop environments [17]:

- *FIAT* (Forward Inter Arrival Time): time between two outgoing packets;
- *BIAT* (Backward Inter Arrival Time): time between two incoming packets;
- *FLOWIAT* (Flow Inter Arrival Time): time between two packets, no matter the direction;
- *Active time*: amount of time a flow is active;
- *Idle time*: amount of time a flow is idle;
- *Flow bytes per second*: number of bytes per second;
- *Flow packets per second*: number of packets per second;
- *Duration*: duration of the flow in seconds.

For all the above features except the last three, we actually compute 4 statistical values: minimum, maximum, mean and standard deviation. Moreover, the active and idle time depends on a configurable threshold, the *activity timeout* T_A. We performed experiments with $T_A = 2$ and $T_A = 5$ s.

Packet Direction and Burst Features —Packet direction and burst features have also been proven to be effective in the context of website fingerprinting on desktop environments [31]. Packet direction indicates whether a packet is going forward, from the source (the Tor client) to the destination, or backward, i.e., in the opposite direction. A burst instead is an uninterrupted sequence of packets in the same direction. After a preliminary analysis, we decided to enrich our feature set with the following features:

- Direction of the first 10 packets (of the flow);
- Incoming Bursts: number of bursts, bursts mean length, length of the longest burst;
- Outgoing Bursts: number of bursts, bursts mean length, length of the longest burst;
- Lengths of the first 10 incoming bursts;
- Lengths of the first 10 outgoing bursts.

Size-Based Features —Event though relay cells are fixed sized, Tor uses variable-length cells for traffic control. As a preliminary analysis, we counted the number of packets for each packet size and we observed that, while there is a large variability in packet sizes, there is a relatively small set of possible packet sizes. Thus, we decided to introduce a feature for each of the ten most frequent packet sizes. These, were (in order of higher frequency) 1500, 595, 583, 2960, 1097, 1384, 151, 1126, 1109 and 233 bytes. We soon decided to discard size 2960, as this exceeds the MTU (1500 byes) and thus represents a reassembled packet. Each feature is a counter of the number of packets of that size observed in the flow.

7   Experimental Evaluation

We performed several experiments using the prototype implementation of our methodology described in the Proof-of-Concept section (see Sect. 6). For each experiment we vary the following settings:

- *Tor's connection padding*: *Reduced* or *Full*, depending on whether we use the dataset with reduced connection padding or full connection padding (see Sect. 6.1);
- *Flow Timeout* (T_F): either 10 or 15 s (see Sect. 5);
- *Activity Timeout* (T_A): either 2 or 5 s (see Sect. 6.2);
- *Presence of the Web Browser app*: Yes/No.

In particular, the last setting indicates whether the traces related to the usage of the web browser app are included in the experiment's dataset or not. The choice of performing experiments for both cases is motivated by the fact that, according to our experiments, the web browser app seems to be the most difficult to recognize among those due to the fact that each class of webpage can potentially have its own pattern that can be similar to apps of the same type.

Thus its inclusion significantly reduces the accuracy of the methodology. Due to space constraints in this paper we discuss only the four most significant experiments (see Table 1). The results of the other experiments are available in the extended version of this work[2] (a brief summary is also reported in this paper in Appendix B). However, from these we drew the same general conclusions drawn from the first four experiments.

Table 1. Experiments discussed in this article (Flow Timeout and Activity Timeout are in seconds).

Experiment	Connection padding	Flow timeout	Activity timeout	Web browser
Experiment 1	Reduced	10	2	Yes
Experiment 2	Reduced	10	2	No
Experiment 3	Full	10	2	Yes
Experiment 4	Full	10	2	No

7.1 Evaluation Methodology

For each experiment we evaluate the performance achieved by our Proof-of-Concept, namely the performance of the classifier. We asses both the overall performance of the classifier and the performance achieved on a per-class basis, so as to highlight whether some apps are more easily recognized than others. The per-class performance are computed in terms of precision, recall, F1 score and accuracy computed for each class in $\mathcal{C}$. The overall classifier performance are computed by averaging the per-class metrics. Note that precision, recall and F1 score are averaged according to two criteria: micro and macro. The two criteria account differently for imbalances in the dataset (i.e., uneven proportion of samples per classes). The micro criteria biases the corresponding metrics towards the most populated classes, while the macro criteria treats all classes equally [28]. Note, that micro precision and micro recall (and thus micro F1 score), are mathematically equivalent. Thus, when presenting the results of the experiments we will only report the micro F1 score.

7.2 Results

In this section we present the results of the experimental evaluation.

Global evaluation —Table 2 shows a comparison of the results obtained in each experiment through this classifier. In all experiments we achieved the best results with the Random Forest classifier. In all experiments we obtained comparable accuracy ($\sim$0.97).

---

[2] https://arxiv.org/abs/1901.04434.

Table 2. Summary of the results of Experiments 1–4.

Experiment	Avg. accuracy	Micro F1	Macro precision	Macro recall	Macro F1
Experiment 1	0.968	0.840	0.834	0.830	0.832
Experiment 2	0.969	0.859	0.859	0.852	0.855
Experiment 3	0.972	0.861	0.857	0.849	0.853
Experiment 4	0.973	0.880	0.877	0.872	0.875

Table 3. Per-class performance of each classifier for Experiment 1.

APP	Random forest				k–NN				SVC			
	PR.	REC.	F1	ACC.	PR.	REC.	F1	ACC.	PR.	REC.	F1	ACC.
Dailymotion	0.83	0.77	0.8	0.96	0.56	0.58	0.57	0.91	0.74	0.72	0.73	0.95
Facebook	0.9	0.84	0.87	0.98	0.62	0.7	0.66	0.94	0.86	0.85	0.86	0.97
Instagram	0.79	0.86	0.82	0.94	0.58	0.67	0.62	0.88	0.77	0.83	0.8	0.94
Replaio_radio	0.99	0.98	0.98	1.0	0.98	0.96	0.97	0.99	0.98	0.98	0.98	0.99
Skype	0.99	0.96	0.97	1.0	0.97	0.94	0.95	0.99	0.98	0.95	0.97	0.99
Spotify	0.67	0.65	0.66	0.94	0.56	0.48	0.52	0.92	0.63	0.66	0.65	0.93
Torbrowser	0.68	0.77	0.72	0.97	0.6	0.47	0.53	0.95	0.67	0.71	0.69	0.96
Twitch	0.83	0.87	0.85	0.97	0.68	0.76	0.71	0.93	0.83	0.83	0.83	0.96
Utorrent	0.9	0.91	0.9	0.98	0.82	0.69	0.75	0.96	0.85	0.84	0.85	0.97
Youtube	0.76	0.69	0.72	0.95	0.61	0.57	0.59	0.93	0.72	0.63	0.67	0.95

Per-app evaluation —Tables 3, 4, 5 and 6 show the per-app result of each experiment. For all classifiers, we observe a certain variability in how accurate the classifier is in recognizing the various apps. Looking at the F1 score, Spotify, Tor Browser and YouTube appear to be the most difficult apps to recognize. Indeed, by looking directly at the data, we observed that these three apps are often confused, one for another. Since both Spotify and YouTube provide streaming contents, they probably generate strongly similar traffic patterns, that mislead the classifiers. The same reasoning probably applies to Tor Browser. Indeed, webpages may embed streaming content, including YouTube videos themselves. Moreover, in experiments 3 and 4, by looking at the F1 score, we observe that the apps that mislead the classifiers the most are Facebook, Instagram and Tor Browser. This is not surprising. Indeed, if we think of the typical usage patterns of the apps that we considered in our experiments, Facebook, Instagram and Tor Browser are the ones with the largest idle periods (the user "think time"), as opposed to the other apps, that mainly provide streaming content (typically, with less frequent and shorter idle periods). Since the connection padding mechanism is activated by idle periods, it is normal to observe a performance degradation when using full connection padding rather than the reduced one.

Result Summary —As expected, all performance metrics slightly improve when we do not consider the Tor Browser app (see Table 2). Indeed, the type of the vis-

Table 4. Per-class performance of each classifier for Experiment 2.

APP	Random forest				k–NN				SVC			
	PR.	REC.	F1	ACC.	PR.	REC.	F1	ACC.	PR.	REC.	F1	ACC.
Dailymotion	0.83	0.78	0.8	0.96	0.56	0.58	0.57	0.9	0.74	0.72	0.73	0.94
Facebook	0.9	0.84	0.87	0.98	0.65	0.71	0.68	0.94	0.86	0.85	0.85	0.97
Instagram	0.79	0.87	0.83	0.94	0.6	0.67	0.63	0.88	0.77	0.82	0.79	0.93
Replaio_radio	0.99	0.98	0.99	1.0	0.98	0.96	0.97	0.99	0.98	0.98	0.98	0.99
Skype	0.99	0.96	0.98	1.0	0.98	0.95	0.96	0.99	0.98	0.96	0.97	0.99
Spotify	0.72	0.74	0.73	0.95	0.6	0.5	0.55	0.92	0.67	0.72	0.69	0.94
Twitch	0.84	0.87	0.85	0.97	0.68	0.76	0.72	0.93	0.84	0.83	0.83	0.96
Utorrent	0.9	0.93	0.91	0.98	0.83	0.71	0.77	0.96	0.87	0.87	0.87	0.97
Youtube	0.77	0.71	0.74	0.95	0.63	0.56	0.59	0.93	0.73	0.66	0.69	0.95

Table 5. Per-class performance of each classifier for Experiment 3.

APP	Random forest				k–NN				SVC			
	PR.	REC.	F1	ACC.	PR.	REC.	F1	ACC.	PR.	REC.	F1	ACC.
Dailymotion	0.87	0.81	0.84	0.97	0.66	0.72	0.69	0.95	0.8	0.77	0.78	0.97
Facebook	0.78	0.72	0.75	0.96	0.48	0.52	0.5	0.91	0.71	0.72	0.72	0.95
Instagram	0.72	0.7	0.71	0.94	0.47	0.47	0.47	0.89	0.67	0.7	0.68	0.93
Replaio_radio	0.95	0.97	0.96	0.99	0.88	0.94	0.91	0.98	0.96	0.96	0.96	0.99
Skype	0.98	0.95	0.97	0.99	0.93	0.92	0.93	0.98	0.98	0.94	0.96	0.99
Spotify	0.82	0.84	0.83	0.96	0.69	0.68	0.68	0.93	0.76	0.78	0.77	0.95
Torbrowser	0.81	0.69	0.75	0.97	0.64	0.35	0.45	0.94	0.78	0.67	0.72	0.97
Twitch	0.86	0.92	0.89	0.98	0.68	0.77	0.72	0.94	0.86	0.87	0.87	0.97
Utorrent	0.99	0.99	0.99	1.0	0.94	0.98	0.96	0.99	0.98	0.99	0.98	1.0
Youtube	0.79	0.88	0.83	0.96	0.68	0.65	0.66	0.92	0.79	0.82	0.8	0.95

ited website strongly impacts on the characteristics of the generated traffic, which makes this app sometimes be confused with other apps. For example, when visiting a webpage with streaming content the Tor Browser app might be confused with a streaming app (such as Spotify or YouTube). A counterintuitive result that we obtained is that apparently the use of Tor's (full) connection padding actually improved the accuracy over the used reduced connection padding. If we look at the per-class results (Tables 3, 4, 5 and 6) we notice that the performance on Facebook and Instagram apps actually worsen significantly. Also the recall of the Tor Browser app worsen significantly, though its precision improves, which means that the proportion of false negatives increases (the app is more often confused with others), while the number of false positives decreases (other apps are less frequently confused with Tor Browser). The fact that these three apps are more often misclassified when using full padding is what we expected. Indeed, as already pointed out, their typical use patterns involve more frequent "think times" and, thus, idle periods, which trigger the connection padding mechanism. On the other hand, the other apps are mainly characterized by a "streaming" pattern, thus involving extremely less frequent idle periods, which explains why for the majority of them the performance does not worsen. However, it does not explain why they improve. Clearly, the padding mechanism has a strong impact

Table 6. Per-class performance of each classifier for Experiment 4.

APP	Random forest				k–NN				SVC			
	PR.	REC.	F1	ACC.	PR.	REC.	F1	ACC.	PR.	REC.	F1	ACC.
Dailymotion	0.88	0.82	0.85	0.97	0.67	0.71	0.69	0.94	0.81	0.77	0.79	0.96
Facebook	0.82	0.73	0.77	0.96	0.51	0.52	0.52	0.91	0.73	0.73	0.73	0.95
Instagram	0.75	0.71	0.73	0.94	0.51	0.49	0.5	0.89	0.69	0.7	0.69	0.93
Replaio_radio	0.95	0.97	0.96	0.99	0.88	0.94	0.91	0.98	0.96	0.96	0.96	0.99
Skype	0.98	0.96	0.97	0.99	0.96	0.92	0.94	0.98	0.97	0.95	0.96	0.99
Spotify	0.84	0.86	0.85	0.97	0.73	0.69	0.71	0.94	0.8	0.81	0.8	0.95
Twitch	0.87	0.92	0.9	0.98	0.71	0.77	0.74	0.94	0.88	0.87	0.87	0.97
Utorrent	0.99	0.99	0.99	1.0	0.96	0.98	0.97	0.99	0.98	0.99	0.99	1.0
Youtube	0.81	0.88	0.84	0.96	0.71	0.65	0.68	0.92	0.8	0.83	0.81	0.95

on the time-based features (see Sect. 6.2), especially the active/idle time. Our guess is that the full padding mechanism is actually activated statistically more often for some of these streaming apps and less often for others, which actually results in a better separation of the corresponding classes. We plan to better investigate this aspect as future work.

8   Conclusion

In this work we have shown that Tor when used on Android devices is vulnerable to app deanonymization. We described a general methodology to perform an attack against a target smartphone which allows to unveil which apps the victim is using. The proposed methodology performs network traffic analysis based on a supervised machine learning approach. It leverages the fact that different apps produce different recognizable traffic patterns even when protected by Tor. We also provided a Proof-of-Concept that implements the methodology, that we employed to assess the accuracy that it can achieve in deanonymizing apps. We performed several experiments achieving an accuracy of 97.3% and a F1 score of 87.5%. We made the software of the Proof-of-Concept, as well as the datasets that we built during the experiments, publicly available, so that it can be used to assess Tor's vulnerability to this attack, compare alternative methodologies and test possible countermeasures.

As future work we plan to experiment with additional machine learning algorithms. Moreover, in this work we adopted a multi-class classifier approach. We plan to extend our experimental evaluation by testing alternative binary-class approaches (such as *one-vs-all* and *one-vs-one*), in which we employ several binary classifiers in place of a single multi-class classifier. Another improvement to this work may be to enlarge the datasets with a richer set of apps and assess the validity of our Proof-of-Concept in a real-world scenario, targeting real users generated traces.

A   User Simulation

This section describes how we simulated the user interaction in our Proof-of-Concept.

Tor Browser. The user activity on the Tor Browser app has been simulated through a python script that visits webpages randomly sampled from a list of the top 10,000 sites extracted from the Majestic Million dataset [5]. The script spend a randomly drawn amount of time on each webpage, before navigating to the next one.

Instagram. To simulate the user interaction with Instagram, we created a new account and added the Socialblade's top 500 most followed profiles [6]. The simulation script generates random swipe inputs on the Instagram app to scroll the main page up and down with random delays. Swipe down inputs are generated with higher probability than swipe up inputs, as a user browsing Instagram posts would typically scroll the page from top to bottom. After a random number of swipes there is a 30% probability that the user decides to visit another random profile, or otherwise a 30% probability that the user will push the like button on the current Instagram post.

Facebook. The simulation of the user interaction with the Facebook app is very similar to that of Instagram. First we create a Facebook account for the user and we add a list of followed pages derived from Socialblade's top 500 most liked Facebook Pages [7]. Similarly to that of Instagram, the simulation script scrolls the posts in the main page of the Facebook app, by generating random swipe inputs with random delays. After a random number of swipes there is a 30% probability that the user pushes the like button on the post showing on the screen.

Skype. Skype calls have been generated by starting calls with an audio source near the smartphone microphone.

UTorrent. The uTorrent app is a Torrent client and, therefore, it does not require a complex user interaction. We simply add some torrent file to the app, and it starts the download.

Dailymotion, Replaio Radio, Spotify, Twitch, YouTube. Also this apps do not require a very complex interaction with the user. We start each app on some streaming content and leave the app in execution.

B   Experiments Result Summary

Table 7 shows the settings of all the experiments that we performed and a summary of the results obtained.

Table 7. Complete set of experiments with results (Flow Timeout and Activity Timeout are in seconds).

Experiment	Connection padding	Flow timeout	Activity timeout	Web browser	Avg. accuracy	Micro F1	Macro precision	Macro recall	Macro F1
Experiment 1	Reduced	10	2	Yes	0.968	0.840	0.834	0.830	0.832
Experiment 2	Reduced	10	2	No	0.969	0.859	0.859	0.852	0.855
Experiment 3	Full	10	2	Yes	0.972	0.861	0.857	0.849	0.853
Experiment 4	Full	10	2	No	0.973	0.880	0.877	0.872	0.875
Experiment 5	Reduced	10	5	Yes	0.969	0.844	0.836	0.833	0.835
Experiment 6	Reduced	10	5	No	0.969	0.860	0.860	0.854	0.857
Experiment 7	Full	10	5	Yes	0.972	0.862	0.858	0.849	0.854
Experiment 8	Full	10	5	No	0.973	0.878	0.876	0.871	0.873
Experiment 9	Reduced	15	2	Yes	0.970	0.852	0.851	0.844	0.847
Experiment 10	Reduced	15	2	No	0.970	0.866	0.871	0.861	0.866
Experiment 11	Full	15	2	Yes	0.975	0.876	0.874	0.859	0.867
Experiment 12	Full	15	2	No	0.976	0.890	0.888	0.878	0.883
Experiment 13	Reduced	15	5	Yes	0.971	0.853	0.851	0.844	0.847
Experiment 14	Reduced	15	5	No	0.972	0.873	0.877	0.868	0.873
Experiment 15	Full	15	5	Yes	0.976	0.878	0.875	0.861	0.868
Experiment 16	Full	15	5	No	0.976	0.893	0.891	0.881	0.886

References

1. Orbot: Tor for android (2018). https://guardianproject.info/apps/orbot/
2. Tcpdump (2018). https://www.tcpdump.org/
3. Androidviewclient (2019). https://github.com/dtmilano/AndroidViewClient
4. Culebra (2019). http://culebra.dtmilano.com/
5. The majestic million (2019). https://majestic.com/reports/majestic-million
6. Socialblade.com top 500 most followed profiles (sorted by followers count) (2019). https://socialblade.com/instagram/top/500/followers
7. Socialblade.com top 500 most liked facebook pages (sorted by count) (2019). https://socialblade.com/facebook/top/500/likes
8. Wireshark (2019). https://www.wireshark.org/
9. AlSabah, M., Bauer, K., Goldberg, I.: Enhancing tor's performance using real-time traffic classification. In: Proceedings of the 2012 ACM Conference on Computer and Communications Security, CCS 2012, pp. 73–84. ACM, New York (2012). https://doi.org/10.1145/2382196.2382208
10. Bissias, G.D., Liberatore, M., Jensen, D., Levine, B.N.: Privacy vulnerabilities in encrypted HTTP streams. In: Danezis, G., Martin, D. (eds.) PET 2005. LNCS, vol. 3856, pp. 1–11. Springer, Heidelberg (2006). https://doi.org/10.1007/11767831_1
11. Chakravarty, S., Barbera, M.V., Portokalidis, G., Polychronakis, M., Keromytis, A.D.: On the effectiveness of traffic analysis against anonymity networks using flow records. In: Faloutsos, M., Kuzmanovic, A. (eds.) PAM 2014. LNCS, vol. 8362, pp. 247–257. Springer, Cham (2014). https://doi.org/10.1007/978-3-319-04918-2_24
12. Conti, M., Mancini, L.V., Spolaor, R., Verde, N.V.: Can't you hear me knocking: identification of user actions on android apps via traffic analysis. In: Proceedings of the 5th ACM Conference on Data and Application Security and Privacy CODASPY 2015, pp. 297–304. ACM, New York (2015). https://doi.org/10.1145/2699026.2699119

13. Dai, S., Tongaonkar, A., Wang, X., Nucci, A., Song, D.: Networkprofiler: towards automatic fingerprinting of android apps, pp. 809–817, April 2013. https://doi.org/10.1109/INFCOM.2013.6566868
14. Finamore, A., Mellia, M., Munafò, M.M., Torres, R., Rao, S.G.: Youtube everywhere: impact of device and infrastructure synergies on user experience. In: Proceedings of the 2011 ACM SIGCOMM Conference on Internet Measurement Conference, pp. 345–360. ACM (2011)
15. Freedom on the Net: 2017 report (2017). https://freedomhouse.org/report/freedom-net/freedom-net-2017
16. Gember, A., Anand, A., Akella, A.: A comparative study of handheld and non-handheld traffic in campus wi-fi networks. In: Spring, N., Riley, G.F. (eds.) PAM 2011. LNCS, vol. 6579, pp. 173–183. Springer, Heidelberg (2011). https://doi.org/10.1007/978-3-642-19260-9_18
17. Habibi Lashkari, A., Draper Gil, G., Mamun, M.S.I., Ghorbani, A.A.: Characterization of tor traffic using time based features. In: Proceedings of the 3rd International Conference on Information Systems Security and Privacy - Volume 1: ICISSP, pp. 253–262. INSTICC, SciTePress (2017). https://doi.org/10.5220/0006105602530262
18. Hintz, A.: Fingerprinting websites using traffic analysis. In: Dingledine, R., Syverson, P. (eds.) PET 2002. LNCS, vol. 2482, pp. 171–178. Springer, Heidelberg (2003). https://doi.org/10.1007/3-540-36467-6_13. http://dl.acm.org/citation.cfm?id=1765299.1765312
19. Juarez, M., Afroz, S., Acar, G., Diaz, C., Greenstadt, R.: A critical evaluation of website fingerprinting attacks. In: Proceedings of the 2014 ACM SIGSAC Conference on Computer and Communications Security CCS 2014, pp. 263–274. ACM, New York (2014). https://doi.org/10.1145/2660267.2660368
20. Liberatore, M., Levine, B.N.: Inferring the source of encrypted http connections. In: Proceedings of the 13th ACM Conference on Computer and Communications Security CCS 2006, pp. 255–263. ACM, New York (2006). https://doi.org/10.1145/1180405.1180437
21. Ling, Z., Luo, J., Wu, K., Yu, W., Fu, X.: Torward: discovery of malicious traffic over tor. In: IEEE INFOCOM 2014 - IEEE Conference on Computer Communications, pp. 1402–1410 (2014)
22. Mittal, P., Khurshid, A., Juen, J., Caesar, M., Borisov, N.: Stealthy traffic analysis of low-latency anonymous communication using throughput fingerprinting. In: Proceedings of the 18th ACM Conference on Computer and Communications Security CCS 2011, pp. 215–226. ACM, New York (2011). https://doi.org/10.1145/2046707.2046732
23. Perry, M.: Tor padding specification (2019). https://gitweb.torproject.org/torspec.git/tree/padding-spec.txt
24. Project, T.: Tor metrics. https://metrics.torproject.org/. Accessed Jan 2019
25. Redondi, A.E.C., Sanvito, D., Cesana, M.: Passive classification of wi-fi enabled devices. In: Proceedings of the 19th ACM International Conference on Modeling, Analysis and Simulation of Wireless and Mobile Systems MSWiM 2016, pp. 51–58. ACM, New York (2016). https://doi.org/10.1145/2988287.2989161
26. Dinledine, R., Mathewson, N., Murdoch, S., Syverson, P.: Tor: the second-generation onion router (2014 draft v1) (2014). https://murdoch.is/papers/tor14design.pdf
27. Saltaformaggio, B., et al.: Eavesdropping on fine-grained user activities within smartphone apps over encrypted network traffic. In: Proceedings of the 10th USENIX Conference on Offensive Technologies WOOT 2016, pp. 69–78. USENIX Association, Berkeley (2016). http://dl.acm.org/citation.cfm?id=3027019.3027026

28. Sokolova, M., Lapalme, G.: A systematic analysis of performance measures for classification tasks. Inf. Process. Manage. **45**(4), 427–437 (2009). https://doi.org/10.1016/j.ipm.2009.03.002
29. Stöber, T., Frank, M., Schmitt, J., Martinovic, I.: Who do you sync you are?: Smartphone fingerprinting via application behaviour. In: Proceedings of the Sixth ACM Conference on Security and Privacy in Wireless and Mobile Networks WiSec 2013, pp. 7–12. ACM, New York (2013). https://doi.org/10.1145/2462096.2462099
30. Taylor, V.F., Spolaor, R., Conti, M., Martinovic, I.: Appscanner: automatic fingerprinting of smartphone apps from encrypted network traffic. In: 2016 IEEE European Symposium on Security and Privacy (EuroS P), pp. 439–454, March 2016. https://doi.org/10.1109/EuroSP.2016.40
31. Wang, T., Cai, X., Nithyanand, R., Johnson, R., Goldberg, I.: Effective attacks and provable defenses for website fingerprinting. In: Proceedings of the 23rd USENIX Conference on Security Symposium SEC 2014, pp. 143–157. USENIX Association, Berkeley (2014). http://dl.acm.org/citation.cfm?id=2671225.2671235

JSLess: A Tale of a Fileless Javascript Memory-Resident Malware

Sherif Saad[1]([⊠]), Farhan Mahmood[1], William Briguglio[1],
and Haytham Elmiligi[2]

[1] School of Computer Science, University of Windsor, Windsor, Canada
{shsaad,babar111,briguglw}@uwindsor.ca
[2] Thompson Rivers University, Kamloops, Canada
helmiligi@tru.ca

Abstract. New computing paradigms, modern feature-rich programming languages and off-the-shelf software libraries enabled the development of new sophisticated malware families. Evidence of this phenomena is the recent growth of fileless malware attacks. Fileless malware or memory resident malware is an example of an Advanced Volatile Threat (AVT). In a fileless malware attack, the malware writes itself directly onto the main memory (RAM) of the compromised device without leaving any trace on the compromised device's file system. For this reason, fileless malware presents a difficult challenge for traditional malware detection tools and in particular signature-based detection. Moreover, fileless malware forensics and reverse engineering are nearly impossible using traditional methods. The majority of fileless malware attacks in the wild take advantage of MS PowerShell, however, fileless malware are not limited to MS PowerShell. In this paper, we designed and implemented a fileless malware by taking advantage of new features in Javascript and HTML5. The proposed fileless malware could infect any device that supports Javascript and HTML5. It serves as a proof-of-concept (PoC) to demonstrate the threats of fileless malware in web applications. We used the proposed fileless malware to evaluate existing methods and techniques for malware detection in web applications. We tested the proposed fileless malware with several free and commercial malware detection tools that apply both static and dynamic analysis. The proposed fileless malware bypassed all the anti-malware detection tools included in our study. In our analysis, we discussed the limitations of existing approaches/tools and suggested possible detection and mitigation techniques.

Keywords: Fileless malware · Unconventional malware · Web vulnerabilities · Javascript · HTML5 · Polymorphic malware

1 Introduction

Fileless malware is a new class of the memory-resident malware family that successfully infects and compromises a target system without leaving a trace on

© Springer Nature Switzerland AG 2019
S.-H. Heng and J. Lopez (Eds.): ISPEC 2019, LNCS 11879, pp. 113–131, 2019.
https://doi.org/10.1007/978-3-030-34339-2_7

the target filesystem or second memory (e.g., hard drive). Fileless malware infects the target's main-memory (RAM) and executes its malicious payload. Fileless malware is not just another memory-resident malware. To our knowledge, Fred Cohen developed the first memory-resident malware (Lehigh Virus) in the early 80s. This usually leads some researchers to believe that fileless malware is not a new malware threat but only a new name for an old threat. However, this is not true, fileless malware has some distinguishing properties. First, malware attacks require some file infection or writing to the hard drive, this includes traditional memory resident malware. Fileless malware infection and propagation does not require writing any data to the target device filesystem. However, it is possible that the malicious payload (e.g., the end goal) of the fileless malware writes data to the hard drive, for example, a fileless ransomware, but again the ransomware propagation and infection are fileless. The second key property of fileless malware is that it depends heavily on using benign software utilities and libraries already installed on the target device to execute the malicious payload. For instance, a fileless ransomware will use cryptographic library and APIs already installed on the target to complete its attack rather than installing a new cryptographic libraries or implement its own.

There are other unique properties of fileless malware, but the most important ones are the fileless infection approach and the use of benign utilities and libraries of the compromised machine to execute the malicious payload. Those two properties of fileless malware make it an effective threat in evading and bypassing sophisticated anti-malware detection systems. This is because most anti-malware relies on scanning the compromised filesystem to detect malware infections. Also, because fileless malware use legitimate software utilities and programs to attack computer systems, it is challenging for anti-malware systems that use dynamic analysis to detect fileless malware. Moreover, being fileless is an anti-forensics technique, since it does not leave any trace after the attack is complete, it is tough for forensics investigator to reverse engineer the malware.

Fileless malware attacks and incidents are already observed in the wild compromising large enterprises. According to KASPERSKY lab, 140 enterprises were attacked in 2017 using fileless malwares [9]. Ponemon Institute reported that 77% of the attacks against companies use fileless techniques [4]. Also, CYREN recently reported that during 2017 there was over 300% increase in the use of fileless attacks. Moreover, they expected that the new generation of Ransomware would be fileless [12]. This expectation proved to be correct when TrendMicro reported the analysis of SOREBRECT Ransomware, the first fileless ransomware attack in the wild [25]. However, we think that it is inaccurate to describe SORE-BRECT Ransomware as fileless malware, since it places an executable file on the compromised machine which injects the malicious payload into a running system process. Then, it deletes the file and any trace on the system logs using a self-destruct routine. Because the infection and the injection of SOREBRECT Ransomware requires placing files on the compromised host, we do not think it is a true fileless malware. Moreover, deleting the files is not enough to hide the trace, file carving techniques could be used to recover the deleted files.

Another common trend in developing fileless malware is the use of Microsoft PowerShell. PowerShell is a command-line shell and scripting language that allows system administrators to manage and automate tasks related to running process, the operating system, and networks. It is preinstalled by default on new Windows versions and it can be installed on Linux and MacOS systems. PowerShell is a good example of a benign and powerful system utility that could be used by fileless malware. Several reports by anti-malware vendors discussed how malware authors take advantages of PowerShell to develop sophisticated fileless malware [15].

In this paper, we summarize our research on fileless malware attacks in modern web applications. We investigate the possibility of developing a fileless malware using modern Javascript features that were introduced with HTML5. In our assessment of the potential threats of fileless malware attacks, we explore the use of benign Javascript and HTML5 features to develop fileless malware. Based on our analysis we implemented **JSLess** as a proof-of-concept fileless Javascript malware that successfully infects a web browser and executes several malicious payloads.

The contribution of this paper is threefold. First, identify the malicious potential of new benign features in web technology and how they could be used to develop fileless malware. Second, design and implement JSLess as a PoC fileless JS malware that uses a new dynamic injection method and advanced evasion techniques to infect modern web apps and execute a variety of attacks. Third, demonstrate the threats of fileless malware in modern web applications by evaluating the proposed fileless malware with several free and commercial malware detection tools that apply both static and dynamic analysis.

This paper is organized as follows; Sect. 2 is a literature review of fileless malware and Javascript malware. In Sect. 3, we explain the new benign features in modern Javascript and HTML5 and there security issues. Then, in Sect. 4 we present our Javascript fileless malware design and implementation. Next, in Sect. 5 we evaluate the evasion behaviors of the JS fileless malware against free and commercial anti-malware tools, then we discuss possible detection and mitigation techniques. Finally, the conclusion and possible future work presented in Sect. 6.

2   Related Work

Code injection attacks have been studied from different perspectives in the literature. The research in this area tried to detect malicious behaviors in Javascripts using various methods, including signature-based analysis, utilizing machine learning algorithms, using honeynets, and applying several de-obfuscation techniques [14]. This section discusses the main research directions in this area and highlights some of the most important contributions in the literature.

Yoon et al. proposed a method to generate unique signatures for malicious Javascripts [29]. The authors used content-based signature generation techniques and utilized the Term Frequency - Inverse Document Frequency (TF-IDF) and

Balanced Iterative Reducing and Clustering using Hierarchies methods to generate the conjunction signatures for Javascripts [29]. Although signature-based analysis can help detect several malicious behaviours, the work in [29] is based on the assumption that the attack type of the input Javascripts is known, which is not always a practical assumption in real-life environments. Moreover, obfuscation remains a challenging problem that reduces the effectiveness of signature-based techniques.

Blanc et al. tried to address the obfuscation problem by applying abstract syntax tree (AST) based methods to characterize obfuscating transformations found in malicious JavaScript [5]. The authors used AST-based methods to demonstrate significant regularities in obfuscated JavaScript programs. The work in [5] is based on generating AST fingerprints (ASTFs) for each JS file present in their learning dataset then manually picking representative subtrees for further processing. The manual intervention in this procedure and relying only on the training datasets without providing a mechanism to update the training set with new samples raise many questions about the feasibility of this solution. Moreover, the work in [5] did not consider the different categories of obfuscation techniques in real-world malicious JavaScript, which was analyzed by Xu et al. in [28]. Similar work was done by AL-Taharwa et al. to detect obfuscation in JavaScript using semantic-based analysis based on the variable length context-based feature extraction (VCLFE) scheme that takes advantage of AST representation [2].

One controversial issue in this area of research is the physical location where the detection mechanism takes place. One approach is to collect and analyze HTTP traffic via local proxy and implement the detection algorithm on the proxy side [18]. Another approach is to implement the detection mechanism on the client side, such as the work done by Sachin et al., who used lightweight JavaScript instrumentation that enables static and dynamic analysis of the visited webpage to detect malicious behavior [21]. Kishor et al. took an extra step and developed an extension that can be installed on the client web browser to detect malicious web contents [11]. Similar work was done by Wang et al., who focused on the browser detection mechanism integrated with HTML5 and Cross Origin resource sharing (CORS) properties [26].

In recent years, JavaScript became a very popular solution for hybrid mobile applications. This recent adoption of technology in mobile applications poses a new risk of malicious code injection attacks on mobile devices. Mao et al. proposed a method to detect anomalous behaviors in hybrid Android apps as anomalies in function call behaviors [14]. The authors instrumented the JavaScript code dynamically in the JavaScript engine to intercept function calls of JavaScript in hybrid apps. They also extracted events from the Android WebView component to enhance the performance of their proposed detection model [14].

Since the feature engineering step is the core of any machine-learning malware detection solution, many researchers focused on developing a feature engineering methodology. Adas et al. proposed a method to extract inspection features from over two million mobile URLs [1]. The authors used a MapReduce/Hadoop based cloud computing platform to train and implement their classifier and evaluate its performance. Although this is a good step towards building a cloud-based classifier, more experiments need to be conducted to evaluate its efficiency with respect to real-time detection of malware. Moreover, the classification model in [1] was trained with features based on the static analysis of the malicious code, which is not an efficient approach in detecting most fileless malwares.

Ndichu et al. developed a neural network model that can be trained to learn the context information of texts [16]. The main contribution of the work in [16] is developing a new feature extraction method and using unsupervised learning algorithms that produce vectors of fixed lengths. These vectors can be used to train a neural network that classifies the JavaScript code as normal or malicious [16]. Similar work was done earlier by Wang et al. using deep learning [27]. Wang et al. used deep features extracted by stacked denoising auto-encoders (SdA) to detect malicious JavaScript codes [27].

Neural networks were not the only machine learning framework used to detect malicious JavaScript codes. Seshagiri et al. used Support Vector Machine (SVM) to detect malicious JavaScript codes [23]. Features were extracted using static analysis of web pages. Although ML is a promising solution, there are many challenges that faces developers during the implementation of such solutions. The main challenge is creating a feature vector that can truly characterize the behaviour of fileless malware. Fileless malwares do not leave clear traces on the victim's machine and therefore are very difficult to identify.

Other research directions are considered in the literature. The following are few examples of different approaches considered by researchers in the last few years. Sayed et al. proposed a model that uses information flow control dynamically at run-time to detect malicious JavaScript [22]. Fange et al. used Long Short-Term Memory (LSTM) to develop a malicious JavaScript detection model [8]. Shen used a high-level fuzzy Petri net (HLFPN) to detect JavaScript malware [20]. Cosovan used hidden markov models and linear classifiers to detect JavaScript-based malware [6]. Last but not least, Maiorca et al. used discriminant and adversary-aware API analysis to detect malicious scripting code [13].

Although the previous work in this research area presented promising results, there are many challenges that prevent accurate detection of fileless malwares in real web applications. To highlight the significance of the threat posed by fileless malwares, this paper presents a practical design and implementation of a fileless malware as a proof-of-concept (PoC) to demonstrate the threats of fileless malware in web applications.

3   Benign Features with Malicious Potentials

With the introduction of HTML5, a new generation of modern web applications become a reality. This is mainly because HTML5 introduced a rich-set of powerful APIs and features that can be used by JavaScript. Some of the new features and APIs in HTML focus on enabling the development of web apps with high connectivity and performance. Further, HTML5 provides a set of APIs that allow web applications written in JavaScript to access information about the host running the web app and also other peripheral devices connected to the host. For instance, a web app developed with HTML5 and JavaScript could have access to the user geolocation, device orientation, mic, and camera.

While these new powerful features were proposed to improve web application development, we found in our analysis of these features that hackers and malware authors could misuse them. Many of these benign features have serious malicious potential. In this section, we will mainly focus on HTML5 features that were proposed to boost web application performance, scalability, and connectivity.

3.1   WebSockets

WebSocket is a new communication protocol that enables a web-client and a web-server to establish a two-way (full-duplex) interactive communication channel over a single TCP connection [17]. It provides bi-directional real-time communication which is an urgent requirement for modern interactive web applications. With WebSocket, the communication method between the web-client and the web-server is not limited to pull-communication [19]. Instead, push-communication and even an interactive communication become possible. For this reason, WebSocket becomes the dominated technology in developing instant messaging apps, gaming applications, streaming services, or any web app which requires data exchange between the client and the server in real-time.

WebSocket is currently supported by all major web browsers such as Chrome, Firefox, Safari, Edge, and IE. Moreover, the WebSocket protocol is supported by common programming languages such as Java, Python, C#, and others. This enables the development of desktop, mobile apps, or even microservices that communicate using WebSocket as a modern and convenient communication protocol.

It is clear that using WebSocket the connectivity of web apps moves to a new level of high quality and reliability. However, WebSocket is considered by web security researchers a security risk [10]. WebSocket enables a new attack vector for malicious actors. Common web attacks such as cross-site scripting (XSS) and man in the middle (MitM) are possible over WebSockets. WebSocket by design does not obey the same-origin policy; this means the web browser will allow a WebSocket script to connect to different web pages even if they do not share the same origin (same URI scheme, host and port number). Again WebSocket by design is not bound by cross-origin resource sharing (CORS). This means a web app running inside the client web browser could request resources that have a different origin from the web app. This flexibility could be easily abused by malicious actors as we will demonstrate in the next section.

3.2   WebWorkers

Originally JavaScript is a single-threaded language which means in any web app there is only a single line of code or statement that can be executed at any given time. As a result, JavaScript cannot perform multiple tasks simultaneously. Web-Worker is a new JavaScript feature that was introduced with HTML5 to improve the performance of the JavaScript application [3]. WebWorker enables JavaScript code to run in a background thread separate from the main execution thread of a web app. In other words WebWorker allows web applications to execute tasks in the background without impacting the user interface as it works completely separate from the UI thread. For this reason, WebWorkers are typically used to run long and expensive operations without blocking the UI. For instance, the code in Listing 1.1 initialize a new web worker object and runs the code in worker.js asynchronously in a new thread.

```
if (typeof(worker) == "undefined") {
    worker = new Worker("worker.js");
}
```

Listing 1.1. WebWorker Initialization Example

WebWorker should be used to do computationally intensive tasks to avoid blocking the UI or any other code executed in the main thread. If a computationally intensive task executes in the main JavaScript thread, the web app will freeze and become unresponsive to the user. WebWorker is currently supported by all major web browsers such as Chrome, Firefox, Safari, Edge, and IE.

As we can see WebWorker is an essential feature for developing a modern and responsive web application. However, the devil is in the details. While Web-Worker seems like a harmless feature, it opens the door for several malicious scenarios and security issues. For example, it allows DOM-based cross-site scripting (XSS) [24]. CORS does not bind it, and hence a web worker could share and access resources from different origins. But in our opinion, the most critical security issue with WebWorker is its ability to insert silent running JavaScript code. This could enable a malicious payload to run in a background thread created by malicious or compromised web apps. One possible example is using WebWorker with a malicious web app to preform cryptocurrency mining without the users' consent. The WebWorker will terminate if the worker completed the execution of the script or if the user closes the web browser or the web app that created the web worker object.

3.3   Service Workers

ServiceWorker is another new appealing JavaScript feature. We could consider ServiceWorker as a special type of WebWoker. ServiceWorker allows running JavaScript code in a separate background thread. This is very similar to Web-Worker but unlike WebWorker, the lifetime of the ServiceWorker is not tied to a specific webpage or even the web browser [7]. This means even if the user navigates away from the web app that created the ServiceWorker or terminated the web browser, the ServiceWorker will continue to run in the background. The ServiceWorker will normally terminate when it's complete (e.g., execute all the computation tasks) or received a termination signal from the web server, or terminate abnormally as a result of a crash, system reboot or shutdown.

ServiceWorker was introduced to enable rich offline experience to the users and improve the performance of modern web apps. The code in Listing 1.2 shows an example that creates a ServiceWorker from the file **sw_demo.js**. Service-Workers share the same security issues and risks that exist in WebWorkers but the lifetime of the security risks are persistent.

```
window.addEventListener('load', () => {
  navigator.serviceWorker.register('/sw_demo.js')
  .then((registration) => {
    // ServiceWorker registered successfully
  }, (err) => {
    // ServiceWorker registration failed
  });
});
```

Listing 1.2. ServiceWorker Registration Example

4   JavaScript Fileless Malware

In this section, we explain how the benign JavaScript features we introduced in Sect. 3 could be used to implement a fileless JavaScript malware. To demonstrate this threat, we design and implement JSLess as a PoC fileless malware. We design JSLess as a fileless polymorphic malware, with a dynamic malicious payload, that applies both timing and event-based evasion.

4.1   Infection Scenarios

In our investigation, we define two main infection scenarios. The first scenario is when the victim (web user) visits a malicious web server or application as illustrated in Fig. 2. In this case, the malicious web server will not show any malicious behaviors until a specific event triggers the malicious behavior. In our demo, the attack posts specific text messages on a common chat room. The message act as an activation command to the malware. When the message is received the malware is injected dynamically into the victim's browser and starts running as part of the script belonging to the public chat room.

The second infection scenario is when the malware compromise a legitimate web application or server to infect the web browsers of the users who are currently visiting the compromised website as illustrated in Fig. 3. In this case, both the website and the website visitors are victims of the malware attack. The malware will open a connection with the malicious server (e.g., C&C server) that hosts the malware to download the malicious payload or receive a command from the malware authors to execute on the victim browser.

Note that in both scenarios the malicious code infection/injection happens on the client side, not the server side.

4.2   Operational Scenario

JSLess delivered to the victim web browser through a WebSocket connection. When the victim visits a malicious web server, the WebSocket connection will be part of the web app on the malicious server. However, if the malware authors prefer to deliver JSLess by compromising a legitimate web app/server to increase in the infection rate, then the WebSocket delivery code could be added into a third-party JavaScript library (e.g. JQuery). Almost all modern web application relies on integrating third-party JavaScript files. The WebSocket delivery code is relatively (see the code in Listing 1.3) and could easily be hidden in a malicious third-party script library that is disguised as legitimate. Alternatively, the code could be inserted via an HTML injection attack on a vulnerable site that does not correctly sanitize the user input.

```
MalWS = new WebSocket('{{WSSurl}}/KeyCookieLog.js');
MalWS.onmessage = function(e) {
    sc = document.createElement('script');
    sc.type = 'text/javascript';
    sc.id = 'MalSocket';
    sc.appendChild(document.createTextNode(e.data));
    B = document.getElementsByTagName("body");
    B[0].appendChild(sc);
};
```

Listing 1.3. Malicious payload delivered with websocket

The WebSocket API is used to deliver the malware source code in JavaScript to the victim browser. Once the connection is opened, it downloads the JavaScript code and uses it to create a new script element which is appended as a child to the HTML file's body element. This causes the downloaded script to be executed by the client's web browser.

Delivering the malware payload over WebSocket and dynamically inject it into the client's web browser provide several advantages to malware authors. The fact that the malware code is only observable when the web browser is executing the code and mainly as a result of a trigger event provides one important fileless behavior for the malware. The malicious code is never written to the victim's file system. Using WebSocket to deliver the malware payload does not raise any red flags by anti-malware systems since it is a popular and common benign feature. Using benign APIs is another essential characteristic of fileless malware.

The fact that JSLess can send any malicious payload for many attack vectors and inject arbitrary JavaScript code with the option to obfuscate the injected malicious code enables the design of polymorphic malware. All of these attributes make JSLess a powerful malware threat that can easily evade detection by anti-malware systems. For instance, a pure JavaScript logger could be quickly injected in the user's browser to captures user's keystroke events and send them to the malware C&C server over WebSocket. Note that benign and native JavaScript keystroke capturing APIs are used which again will not raise any red flags. Figure 1 shows an example of an injected JavaScript key logger that captures keystroke events and send it to the malware C&C server over WebSockect.

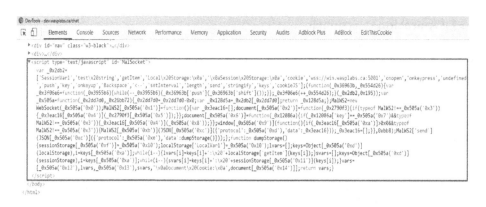

Fig. 1. Obfuscated JavaScript code injected in the body of web page which opens a secure WebSocket connection with Remote C&C Server to send the user's keystrokes information to attacker

To utilize the victim system's computation power or run the malicious scripts in a separate thread from the main UI thread, JSless takes advantage of Web-Workers. This allows JSless to run malicious activities that are computationally intensive, such as cryptocurrency mining. The WebWorker script is downloaded from the C&C server. The JavaScript code in Listing 1.4 shows how the malicious WebWorker code could be obtained as a blob object and initiated on the victim's browser. In conjunction with the importScripts and createObjectURL functions, we were able to load a script from a different domain hosted on the different server and executed it in the background of the benign web app.

```
blob = new Blob(["self.importScripts('{{HTTPSurl}}/foo.js');"
    ],
        {type: 'application/Javascript'});

w = new Worker(URL.createObjectURL(blob));
```
Listing 1.4. Breaking Same-origin Policy with ImportScripts()

Until this point one limitation of JSless malware-framework is that fact that the malware will terminate as soon as the user closes his web browser or navigates away from the compromised/malicious web server. This limitation is not specific to JSless, it is the common behaviors of any fileless malware. In fact, many malware authors sacrifice the persistence of their malware infection by using fileless malware to avoid detection and bypass anti-malware systems. However, that does not mean fileless malware authors are not trying to come up with new methods and techniques to make their fileless malware persistent. In our investigation to provide persistence for JSless even if the user navigates away from the compromised/malicious web page or closes the web browser, we took advantage of the ServiceWorker API to implement a malware persistence technique with minimal footprint.

To achieve malware persistence, we used the WebSocket API to download a script from the malicious server. After downloading the ServiceWorker registration code from the malicious server as shown in Listing 1.1, it registers a sync event as shown in Listing 1.5, cause the downloaded code to execute and stay alive even if the user has navigated away from the original page or closed the web browser. The malicious code will continue to run and terminate normally when it is completed or abnormally as result of exception, crash or if the user restarts his machine. Note that when we use ServiceWorker, a file is created and temporarily stored on the client machine while the ServiceWorker is running. This is the only case where JSless will place a file on the victim machine, and it is only needed for malware persistence.

```
self.addEventListener('sync', function (event) {
  if (event.tag === 'mal-service-worker') {
   event.waitUntil(malServiceWorker()
   .then((response) => {
    // Service Worker task is done
   }));
  }
});

function malServiceWorker() {
 // Malicious activity can be performed here
}
```

Listing 1.5. ServiceWorker Implementation for malicious purpose

In our proof-of-concept implementation for the malware persistence with ServiceWorker, we implemented a MapReduce system. In this malicious MapReduce system, all the current infected web browsers receive the map function and a chunk of the data via WebSocket. The map function executes as a ServiceWorker and operates over the data chunks sent by the malicious server. When the ServiceWorker finishes executing the map function, it returns the result to the malicious server via WebSocket. When the malicious server receives the results from the ServiceWorker, it performs the reduce phase and returns the final result to the malware author.

4.3   Attack Vectors

The ability to inject and execute arbitrary JavaScript code allows JSless to support a wide variety of malicious attacks. Here are the most common attacks that JSless could execute:

Data Stealing. On infection JSless can easily collect keystrokes, cookie and web storage data, as demonstrated in our PoC. Also, it could control multimedia devices and capture data from a connected mic or webcam using native browser WebRTC APIs.

DDoS. JSless malicious C&C server could orchestrate all the currently infected web browsers to connect to a specific URL or web server to perform a DDoS attack. In this case, JSless constructs a botnet of infected browsers to execute the DDoS attack.

Resource Consumption Attack. In this case, JSless could use the infected users' browser to run computationally intensive tasks such as cryptocurrency mining, password cracking, etc. The MapReduce system we implement as part of JSless is an example of managing and running computationally intensive tasks. Also, beside the above attacks which we have implemented in our JSless it is possible to perform other attacks like Click Fraud, RAT-in-the-Browser (RitB) Attacks, and many other web-based attacks.

5   Experiment and Evaluation

In order to assess the identified JavaScript/HTML5 vulnerabilities and threats, we developed JSless as a proof-of-concept fileless malware that is completely written in JavaScript. We used the second injection scenario to test our fileless malware implementation. For this purpose, we also implemented a web app that JSless will compromise to infect the web browser of any user using the web app. The web app is a shared chat board that allows users to register, post and receive messages to/from a shared chat board. The web app and the JSless C&C server are implemented in JavaScript using MEAN stack (MongoDB, ExpressJS, AngularJS, and Node.js). The source code for the fileless malware and the target web app is available on our GitHub/bitbucket repository for interested researchers and security analysts.

For the actual test, we deployed the target web app and the JSless C&C server on Amazon Web Services (AWS). We used two AWS instances with two different domains, one to host the target web app and the second to host JSLess C&C server. We mainly tested two attack vectors, the data stealing attack and the resource consumption attack.

5.1   JS Malware Detection Tools

To our surprise, few anti-malware systems try to detect JavaScript malware. We identified seven tools that we considered promising based on the techniques and the technology they use for detection. Most of the tools apply both static and dynamic analysis. Some of those tools are commercial, but they provide a free trial period that includes all the commercial feature for a limited time. Table 1 shows the list of tools we used in our study.

None of the tools were able to detect JSless malicious behaviors.

Table 1. JavaScript and web app malware detection tools

Tool name	Detection technique	License	Website	Detect JSLess
ReScan.pro	Static & dynamic	Commercial	https://rescan.pro/	NO
VirusTotal	Static & dynamic	Free & commerical	https://www.virustotal.com/	NO
SUCURI	Static	Commercial	https://sucuri.net/	NO
SiteGuarding	Static	Commercial	https://www.siteguarding.com/	NO
Web Inspector	Static & dynamic	Free	https://app.webinspector.com/	NO
Quttera	Static & dynamic	Free & commercial	https://quttera.com/	NO
AI-Bolit	Static & dynamic	Free & commercial	https://revisium.com/aibo/	NO

5.2 Detection and Mitigation

By reviewing the results from the detection tools and how those tools work, it is obvious that detecting JSLess is not possible. The use of WebSocket to inject and run obfuscated malicious code, make it almost impossible to any static analysis tool to detect JSLess, since the malicious payload does not exist at the time of static analysis. The use of benign JavaScript/HTML5 APIs and features, in addition to the dynamic injection behaviors also make it very difficult for the current dynamic analysis tools to detect JSLess. Blocking or preventing new JavaScript/HTML5 APIs is not the solution and it is not an option. In our opinion, a dynamic analysis technique that implements continuous monitoring and context-aware is the only approach that we think could detect or mitigate fileless malware similar to JSLess.

5.3 Tools Analysis Results

ReScan.Pro. It is a cloud-based web application scanner which takes URL of the website and generates a scan report after filtering the website for web-based malware and other web security issues. It explores the website URLs and checks for infections, suspicious contents, obfuscated malware injections, hidden redirects and other web security threats present. In-depth and comprehensive analysis of ReScan.Pro based on three main features.

1. *Static Page Scanning:* combination generic signature detection technique and heuristic detection. It uses signature and pattern-based analysis to identify malicious code snippets and malware injections. It also looks for malicious and blacklisted URLs in a proprietary database.
2. *Behavioral Analysis:* imitates the website user's behavior to evaluate the intended action of implemented functionality.
3. *Dynamic Page Analysis:* performs dynamic web page loading analysis which includes deobfuscation techniques to decode the encoded JavaScript in order to identify the runtime code injects and it also checks for malware in external JavaScript files.

We ran the experiment with the ReScan.Pro to test if it will detect the malicious activities of JSless malware. It generated a well defined report after analyzing the website with its static and dynamic features. The produced result shows that the website is clean and no malicious activity has been found. ReScan.Pro could not detect our JavaScript fileless malware.

Web Inspector. This tool runs a website security scan and provides a malware report which has more information than most other tools. Its security scanner is bit different from others because it performs both malware and vulnerabilities scans together. For scanning a website, it just requires a user to provide the website URL and click on the 'Start the Scan' button. It starts scanning the website and generates the report within minutes. This tool provides five different detection technologies such as (1) Honeypot Engine, (2) Antivirus Detection, (3) BlackList Checking, (4) SSL Checking, and (5) Analyst Research. The Honeypot Engine has special algorithms for Exploit Packs and multi-redirect malware detection and it gives full web content scan using a real browser clone with popular plugins. Web inspector shows a threat report which includes Blacklists, Phishing, Malware Downloads, Suspicious code, Heuristic Viruses, Suspicious connections, and worms.

As described above, Web Inspector provides a report on full web content scanning by applying various techniques to detect malware. However, we noticed that our JavaScript fileless malware was able to successfully deceive this malware detection tool as well.

Sucuri. Sucuri is yet another tool that offers a website monitoring solution to evaluate any website's security with a free online scanner. This scanning tool searches for various indicators of compromise, which includes malware, drive-by downloads, defacement, hidden redirects, conditional malware, etc. To match more signatures and generate fewer false positives, it uses static techniques with intelligent signatures which are based on code anomalies and heuristic detection. Server side monitoring is another service provided by them which can be hosted on the compromised server to look for backdoors, phishing attack vulnerabilities, and other security issues by scanning the files present on the server. Moreover, Sucuri provides a scanning API as a paid feature to scan any site and get a result similar to what is provided on its internal malware scanners.

Testing with Sucuri online scanner, we see it displays that there is "No Malware Found" as well as a seek bar indicating a medium security risk. However, this is due to Insecure SSL certificates, not from the detection of our fileless malware.

Quttera. Quttera is a popular website scanner that attempts to identify malware and suspicious activities in web application. Its malware detector contains non-signature based technology which attempts to uncover traffic re-directs, generic malware, and security weakness exploits. It can be accessed from any computer or mobile device through a web browser. It also provides real-time detection of shell-codes, obfuscated JavaScript, malicious iframes, traffic redirect and other online threats.

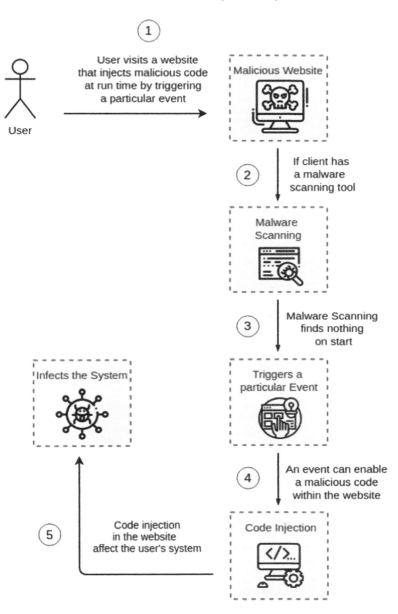

Fig. 2. JavaScript fileless malware first infection scenario

VirusTotal. VirusTotal is a free malware inspection tool which offers a number of services to scan websites and files leveraging a large set of antivirus engines and website scanners. This aggregation of different tools covers wide variety of techniques, such as heuristic, signature based analysis, domain blacklisting

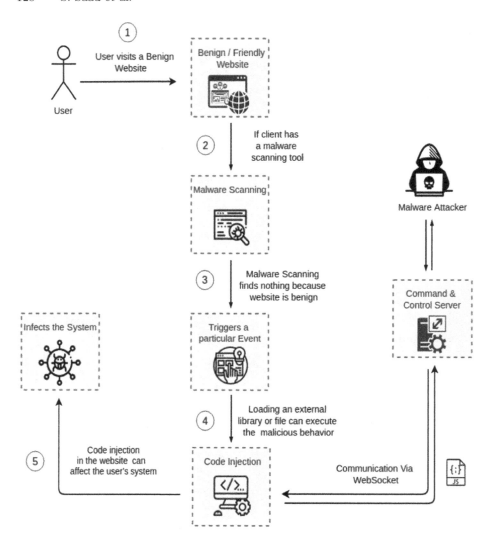

Fig. 3. JavaScript fileless malware second infection scenario

services, etc. A detailed report is provided after completing the scan which not only indicates the malicious content present in a file or website but also exhibits the detection label by each engine.

We scan our compromised web app with VirusTools using 66 different malware detection engine, and none of those 66 engines was able to detect that the web app is compromised.

AI-BOLIT is an antivirus malware scanner for websites and hosting. It uses heuristic analysis and other patented AI algorithms to find malware from any kind of scripts and templates. We used it to scan our JSLess malware scripts. However, it failed to detect JSLess and it generated false positive when it consider some of the core modules of NodeJS as malicious JavaScripts.

6 Conclusion and Future Work

In this paper, we confirmed several threat-vectors that exist in new JavaScript and HTML5. We demonstrate how an attacker could abuse benign features and APIs in JavaScript and HTML5 to implement fileless malware with advanced evasion capabilities. We showed a practical implementation of a fileless JavaScript malware that to our knowledge the first of its kind. The proof-of-concept implementation of the proposed JS fileless malware successfully bypasses several well-known anti-malware systems that are designed to detect JavaScript and web malware. In addition, third-party malware analysts team confirmed our finding and prove that the proposed malware bypasses automated malware detection systems. From this particular study, we conclude that the current static and dynamic analysis techniques are limited if not useless against fileless malware attacks. Moreover, fileless malware attacks are not limited to PowerShell and Windows environment. In our opinion, any computing environment that enables running and executing arbitrary code could are vulnerable to fileless attacks.

Our future work could be summarized in three different directions. First, we will continue extending the malicious behaviors of JSLess and investigate the possibility of more advanced attacks using other new benign features and APIs from JavaScript and HTML5. Second, we will design a new detection technique to detect advanced JS malware and mainly fileless JS malware like the proposed JSLess. We plan to implement behaviors and dynamic analysis approach that continually monitor and analysis Javascript and Browser activities. Finally, our third research direction will focus on investigating fileless malware threat in unconventional computing environments, such as the Internet of Things, in-memory computing environments (e.g., Redis, Hazelcast, Spark, etc.). We hope our research will help to raise awareness of the emerging unconventional malware threats.

References

1. Adas, H., Shetty, S., Tayib, W.: Scalable detection of web malware on smartphones. In: 2015 International Conference on Information and Communication Technology Research (ICTRC), pp. 198–201, May 2015
2. AL-Taharwa, I.A., et al.: RedJsod: a readable JavaScript obfuscation detector using semantic-based analysis. In: 2012 IEEE 11th International Conference on Trust, Security and Privacy in Computing and Communications, pp. 1370–1375, June 2012
3. Arias, D.: Speedy introduction to web workers, August 2018. https://auth0.com/blog/speedy-introduction-to-web-workers/
4. Barkly. The 2017 state of endpoint security risk (2017). https://www.barkly.com/ponemon-2018-endpoint-security-risk

5. Blanc, G., Miyamoto, D., Akiyama, M., Kadobayashi, Y.: Characterizing obfuscated JavaScript using abstract syntax trees: experimenting with malicious scripts. In: 2012 26th International Conference on Advanced Information Networking and Applications Workshops, pp. 344–351, March 2012

6. Cosovan, D., Benchea, R., Gavrilut, D.: A practical guide for detecting the Java script-based malware using hidden Markov models and linear classifiers. In: 2014 16th International Symposium on Symbolic and Numeric Algorithms for Scientific Computing, pp. 236–243, September 2014

7. Google Developers. Introduction to service worker—web, May 2019. https://developers.google.com/web/ilt/pwa/introduction-to-service-worker

8. Fang, Y., Huang, C., Liu, L., Xue, M.: Research on malicious JavaScript detection technology based on LSTM. IEEE Access **6**, 59118–59125 (2018)

9. Global Research and Analysis Team: KASPERSKY Lab. Fileless attack against enterprise network, White Paper (2017)

10. INFOSEC. Websocket security issues, December 2014. https://resources.infosecinstitute.com/websocket-security-issues/

11. Kishore, K.R., Mallesh, M., Jyostna, G., Eswari, P.R.L., Sarma, S.S.: Browser JS guard: detects and defends against malicious JavaScript injection based drive by download attacks. In: The Fifth International Conference on the Applications of Digital Information and Web Technologies (ICADIWT 2014), pp. 92–100, February 2014

12. Magnusardottir, A.: Fileless ransomware: how it works & how to stop it?, June 2018. https://www.infosecurityeurope.com/en/Sessions/58302/Fileless-Ransomware-How-It-Works-How-To-Stop-It

13. Maiorca, D., Russu, P., Corona, I., Biggio, B., Giacinto, G.: Detection of malicious scripting code through discriminant and adversary-aware API analysis. In: Armando, A., Baldoni, R., Focardi, R. (eds.) Proceedings of the First Italian Conference on Cybersecurity (ITASEC17), Venice, Italy, 17–20 January 2017. CEUR Workshop Proceedings, vol. 1816, pp. 96–105. CEUR-WS.org (2017)

14. Mao, J., Bian, J., Bai, G., Wang, R., Chen, Y., Xiao, Y., Liang, Z.: Detecting malicious behaviors in JavaScript applications. IEEE Access **6**, 12284–12294 (2018)

15. McAfee. Fileless malware execution with powershell is easier than you may realize, March 2017. https://www.mcafee.com/enterprise/en-us/assets/solution-briefs/sb-fileless-malware-execution.pdf

16. Ndichu, S., Ozawa, S., Misu, T., Okada, K.: A machine learning approach to malicious JavaScript detection using fixed length vector representation. In: 2018 International Joint Conference on Neural Networks (IJCNN), pp. 1–8, July 2018

17. Mozilla Developer Network. Glossary: websockets (2015). https://developer.mozilla.org/en-US/docs/Glossary/WebSockets

18. Oh, S., Bae, H., Yoon, S., Kim, H., Cha, Y.: Malicious script blocking detection technology using a local proxy. In: 2016 10th International Conference on Innovative Mobile and Internet Services in Ubiquitous Computing (IMIS), pp. 495–498, July 2016

19. Kaazing Corporation Peter Lubbers & Frank Greco. HTML5 websocket: a quantum leap in scalability for the web. www.websocket.org/quantum.html

20. Shen, V.R.L., Wei, C.-S., Juang, T.T.-Y.: JavaScript malware detection using a high-level fuzzy Petri net, pp. 511–514, July 2018

21. Sachin, V., Chiplunkar, N.N.: SurfGuard JavaScript instrumentation-based defense against drive-by downloads. In: 2012 International Conference on Recent Advances in Computing and Software Systems, pp. 267–272, April 2012

22. Sayed, B., Traoré, I., Abdelhalim. A.: Detection and mitigation of malicious JavaScript using information flow control. In: 2014 Twelfth Annual International Conference on Privacy, Security and Trust, pp. 264–273, July 2014
23. Seshagiri, P., Vazhayil, A., Sriram, P.: AMA: static code analysis of web page for the detection of malicious scripts. Procedia Comput. Sci. **93**, 768–773 (2016). Proceedings of the 6th International Conference on Advances in Computing and Communications
24. Netsparker Security Team. DOM based cross-site scripting vulnerability, May 2019. https://www.netsparker.com/blog/web-security/dom-based-cross-site-scripting-vulnerability/
25. TrendMicro. Analyzing the fileless, code-injecting sorebrect ransomware, June 2017. https://blog.trendmicro.com/trendlabs-security-intelligence/analyzing-fileless-code-injecting-sorebrect-ransomware/
26. Wang, C., Zhou, Y.: A new cross-site scripting detection mechanism integrated with HTML5 and CORS properties by using browser extensions. In: 2016 International Computer Symposium (ICS), pp. 264–269, December 2016
27. Wang, Y., Cai, W.-D., Wei, P.: A deep learning approach for detecting malicious JavaScript code. Secur. Commun. Netw. **9**, 1520–1534 (2016)
28. Xu, W., Zhang, F., Zhu, S.: The power of obfuscation techniques in malicious JavaScript code: a measurement study. In: 2012 7th International Conference on Malicious and Unwanted Software, pp. 9–16, October 2012
29. Yoon, S., Jung, J., Noh, M., Chung, K., Im, C.: Automatic attack signature generation technology for malicious JavaScript. In: Proceedings of 2014 International Conference on Modelling, Identification Control, pp. 351–354, December 2014

Security Protocol and Tool

A Physical ZKP for Slitherlink: How to Perform Physical Topology-Preserving Computation

Pascal Lafourcade[1] , Daiki Miyahara[2,4] , Takaaki Mizuki[3] ,
Tatsuya Sasaki[2], and Hideaki Sone[3]

[1] LIMOS, University Clermont Auvergne, CNRS UMR 6158,
Clermont-Ferrand, France
[2] Graduate School of Information Sciences, Tohoku University, Sendai, Japan
daiki.miyahara.q4@dc.tohoku.ac.jp
[3] Cyberscience Center, Tohoku University, Sendai, Japan
[4] National Institute of Advanced Industrial Science and Technology, Tokyo, Japan

Abstract. We propose a new technique to construct physical Zero-Knowledge Proof (ZKP) protocols for games that require a single loop draw feature. This feature appears in Slitherlink, a puzzle by Nikoli. Our approach is based on the observation that a loop has only one hole and this property remains stable by some simple transformations. Using this trick, we can transform a simple big loop, visible to anyone, into the solution loop by using transformations that do not disclose any information about the solution. As a proof of concept, we apply this technique to construct the first physical ZKP protocol for Slitherlink.

Keywords: Physical Zero-Knowledge Proof · Slitherlink · Physical Topology Preserving Computation

1 Introduction

Zero-Knowledge Proof (ZKP) systems are powerful cryptographic tools that were introduced by Goldwasser, Micali, and Rackoff in [10]. It was then shown that for any NP-complete problem, there exists an interactive ZKP protocol [9]. Later, one of the first physical ZKP protocols was introduced by Naor et al. in [11] for a popular puzzle, Sudoku. In the mentioned article, a prover wants to prove to a verifier that he/she knows the solution of a Sudoku puzzle instance using only physical objects; to this end, in that paper the authors used only cards. Recently in [21], better ZKP protocols have been proposed in terms of numbers of cards used and complexity. They used envelopes and physical tricks to improve the original protocol.

Nikoli[1] is a Japanese company famous for designing puzzles. The list of puzzles created by Nikoli contains more than 40 different kinds of puzzles including

---

[1] http://www.nikoli.com/.

© Springer Nature Switzerland AG 2019
S.-H. Heng and J. Lopez (Eds.): ISPEC 2019, LNCS 11879, pp. 135–151, 2019.
https://doi.org/10.1007/978-3-030-34339-2_8

Sudoku. In this paper, we focus on *Slitherlink* that was introduced in 1989 in issue the 26th of Nikoli's Puzzle Times. It is also known as *Loop-the-Loop*. It is explained on Nikoli's web site as follows: *"Getting the loop right is absorbing and addictive. Watch out not to get lost in Slitherlink. It's amazing to see how endless patterns can be made using only four numbers (0, 1, 2 and 3)"*. Slitherlink was proven to be NP-complete in [23] and other variants in [16]. It means that applying the technique of [9] to construct a ZKP is possible.

Our aim is to propose a physical ZKP protocol for this game. Slitherlink is not like other Nikoli's games since it requires to draw a **single** loop to solve the puzzle. This feature of the game is a challenge that was not present in the previous physical ZKPs for Nikoli's puzzles [4–6,8,11,21].

Contributions: We introduce a new technique to construct a ZKP protocol for a puzzle where constructing a single loop is one of the requirements of the solution. The difficulty is to avoid leaking any information regarding the solution to the verifier. For this, we use a topological point of view; more precisely, we use the notion of homology that defines and categorizes holes in a manifold. The main idea is that after any continuous transformations, the number of holes always remains the same. Using this simple idea, we construct transformations that preserve the number of loops in the solution. First, the verifier checks that the initial configuration has only a single big loop. Then, by transforming in several steps this trivial big loop into the solution, the prover convinces step after step that the solution has only one loop at the end by proving that the transformation does not break the loop or introduce an extra hole. This construction is applied to Slitherlink in this article but it can be used for any other puzzles that require such type of features in their rules.

Related Works: Since Naor et al. [11] introduced the first physical ZKP protocol for the Sudoku, physical ZKPs for other puzzles (proven to be NP-complete) have been proposed, e.g., Nonogram [6], Akari, Takuzu, Kakuro, Kenken [4], Makaro [5], and Norinori [8]. All these ZKPs deal with numbers. For example, in Sudoku, a prover has to show the verifier that each column, row, and subgrid contain all the numbers from one to nine.

Physical objects enable us to perform secure computation without relying on computers: such examples are a PEZ dispenser [2], tamper-evident seals [18], and a deck of cards [3]. Among them, secure computation with a deck of cards, called *card-based cryptography*, has been widely studied. Especially, for secure computation of logical AND function, the number of required cards have been reduced in [7,15,17,19,22], and necessary and sufficient numbers of cards have been provided in [13,15].

However, these works do not deal with proving the topological feature of having a single loop in the solution.

Outline: In Sect. 2, we define the rules of Slitherlink, the formal definition of ZKP, and the notation used in this paper. In Sect. 3, we describe our ZKP protocol for Slitherlink. In Sect. 4, we show the security proofs of ZKP.

2 Preliminaries

Rules of Slitherlink

Slitherlink is one of the most famous pencil puzzles published in the puzzle magazine *Nikoli*. The puzzle instance consists of lattice-like dots where some squares contain numbers between 0 and 3. The goal of the puzzle is to draw lines that satisfy the following rules [1]:

1. Connect vertical/horizontal adjacent dots with lines to make a single loop.
2. Each number indicates the number of lines that should surround its square, while empty squares may be surrounded with any number of lines.
3. The loop never crosses itself and never branches off.

Figure 1 shows an example of a Slitherlink puzzle and its solution; one can easily verify that all conditions are satisfied.

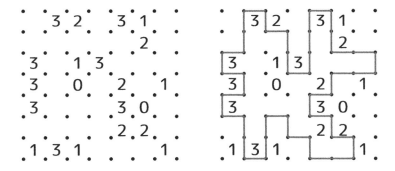

Fig. 1. Example of a standard Slitherlink challenge, and its solution.

Zero-Knowledge Proof

A *Zero-Knowledge Proof (ZKP)* is a secure two-party protocol between a prover P and a verifier V. Formally, they both have an instance of $\mathcal{I}$ of a problem and only P knows the solution w. The prover P wants to convince V that he/she knows w without revealing any information about w. Such a proof is called a *zero-knowledge proof*, if it satisfies the following three properties.

Completeness. If P knows w, then P can convince V.

Extractability. If P does not know w, then P cannot convince V.

Zero-Knowledge. V cannot obtain any information about w. Assuming a probabilistic polynomial time algorithm $M(\mathcal{I})$ not containing w if outputs of the protocol and $M(\mathcal{I})$ follow the same probability distribution, the zero-knowledge property is satisfied.

Notations

We use the following physical cards: ♣♣ ⋯ ♡♡; the black ♣ and red ♡ cards are called *binary cards*. The backs of all cards are identical and denoted by ?. In our construction, binary cards are used to encode the existence of a line while number cards are used for rearranging the positions of cards, as shown later.

Encoding: We encode Boolean values with two binary cards as follows: ♣♡ = 0 and ♡♣ = 1. Two face-down cards encoding 0 and 1 are called a *0-commitment* and a *1-commitment*, which are denoted by 0 and 1, respectively.

In our protocol, a 0-commitment placed on a gap between two adjacent dots means that there is no line on the gap, and a 1-commitment means that there is a line on the gap. With this encoding, we can represent a loop that is made of several lines. Note that given an x-commitment for $x \in \{0, 1\}$, swapping the two cards consisting the commitment results in an $\bar{x}$-commitment; thus, negation can be easily done.

Shuffle: Given a sequence of m face-down cards $(c_1, c_2, \ldots, c_m)$, a *shuffle* results in a sequence $(c_{r^{-1}(1)}, c_{r^{-1}(2)}, \ldots, c_{r^{-1}(m)})$, where $r \in S_m$ is a uniformly distributed random permutation and S_m denotes the symmetric group of degree m.

Pile-Shifting Shuffle: The goal of this operation, which is also called Pile-Shifting Scramble [20], is to *cyclically* shuffle piles of cards. That is, given m piles, each of which consists of the same number of face-down cards, denoted by $(pile_1, pile_2, \ldots, pile_m)$, applying a Pile-Shifting Shuffle results in $(pile_{s+1}, pile_{ss+2}, \ldots, pile_{s+m})$:

$$\underbrace{?}_{pile_1} \underbrace{?}_{pile_2} \cdots \underbrace{?}_{pile_m} \rightarrow \underbrace{?}_{pile_{s+1}} \underbrace{?}_{pile_{s+2}} \cdots \underbrace{?}_{pile_{s+m}},$$

where s is uniformly and randomly chosen from $\mathbb{Z}/m\mathbb{Z}$. To implement Pile-Shifting Shuffle, we use physical cases that can store a pile of cards, such as boxes and envelopes; a player (or players) cyclically shuffle them by hand until nobody traces the offset. It can be done by physical object as the one created for the physical ZKP for Sudoku in [21].

Pile-Scramble Shuffle: Pile-Scramble Shuffle is a well-known shuffle operation which was first used in [12]. As mentioned above, let us denote m piles by $(pile_1, pile_2, \ldots, pile_m)$. For such a sequence of piles, applying a Pile-Scramble Shuffle results in $(pile_{r^{-1}(1)}, pile_{r^{-1}(2)}, \ldots, pile_{r^{-1}(m)})$, where $r \in S_m$ is a uniformly distributed random permutation. A Pile-Scramble Shuffle uses similar material as Pile-Shifting Shuffle but its operation is similar to Shuffle.

Chosen Pile Cut: It was proposed in [14]. *Chosen Pile Cut* enables a prover to choose a pile $pile_i$ from m piles $(pile_1, pile_2, \ldots, pile_m)$ without revealing i to a verifier. The Chosen Pile Cut proceeds as follows, given m piles along with m additional cards:

1. The prover P holds $m-1$ ♣s and one ♡. Then, P places m cards with their faces down below the piles such that only the i-th card is ♡:

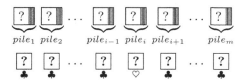

2. Regarding the cards in the same row as a pile, apply Pile-Shifting Shuffle to the piles (denoted by $\langle \cdot \mid \ldots \mid \cdot \rangle$):

$$\left\langle \underbrace{\boxed{?}}_{pile_1} \middle| \underbrace{\boxed{?}}_{pile_2} \middle| \ldots \middle| \underbrace{\boxed{?}}_{pile_m} \right\rangle \rightarrow \underbrace{\boxed{?}}_{pile_{s+1}} \underbrace{\boxed{?}}_{pile_{s+2}} \ldots \underbrace{\boxed{?}}_{pile_{s+m}},$$

where s is generated uniformly at random from $\mathbb{Z}/m\mathbb{Z}$ by this shuffle action.

3. Reveal all the cards in the second row. Then, one ♡ appears, and the pile above the revealed ♡ is $pile_i$, and hence, we can obtain the desired $pile_i$.

Owing to the Pile-Shifting Shuffle in Step 2, revealing cards leaks no information about i and thus, Chosen Pile Cut leaks no information about i, the index of the chosen pile.

3   Zero-Knowledge Proof for Slitherlink

In this section, we construct our physical zero-knowledge proof protocol for Slitherlink. The outline of our protocol is as follows.

Input Phase: The verifier V puts a 1-commitment (i.e., two face-down cards encoding 1) on every gap on the boundary of the puzzle board and 0-commitments on all the remaining gaps. In other words, V creates a single big loop whose size is the same as the board.

Topology-Preserving Computation Phase: The prover P transforms the shape of the loop according to the solution. After this phase, V is convinced that the placement of 1-commitments satisfies Rules 1 and 3 of Slitherlink without the disclosure of any information about the shape.

Verification Phase: V verifies that the placement of 1-commitments satisfies Rule 2 of Slitherlink.

We introduce some subprotocols in Sect. 3.1 before presenting our protocol in Sect. 3.2.

3.1 Subprotocols

Chosen Pile Protocol: This is an extended version of the Chosen Pile Cut [14] explained in Sect. 2. Given m piles with $2m$ additional cards, this protocol enables P to choose the i-th pile and regenerate the original sequence of m piles.

1. Using $m - 1$ ♣s and one ♡, the prover P places m cards with their faces down below the given piles such that only the i-th card is ♡:

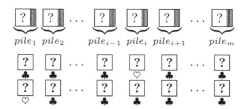

   We further put m cards below the cards such that only the first card is ♡:

2. Considering the cards in the same row as a pile, apply a Pile-Shifting Shuffle to the sequence of piles:

   where s is generated uniformly at random from $\mathbb{Z}/m\mathbb{Z}$.
3. Reveal all the cards in the second row. Then, one ♡ appears, and the pile above the revealed ♡ is the i-th pile (and hence, P can obtain $pile_i$). When this protocol is invoked, certain operations are applied to the chosen pile. Then, the chosen pile is placed back to the i-th position in the sequence.
4. Remove the revealed cards, i.e., the cards in the second row. Then, apply a Pile-Shifting Shuffle:

   where s' is generated uniformly at random from $\mathbb{Z}/m\mathbb{Z}$.

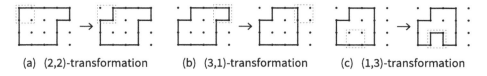

(a) (2,2)-transformation   (b) (3,1)-transformation   (c) (1,3)-transformation

Fig. 2. Three transformations.

5. Reveal all the cards in the second row. Then, one $\boxed{\heartsuit}$ appears, and the pile above the revealed $\boxed{\heartsuit}$ is $pile_1$. Therefore, by shifting the sequence of piles, we can obtain a sequence of piles whose order is the same as the original one without revealing any information about the order of input sequence.

Verifying-Degree Protocol: This protocol can verify that the "degree" of a target vertex (dot) is not four. Here, *degree* means the number of 1-commitments placed around a target vertex. Thus, the prover P wants to prove that there is at least one 0-commitment around the target vertex (when only P knows what the four commitments around the target are).

The Verifying-Degree Protocol proceeds as follows.

1. Given four commitments that are placed around the target vertex, these can be regarded as a sequence of 4 commitments:

2. By using Chosen Pile Protocol, P chooses one of the 0-commitments. Open the chosen pile to show that it is 0. Now, V is convinced that the degree of the target vertex is not four. Then, V turns over all the opened cards. Because only a 0-commitment is always opened, no information about the four commitments is disclosed.
3. V performs the remaining steps in the Chosen Pile Protocol. Then, all the cards are placed back to their original positions.

Topology-Preserving Computation: This protocol changes a given loop into another loop by one of the three transformations given in Fig. 2. Each transformation changes the lines surrounding a square, represented by dash line in Fig. 2.

Remember that a line is expressed by a commitment (i.e., two face-down binary cards) in our protocol. Therefore, for example, a $(2, 2)$-transformation means.

This can be implemented by swapping two cards of each commitment. (Remember that swapping the two cards performs negation of a commitment.) A (3, 1)-transformation and a (1, 3)-transformation can also be implemented by swapping two cards of each commitment:

Now, P wants to apply one of the three transformations while the applied transformation is hidden from V. Furthermore, P needs to show that the commitments around a target square are "transformable." Note that the three transformations are applicable to four commitments around a square if and only if there exists a 0-commitment facing a 1-commitment.

Topology-Preserving Computation proceeds as follows.

1. Pick four commitments around a target square:

2. P chooses a 0-commitment facing a 1-commitment using Chosen Pile Protocol.
3. V reveals the chosen commitment and the commitment that is two piles away from it:

Then, V checks that the two commitments are a 0-commitment and a 1-commitment to be convinced that any transformation can be applied.
4. After turning over all the opened cards, V performs the remaining steps in the Chosen Pile Protocol to place all the cards back to their original positions.
5. Swap the two cards of each of the four commitments. (Remember that this results in negating all the four commitments, and hence, a transformation is applied.)
6. V applies a Verifying-Degree Protocol to each of the four dots of the target square. Then, V is convinced that no dots of degree four have been obtained as the result of transformation. This guarantees that the loop was not split and thus, it remains a single loop.

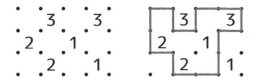

Fig. 3. Small example of Slitherlink challenge, and its solution.

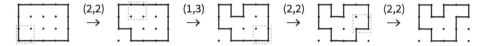

Fig. 4. Transformation process.

3.2   Our Construction

As mentioned at the beginning of this section, the main idea behind our protocol is that the verifier V first creates a big loop and then the prover P transforms the loop into the solution loop one by one. Let us consider a puzzle instance shown in Fig. 3 as an example. Our protocol transforms the loop as illustrated in Fig. 4.

We are now ready to present the full description of our zero-knowledge proof protocol for Slitherlink.

Input Phase: The verifier V puts a 1-commitment on every gap on the boundary of the puzzle board and 0-commitments on all the other gaps. This placement corresponds to the single loop with the same size as the board. The following is an example of the placement of (2×2)-square puzzle board:

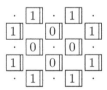

P will apply Topology-Preserving Computation to these commitments to transform the shape of the loop into the solution. Here, P needs to hide the target square. Therefore, we make a sequence of piles from the placed cards, pick the four target commitments using the Chosen Pile Protocol, and apply Topology-Preserving Computation. To properly pick the four commitments, a sequence of piles is formed, as follows.

We first expand the puzzle board by adding dots around the original board. (For explanation, the expanded dots are denoted by ⊙.)

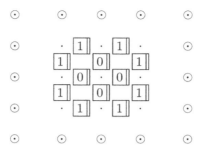

Note that the expanded area is unrelated to the actual puzzle board. V puts dummy commitments on the gaps at the expanded area other than the right and the bottom ends. Each dummy commitment consists of two black cards ♣♣ to prevent the loop from spreading over the expanded area. We denote the dummy commitment by ♣.

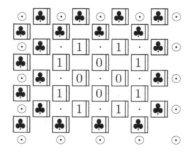

Next, V makes a sequence of 4-card piles as follows. For each square, V first makes a pile from the commitments placed on the left and the top (the commitment on the gap between each vertically consecutive dots is placed on the commitment on its upper right).

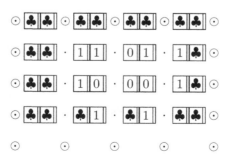

Then, pick 4-card piles from top to bottom:

♣♣♣♣♣♣ ⋯ ♣1♣1♣♣

to make a sequence of piles:

$$\boxed{?}\,\boxed{?}\,\boxed{?}\,\cdots\,\boxed{?}\,\boxed{?}\,\boxed{?}$$

Topology-Preserving Computation Phase: In this phase, P applies transformations (explained in Sect. 3.1) to stepwise change the big loop to the solution loop. Let n be the size of the puzzle instance, namely the number of squares on the puzzle board. Then, note that P can make the solution loop by at most n transformations.

1. P applies the following exactly $n-1$ times such that either the resulting loop is already the solution, or one more transformation will end up the solution. (This is possible because successive two transformations (of the same) to the same square keep the loop unchanged.)
   (a) P applies the Chosen Pile Protocol to the sequence of 4-card piles: P picks a 4-card pile composed of left and top edges of the square that P wants to transform. The other edges can be picked by counting the distance from the chosen pile[2].
   (b) P applies the Topology-Preserving Computation to the four picked commitments.
   (c) V performs the remaining steps in the Chosen Pile Protocol to place the cards back to their original positions.
2. P applies one more transformation or does not change the solution loop so that V does not learn which action occurs, as follows.
   (a) Similarly to Step 1 (a) above, P picks four commitments around the target square.
   (b) By using the method explained in Topology-Preserving Computation, V confirms that any transformation is applicable.
   (c) V arranges the four commitments vertically and makes a pile from each column:

$$\begin{array}{cc}\boxed{?}&\boxed{?}\\\boxed{?}&\boxed{?}\\\boxed{?}&\boxed{?}\\\boxed{?}&\boxed{?}\end{array}\quad\rightarrow\quad\boxed{?}\,\boxed{?}$$

   Note that swapping two piles results in inverted value of each commitment. Thus, it is equivalent to applying a transformation.
   (d) Using the Chosen Pile Cut, if P wants to transform the target square, then P chooses the right pile; otherwise, the left pile is chosen.
   (e) Rearrange the cards vertically such that the chosen pile is placed at left:

$$\underbrace{\boxed{?}\quad\boxed{?}}_{\text{Chosen pile}}\quad\rightarrow\quad\begin{array}{cc}\boxed{?}&\boxed{?}\\\boxed{?}&\boxed{?}\\\boxed{?}&\boxed{?}\\\boxed{?}&\boxed{?}\end{array}$$

---

[2] In the above example, the bottom edge corresponds to the pile which is 4 piles away from the chosen pile. Note that the distance between any two piles never changes because only Pile-Shifting Shuffle is applied.

(f) V makes four commitments from each row, performs the remaining steps in the Chosen Pile Protocol, and places each commitment back to their original position.

3. Finally, all cards are placed on the puzzle board and the cards at the dummy area are removed.

Verification Phase: V is now convinced that the placement of 1-commitments is a single loop (Rule 1) and it never branches off (Rule 3). Therefore, V only needs to verify that the placement satisfies Rule 2 of Slitherlink.

Now, V verifies that the number on each square is equal to the number of lines surrounding it. The verification proceeds as follows, where we virtually assume that the board is colored like a checkered pattern so that all squares in the first row are alternation of blue and yellow, those in the second row are alternation of yellow and blue, and so on.

1. V picks all left cards (if the square is virtually blue) or all right cards (if the square is yellow) of four commitments around a square on which a number is written:

$$\boxed{?}\boxed{?}\boxed{?}\boxed{?}.$$

2. P shuffles the four cards.
3. V reveals the four cards.
   - If V picked all the left cards of four commitments in Step 1, V checks that the number of red cards $\boxed{\heartsuit}$ is equal to the number on the square.
   - If V picked all the right cards of four commitments in Step 1, V checks that the number of black cards $\boxed{\clubsuit}$ is equal to the number on the square.
4. Apply Steps 1 to 3 to all other numbered squares. (Note that a commitment is related to at most one blue numbered square and one yellow numbered square.)

Our protocol uses $6(p+2)(q+2)+8$ cards in total, where we have a $p \times q$ board.

4   Security Proofs for Our Construction

In this section, we show that our construction satisfies the completeness, extractability, and zero-knowledge properties.

Completeness: In the input phase, V is convinced that 1-commitments are placed in a single loop because V does the operations by himself/herself, and hence, V is convinced that the placement satisfies Rules 1 and 3 of Slitherlink. As explained in Sect. 3.1, the transformations are applied to only applicable squares. Thus, every transformation is performed while preserving Rules 1 and 3. By verifying that the placement satisfies Rule 2 in verification phase, V is convinced that P knows the solution. Therefore, if P has a solution for the puzzle then P can always convince V.

Remember that P uses only (3, 1), (1, 3), and (2, 2)-transformations in the Topology-Preserving Computation to transform a single loop into the shape of the solution. We now prove that this is possible in Theorem 1.

Theorem 1. *Let n be the number of squares in the puzzle instance (namely, the big loop), and let k be the number of squares inside its solution loop. By applying a transformation to the loop exactly $n - k$ times, the big loop can be transformed into the solution loop.*

To prove Theorem 1, we first show Lemmas 1 and 2.

Lemma 1. *The resulting placement of 1-commitments after the Topology-Preserving Computation always represents a single loop.*

Proof. Remember Steps 2 and 6 in the Topology-Preserving Computation: Due to Step 2, the target square is guaranteed to be none of the following two ones (up to rotations).

That is, one of (2, 2), (3, 1), and (1, 3)-transformations is always applied to the target square.

Due to the execution of the Verifying-Degree Protocol in Step 6, the following two transformations that make a loop split cannot occur.

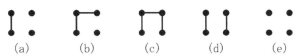

Therefore, it remains a single loop.   □

Lemma 2. *For any single loop, there is always a (3, 1), (1, 3), or (2, 2)-transformation that increases the number of squares inside the loop by exactly one.*

Proof. Consider a single loop; let ℓ be the number of squares inside the loop. To prove this lemma, we show that there always exists a square on the board such that a (3, 1), (1, 3), or (2, 2)-transformation can be applied to the square such that ℓ increases. Note that the loop remains single after the application of the transformation by Lemma 1.

If $\ell \leq 2$, a (1, 3)-transformation increases the number of squares by one. Thus, one may assume that $\ell \geq 3$. Then, any square outside the loop can be classified in one of the following five types (up to rotations):

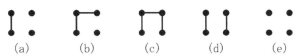

(a)   (b)   (c)   (d)   (e)

If none of (a), (b), and (c) exists, all squares outside the loop are either (d) or (e), and hence, it would not be a single loop. Therefore, at least one square of type (a), (b), or (c) must exist outside the loop.

Applying a $(3, 1)$, $(1, 3)$, or $(2, 2)$-transformation to such an external square results in increasing ℓ by one.   □

By these lemmas, Theorem 1 can be proved.

Proof of Theorem 1. By Lemmas 1 and 2, we can always increase the number of squares inside the solution loop by a transformation. Therefore, we can repeat the transformation so that the solution loop becomes the big loop. This means that, conversely, the big loop can be transformed into the solution loop by applying $(3, 1)$, $(1, 3)$, or $(2, 2)$-transformation exactly $n - k$ times.   □

Extractability: Only the person who knows the solution can transform the loop so that the shape satisfies Rule 2. Therefore, V can detect any illegal prover in Verification Phase. Thus, if the prover does not know the solution for a puzzle, then V will be never convinced, irrespective of P's behavior.

More formally, to prove the extractability, we are required to show that any shape that does not satisfy Rule 1, 2, or 3 is always rejected during the protocol.

Theorem 2. *If the prover does not know the solution for the Slitherlink puzzle, then the verifier always rejects regardless of the prover's behavior.*

To prove Theorem 2, we show that the resulting loop after the Topology-Preserving Computation always satisfies Rules 1 and 3 (as in Lemma 1) and any single loop that does not satisfy Rule 2 is always rejected in Verification Phase (as in Lemma 3). Therefore, any single loop except for the solution is always rejected.

Lemma 3. *Any (single) loop that does not satisfy Rule 2 is always rejected in Verification Phase.*

Proof. Consider any (single) loop that does not satisfy Rule 2, i.e., there are four commitments surrounding a numbered square such that the number of 1-commitments among them is not equal to the number. Due to Step 3 in Verification Phase, all the left (or right) cards of four commitments are turned over (after shuffling them), and hence, the number of 1-commitments is revealed. This means that the verifier can always reject any (single) loop that does not satisfy Rule 2.   □

Proof of Theorem 2. By Lemma 1, the resulting loop after the Topology-Preserving Computation is always single, i.e., it satisfies Rules 1 and 3. By Lemma 3, if it does not satisfy Rule 2, the verifier always rejects it in Verification Phase. That is, any loop except for the solution cannot go through Verification Phase.   □

Zero-Knowledge: In our construction, all the opened cards have been shuffled before being opened. Therefore, all distributions of opened cards can be simulated by a simulator $M(\mathcal{I})$ who does not know the solution. For example, at Step 3 in Verification Phase, the Pile-Scramble Shuffle have been applied to opened commitments; thus, this is indistinguishable from a simulation putting randomly 1-commitments such that the number of them is equal to the number of the square.

5   Conclusion

In this study, we introduced a new technique that can transform a single loop encoded with physical objects into a new geometrical figure while preserving the single loop. Furthermore, by using this secure computation, we constructed the first physical zero-knowledge proof protocol for Slitherlink.

As we mentioned in Sect. 1, our construction can be used for other puzzles that require a feature of drawing a single loop. For example, *Masyu* published by Nikoli has the same rule as Slitherlink, i.e., we should draw a single loop that never crosses itself and never branches off. Therefore, we can easily construct a physical ZKP protocol for Masyu by executing Topology-Preserving Computation (and then verifying the other rules).

Because physical ZKP protocols should be executed by humans' hands, we usually consider the size of puzzle instance to be bounded by a constant. This differs from conventional ZKP protocols (relying on computers). Note that people enjoying a pencil puzzle will not use a computer to solve it, and hence, physical ZKP protocols are useful and effective for ordinally people.

Acknowledgement. We thank the anonymous referees, whose comments have helped us to improve the presentation of the paper. This work was supported by JSPS KAKENHI Grant Number JP17K00001 and JP19J21153.

References

1. Nikoli, Slitherlink. http://www.nikoli.co.jp/en/puzzles/slitherlink.html
2. Balogh, J., Csirik, J.A., Ishai, Y., Kushilevitz, E.: Private computation using a PEZ dispenser. Theor. Comput. Sci. **306**(1–3), 69–84 (2003)
3. Boer, B.: More efficient match-making and satisfiability *the five card trick*. In: Quisquater, J.-J., Vandewalle, J. (eds.) EUROCRYPT 1989. LNCS, vol. 434, pp. 208–217. Springer, Heidelberg (1990). https://doi.org/10.1007/3-540-46885-4_23
4. Bultel, X., Dreier, J., Dumas, J.G., Lafourcade, P.: Physical zero-knowledge proofs for Akari, Takuzu, Kakuro and KenKen. In: Demaine, E.D., Grandoni, F. (eds.) FUN 2016. LIPIcs, vol. 49, pp. 8:1–8:20 (2016)
5. Bultel, X., et al.: Physical zero-knowledge proof for Makaro. In: Izumi, T., Kuznetsov, P. (eds.) SSS 2018. LNCS, vol. 11201, pp. 111–125. Springer, Cham (2018). https://doi.org/10.1007/978-3-030-03232-6_8

6. Chien, Y.-F., Hon, W.-K.: Cryptographic and physical zero-knowledge proof: from Sudoku to Nonogram. In: Boldi, P., Gargano, L. (eds.) FUN 2010. LNCS, vol. 6099, pp. 102–112. Springer, Heidelberg (2010). https://doi.org/10.1007/978-3-642-13122-6_12

7. Crépeau, C., Kilian, J.: Discreet solitary games. In: Stinson, D.R. (ed.) CRYPTO 1993. LNCS, vol. 773, pp. 319–330. Springer, Heidelberg (1994). https://doi.org/10.1007/3-540-48329-2_27

8. Dumas, J.-G., Lafourcade, P., Miyahara, D., Mizuki, T., Sasaki, T., Sone, H.: Interactive physical zero-knowledge proof for Norinori. In: Du, D.-Z., Duan, Z., Tian, C. (eds.) COCOON 2019. LNCS, vol. 11653, pp. 166–177. Springer, Cham (2019). https://doi.org/10.1007/978-3-030-26176-4_14

9. Goldreich, O., Kahan, A.: How to construct constant-round zero-knowledge proof systems for NP. J. Cryptol. 9(3), 167–189 (1991)

10. Goldwasser, S., Micali, S., Rackoff, C.: The knowledge complexity of interactive proof-systems. In: STOC 1985, pp. 291–304. ACM (1985)

11. Gradwohl, R., Naor, M., Pinkas, B., Rothblum, G.N.: Cryptographic and physical zero-knowledge proof systems for solutions of sudoku puzzles. In: Crescenzi, P., Prencipe, G., Pucci, G. (eds.) FUN 2007. LNCS, vol. 4475, pp. 166–182. Springer, Heidelberg (2007). https://doi.org/10.1007/978-3-540-72914-3_16

12. Ishikawa, R., Chida, E., Mizuki, T.: Efficient card-based protocols for generating a hidden random permutation without fixed points. In: Calude, C.S., Dinneen, M.J. (eds.) UCNC 2015. LNCS, vol. 9252, pp. 215–226. Springer, Cham (2015). https://doi.org/10.1007/978-3-319-21819-9_16

13. Kastner, J., Koch, A., Walzer, S., Miyahara, D., Hayashi, Y., Mizuki, T., Sone, H.: The minimum number of cards in practical card-based protocols. In: Takagi, T., Peyrin, T. (eds.) ASIACRYPT 2017. LNCS, vol. 10626, pp. 126–155. Springer, Cham (2017). https://doi.org/10.1007/978-3-319-70700-6_5

14. Koch, A., Walzer, S.: Foundations for actively secure card-based cryptography. IACR Cryptology ePrint Archive 2017, 423 (2017)

15. Koch, A., Walzer, S., Härtel, K.: Card-based cryptographic protocols using a minimal number of cards. In: Iwata, T., Cheon, J.H. (eds.) ASIACRYPT 2015. LNCS, vol. 9452, pp. 783–807. Springer, Heidelberg (2015). https://doi.org/10.1007/978-3-662-48797-6_32

16. Kölker, J.: Selected slither link variants are NP-complete. J. Inf. Process. 20(3), 709–712 (2012)

17. Mizuki, T., Sone, H.: Six-card secure AND and four-card secure XOR. In: Deng, X., Hopcroft, J.E., Xue, J. (eds.) FAW 2009. LNCS, vol. 5598, pp. 358–369. Springer, Heidelberg (2009). https://doi.org/10.1007/978-3-642-02270-8_36

18. Moran, T., Naor, M.: Basing cryptographic protocols on tamper-evident seals. In: Caires, L., Italiano, G.F., Monteiro, L., Palamidessi, C., Yung, M. (eds.) ICALP 2005. LNCS, vol. 3580, pp. 285–297. Springer, Heidelberg (2005). https://doi.org/10.1007/11523468_24

19. Niemi, V., Renvall, A.: Secure multiparty computations without computers. Theor. Comput. Sci. 191(1–2), 173–183 (1998)

20. Nishimura, A., Hayashi, Y., Mizuki, T., Sone, H.: Pile-shifting scramble for card-based protocols. IEICE Trans. Fundam. Electron. Commun. Comput. Sci. 101(9), 1494–1502 (2018)

21. Sasaki, T., Mizuki, T., Sone, H.: Card-based zero-knowledge proof for Sudoku. In: Ito, H., Leonardi, S., Pagli, L., Prencipe, G. (eds.) Fun with Algorithms 2018. LIPIcs, vol. 100, pp. 29:1–29:10. Schloss Dagstuhl - Leibniz-Zentrum fuer Informatik (2018)

22. Stiglic, A.: Computations with a deck of cards. Theor. Comput. Sci. **259**(1–2), 671–678 (2001)
23. Yato, T., Seta, T.: Complexity and completeness of finding another solution and its application to puzzles. IEICE Trans. Fundam. Electron. Commun. Comput. Sci. (Inst. Electron. Inf. Commun. Eng.) **E86–A**(5), 1052–1060 (2003)

Secure Best Arm Identification
in Multi-armed Bandits

Radu Ciucanu[1]([⊠]), Pascal Lafourcade[2], Marius Lombard-Platet[3,4],
and Marta Soare[1]

[1] INSA Centre Val de Loire, Univ. Orléans, LIFO EA 4022, Orléans, France
radu.ciucanu@insa-cvl.fr, marta.soare@univ-orleans.fr
[2] Université Clermont Auvergne, LIMOS CNRS UMR 6158, Aubière, France
pascal.lafourcade@uca.fr
[3] Département d'informatique de l'ENS, École normale supérieure, CNRS,
PSL Research University, Paris, France
marius.lombard-platet@ens.fr
[4] Be-Studys, Geneva, Switzerland

Abstract. The stochastic multi-armed bandit is a classical decision making model, where an agent repeatedly chooses an action (pull a bandit arm) and the environment responds with a stochastic outcome (reward) coming from an unknown distribution associated with the chosen action. A popular objective for the agent is that of identifying the arm with the maximum expected reward, also known as the *best-arm identification* problem. We address the inherent privacy concerns that occur in a best-arm identification problem when outsourcing the data and computations to a *honest-but-curious* cloud.

Our main contribution is a distributed protocol that computes the best arm while guaranteeing that (i) no cloud node can learn at the same time information about the rewards and about the arms ranking, and (ii) by analyzing the messages communicated between the different cloud nodes, no information can be learned about the rewards or about the ranking. In other words, the two properties ensure that the protocol has no security single point of failure. We rely on the partially homomorphic property of the well-known Paillier's cryptosystem as a building block in our protocol. We prove the correctness of our protocol and we present proof-of-concept experiments suggesting its practical feasibility.

Keywords: Multi-armed bandits · Best arm identification · Privacy · Distributed computation · Paillier cryptosystem

1 Introduction

In a stochastic multi-armed bandit model, a learning agent sequentially needs to decide which *arm* (option/action) to pull from K arms with unknown associated

---

This project is partially funded by the European Union's Horizon 2020 Research and Innovation Programme under Grant Agreement No. 826404.

User

Budget N

Best arm learned
for budget N

K arms

Data Owner

Fig. 1. System architecture.

values available in the learning environment. After each pull, the environment responds with a feedback, in the form of a stochastic *reward* from an unknown distribution associated with the arm chosen by the agent. This is a dynamic research topic with a wide range of applications, including clinical trials for deciding on the best treatment to give to a patient [17], on-line advertisements and recommender systems [12], or game playing [4,11,14].

In this paper, we focus on a popular objective in multi-armed bandits, that of *best arm identification*: given a set of K arms and a limited budget of N pulls, the goal of the agent is to design a budget-allocation strategy that maximizes the probability of identifying the arm with the maximum expected reward. This problem has been extensively studied in the machine learning community [1, 3,7,8,10,16], but to the best of our knowledge, there is no previous work that considers this problem from a privacy-preserving viewpoint. Next, we illustrate the problem via a motivating example.

Use Case Example. A classical real-world application of the *best-arm identification* problem is as follows. Before launching a new product on the market, companies can create several versions of the product that are put into a testing phase. By *product*, we refer here to any type of object/service that might be offered by a company and that may contain (or be obtained as a result of analyzing) private data. Each version of the product has distinguishing characteristics and the company surveys potential customers about the version they prefer. The company's objective is that once the testing phase is over, it can put on the market the version that is likely to yield the best sales. The goal of the best-arm identification problem is to define algorithms that maximize the probability of identifying the best arm (here, the best version among the K alternative versions), given a limited budget of N observations (here, customer surveys). Therefore, best-arm identification algorithms are a good fit for the product testing phase.

Now, imagine the scenario where a company collected over the years a large quantity of customer surveys that it no longer needs for its purposes. This data may actually be useful for other smaller companies that cannot afford doing their own customer surveys, but nonetheless want to simulate the test of different versions of their product. This brings us to the system architecture depicted in Fig. 1. The *data owner* is the company that owns a large quantity of customer surveys that it wants to monetize. The *user* is the small company that wants to simulate the testing of different versions of its product, without conducting its own customer survey. It may actually be cheaper to pay a limited budget to reuse pieces of existing data, rather than doing a new survey with real customers.

The interaction between the data owner and the user is done using some *public cloud*, where initially the data owner outsources its data, then the users interact directly with the cloud. More precisely, each user allocates some budget to the cloud and reuses the available surveys for deciding which version of its own product should be put on the market. The budget would refer here to the number of survey answers the user wants the cloud to use before outputting the best option. As a simplified example, assume that the available data consists of user preferences about the characteristics of security devices they would buy for protecting their homes. There are 1M surveys available and consulting a survey costs 0.1$. If a small company wants to know which type of device people from their market are more likely to buy, the precision of the answer it receives from the cloud depends on the paid budget. If it pays 100$, it is more likely to get a clearer image about the type of device that is the most likely to be purchased, than if it pays 5$. But in both cases the obtained information is not 100% sure because only a sample of the available data is consulted.

The aforementioned use case can be easily reformulated to other real-world scenarios, such as health or medical data, cosmetics (e.g., trials for finding the best anti-wrinkle cream), data concerning political preferences, education and employment records, to name a few.

As already mentioned, we consider a scenario where the multi-armed bandits (i.e., the *data*) as well as the best arm identification algorithm (i.e., the *computation*) are outsourced to some public cloud. We assume that the cloud is *honest-but-curious*: it executes tasks dutifully, and try to gain information on the ranking of the arms and their associated values from the data they receive. We address the privacy concerns that occur when outsourcing the data and computations.

Indeed, the externalized data can be communicated over an untrustworthy network and processed on some untrustworthy machines, where malicious public cloud users may learn private data that belongs only to the data owner. This is why we require the data owner to encrypt all information about the arms before outsourcing the data to the public cloud.

Moreover, each cloud user observes a result of the best arm identification algorithm that is proportional to the budget that the user pays. It should be impossible for a malicious cloud user to compose observations of several runs of the best arm identification algorithm in order to learn the best arm with a higher confidence, and then sell this information to some other user.

Summary of Contributions and Paper Organization. In Sect. 2, we give background information on the problem of best-arm identification in multi-armed bandits.

In Sect. 3, we first present the considered security model, then the needed security tools, and finally the distributed security protocol, that is the main contribution of the paper. We rely on the partial homomorphic property of Paillier's cryptosystem [15] as a building block in our protocol. The difficulty of our setting comes from the fact that we need additions, multiplications, and comparisons to solve the best arm identification problem, whereas a partially homomorphic cryptosystem such as Paillier's provides only homomorphic additions. Therefore, in our protocol we distribute the computation among several participants and insure that each of them can only learn the specific information needed for performing their task, and no any other information. Thus, we show that our distributed protocol has no single point of failure, in the *honest-but-curious* cloud model. The overhead due to the security primitives of our protocol depends only on the number of arms K and not on the budget N. This is a desirable property because in practice the budget N (i.e., the number of arm pulls that we are allowed to do) is often much larger than the number of arms K among which we can choose.

We prove the security of our protocol in Appendix A, and we present proof-of-concept experiments suggesting its feasibility in Sect. 4. We discuss related work in Sect. 5, and conclusions and future work in Sect. 6.

2   Primer on Multi-armed Bandits

The problem of *best arm identification in multi-armed bandits* [1] has been initially formulated in the domain of real numbers. We slightly revisit the initial formulation of the problem in order to manipulate integers. The reason behind this adaptation is that later on in our protocol, we rely on public key cryptography tools to add security guarantees to a state-of-the-art best arm identification algorithm.

Input. The input is twofold:

- Number of arms K. Each arm $i \in \{1, \ldots, K\}$ is associated to a reward value $x(i)$ and a reward function r that returns a random integer in an interval $[x(i) - \epsilon, x(i) + \epsilon]$ according to a uniform probability distribution. Whereas each arm i is associated to its specific value $x(i)$, the value of ϵ is common to all arms. The intervals associated to different arms may be overlapping, which makes the setting non-trivial. The best arm i^* is $\arg\max_{i \in \{1,\ldots,K\}} x(i)$.
- Budget N that means how many arm pulls (and implicit reward observations) the user is allowed to do.

Note that for designing a budget-allocation strategy between the arms, only the number of arms K and the budget N are known. There is no initial information about the reward associated to each arm.

Output. The estimated best arm $\widehat{i^*}_\alpha$ that can be learned after making N arm pulls (and subsequent reward observations) according to some allocation strategy α, which defines how the budget is divided between the K arms. The challenge is to design a budget-allocation strategy α that makes the best possible use of the budget. In other words, when selecting the arms to be pulled according to α, the observed rewards allow to acquire as much useful information as possible for identifying i^*.

Performance Measure. We call *simple regret* R_N the difference between the value of the (true) best arm i^* and the arm $\widehat{i^*}_\alpha$ estimated as being the best arm by an allocation strategy α after N arm pulls. Thus, we compare the gap between the value of the identification made by strategy α and that of an *oracle* strategy that knows the values of the arms beforehand. Formally, the performance of strategy α after using a budget N is $R_N(\alpha) = x(i^*) - x(i_\alpha^*)$.

Example. We have 3 arms with associated reward values in intervals $[3, 23]$, $[25, 45]$, and $[40, 60]$. This means that $x(1) = 13, x(2) = 35, x(3) = 50$, and $\epsilon = 10$. Assuming a budget of 3, the user may choose to spend one pull for each arm and observe rewards of (for instance) 23, 44, and 41, respectively. Hence, the user could wrongly think that arm 2 is the best, thus getting a regret of $50 - 35 = 15$.

Obviously, increasing the budget would increase the number of pulls that can be done, hence it would increase the chances of correctly identifying the best arm. This can be easily done in the presence of an infinite budget, but the challenge is to identify the best arm using as few pulls as possible, or in other words, to maximize the probability of correctly identifying the best arm while having a limited budget.

Successive Rejects (SR) [1]. The algorithm takes as input the number of arms K and the budget N. Initially, all K arms are candidates. SR divides the budget in $K-1$ phases. At the end of each phase, a decision is made. The phases' lengths are fixed such that the available budget is not exceeded and the probability of wrongly identifying the best arm is minimized.

More precisely, at each phase $j \in \{1, \ldots, K-1\}$, each still candidate arm in A_j is pulled n_j times according to the fixed allocation (cf. Algorithm 1). At the end of each phase, the algorithm rejects the arm with the lowest sum of observed rewards, that is the arm estimated to be the worst. If there is a tie, SR randomly selects the arm to reject among the worst arms. Then, at the next phase, the remaining arms are again uniformly pulled according to the fixed allocation. Thus, the worst arm is pulled n_1 times, the second worst is pulled $n_2 + n_1$ times, and so on, with the best and the second-best arm being pulled $n_{K-1} + \ldots + n_1$ times. The estimated best arm is the unique arm remaining after phase $K - 1$.

We consider the sums of observed rewards per arm when deciding which arm to reject instead of empirical means as in the original version [1] as a simplification. Indeed, each candidate arm is pulled the same number of times in each phase, hence the ranking of the arms is identical regardless of whether we look at sums or means.

Example. Let a multi-armed bandit with 4 arms and $x(1) > x(2) > x(3) > x(4)$, with budget $N = 500$ pulls. We have $\overline{log}(4) = \frac{1}{2} + \sum_{i=2}^{4} \frac{1}{i} = \frac{19}{12}$ and:

Phase 1: each arm 1, 2, 3, 4 is pulled $n_1 = \lceil \frac{12}{19} \frac{500-4}{4+1-1} \rceil = 79$ times
Phase 2: each arm 1, 2, 3 is pulled $n_2 = \lceil \frac{12}{19} \frac{500-4}{4+1-2} \rceil - n_1 = 26$ times
Phase 3: each arm 1, 2 is pulled $n_3 = \lceil \frac{12}{19} \frac{500-4}{4+1-3} \rceil - (n_1 + n_2) = 52$ times.

In other words, arm 4 is pulled 79 times, arm 3 is pulled $79 + 26 = 105$ times, each arm 1, 2 is pulled $79 + 26 + 52 = 157$ times, totalling $79 + 105 + 2 \times 157 = 498$ pulls.

Algorithm 1. SR algorithm (adapted from [1])

1: $A_1 \leftarrow \{1, \dots, K\}$	▷ Initialization
2: **for all** $i \in A_1$ **do**	
3: $sum[i] \leftarrow 0$	
4: $\overline{\log}(K) \leftarrow \frac{1}{2} + \sum_{i=2}^{K} \frac{1}{i}$	
5: $n_0 \leftarrow 0$	
6: **for** j from 1 to $K - 1$ **do**	▷ Successive rejects
7: $n_j \leftarrow \left\lceil \frac{1}{\overline{\log}(K)} \frac{N-K}{K+1-j} \right\rceil - \sum_{l=0}^{j-1} n_l$	
8: **for all** $i \in A_j$ **do**	
9: **loop** n_j times	
10: $r \leftarrow$ random integer from $[x(i) - \epsilon, x(i) + \epsilon]$	
11: $sum[i] \leftarrow sum[i] + r$	
12: $A_{j+1} \leftarrow A_i \backslash \arg \min_{i \in A_j} sum[i]$	
13: **return** A_K	

3   Secure Protocol

3.1   Security Model

We assume that the reward functions associated to the arms as well as the best arm identification algorithm are outsourced to some cloud. We assume that the cloud is honest-but-curious i.e., it executes tasks dutifully, but tries to extract as much information as possible from the data that it sees. The user indicates to the cloud her budget and receives the best arm that the cloud can compute using the user's budget. The user does not have to do any computation, except for eventually decrypting $\widehat{i^*}$ if she receives this information encrypted from the cloud. We expect the following security properties:

1. No cloud node can learn at the same time information about the rewards and about the ranking of the arms.
2. By analyzing the messages communicated between the different cloud nodes, no information can be learned about the rewards or about the ranking.

The two aforementioned properties essentially ensure that the desired protocol has no security single point of failure. In particular, the first property says that (i) there may be some cloud node that knows the ranking of the arms (hence also the best arm), but it is not allowed to know which rewards are associated to these arms, and (ii) there may also be some cloud node that knows some rewards, but it is not allowed to know which arms are associated to these rewards. If all cloud nodes collude, the cloud can learn the rewards associated to the arms[1]. We do not consider collusions in our model.

---

[1] In case of collusions, if several users spent successive budgets to learn the best arm among the same set of arms, the cloud could compose the observed rewards. Hence the cloud could compute the best arm using as budget the total budget of the users and leak this information to some malicious user.

3.2   Security Background

We use Pailler's public key encryption scheme [15]. We first recall the definition of public-key encryption. Pailler's encryption scheme is IND-CPA secure. We recall the definition of IND-CPA before presenting the scheme itself that has an additive homomorphic property that we use in our protocol.

Definition 1 (PKE). *Let η be a security parameter. A public-key encryption (PKE) scheme is defined by $(\mathcal{G}, \mathcal{E}, \mathcal{D})$:*

$\mathcal{G}(\eta)$: *returns a public/private key pair* $(\mathsf{pk}, \mathsf{sk})$.
$\mathcal{E}_{\mathsf{pk}}(m)$: *returns the ciphertext c.*
$\mathcal{D}_{\mathsf{sk}}(c)$: *returns the plaintext m.*

We also recall the notion of negligible function in order to define the IND-CPA security notion.

Definition 2. *A function $\gamma \colon \mathbb{N} \to \mathbb{N}$ is negligible in η, and is noted $negl(\eta)$, if for every positive polynomial $p(\cdot)$ and sufficiently large η, $\gamma(\eta) < 1/p(\eta)$.*

Let $\Pi = (\mathcal{G}, \mathcal{E}, \mathcal{D})$ be a PKE scheme, $\mathcal{A}$ be a probabilistic polynomial-time adversary. For $b \in \{0, 1\}$, we define the IND-CPA-b experiment where $\mathcal{A}$ has access to the oracle $\mathcal{E}_{\mathsf{pk}}(LR_b(\cdot, \cdot))$ taking (m_0, m_1) as input and returns $\mathcal{E}_{\mathsf{pk}}(m_0)$ if $b = 0$, $\mathcal{E}_{\mathsf{pk}}(m_1)$ otherwise. $\mathcal{A}$ tries to guess the bit b chosen in the experiment. We define the advantage of $\mathcal{A}$ against the IND-CPA experiment by: $\mathsf{Adv}_{\Pi, \mathcal{A}}^{\text{ind-cpa}}(\eta) = \big| \Pr[1 \leftarrow \mathsf{Exp}_{\Pi, \mathcal{A}}^{\text{IND-CPA-1}}(\eta)] - \Pr[1 \leftarrow \mathsf{Exp}_{\Pi, \mathcal{A}}^{\text{IND-CPA-0}}(\eta)] \big|$. We said that Π is IND-CPA if this advantage is negligible for any probabilistic polynomial-time $\mathcal{A}$. Paillier's cryptosystem is an IND-CPA scheme. We give the key generation, the encryption and decryption algorithms.

Key Generation. We denote by $\mathbb{Z}_n$, the ring of integers modulo n and by $\mathbb{Z}_n^\times$ the set of invertible elements of $\mathbb{Z}_n$. The public key pk of Paillier's cryptosystem is (n, g), where $g \in \mathbb{Z}_{n^2}^\times$ and $n = pq$ is the product of two prime numbers such that $gcd(p, q) = 1$. The corresponding private key sk is (λ, μ), where λ is the least common multiple of $p - 1$ and $q - 1$ and $\mu = (L(g^\lambda \mod n^2))^{-1} \mod n$, where $L(x) = (x - 1)/n$.

Encryption Algorithm. Let m be a message such that $m \in \mathbb{Z}_n$. Let g be an element of $\mathbb{Z}_{n^2}^\times$ and r be a random element of $\mathbb{Z}_n^\times$. We denote by $\mathcal{E}_{\mathsf{pk}}(\cdot)$ the encryption function that produces the ciphertext c from a given plaintext m with the public key $\mathsf{pk} = (n, g)$ as follows: $c = g^m \cdot r^n \mod n^2$.

Decryption Algorithm. Let c be a ciphertext such that $c \in \mathbb{Z}_{n^2}^\times$. We denote by $\mathcal{D}_{\mathsf{sk}}(\cdot)$ the decryption function of c with the secret key $\mathsf{sk} = (\lambda, \mu)$ defined as follows: $m = L\left(c^\lambda \mod n^2\right) \times \mu \mod n$.

Paillier's cryptosystem is a partial homomorphic encryption scheme. Let m_1 and m_2 be two plaintexts in $\mathbb{Z}_n$. The product of the two associated ciphertexts

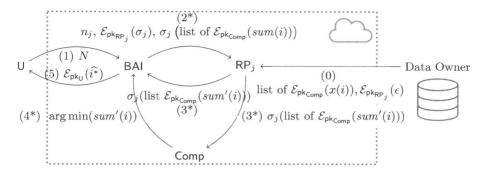

Fig. 2. Workflow of the secure algorithm. We use numbers to indicate the order of the steps. The steps annotated with * are repeated for each phase $j \in \{1, K-1\}$. For the communications $\mathsf{BAI} \to \mathsf{RP}_j$, $\mathsf{RP}_j \to \mathsf{BAI}$, and $\mathsf{RP}_j \to \mathsf{Comp}$, the list concerns all the arms that are still candidates i.e., the set A_j.

with the public key $\mathsf{pk} = (n, g)$, denoted $c_1 = \mathcal{E}_{\mathsf{pk}}(m_1) = g^{m_1} \cdot r_1^n \mod n^2$ and $c_2 = \mathcal{E}_{\mathsf{pk}}(m_2) = g^{m_2} \cdot r_2^n \mod n^2$, is the encryption of the sum of m_1 and m_2, i.e., $\mathcal{E}_{\mathsf{pk}}(m_1) \cdot \mathcal{E}_{\mathsf{pk}}(m_2) = \mathcal{E}_{\mathsf{pk}}(m_1 + m_2 \mod n)$.

We also remark that: $\mathcal{E}_{\mathsf{pk}}(m_1) \cdot \mathcal{E}_{\mathsf{pk}}(m_2)^{-1} = \mathcal{E}_{\mathsf{pk}}(m_1 - m_2)$.

3.3 Secure Algorithm

We revisit the successive rejects (SR) algorithm in order to satisfy the properties outlined in Sect. 3.1. We consider K arms. We note $[\![n]\!]$ the set of the n first integers: $[\![n]\!] = \{1, \ldots, n\}$. Recall that SR has $K-1$ phases and at each phase j, it uses a budget of n_j to pull each of the still candidate arms. At the end of each phase, SR rejects the worst arm, based on all pulls observed since the beginning.

In the sequel, each time we refer to some $(\mathsf{pk}, \mathsf{sk})$, and associated encryption/decryption functions, we assume they are done using Paillier's cryptosystem [15]. In particular, we rely on the homomorphic addition property of Paillier's cryptosystem i.e., $\mathcal{E}_{\mathsf{pk}}(x + y) = \mathcal{E}_{\mathsf{pk}}(x) \cdot \mathcal{E}_{\mathsf{pk}}(y)$.

In our security protocol, we assume $K + 3$ participants:

- DO is the Data Owner, who is not in the cloud. DO sends the encrypted arm values $\mathcal{E}_{\mathsf{pk}_{\mathsf{Comp}}}(x_i)$ and $\mathcal{E}_{\mathsf{pk}_{\mathsf{RP}_j}}(\epsilon)$ for $i \in [\![K]\!]$ and $j \in [\![K-1]\!]$.
- U is the User, a participant that is not in the cloud. The user generates $(\mathsf{pk}_{\mathsf{U}}, \mathsf{sk}_{\mathsf{U}})$ and shares pk_{U} and the budget N with the cloud. The cloud nodes compute $\widehat{i^*}$ and at the end BAI sends $\mathcal{E}_{\mathsf{pk}_{\mathsf{U}}}(\widehat{i^*})$ to the user, who is able to decrypt it using her secret key sk_{U}.
- BAI (Best-Arm Identification) is the node responsible for executing the $K-1$ phases of the SR algorithm. BAI generates $K-1$ uniformly selected permutations σ_j of $[\![K+1-j]\!]$ (as there are $K+1-j$ candidate arms at round j). Each σ_j is shared with the node RP_j, but not with Comp. At each phase, BAI knows which arm is the worst and should be rejected, and after the last phase

Table 1. What each cloud node knows and does not know.

Node	BAI	Comp	RP_j
Does know	• ranking of arms (including best arm)	• sums of rewards	• arms still candidate at phase j • arms already rejected before phase j • sums of rewards added at phase j
Does not know	• sums of rewards of any arm (Theorem 1)	• mapping between sums of rewards and the arms that produced them (Theorem 3) • ranking of arms (including best arm) (Theorem 2)	• ranking of arms (including best arm) (Theorems 4 and 5) • sums of rewards from phases $1, \ldots, j - 1, j + 1, \ldots, K - 1$ (Theorem 6)

it knows which arm is the best. However, BAI does not know which rewards are associated to the arms because the rewards are encrypted with $\mathsf{pk_{Comp}}$.
- Comp is the node responsible of choosing the worst one among the sums of rewards associated to the candidate arms. Comp generates $(\mathsf{pk_{Comp}}, \mathsf{sk_{Comp}})$ and shares $\mathsf{pk_{Comp}}$ with all other cloud nodes and DO.
- $RP_1, \ldots, RP_{K-1}$ are $K - 1$ nodes, each of them knowing the value ϵ that is needed to generate a reward for each arm. Each node RP_j generates $(\mathsf{pk_{RP_j}}, \mathsf{sk_{RP_j}})$ and shares $\mathsf{pk_{RP_j}}$ with BAI and DO.

The algorithm, which is summarized in Algorithm 2, consists of:

- Initialization done by BAI is:
  - Based on the total budget N, compute $n_1, \ldots, n_{K-1}$ that is the number of times each of the candidate arms should be pulled at phase $1, \ldots, K - 1$, respectively.
  - Uniformly select a permutation σ_1 of $[\![K]\!]$ and send $\mathcal{E}_{\mathsf{pk_{RP_1}}}(\sigma_1)$ to RP_1. A new permutation σ_j on $[\![K + 1 - j]\!]$ is randomly selected at each round, and sent to RP_j.
  - For each arm i, compute $sum[\sigma_1(i)] = \mathcal{E}_{\mathsf{pk_{Comp}}}(0)$.
  During the $K - 1$ phases of the algorithm, these encrypted sums are updated by the nodes RP_j.
- $K - 1$ phases where nodes BAI, RP_j, and Comp interact as shown in Fig. 2. We add the following specifications:
  - Each RP_j updates the encrypted sums using the homomorphic addition property of the Paillier's cryptosystem: for a round j and a candidate arm i with sum $sum[\sigma_j(i)]$, we get the updated sum $sum'[\sigma_j(i)]$ by homomorphically adding $\left(\mathcal{E}_{\mathsf{pk_{Comp}}}(x(\sigma_j(i))) \right)^{n_j} \times \prod_{l=1}^{n_j} \mathcal{E}_{\mathsf{pk_{Comp}}}(k_l)$ to $sum[\sigma_j(i)]$, where k_l is uniformly selected in $[-\epsilon, \epsilon]$ by RP_j.

- When Comp computes the index of the worst arm, if two or more arms have the same worst sum of rewards, then Comp selects uniformly at random one of these arms as the worst one. This ensures that the index of the worst arm has a uniform distribution.

Algorithm 2. Secure SR algorithms

1: **function** SETUP_BAI(N) ▷ Step 1 ▷ j tracks the round number, sum contains the sum of rewards of each competing arm. Both are stored in BAI state.

2:     **for** j from 1 to K-1 **do**

3:         $n_j \leftarrow \left\lceil \frac{1}{log(K)} \frac{N-K}{K+1-j} \right\rceil - \sum_{l=0}^{j-1} n_l$

4:     **for all** $i \in [\![K]\!]$ **do**

5:         $sum[i] \leftarrow \mathcal{E}_{\mathsf{pk}_{\mathsf{Comp}}}(0)$

6:     $j \leftarrow 1$

7: **function** START_ROUND_BAI   ▷ Step 2*

8:     $\sigma_j \leftarrow$ random permutation of $[\![K - j + 1]\!]$

9:     save σ_j in BAI state

10:     **return** $\sigma_j(sum), \mathcal{E}_{\mathsf{pk}_{\mathsf{RP}_j}}(\sigma_j), n_j$

11: **function** ROUND_RP$_j(\sigma_j(sum), \mathcal{E}_{\mathsf{pk}_{\mathsf{RP}_j}}(\sigma_j), n_j)$ ▷ Step 3*

12:     Decrypt $\mathcal{E}_{\mathsf{pk}_{\mathsf{RP}_j}}(\sigma_j)$, retrieve σ_j and un-permute $\sigma_j(sum)$ to get sum

13:     **for** each arm in sum **do**

14:         Homomorphically add to sum[arm] the rewards from n_j pulls of the arm

15:     **return** $\sigma_j(sum)$

16: **function** ROUND_Comp($\sigma_j(sum)$)   ▷ Step 4*

17:     Decrypt each element of $\sigma_j(sum)$

18:     $x_{min} \leftarrow$ the index of a lowest element of the decrypted list, randomly chosen amongst all lowest elements

19:     **return** x_{min}

20: **function** END_ROUND_BAI($\sigma_j(sum), x_{min}$)   ▷ After Step 4*, before next round

21:     $u_{min} \leftarrow \sigma_j^{-1}(x_{min})$

22:     Remove arm u_{min} from the list of participants, and from sum to reflect so

23:     $j{+}{+}$

24: **function** RESULT   ▷ Step 5

25:     Get the only remaining competing arm $\widehat{i^*}$ from sum in BAI state

26:     **return** $\mathcal{E}_{\mathsf{pk}_{\mathsf{U}}}(\widehat{i^*})$

We summarize in Table 1 what each cloud node knows and does not know, in order to satisfy the desired security properties. We formally prove the security properties in Appendix A. Next, we briefly outline why we need so many nodes:

- Assuming that all RP_j nodes are a single one, this node would know all rewards since the beginning of the algorithm hence it would learn the ranking of the arms.
- Assuming that Comp and RP_j are the same, then it would leak which arm is associated to which sum, hence the best arm could be leaked.
- Assuming that Comp and BAI are the same, then BAI would learn the plain rewards in addition to the ranking that it already knows.
- Assuming that BAI and RP_j are the same, then it would leak to BAI the sum of rewards associated to each arm.

3.4   Complexity

We give here a brief description of the complexity, in terms of the number of calls to $\mathcal{E}$ and $\mathcal{D}$ (the costliest operations).

- At Step 0, DO computes $\forall i \in [\![K]\!], \mathcal{E}_{\mathsf{pk}_{\mathsf{Comp}}}(x(i))$. It also encrypts ϵ for each RP_j, thus having $O(K)$ complexity.
- At Step 2, BAI computes a new encrypted permutation, that can be encoded as $[\mathcal{E}_{\mathsf{pk}_{\mathsf{RP}_j}}(\sigma_j(1)), \ldots, \mathcal{E}_{\mathsf{pk}_{\mathsf{RP}_j}}(\sigma_j(K + 1 - j)]$, thus having $O(K - j) = O(K)$ complexity.
- At Step 3, RP_j computes the added rewards. Given the algorithm in Sect. 3.3, this step has $O(K)$ complexity.
- At Step 4, Comp decrypts all partial sums, with a complexity of $O(K)$, before sending the argmin to BAI.

Steps 2, 3, 4 are repeated $K - 1$ times. The total complexity of these three steps is then $O(K^2)$, and the total complexity of the algorithm is $O(K^2)$.

Note that the complexity of the algorithm is independent from the total budget N, which is a great advantage as typical budgets for these kinds of problems are often elevated and usually much larger than the number of arms. More precisely, the complexity related to N is hidden by the complexity of the encryptions.

4   Experiments

We report on a proof-of-concept experimental study of our proposed protocol. We implemented and compared:

- SR: the successive rejects algorithm, adapted from [1]. We give the pseudocode of SR in Fig. 1.
- SR-secured: our proposed protocol, which adds security guarantees to SR. We describe SR-secured in Sect. 3.3 and we outline its workflow in Fig. 2.

We implemented the algorithms in Python 3. Our code is available on a public git repository[2]. For SR-secured, we used phe[3], an open-source Python 3 library for partially homomorphic encryption using the Paillier's cryptosystem.

---

[2] https://gitlab-sds.insa-cvl.fr/vciucanu/secure-bai-in-mab-public-code.
[3] https://python-paillier.readthedocs.io/en/develop/.

We summarize the results in Fig. 3 and we discuss them next. We carried out these experiments on a laptop with Intel Core i5 3.10 GHz and 8 GB of RAM. We used 2048 bits keys. The results are averaged over 100 runs.

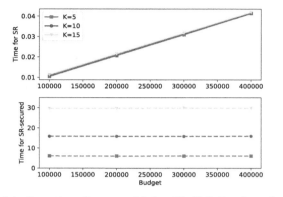

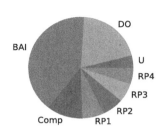

(a) Run time (in seconds) for SR (full lines), and for SR-secured (dashed).

(b) Time share during SR-secured execution, for $N{=}400000$ and $K{=}5$.

Fig. 3. Experimental results.

Run Time Comparison SR vs SR-Secured. In each half of Fig. 3(a), we have 12 points, corresponding to the pairwise combinations between 4 budget values N (100000, 200000, 300000, 400000) and 3 values for the number of arms K (5, 10, 15). We split the figure in two plots with different Y axis because the observed times are in the order of tens of milliseconds for SR and tens of seconds for SR-secured. For SR, we observe that the time varies more on N and less on K, which makes sense because the operations depending on N (i.e., picking random numbers in the rewards generation) are more expensive than the operations depending on K (i.e., additions and multiplications). On the other hand, for SR-secured, the slight run time increase depending on N is barely visible (hence the curves look rather constant) because of the three-orders-of-magnitude overhead that is a natural consequence of the high number of encryptions and decryptions performed by SR-secured. As explained in Sect. 3.3, each participant and encryption/decryption from SR-secured is useful for the protocol in order to guarantee the desired security properties. We stress that the time of SR-secured barely grows when increasing the budget N, which confirms the essential property that we outlined in the complexity discussion: the number of cryptographic primitives does not depend on N. Hence, we were easily able to run SR-secured for large budgets as we show in the figure. We conclude from this experiment that SR-secured retains the scalability of SR while adding an overhead (depending on K and not on N) due to the security primitives. Obviously, both algorithms compute exactly the same result i.e., the best arm.

Moreover, before running this time comparison study, we carefully checked that all intermediate sums and arm rankings are identical for SR and SR-secured, despite the encryptions and decryptions that the latter algorithm performs.

Zoom on SR-Secured. In Fig. 3(b) we highlight how the total time taken by SR-secured is split among the participants. We obtained this figure for $N = 400000$ and $K = 5$, hence there are 4 phases, thus 4 participants RP_1, RP_2, RP_3, RP_4 in addition to Comp, BAI, the data owner DO, and the user U. First, notice that the shares of U and DO of the total time are relatively small, which is a desired property. Indeed, we require the DO only to encrypt her knowledge of the arms before outsourcing such encrypted data to the cloud (step 0 in Fig. 2). This could be actually done only once at the beginning and then all runs of the best-arm identification algorithm can be done using the same encrypted data, regardless of the user that pays for such a run. Moreover, we require U to not do any computation effort other than decrypting the result of the best-arm identification algorithm that the cloud returns to her (step 5 in Fig. 2). Among the cloud participants, we observe that BAI takes the lion's share of the total running time. This is expected because the role of BAI is similar to a controller that interacts with all other cloud participants. In what concerns Comp and the RP_j, their shares are quite similar. We observed the same behavior regardless of the chosen N and K on which we zoom.

5 Related Work

To the best of our knowledge, our work is the first that relies on public-key encryption in order to add privacy guarantees to best-arm identification algorithms for multi-armed bandits.

There is a recent line of research on multi-armed bandits using differential privacy techniques [5,6], which are based on adding an amount of noise to the data to ensure that the removal or addition of a single data item does not affect the outcome of any data analysis. These works have either focused on strategies to obtain: (i) privacy-preserving input guarantees i.e., make the observed rewards unintelligible to an outside user [9], or (ii) privacy-preserving output guarantees i.e., protect the chosen actions and their associated rewards from revealing private information [13,18].

There are some fundamental differences between this line of work based on differential privacy and our work based on public-key encryption. First, the considered multi-armed bandit problems are different. Indeed, we focus on identifying the best arm, which is equivalent to minimizing the *simple regret*, that is the difference between the values associated to the arm that is actually the best and the best arm identified by the algorithm. On the other hand, the aforementioned works consider the *cumulative regret* minimization that roughly consists of minimizing the difference between the rewards observed after pulling N times the best arm and the rewards observed during the N pulls done by the algorithm.

A second difference is as follows. On the one hand, our secured algorithm based on *public-key encryption* is guaranteed to return exactly the same result as the (non-secured) SR algorithm [1] on which we rely as a building block in our protocol. On the other hand, the result of a *differentially-private* algorithm contains by definition some noise, hence it is different from the result of the algorithm without privacy guarantees.

Third, by construction, the performance measure (the regret) of our secure algorithm remains the same as for the non-secured version, since both versions use the same arm-pulling strategies (that is, the performed encryptions/decryptions have no influence on the choice of arms to be pulled). The price we pay for making the algorithm secure comes only in the form of additional time needed for the encryptions and decryptions. In contrast, in the differential privacy approach, noise is introduced in the inputs/outputs in order to guarantee that the algorithms are differentially private and this has a direct impact on the arm-selection strategies. Therefore, the performance of the differential private versions of the algorithms suffers an increased regret with respect to their non-secured versions by an additive [18] or a multiplicative factor [9,13].

6 Conclusions and Future Work

We studied the problem of best-arm identification in multi-armed bandits and we addressed the inherent privacy concerns that occur when outsourcing the data and computations to a public cloud. Our main contribution is a distributed protocol that computes the best arm while guaranteeing that (i) no cloud node can learn at the same time information about the rewards and about the ranking of the arms and (ii) by analyzing the messages communicated between the different cloud nodes, no information can be learned about the rewards or about the ranking. To do so, we relied on the partially homomorphic property of Paillier's cryptosystem. The overhead due to the security primitives of our protocol depends only on the number of arms K and not on the budget N. Our experiments confirmed this property.

Looking ahead to the future work, there are many directions for further investigation. For example, we plan to investigate whether we can leverage an addition-homomorphic cryptosystem other than Paillier's, which may be more efficient in practice and could help us reduce the run time gap between the secured and the non-secured algorithms that we observed in our proof-of-concept experimental study. Additionally, we plan to add privacy guarantees to other multi-armed bandit settings e.g., cumulative regret minimization [2] or best-arm identification in linear bandits [16], where the rewards of the arms depend linearly on some unknown parameter.

A   Security Proofs

In this section, we prove that our secure algorithm presented in Sect. 3.3 satisfies the two desirable security properties outlined in Sect. 3.1: we prove the first property from Sects. A.2 to A.4, and the second property in Sect. A.5.

A.1   Notations and Security Hypothesis

For a node A, we note $data_A$ the data to which A has access and $\mathcal{A}^{pb}(d)$ the answer of a Probabilistic Polynomial-Time (PPT) adversary $\mathcal{A}$ having knowledge of d, trying to solve the problem pb. We recall that, in our notation conventions, $[\![K]\!]$ denotes the set of positive integers lower than or equal to K: $[\![K]\!] = \{1, \ldots, K\}$.

Lemma 1. *For a list $l = [l_1, \ldots, l_n]$, a permutation σ and the permuted list $\sigma(l) = [l_{\sigma(1)}, \ldots, l_{\sigma(n)}]$, a PPT adversary $\mathcal{A}(l_\sigma)$ cannot invert one element with probability better than random. More specifically, $P\left[\mathcal{A}^{\sigma^{-1}}(\sigma(l)) \in \{i, \sigma^{-1}(i)\}_{i \in [\![K]\!]}\right] = \frac{1}{K}$ where $\mathcal{A}$ returns a tuple $(i, g(i))$ and $g(i)$ is $\mathcal{A}$'s guess for the preimage of i.*

Proof. This is immediate, as all preimages are equally likely if σ is uniformly selected. □

Lemma 2. *Let $\mathcal{A}$ be a PPT adversary. Consider the adversarial game in which $\mathcal{A}$ choses three messages m_0, m_1, z and sends them to the challenger $\mathcal{C}$. $\mathcal{C}$ choses a random bit b, and returns a tuple (c_0, c_1, s) where $c_0 = \mathcal{E}_{pk}(m_0), c_1 = \mathcal{E}_{pk}(m_1)$, and $s = \mathcal{E}_{pk}(m_b + z) = c_b \cdot \mathcal{E}_{pk}(z)$. $\mathcal{A}$ must then guess the value of b.*

If $\mathcal{E}_{pk}(\cdot)$ is IND-CPA secure, then $\mathcal{A}$ does not have any advantage in this adversarial game: $2\left|P\left[\mathcal{A}(c_0, c_1, s) = b\right] - \frac{1}{2}\right| < negl(\eta)$.

Proof. Assume there is a PPT adversary $\mathcal{O}$ able to win the game with significant advantage $x + negl(\eta)$: then $\mathcal{O}$ can guess b with probability $\frac{1}{2} + \frac{x}{2} + negl(\eta)$. We then prove that an PPT adversary $\mathcal{A}$ can break the IND-CPA property of Paillier. We can assume that when $\mathcal{O}$ is given c_0, c_0', s as input (where c_0' is another encryption of m_0), then the advantage of $\mathcal{O}$ is negligible: this gives us a lower bound of the advantage of $\mathcal{O}$ in a more general adversarial game.

Let us consider an IND-CPA game and an adversary $\mathcal{A}$, in which $\mathcal{A}$ choses m_0, m_1 and sends them to the challenger. The challenger randomly selects the bit b and sends back $c_b = \mathcal{E}_{pk}(m_b)$. Then, $\mathcal{A}$ selects a message z and computes $\mathcal{E}_{pk}(z)$, before computing $s = \mathcal{E}_{pk}(m_b) \cdot \mathcal{E}_{pk}(z)$. $\mathcal{A}$ also computes $c_0' = \mathcal{E}_{pk}(m_0)$. Then, $\mathcal{A}$ calls $\mathcal{O}(c_0', c_b, s)$, retrieves (in polynomial time) from $\mathcal{O}$ the guessed value b^*, and returns b^*.

If $b = 0$, then $\mathcal{A}$ has actually called $\mathcal{O}(c_0', c_0, s)$, which guesses the correct b^* with probability $\frac{1}{2} + negl(\eta)$. On the other hand, if $b = 1$, then $\mathcal{A}$ has actually called $\mathcal{O}(c_0', c_1, s)$, which gives the correct b^* with probability $\frac{1}{2} + \frac{x}{2} + negl(\eta)$.

b being randomly chosen, $\mathcal{A}$ correctly guesses b with probability $\frac{1}{2} \cdot \frac{1}{2} + \frac{1}{2} \cdot \left(\frac{1}{2} + \frac{x}{2}\right) + negl(\eta) = \frac{1}{2} + \frac{x}{4} + negl(\eta)$, thus yielding to $\mathcal{A}$ an advantage of $\frac{x}{2} + negl(\eta)$ in the IND-CPA game, in polynomial time. This is a contradiction with the fact that Paillier is IND-CPA secure. □

A.2   Security Proofs for BAI

Lemma 3. *From the data obtained at round j, a honest-but-curious BAI does not know the sum of the rewards of any arm. More precisely, for R the set of possible rewards, $\frac{|R|}{|R|-1}\left|P\left[\mathcal{A}^{reward}(data_{BAI^j}) \in \{i, reward(i)\}_{i \in [\![K+1-j]\!]}\right] - \frac{1}{|R|}\right| <$*

$negl(\eta)$ where $A^{reward}(data_{\mathsf{BAI}^j})$ returns a tuple $(i, g_{reward}(i)))$, with $g_{reward}(i)$ being $\mathcal{A}$'s guess of the sum of rewards of i.

Proof. At round j, BAI has access to the permuted list of the encrypted partial sums, as well as to the permutation σ_j and the index i_{min_j} of the lowest-ranking element from round j. From the first two arguments, BAI can access to the (unpermuted) list of the encrypted partial sums of the arms rewards $se_j = \left[\mathcal{E}_{\mathsf{pk_{Comp}}}(sum_{\alpha_1}), \dots, \mathcal{E}_{\mathsf{pk_{Comp}}}(sum_{\alpha_{K+1-j}}) \right]$, where the α_i are the arms still present in the algorithm at step j. So we can equivalently say that $data^j_{\mathsf{BAI}} = [se_j, i_{min_j}]$.

Assume that there exists a PPT adversary $\mathcal{O}$ able to break the above inequality, with advantage $x + negl(\eta)$: given $[se, i_{min_j}]$ as input, $\mathcal{O}$ returns some tuple (i, g_{reward}) where g_{reward} is the guessed reward of the arm α_i. The guess is correct with probability $\frac{1}{|R|} + \frac{|R|-1}{|R|}x + negl(\eta)$. Also note that, on average, $i = 1$ with probability $\frac{1}{K+1-j}$.

Let us consider a classical IND-CPA game as previously defined. When $\mathcal{A}$ receives $\mathcal{E}_{\mathsf{pk}}(m_b)$, they randomly chose $K - j$ cleartexts $r_1, \dots, r_{K-j}$ and compute their ciphertexts $\mathcal{E}_{\mathsf{pk}}(r_1), \dots, \mathcal{E}_{\mathsf{pk}}(r_{K-j})$. Then, $\mathcal{A}$ calls the oracle $\mathcal{O}(\mathcal{E}_{\mathsf{pk}}(m_b), \mathcal{E}_{\mathsf{pk}}(r_1), \dots, \mathcal{E}_{\mathsf{pk}}(r_{K-j}))$ which returns (i, g_{reward}). If $i = 1$ and $g_{reward} \in \{m_0, m_1\}$ then $\mathcal{A}$ returns 0 or 1, respectively. Otherwise $\mathcal{A}$ returns a random guess.

Finally, $\mathcal{A}$ returns the good answer with probability $\frac{1}{K+1-j} \left(\frac{1}{|R|} + \frac{|R|-1}{|R|}x + negl(\eta) \right) + \left(1 - \frac{1}{K+1-j} \left(\frac{1}{|R|} + \frac{|R|-1}{|R|}x + negl(\eta) \right) \right) \frac{1}{2}$, i.e. with probability $\frac{1}{2} + \frac{1}{2}\frac{1}{K+1-j} \left(\frac{1}{|R|} + \frac{|R|-1}{|R|}x \right) + negl(\eta)$, which yields an advantage of $\frac{1}{K+1-j} \left(\frac{1}{|R|} + \frac{|R|-1}{|R|}x \right) + negl(\eta)$ to $\mathcal{A}$. Hence, $\mathcal{A}$ has a non-negligible advantage in the IND-CPA game, which is a contradiction with the fact that Paillier's cryptosystem is IND-CPA secure. □

Theorem 1. *From the data obtained up to round j, a honest-but-curious BAI does not know the sum of the rewards of any arm. More precisely, for R the set of possible rewards, $\frac{|R|}{|R|-1} \times \left| P \left[A^{reward}(data_{\mathsf{BAI}^{\le j}}) \in \{i, reward(i)\}_{i \in [\![K]\!]} \right] - \frac{1}{|R|} \right| < negl(\eta)$ where the data $data_{\mathsf{BAI}^{\le j}}$ is the data obtained by BAI during the first j rounds and $reward(i)$ is the reward of the i-th arm.*

Proof. We notice that $data_{\mathsf{BAI}^{\le j}}$ is equal to $[data_{\mathsf{BAI}^1}, \dots, data_{\mathsf{BAI}^j}] = [[se_1, i_{min_1}], \dots, [se_j, i_{min_j}]]$. We know that each ciphertext from se_{j+1} results from the homomorphic addition of one ciphertext from se_j and one other unknown ciphertext[4]. Given Lemma 2, the set $[se_j, se_{j+1}]$ is indistinguishable from the set $[se_j, se'_{j+1}]$ where se'_{j+1} is a list of ciphertexts, unrelated to the ones in se_j. Hence, $data_{\mathsf{BAI}^{\le j}}$ is indistinguishable from the list $[se_1, se'_2, \dots, se'_j, i_{min_1}, \dots, i_{min_j}]$, where se'_i is a list of ciphertexts unrelated to se'_j or se_1.

Assume that there exists a PPT adversary $\mathcal{O}$ able to break the above inequality, with an advantage of $x + negl(\eta)$. The data available to $\mathcal{A}$ basically consists of j iterations, of various sizes, of the problem addressed in Lemma 3. Then, if

---
[4] Namely, the ciphertext of the rewards of the arm i at round j.

$\mathcal{A}$ can solve our current adversarial game with non negligible advantage, $\mathcal{A}$ can immediately solve the problem in Lemma 3 with non negligible advantage (from one set of ciphertexts, $\mathcal{A}$ will generate other sets, and immediately places itself in the current problem). Because a non negligible advantage to the above problem breaks IND-CPA security, we conclude to a contradiction.   □

A.3   Security Proofs for Comp

Lemma 4. *Let* $j \in [\![K - 1]\!]$. *From the data received at the round* j, *a honest-but-curious* Comp *cannot infer the ranking of any arm. More specifically,*
$P\left[\mathcal{A}^{rank}(data_{\mathsf{Comp}^j}) \in \{i, ranking(i)\}_{i \in [\![K+1-j]\!]}\right] = \frac{1}{K+1-j}.$

Proof. We have $data_{\mathsf{Comp}} = se_{\sigma_j} = [\mathcal{E}_{\mathsf{pk}_{\mathsf{Comp}}}(sum_{\sigma_j(\alpha_1)}), \ldots, \mathcal{E}_{\mathsf{pk}_{\mathsf{Comp}}}$ $(sum_{\sigma_j(\alpha_{K+1-j})})]$, which can be decrypted by Comp to $s_{\sigma_j} = [sum_{\sigma_j(\alpha_1)}, \ldots,$ $sum_{\sigma_j(\alpha_{K+1-j})}]$ where the α_i are the arms still present at round j. From this list of scores, Comp can infer the ranking of the permuted arms, i.e., compute the ranking any $A_{\sigma_j(i)}$ in polynomial time.

Assume there exists a PPT adversary $\mathcal{A}_{\mathrm{rank}}$ capable of breaking the above equality. If $\mathcal{A}$ is able to predict the ranking of the arm i with advantage better than random, then $\mathcal{A}$ knows the ranking of A_i, namely $ranking(A_i)$. Knowing the ranking of all $A_{\sigma_j(i)}$, with probability better than random, $\mathcal{A}$ is then able to compute $\sigma_j^{-1}(i)$ with advantage better than random by identifying which $A_{\sigma_j(i)}$ matches A_i. Hence a contradiction with Lemma 1.   □

Theorem 2. *Let* $j \in [\![K - 1]\!]$. *From the data received until the round* j, *A honest-but-curious* Comp *cannot infer the ranking of any arm. More specifically,*
$P\left[\mathcal{A}^{rank}(data_{\mathsf{Comp}^{\leq j}}) \in \{i, ranking(i)\}_{i \in [\![K]\!]}\right] = \frac{1}{K+1-j}.$

Proof. The proof is based on the proof of Lemma 4, with additional arguments similar to the ones of the proof of Theorem 1: because of Lemma 2, we can assume that we have j independent sets of unrelated permuted data. If an adversary $\mathcal{A}$ can break the above equality with non-negligible advantage in PPT, then we can construct an adversary who breaks the equality of Lemma 4 with non-negligible advantage, in PPT, which breaks Lemma 1, so we get a contradiction.   □

Lemma 5. *Let* $j \in [\![K - 1]\!]$. *From the data received at round* j, *a honest-but-curious* Comp *does not know the correspondence between sums of rewards and arms. More specifically,* $P\left[\mathcal{A}^{rwd}(data_{\mathsf{Comp}^j}) \in \{i, reward(i)\}_{i \in [\![K+1-j]\!]}\right] = \frac{1}{K+1-j}.$

Proof. Assume that Comp is able, from s_{σ_j}, to infer the sum of rewards of the arm A_k with probability better than $\frac{1}{K+1-j}$. Because Comp knows the sum of rewards of the permuted arms $A_{\sigma_j(\alpha_i)}$ for all $i \in [\![K+1-j]\!]$, then by matching these rewards with the sum of the rewards of A_i, Comp is able to compute $\sigma_j(i)$ with a probability better than random. Hence, Comp breaks Lemma 1.   □

Theorem 3. *Let* $j \in [\![K-1]\!]$. *From the data received until round* j, *a honest-but-curious* Comp *does not know the correspondence between sums of rewards and arms. More specifically,* $P\left[\mathcal{A}^{rwd}(data_{\mathsf{Comp}^{\leq j}}) \in \{i, reward(i)\}_{i \in [\![K]\!]}\right] = \frac{1}{K}.$

Proof. Similar to the proof of Theorem 2.   □

A.4   Security Proofs for the RP_j

Theorem 4. *A honest-but-curious* RP_j *does not know the ranking of the* $K - j + 1$ *best ranking arms, for* $j \in [\![K - 1]\!]$. *More specifically,* $\forall j \in [\![K - 1]\!], \forall i \in [\![K + 1 - j]\!]$, *and* $ranking_j(i)$ *is the ranking of the i-th arm at round* j,
$$\frac{K+1-j}{K-j} \left| P\left[\mathcal{A}^{rank}(data_{\mathsf{RP}_j}) \in \{i, ranking_j(i)\}_{i\in[\![K+1-j]\!]}\right] - \frac{1}{K+1-j} \right| < negl(\eta).$$

Proof. We have $data_{\mathsf{RP}_j} = [se_{\sigma_j}, \mathcal{E}_{\mathsf{pk}_{\mathsf{RP}_j}}(\sigma_j), n_j]$, where $se_{\sigma_j} = \sigma_j([\mathcal{E}_{\mathsf{pk}_{\mathsf{Comp}}}(sum_{\alpha_1}), \ldots, \mathcal{E}_{\mathsf{pk}_{\mathsf{Comp}}}(sum_{\alpha_{K-j}})])$, the permuted list of encrypted sums of rewards. RP_j can further 'un-permute' se_{σ_j} to $se = [\mathcal{E}_{\mathsf{pk}_{\mathsf{Comp}}}(sum_{\alpha_1}), \ldots, \mathcal{E}_{\mathsf{pk}_{\mathsf{Comp}}}(sum_{\alpha_{K-j}})]$, the list of encrypted sums of rewards. Note that n_j does not carry any information about the partial sum, as one can simulate any se with the same n_j, so does not carry significant information to our problem.

Assume that RP_j can guess the ranking of one element with advantage $x + negl(\eta)$: there exist a PPT oracle $\mathcal{O}$ taking as input se, and outputs $(i, v(i))$, with $i \in [\![K + 1 - j]\!]$. Furthermore, we have $\widehat{v}(i) = ranking_j(i)$ with probability $\frac{1}{K+1-j} + \frac{K-j}{K+1-j}x + negl(\eta)$. Note that, on average, $i = 1$ with probability $\frac{1}{K+1-j}$. Let us consider an IND-CPA game, in which the strategy of $\mathcal{A}$ is the same as the one in the proof of Lemma 3 (i.e., generate enough ciphertexts so they can call $\mathcal{O}$). Then, following the same reasoning we get that $\mathcal{A}$ has an advantage of
$$\frac{1}{K+1-j}\left(\frac{1}{K+1-j} + \frac{K-j}{K+1-j}x\right) + negl(\eta)$$ in the IND-CPA game, which is a contradiction with the IND-CPA property of Paillier's. □

Theorem 5. *A honest-but-curious* RP_j *does not know the ranking of the* $j - 1$ *lowest ranking arms. More specifically,* $\forall j \in \{3, \ldots, K - 1\}, \forall i \in [\![j - 1]\!]$, *and* $ranking(i)$ *the ranking of the i-th arm,*
$$\frac{j-1}{j-2}\left| P\left[\mathcal{A}^{rank}(data_{\mathsf{RP}_j}) \in \{i, ranking(i)\}_{i\in[\![K+1-j]\!]}\right] - \frac{1}{j-1} \right| < negl(\eta).$$

Proof. This is straightforward as RP_j does not receive any information about the sums of the j lowest ranking arms. Furthermore, we must impose $j \geq 3$ because it is clear that RP_1 and RP_2 know the ranking of the lowest ranking arm. □

Theorem 6. *Except for* RP_1, *a honest-but-curious* RP_j *does not know the sums of rewards at step* j. *More precisely, for* R *the set of possible rewards,* $\forall i \in [\![K + 1 - j]\!]$, $\frac{|R|}{|R|-1}\left| P\left[\mathcal{A}^{reward}(data_{\mathsf{RP}_j}) \in \{i, reward_j(i)\}_{i\in[\![K+1-j]\!]}\right] - \frac{1}{|R|} \right| < negl(\eta).$

Proof. Assume that a PPT adversary $\mathcal{A}$ breaks the above inequality: there exists a PPT oracle $\mathcal{O}(c_1, \ldots, c_K)$, that returns the tuple (i, m_i) where m_i is the cleartext of c_i with advantage $x + negl(\eta)$. Then we prove that the adversary breaks the IND-CPA property of Paillier's cryptosystem. Note that, on average, $i = 1$ with probability $\frac{1}{n}$, and that a decryption is correct with probability $\frac{1}{|R|} + \frac{|R|-1}{|R|}x + negl(\eta)$.

If we consider an IND-CPA game where the strategy of $\mathcal{A}$ is the same as in the proof of Lemma 3 (i.e., generate enough ciphertexts so they can call $\mathcal{O}$), we get that $\mathcal{A}$ has an advantage of $\frac{1}{n|R|} + \frac{|R|-1}{n|R|}x$ in the IND-CPA game, which is a contradiction with Paillier being IND-CPA secure. □

A.5   Security Proof for an External Observer

Theorem 7. *An external observer, having access to the set M of all the messages exchanged during the protocol, cannot infer anything about the sum of rewards of any arm. More specifically, any such observer is bound by the inequality mentioned in Theorem 1, with* $data_{\mathsf{BAI} \leq j}$ *being replaced by M.*

Proof. Assume that there exists an adversary $\mathcal{O}$ able to break the above inequality, given M, in PPT. We then prove that an adversary $\mathcal{A}$ is able to break IND-CPA security of Pailler's scheme in PPT.

Let us consider a classical IND-CPA challenge, in which $\mathcal{A}$ choses two rewards r_0, r_1 and sends them to the challenge. The challenger returns $\mathcal{E}_{\mathsf{pk}_{\mathsf{Comp}}}(r_b)$, where b is a uniformly random bit. Then, $\mathcal{A}$ simulates a secure multi-armed bandit protocol, with 2 arms, so that at the end of round 1, one of the arms has for encrypted sum of rewards the value $\mathcal{E}_{\mathsf{pk}_{\mathsf{Comp}}}(r_b)$, the other being random. This is possible because in this simulation, $\mathcal{A}$ can set herself the rewards x_i of each arm, as well as the budget for round 1. Furthermore, knowing the cleartext of every encrypted value at any time, $\mathcal{A}$ can simulate the full protocol by herself (especially, she can simulate Comp execution). This simulation yields a set of messages M.

Now, calling $\mathcal{O}(M)$, $\mathcal{A}$ will retrieve in PPT, with some non-negligible advantage, some information about the sums of rewards of one of the arms. With probability $\frac{1}{2}$, this information will be about the arms of r_b, thus giving, in PPT, a non-negligible advantage in the IND-CPA game, as $\mathcal{A}$ is able to find the value of b with some advantage. This is a contradiction with the fact that Paillier is IND-CPA secure.   □

Theorem 8. *An external observer, having access to the set M of all the messages exchanged during the protocol, cannot infer anything about the ranking of any arm:* $\frac{K}{K-1} \left| P\left[\mathcal{A}^{rwd}(M) \in \{i, ranking(i)\}_{i \in \llbracket K \rrbracket} \right] - \frac{1}{K} \right| < negl(\eta)$.

Proof. It is obvious that such an observer can deduce the permuted list of rankings by listening to data exchanged at step 4. However, from the data of one round, it is impossible to know more: the data from one round is an encrypted permuted sum of rewards S, the lowest permuted index i, and the same sum, with the lowest element removed S' (steps 3, 4, 2). This is equivalent of having knowledge of S and i only. If an adversary $\mathcal{O}$ breaks the inequality with S and i, then we can break IND-CPA.

Let $\mathcal{A}$ be the adversary, picking $K + 1$ messages such that $m_0 < m_i' < m_1$, and a permutation σ. Sending m_0 and m_1, they receive $c_b = \mathcal{E}_{\mathsf{pk}}(m_b)$, and also compute $c_i' = \mathcal{E}_{\mathsf{pk}}(m_i')$. Then, if $\mathcal{O}(\sigma([c_b, c_2', \ldots, c_k']), \sigma(0)) = 0$, $\mathcal{A}$ returns 0, else 1. If $\mathcal{O}$ has a non-negligible advantage x, we prove similarly to the other proofs that $\mathcal{A}$ has a advantage of $\frac{x}{2}$ in the IND-CPA game, which is a contradiction.

Now, because of Lemma 2, having access to all messages does not change anything. This is because each new round is indistinguishable from a simulation run by $\mathcal{A}$, so an advantage in the "all-rounds" game would yield an advantage in the "one-round" game.   □

References

1. Audibert, J., Bubeck, S., Munos, R.: Best arm identification in multi-armed bandits. In: Conference on Learning Theory (COLT) (2010)
2. Auer, P., Cesa-Bianchi, N., Fischer, P.: Finite-time analysis of the multiarmed bandit problem. Mach. Learn. **47**, 235–256 (2002)
3. Chen, S., Lin, T., King, I., Lyu, M.R., Chen, W.: Combinatorial pure exploration of multi-armed bandits. In: Conference on Neural Information Processing Systems (NIPS) (2014)
4. Coquelin, P., Munos, R.: Bandit algorithms for tree search. In: Conference on Uncertainty in Artificial Intelligence (UAI) (2007)
5. Dwork, C.: Differential privacy. In: International Colloquium on Automata, Languages and Programming (ICALP) (2006)
6. Dwork, C., Roth, A.: The algorithmic foundations of differential privacy. Found. Trends Theor. Comput. Sci. **9**, 211–407 (2014)
7. Even-Dar, E., Mannor, S., Mansour, Y.: Action elimination and stopping conditions for the multi-armed bandit and reinforcement learning problems. J. Mach. Learn. Res. **7**, 1079–1105 (2006)
8. Gabillon, V., Ghavamzadeh, M., Lazaric, A.: Best arm identification: a unified approach to fixed budget and fixed confidence. In: Conference on Neural Information Processing Systems (NIPS) (2012)
9. Gajane, P., Urvoy, T., Kaufmann, E.: Corrupt bandits for preserving local privacy. In: Algorithmic Learning Theory (ALT) (2018)
10. Kaufmann, E., Cappé, O., Garivier, A.: On the complexity of best-arm identification in multi-armed bandit models. J. Mach. Learn. Res. **17**, 1–42 (2016)
11. Kocsis, L., Szepesvári, C.: Bandit based Monte-Carlo planning. In: Fürnkranz, J., Scheffer, T., Spiliopoulou, M. (eds.) ECML 2006. LNCS (LNAI), vol. 4212, pp. 282–293. Springer, Heidelberg (2006). https://doi.org/10.1007/11871842_29
12. Li, L., Chu, W., Langford, J., Schapire, R.E.: A contextual-bandit approach to personalized news article recommendation. In: International Conference on World Wide Web (WWW) (2010)
13. Mishra, N., Thakurta, A.: (Nearly) optimal differentially private stochastic multi-arm bandits. In: Conference on Uncertainty in Artificial Intelligence (UAI) (2015)
14. Munos, R.: From bandits to Monte-Carlo tree search: the optimistic principle applied to optimization and planning. Found. Trends Mach. Learn. **7**, 1–129 (2014)
15. Paillier, P.: Public-key cryptosystems based on composite degree residuosity classes. In: Stern, J. (ed.) EUROCRYPT 1999. LNCS, vol. 1592, pp. 223–238. Springer, Heidelberg (1999). https://doi.org/10.1007/3-540-48910-X_16
16. Soare, M., Lazaric, A., Munos, R.: Best-arm identification in linear bandits. In: Conference on Neural Information Processing Systems (NIPS) (2014)
17. Thompson, W.R.: On the likelihood that one unknown probability exceeds another in view of the evidence of two samples. Biometrika **25**, 285–294 (1933)
18. Tossou, A.C.Y., Dimitrakakis, C.: Algorithms for differentially private multi-armed bandits. In: AAAI Conference on Artificial Intelligence (2016)

CATCHA: When Cats Track Your Movements Online

Prakash Shrestha[1]($^{(\boxtimes)}$), Nitesh Saxena[1], Ajaya Neupane[2], and Kiavash Satvat[3]

[1] University of Alabama at Birmingham, Birmingham, AL 35294, USA
{prakashs,saxena}@uab.edu
[2] University of California, Riverside, CA 92521, USA
ajaya@ucr.edu
[3] University of Illinois at Chicago, Chicago, IL 60607, USA
ksatva2@uic.edu

Abstract. Any website can record its users' mouse interactions within that site, an emerging practice used to learn about users' regions of interests usually for personalization purposes. However, the dark side of such recording is that it is oblivious to the users as no permissions are solicited from the users prior to recording (unlike other resources like webcam or microphone). Since mouse dynamics may be correlated with users' behavioral patterns, any website with nefarious intentions ("cat") could thus try to surreptitiously infer such patterns, thereby compromising users' privacy and making them prone to targeted attacks. In this paper, we show how users' personal information, specifically their *demographic characteristics*, could leak in the face of such mouse movement eavesdropping. As a concrete case study along this line, we present *CATCHA*, a mouse analytic attack system that gleans potentially sensitive demographic attributes—*age group*, *gender*, and *educational background*—based on mouse interactions with a *game CAPTCHA* system (a simple drag-and-drop animated object game to tell humans and machines apart).

CATCHA's algorithmic design follows the machine learning approach that predicts unknown demographic attributes based on a total of 64 mouse dynamics features extracted from within the CAPTCHA game, capturing users' innate cognitive abilities and behavioral patterns. Based on a comprehensive data set of mouse movements with respect to a simple game CAPTCHA collected in an online environment, we show that CATCHA can identify the users' demographics attributes with a high probability (*almost all attributes with more than 85%*), significantly better than random guessing (50%) and in a very short span of interaction time (*about 14 s*). We also provide a thorough statistical analysis and interpretation of differentiating features across the demographics attributes that make users susceptible to the CATCHA attack. Finally, we discuss potential extensions to our attack using other user interaction paradigms (e.g., other types of CAPTCHAs or typical web browsing interactions, and under longitudinal settings), and provide potential mitigation strategies to curb the impact of mouse movement eavesdropping.

A. Neupane and K. Satvat—Work done at UAB.

S.-H. Heng and J. Lopez (Eds.): ISPEC 2019, LNCS 11879, pp. 172–193, 2019.
https://doi.org/10.1007/978-3-030-34339-2_10

1   Introduction

Behavioral modeling of users is important for web services providers [43]. On one end, it facilitates the web services to personalize their offerings for an individual user, likely benefiting both the services and their users since the information fetched and delivered to the users can be tailored according to their personal needs. The websites can also learn users' interests which may help them with their monetization activities by pushing targeted advertisements and other dynamic content to the users. On the other end, however, such behavioral tracking raises a serious privacy concern as the websites would learn users' personal, potentially sensitive, information which users may not want to disclose, or be fully aware of its exposure [48]. Besides the breach of privacy, if potentially malicious websites can infer users' private behavioral information in this fashion, they could use it to launch targeted attacks against the users which can hamper their security, safety and well-being.

As a case in point, this paper investigates the notion of behavioral modeling, specifically privacy leakage, based on one of the most rudimentary and apparently inconspicuous modes of user-to-web interactions, the *mouse*. Any website can record its users' mouse interactions (clicks, movements, scrolls, etc.) *within that site*, specifically using the JavaScript functionality. On the benign front, such a monitoring of users' mouse dynamics seems to be an emerging practice used to learn about users' regions of interests on the site usually for personalization purposes and to improve user experience. For example, mouse movement information can be used to detect where exactly on the web UI the user might be gazing at, which may capture the information the user is interested in [9]. Similarly, mouse dynamics has also been demonstrated as a viable behavioral biometrics modality, using which users may be transparently authenticated to the web services [55]. Third party companies (e.g., Mouse Flow [38]) already record mouse movements for marketing purposes. And, even big companies (e.g., Facebook) seem to be considering plans to monitor mouse movements remotely in order to offer improved services to their users [52].

However, a detrimental side of such mouse interaction recording is that it is invisible to the users as no permission models exist in the currently deployed web browsers to solicit users' consent prior to such recording can take place. This practice lies in stark contrast to access control models adopted for other sensitive resources such as webcam, microphone or location (GPS), where user approval is necessary before the website can gain access to the data collected by these sensors. The choice of such permission models is perhaps explainable—*mouse interactions do not appear to be explicitly sensitive* in contrast to the other sensors cited above. However, since mouse dynamics are *implicitly* correlated with users' behavioral traits [22], any website with nefarious intentions ("cat") could therefore still surreptitiously infer such traits, in turn compromising users' privacy and making them susceptible to targeted attacks exploiting the learned behavioral information.

Given the differences in the way the users from different demographic groups (e.g., gender, age group) move the mouse cursors due to the intrinsic differences in the users' cognitive level, experience, risk-taking behavior, and motor ability [6,7,22,42,49,53,54], we set out to analyze mouse movements of users when they are solving game CAPTCHAs and intend to build user models based on their gender, age, and education. Specifically, we intend to demonstrate how users' personal information, namely, their *demographic characteristics*, could implicitly leak in the face of such mouse movement eavesdropping. As a concrete case study in this research line, we present *CATCHA*, a mouse analytic privacy attack system that surreptitiously extracts potentially sensitive demographic attributes—*gender, age group*, and *education level*—based on mouse interactions with a *game CAPTCHA* system, a mouse-based animated object game to tell humans and machines apart. In particular, we focus on a simple game-based CAPTCHA that requires the user to identify the answer object(s) from a set of moving objects, and drag-drop them to the corresponding target object(s). A start-up company, named "are you a human", had released and deployed a series of such game CAPTCHAs [51]. These CAPTCHAs have also been extensively studied by researchers [19,34,35].

Although the studied demographic attributes may seem minor (or non-sensitive) at first hand, an involuntary disclosure of such demographic attributes through our attack is a major concern since it *not only breaches people's privacy but also opens up room for targeted scams against users*. For example, specific targeted attacks can be launched against people of one given gender (e.g., sexual harassment against females, gender discrimination in job search) and age group (phishing scams against elderly or cyber-bullying of children) [8,10,21,32]. The attack possibilities are endless and already deployed by cyber-criminals in the wild.

Game CAPTCHAs seem like a representative platform to study mouse dynamics privacy leakage. They involve well-defined, although short, mouse interactions such as dragging and dropping which, as we will show, would surprisingly leak demographic cues about users. These CAPTCHAs may offer improved usability and security over text CAPTCHAs (especially against CAPTCHA farming attacks) as shown in the literature [19,34,35]. Due to these properties, they have already been deployed in the past [25,51] and may get deployed at large scale in the future, enabling mouse dynamics privacy leakage. Arbitrary, potentially malicious, websites can also deploy such CAPTCHAs in the name of improved web security but with a hidden goal of inferring private demographic characteristics of users visiting such websites.

Our Contributions: Our contributions are two-fold:

1. *Design and Implementation of CATCHA, a Mouse Analytic Attack System:* The CATCHA algorithmic design follows the machine learning methodology that predicts demographic attributes based on several (64 in total) mouse dynamics features extracted from within the CAPTCHA game, capturing users' innate cognitive abilities and behavioral patterns.
2. *Comprehensive Evaluation of CATCHA:* Based on a comprehensive data set of mouse movements with respect to a simple game CAPTCHA collected in an online environment [36], we show that CATCHA can identify the users'

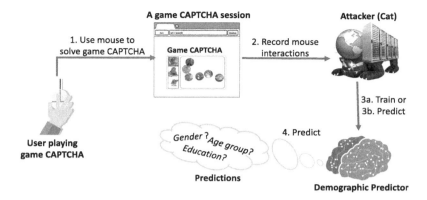

Fig. 1. High level overview of CATCHA.

demographic attributes with a high probability (with the accuracy of >85%), significantly better than random guessing (50%), in a short interval of time. We also provide a thorough statistical analysis and interpretation of features that make users susceptible to the CATCHA attack.

Broader Significance of Our Work: While we focus on game CAPTCHAs as our mouse dynamics privacy leakage platform, we also discuss potential extensions to our attack using other user interaction objects (e.g., other types of CAPTCHAs or web browsing interactions). We also provide potential mitigation strategies and future directions involved in curbing the impact of mouse movement eavesdropping. Overall, our work serves to demonstrate a practical attack vector that could be exploited by third-party online companies and malicious actors to breach people's privacy using one of the most fundamental and apparently inconspicuous modes of human-computer interaction ("mouse"), to raise people's awareness and to bootstrap work on mitigation against such threats. Although we use game CAPTCHA as a representative example to demonstrate the threat in question, our work should not be viewed as an attack against the CAPTCHA scheme itself, but rather as a form of a side channel privacy vulnerability based on mouse dynamics. Further, a benign application of our demographic prediction model could be towards validating the user information in a given domain. For example, an adult website can utilize the prediction model to see whether the user is indeed above age of 18. In fact, many websites can utilize the prediction models to validate the demographic information provided by the user.

2   Attack Premise and Overview

JavaScript, one of the core web technologies, comes with a wide variety of functionality that enables web developers or website owners to access various resources such as webcam and microphone at user's end through the browser.

Since these resources are sensitive in nature, browsers have integrated a permission model that secures access to these sensitive resources [20,46]. The permission model mandates the website to ask permission of the user before accessing any such resources through the browser that it considers sensitive to the user. Moreover, recently some browsers (Chrome, Firefox) started adding a new functionality, named privacy UI, that allows a user to be always aware of the use of any sensitive resources such as microphone or webcam [5,17]. The permission model and privacy UI consider certain set of resources as sensitive explicitly while it considers some other set of resources as non-sensitive to the users. Most important to our work, mouse movements (and key presses) at user's end are not protected by this permission model. Any web-developer can design a website in such a way that it can capture and store mouse movement (and key press) events without the consent of the user.

The website can utilize these mouse events to extract various personal information about the user that it can later use for their own purposes, thereby compromising the privacy of the users. For instance, mouse movements can be related to the focus of the eyes and the direction in which the user is looking at [44]. This may reveal the information about the content on the website that he is interested in and any e-commerce website may know which products the user is focusing on. It is also possible to recognize a particular user based on his mouse movements traits [55]. So, it may also be possible to estimate other demographic properties such as age, gender, and education from such mouse movements data (our primary study goal). These attributes, although look generic, can be utilized by the attackers for various nefarious purposes – targeted attacks against people of one gender (e.g., sexual harassment against females, gender discrimination in job), and age group (phishing scams against elderly or cyber-bullying of children) [8,10,21,32].

As a case study on demographic information leakage through mouse movements tracking, we design the CATCHA attack (high level overview is shown in Fig. 1) following the machine learning approach. The *demographic predictor* (classification model) of CATCHA can be built offline utilizing the mouse interactions with respect to game CAPTCHA from one set of the users, perhaps recruited by the attacker himself, and using this predictor, another set of users (victims) can be attacked. We evaluate the performance of CATCHA using the dataset collected in the study of *Gametrics* [36] (details presented in Sect. 3).

Specifically, as a real-world case, we study the scenario where a user willingly provides his demographic information to a widely used website *W1* (say Google or Facebook). During his interaction with *W1*, the mouse movement data is collected and used to build the demographic prediction model. The widely adopted web-service typically complies with the privacy policy that none of the personally identifiable information would be shared with any third party services, such as publishers, advertisers, developers, researchers, or law enforcement, without the consent from the user. They can only share aggregated statistics including demographic prediction model with third-party services that help them improve their services [26,28]. However, the demographic prediction model can be shared with and used by any secondary website $W2$ (say Macys, Forever-21 and others) to enhance their market through personalize marketing. The shopping stores such as Macys, Forever-21, generally compel the users to register at their stores with emails (or phone numbers) by providing several offers/discounts on their purchase. Later, they target those users for marketing by sending emails/texts with ads of their products [12,29]. At such stores, specifically with $W2$, the user does not wish to explicitly/voluntarily share his personal information. However, $W2$ can utilize our demographic prediction model to predict the demographics of the users and craft the emails/texts so that they can connect with their customers in the best possible way by advertising related products. The secondary websites can also use our prediction model as a lie detector. The users may intentionally provide false information, potentially because they do not wish to share their actual personal information with such websites. They can use our demographic prediction model for detecting false information, correct the user's information, and use it for personalized marketing. Further, such websites may also turn into malicious entities and utilize those predicted demographic attributes for various nefarious purposes.

3   Game CAPTCHA Review and Dataset

Game CAPTCHA: *Gametrics*(game-based biometric) is a behavioral biometric based authentication system that authenticates a user based on the unique way of solving a game challenge. The design of *Gametrics* is based on the notion of a game CAPTCHA scheme called *Dynamic Cognitive Game* (DCG) introduced in [35]. The purpose of DCG was to build a CAPTCHA scheme, not an authentication scheme. DCG games consist of floating and static objects as shown in Appendix Fig. 4. And, the task of the user is to find some relation of moving object(s) with one of the static objects, which is considered as target location, and drag-drop the moving object to their target location. The authors of *Gametrics* utilized such simple interactive game to extract unique biometric features that capture cognitive abilities and mouse dynamics of the users and used these features to successfully authenticate the users. Contrary to the work of *Gametrics*, although we utilize a similar set of features on their dataset, our goal is to extract the demographic attributes of the user based on the cognitive abilities and mouse dynamics of the user, *not user authentication*.

Game CAPTCHA Dataset: The *Gametrics* dataset contains data samples, particularly mouse interactions while its users were solving game CAPTCHA, from the users in both online and lab settings. Their study required participants to go through a tutorial on a game CAPTCHA and fill up a demographic form. The participants were then asked to solve several instances of game challenges.

For the online study, *Gametrics'* work utilized the Amazon Mechanical Turk (AMT) service to recruit participants. They created three Human Intelligence Tasks (HITs) distributed over three days. From the first HIT, they collected 98 valid submissions that constitute 5839 game challenges. The participants had to solve 60 instances of challenges. For each participant, the order of presenting

Table 1. Summary of CAPTCHA dataset and demographics of its participants [36].

(a) *Summary of CAPTCHA dataset.*

		# of Users	Completed Challenges
Online-study	Day 1	98	5839
	Day 2	62	2209
	Day 3	29	1028
Lab-study		20	1200

(b) *Demographics of the partici-pants.*

	Online study	Lab study
Gender (%)		
Male	58.2	65
Female	41.8	35
Age (%)		
<25	21.4	40
25-34	38.8	45
≥35	39.8	15
Education (%)		
High School	26.5	25
Bachelor	58.2	40
Graduate	15.3	30

the challenges was random. For the next two days, authors of *Gametrics* sent out an email to the participants asking them to participate in the follow-up study. On the second day, 62 participants performed the study completing 2209 game challenges and on the third day, only 29 performed the study with the submission of 1028 challenges. The follow-up study asked participants to solve 36 challenges. There were 98 participants in online study and they completed 9076 game challenges with an average(std) completion time of 7.38(3.22) s. For the lab study, *Gametrics'* work collected data from volunteers at the University following a similar protocol as the online study. Total 20 volunteers participated in the lab study and completed 1200 game challenges. Each of the participant solved 60 game challenges using the *same mouse/computer*. Table 1a summarized the dataset collected in the *Gametrics'* study.

Crucial to our work, Table 1b shows the demographics information of the participants in the study of *Gametrics*. The second and third column show the demographics of online and lab participants, respectively. Participants were from various age groups and educational level. We categorize them to the classes of our interest relevant to our work. Since all the participants of Gametrics' online study use their own computer, browser, and mouse, different mouse or hardware were involved in creating the mouse movements data as in a real world scenario. The use of variety of mice/hardware may have impacted the performance of the prediction models. To verify that the performance of prediction models are resulted from the participants' interaction, specifically the common traits in demographics, rather than the diverse nature of mice/hardware, we performed analysis on the dataset collected in the lab study where all the samples were collected using the same mice/hardware.

4   CATCHA Design and Implementation

4.1   Demographic Attributes of Interest

We are interested in extracting information about the users' gender, age group, and education level based on their mouse interactions. We categorize each attribute into two to three classes (i.e., possible values for an attribute) as shown in Table 2. For example, there are two classes in our classification for gender – male and female. For age, we consider two sets of classes. The first set consists of two classes: (a) age <35 that covers teenagers to adult, and (b) age ≥35 that covers the users over middle age. The second set consists of three classes: (a) age <25 that covers the users from teenagers to young adults, (b) age between 25–34 that covers the adult users, and (c) age ≥35 that covers users above the middle age. The purpose of these groupings of age is to see whether age can be classified within finer grained age groups through mouse interactions.

Table 2. Various attributes considered in our analysis with brief description of their corresponding classes. First column "Attribute Code" shows the unique code for a demographic attribute to indicate various values (column "Class Description") it can hold.

Attribute code	Attribute (# of classes)	Class description
Gender	Gender (2)	Male and Female
Age-2	Age (2)	<35 and ≥35
Age-3	Age (3)	<25, (25 − 34), and ≥35
Edu-Highschool	Education (2)	Highschool and Other
Edu-Bachelor	Education (2)	Bachelor and Other
Edu-All	Education (3)	Highschool, Bachelor, and Graduate (Master and PhD)

With respect to education, we consider three education levels – highschool, bachelor, and graduate (masters and PhD), and create three sets of classes combination for classification. In the first set, education is grouped into two classes: *highschool* and rest of the education levels (bachelor and graduate) belonging to *other*. Also, in the second set, education is grouped into two classes: *bachelor* and rest of the educational levels (highshool and graduate) classified to *other*. Whereas, in the third set, all three levels of education are grouped separately into individual classes: *highschool, bachelor*, and *graduate*. The purpose of these three different groupings is to see whether one level of education can be recognized from the rest of the education levels, and also whether these education levels are distinguishable between each other based on mouse interactions. Table 2 summarizes these attributes under consideration for classification.

4.2   Feature Extraction

Due to the intrinsic differences in the users' cognitive level, experience, risk-taking behavior, and motor ability across demographic groups, the mouse usage behavior differs across demographic groups [6,7,22,42,49,53,54]. To capture this *demographic-level differences* on the mouse usage behavior (the premise behind our CATCHA attack), we extracted 64 features that capture cognitive and mouse interaction characteristics of the users while playing the game CAPTCHA similar to *Gametrics* (listed in Table 1 of [36]). All these features may not contribute to distinguishing a particular demographic attribute. So, we perform statistical analysis on these features extracted from the game CAPTCHA dataset to see the features that are statistically significant across the demographic attributes and later use these statistically significant features for our design and analysis of CATCHA.

4.3   Classification Models

We tested various machine learning algorithms including Random Forest, Naive Baiyes, Logistic Regression, Support Vector Machine, and K-Nearest Neighbor with our datasets. Since Random Forest outperformed all other models, we utilize Random Forest classifier to build our demographic prediction model underlying CATCHA system. Random Forest can estimate the importance of features, and is robust against noise [33]. We design and implement several classification models evaluating and improving the performance of CATCHA system in predicting various demographic attributes. As a preliminary study, we first design a classification model utilizing all the samples collected from the users in all three days and apply 10-fold cross validation. Specifically, we build two classification models. In the first model, features from each individual CAPTCHA challenge ("single-game") are used. In the second model, we paired two consecutive CAPTCHA challenges from a user and used features from each of such paired challenges ("two-games"). The two-game setting is equivalent to solving two challenges simultaneously or a longer challenge that combines two challenges into one single challenge. In the two-game setting, features from individual game CAPTCHA are extracted and then averaged to compute the combined features. For each of these models, two different sets of features are used; first, all 64-features (*"all-features"*), and second, only the features that are statistically significant (*"stat-features"*) across the demographic attribute. The purpose of these cross-fold validation models is to see if it is possible to predict demographic attributes of the users based on their mouse interaction while playing a game CAPTCHA challenge, and also to see the impact of using only stat-features on the classification performance. In the rest of the classification models, we utilize only the *stat-features*, features that are statistically significant across the demographic attribute. The reason behind using only the stat-features is explained later in Sect. 5.3.

In a real world scenario, the classification model (*train-test model*) is first trained with one set of data samples (training set) and later used against another set of data samples (testing set). In order to see whether demographic information leakage through mouse interactions is feasible in the real world, we build several train-test models. In the first model, we use features from *single-game* while the features from *two-games* is used in the second model. Each of these models is trained with two different training sets. The first training set, *"One-day"*, is created from the game challenges collected in first day, and the second training set, *"Two-days"*, is created by combining game challenges from the first and second (or third) days. Then the classifiers are tested against the game challenges from the remaining day. Hence, second training set has a larger pool of samples than the first training set. The purpose of second training set is to see whether increasing the training set size when building an attribute classifier improves its performance.

In all these models, the training samples corresponding to each attribute were *balanced* while building the classification models, i.e., the same number of instances were present in each class considered in the classification. Although our data samples are skewed as shown in Table 1b, since the prediction model is built with balanced data, each class has an equal probability for a random guess. The employed approach may look relatively simplistic, however, it involves a crucial challenge of finding the cognitive and the mouse-related behavioral characteristics that correlate with the users' demographic attributes. We address this challenge by employing an extensive set of statistical hypotheses testing across different demographic groups (see Sect. 5.2). Further, we believe that employing a relatively simple approach is a strength of our work, as it can be easily, yet effectively, exploited by a real-world, low-capability attacker.

5   Analysis and Results

5.1   Performance Metrics

In order to measure the performance of CATCHA classification models in predicting a demographic attribute of a user, we use false positive rate (FPR), false negative rate (FNR), precision, recall and F-measure (F1 score). False Positive (FP) indicates the number of times a user is incorrectly classified to a particular attribute, and False Negative (FN) indicates the number of times a user is incorrectly classified to a different attribute. Precision measures the amount of extracted demographic attribute that are relevant to the user. Recall measures the amount of relevant demographic attribute that are correctly extracted. F1-score (or F-Measure) is the harmonic mean of precision and recall. To make our classification more accurate, we would like to have low FPR and low FNR with high F1-score/F-Measure.

5.2   Statistical Analysis of Dataset

We perform statistical analysis to measure the contrast in mouse movements when users belong to different demographic groups. For the same, we first computed several features representing these groups and measured the differences in mean values of the features between these groups. The presence of statistically significant differences on certain features between these groups will depict the features' strength in creating machine-learning based classification models. Also, removing the features without statistically significant differences in building classification models may improve their computation time, and performance.

Table 3. The statistical tests performed on feature sets of various demographic attributes, and the list of features which show statistically significant differences in the distribution of data representing different classes. The numeric values indicate the number of statistic measures (out of mean, standard deviation, minimum, and maximum) on the features that are statistically significant. Symbol '$*$' represents the statistical significant single-valued feature (p-value < 0.0007). Time, Time first action, Time first drag, and Total distance are single-valued features. Empty cells show the features that are not statistically significant.

Attribute Code	Statistical Test	Time	Time first action	Time first drag	Time between drags	Speed drag	Speed move	Acceleration drag	Acceleration move	Difference timestamp	Move silence	Drag silence	Pause and drag	Pause and drop	Angle	Drag distance to real distance	Move distance to distance	Distance click object center	Distance drop target center	Total distance
Gender	M-W Test	$*$			4	4	3	4	4	3	2	3		4	1	2	3	1	3	
Age-2	M-W Test	$*$	$*$	$*$	2	4	3	4	4	3	2	4	3	3	3				4	
Age-3	K-W Test	$*$	$*$	$*$	2	4	3	4	4	3	2	4	3	3	3		3	1	4	$*$
Edu-Highschool	M-W Test	$*$		$*$	4	3	3	3	4	4	4	4		3	3			1		
Edu-Bachelor	M-W Test	$*$		$*$	2		2	2	2	4	3	4	2	3	3			1		
Edu-All	K-W Test	$*$		$*$	4	4	4	4	4	4	4	4	4	4	2	3	3		4	$*$

For statistical analysis, first, we performed Kolmogorov-Smirnov (K-S) test to determine the normality of data distribution. The null hypothesis in K-S is that the observed distribution fits the normal distribution. However, the K-S tests of our dataset for all groups were statistically significant ($p < 0.05$), and hence rejected the null hypothesis showing the distribution did not fit the normal distribution. So, we used Kruskal-Wallis H test (K-W), a rank-based non-parametric test, to determine if there are statistically significant differences between three or more groups (independent variables) on the feature vectors (dependent variables) representing them. Similarly, we used Mann-Whitney U test (M-W) to compare differences between two groups on their feature vectors. We performed the analysis on all the features extracted for all the demographic attributes (see Table 2). Since we were making 64 feature-vector comparisons in each attribute, we applied Bonferroni correction on p-value to prevent Type I error, and considered only the comparisons with p-value < 0.0007 as statistically significant. Table 3 lists the results obtained after the statistical analysis. The features with statistically significant differences between two classes were used for building automated demographic predictor (see Sect. 4.3).

5.3   CATCHA Performance

Cross-Validation Model: The performance of CATCHA when using features from *single-game* and *two-games* with cross-fold validation approach is presented below.

Single Game Challenge: When all-features are used, we achieved the classification accuracies (F1-Scores) reasonably higher when compared to the random guessing accuracies for each demographic attribute (as shown in first part, *"All-features"*, of Appendix Table 6a). For gender, we achieved classification accuracy of 73.34% while random guessing accuracy is 50%. We achieved accuracies of 71.23% and 63.20% for Age-2 and Age-3 while their random guessing accuracies are 50% and 33.33%, respectively. For Edu-Highschool, Edu-Bachelor and Edu-All, we achieved accuracies (random guessing accuracies) of 71.65% (50%), 70.46% (50%), and 76.88% (33.33%), respectively. This shows that the accuracies of demographic attributes extraction are reasonably higher than that of the random guessing models when all-features from a single game challenge are used. When stat-features are used, across all demographic attributes, we found the accuracy of classification model (as shown in second part, *"Stat-features"*, of the Appendix Table 6a) consistently similar to the accuracy of corresponding classifier that uses all-features (can be visualized in Fig. 2). This indicates the features that are found to be statistically non-significant across a demographic attribute do not add any information to the classification models at the time of training and hence, can be discarded.

Table 4. Two Game Challenges. Performance (all presented in %) of two classification models - (a) cross-validation, and (b) train-test, corresponding to various demographic attributes when using two CAPTCHA game(s). The last column "Random" shows the random guessing accuracy of the classifier. Highlighted cells show the attribute predictions with FPRs/FNRs of less than 15%, and F1-Scores of at least 85%.

(a) *Cross-validation Model*

	Attribute Code	FPR	FNR	Prec.	Recall	F1-Score (Random)
All-features	Gender	11.24	11.24	88.82	88.76	88.76 (50.00)
	Age-2	12.35	12.35	87.68	87.65	87.64 (50.00)
	Age-3	11.19	22.37	77.68	77.63	77.58 (33.33)
	Edu-Hishschool	13.59	13.59	86.41	86.41	86.41 (50.00)
	Edu-Bachelor	13.71	13.71	86.32	86.29	86.29 (50.00)
	Edu-All	11.18	22.35	77.70	77.65	76.60 (33.33)
Stat-features	Gender	13.75	13.75	86.27	86.25	86.24 (50.00)
	Age-2	12.59	12.59	87.46	87.41	87.40 (50.00)
	Age-3	11.09	22.18	77.88	77.82	77.75 (33.33)
	Edu-Hishschool	14.07	14.07	85.95	85.93	85.93 (50.00)
	Edu-Bachelor	14.16	14.16	85.87	85.84	85.84 (50.00)
	Edu-All	11.05	22.09	77.93	77.91	77.85 (33.33)

(b) *Train-test Model*

	Attribute Code	FPR	FNR	Prec.	Recall	F1-Score (Random)
One-day	Gender	18.68	18.68	81.41	81.32	81.31 (50.00)
	Age-2	19.30	19.30	80.84	80.70	80.68 (50.00)
	Age-3	15.58	31.16	69.26	68.84	68.19 (33.33)
	Edu-Hishschool	16.15	16.15	84.23	83.85	83.80 (50.00)
	Edu-Bachelor	16.72	16.72	83.48	83.28	83.25 (50.00)
	Edu-All	15.83	31.65	68.66	68.35	67.95 (33.33)
Two-days	Gender	9.06	9.06	90.95	90.94	90.94 (50.00)
	Age-2	11.07	11.07	88.97	88.93	88.92 (50.00)
	Age-3	9.60	19.19	81.34	80.81	80.76 (33.33)
	Edu-Hishschool	11.37	11.37	88.73	88.63	88.62 (50.00)
	Edu-Bachelor	12.45	12.45	87.61	87.55	87.55 (50.00)
	Edu-All	9.44	18.88	81.25	81.12	80.96 (33.33)

Two Game Challenges: Table 4a shows the results of cross-fold validation approach when combining two game challenges to extract the features for both all-features and stat-features. When using all-features from two game challenges, classification accuracies increase by 14–16% across most of the demographic attributes comparing to the accuracies of the models using all-features from single game challenge. Also, when stat-features from the merging of two game challenges are used, classification accuracies increase by 14–19% comparing to the accuracies when using stat-features from the single game challenge. With these improvements on the accuracies when using features from the merge of two game challenges, it has made the classification models of each demographic attributes further better than its corresponding random guessing models. This can be visualized through Fig. 2. As can be seen from the figure that stat-features provide nearly similar performance result as that by all-features. Since statistically non-significant features do not seem to provide any fruitful information at the time of training the classifiers in both single game challenge setting and merge of two game challenges setting, we consider only stat-features in rest of our analysis and by using *features*, we are referring to stat-features.

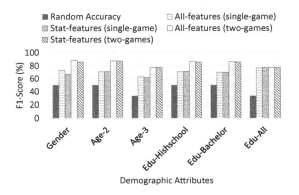

Fig. 2. Performance (F1-Score) of classification models (<u>cross-validation</u>) corresponding to various demographic attributes (along X-axis) when using all-features and stat-features from a single game challenge (single-game) and the combination of two game challenges (two-games).

Train-Test Model. Here, we present the performance of the CATCHA system when using features from *single-game* and *two-games* using the train-test model.

Single Game Challenge: As mentioned earlier, two different classification models were built within this model. The first classification model is trained with *One-day* training set and tested against game challenges from second and third days. All the results are average of results when tested against game challenges from second day and third day. With this model, for gender, we achieved the average accuracy of 64.40%, fairly better than the random guessing accuracy of 50%. For Age-2 and Age-3, we achieved average accuracies of 66.31% and 47.47%, respectively, which are higher than the random guessing accuracies of 50% and 33.33%, respectively. Similarly, for other demographic attributes, we achieved the accuracies reasonably better than random guessing accuracies. For Edu-Highschool, Edu-Bachelor, and Edu-All, we achieved accuracies of 70.41%, 65.23%, and 66.91%, respectively while their random guessing accuracies are respectively 50%, 50%, and 33.33%. These results are also presented in first part, *"One-day"*, of Appendix Table 6b.

The second classification model is trained using *Two-days* training set. Two days can be either first and second days or first and third days. The model is then tested against the game instances from remaining day. Like "One-day" approach, results are also average of results for game instances from second and third days. Using this approach, we achieved an average accuracy of 66.02% for gender while it was 64.40% when model was trained with game challenges from first day. The accuracies of 70.34% and 59.23% were achieved for Age-2 and Age-3, while they were 66.25% and 47.47%, respectively when using samples from only first-day. In a similar way, accuracies of classification models corresponding to rest of the demographic attributes (Edu-Highschool, Edu-Bachelor, and Edu-All) increase by (2–12)% as compared to the corresponding classification accuracies when game instances from only first day were used as training set. These results are also shown in second part, *"Two-days"*, of Appendix Table 6b.

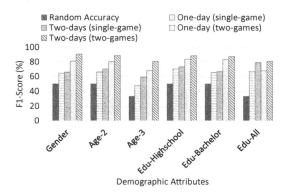

Fig. 3. Performance (F1-Score) of classification models (train-test) corresponding to various demographic attributes (along X-axis) when using a single game challenge (single-game) and combination of two game challenges (two-games) and when game instances from one-day and two-days are used as training set.

Two Game Challenges: Table 4b shows the results of applying the train-test model when using features from two game challenges. First row "One-day" shows the performance of classification models when samples from first day are used as training set and samples from second and third days are used as testing set. Using this approach, we achieved accuracy of 81.31% for gender while it was 64.40% when using features from single game challenge. For Age-2 and Age-3, classification accuracies increase from the accuracies when using single game challenge, specifically from 66.25% to 80.68% and 47.47% to 68.19%, respectively. Similarly, accuracies increase from 70.41% to 83.80%, 65.23% to 83.25%, and

66.91% to 67.95% for Edu-Highschool, Edu-Bachelor, and Edu-All, respectively. Overall, classification accuracies increase by (2–22)% when features from two game challenges are used comparing to the accuracies when single game challenge was used. Now, looking at the results in second part "Two-day", classification accuracies further improve by (4–13)%. For an instance, for gender accuracy improves from 81.32% to 90.94% while for Age-2 and Age-3 they improve from 80.68% to 88.92%, and 68.19% to 80.76%, respectively. We also achieved similar results for other demographic attributes as shown in Table 4b. We can see from this table that CATCHA achieves significantly high accuracies of at least 85% (shown in highlighted cells) compared to those of the random guessing model across all the attributes with two classes.

Thus, merging two game challenges enhances the performance of classifiers implemented in our CATCHA attack, since it provides more informative features to the classifiers at the time of training. Increasing the training samples also improves the results of classification as it provide a larger data that in turn enable the classifier to learn more distinguishable features. This can be visualized in Fig. 3 which shows the performance (F1-Score) of classifiers corresponding to various demographic attributes when single game challenge and two-game challenges were used. It also presents the results for the models when trained with one-day dataset and two-day dataset.

Train-Test Model on Lab Dataset. Table 5 shows the classification accuracies of prediction model when using the lab dataset (same mice hardware for all users). When using single game challenge, classification accuracies were – Gender: 69.52%, Age-2: 79.15%, Age-3: 60.81%, Edu-Highschool: 70.25%, Edu-Bachelor: 67.01%, and Edu-All: 59.77%. These accuracies are reasonably higher than random guessing accuracies (shown in last column "Random"). When two game challenges were used, the accuracies increased by (0–5)% from the accuracies when single game challenge was used.

This result shows that the classification accuracy of the prediction model still remains intact when the same mouse/hardware is used to generate the

Table 5. Accuracies (all presented in %) of prediction models corresponding to various demographic attributes using the lab-study dataset when using single and two CAPTCHA game(s). In lab-study, same mouse (desktop machine) was used by all the participants to solve the game challenges.

Attribute code	Single-game	Two-games	Random
Gender	69.52	71.73	50.00
Age-2	79.15	79.68	50.00
Age-3	60.81	65.70	33.33
Edu-Highschool	70.25	73.90	50.00
Edu-Bachelor	67.01	68.07	50.00
Edu-All	59.77	62.58	33.00

mouse movement data. This indicates that the reasonably high classification accuracy of prediction model compared to the random guessing accuracy is obtained because of the participants' behavioral differences while solving the game challenges *rather than* the diverse nature of mice/hardware.

6   Discussion and Future Work

Extension to the Threat: The threat of personal attribute leakage based on mouse interactions may further be extended in two different ways: first, based on the mechanism using which the leakage happens, i.e., type of interactions, and second, based on the type of leakage. Several browser interactions such as solving CAPTCHA games (other than the game CAPTCHA considered in our study), or even normal browsing behavior may be utilized to derive several user characteristics. For instance, it may be possible to learn users' personal traits utilizing the mouse behavior while solving *Google No CAPTCHA reCAPTCHA* [27], a popular free service offered by Google to recognize a machine and a human [45]. The underlying technique, advanced risk analysis, of Google reCAPTCHA, considers the user's mouse interactions at the website along with various browser characteristics to differentiate the machine from the human [45]. Google or potentially a malicious website hosting Google reCAPTCHA may then utilize such personal traits for their own benefits. Similar to Google reCAPTCHA, the threat may also apply to *FunCaptcha* [18], a simple interactive game CAPTCHA that requires the user to orient the image in correct position through a few mouse interactions. Other than the demographic attributes considered in our work, it may be possible to deduce various other personal attributes, such as race, marital status, or religion, of the user utilizing mouse dynamics. Moreover, emotional status of the user at the time of browsing may also be learned through his mouse activities. However, further research is needed towards the extension of CATCHA threat by utilizing different types of mouse interactions or by extracting several other personal attributes of the user.

Potential Defenses and Challenges: One approach to securing mouse movement tracking may be to block JavaScript (*JS*) mouse API on the browser that disables the mouse movements tracking and in turn fixes the problem of information leakage. However, this may not be a viable solution since there are several legitimate use cases of mouse API other than mouse tracking such as in presenting dynamic web contents. Therefore, blocking *JS* mouse API would prevent these use cases, reducing the web functionality. Further, websites may use other techniques (e.g., plugins) to track mouse movements, although they may have poorer performance in tracking mouse movements compared to the performance of *JS* API. Another approach may be to integrate mouse movement recording with already available permission model that requires users' consent prior to allowing access to sensitive resources, such as webcam, microphone or location. These models will prompt the user for granting permission for mouse movement tracking and make user aware of mouse activities being potentially tracked. Further, whenever such mouse movement tracking is taking place, clearly informing and alerting the user about ongoing tracking could be a viable defense [41]. One fundamental challenge with this approach is that, although users may become aware of such tracking, they may not be aware of the actual privacy risks and may be fooled to grant permissions. Further research must be conducted to validate the feasibility of such models in protecting the mouse data privacy leakage.

7   Related Work

An extensive amount of research has been performed to profile users and create their fingerprints [13,31,39,40]. Some researchers used the Javascript engine to obtain client information [40]. The others tracked the user based on JavaScript execution characteristics in the client's browser [39]. Eckersley [13] placed the effectiveness of browser fingerprinting under scrutiny by collecting 470,161 fingerprints from the visitors of a given website [14]. Hu et al. [24] tried to exploit users' web browsing behavior to infer their demographic information including age and gender. Laperdrix et al. [31] explored and reported on effectiveness of the browser fingerprinting in context of HTML5 and browser's Canvas. However, one drawback of browser-based fingerprinting or demographic prediction is that they remain changeable over the course of time due to the variety of issues such as browser/plugin upgrades and other changes in the environmental variables. Moreover, the system may be defeated easily by a privacy-conscious user by the use of NoScript or Torbutton plugins [1,47].

Many studies have been conducted on keystroke rhythm and their dynamics to either authenticate users or draw personal and demographic information [4,11,16,30]. Epp et al. [15] tried to identify users' emotional states (e.g., relaxation, sadness, anger, excitement) using keystroke dynamics and proposed an emotional-aware system. Fairhurst and Costa-Abreu [16] tried to infer users' characteristics on social networks based on keystroke dynamics and reported preliminary results.

Although, an extensive number of researches have been conducted in the area of mouse movement dynamics and user authentication [2,3,23], no study to our knowledge has been done on the attack side, like CATCHA, to draw users' demographic map. Olejnik and Castelluccia [41] studied the presence of mouse movement scripts for the purpose of user profiling and users tracking. The paper offered the MouseIndicator extension for the mitigation, which can serve as a potential defense against the CATCHA attack also. As a benign use case of mouse tracking, Wang et al. [50] and Monaro et al. [37] investigate the clicking habits of the users, and demonstrate that mouse behavior can be used to detect the fake profiles.

To the best of our knowledge, the most relevant study to ours is performed by Hertzum and Hornbaek [22] where they tried to analyze the effects of aging on the use of mouse and touchpad between three different age groups. However, our study significantly differs from the study in [22], since their study has only been conducted to differentiate the age group, but our study offers a practical attack scenario using a simple game CAPTCHA task and addresses a wide range of demographic features.

8   Conclusion

In this paper, we presented CATCHA, an attack system that can retrieve the users' personal information, specifically various demographic attributes such as gender, age group, and education level based on the innocuous-looking mouse movements while solving a simple game CAPTCHA. CATCHA leverages several mouse dynamic features that capture users' inherent cognitive and behavioral abilities, and builds a machine learning model to predict demographic attributes. We built and evaluated the CATCHA demographic predictor utilizing a comprehensive dataset of mouse interactions with a simple game CAPTCHA collected in an online setting, and achieved sufficiently high accuracies, significantly better than that corresponding to a random guessing classifier model. This underscored the threat of leaking various personal attributes through users' mouse movement characteristics when performing a commonly-occurring security task over the web (solving a CAPTCHA), unbeknownst to the users. Further, the CATCHA threat may become even more devastating if it can be extended to the next level, e.g., by using different modes of interactions (solving other CAPTCHA challenges or normal browsing behavior, and over longitudinal settings) to infer the user's attributes or by inferring attributes other than demographics considered in this work. Overall, our work highlighted the fact that mouse tracking through websites is detrimental to users' privacy, and motivated the design of a robust, yet usable security mechanism that protects the web users' privacy against CATCHA like mouse-based attacks without affecting the user-to-browser experience.

Appendix

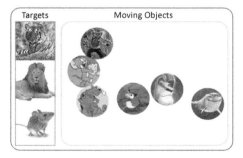

Fig. 4. An instance of game CAPTCHA. Targets (left) are static and moving objects (right) are mobile. The task of the user is to drag-drop a subset of moving objects to their corresponding target locations.

Table 6. Single game challenge. Performance (all presented in %) of two classification models - (a) cross-validation, and (b) train-test, corresponding to various demographic attributes when using single CAPTCHA game. The figures within the parenthesis ("Random") in the last column show the random guessing accuracy of the classifier.

(a) *Cross-validation Model*

	Attribute Code	FPR	FNR	Prec.	Recall	F1-Score (Random)
All-features	Gender	26.64	26.64	73.42	73.36	73.34 (50.00)
	Age-2	28.76	28.76	71.28	71.24	71.23 (50.00)
	Age-3	18.38	36.76	63.24	63.24	63.20 (33.33)
	Edu-Hishschool	28.35	28.35	71.65	71.65	71.65 (50.00)
	Edu-Bachelor	29.52	29.52	70.54	70.48	70.46 (50.00)
	Edu-All	11.52	23.05	76.97	76.95	76.88 (33.33)
	Prof-Computer	25.66	25.66	74.35	74.34	74.34 (50.00)
	Prof-Business	26.29	26.29	74.43	73.71	73.52 (50.00)
	Prof-All	9.76	19.52	80.78	80.48	80.43 (33.33)
Stat-features	Gender	32.68	32.68	67.36	67.32	67.30 (50.00)
	Age-2	28.65	28.65	71.37	71.35	71.34 (50.00)
	Age-3	18.97	37.95	62.02	62.05	62.01 (33.33)
	Edu-Hishschool	28.48	28.48	71.54	71.52	71.52 (50.00)
	Edu-Bachelor	29.88	29.88	70.17	70.12	70.10 (50.00)
	Edu-All	11.23	22.47	77.53	77.53	77.47 (33.33)
	Prof-Computer	27.05	27.05	72.95	72.95	72.95 (50.00)
	Prof-Business	28.52	28.52	72.18	71.48	71.26 (50.00)
	Prof-All	9.84	19.67	80.57	80.33	80.26 (33.33)

(b) *Train-test Model*

	Attribute Code	FPR	FNR	Prec.	Recall	F1-Score (Random)
One-day	Gender	35.56	35.56	64.51	64.44	64.40 (50.00)
	Age-2	33.69	33.69	66.40	66.31	66.25 (50.00)
	Age-3	26.15	52.30	47.74	47.70	47.47 (33.33)
	Edu-Hishschool	29.58	29.58	70.46	70.42	70.41 (50.00)
	Edu-Bachelor	34.61	34.61	65.64	65.39	65.23 (50.00)
	Edu-All	16.39	32.79	67.70	67.21	66.91 (33.33)
	Prof-Computer	33.83	33.83	66.24	66.17	66.13 (50.00)
	Prof-Business	37.99	37.99	62.14	62.01	61.90 (50.00)
	Prof-All	14.41	28.82	71.40	71.18	70.97 (33.33)
Two-days	Gender	33.96	33.96	66.07	66.04	66.02 (50.00)
	Age-2	29.62	29.62	70.47	70.38	70.34 (50.00)
	Age-3	20.28	40.55	59.41	59.45	59.23 (33.33)
	Edu-Hishschool	26.70	26.70	73.30	73.30	73.30 (50.00)
	Edu-Bachelor	33.16	33.16	66.94	66.84	66.80 (50.00)
	Edu-All	10.31	20.63	79.47	79.37	79.24 (33.33)
	Prof-Computer	32.67	32.67	67.40	67.33	67.31 (50.00)
	Prof-Business	31.73	31.73	68.64	68.27	68.10 (50.00)
	Prof-All	9.20	18.40	81.88	81.60	81.46 (33.33)

References

1. InformAction: Noscript - JavaScript/Java/Flash blocker for a safer Firefox experience! - what is it? (2017). https://noscript.net/. Accessed 28 Oct 2017
2. Ahmed, A.A.E., Traore, I.: Anomaly intrusion detection based on biometrics. In: IEEE SMC Information Assurance Workshop (2005)
3. Ahmed, A.A.E., Traore, I.: A new biometric technology based on mouse dynamics. IEEE Trans. Dependable Secur. Comput. **4**, 165–179 (2007)

4. Bergadano, F., Gunetti, D., Picardi, C.: Identity verification through dynamic keystroke analysis. Intell. Data Anal. **7**, 469–496 (2003)
5. Chrome Blog: Everyone can now track down noisy tabs (2017). https://goo.gl/mojwB2. Accessed 19 May 2017
6. Brodic, D., Petrovska, S., Jankovic, R., Amelio, A., Draganov, I.: User-centric analysis of the CAPTCHA response time: a new perspective in artificial intelligence. ERCIM News **109**, 49–50 (2017)
7. Bursztein, E., Bethard, S., Fabry, C., Mitchell, J.C., Jurafsky, D.: How good are humans at solving CAPTCHAs? A large scale evaluation. In: IEEE Security and Privacy (S&P) (2010)
8. Carlson, E.L.: Phishing for elderly victims: as the elderly migrate to the internet fraudulent schemes targeting them follow. Elder LJ (2006)
9. Chen, M.C., Anderson, J.R., Sohn, M.H.: What can a mouse cursor tell us more?: correlation of eye/mouse movements on web browsing. In: Extended Abstracts on Human Factors in Computing Systems (2001)
10. Datta, A., Tschantz, M.C., Datta, A.: Automated experiments on ad privacy settings. Priv. Enhancing Technol. **2015**, 92–112 (2015)
11. Dowland, P.S., Furnell, S.M.: A long-term trial of keystroke profiling using digraph, trigraph and keyword latencies. In: Deswarte, Y., Cuppens, F., Jajodia, S., Wang, L. (eds.) SEC 2004. ITIFIP, vol. 147, pp. 275–289. Springer, Boston, MA (2004). https://doi.org/10.1007/1-4020-8143-X_18
12. Eccles, L.: Money mail reveals why shops want your email address (2016). https://goo.gl/9jFtfr. Accessed 24 Sept 2018
13. Eckersley, P.: How unique is your web browser? In: Atallah, M.J., Hopper, N.J. (eds.) PETS 2010. LNCS, vol. 6205, pp. 1–18. Springer, Heidelberg (2010). https://doi.org/10.1007/978-3-642-14527-8_1
14. Eckersley, P.: Panopticlick (2010). https://panopticlick.eff.org. Accessed 28 Oct 2017
15. Epp, C., Lippold, M., Mandryk, R.L.: Identifying emotional states using keystroke dynamics. In: SIGCHI Conference on Human Factors in Computing Systems. ACM (2011)
16. Fairhurst, M., Da Costa-Abreu, M.: Using keystroke dynamics for gender identification in social network environment. In: Imaging for Crime Detection and Prevention 2011 (ICDP 2011). IET (2011)
17. Firefox: Mute sound in Firefox tabs (2017). https://goo.gl/KeA80E. Accessed 19 May 2017
18. FunCaptcha: reCAPTCHA: easy on humans, hard on bots (2017). https://www.funcaptcha.com/. Accessed 13 May 2017
19. Gao, S., Mohamed, M., Saxena, N., Zhang, C.: Emerging image game CAPTCHAs for resisting automated and human-solver relay attacks. In: Annual Computer Security Applications Conference (2015)
20. Google Chrome: Change website permissions - google chrome (2017). https://goo.gl/OhoO5H. Accessed 19 May 2017
21. Henry, N., Powell, A.: Embodied harms gender, shame, and technology-facilitated sexual violence. Violence Against Women **21**, 758–779 (2015)
22. Hertzum, M., Hornbæk, K.: How age affects pointing with mouse and touchpad: a comparison of young, adult, and elderly users. Int. J. Hum.-Comput. Interact. **26**, 703–734 (2010)
23. Hocquet, S., Ramel, J., Cardot, H.: Users authentication by a study of human computer interactions. In: Proceedings of the Eighth Annual (Doctoral) Meeting on Health, Science and Technology (2004)

24. Hu, J., Zeng, H.J., Li, H., Niu, C., Chen, Z.: Demographic prediction based on user's browsing behavior. In: International Conference on World Wide Web (2007)
25. HuffingtonPost: 'are you a human' CAPTCHA game brings fun to web security (2018). https://goo.gl/aEWa4e. Accessed 27 March 2018
26. Facebook Inc.: Data policy (2018). https://www.facebook.com/policy.php. Accessed 19 Sept 2018
27. Google Inc.: reCAPTCHA: Easy on humans, hard on bots (2017). https://goo.gl/oL49TZ. Accessed 17 May 2017
28. Google Inc.: Privacy policy - Google (2018). https://goo.gl/fwnohr. Accessed 19 Sept 2018
29. James, M.S.: Why do they want my phone number? (2016). https://goo.gl/EWoyqT. Accessed 24 Sept 2018
30. Joyce, R., Gupta, G.: Identity authentication based on keystroke latencies. Commun. ACM **33**, 168–176 (1990)
31. Laperdrix, P., Rudametkin, W., Baudry, B.: Beauty and the beast: diverting modern web browsers to build unique browser fingerprints. In: IEEE Symposium on Security and Privacy (SP) (2016)
32. Li, Q.: Cyberbullying in schools: a research of gender differences. Sch. Psychol. Int. **27**, 157–170 (2006)
33. Maxion, R.A., Killourhy, K.S.: Keystroke biometrics with number-pad input. In: Dependable Systems and Networks (DSN) (2010)
34. Mohamed, M., Gao, S., Saxena, N., Zhang, C.: Dynamic cognitive game captcha usability and detection of streaming-based farming. In: Workshop on Usable Security (USEC), co-located with NDSS (2014)
35. Mohamed, M., et al.: A three-way investigation of a game-CAPTCHA: automated attacks, relay attacks and usability. In: ACM Symposium on Information, Computer and Communications Security (2014)
36. Mohamed, M., Saxena, N.: Gametrics: towards attack-resilient behavioral authentication with simple cognitive games. In: Annual Conference on Computer Security Applications (2016)
37. Monaro, M., Gamberini, L., Sartori, G.: The detection of faked identity using unexpected questions and mouse dynamics. PloS One (2017)
38. Mouseflow (2017). https://mouseflow.com/. Accessed 13 May 2017
39. Mowery, K., Bogenreif, D., Yilek, S., Shacham, H.: Fingerprinting information in JavaScript implementations. In: Proceedings of W2SP (2011)
40. Mulazzani, M., et al.: Fast and reliable browser identification with JavaScript engine fingerprinting. In: Web 2.0 Workshop on Security and Privacy (W2SP) (2013)
41. Olejnik, L., Castelluccia, C.: Of mice and men: mouse movements tracking and browser UI protections
42. Pentel, A.: Predicting age and gender by keystroke dynamics and mouse patterns. In: Conference on User Modeling, Adaptation and Personalization (2017)
43. Radinsky, K., Svore, K.M., Dumais, S., Teevan, J., Bocharov, A., Horvitz, E.: Modeling and predicting behavioral dynamics on the web (2012)
44. Rodden, K., Fu, X.: Exploring how mouse movements relate to eye movements on web search results pages. In: Web Information Seeking and Interaction (2007)
45. Sivakorn, S., Polakis, I., Keromytis, A.D.: I am robot: (deep) learning to break semantic image CAPTCHAs. In: IEEE European Symposium on Security and Privacy (EuroS&P) (2016)
46. The WindowsClub: how to setup Firefox permission manager for websites (2017). https://goo.gl/PNOozZ. Accessed 19 May 2017

47. Tor: Tor project: Torbutton (2017). https://www.torproject.org/docs/torbutton. Accessed 13 May 2017
48. Ur, B., Leon, P.G., Cranor, L.F., Shay, R., Wang, Y.: Smart, useful, scary, creepy: perceptions of online behavioral advertising. In: Symposium on Usable Privacy and Security (2012)
49. Walker, N., Millians, J., Worden, A.: Mouse accelerations and performance of older computer users. In: Human Factors and Ergonomics Society Annual Meeting. SAGE Publications (1996)
50. Wang, G., Konolige, T., Wilson, C., Wang, X., Zheng, H., Zhao, B.Y.: You are how you click: clickstream analysis for sybil detection. In: USENIX Security Symposium (2013)
51. Wordpress: Are you a human - the fun spam blocker (2017). https://goo.gl/pszcYQ. Accessed 13 May 2017
52. WSJ: Facebook tests software to track your cursor on screen (2013). https://goo.gl/tM3zxu
53. Yamauchi, T.: Mouse trajectories and state anxiety: feature selection with random forest. In: IEEE Affective Computing and Intelligent Interaction (ACII) (2013)
54. Yamauchi, T., Seo, J.H., Jett, N., Parks, G., Bowman, C.: Gender differences in mouse and cursor movements. Int. J. Hum.-Comput. Interact. **31**, 911–921 (2015)
55. Zheng, N., Paloski, A., Wang, H.: An efficient user verification system via mouse movements. In: Conference on Computer and Communications Security (2011)

Designing a Code Vulnerability Meta-scanner

Raounak Benabidallah$^{(\boxtimes)}$, Salah Sadou, Brendan Le Trionnaire,
and Isabelle Borne

Université Bretagne Sud, IRISA, Vannes, France
{Raounak.Benabidallah,Salah.Sadou,Brendan.LeTrionnaire,
Isabelle.Borne}@univ-ubs.fr

Abstract. The concept of "secure by design" is based on preventive software security and aims at avoiding vulnerabilities as soon as possible. However, finding vulnerabilities manually is a time-consuming and error-prone process. Thus, the use of code scanner tools becomes a good practice for developers. Unfortunately, existing code scanner tools produce too many false positives, which complicates the cycle development task.

In this paper, we present an approach to construct a code vulnerability scanner upon existing scanner tools. The aim of such a scanner, called code vulnerability meta-scanner (CVMS), is to be more efficient and reduce the number of false positives. Our experimental results show that none of the scanners strictly subsumes another, and none of them is better than all the others for all the vulnerabilities. So, we propose a method that combines their results with respect to their performances. We experimented our approach using three existing scanner tools (Fortify, Yag Suite and SpotBug). Then, we used the resulted CVMS to annotate a well-known Java application corpus, namely Qualitas Corpus. These experiment results demonstrated that the CVMS performs better than the scanners on which it is constructed.

1 Introduction

Most attacks on software systems are possible due to the existence of vulnerabilities in their source code. Vulnerabilities may be defects in design or implementation, or simply a code erosion due to a poor maintenance activity [22]. Good software engineering methods, the use of a secure design environment, the choice of appropriate languages and programming rules can reduce the number of vulnerabilities in the code. However, these good practices are still relatively uncommon and do not guarantee to avoid vulnerabilities. Thus, more research works are needed to help developers in vulnerability identification.

Identifying vulnerabilities in a source code is a complex and costly activity. Several techniques were already proposed to identify code vulnerabilities. The most intuitive one is the source code review. This kind of analysis is recognized as one of the most effective defense strategies [13] and is therefore essential in the

© Springer Nature Switzerland AG 2019
S.-H. Heng and J. Lopez (Eds.): ISPEC 2019, LNCS 11879, pp. 194–210, 2019.
https://doi.org/10.1007/978-3-030-34339-2_11

software development life cycle. However, finding vulnerabilities manually is a time-consuming and error-prone process. Furthermore, it requires security expertise that remains rare among developers. To address this problem, researchers and industrialists have put a lot of effort into finding new methods. One of the most widespread techniques consists in mining program patches in order to collect vulnerabilities [10]. The idea here is to consider the piece of code targeted by the patch as the prototype of a vulnerability, and once the patch is applied, the resulting code can be considered as cleared of this vulnerability [1]. However, there are several ways to fix a vulnerability and a patch represents only one possible solution. Furthermore, considering the code as vulnerable before the patch and as not vulnerable after is an incorrect assumption. Indeed, after applying the patch we have no guarantee that the vulnerability has been correctly fixed nor that the code does not contain other types of vulnerabilities.

Another method widely used by industrialists and researchers is to use code scanners to identify vulnerabilities. Several works proposed code scanner tools [15]. However, existing scanner tools find too many false positives, which makes the maintenance activity hard and thus error-prone.

Through this paper, we propose an approach to build code vulnerability scanners to identify vulnerabilities with better accuracy than existing tools and with fewer false positives. This approach jointly use several existing code vulnerability scanner tools in order to construct a better one. Our approach is based on the emergence theory: the whole is more than the sum of its parts.

This paper introduces the following contributions:

- A new method that merges existing scanners to benefit from the effectiveness of each scanner tool and provides a more efficient one.
- A new vulnerability categorization to compare performances and results of different scanner tools for a best joint use.
- Tagging a well-known software corpus with its held vulnerabilities. This will be very useful for experiments on software vulnerabilities.

The remainder of the paper is organized as follows: in the next section, we describe the proposed approach to design a code vulnerability meta-scanner. In Sects. 3 to 7, we detail all the steps that allow the accomplishment of the design methodology. In Sect. 8, we give the results of the different experiments we conducted and discuss the results obtained. In Sect. 9, we discuss some related works. We conclude the paper in Sect. 10 and give the link to the generated data.

2   General Approach

The scanners built with our approach are based on the following idea: listen to advice from different code vulnerability scanner tools to build a consistent decision. The process describing this approach is defined by Fig. 1.

The existence of a vulnerability is suspected as soon as one of the scanners reports it. However, before making a decision, we must consult the result of the other scanners concerning this vulnerability in the same portion of code.

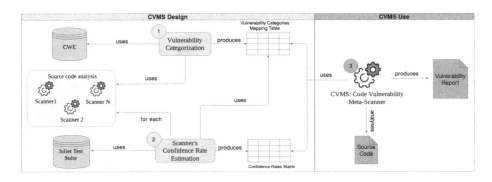

Fig. 1. General approach for Code Vulnerability Meta-Scanner construction

Somehow, it is as if we are organizing a vote for scanners with the following question: is there vulnerability x in the y portion of code? The answer can only be *yes* or *no*. However, the organization of such a vote, in an automatic manner, raises several problems:

1. The same vulnerability is not identified in the same way by the different scanners.
2. The accuracy level of the different scanners differs from one vulnerability to another.
3. How to aggregate the above information to produce the vote result?

Vulnerability Categorization step shown in Fig. 1 aims at providing a common vulnerability referencing for different scanners. It is based on CWE categorization in order to provide a pragmatic mapping between information given by each scanner and the corresponding vulnerabilities in a common categorization. This step answers the problem (1) by providing the scanners with a same categorization of vulnerabilities.

The second step of our approach consists in estimating the scanners confidence rate. For that aim, we benchmark each scanner using the Juliet test suite [7] in order to determine its performance for each vulnerability. We consider the accuracy as a confidence rate (solution to problem 2).

The last step of our approach consists in using the elements built in the previous steps when analyzing the same code with different scanners in order to determine the existence of some vulnerabilities. For each part of the code (in our case a method), we collect the results of each scanner to aggregate them as a vote weighted by the confidence rate of the scanners (solution to problem 3).

In the following, we describe all the elements necessary for the accomplishment of our approach.

3   Vulnerability Benchmark Corpus

The proposed approach is essentially based on a pragmatic use of existing scanner tools. We need to evaluate their performances in order to combine them effectively. One of the most effective ways to evaluate static analysis tools is by using them in the analysis of a portion of code, then comparing their results with the actual vulnerabilities. Therefore, we need to choose the appropriate code to be analyzed. In our work, we mainly need a benchmark with vulnerable and non-vulnerable code. The objective is not only to evaluate the scanner's performance in identifying vulnerabilities but also to estimate its effectiveness in avoiding false alerts (false positives). We have selected the Juliet Test Suite because it satisfies the identified needs. Juliet Test Suite was created by the National Security Agency's (NSA) Center for Assured Software (CAS) and developed specifically for assessing the effectiveness of static analysis tools [20]. It consists of a collection of C/C++ and Java programs with known flaws. The test cases use MITRE's [18] Common Weakness Enumeration (CWE [17])[1] as a basis for naming and organizing. The most specific CWE entry is used for the target flaw. The test cases cover 113 CWE entries, but only 11 of the 2011 CWE/SANS Top 25 Most Dangerous Software Errors which are the only ones detectable by static code analysis.

Once the choice of the test suite made, we need to define the level of granularity to use when reporting security alerts. Granularity represents the entity that will be presented to developers for analysis [14]. Different levels of granularity offer different advantages [19]. For instance, the line of code granularity can be considered as a precise alert but this granularity is too fine for developers to identify an issue [14]. Most of the studies adopt the component file granularity level following the findings of Morrison et al. [19]. However, we suspect that this level may not be accurate in case of vulnerability studies, especially if the files are very large. Indeed, in the latter case, the analysis becomes expensive in execution time or error-prone if human analysis is used. For this reason, we propose to use the method of a class as the smallest granularity. This should be a good compromise between the number of lines of code to analyze and the information we may deduce from them.

In the reminder of the paper, we will use the term *individual* to represent a method of a class.

4   Code Vulnerability Scanner Tools

The static analysis tools need to be selected based on the two following criteria:

- The first selection criterion concerns the vulnerability coverage quality of the scanners. The idea is to choose scanners that do not cover exactly the same vulnerabilities.
- The second corresponds to the vulnerability detection method used by the scanner tools. Even if we are restricted to methods based on source code static analysis, we found several techniques in this area (vulnerability modeling, AI,

---

[1] CWE: CWE is a community-developed list of common software security weaknesses. It serves as a common language, a measuring stick for software security tools, and as a baseline for weakness identification, mitigation, and prevention efforts.

etc.). It is therefore interesting to vary the used techniques in order to mitigate the individual weaknesses of the selected scanners.

For our experiments, we have eliminated some tools for their unavailability (in terms of price, documentation, etc.) and others for the lack of additional information they provide. We selected the following three scanners: Find Security Bugs (also named SpotBugs) [5], Fortify Static Code Analyzer [8] and Yag suite [23]. Table 1 summarizes the vulnerabilities from the Juliet test suite that are covered by at least one of the three selected scanners. The vulnerabilities are sorted by their CWE identity number.

Table 1. Vulnerabilities from Juliet covered by the selected scanner tools

Vulnerabilities scanners	23	36	78	80	81	83	88	89	90	113	134	256	259	315	319	321	325
Fortify	X	X	X	X	X	X	X	X	-	-	-	X	X	-	X	X	X
Yag Suite	X	X	X	X	X	X	-	X	X	X	-	-	-	X	-	-	-
SpotBugs	-	-	X	-	X	X	-	X	X	X	X	-	X	-	-	X	-

Vulnerabilities scanners	327	328	329	330	338	470	506	510	534	535	539	566	601	606	614	643	1004
Fortify	X	-	-	-	-	-	X	X	-	-	-	X	X	-	-	-	-
Yag Suite	X	-	-	X	X	X	-	-	X	X	X	-	X	X	X	-	-
SpotBugs	X	X	X	X	X	-	X	-	-	X	X	-	X	-	-	X	X

Here is a small description of each selected scanner:

- *Find Security Bugs* or *SpotBugs* is an open source tool for static source code analysis. SpotBugs relies on vulnerability modeling and manages a knowledge base containing 128 vulnerability patterns [4].
- *Fortify Static Code Analyzer* (SCA) uses multiple algorithms and an expansive knowledge base of secure coding rules to analyze source code. To process a code, Fortify SCA converts source code into an intermediate enhanced structure for security analysis. The analysis engine, which consists of multiple specialized analyzers, uses secure coding rules to analyze the source code in order to find coding practice violations. Fortify SCA also provides a rule builder to extend and expand static analysis capabilities with some specific rules [9].
- *Yag Suite* is a software suite based on machine learning techniques for vulnerability prediction. One of the strengths of this tool is that it assesses the relevance of each identified vulnerability and estimates its criticality. In addition, the knowledge base is refined according to the application domain by integrating some user's answers [23].

5   Vulnerability Categorization

Vulnerability scanners are widely used for automatic code review but they do not completely cover the same set of vulnerabilities. In order to increase their coverage rate, we propose to combine their results. However, we have first to tackle a challenging problem: each scanner represents, identifies and classifies vulnerabilities using its own denomination [26]. For instance, the Cross-Site Scripting vulnerability (XSS) is called "Insecure Interaction - CWE ID 079" by Fortify, "XSS-Servlet" by Spotbugs, and "xss.stored" by Yag Suite. Due to this diversity of responses for the same vulnerability, it is very difficult to use together different scanner tools for a common purpose.

Moreover, to compare the effectiveness of different scanner tools, we can rely on the Common Weakness Enumeration (CWE) [17] classification to categorize the vulnerabilities and on Juliet as a test suite corpus. Unfortunately, while it is obvious but tedious to find the most abstract CWE identifier that corresponds to the definitions given by the scanner tools, it is not easy to find its corresponding identifier in Juliet. Indeed, Juliet test cases are created for all appropriate flaw types and each one is named using the most relevant CWE entry. For instance, the XSS vulnerability (CWE-79) may correspond to at least one of the following identifiers in Juliet:

- CWE-80: Improper Neutralization of Script-Related HTML Tags in a Web Page (Basic XSS);
- CWE-81: Improper Neutralization of Script in an Error Message Web Page;
- CWE-83: Improper Neutralization of Script in Attributes in a Web Page;

Having such details to distinguish two vulnerabilities is not always helpful. Indeed, the evaluation of a scanner is usually done by comparing its results with the actual vulnerabilities. However, evaluating the scanners by confronting them to Juliet and comparing the CWE identifiers is not always adequate. As previously shown, a security alert returned by a scanner could cover several vulnerabilities of Juliet when: (i) Juliet's test cases correspond to less abstract vulnerabilities than those returned by the scanner; (ii) The vulnerabilities are strongly related to each other.

To ensure efficient evaluation and compare the performance of scanners, we proceed to the categorization of the vulnerabilities covered by the scanner tools with respect to Juliet suite corpus definitions and CWE categorization. This process consists in creating a unique and common reference for the scanners, gathering all the correct correspondences between the results of the scanners and the Juliet test cases. Our process involves three steps:

1. Juliet analysis: the aim is to collect all the vulnerabilities defined in Juliet and covered by the used scanner tools.
2. CWE identifier mapping: for each vulnerability definition given by each scanner tool, found its corresponding CWE identifier.
3. Propose a common categorization: group definitions from Juliet which are related to the same vulnerability in a common and meaningful definition.

Concretely, in the last step of our process, we start from each label returned by each scanner tool then analyze all the individuals where the corresponding vulnerability was detected. To facilitate this task, we rely on the CWE categorization to verify the mapping between scanner results and vulnerability identifiers on Juliet. The categorization CWE was set up by the MITRE [17] and consists of hierarchical organization between the vulnerabilities. The roles assigned to the identifiers represent several levels of abstraction, presented in the following from the more abstract to the more concrete:

- Category: a CWE entry that contains a set of other entries that share a common characteristic;
- Class: a weakness that is described in a very abstract fashion, typically independent from any specific language or technology. Moreover, this relationship is confirmed by the categorization proposed by CWE.
- Base: a weakness that is described in an abstract fashion, but with sufficient details to infer specific methods for detection and prevention.
- Variant: a weakness that is described at a very low level of detail, typically limited to a specif language or technology.

Moreover, the links between the different levels are represented by multiple relationships such as "MemberOf", "ParentOf", "ChildOf", "CanAlsoBe", etc. We have used all this information to draw the possible paths between vulnerability identifiers. Nevertheless, by closely analyzing the invalid matches, we noticed that there were several scanner responses that were correct according to the CWE definitions but no link was created in the CWE categorization. This is mainly due to the fact that the categorization was done in a subjective way [29]. As a result, this categorization could not be considered as a standard. Thus, the mapping we propose in this paper serves as a complement to CWE categorisation.

Table 2 summarizes the categorisation we propose for some Juliet's vulnerability definitions. We only consider vulnerabilities that have been detected by at least one of the scanner tools we selected for our experiment, namely Fortify, SpotBugs or Yag Suite. According to our knowledge of other vulnerability scanner tools (mostly free access), the vulnerabilities covered by the three used scanners almost encompass the vulnerabilities that existing code scanner tools can detect. Thus, the mapping table that we propose remains sufficiently reusable in the case of another group of code scanner tools. If in the future, a new code scanner tool arrives with some vulnerabilities not covered yet, this mapping table will need to be completed.

To facilitate the addition of a vulnerability to our mapping table, we give more details on how we proceed on an example of a vulnerability, namely Path Traversal (Category 1). By analyzing the results of the scanner tools on Juliet test cases implementing CWE-23 and CWE-36 flaws, we noticed that Fortify returned the message "Risk Management Resource - CWE ID 022", Yag suite returned the message "Injection.path" while Spotbugs did not detect any vulnerability that can match with this category. When looking for these definitions in CWE, we found that the CWE-22 is the one that matches the best.

Table 2. Proposed vulnerability categorization

Category number	Category description	Associated to in Juliet Test Suite
1	Path traversal CWE-22	CWE-23: Relative path traversal CWE-36: Absolute path traversal
2	Os command injection CWE-78	CWE-78 CWE-506: Embedded malicious code CWE-88: Argument injection or modification
3	XSS: Improper neutralization Of input during Web Page Generation CWE-79	CWE-80: XSS CWE-81: XSS Error Message Servlet File CWE-83: XSS Attribute Servlet connect tcp CWE-535: Info exposure shell error servlet
4	SQL injection CWE-89	CWE-89
5	Injection LDAP CWE-90	CWE-90
6	Uncontrolled format string CWE-134	CWE-134
7	Use of broken or risky Cryptographic Algorithm CWE-327	CWE-256: Plaintext storage pwd CWE-319: Cleatext Tx sensitive info CWE-321: Hard coded cryptographic key CWE-325: Missing required cryptographic step CWE-327 CWE-328: Reversible One-Way Hash CWE-329: Not Using a Random IV with CBC Mode
8	Use of insufficiante random values CWE-330	CWE-330 CWE-338: Use of Cryptographically Weak Pseudo-Random Number Generator (PRNG)
9	Use if externally controlled Input to select classes or code (unsafe reflection) CWE-470	CWE-470
10	Open redirect to untrusted site CWE-601	CWE-601
11	Unchecked loop CWE-606	CWE-606
12	XPATh injection CWE-643	CWE-643
13	Use of hard coded credentials CWE-798	CWE-256: Plaintext storage pwd CWE-259: Hard codded password CWE-319: Cleatext Tx sensitive info CWE-321: Hard coded cryptographic key
14	Reliance on untrusted Inputs in a security decision CWE-807	CWE-510: Trapdoor
15	Incorrect authorization CWE-863	CWE-566: Authorization Bypass Through User-Controlled SQL Primary Key
16	Sensitive cookies in HTTPs session	CWE-614: Sensitive cookies in HTTPs session without 'secure' attribute CWE-539: Information exposure through persistent cookies CWE-315: Cleatext storage of sensitive information in a cookie CWE-113: HTTP response splitting CWE-1004: Sensitive Cookie Without 'HttpOnly' Flag

However, CWE-22 covers two other sub-categories CWF-23 and CWE-36 which correspond, respectively, to the relative and absolute paths. Moreover, this relationship is confirmed by the categorization proposed by CWE. Indeed, the links between the vulnerability CWE-22 and the vulnerabilities CWE-36 and CWE-23 are represented in the CWE categorization by the "parentOf" relationship.

6   Scanners Confidence Rates Estimation

In order to detect the vulnerabilities of an individual, we must confront it with each scanner tool. However, during our first experiments, we noticed that the performance of each of them depends on the targeted vulnerability. Thus, none of the scanner tools is better than all the others for all the vulnerabilities. So when the confrontation of an individual with the scanner tools gives divergent results, we need complementary information to conclude. We believe that the accuracy of detecting a given vulnerability by a given scanner tool can be very useful for decision making. This accuracy will be treated as a confidence rate assigned to the scanner result regarding the intended vulnerability. To determine the confidence rate associated to each vulnerability according ti each scanner tool, we used the Juliet Test Cases. So, for each scanner tool and for each vulnerability category it detect we calculated its accuracy as follows:

$$Accuracy = \frac{TP + TN}{TP + FP + TN + FN} \tag{1}$$

where:

- TP (True Positives) represents the number of well detected individuals with the vulnerability in question.
- TN (True Negatives) represents the number of individuals considered not containing the vulnerability in question, and this is really the case.
- FP (False Positives) is the number of individuals that the scanner tool considered containing the vulnerability whereas they do not.
- FN (False Negatives) is the number of individuals that the scanner tool considered not containing the vulnerability whereas they do.

Table 3 summarizes the confidence rates obtained with the three scanner tools for the proposed vulnerability categories. In this table, we notice that the classification accuracy varies between 0.26 to 0.82 for Fortify, and between 0.47 to 1 for Yag Suite and SpotBugs. These ranges of variation confirm the need to assign weights by category of vulnerabilities.

Furthermore, scanner tools that do not detect a category may have a positive weight ($>= 0$). This is due to the number of individuals that do not contain the targeted vulnerability and where the scanner detects nothing (TN). Indeed, among the test cases, some have been generated for the target flaw but without the vulnerability. This is to assess the ability of the scanner tool to discriminate between vulnerable and non-vulnerable cases. In this case, a scanner tool that does not detect the vulnerability will pass the test and this will increase its number of true negatives. To solve this problem, we simply ignore the result of such a scanner tool for this vulnerability by setting its confidence rate to 0.

Table 3. Scanner tools confidence rates per vulnerability category

Category number	Fortify	Yag Suite	SpotBugs	Our Approach
1	**0.82**	0.64	0.55	**0.82**
2	0.42	0.61	0.56	**0.63**
3	**0.76**	0.74	0.67	0.75
4	**0.8**	0.75	0.69	0.77
5	–	0.64	**0.76**	**0.76**
6	–	–	**0.83**	**0.83**
7	0.33	0.57	**0.71**	0.57
8	–	**1.0**	**1.0**	**1.0**
9	–	**0.64**	–	**0.64**
10	**0.82**	–	0.8	**0.82**
11	–	**0.70**	–	0.7
12	–	–	**0.84**	**0.84**
13	0.54	–	**0.66**	**0.66**
14	0.26	–	–	0.26
15	**0.82**	–	–	**0.82**
16	–	**0.71**	**0.71**	**0.71**

7 Code Vulnerability Identification

The purpose of code vulnerability identification is not only to classify a code as vulnerable or not, but rather to find the vulnerabilities it contains. Indeed, the same method may contain different categories of vulnerabilities. Therefore, it is important to lead the developer to the vulnerability categories that should be analyzed and/or corrected. We do not care if the same vulnerability appears more than once. The aim is to indicate the presence of some vulnerability categories but not their number of occurrences.

The presence or absence of a given vulnerability category in a given individual (a method of a class) is calculated using the confidence rate (noted C bellow) previously attributed to the scanner tools. For each individual, the presence or absence of a given vulnerability is calculated as follows:

$$
V(v) = \begin{cases} 1 & \text{if } \sum_{i=0}^{K} C(v)_{i+} > \sum_{j=0}^{M} C(v)_{j-} \quad i,j \in \{Scanners\} \\ 0 & \text{if } \sum_{i=0}^{K} C(v)_{i+} < \sum_{j=0}^{M} C(v)_{j-} \end{cases}
$$

where:

- v represents the category of vulnerabilities;

- $C_{i+}(v)$ is the weight of the ith scanner which has detected the vulnerability v in the individual;
- $C_{j-}(v)$ is the weight of the jth scanner which has not detected the vulnerability v in the individual;
- K and M represent the number of scanners that have/have not detected the vulnerability v respectively.

In other words, for each individual and for each vulnerability, we assign a value "1" when the weights of the scanner tools that have detected this vulnerability are greater than the weights of the scanner tools that did not detect it.

8   Experimentation

The main objective of this experiment is to validate the approach of constructing a meta-scanner. This is done by comparing the results of our CVMS with those of scanner tools. The goal is to check whether our approach gives better results than the scanner tools applied each one apart. The second objective is to apply the meta-scanner on a real Java source code to show that the approach gives accurate results.

8.1   CVMS VS Individual Scanner Tools

First, we apply our approach on Juliet Test Suite in order to evaluate its effectiveness and compare its results with those from the selected scanner tools. The comparison is made on vulnerability categories. For this, we compute the approach accuracy for each vulnerability category (see column 5 of Table 3). As shown in the Table 3, we can notice that our approach results often converge towards the results of the scanners having the best accuracy for the considered vulnerability categories.

Nevertheless, some exceptions need to be highlighted, especially for category 7 where our approach has an accuracy of 0.57. This is due to the fact that the sum of the weights of the two weakest scanner tools is stronger than the third. For the rest of categories, we record a similar performance as the most efficient scanner tools.

In a second step, we compare the macro-average performances of the scanner tools independently of the vulnerability category. Table 4 presents the overall benchmarking results (precision, recall and F-Measure). The precision focuses on the balance between True Positives (TP) and False Positives (FP) and the recall focuses on the True Positives rate. The F-Measure is an average between precision and recall. As we can see from this table, our approach presents the higher F-Measure.

We also note that Yag Suite has the best accuracy rate. Recall that this scanner tool has the advantage of evaluating the relevance of vulnerabilities. Indeed, this tool is not aimed at the simple detection of vulnerability but rather the reduction of the number of FPs. To reduce this rate, we have set the relevance threshold at 30%, which leads to ignore any security alerts with a percentage of relevance below this limit. As a result, the precision value is very high but the value of the recall is very low.

Thus, based on the Juliet test suite, we can conclude that our approach globally gives better results than the scanner tools taken individually in terms of number of vulnerabilities and performances.

Table 4. Evaluation results

Scanner tools	Precision	Recall	F-Measure	Accuracy
Fortify	0.67	**0.31**	**0.43**	0.71
Yag Suite	**0.91**	0.14	0.25	0.7
Spotbugs	0.74	0.18	0.29	0.7
Our approach	0.87	0.31	**0.46**	**0.75**

8.2   CVMS on Real Java Source Code

The second step of our experiments aims to use the CVMS for the detection of vulnerabilities in Java real code. In order to evaluate our approach performances, we need a large number of applications, covering different domains, having different sizes and designed by developers with different expertise. These criteria have led us to use a validated corpus in software engineering, widely used by researchers, namely the Qualitas Corpus [24]. The Qualitas Corpus is a curated collection of open-source Java systems. The corpus was developed by Tampero et al. [24] in order to reduce the cost of large empirical studies of code. The Qualitas corpus provides a huge contribution for experimentation in software engineering. However, there are several studies, such as experiments that rely on Abstract Syntax Tree (AST) or bytecode, where a compiled corpus is needed. Thus, Ricardo et al. [25] provides a compiled version of Qualitas called Qualitas.class Corpus. The corpus contains a collection of systems, each one of them includes one or more projects. Qualitas has a total of 111 systems and 802 internal projects and is considered as the largest curated corpus for code analysis studies.

For compatibility issues between scanners and some applications from Qualitas, we started our experiments on a subset of the Qualitas applications that represents 41 Java systems containing more than 170k methods. The results show that our approach detected 957 vulnerabilities divided into 12 categories. Table 5 presents all the categories with the corresponding occurrence number.

In order to validate Qualitas results, we performed a manual checking on a part of the corpus. For this aim, we randomly selected 10% of the individuals (methods) based on a stratified sampling that focuses on the following factors: (i) non-vulnerable code/vulnerable code, and (ii) vulnerable code with category

Table 5. Vulnerability categories discovered

Category number	1	2	3	4	5	6	7	8	9	10	11	12	13	14	15	16
Occurrences	671	5	0	2	2	0	0	64	59	1	0	3	15	108	25	2

1/.../vulnerable code with category 16. This phase ensures the distributional balance of these factors within the selected population. The results of this operation are given in the Table 6.

Table 6. Performance measures on the annotation of Qualitas Corpus with vulnerabilities

Accuracy	0.99
Precision	0.85
Recall	0.89
F-measure	0.87

The results obtained give very encouraging performances. For research work aiming at constructing prediction models, these performances are generally acceptable. Thus, we can say that our approach guarantees accurate results on real Java source code.

8.3 Discussion

The approach we proposed is based on the use of existing scanner tools. As the performance of our approach strongly depends on the efficiency of the scanners, it is very important to take performing scanner tools. The other parameter that could increase the quality of the results is the variety of approaches used by the selected scanners (static analysis, dynamic analysis, penetration test, etc.). With a larger number of scanner tools covering a wider variety of analysis approaches, we hope to increase the quality of the obtained results.

Comparing the sum of positive weights (scanners that responded positively) and negative ones (scanners that answered negatively) allows us to use the voting technique to decide whether or not an individual is vulnerable. However, other solutions can be used to take this decision such as fuzzy logic or Bayesian networks.

8.4 Threat to Validity

We present threats to validity of our experimentation from two points of view: internal threats and external threats.

- Internal threats: the use of accuracy as a measure of scanner tools performance could alter the results. Indeed, when the number of individuals without a vulnerability is important, this increases considerably the number of true negatives. As explained before, if this result is taken into consideration for scanner tools that do not even detect the vulnerability, the result is biased. To overcome this problem, we ignore the responses of the scanner tools that are not supposed to detect the vulnerability.
- External threats: the corpus we chose concerns applications written in Java. As a consequence, the results we obtained may be different in the case of applications written with another programming language. In addition, the choice of scanner tools has imposed a subset of vulnerabilities covered by Juliet test suite. The choice of other scanner tools will give another subset, so it will be difficult to compare the obtained results with ours. As mentioned before, this paper describes a bootstrap process designed to build a meta-scanner from many independent scanners, we chose the Juliet Test Suite as a reference for performance measurements. Thus, the use of another test corpus may give other performance results.

9   Related Work

Our work is related to work on the assessment of vulnerability analysis tools and to work on combining several tools to build a better one. Below, we will present some of these works.

9.1   Scanner Tool Evaluation

Several works have been focused on comparing existing scanners in order to identify the most effective for each type of analysis.

For instance, Autunes et al [3] proposed an approach to benchmark the effectiveness of static analysis tools and automatic penetration testing. The study focused mainly on SQL injections in web services. The authors showed that static analysis approaches are more efficient than automated penetration testing. They also found that both methods returned a lot of false positives. Part of our work concerned tools evaluation and also has led us to the same conclusion. However we did not focus only on one type of vulnerability in particular. Our goal was to cover as many vulnerabilities as possible.

There are several other works on the evaluation of tools targeting vulnerability detection [2,6,11,27]. Each of them showed which tool or technique gave better results than the others, but none of them really showed how the comparison is made. Indeed, from one scanner tool to another, the results are returned differently even for the same vulnerability. Hence it is important to have a common reference allowing to compare the scanner tools effectively. In this work, we give all the details of this process in order to make it replicable by other researchers. In addition, the study we made on the selected scanner tools aims at a better joint use for a given goal rather than really comparing them.

9.2   Combining Multiple Scanner Tools

Rutar, et al. [12] conducted a case study using five bug-finding tools to analyse a variety of Java programs. Their experiments showed that the tools discovered non-overlapping bugs. To exploit the number of warnings returned for each individual, they proposed a meta-tool that combines the results of the tools based on the alert frequency for the same individual. Alerts are not reviewed manually. We therefore have no information on the relevance of the results returned by the tools.

Meng et al. [16] also proposed an approach to merge results from different static analysis tools. The authors apply two policies to rank the results so that critical alerts come before unnecessary and false reports. Wang et al. [28] proposed a web service based approach that encapsulates multiple static analysis tools. The user has the possibility to analyse a source code without downloading any analyzing tools. The results are merged and refined by removing defect redundancies. This approach was validated in term of running time. This aspect may be important in some cases, but not really in our case.

Each of the above works focus on a given property of the proposed tool, but no one considered the accuracy of the combination. Indeed, they do not classify the returned results in term of false and true positive. In our work, we mainly focused on the accuracy of the results returned by our CVMS.

Nunes et al. [21] focused on the problem of how to combine several static analysis tools for a given goal. In this work, the authors considered four criticality levels of software development scenarios. For each scenario, they used the most adequate metric to rank all possible tool combinations. Thus, the best solution can be a single tool or a combination of certain tools. Unlike previous works, Nunes et al. do make a distinction between true positives (TP) and false positives (FP). For a given combination, the union of FPs returned by the concerned scanners is considered as positive instances and the union of all FPs becomes part of the negative instances. However, as pointed out by the authors, combining the results in this way considerably increases the number of false alerts. In this work, the variability lies in the selected subset of tools. The aggregation of the results returned by all the tools remains the same. In our case, we start from the same set of tools to propose the best way to aggregate them.

10   Conclusion

In this paper, we presented an approach to build a code vulnerability meta-scanner using several existing scanner tools. We mainly focused on how to aggregate the scanner tools in order to improve their effectiveness. Thus, we proposed an heuristic that combines the scanners based on their accuracy in identifying each category of vulnerabilities. For this aim, we proposed a categorization which helps to compare results from different scanner tools.

We experimented our approach using three scanner tools, namely Fortify, SpotBugs and Yag Suite. Then, we compared the efficiency of the constructed CVMS with the performance of the scanners separately. The results show that the combination of several scanners allows, on the one hand, to cover a larger set of vulnerabilities than individual scanner tools. On the other hand, the performance of our CVMS converges towards the best scanner for each type of vulnerability.

Moreover, we used the resulting CVMS to identify the vulnerabilities of a widely used corpus in software engineering, namely Qualitas Corpus. The meta-scanner has shown its usefulness and effectiveness on real Java code. This experience allowed us to build a corpus of Java code (extracted from Qualitas) tagged with the vulnerabilities it contains. This result is very useful for researchers in the field of software vulnerabilities. So, we made it available through the following link: "https://github.com/Brendan-LT/qualitas-vulnerabilities"

The first results obtained with our approach prove its efficiency but many improvements can be implemented. We mention many of them in this paper, including the use of a larger number of scanners for better accuracy. It should be noted that the approach we present can be applied to different types of analysis such as dynamic analysis using scanners based on dynamic methods or a hybrid analysis by integrating static and dynamic scanners.

A CVMS constructed with our approach can be used as a code scanner tool but this requires to have at least three different scanner tools and the process is maybe expensive for a maintenance phase. The next step we planed for work is to use the data obtained with our CVMS (tagged corpus) to propose prediction models that allow automatic identification of vulnerabilities.

References

1. Alves, H., Fonseca, B., Antunes, N.: Software metrics and security vulnerabilities: dataset and exploratory study. In: 2016 12th European Dependable Computing Conference (EDCC), pp. 37–44, September 2016
2. Antunes, N., Vieira, M.: Comparing the effectiveness of penetration testing and static code analysis on the detection of SQL injection vulnerabilities in web services. In: 2009 15th IEEE Pacific Rim International Symposium on Dependable Computing, pp. 301–306, November 2009
3. Antunes, N., Vieira, M.: Benchmarking vulnerability detection tools for web services. In: 2010 IEEE International Conference on Web Services, pp. 203–210, July 2010
4. Arteau, P.: Bugs Patterns. https://find-sec-bugs.github.io/bugs.htm
5. Arteau, P.: Find Security Bugs. https://find-sec-bugs.github.io
6. Austin, A., Williams, L.: One technique is not enough: a comparison of vulnerability discovery techniques. In 2011 International Symposium on Empirical Software Engineering and Measurement (ESEM), pp. 97–106 (2011)
7. Boland, T., Black, P.E.: Juliet 1.1 C/C++ and Java test suite. Computer **45**(10), 88–90 (2012)
8. Micro Focus. Fortify static code analyzer. https://www.microfocus.com/fr-fr/products/static-code-analysis-sast/overview
9. Micro Focus. Fortify Static Code Analyzer (SCA) Static Application Security Testing. https://www.microfocus.com/media/data-sheet/fortify_static_code_analyzer_static_application_security_testing_ds.pdf

10. Fonseca, J., Vieira, M.: Mapping software faults with web security vulnerabilities. In: 2008 IEEE International Conference on Dependable Systems and Networks with FTCS and DCC (DSN), pp. 257–266, June 2008
11. Fonseca, J., Vieira, M., Madeira, H.: Testing and comparing web vulnerability scanning tools for SQL injection and XSS attacks. In: 13th Pacific Rim International Symposium on Dependable Computing (PRDC 2007), pp. 365–372, December 2007
12. Foster, J.S., Almazan, C.B., Rutar, N.: A comparison of bug finding tools for Java. In: 15th International Symposium on Software Reliability Engineering(ISSRE), pp. 245–256 (2004)
13. Howard, M., David, L.B.: Writing Secure Code for Windows Vista^{TM}, 1st edn. Microsoft Press, Redmond (2007)
14. Jimenez,, M.: Evaluating vulnerability prediction models. Ph.D. thesis, Université du Luxembourg (2018)
15. Livshits, V.B., Lam, M.S.: Finding security vulnerabilities in java applications with static analysis. In: Proceedings of the 14th Conference on USENIX Security Symposium - Volume 14, SSYM 2005, p. 18. USENIX Association, Berkeley (2005)
16. Meng, N., Wang, Q., Wu, Q., Mei, H.: An approach to merge results of multiple static analysis tools (short paper). In: 2008 The Eighth International Conference on Quality Software, pp. 169–174, August 2008
17. Mitre. Common Weakness Enumeration (2019). https://cwe.mitre.org/
18. Mitre (2019). https://www.mitre.org/
19. Morrison, P., Herzig, K., Murphy, B., Williams, L.: Challenges with applying vulnerability prediction models. In: Proceedings of the 2015 Symposium and Bootcamp on the Science of Security, HotSoS 2015, pp. 4:1–4:9. ACM, New York (2015)
20. NSA. Juliet Test Suite v1.2 for Java (2012). https://samate.nist.gov
21. Nunes, P., Medeiros, I., Fonseca, J., Neves, N., Correia, M., Vieira, M.: On combining diverse static analysis tools for web security: an empirical study. In: 2017 13th European Dependable Computing Conference (EDCC), pp. 121–128, September 2017
22. OWASP. Vulnerability (2016). https://www.owasp.org/index.php/Category: Vulnerability
23. YAGAAN Software Security. Yag Suite (2017). https://www.yagaan.com/ products.html#yag-approche
24. Tempero, E., et al.: Qualitas corpus: a curated collection of Java code for empirical studies. In: 2010 Asia Pacific Software Engineering Conference (APSEC 2010), pp. 336–345, December 2010
25. Terra, R., Miranda, L.F., Valente, M.T., Bigonha, R.S.: Qualitas.class corpus: a compiled version of the Qualitas Corpus. Softw. Eng. Notes **38**(5), 1–4 (2013)
26. Venter, H.S., Eloff, J.H.P., Li, Y.L.: Standardising vulnerability categories. Comput. Secur. **27**(3), 71–83 (2008)
27. Vieira, M., Antunes, N., Madeira, H.: Using web security scanners to detect vulnerabilities in web services. In: 2009 IEEE/IFIP International Conference on Dependable Systems Networks, pp. 566–571, June 2009
28. Wang, Q., Meng, N., Zhou, Z., Li, J., Mei, H.: Towards SOA-based code defect analysis. In: 2008 IEEE International Symposium on Service-Oriented System Engineering, pp. 269–274, December 2008
29. Zhang, Y., Wu, Q., Yang, G., Wen, T.: ASVC: an automatic security vulnerability categorization framework based on novel features of vulnerability data. J. Commun. **10**(2), 107–116 (2015)

Access Control and Authentication

Using IFTTT to Express and Enforce UCON Obligations

Antonio La Marra[1], Fabio Martinelli[1], Paolo Mori[1], Athanasios Rizos[1,2(✉)], and Andrea Saracino[1]

[1] Istituto di Informatica e Telematica, Consiglio Nazionale delle Ricerche, Pisa, Italy
{antonio.lamarra,fabio.martinelli,paolo.mori,athanasios.rizos, andrea.saracino}@iit.cnr.it
[2] Department of Computer Science, University of Pisa, Pisa, Italy

Abstract. If This Then That (IFTTT) is a free and widely used web-based platform where it is possible to create applet chains (Applets) of simple conditional statements that combine different web and smart services. In this paper we propose a methodology to express Usage Control (UCON) obligations in such a way that they can contain valid data in order to trigger such applet chains. The obligations that follow the response of access requests coming from UCON, become a trigger to the IFTTT platform and this enables a more abstract and non application specific mixture of them without each one losing their abstract structure. We will present the architecture and workflow of our approach, also together with a couple of use cases and the evaluation of an implementation of UCON together with a real IFTTT Applet.

Keywords: Access Control · IFTTT · Internet of Things · Obligations · Usage Control · XACML

1 Introduction

Over the last years, Internet of Things (IoT) devices have started to play a significant role to our daily life. According to Ericsson [3], in 2020 we should expect the total number of IoT devices to reach 50 billions. This number becomes even more dramatic if we consider the Internet of Everything (IoE) paradigm, which also includes user devices such as smartphones, smartwatches, tablets and thus the interaction of the user itself. Managing complex IoT systems is further complicated by the presence of different communication protocols, application standards, architectures and interaction models, which make the management of security in this environment an extremely challenging task. Still, such a task is mandatory, considering both issues for captured and processed data, and the effect of IoT devices actions in the physical world.

This work has been partially funded by EU Funded projects H2020 NeCS, GA #675320, H2020 C3ISP, GA #700294 and EIT Digital HC&IoT.

© Springer Nature Switzerland AG 2019
S.-H. Heng and J. Lopez (Eds.): ISPEC 2019, LNCS 11879, pp. 213–231, 2019.
https://doi.org/10.1007/978-3-030-34339-2_12

To manage security and privacy in IoT environments, Usage Control (UCON) has been successful used as a control tool able to handle seamless access management and data protection [8]. UCON is an extension of traditional eXtensible Access Control Markup Language (XACML)-based Attribute-Based Access Control (ABAC) which enforces continuity of access decision, by evaluating and enforcing policies based on mutable attributes [9]. XACML is an Extensible Markup Language (XML)-based language standardized by OASIS[1] with a very high expressiveness potential, hence fitting the flexibility requirements of complex environments, such as IoE ones. To further increase its expressiveness, XACML pairs standard ABAC constructs such as authorizations and prohibitions with *Obligations*, i.e. mandatory actions that have to be performed in conjunction with the policy enforcement [4].

Currently, XACML does not provide a standard for the description of obligation semantic. While the intention is the one of non imposing constraints on format of the represented information, the direct consequence is that every obligation management engine has to be developed ad-hoc. Having a standard semantic for representation which is meaningful at least in an application macro-environment, such as IoE, can push developers and policy editors to use common expressions to represent and enforce obligations. In particular, it is possible to express obligations as commands for an inter-operable service or platform used by a multitude of IoT/IoE devices, such as If This Then That (IFTTT)[2]. IFTTT is a free web-based platform used to create applet chains of conditional statements in IoT settings. Each applet chain, also called *Recipe* or *Applet*, is triggered by changes that happen within various web-services and as a result does specific actions on other web-services. Expressing triggers through UCON obligations will allow the device receiving the policy evaluation decision to easily execute the obligations, without hard-coding the actual obligation interpretation, demanded to the specific UCON applet.

In this paper we present the application of IFTTT triggers to express and enforce UCON obligations. The paper will describe a novel architecture where the standard UCON framework is combined with the IFTTT platform services. Our framework, is providing a standardized format of obligations so that they can trigger valid IFTTT *Applets*. The proposed framework is designed to be independent from the specific device implementation, specific application and transport level communication protocols. Thus, the proposed framework does not alter the XACML model and workflow, whereas we enhance its capabilities by proposing a standardized way of expressing obligations, reusing pre-existing components, being thus non intrusive. The paper will discuss the full operative workflow, detailing both UCON and IFTTT operation parts, proposing two relevant use cases and a set of performance experiments to demonstrate the viability. Moreover, our framework does not interfere with the execution of the IFTTT *Applets* and does not require any modification in the model of UCON.

---

[1] https://www.oasis-open.org/committees/xacml/.
[2] https://www.ifttt.com/.

The rest of the paper is organized as follows: In Sect. 2 we report background information about IFTTT and UCON. Section 3 details the architecture and the operative workflow. Section 4 provides some relevant use cases and also details the results of the performance analysis. In Sect. 5 we report and compare with related work in access control management in IoT/IoE. Finally, Sect. 6 concludes by proposing future directions.

2   Background

In this section we provide some background knowledge about IFTTT and UCON.

2.1   IFTTT

IFTTT creates chains of simple conditional statements that are called *Applets* and are triggered by changes that happen within web-services. An example is, when a user likes a video on Youtube, to add it to his/her Spotify account. After an *Applet* is triggered, there is an action that happens on another web-service. In fact, given a certain set of criteria, IFTTT gathers web-services in one place so that they can easily interact between each other [15]. IFTTT consists of the following structure:

Services: The basic building block of IFTTT. They describe data and actions controlled by an Application Programming Interface (API), and each service has a specific set of *Triggers* and *Actions*.

Triggers: The *"This"* part of the *Applet*, causing thus the triggering of the *Action*.

Actions: The *"That"* part of the *Applet* which is the result of a *Trigger*.

Applets/Recipes: The complete part of an example when a successful *Trigger* that leads to the execution of an *Action*.

Ingredients: The data that are available after the triggering to guide the *Action*.

An advantage of IFTTT is that it can work with various platforms and devices in IoT. In order to create an *Applet*, the only necessary step is to mix *Ingredients* in such a way that they make sense so that the *Trigger* can interact correctly with the *Applet*. Then, there must be a definition of the pieces of information utilized by each *Trigger* and *Action*. A drawback of IFTTT is that it allows only a single *Trigger* and a single *Action*. The same *Trigger* can be used for other *Actions* but not inside the same *Applet*.

There are various competitors of IFTTT and in Table 1 we see a summary of the pros and cons of them. More in detail, the biggest competitor of IFTTT is Microsoft Flow. It is free for up to 750 runs/month, it can allow multi step connection and works with many apps including Gmail, Facebook etc. and can be accessed either via apps or browsers. The cons are that, up to now, the apps are around 226 and it does not work with physical devices. But, it also supports Do/While and For/Each loops whereas IFTTT supports only If conditionals. Hence, it is more difficult and complicated to operate. Another

Table 1. Comparison of IFTTT and its alternatives

Name	Cost	Connections	Apps/devices	Number of services	Access
IFTTT	Free	One-to-One	Yes/Yes	>600	App/Browser
Microsoft Flow	Free/Paid	Multiple	Yes/No	226	App/Browser
Zapier	Free/Paid	Multiple	Yes/No	>1500	Browser
Yonomi	Free	Multiple	No/Yes	200	App
Stringify	Free	Multiple	Yes/Yes	70	App/Browser
Workflow	Free	Multiple	Yes(iOS)/No	N/A	App

example is `Zapier` that works only with apps and not physical devices. It allows multi step connection between devices and has a simple free usage up to 100 runs/month and also paid plans of use. On the contrary, `Yonomi` works only with physical devices and not with apps, but allows multi-step connection between the about 100 compatible devices, it is free and focuses more on home applications. Furthermore, `Stringify` is also free and can host multiple connections but has only about 70 services and cannot be accessed via a browser like IFTTT but only via an app. Finally, there is also `Workflow` that works only with iOS apps and allows multiple step systems. It is again free but there is not a list of compatible services but only the most famous iOS apps are used like Safari, Photo Gallery, Facebook etc.

2.2 Usage Control

The UCON model [16] extends traditional access control models [17]. It introduces mutable attributes and new decision factors besides authorizations which are obligations and conditions. Mutable attributes represent features of subjects, objects, and environment that can change their values as a consequence of the operation of the system [6]. Since mutable attributes change their values during the usage of an object, UCON model allows to define and evaluate policies before and continuously during the access.

The main block of UCON framework is the *Usage Control System (UCS)* surrounded by the *Controlled Systems* and the *Attribute Environment* as shown in Fig. 1. UCS has its own components which are the following [12]:

Policy Decision Point (PDP): This component takes as an input an access (usage) request and an access (usage) policy returning one of the following decisions: *Permit, Deny, Indeterminate.*

Policy Information Point (PIP): This component retrieves attributes related to subject, object and environment of received access requests. Each PIP acts as the interface between the UCS and a specific Attribute Manager (AM) which is a non controlled component that has the values of the attributes that have to be acquired by each PIP [1]. Each PIP has custom implementation for each specific application, AM and the kind of attribute that should be retrieved.

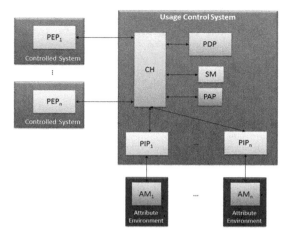

Fig. 1. Usage Control framework diagram.

Session Manager (SM): This component is a database which stores all the active sessions, with the necessary information to perform policy reevaluations.

Context Handler (CH): This component is the main core of the UCS, where it is responsible of routing messages among the various components. Firstly, it has to forward the access request to the various PIPs for attribute retrieval, then the complete access to the PDP and as a result to return the decision to the Policy Enforcement Point (PEP). Finally, it receives notification from PIPs when the value of an attribute changes, forwarding to the PDP the new value for policy reevaluation.

Communication between Policy Enforcement Point (PEP) and UCS is performed via the following actions [10]:

TryAccess: Action invoked by the PEP to send to the UCS the request to perform an action or access a resource, to be evaluated against a policy. The UCS will respond with a Permit or Deny decision, eventually collecting the needed attributes from the PIPs. If the answer is Permit, this response is also containing the Session ID for the session that is about to start.

StartAccess: Action invoked by the PEP having the SessionID as a parameter. This is the actual start of using the service requested. There is again evaluation from the PDP and after an affirmative response the CH confirms the session to the SM as active.

EndAccess: Action invoked when the usage of the resource terminates. When received by the UCS, it deletes the session details from the SM and communicates to the PIPs that the attributes related to that policies are not needed anymore, unless other sessions are using it.

RevokeAccess: Occurs when a change of a mutable attribute causes a policy reevaluation, which ends in a deny. The PEP is thus notified and the corresponding usage session is terminated.

```
<Policy xmlns="urn:oasis:names:tc:xacml:3.0:core:schema:wd−17"          1
PolicyId="policyIfttt" RuleCombiningAlgId="..." Version="3.0">          2
<Description>Description</Description>                                  3
                                                                        4
<Rule Effect="Permit" RuleId="rule−permit">                            5
<Target>Target</Target>                                                6
                                                                        7
<Condition DecisionTime="pre">Condition                                8
<ObligationExpressions>                                                9
<ObligationExpression                                                  10
ObligationId="urn:oasis:names:tc:xacml:1.0:example:obligation:oblig"    11
FulfillOn="Permit">                                                    12
<AttributeAssignment                                                   13
AttributeId="urn:oasis:names:tc:xacml:1.0:example:attribute:text"       14
DataType="http://www.w3.org/2001/XMLSchema#string"> PAYLOAD            15
</AttributeAssignment>                                                 16
</ObligationExpression>                                                17
</ObligationExpressions>                                               18
</Condition>                                                           19
<Condition DecisionTime="ongoing">Condition</Condition>                20
<Condition DecisionTime="post">Condition</Condition>                   21
</Rule>                                                                22
<Rule Effect="Deny" RuleId="rule−deny">                                23
<Description>Description</Description>                                  24
<ObligationExpressions>                                                25
<ObligationExpression FulfillOn="Deny" ObligationId="PAYLOAD"/>        26
</ObligationExpressions>                                               27
</Rule>                                                                28
                                                                       29
</Policy>                                                              30
```

Listing 1.1. Examples of the two types of obligations.

Obligations are predicates which define requirements that must be fulfilled before the access *Pre-Obligations*, while a session is in progress *Ongoing-Obligations* or after the session has ended *Post-Obligations*. In real world implementations, obligations are agreed before obtaining the rights and at that time obligation-related authorization rules are checked. For example, a subject may have to accept terms and conditions before obtaining the rights for accessing certain resources. Summarizing, on both XACML and XACML with Continuous Usage Control Features (U-XACML), obligations are part of the policy and they are written in the same way as a tag of the policy. The obligations have two different targets. The first target is to force the update of the values of specific attributes according to the value included in the obligation. This part has to be in a specific format like the other attribute values in the policy file. The second target is to force the PEP to perform specific actions. This part is not standardized meaning that the obligation contains plain text and the PEP must extract and enforce the obligation. Thus, the PEP has to be specifically programmed for extracting and enforcing each obligation. The obligation must be executed by the subject before accessing or during the access. Although one obligation can be used in many scenarios, e.g. sending an email, every time that the obligation is different it means that it is application specific and the requirements must be defined specifically for each use-case. In XACML, the obligation is included in a separate tag called *ObligationExpressions*. The obligation can be executed when a *rule* or a *condition* is executed. The difference between U-XACML and XACML is the existence of the pre, ongoing and post conditions. This indicates that, in UCON, an obligation can be performer after any of the actions described above (e.g. TryAccess, StartAccess etc.). An example of UCON policy with obligations is reported on Listing 1.1. This policy presents two different obligations, inside the two different rules of "Permit" and "Deny" respectively. The first obligation is of type **AttributeAssignment** and it is used to issue a specific attribute value to the PIP. The second one is plain text and each PEP has to be specifically programmed to successfully extract and enforce it.

3   Enforcing UCON Obligations via IFTTT

In this section we report the description of the proposed framework for evaluating UCON policies and enforcing obligations via IFTTT. We will describe the workflow, the implementation and the process of including IFTTT *Triggers* in the standard XACML.

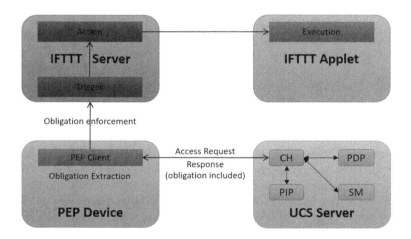

Fig. 2. Logical architecture

3.1   Architecture

Our goal is to create such an obligation format that the PEP can execute IFTTT *Applets* without the need of specific PEP per *Applet*. To this aim, we propose a framework that is implementing the PEP on a smart-device so as to perform access requests and receive the responses to and from the UCS respectively. If in the response of the UCS there is an obligation, the PEP has to extract and enforce it by performing the corresponding *Trigger* to an IFTTT *Applet*. The components of the proposed framework are shown in Fig. 2. Firstly, the UCS has to be installed on a smart-device which can be any appliance, computer, smartphone that is able to run an operating system capable of installing and running third party applications. Such a device can be a RaspberryPi or a smart-TV. Then, UCS has to communicate with the device that hosts the PEP. Other smart but not very powerful IoT devices, such as a smart temperature or light sensors, can be used from the various PIPs in order to acquire information about attribute values by the AMs and provide it to the UCS. The PEP can either reside in the same device as the UCS or in a separate device. The interpretation of the obligation coming from the UCS, is to the values that are necessary for the IFTTT *Trigger* and the enforcement is to perform the triggering of the *Applet*. The triggering happens via a web request from the PEP with the IFTTT by making a web request that enforces the obligation. This means that the PEP must have access to the Internet so as to communicate with the IFTTT servers. Then, the IFTTT server is responsible to execute the *Applet* when receiving the *Trigger* of the obligation. After that, the necessary information will be extracted from the IFTTT server and the *Action* service will be executed.

3.2   Workflow

The complete workflow of our framework is presented in Fig. 3. This figure describes the communication between the PEP and UCS from sending the request until the obligation enforcement and the triggering of the *Applet*. For better understanding we will describe the workflow in two parts. These parts are (i) the communication between the PEP and the UCS (tasks 1–3, 7–9, 13–16) and (ii) obligation enforcement for by the PEP to IFTTT (tasks 4–6, 10–12, 17–19).

Communication Between PEP and UCS: As shown in Fig. 3, the PEP primarily initiates communication with the UCS by performing the *TryAccess* action for evaluation of the request (task 1). Then, the CH component of the UCS receives the request and the values of the attributes from the various PIPs. All the previous, are sent to the PDP for evaluation where the answer is *Permit* or *Deny* according to their compliance with the policy that arrives together with the request (task 2). If the answer is *Deny*, the PEP is informed about it (task 3). But, if the answer is *Permit*, the SM starts keeping a record of the session by assigning a unique ID to it and the PEP is informed that the access was initially granted and retrieves the session ID (task 3). In both cases, if there is an obligation in the response, the PEP has to extract and enforce it. The PEP, then, starts the actual usage of the resources by performing the *StartAccess* action to the UCS for the session with the specific ID (task 7). After another evaluation from the PDP (task 8), if the answer is *Permit* or *Deny* there may be an obligation in the response to the PEP, whereas the PEP is responsible for

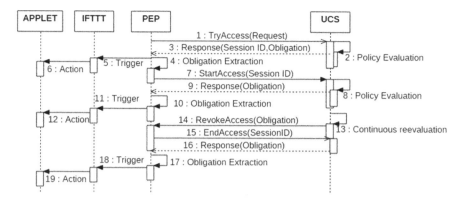

Fig. 3. Sequence diagram of the proposed framework

interpreting and enforcing it (task 9). For more information about the procedure inside UCS component, readers can refer to [9]. Moreover, while a session is in progress, there is a continuous re-evaluation of the session (task 13). In the case of policy violation, the UCS performs the *RevokeAccess* and the sends the appropriate message to the PEP (task 14). On the contrary, if the subject wants to terminate the session while it is on progress, the PEP has to inform the UCS about it by performing the *EndAccess* action (task 15) and receive the answer (task 16). Both in *RevokeAccess* or an *EndAccess* the message from UCS to the PEP may include, as previously, an obligation so after Task 14 or Tasks 15, 16 the Tasks 17–19 of the obligation happen. We can see that obligations can be performed after every action of UCON, and they must include all the necessary information so that the PEP can trigger the *Applet*.

Communication Between PEP and IFTTT: The PEP must not only communicate with the UCS, but also to extract the obligations and enforce them by triggering the IFTTT *Applet*. About obligation enforcement, firstly the IFTTT *Applet* has to be created in the IFTTT platform and the *Trigger* has to be a web request service. The *Applet* is executed by making the web request from the PEP to the IFTTT platform and, if the data received are correct, the platform performs the *Action*. The type of the *Action* depends on what the creator of the *Applet* selected and is not controlled by the UCS. The role of the PEP is to extract the information related to the obligation. For the tasks that may include obligations, the PEP must firstly extract the information included in the obligation (tasks 4, 10, 17). The next step is to enforce the obligation by performing the corresponding *Trigger* of the IFTTT *Applet* that has to run. To do so, the PEP has to create and send the appropriate web request to the IFTTT server (tasks 5, 11, 18). The correctness of the web request is verified by the IFTTT server and it is not controlled by the PEP (tasks 6, 12, 19).

3.3   Obligation Standardization

According to the OASIS standard [14], obligation, as part of a policy for access control, is a XACML tag that describes when the obligation will be triggered. If it is triggered on a Permit or on a Deny it must be included in the appropriate policy rule. Furthermore, in U-XACML, the format of the obligation does not change compared to XACML [4]. But, in U-XACML, according to the time of execution, the corresponding obligation *Pre, OnGoing* must be included in the appropriate condition (Pre, Ongoing) respectively. In our case, we consider the enforcement of obligations that have not attribute updates targeting the PIPs, but obligations that target the PEP and include the necessary data of an IFTTT *Trigger*. When an obligation targets the PEP, the payload that the PEP has to extract and enforce is included in the "ObligationId" as a string variable that has no specific type. In our framework, this string has the form of a JavaScript Object Notation (JSON) structure that includes the names and the values of the variables that are necessary to perform the IFTTT *Trigger*. As an example, we consider a couple of obligations that happen (a) after a successful set of *TryAccess* action followed by a successful *StartAccess* ($Oblig_1$) and (b) after a *RevokeAcess* ($Oblig_2$). In Listing 1.2, we can see a simplified version of a policy written in U-XACML focusing on the obligation part. The first obligation example is an expression of ($Oblig_1$) and the second obligation part is an expression of ($Oblig_2$). Both are included inside the corresponding policy rules. We can see the *ObligationId* string, expressed in such a format of JSON structure so that it can be included in the U-XACML file without issues including the IFTTT payload.

The string of the obligation which JSON formatted includes the specific values for the *Trigger* of the IFTTT to happen. The *Trigger* is a web-request. For this action we selected the *Webhooks*[3] service when we created the *Applet* in the IFTTT platform. Webhooks service provides the ability for a web request to be the *Trigger* of the *Applet* but generalizing, any other IFTTT service could be used supposing that the PEP of UCON is changed accordingly. The *Webhooks* services gives to each IFTTT acccount a unique *Key* that should be included in every request for identification purposes. Since the *Key* remains the same for all the different *Applets* of each user of the same *Webhooks* service account, the only way to distinguish each application between each other, is done via the unique *EventName* that every instance of the *Webhooks* service must have. *Webhooks* gives also the opportunity to include some payload variables in the web-request. The *Payload* can include values of attributes, plain text, or everything other information acquired by the UCS or the PEP. In total, in order for the obligations to include the IFTTT data for the *Trigger* as shown in Listing 1.2, they must include the *(Key, EventName, Payload)* values. Summarizing, for the two types of obligations mentioned above, the requirements and decision that has to be issued by the UCS to the PEP, are the following:

---

[3] https://www.ifttt.com/maker_webhooks.

```
<Policy xmlns="urn:oasis:names:tc:xacml:3.0:core:schema:wd−17"      1
PolicyId="policyIfttt" RuleCombiningAlgId="..." Version="3.0">     2
<Description>Description</Description>                              3
                                                                   4
<Rule Effect="Permit" RuleId="rule−permit">                       5
<Target>Target</Target>                                            6
<Condition DecisionTime="pre">Condition</Condition>               7
<Condition DecisionTime="ongoing">Condition                       8
<ObligationExpressions>                                            9
<ObligationExpression FulfillOn="Permit"                          10
ObligationId="{\"EventName\":\"ucon_oblig_enforc\",               11
\"Key\":\"bhOEWZ5qcbgMoa_w4−Nny_\",                               12
\"Value1\":\"UCON_request_for_access_happened\",                 13
\"Value2\":\"with_result\",                                       14
\"Value3\":\"PERMIT\"}"/>                                         15
</ObligationExpressions>                                           16
</Condition>                                                       17
<Condition DecisionTime="post">Condition</Condition>             18
</Rule>                                                            19
                                                                  20
<Rule Effect="Deny" RuleId="rule−deny">                          21
<Description>Description</Description>                            22
<ObligationExpressions>                                          23
<ObligationExpression FulfillOn="Deny"                           24
ObligationId="{\"EventName\":\"ucon_oblig_enforc\",              25
\"Key\":\"bhOEWZ5qcbgMoa_w4−Nny_\",                              26
\"Value1\":\"UCON_REVOKE_happened\",                            27
\"Value2\":\"because_the_result_was\",                          28
\"Value3\":\"DENY\"}"/>                                         29
</ObligationExpressions>                                          30
</Rule>                                                           31
</Policy>                                                         32
```

Listing 1.2. Simplified example of policy including obligation in XACML.

$$-\text{TryAccess} \wedge \text{StartAccess} \rightarrow \text{Permit} \rightarrow Oblig_1$$
$$-\text{RevokeAccess} \rightarrow \text{Deny} \rightarrow Oblig_2$$
$$Oblig_1 = (\text{Key1,EventName1,Payload1}),\ Oblig_2 = (\text{Key2,EventName2,Payload2})$$

Every time that the PEP executes correctly the web request, the *Applet* should run and users should see this in the IFTTT panel and also monitor that the *Action* happened. The execution can also be monitored the control panel of the IFTTT platform account related to the *Applet* that was executed.

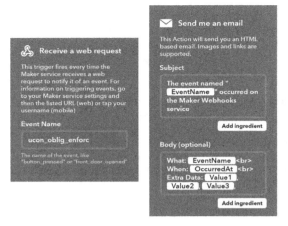

Fig. 4. Example of *Applet* structure

3.4 Implementation

The UCS comes as a JAR or WAR file, to be deployed on the device(s) intended to evaluate the access decisions. The *Trigger* was the *Webhooks* service, whereas the *Action* service was the "Send me an email" service of IFTTT platform that sends an email to the owner of the account of the *Applet*. In Fig. 4 there are shown the two services of the *Applet*. On the left, there is the *Trigger* part which provides a box for specifying the unique *EventName* of the *Webhooks* service. On the right part there is the *Action* service that includes the subject and the body of the email structure. On both the subject and the body of the email plain text can be combined with data coming from variables. These data may be included in the obligation (e.g. EventName, Value1-3) as they are described in Listing 1.2. The data may be also variables that the IFTTT platform provides, such as the "OccuredAt" in Fig. 4 that gives the timestamp of the execution of the *Applet*.

For this *Applet* we consider two obligations that must be filled with details according the standardization of the previous section. The first one happens after a succesful *StartAccess* action ($Oblig_1$) and the second one happens after a *RevokeAccess* action ($Oblig_2$). The *Key* is obtained by the *Webhooks* service and the unique *EventName* is set up in the *Trigger* service as shown on the left part of Fig. 4. There is the possibility of either executing the same instance of the *Webhooks* service with a different *Payload*, or creating two difference instances for each obligation ($Oblig_1$, $Oblig_2$). In the first case, which is the one used in this paper, the *EventName* is the same and the *Payload* only changes, and in the second case both the *EventName* and the *Payload* change. In Listing 1.2 we present the examples of the obligations. It is worth noticing that the *Payload* includes three values. Whenever the UCS sends an obligation to the PEP, this obligation must include the *Key*, the *EventName* and the values. The link that the web-request has to be sent to has the following format in order for the *Trigger* to be successful.

$$\text{https://maker.ifttt.com/trigger/A/with/key/B , A} \leftarrow EventName \text{ , B} \leftarrow Key$$

This is necessary because in the case of creating multiple *Applets*, both the IFTTT and the PEP must distinguish them. The three values that are included in the obligation, explain in plain text what happened in UCON part and show the difference between $Oblig_1$ and $Oblig_2$. Hence, every time that the *Applet* is executed, the recipient of the email can distinguish which obligation has been enforced.

4   Experimental Evaluation

In this section, we present two relevant use cases for application of the proposed framework. Furthermore, a set of experiments to evaluate the performance overhead introduced and demonstrate the viability of our approach is reported.

4.1   Examples of Use-Cases

The first example is advanced management through policy enforcement for remote urban farming in smart greenhouses. One of the motivations to consider this use case is that there are several pre-existing examples of IFTTT *Applets* designed[4] to manage watering and other smart devices in a greenhouse, which can be exploited to enforce UCON obligations. The representation of the scenario is shown in Fig. 5. The policy here for UCON is to monitor via smart-sensors various attributes of a greenhouse, e.g. humidity, temperature through the proposed framework and provide access to a smart-heating device to perform a scheduled heating of the plants. The obligations are targeting to the watering schedule of the smart-watering device that is responsible for watering the plants. The goal in this example is to maintain the temperature and humidity levels of the greenhouse to the desired values via controlling the smart-heating with UCS and change the schedule of the smart-watering device with IFTTT via the obligations coming from UCS. More in detail, the PEP is in the smart-heating device and asks for permission to operate on the smart-greenhouse. The PEP communicates with the UCS in order to request access to operate. The UCS monitors the values of the humidity, temperature and provides the answer. There are also other smart-sensors that can be used such as the availability of electricity/batteries etc. After a successful request, in the response sent by the UCS after the *StartAccess* action, there is an obligation including a schedule for the smart-watering device to operate less frequently. When the PEP receives this obligation, it has to enforce it by performing the web-request to the IFTTT platform containing the schedule for the smart-watering device. When the IFTTT

---

[4] https://ifttt.com/greeniq.

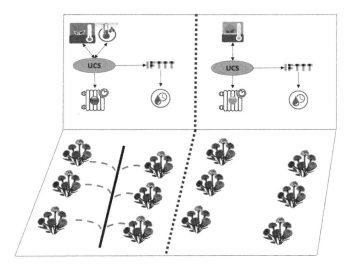

Fig. 5. Example of UCON obligation via IFTTT in a smart-greenhouse installation.

executes the *Applet* the smart-watering device is operating on the defined schedule. In the meantime, if the weather is too hot or the smart-heating device is operating for too long, the UCS, during the continuous re-evaluation procedure, receives this information from the smart-temperature sensor. Thus, understands that there is a policy violation that may affect the plants inside the smart-greenhouse. So, the UCS performs the *RevokeAccess* to the PEP (smart-heating device) to stop operating. An obligation is also included that provides a schedule targeting the smart-watering device which has to operate more intensively so that the temperature decreases and the humidity level increases. This obligation is extracted and enforced by the PEP and is sent to the IFTTT platform. Summarizing, in the case of the obligation after the *StartAccess* the smart-heating device operates and the watering schedule is less intensive. In the case of the obligation after the *RevokeAccess* the smart-heating device stops operating and the watering schedule is more dense so as to lower the temperature and provide better conditions in the greenhouse.

Another example is smart management through policy enforcement for controlling a smart-office. The goal of this scenario is to continuously monitor the presence of the people inside an office and the air quality of the room while they are inside. The motivation in this example is the optimized use of the appliances that control the convenience of the people inside an office (such as air quality, temperature etc.). Frequently we face the situation that when there are several people in an office during meetings, the air quality is not optimal disturbing, thus, the meeting and make the people feel annoyed. The policy in this example is the control by the UCS of the access of the smart-heating device operation inside the room as scheduled and the operation of the ventilation system by the IFTTT platform through obligations. The control of the access is based on the

Fig. 6. Example of UCON obligation via IFTTT in a smart-office installation for monitoring air quality.

continuous monitoring of attributes such as temperature and air quality provided by smart-devices installed inside the office. The UCS can be in this case installed in a RaspberryPi that also provides sensors about air-quality[5]. The representation of this scenario is shown in Fig. 6 where there are shown two cases of this scenario. On the left there is the case with a few people inside the office. The PEP is installed in the smart-heating device and request for access from the UCS to operate as scheduled. The UCS monitors the attributes of the temperature and air-quality and provides the answer. In the response of the UCS after the *StartAccess* there is an obligation for the IFTTT to force the stop of the ventilation system. On the right there is the case with too many people inside the office. In this case, there is a policy violation because the attributes indicate that the condition inside the office is not comfortable. Then, independently from the schedule of the smart-heating, UCS issues the *RevokeAccess* action to force the smart-heating device to stop. The obligation that comes together with the *RevokeAccess* and must be enforced, forces, through the execution of the IFTTT *Applet*, the smart-ventilation system to start operating. In this example, the first obligation comes with the response after a successful *StartAccess* and forces through the IFTTT the smart-ventilation system to stop. The second obligation comes with the *RevokeAccess* and forces through the IFTTT the smart-ventilation system to operate.

4.2   Testbed and Timing Evaluation

For evaluating the viability of our framework, we selected to create the following testbed. We used a virtual machine with Ubuntu 18.04 installed on a PC with constrained settings in terms of the enabled CPU cores and the amount of RAM used. In particular we used 2 cores of an i7-6700HQ CPU and 1 GB of RAM. In this virtual machine we ran both the UCS and the PEP applications. When receiving an obligation, the PEP was forced to trigger an IFTTT *Applet* that was created for this scope. We have selected to study the performance of our

---

[5] http://bit.ly/2MlxI4i.

framework by monitoring both the timings that UCON actions happen and the timings that our system needs to extract, create and send the web request of the obligation. However, since we cannot interfere with the time that actually the *Applet* is executed in the IFTTT platform or the synchronizing settings of the email recipient, we do not consider them in our timing evaluation. Although the execution of the *Applet* is related to the traffic of the IFTTT servers, we did not face in any experiment times larger than 1–2 min. Our evaluation is based on the number of the attributes that our system has starting from a simple case with one attribute until a case with 40 attributes. We executed every experiment five times and took the average out of them, while increasing the number of the attributes to multiples of 5. The results of the execution are shown in Table 2. In this table we can see that the number of attributes increases the time that the UCS need to evaluate the *TryAccess* and *StartAccess* request. Both these timings if added together lead to the summary that from the time that the PEP sends the request via the *TryAccess* until the time it has back the response of the *StartAccess* by the UCS, the time varies from 400 ms in the case of one attribute until 650 ms seconds in the case of 40 attributes whereas it increases in a linear way. Nevertheless, we observe that the average time that the PEP needs to extract and enforce the obligation is independent from the number of attributes and equal to 450–700 ms in every case. This is something that was expected since the attribute values are used only by the UCS for the re-evaluation but to summarize we can identify that in any case the overall time from the time that the PEP starts a request until the time that the obligation *Trigger* has happened is a bit more than one second.

Table 2. Timings in milliseconds (ms) over the number of attributes

Time (ms)/attribute no.	1	5	10	15	20	25	30	35	40
UCON Tryaccess	312.6	387.8	380.6	358	380	393.6	433.4	476.2	477.8
UCON Startaccess	79	94.2	76.8	98.2	90.6	127	106.2	131.4	169.8
Permit Oblig. Enforcement	739.8	728.8	688.2	675.4	666.8	590.8	523.6	512.2	559.6
UCON RevokeAccess	52	70.2	72.8	92.6	103.8	121.4	115.6	170.4	146.4
Revoke Oblig. Enforcement	685.6	714.2	715.4	701.6	729.8	719	713.6	734.2	727

In addition to the previous, we can see that the time for UCS to execute the *RevokeAccess* varies from 50 ms to 150 ms from 1 to 40 attributes respectively. The time that the PEP needs to extract end enforce the obligation in this case, remains similar to the one of the previous case and between 600–700 ms.

In Fig. 7, we show the total timings for firstly handling a request and secondly handling a revoke. In the first case, which is marked with a dashed line, we report the time that from sending the *TryAccess* from the PEP to the UCS, until the time that the obligation is executed by the PEP to the IFTTT. We can identify that the total time does not change much when the attribute number

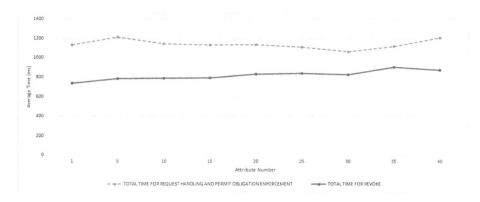

Fig. 7. Timings for handling a request and a revoke of access

is increasing which reveals a stability in the timings aroun 1100–1200 ms. In the second case, which is marked with a continuous line, we report the time that the *RevokeAccess* is triggered until the time that the obligation is executed by the PEP. Again, we can see that the increased number of the attributes does not change significantly the timings.

5   Related Work

An application of UCON in IoT environments has been presented in [11]. The authors propose a distributed model of the standard UCON framework, discussing a smart home use case. An implementation specific for IoT communication protocols is presented in [7], where the authors present an integration of the UCON paradigm in the Message Queue Telemetry Transport (MQTT) workflow. The focus of these works, however, is not centered on obligations, they only exploit in an appropriate way the authorization constructs. On the side of IFTTT an effort to create simple policy algorithms for IoT is presented in [13]. This work focuses more on the policy specification and how it could be predicted according to the user features and the specific IoT domain. This work, does not study the way the policies are written, or the obligation format and context but focuses more on the part of how to create a policy according to what is happening in a specific IoT domain. Furthermore, enforcement mechanisms are not considered in their analysis. In [19], the author describes the development of a specific framework that can modify the concepts of the IFTTT platform so as to provide services that can be used in order to make home automation systems more secure. This work, though, creates specific services in the IFTTT platform and also depends only on the security mechanisms of IFTTT without any control on the installed environment and, also, no continuous way of evaluation or policy enforcement. In [18], the authors describe also some possible security and privacy risks in the *Applets* of IFTTT. Concerning the XACML model for policies, in [5], the authors present a description of obligation expression based on examples in Grid and networking security. The work is very specific to this limited environments and does not provide a way to formalize the obligations semantic. Finally, in [2], the authors present a variation of XACML specific for obligation extraction. Firstly, they propose a method of creating a new file for obligations in XACML which is produced by the initial file but they do not give a clear description of how the obligation part should be constructed so as to be easily readable by both the PDP and the PEP. Though interesting, their approach is not based on standard XACML, differently from our solution that integrates in XACML 3.0 policies without requiring any modification to the standard architecture and workflow.

6   Conclusion

Obligations is a powerful access and usage control tool which enables a capillary control which goes beyond evaluating the right to perform or not an action. However, in the XACML 3.0 specific semantic for standardized obligation representation and enforcement is not considered. In this work we have proposed a way to define an obligation semantic that is specific to IoT environments, using IFTTT triggers to be enforced by PEPs that are directly connected to IFTTT *Applets*. We have reported two specific use cases which motivate our work and reported performance results to demonstrate the viability of the proposed approach, detailing how the proposed solution is not disruptive for the standard UCON workflow, enabling seamless integration.

As future directions we plan to perform an implementation on a larger testbed with several coexistent IFTTT *Applets* and a wider number of attributes. Furthermore, we plan to extend the standardization effort, giving a formal definition of the grammar to be used for defining IFTTT obligations.

References

1. Carniani, E., D'Arenzo, D., Lazouski, A., Martinelli, F., Mori, P.: Usage control on cloud systems. Future Gen. Comput. Syst. **63**(C), 37–55 (2016). https://doi.org/10.1016/j.future.2016.04.010
2. Chadwick, D., Lischka, M.: Obligation standardization. In: W3C Workshop on Access Control Application Scenarios, pp. 1–5 (2009). https://www.w3.org/2009/policy-ws/papers/Chadwick.pdf
3. Collina, M., Corazza, G.E., Vanelli-Coralli, A.: Introducing the QEST broker: scaling the IoT by bridging MQTT and REST. In: 2012 IEEE 23rd International Symposium on Personal, Indoor and Mobile Radio Communications - (PIMRC), pp. 36–41, September 2012. https://doi.org/10.1109/PIMRC.2012.6362813
4. Colombo, M., Lazouski, A., Martinelli, F., Mori, P.: A proposal on enhancing XACML with continuous usage control features. In: Desprez, F., Getov, V., Priol, T., Yahyapour, R. (eds.) Grids. P2P and Services Computing, pp. 133–146. Springer, Heidelberg (2010). https://doi.org/10.1007/978-1-4419-6794-7_11

5. Demchenko, Y., Koeroo, O., de Laat, C., Sagehaug, H.: Extending XACML authorisation model to support policy obligations handling in distributed application. In: Proceedings of the 6th International Workshop on Middleware for Grid Computing, MGC 2008, pp. 5:1–5:6. ACM, New York (2008). https://doi.org/10.1145/1462704.1462709

6. Faiella, M., Martinelli, F., Mori, P., Saracino, A., Sheikhalishahi, M.: Collaborative attribute retrieval in environment with faulty attribute managers. In: 2016 11th International Conference on Availability, Reliability and Security (ARES), pp. 296–303, August 2016. https://doi.org/10.1109/ARES.2016.51

7. La Marra, A., Martinelli, F., Mori, P., Rizos, A., Saracino, A.: Improving MQTT by inclusion of usage control. In: Wang, G., Atiquzzaman, M., Yan, Z., Choo, K.K.R. (eds.) SpaCCS 2017. LNCS, vol. 10656, pp. 545–560. Springer, Cham (2017). https://doi.org/10.1007/978-3-319-72389-1_43

8. La Marra, A., Martinelli, F., Mori, P., Rizos, A., Saracino, A.: Introducing usage control in MQTT. In: Katsikas, S.K., et al. (eds.) SECPRE 2017, CyberICPS 2017. LNCS, vol. 10683, pp. 35–43. Springer, Cham (2018). https://doi.org/10.1007/978-3-319-72817-9_3

9. Lazouski, A., Martinelli, F., Mori, P.: Survey: usage control in computer security: a survey. Comput. Sci. Rev. **4**(2), 81–99 (2010). https://doi.org/10.1016/j.cosrev.2010.02.002

10. Lazouski, A., Martinelli, F., Mori, P., Saracino, A.: Stateful data usage control for Android mobile devices. Int. J. Inf. Secur. 1–25 (2016). https://doi.org/10.1007/s10207-016-0336-y

11. Marra, A.L., Martinelli, F., Mori, P., Saracino, A.: Implementing usage control in internet of things: a smart home use case. In: 2017 IEEE Trustcom/BigDataSE/ICESS, pp. 1056–1063, August 2017. https://doi.org/10.1109/Trustcom/BigDataSE/ICESS.2017.352

12. Martinelli, F., Mori, P.: On usage control for GRID systems. Future Gen. Comput. Syst. **26**(7), 1032–1042 (2010). https://doi.org/10.1016/j.future.2009.12.005

13. Nadkarni, A., Enck, W., Jha, S., Staddon, J.: Policy by Example: An Approach for Security Policy Specification. arXiv preprint arXiv:1707.03967 (2017)

14. OASIS Standard: eXtensible Access Control Markup Language (XACML) Version 3.0, January 2013. http://docs.oasis-open.org/xacml/3.0/xacml-3.0-core-spec-os-en.html

15. Ovadia, S.: Automate the Internet with "If This Then That" (IFTTT). Behav. Soc. Sci. Libr. **33**(4), 208–211 (2014). https://doi.org/10.1080/01639269.2014.964593

16. Park, J., Sandhu, R.: Towards usage control models: beyond traditional access control. In: Proceedings of the Seventh ACM Symposium on Access Control Models and Technologies, SACMAT 2002, pp. 57–64. ACM, New York (2002). https://doi.org/10.1145/507711.507722

17. Samarati, P., de Vimercati, S.C.: Access control: policies, models, and mechanisms. In: Focardi, R., Gorrieri, R. (eds.) FOSAD 2000. LNCS, vol. 2171, pp. 137–196. Springer, Heidelberg (2001). https://doi.org/10.1007/3-540-45608-2_3

18. Surbatovich, M., Aljuraidan, J., Bauer, L., Das, A., Jia, L.: Some recipes can do more than spoil your appetite: analyzing the security and privacy risks of IFTTT recipes. In: Proceedings of the 26th International Conference on World Wide Web, WWW 2017, pp. 1501–1510. International World Wide Web Conferences Steering Committee, Republic and Canton of Geneva, Switzerland (2017). https://doi.org/10.1145/3038912.3052709

19. Vorapojpisut, S.: A lightweight framework of home automation systems based on the IFTTT model. JSW **10**(12), 1343–1350 (2015)

Evaluation of Software PUF
Based on Gyroscope

Kazuhide Fukushima[1]([⊠]), Ayumu Yoshimura[2], Shinsaku Kiyomoto[1],
and Norikazu Yamasaki[2]

[1] KDDI Research, Inc., 2–1–15 Ohara, Fujimino, Saitama 356–8502, Japan
ka-fukushima@kddi-research.jp
[2] Tamagawa University, 6–1–1 Tamagawagakuen, Machida, Tokyo 194–8610, Japan

Abstract. The Physically Unclonable Function (PUF), which extracts
a unique device identification based on variations in manufacturing processes, has recently attracted attention. IoT devices, including sensor
monitors and wearables, have come into widespread use, and various
kinds of devices have access to a range of services. Device authentication
and management of key to encryption communication data are essential
for a secure service. We can realize secure authentication based on device
identification extracted by a PUF. For example, PUF is used as a key generator to avoid storing the encryption key in a device. However, existing
PUFs require dedicated hardware or software (driver) to extract device
identification. Thus, it may not be possible to apply existing PUFs to
IoT devices in a situation where there are a variety of devices and many
device manufacturers. We can use characteristic values of existing sensors in an IoT device as an alternative to PUF. In this paper, we expand
an existing software PUF based to support characteristic values extract
from a gyroscope, and evaluate the entropy and robustness. We found
that the same device identifier can be reliably extracted from a gyroscope
even under conditions of high and low temperature, and low-pressure. No
changes in the characteristic values of the gyroscope due to degradation
with age were found over a wearing period exceeding than three years.
The device identifier has up to 81.2 bits entropy with no error-correcting
mechanism. It has up to 57.7 bits entropy when error-correction of one
bit is applied to each characteristic value by a Fuzzy extractor.

Keywords: IoT devices · Sensor monitors · Wearables · Gyroscope ·
Physically Unclonable Function · Software PUF

1 Introduction

IoT devices, including sensor monitors and wearables, have come into widespread
use. Rapid growth of the IoT market is expected in the areas of automobiles and
transportation, where the use of connected-vehicles is expanding, the medical

---

A. Yoshimura—He currently belongs to TDC SOFT Inc.

S.-H. Heng and J. Lopez (Eds.): ISPEC 2019, LNCS 11879, pp. 232–247, 2019.
https://doi.org/10.1007/978-3-030-34339-2_13

field, where we see growth in the use of digital devices for healthcare, and in industry (including factories, infrastructure, and logistics), where we are witnessing the expansion of smart factories and smart cities. IHS Markit [18] predicts that the number of connected IoT devices worldwide will increase by 12% on average annually. There were nearly 27 billion devices in 2017, and this number will surge to 125 billion by 2030. Google has released Wear OS [14] for wearables and announced the release of Android Things [15], which is an Android-based platform for smart speakers and smart displays. Users can add new features to their smartphones and IoT devices by installing applications. However, an attacker may be able to analyze applications and find a secret key to decrypt protected content or obtain authentication information illegally.

One approach is to generate a unique key dynamically based on the device information of a smartphone or IoT device. For example, the MAC address of a Wi-Fi adapter and Bluetooth adapter has been used as the input to a key generation function. However, the MAC address can be easily modified in a device where the administrator privilege is compromised. Furthermore, the current version of Android and iOS prohibit general applications from getting the MAC address. Android 6.0 (API level 23) or later returns a fixed value 02:00:00:00:00:00 for `WifiInfo.getMacAddress()` and `BluetoothAdapter.getAddress()`, which are ways of getting the MAC address of the Wi-Fi and Bluetooth adapter respectively [13]. iOS7 or later returns the same value for similar APIs [2]. Protection of the key generation algorithm is another critical issue. The Android SDK contains an obfuscation too called Pro-Guard [24] to protect against unauthorized analysis and modification. Nonetheless, this mechanism offers only limited protection since it relies solely on a software mechanism.

Another approach is hardware-based protection, and one idea is to use tamper-proof hardware. Mobile phones have a tamper-proof module, such as a user identity module (UIM) [1] or subscriber identity module (SIM) [37]. These modules provide secure storage for service-subscriber keys and ensure secure computational capability. The serial number of the SIM card can be used as a valid identifier. Android provides the `getSimSerialNumber()` method to get the identifier. The Trusted Computing Group (TCG) has established technology specifications for the Trusted Platform Module (TPM) that is available in smartphones and PCs [38]. The TPM provides the cryptographic functions to enhance the security of the platform, and it is used as a root of trust. However, most IoT devices, including sensor monitors and wearables, do not have dedicated hardware.

The Physically Unclonable Function (PUF), which generates unique device identifiers based on variations in the manufacturing process, is a promising alternative. We can use the device identifier as a key. The device identifier generated by the PUF is hard to analyze since it does not appear in digital format on the device. The existing PUFs depend on additional and dedicated hardware. Thus, they are impractical for use in IoT devices due to the strict limitations on production cost and power consumption. The Static Random-Access Memory (SRAM) PUF and Dynamic Random-Access Memory (DRAM) PUF utilize existing hardware. Still, they are not feasible since they require low-level software, i.e., a driver.

Smartphones and IoT devices have various sensors and hardware such as an accelerometer, gyroscope, proximity sensor, microphone, speaker, and camera. Most wearables have an accelerometer and gyroscope to act according to users' behavior. In this paper, we evaluate the robustness and identification capability of a software PUF that utilizes the characteristic values extracted from a gyroscope. The software PUF based on sensors is widely available on IoT devices, including sensor monitors and wearables.

2   Related Work

The Physically Unclonable Function (PUF) [32] is a function that extracts unique identifiers based on variations in the manufacturing process. It uses slight differences in electronic, optical, or magnetic characteristics. The Arbiter PUF utilizes different signal propagation delays over identical paths [11,25], and the Glitch PUF is based on glitches that are caused by variation in the delay between the input and output signals of each gate [35]. Butterfly PUF, proposed by Kumar et al. [23], uses the initial state of flip-flops. The ClockPUF proposed by Yao et al. [40] extracts the variation in pairwise skews between sinks of a clock network. Gassend et al. proposed the Ring Oscillator PUF based on the variation in the oscillating frequency of the ring oscillator [10]. Finally, Tuyls et al. proposed the Coating PUF based on the capacitance of the coating materials containing dielectric particles [39]. PUFs are categorized into strong PUFs, which include the arbiter PUF, and weak PUFs, which include the butterfly PUF. Strong PUFs takes a challenge as an input and outputs a response calculated with their characteristics. Weak PUFs takes no or one fixed challenge and outputs a fixed characteristic value. These PUFs depend on additional and dedicated hardware; thus, they are not practical for use in smartphones or IoT devices.

Some PUFs based on existing hardware have been proposed. An SRAM PUF utilizes the initial data in memory when the power is turned on [7,27,28]. Krishna et al. proposed a memory-cell-based PUF that uses intrinsic process variations in the read and write reliability of cells in static memory [22]. Liu et al. proposed a DRAM PUF that uses decay time and output stability [26]. Keller et al. proposed a PUF based on the influence of temperature and time on the charge decay [19]. A DRAM PUF proposed by Tehranipoor [36] uses initial data similar to an SRAM PUF. However, the SRAM and DRAM PUFs are still impractical in smartphones or IoT devices. They require dedicated drivers to extract the characteristic features of devices, which imposes an additional cost.

Another approach is to establish features of PUF using existing hardware that can be manipulated with a standard application program interface (API). We call this sort of PUF a *software PUF*. The software PUF is flexible in terms of its introduction into a system since it can be installed as software. Cao et al. [3]

proposed a software PUF based on a CMOS image sensor for coherent sensor-level authentication. Kim and Lee [20] proposed a software PUF based on the fixed pattern noise of a CMOS image sensor. Fukushima et al. [9] proposed a software PUF based on sensors in smartphones and IoT devices. The software PUF can extract the characteristic values of sensors through the standard API of the OS.

Some application studies are using PUFs. Che et al. [6] shows the requirements for PUF-based authentication and proposed a PUF-based authentication protocol designed for resource-constrained devices. Rahim et al. [33] combined a blockchain and software PUF authentication mechanism to establish a real-time and non-repudiable access to IoT devices in a smart home. Chatterjee et al. proposed certificate-less authentication and key exchange schemes based on PUF and identity-based encryption (IBE) [4], and applied the scheme to the handshake protocol in the SSL/TLS layer [5].

3   Software PUF Based on Sensors

Fukushima et al. [9] proposed a sensor-based software PUF for IoT devices, including sensor monitors and wearables. The software PUF acquires the maximum and minimum values of sensors as the characteristic values of the sensors and generates device identifiers based on these characteristic values. They demonstrated that the software PUF based on an accelerometer is practical by showing it has enough identification capability and robustness. We expand their software PUF to support characteristic values extract from a gyroscope, and evaluate the entropy and robustness.

We describe the software PUF [9] to generate a device identifier based on the characteristic values of the sensors in Sect. 3.1. Section 3.2 describes the features of a gyroscope.

3.1   Device Identifier Generation

The identifier generation process consists of the acquisition of the characteristic values of the sensors (step 1) and identifier generation using a one-way function (step 2).

Step 1 Acquisition of the Characteristic Values of the Sensors. The software PUF requires the maximum values and minimum values of the accelerometer and gyroscope. A user needs to sharply shake and twist his/her arm while wearing or holding the device. This process stores the tentative maximum and minimum values of sensors. These tentative values are updated when the current sensor value is larger or smaller than the tentative maximum or minimum value, respectively. We consider the tentative values to be the actual maximum and minimum values after a user shakes the device for a specified time (a few seconds), and the tentative values are stable. We show a sample implementation of this step in the appendix.

Fig. 1. Gyroscope in wearable device

Step 2 Generation of Device Identifier. The software PUF uses a one-way function to generate a device identifier from the concatenated characteristic values extracted from sensors. A device identifier has to vary with each application or service when the identifier is used as a key. In this case, applications or services can use a seed s as an auxiliary input to the one-way function to fulfill the requirement.

We can use a fuzzy extractor [8] to deal with minor deviations in the characteristic values of the sensors. The fuzzy extractor generates and registers a secure sketch SS for future identifier extractions in the registration phase. It generates the random number r, encoded with an error-correcting code C. The secure sketch SS is the exclusive-or of the characteristic value of sensor w, and $C(r)$ or $SS = w \oplus C(r)$. The random number r is disposed of one the registration process is complete. In the device identifier generation phase, the fuzzy extractor recovers the original characteristic value w from the secure sketch SS calculated from the current characteristic value w' in the device. It calculates $C(r)$ as

$$C(r) = \mathsf{ErrCx}(SS \oplus w') = \mathsf{ErrCx}[C(r) \oplus (w \oplus w')],$$

where ErrCx is the error-correcting function and $w \oplus w'$ denotes the minor deviation of the characteristic values of the sensor. Finally, the fuzzy extractor generates the device identifier as

$$\mathsf{DeviceID}(w', s) = h(w \oplus s) = h(SS \oplus C(r) \oplus s)$$

using the one-way function h.

The sensor values for each axis can be considered as independent. Thus, the software PUF separately applies the fuzzy extractor to each characteristic value (maximum and minimum values for each of the axes, x, y, and z).

3.2 Gyroscope

A three-axis gyroscope measures the angular velocities around the x, y, and z-axes. Figure 1 shows the rotation direction around these axes. Many wearables have a gyroscope that can measure up to 2,000 degree/s (34.9 rad/s).

Table 1. Maximum and minimum values of angular velocity

(a) Gyroscope of a smartwatch

	Maximum	Minimum
x-axis	34.999954 rad/s	-34.998978 rad/s
y-axis	34.994186 rad/s	-35.004745 rad/s
z-axis	34.967545 rad/s	-35.031387 rad/s

(b) Gyroscope of another smartwatch

	Maximum	Minimum
x-axis	35.018036 rad/s	-34.980896 rad/s
y-axis	35.009125 rad/s	-34.989807 rad/s
z-axis	34.989014 rad/s	-35.009920 rad/s

The maximum and minimum values of the gyroscope around each axis differ from one device to another. Thus, these values can be used to generate device identification data. We construct a six-dimensional data set that consists of the maximum and minimum values around the x, y, and z-axes and extracts digits that have enough variety. The characteristic values of the gyroscope can be obtained by concatenating these digits.

4 Experiment

We implemented the software PUF based on a gyroscope as a Wear OS application. The software PUF application is executed on an LG Watch Urbane smartwatch to evaluate the entropy and robustness of the device identifier.

The LG Watch Urbane runs on the Wear OS 2.24.0.248902549 that is compatible with Android OS 7.1.1 and it has a gyroscope that can measure from $-2,000$ degree/s $(-34.9$ rad/s) to 2,000 degree/s (34.9 rad/s). Table 1 shows an example. The number in the fourth decimal place and the following digits have enough variety. Thus, the PUF application extracts the numbers in the fourth to sixth decimal place as a character string with three figures from each of the maximum and minimum values of angular velocities around the x, y, and z-axes. The application can acquire a characteristic value of the accelerometer with 18 characters by concatenating these six character strings.

The software PUF application generates a device identifier with 128-bit length from the characteristic value of a gyroscope by using SHA-256 and truncating the last 128 bits. We do not use the fuzzy extractor in the application since it can reliably extract the identical characteristic values from the gyroscope.

Figure 2 shows a photo of the PUF application on the LG Watch Urbane. The application regenerates and displays the generated device identifier whenever the tentative maximum and minimum values of sensors are updated. The tentative maximum and minimum values are reset to zero when the user presses the reset button (RST). The application stores the device identifier when the register button (REG) is pressed and deletes the identifier when the unregister button (URG) is pressed. We can use this function to evaluate the robustness of the device identifier. The application compares the generated identifier and stored identifier and displays "OK" if they are identical or "NG" otherwise.

Fig. 2. Screenshot of gyroscope-based software PUF

5   Evaluation

We evaluate the compatibility of the software PUF based on a gyroscope with the requirements for PUFs. Then, we evaluate the robustness and entropy of the device identifier generated by the accelerometer-based PUF.

5.1   Compatibility with Requirements

Maes and Verbauwhede [29] showed the requirements for PUFs: evaluable, unique, reproducible, unpredictable, one-way, unclonable and tamper evident. We show the compatibility of the software PUF based on a gyroscope in relation to these requirements.

Evaluable. The software PUF based on a gyroscope uses the characteristic values of the existing sensors, and these values can be acquired through the existing APIs. The software PUF can be implemented as a general application at a minimal cost. Furthermore, the software PUF uses only the extraction and concatenation of character strings, one-way function, and optional exclusive-or and operations for the error-correcting code. Thus, the PUF is feasible in resource-restricted devices.

Unique. The device identifier generated by the software PUF based on a gyroscope is unique since it has high entropy. We evaluate the entropy of the software PUF in Sect. 5.2.

Reproducible. The device identifier generated by the software PUF based on a gyroscope is reproducible since it has high robustness. We evaluate the robustness of the software PUF in Sect. 5.3.

Unpredictable. The software PUF based on a gyroscope is a weak PUF and does not apply to the challenge-response model. Thus, we cannot evaluate the unpredictability of the sensor-based software PUF. However, we can construct a strong PUF that protects against side-channel analysis and machine learning attacks [34].

One-way. The software PUF based on a gyroscope uses a one-way function to generate the device identifier from the characteristic values. The one-way function guarantees this requirement for the sensor-based software PUF.

Unclonable and Tamper Evident. The software PUF based on a gyroscope acquires the characteristic values of sensors using software (application) and generates the device identifier. Thus, we need to protect against the acquisition and modification of the characteristic values and generated device identification. For example, attackers can make a clone of the software PUF by acquiring the characteristic values of the sensor. They can also modify the values of the sensors or the generated device identifier in the memory. Thus, we obviously have to protect against these attacks by applying memory protection techniques [12,30,31]. Attackers may modify the identifier generation algorithm so that it outputs an arbitrary identifier. We also have to protect against these attacks by applying software tamper-proof techniques to prevent modification of the application.

5.2 Identification Capability

We have evaluated the quadratic Renyi entropy of the device identifier extracted from a gyroscope. The quadratic Renyi entropy is defined as:

$$H_2(C) = -\log_2 \left(\sum_{w \in C} p_C(w)^2 \right).$$

$H_2(C)$ is a particular case ($\alpha = 2$) of the Renyi entropy $H_\alpha(C)$, which is defined as:

$$H_\alpha(C) = \frac{1}{1-\alpha} \log_2 \left(\sum_{w \in C} p_C(w)^\alpha \right).$$

The Shannon entropy is defined as

$$H(C) = - \sum_{w \in C} p_C(w) \log_2 p_C(w).$$

The Renyi entropy and Shannon entropy have the relationship: $\lim_{\alpha \to 1} H_\alpha(C) = H(C)$ and is non-increasing with respect to α. The quadratic Renyi entropy is smaller than or equal to the Shannon entropy, or $H_2(\mathcal{C}) \leq H(\mathcal{C})$. The equality holds when C is chosen according to the uniform distribution. Thus, the quadratic Renyi entropy gives an upper-bound of the Shannon entropy.

The $\sum_{w \in C} p_C(c)^2$ is the probability that the two characteristic values are identical, and the quadratic Renyi entropy is referred to as the collision entropy. The quadratic Renyi entropy can be written as

$$H_2(C) = -\log_2 p_D(0)$$

with the probabilistic mass function of the distance D between two characteristic values $p_D(d)$. The quadratic Renyi entropy has been used to evaluate the entropy

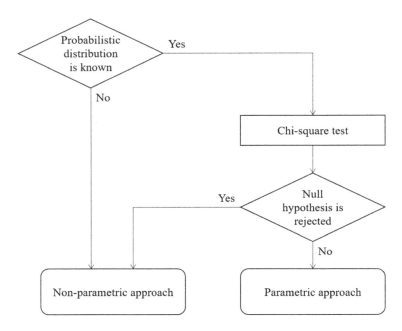

Fig. 3. Flowchart to select approach to estimate probability $p_D(0)$

of biometric information [16, 17]. However, it is difficult to predict the probability $p_D(d)$ directly with a limited number of samples. Thus, we need to estimate $p_D(d)$.

Figure 3 shows a flowchart to select an approach to estimate the probability $p_D(0)$. Fukushima et al. [9] the evaluate the entropy of a device identifier extracted by the software PUF based on an accelerometer-based on a non-parametric approach [21]. The experimental distribution of the Hamming distance between characteristic values matches the theoretical binomial distribution well in our evaluation (Figs. 4 and 5). We derive a parameter p of a binomial distribution $\tilde{p}$ based on a maximum likelihood estimation technique. Then, the chi-squared test is used to determine whether the experimental distribution is in conformance with a binomial distribution with parameters n and $\tilde{p}$. We can calculate the quadratic Renyi entropy using the probabilistic mass function of the binomial distribution (Eq. (1)) if the null hypothesis is not rejected. We need to use a non-parametric approach [21] if the probabilistic distribution of the Hamming weight is unknown or the null hypothesis is rejected.

The probability $p_D(d)$ can be calculated as:

$$p_D(d) = \binom{n}{d} \tilde{p}^d (1 - \tilde{p})^{n-d}$$

in the situation where the Hamming weight between characteristic value D follows a binomial distribution with parameters n and $\tilde{p}$, where n is the bit-length of a characteristic value. We have

$$p_D(0) = (1 - \tilde{p})^n$$

and the quadratic Renyi entropy can be calculated as:

$$H_2(C) = -n \log_2(1 - \tilde{p}). \tag{1}$$

We exhaustively compared the 36 characteristic values extracted from six wearable devices. A total of 630 $(= 36(36-1)/2)$ samples are used to estimate the distribution of the Hamming distance. Our experiment evaluates the quadratic Renyi entropy of characteristic values extracted from (1) three decimal digits in the fourth to sixth decimal place and (2) four decimal digits in the third to the sixth decimal place, from the maximum and minimum values of the gyroscope.

Characteristic Value Based on Three Decimal Digits. We can extract a 10-bit characteristic value from three decimal digits from 000 to 999. The blue bar graph in Fig. 4 shows the distribution measured Hamming distance between extracted characteristic values, and the light blue bar graph shows the ideal binomial distribution with parameters $n = 10$ and $\tilde{p} = 0.4978$ that is derived from the actual distribution. The chi-square with 10 degrees of freedom is 9.40, and the corresponding p-value is 0.498; thus, the null hypothesis is not rejected. We conclude that the distribution of the Hamming distance follows the binomial distribution. Each characteristic value has 9.94 bits of the quadratic Renyi entropy, and we can extract a device identifier with 59.6 bits of entropy from a gyroscope with a six-dimensional characteristic value.

Four Decimal Digits Based on Four Decimal Digits. We can extract a 14-bit characteristic value from four decimal digits from 0000 to 9999. The blue bar graph in Fig. 5 shows the distribution measured Hamming distance between extracted characteristic values, and the light blue bar graph shows the ideal binomial distribution with parameters $n = 14$ and $\tilde{p} = 0.4882$ that is derived from the actual distribution. The chi-square value with 14 degrees of freedom is 9.34, and the corresponding p-value is 0.809; thus, the null hypothesis is not rejected. We conclude that the distribution of the Hamming distance follows the binomial distribution. Each characteristic value has 13.5 bits of the quadratic Renyi entropy, and we can extract a device identifier with 81.2 bits of entropy from a gyroscope with a six-dimensional characteristic value.

We can consider the distribution of the Hamming distance of characteristic values as a binomial distribution in both cases. Equation (1) can be used to evaluate the quadratic Renyi entropy of the characteristic values extracted from a gyroscope. A device identifier extracted from a gyroscope has 81.2 bits of entropy when we utilize four decimal digits of the characteristic values extracted from a gyroscope.

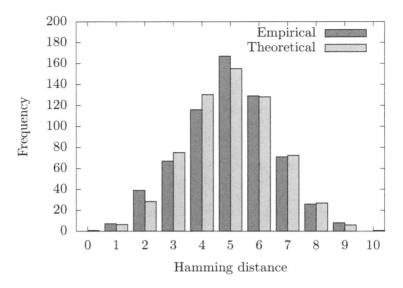

Fig. 4. Distribution of Hamming distance between characteristic values extracted from four decimal digits (Color figure online)

We discuss the trade-off between identification capability and robustness in the case where the sensor-based software PUF uses the fuzzy extractor. The entropy loss of each characteristic value of the sensors is at least $\log_2 \left(\sum_{k=0}^{t} \binom{n}{k} \right)$ bits according to the Hamming bound. n is the bit length of the encoded characteristic value, and t is the correction capability of the error-correcting code. The total entropy loss is at least $6 \log_2 \left(\sum_{k=0}^{t} \binom{n}{k} \right)$ bits. Table 2 shows the relationship between the correction capability of the error-correcting code and the upper bound of the total entropy of the device identifier generated by the sensor-based software PUF. It also compares the entropy of identifiers extracted by the existing scheme [9] and our proposed scheme. The device identifier generated by the gyroscope-based PUF can achieve more than 60 bits of entropy when the fuzzy

Table 2. Entropy loss due to error-correction

Capability	Entropy [9]	Entropy (Our)
0	91.7	81.2
1	66.6	57.7
2	48.1	40.8
3	33.4	27.9
4	21.8	18.0
5	12.5	10.6

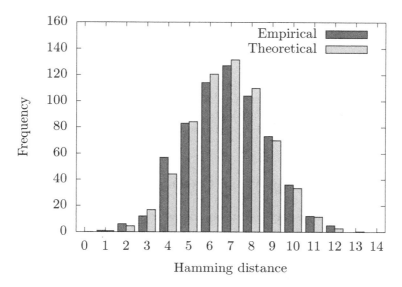

Fig. 5. Distribution of Hamming distance between characteristic values extracted from four decimal digits (Color figure online)

extractor is not used, or when the fuzzy extractor uses the error-correcting code with one-bit correction capability.

5.3 Robustness

The software PUF based on a gyroscope can generate an identical device identifier within the same device without the fuzzy extractor. We were able to confirm that the device identifier generated by the accelerometer-based PUF is consistent from the fact that the same user could generate the same identifier more than 1,000 times. Furthermore, more than ten users can generate the same device identifier within the same device. The accelerometer-based PUF generates the same device identifier regardless of the surrounding temperature. Finally, it generates the same identifier after placing the device in −15 °C and 90 °C, and at 2,000 m above sea level on a mountain. No changes in the characteristic values of the gyroscope due to degradation with age were found when the device was worn for a period exceeding three years.

6 Conclusion

We expanded an existing software PUF [9] to support characteristic values extracted from a gyroscope. The software PUF based on a gyroscope is widely applicable to smartphones and IoT devices. Our experimental results show that the software PUF based on a gyroscope is practical due to enough identification capability (entropy of 81.2 bit) and robustness. The software PUF [9] extracts a device identifier with an entropy of up to 91.7 bits from an accelerometer. The combination of device identifiers from an accelerometer and gyroscope can achieve higher identification capability as a key for a secret key cryptosystem. However, the software PUF based on gyroscope has a limitation that a user has to sharply twist the arm wearing or holding a device to extract the device identifier. In future research, we will endeavor to make extraction of device identifier from sensors easier for users and study security measures against physical attacks.

A Implementation on Wear OS Device

Figure 6 shows a sample implementation designed to acquire the maximum and minimum values of the gyroscope in a wearable device with Wear OS. The fields maxX, minX, maxY, minY, maxZ, and minZ are fields that store the tentative maximum and minimum values of the angular velocities around the x, y and z-axes. The method onSensorChanged is called when the sensor values have changed. We retrieve the event from the gyroscope by using the if statement. The angular velocities around the x, y, and z-axes are stored in the values array. The same code where Sensor.TYPE_GYROSCOPE is replaced with Sensor.TYPE_ACCELEROMETER can acquire the maximum and minimum values of accelerations along each axis.

```
@Override
public void onSensorChanged(SensorEvent event) {
    if (event.sensor.getType() == Sensor.TYPE_GYROSCOPE) {
        boolean upd = false;
        float x = event.values[0];
        float y = event.values[1];
        float z = event.values[2];
        if (x > maxX) { maxX = x; upd = true; }
        if (x < minX) { minX = x; upd = true; }
        if (y > maxY) { maxY = y; upd = true; }
        if (y < minY) { minY = y; upd = true; }
        if (z > maxZ) { maxZ = z; upd = true; }
        if (z < minZ) { minZ = z; upd = true; }
        if (upd) {
            // Regenerate device identifier using updated values
            deviceId = generateDeviceId();
        }
    }
}
```

Fig. 6. Acquisition of maximum and minimum values of the gyroscope [9]

The software PUF based on a gyroscope needs to set the highest sampling frequency on the sensors so that we can efficiently acquire the maximum and minimum values. We can set the sampling frequency through the `registerListener` method in Android. The method registers `SensorEventListener` that is used to receive notifications from the `SensorManager` when the sensor values have changed. The notification frequency is highest, and the period is a few milliseconds if `SENSOR_DELAY_FASTEST` is passed to the method.

References

1. 3GPP2: Removable User Identity Module (R-UIM) for cdma2000 Spread Spectrum Systems (2000). https://www.3gpp2.org/Public_html/Specs/CS0023-0.pdf
2. Apple: What's New in iOS 7.0 - Apple Developer (2013). https://developer.apple.com/library/ios/releasenotes/General/WhatsNewIniOS/Articles/iOS7.html
3. Cao, Y., Zhang, L., Zalivaka, S.S., Chang, C., Chen, S.: CMOS image sensor based physical unclonable function for coherent sensor-level authentication. IEEE Trans. Circ. Syst. I: Regular Pap. **62**(11), 2629–2640 (2015). https://doi.org/10.1109/TCSI.2015.2476318
4. Chatterjee, U., et al.: Building PUF based authentication and key exchange protocol for IoT without explicit CRPs in verifier database. IEEE Trans. Dependable Secur. Comput. **16**(3), 424–437 (2019). https://doi.org/10.1109/TDSC.2018.2832201
5. Chatterjee, U., et al.: PUFSSL: an OpenSSL extension for PUF based authentication. In: 2018 IEEE 23rd International Conference on Digital Signal Processing (DSP), pp. 1–5, November 2018. https://doi.org/10.1109/ICDSP.2018.8631814
6. Che, W., Saqib, F., Plusquellic, J.: PUF-based authentication. In: 2015 IEEE/ACM International Conference on Computer-Aided Design (ICCAD), pp. 337–344, November 2015. https://doi.org/10.1109/ICCAD.2015.7372589
7. Chopra, J., Colopy, R.: SRAM Characteristics as Physical Unclonable Functions (2009). http://www.wpi.edu/Pubs/E-project/Available/E-project-031709-141338/
8. Dodis, Y., Ostrovsky, R., Reyzin, L., Smith, A.: Fuzzy extractors: how to generate strong keys from biometrics and other noisy data. SIAM J. Comput. **38**(1), 97–139 (2008). https://doi.org/10.1137/060651380
9. Fukushima, K., Hidano, S., Kiyomoto, S.: Sensor-based wearable PUF. In: Proceedings of the 13th International Joint Conference on e-Business and Telecommunications - Volume 4: SECRYPT, (ICETE 2016), pp. 207–214. INSTICC, SciTePress (2016). http://www.scitepress.org/DigitalLibrary/Link.aspx?doi=10.5220/0005946702070214
10. Gassend, B., Clarke, D., van Dijk, M., Devadas, S.: Silicon physical random functions. In: Proceedings of the 9th ACM Conference on Computer and Communications Security, CCS 2002, p. 148 (2002). https://doi.org/10.1145/586110.586132
11. Gassend, B., Clarke, D., Lim, D., van Dijk, M., Devada, S.: Identification and authentication of integrated circuits. Concurrency Comput.: Practice Exp. **16**(11), 1077–1098 (2004)
12. Goldreich, O., Ostrovsky, R.: Software protection and simulation on oblivious RAMs. J. ACM **43**(3), 431–473 (1996). https://doi.org/10.1145/233551.233553

13. Google: Android 6.0 changes, access to hardware identifier (2015). http://developer.android.com/intl/ja/about/versions/marshmallow/android-6.0-changes.html#behavior-hardware-id
14. Google: Wear OS (2018). https://wearos.google.com/
15. Google: Android Things (2019). https://developer.android.com/things/
16. Hidano, S., Ohki, T., Takahashi, K.: Evaluation of security for biometric guessing attacks in biometric cryptosystem using fuzzy commitment scheme. In: Proceedings of 2012 International Conference of the Biometrics Special Interest Group, BIOSIG, pp. 1–6 (2012)
17. Hidano, S., Ohki, T., Komatsu, N., Takahashi, K.: A metric of identification performance of biometrics based on information content. In: Proceedings of 11th International Conference on Control, Automation, Robotics and Vision, ICARCV 2010, pp. 1274–1279 (2010). https://doi.org/10.1109/ICARCV.2010.5707961
18. IHS Markit: Number of Connected IoT Devices Will Surge to 125 Billion by 2030, IHS Markit Says (2015). http://www.statista.com/statistics/266210/
19. Keller, C., Gurkaynak, F., Kaeslin, H., Felber, N.: Dynamic memory-based physically unclonable function for the generation of unique identifiers and true random numbers. In: Proceedings of IEEE International Symposium on Circuits and Systems, vol. 3, pp. 2740–2743 (2014). https://doi.org/10.1109/ISCAS.2014.6865740
20. Kim, Y., Lee, Y.: CamPUF: physically unclonable function based on CMOS image sensor fixed pattern noise. In: Proceedings of the 55th Annual Design Automation Conference, DAC 2018, pp. 66:1–66:6. ACM, New York (2018). https://doi.org/10.1145/3195970.3196005
21. Kokonendji, C.C., Kiesse, T.S., Zocchi, S.S.: Discrete triangular distributions and non-parametric estimation for probability mass function. J. Nonparametric Stat. 19(6–8), 241–254 (2007). https://doi.org/10.1080/10485250701733747
22. Krishna, A.R., Narasimhan, S., Wang, X., Bhunia, S.: MECCA: a robust low-overhead PUF using embedded memory array. In: Preneel, B., Takagi, T. (eds.) CHES 2011. LNCS, vol. 6917, pp. 407–420. Springer, Heidelberg (2011). https://doi.org/10.1007/978-3-642-23951-9_27
23. Kumar, S.S., Guajardo, J., Maes, R., Schrijen, G.J., Tuyls, P.: The butterfly PUF protecting IP on every FPGA. In: Proceedings of 2008 IEEE International Workshop on Hardware-Oriented Security and Trust, HOST 2008, pp. 67–70 (2008). https://doi.org/10.1109/HST.2008.4559053
24. Lafortune, E.: ProGuard (2002). https://www.guardsquare.com/en/products/proguard
25. Lee, J., Lim, D.L.D., Gassend, B., Suh, G., Dijk, M.V., Devadas, S.: A technique to build a secret key in integrated circuits for identification and authentication applications. In: Proceedings of 2004 Symposium on VLSI Circuits, pp. 176–179 (2004). https://doi.org/10.1109/VLSIC.2004.1346548
26. Liu, W., Zhang, Z., Li, M., Liu, Z.: A trustworthy key generation prototype based on DDR3 PUF for wireless sensor networks. In: Proceedings of 2014 International Symposium on Computer, Consumer and Control, IS3C 2014, pp. 706–709 (2014). https://doi.org/10.1109/IS3C.2014.188
27. Maes, R., Tuyls, P., Verbauwhede, I.: A soft decision helper data algorithm for SRAM PUFs. In: Proceedings of IEEE International Symposium on Information Theory, ISIT 2009, pp. 2101–2105 (2009). https://doi.org/10.1109/ISIT.2009.5205263
28. Maes, R., Tuyls, P., Verbauwhede, I.: Low-overhead implementation of a soft decision helper data algorithm for SRAM PUFs. In: Clavier, C., Gaj, K. (eds.) CHES

2009. LNCS, vol. 5747, pp. 332–347. Springer, Heidelberg (2009). https://doi.org/10.1007/978-3-642-04138-9_24

29. Maes, R., Verbauwhede, I.: Physically unclonable functions: a study on the state of the art and future research directions. In: Sadeghi, A.R., Naccache, D. (eds.) Towards Hardware-Intrinsic Security. ISC, pp. 3–37. Springer, Heidelberg (2010). https://doi.org/10.1007/978-3-642-14452-3_1

30. Nakano, Y., Cid, C., Kiyomoto, S., Miyake, Y.: Memory access pattern protection for resource-constrained devices. In: Mangard, S. (ed.) CARDIS 2012. LNCS, vol. 7771, pp. 188–202. Springer, Heidelberg (2013). https://doi.org/10.1007/978-3-642-37288-9_13

31. Ostrovsky, R.: Efficient computation on oblibious RAMs. In: Proceedings of the 22nd Annual ACM Symposium on Theory of Computing, STOC 1990, pp. 514–523 (1990). https://doi.org/10.1145/233551.233553

32. Pappu, R., Recht, B., Taylor, J., Gershenfeld, N.: Physical one-way functions. Science **297**, 2026–2030 (2002). https://doi.org/10.1126/science.1074376

33. Rahim, K., Tahir, H., Ikram, N.: Sensor based PUF IoT authentication model for a smart home with private blockchain. In: 2018 International Conference on Applied and Engineering Mathematics (ICAEM), pp. 102–108, September 2018. https://doi.org/10.1109/ICAEM.2018.8536295

34. Santiago, L., et al.: Realizing strong PUF from weak PUF via neural computing. In: 2017 IEEE International Symposium on Defect and Fault Tolerance in VLSI and Nanotechnology Systems (DFT), pp. 1–6, October 2017. https://doi.org/10.1109/DFT.2017.8244433

35. Suzuki, D., Shimizu, K.: The glitch PUF: a new delay-PUF architecture exploiting glitch shapes. In: Mangard, S., Standaert, F.-X. (eds.) CHES 2010. LNCS, vol. 6225, pp. 366–382. Springer, Heidelberg (2010). https://doi.org/10.1007/978-3-642-15031-9_25

36. Tehranipoor, F., Karimina, N., Xiao, K., Chandy, J.: DRAM based intrinsic physical unclonable functions for system level security. In: Proceedings of the 25th edition on Great Lakes Symposium on VLSI, GLSVLSI 2015, pp. 15–20 (2015). https://doi.org/10.1145/2742060.2742069

37. The 3rd Generation Partnership Project (3GPP): Specification of the Subscriber Identity Module - Mobile Equipment (SIM-ME) Interface (1990). http://www.3gpp.org/ftp/Specs/html-info/1111.htm

38. Trust Computing Group: Trusted Platform Module (2016). http://www.trustedcomputinggroup.org/developers/trusted_platform_module

39. Tuyls, P., Schrijen, G.-J., Škorić, B., van Geloven, J., Verhaegh, N., Wolters, R.: Read-proof hardware from protective coatings. In: Goubin, L., Matsui, M. (eds.) CHES 2006. LNCS, vol. 4249, pp. 369–383. Springer, Heidelberg (2006). https://doi.org/10.1007/11894063_29

40. Yao, Y., Kim, M., Li, J., Markov, I.L., Koushanfar, F.: ClockPUF: physical unclonable functions based on clock networks. In: 2013 Design, Automation Test in Europe Conference Exhibition (DATE), pp. 422–427, March 2013. https://doi.org/10.7873/DATE.2013.095

White-Box Implementation of the KMAC Message Authentication Code

Jiqiang Lu[1(✉)], Zhigang Zhao[2], and Huaqun Guo[2]

[1] School of Cyber Science and Technology, Beihang University,
37 Xueyuan Road, Beijing 100083, China
lvjiqiang@hotmail.com, lvjiqiang@buaa.edu.cn
[2] Institute for Infocomm Research, Agency for Science, Technology and Research,
1 Fusionopolis Way, Singapore 138632, Singapore
{zzhao,guohq}@i2r.a-star.edu.sg

Abstract. In 2016, US NIST released the KMAC message authentication code, which is actually a keyed variant of the new-generation hash function standard SHA-3. Following the increasing use of SHA-3, it is highly anticipated that KMAC will also be increasingly widely used in various security applications. Due to the distinctions between sponge hash functions and Merkle-Damgård hash functions, white-box implementations of KMAC and HMAC are rather different. In this paper, we present an efficient white-box implementation of KMAC with strong resistance against both key extraction and code lifting attacks, which can still work with an updated user key. It has a storage complexity of about 107.7 MB, and has a running time of about 1.5 ms on a DELL Precision T5610 workstation, about 375 times slower than the original KMAC implementation without white-box protection. There are implementation variants with different trade-offs between security and performance. This is the first published white-box implementation of KMAC to the best of our knowledge, and our implementation methods can be applied to similar sponge constructions.

Keywords: White-box cryptography · Message authentication code (MAC) · Hash function · Sponge construction · SHA-3 · KMAC

1 Introduction

In 2005, serious collision attacks [29,30] were published on then hash function standards MD5 [28] and SHA-1 [24]. As a consequence, US NIST announced the

---

J. Lu—The author was with Institute for Infocomm Research (Singapore) when the work was partially completed.
This work was supported by the National Research Foundation (NRF), Prime Minister's Office, Singapore, under its National Cybersecurity R&D Programme (Award No. NRF2014NCR-NCR001-31) and administered by the National Cybersecurity R&D Directorate, and was supported also by a grant (No. ZG216S1992) of Beihang University.

S.-H. Heng and J. Lopez (Eds.): ISPEC 2019, LNCS 11879, pp. 248–270, 2019.
https://doi.org/10.1007/978-3-030-34339-2_14

public SHA-3 competition to develop an alternative but dissimilar cryptographic hash standard in 2007, selected the candidate Keccak [4] in 2012, and finally approved it as the new-generation SHA-3 hash standard [26] in 2015. SHA-3 is based on the sponge construction method [3], which is quite different from the Merkle-Damgård construction method [13,20] that earlier hash functions like MD5 and SHA-1/2 [25] are based on. SHA-3 has been adopted by real-life applications like Ethereum [31], owing to its technical advantages.

The HMAC [2] message authentication code (MAC) was proposed in 1996 mainly for use with a Merkle-Damgård hash function like SHA-1/2, because a Merkle-Damgård hash function cannot be readily transformed into a secure MAC for authenticity by prepending a key to message, due to length extension attack, that is, an attacker can append one or more message blocks and is able to compute the resulting MAC. HMAC uses a nested structure to prevent length extension attacks, however, a sponge hash function can prevent length extension attacks itself, mainly because the internal states are not fully released as output; and thus HMAC would be not efficient with a sponge hash function. In 2016, NIST released the KMAC algorithm for use with SHA-3 to provide authenticity, which is actually a keyed variant of SHA-3, simply by prepending a padded key to message.

White-box cryptography [11,12] was introduced in 2002, with its applications to the AES [23] and DES [22] block ciphers. It works under the so-called white-box model, which assumes an attacker to have access to the execution details and execution environment of a software implementation, giving the attacker more power than the black-box and grey-box models. For white-box cryptography, the primary security threat is key extraction attack, which aims to extract the key used in white-box implementation; and another serious security threat is what we call code lifting attack, which aims to use white-box implementation to generate the output for an unauthorised input. Nowadays, white-box cryptography has many real-life application scenarios like TV boxes, mobile phones and game consoles, where the owner/user of a client service device may compromise the underlying security mechanism for illegal use of the service, and many IT companies like Apple and Microsoft already use or plan to use white-box cryptography solutions. At present, there are mainly two research directions on white-box cryptography: One is the design and analysis [1,6,10–12,16,18,19,32,33] of white-box implementations of existing cryptographic algorithms, and it has been well understood that this line of white-box implementation designs is hardly impossible to achieve a full security but can still provide some level of protection more or less; the other research direction is the design and analysis [7–9,14] of completely new white-box primitives that aim to achieve a full security efficiently. Both the directions have their respective application scenarios in reality.

Our work in this paper falls in the first research direction of white-box cryptography. We observe that the following two particular distinctions between Merkle-Damgård and sponge hash functions make a huge difference to white-box implementations of the corresponding MACs: (1) The compression function of a Merkle-Damgård hash function like SHA-1/2 is one-way (i.e. irreversible), while the state transformation function of a sponge hash function like SHA-3 is usually a permutation, which is bijective and reversible; and (2) A Merkle-Damgård hash function like SHA-1/2 usually involves a message expansion function, while a sponge hash function does not involve a message expansion function. The first distinction makes it rather simple to design an efficient white-box implementation against only key extraction attacks for HMAC-SHA-1/2 [15,17,19], while it is complex for KMAC; and the second distinction requires much less additional cost to design a white-box implementation against both key extraction and code lifting attacks for KMAC than for HMAC-SHA-1/2, on the basis of their respective white-box implementation against only key extraction attacks. Finally, we present an efficient white-box implementation of KMAC with strong resistance against both key extraction and code lifting attacks, by protecting every 64-bit state word with a 64-bit mixing bijection [11,12] and a layer of sixteen 4-bit encodings [11,12], merging several adjacent operations of the round function, building white-box implementations of basic operations with great security, and using an iterative process at different phases of KMAC. The implementation has a storage complexity of about 107.7 MB, and has a running time of about 1.5 ms on a DELL Precision T5610 workstation, about 375 times slower than the original KMAC implementation without white-box protection; and the same implementation can be reused when the key is updated. Besides, there are security–performance trade-offs.

The remainder of the paper is organised as follows. In the next section, we describe the notation, the sponge construction method, SHA-3 and KMAC. In Sect. 3, we discuss white-box KMAC and HMAC. We describe our white-box implementation schema of KMAC in Sect. 4, present white-box implementations of its basic operations in Sect. 5, give the white-box KMAC implementation in Sect. 6, and evaluate its security and performance in Sects. 7 and 8, respectively. Section 9 discusses possible implementation variants. Section 10 concludes this paper.

2   Preliminaries

In this section, we give the notation used throughout this paper, and briefly describe the sponge construction method, SHA-3 and KMAC.

2.1   Notation

In all descriptions we assume that the bits of a value are numbered from left to right, starting with 0. We use the following notation throughout this paper.

$\oplus$ bitwise exclusive OR (XOR)
$\&$ bitwise AND
$\neg$ the complement (NOT)
$\lll$ left rotation of a bit string
$\|$ bit string concatenation
$\circ$ functional composition. When composing functions X and Y, X $\circ$ Y denotes the function obtained by first applying X and then applying Y

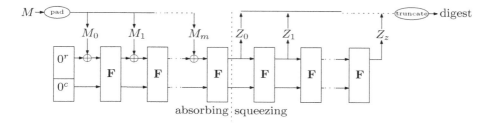

Fig. 1. The sponge construction

2.2 The Sponge Hash Function Construction Method

The sponge construction was proposed by Bertoni et al. [3]. As illustrated in Fig. 1, for some positive integers r and c, a sponge construction maps binary strings with bit length of a multiple of r into binary strings of any requested length (i.e. $\mathbb{Z}_2^{r,*}$ to $\mathbb{Z}_2^\infty$), by calling a transformation $\mathbf{F} : \mathbb{Z}_2^{r+c} \to \mathbb{Z}_2^{r+c}$, where r is called the bitrate (of the sponge construction), c is called the capacity (of the sponge construction) which should be twice the length of the requested digest, and $\mathbf{F}$ is often referred to as the state transformation function (of the sponge construction). Note that a message M should be padded first to reach a bit length of a minimum multiple of r, and then divided into a number of r-bit blocks $M_0, M_1, \cdots, M_m$; and the digest Z is made up of r-bit blocks $Z_0, Z_1, \cdots, Z_z$ with the last block being truncated to meet the requested digest length if necessary.

A sponge construction consists of two phases at a high level: absorbing phase and squeezing phase. The absorbing phase processes a message, and the squeezing phase outputs a (message) digest (or hash value).

2.3 The SHA-3 Hash Function Family

SHA-3 [26] is a family of four cryptographic hash functions and two extendable-output functions. Below we focus on the SHA-3 hash function member with a 256-bit digest, that is SHA3-256, and we refer the reader to [26] for a detailed specification.

For SHA3-256, the capacity $c = 512$, the bitrate $r = 1088$, the digest length is 256, and a message is padded by appending first three bits '011', then as many zeros as minimally required and finally one-bit '1' to reach a bit length of a multiple of r, where the first two the SHA-3 hash functions from the SHA-3 extendable-output functions.

For all SHA3 members, the state transformation function $\mathbf{F}$ is a permutation operating on binary strings of 1600 bits (that is $r + c$) long. A 1600-bit state is represented as a $5 \times 5 \times 64$ bit array of three dimensions, denoted by $A = \{A[x, y, z] | 0 \le x \le 4, 0 \le y \le 4, 0 \le z \le 63\}$. The state transformation function $\mathbf{F}$ consists of the following five elementary operations, where $\widehat{A} = \{\widehat{A}[x, y, z] | 0 \le x \le 4, 0 \le y \le 4, 0 \le z \le 63\}$ is a $5 \times 5 \times 64$ bit array variable:

– $\theta : \theta(A) = \widehat{A}$ is defined as the following three steps:
  1. For $0 \le x \le 4$ and $0 \le z \le 63$:

$$C[x, z] = \bigoplus_{y=0}^{4} A[x, y, z]. \tag{1}$$

  2. For $0 \le x \le 4$ and $0 \le z \le 63$:

$$D[x, z] = C[(x-1) \bmod 5, z] \oplus C[(x+1) \bmod 5, (z-1) \bmod 64]. \tag{2}$$

  3. For $0 \le x \le 4, 0 \le y \le 4, 0 \le z \le 63$: $\widehat{A}[x, y, z] = A[x, y, z] \oplus D[x, z]$.
– $\rho : \rho(A) = \widehat{A}$ is defined as the following three steps:
  1. For $0 \le z \le 63$: $\widehat{A}[0, 0, z] = A[0, 0, z]$.
  2. $(x, y) = (1, 0)$.
  3. For $t = 0$ to 23:
     (a) For $0 \le z \le 63$:

$$\widehat{A}[x, y, z] = A[x, y, (z - \frac{(t+1) \times (t+2)}{2}) \bmod 64]. \tag{3}$$

     (b) $(x, y) = (y, (2x + 3y) \bmod 5)$.
– $\pi : \pi(A) = \widehat{A}$ is defined as follows:
  • For $0 \le x \le 4, 0 \le y \le 4, 0 \le z \le 63$:

$$\widehat{A}[x, y, z] = A[(x + 3y) \bmod 5, x, z]. \tag{4}$$

– $\chi : \chi(A) = \widehat{A}$ is defined as follows:
  • For $0 \le x \le 4, 0 \le y \le 4, 0 \le z \le 63$:

$$\widehat{A}[x, y, z] = A[x, y, z] \oplus ((A[(x+1) \bmod 5, y, z] \oplus 1) \times A[(x+2) \bmod 5, y, z]). \tag{5}$$

– $\iota : \iota(A, i) = \widehat{A}$ is defined as the following four steps, where i is the round index $(0 \le i \le 23)$, and $RC_i = RC_i[0] || RC_i[1] || \cdots || RC_i[63]$ are 64-bit round constants generated by a function $\mathbf{rc}(\cdot)$:
  1. For $0 \le x \le 4, 0 \le y \le 4, 0 \le z \le 63$: $\widehat{A}[x, y, z] = A[x, y, z]$.
  2. $RC = 0^{64}$.
  3. For $j = 0$ to 6: $RC_i[2^j - 1] = \mathbf{rc}(j + 7i)$.
  4. For $0 \le z \le 63$:

$$\widehat{A}[0, 0, z] = \widehat{A}[0, 0, z] \oplus RC_i[z]. \tag{6}$$

The round function of SHA-3 is defined to be $\iota(\chi(\pi(\rho(\theta(A)))), i)$, where i is the round index $(0 \le i \le 23)$. The state transformation function $\mathbf{F}$ of SHA-3 is an iteration of the round function 24 times with the round index i from 0 to 23 sequentially, defined as $A = \iota(\chi(\pi(\rho(\theta(A)))), i)$ for $i = 0$ to 23.

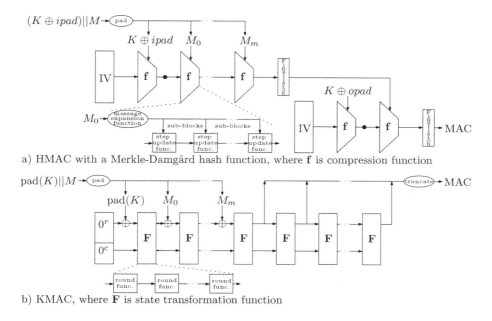

a) HMAC with a Merkle-Damgård hash function, where **f** is compression function

b) KMAC, where **F** is state transformation function

Fig. 2. General structures of KMAC and HMAC

2.4   The KMAC Message Authentication Code

The KMAC [27] message authentication code was released in 2016, which is actually a keyed SHA-3. KMAC is defined as $\mathrm{KMAC}(K, M) = \mathbf{H}(\mathrm{pad}(K)\|M)$, where $\mathbf{H}$ is a member of the Keccak hash family, and K is a 128- or 256-bit user key. That is, the padded key together with the original message is treated as the input message in Keccak, with the first r-bit message block being the padded key.

3   Distinctions Between White-Box Implementations of KMAC and HMAC

In this section, we discuss two main distinctions between white-box implementations of KMAC and HMAC. Figure 2 illustrates general structures of KMAC and HMAC (instantiated with a Merkle-Damgård hash function). Although functioning differently, structurally speaking at a high level, the compression function in the Merkle-Damgård construction method is similar to the state transformation function in the sponge construction method, and the step update function in a Merkle-Damgård hash function like SHA-1/2 is similar to the round function in a sponge hash function like SHA-3, but they make a huge difference to white-box implementations of KAMC and HMAC:

1. The core of the Merkle-Damgård construction method is a one-way compression function which maps from a domain to a range that is smaller than the

domain. The core of the sponge construction method is a state transformation function which maps from a domain to a range that is equal to the domain, which is usually a permutation like that used in SHA-3. In other words, the compression function of a Merkle-Damgård hash function is irreversible, while the state transformation function of a sponge hash function is usually bijective and thus reversible.

As a consequence, if only key extraction attack is concerned, there is a very simple and efficient white-box implementation for HMAC-SHA-1/2, as described or mentioned in [15,17,19], that is, computing the two internal states immediately after the processes of the two key blocks and then releasing them as starting values for white-box HMAC implementation. It is feasible because the two key blocks are the first blocks of the two different hash computations. This simple white-box implementation reaches the full security against key extraction attack as long as the underlying hash function is one-way, since none can reverse the two released initial values to extract the keys under a one-way function.

However, the simple white-box implementation of HMAC-SHA-1/2 does not apply to KMAC at all, since the release of an internal state of KMAC would enable one to extract the key easily, by reversing the state transformation function $\mathbf{F}$, as $\mathbf{F}$ is a permutation. That indicates that a white-box KMAC implementation should protect the internal states even it aims to resist only key extraction attack, which makes it very close to a white-box KMAC protection against both key extraction and code lifting attacks, with slight extra cost to protect against code lifting.

2. A Merkle-Damgård hash function usually involves a message expansion function, which first divides a message block into a number of smaller sub-blocks, then extends the sub-blocks into a larger number of sub-blocks of the same length as the original sub-blocks preferably in a non-linear manner like SHA-2, and finally processes the original and extended sub-blocks with a compression function that usually consists of an iteration of a step update function, with each step processing a sub-block. However, a sponge hash function like SHA-3 does not involve a message expansion function, and a message block is input once as a whole at the beginning of a state update function.

As a consequence, to design a general white-box implementation against both key extraction and code lifting attacks under one message block, we cannot iteratively use a white-box implementation of the step update function to process the message sub-blocks for a Merkle-Damgård hash function, due to the generally different protection effects on the message sub-blocks, unless forcing them to be protected with the same white-box protections at the sacrifice of generality. However, the round function of KMAC takes only an earlier internal state and some fixed constants as input, without message or key, and as a result we may be able to somehow use iteratively a white-box implementation of the round function for KMAC within the 24-round process of a message block.

Code lifting attacks require us to protect the correspondence between message and digest (i.e. hash value), so that an attacker cannot produce a correct (original message, original digest) pair which the white-box implementation does not produce before, but the problem that an attacker can produce a correct (protected message, protected digest) pair from a white-box implementation does not belong to this area.

4   White-Box Implementation Schema of KMAC

In this section, we describe our white-box implementation method of KMAC to prevent key extraction and code lifting attacks to some extent. We use 64×64-bit mixing bijections and 4-bit encodings generally. A mixing bijection is generally a linear or affine bijective transformation to provide diffusion property, with the linear form being usually a matrix multiplication [11] and the affine form being usually a matrix multiplication followed by an XOR with a constant [12]; and an (external) encoding [11,12] is generally a non-linear bijective transformation to provide confusion property, with the most being used form being an substitution table.

4.1   Implementation Method

Our white-box KMAC implementation merges a few adjacent operations of the round function and uses an iterative process at a few phases of KMAC to efficiently generate a variable-length digest on a message with an arbitrary length, as follows.

1. To deal with the variable length of an arbitrary message, we use an iterative manner to process the 1088-bit message block(s) of a message; specifically, the white-box implementation output of the **F** function of a message block should be of the same format as the white-box implementation output of the **F** function of the previous message block (if any), so that it can be iterated for different 1088-bit message blocks.
2. Within the process of a 1088-bit message block, the round function of **F** only takes the previous internal state as input, plus a round constant. We use another iterative process to process the 24 rounds of the **F** function, and most of the five operations of the round function can be iteratively reused in different rounds, except that the operations with the round constants are dedicated respectively to the rounds.
3. We deal with a variable-length digest of more than one blocks long, and iterate the while-box implementation for a message block in the squeezing phase. The white-box implementation of the **F** function for producing a digest is an iteration of the white-box implementation of the **F** function for processing a message block, with message input operation being removed, using the same set of white-box protections for both the input and output of the **F** function of a message block. Thus, there is no message input in the squeezing phase, and we can reuse the white-box implementation in the absorbing phase.

4. The white-box KMAC implementation treats a 64-bit lane (that is, $A[x, y] = (A[x, y, 0]|| \ A[x, y, 1]||| \cdots ||A[x, y, 63]))$ as the basic unit, and treats all the five elementary operations of the round function as some operations on 64-bit lanes. More specifically:

   - $C[(x+1) \bmod 5, (z-1) \bmod 64]$ of Eq. (2) is equivalent to $C[(x+1) \bmod 5] \lll 1$, where $C[(x + 1) \bmod 5] = (C[(x + 1) \bmod 5, 0]||C[(x + 1) \bmod 5, 1]||| \cdots ||C[(x + 1) \bmod 5, 63])$.
   - $A[x, y, (z - \frac{(t+1) \times (t+2)}{2}) \bmod 64]$ of Eq. (3) is equivalent to $A[x, y] \lll (\frac{(t+1) \times (t+2)}{2} \bmod 64)$.
   - $\widehat{A}[x, y, z] = A[(x + 3y) \bmod 5, x, z]$ of Eq. (4) is equivalent to a reordering of the positions of the 64-bit lanes $A[x, y]$. Thus, the operation π can be combined together with the previous operation ρ.
   - The operation $(A[(x+1) \bmod 5, y, z] \oplus 1) \times A[(x+2) \bmod 5, y, z]$ of Eq. (5) is equivalent to $(\neg A[(x+1) \bmod 5, y, z]) \& A[(x+2) \bmod 5, y, z]$; or simply $(\neg A[(x + 1) \bmod 5, y]) \& A[(x + 2) \bmod 5, y]$ on two 64-bit lanes.
   - All other operations like the $\oplus$ operation in Eq. (1) are relatively simple when implemented on 64-bit lanes.

   Thus, white-box KMAC involves only bitwise operations on 64-bit words.

5. We merge a few adjacent operations of the round function in the white-box KMAC implementation, as follows.

   - White-box implementation of the equivalent $C[(x + 1) \bmod 5] \lll 1$ of $C[(x + 1) \bmod 5, (z - 1) \bmod 64]$ in Eq. (2) is merged into the white-box XOR operation in Eq. (2), where $C[(x + 1) \bmod 5] = (C[(x + 1) \bmod 5, 0]||C[(x + 1) \bmod 5, 1]||| \cdots ||C[(x + 1) \bmod 5, 63])$. That is, our white-box implementation of $D[x] = C[(x-1) \bmod 5] \oplus (C[(x+1) \bmod 5] \lll 1)$ is implemented by incorporating the $\lll 1$ operation inside the white-box XOR operation.
   - The ρ and π operations are merged with Step 3 of θ. Specifically, let $(A[x, y], D[x])$ and $\widehat{A}[x, y]$ denote respectively the input and output for the merged operation $(\theta : \text{Step 3}) \circ \rho \circ \pi$, since $A[x, y, (z - \frac{(t+1) \times (t+2)}{2}) \bmod 64]$ of Eq. (3) is equivalent to $A[x, y] \lll (\frac{(t+1) \times (t+2)}{2} \bmod 64)$, then the output $\widehat{A}[x, y]$ is $\widehat{A}[0, 0] = A[0, 0] \oplus D[0]$ if $(x, y) = (0, 0)$, and is $\widehat{A}[x, y] = (A^{((x+3y) \bmod 5, x)} \lll (\frac{(t+1) \times (t+2)}{2} \bmod 64)) \oplus (D[(x + 3y) \bmod 5] \lll (\frac{(t+1) \times (t+2)}{2} \bmod 64))$ if $(x, y) \neq (0, 0)$, where both the $\lll (\frac{(t+1) \times (t+2)}{2} \bmod 64)$ operations are incorporated inside the white-box XOR operation, and t is determined under $((x + 3y) \bmod 5, x)$ in Eq. (3).
   - The ι operation is merged with the χ operation. Specifically, let $(A^{(x,y)}, A^{(x+1 \bmod 5, y)}, A^{(x+2 \bmod 5, y)})$ and $\widehat{A}[x, y]$ denote respectively the input and output for the merged operation $\chi \circ \iota$, then the output $\widehat{A}[x, y]$ is $\widehat{A}[x, y] = A^{(x,y)} \oplus (A^{(x+1 \bmod 5, y)} \oplus A^{(x+2 \bmod 5, y)})$ if $(x, y) \neq (0, 0)$, and is $\widehat{A}[0, 0] = (A^{(0,0)} \oplus (A^{(1,0)} \oplus A^{(2,0)})) \oplus RC_i$ if $(x, y) = (0, 0)$, where RC_i is the 64-bit constant used in the i-th round and is incorporated inside the white-box implementation of the outer XOR operation.

As a result, our white-box KMAC implementation involves the following five operations: $X \oplus Y$, $X \oplus (Y \lll \alpha)$, $(X \lll \alpha) \oplus (Y \lll \alpha)$, $X \oplus Y \oplus RC_i$ and $(\neg X)\&Y$, which can be summarised as the following three basic operations: $(X \lll \alpha) \oplus (Y \lll \beta)$, $X \oplus Y \oplus RC_i$ and $(\neg X)\&Y$, where X and Y are 64-bit variables and $0 \leq \alpha, \beta < 64$.

4.2 Protecting Message Against Code Lifting

To protect a 1088-bit message block M_l against code lifting to some extent ($l \geqslant 0$), the server generates its white-box form in the following way.

1. Generate a group of 17 64×64-bit mixing bijections $\mathbf{MB}_0 = \{\mathbf{MB}_0^{(x,y)} | 0 \leq x \leq 4, 0 \leq y < 4\}$. (Note that here $0 \leq y < 4$, since a message block M_l is only 1088 bits long.)
2. Generate a group of 272 4-bit (external) encodings $\mathbf{e}_{0,0-15} = \{\mathbf{e}_{0,j}^{(x,y)} | 0 \leq x \leq 4, 0 \leq y < 4, 0 \leq j \leq 15\}$.
3. The white-box form of M_l is $\mathbf{e}_{0,0-15}(\mathbf{MB}_0(M_l))$.

4.3 Protecting Key Against Key Extraction

To protect against key extraction to some extent, the server computes $\mathbf{F}(\text{pad}(K)||0^c)$ and then generates its white-box form in the following way.

1. Generate a group of 25 64×64-bit mixing bijections $\mathbf{MB}_1 = \{\mathbf{MB}_1^{(x,y)} | 0 \leq x \leq 4, 0 \leq y \leq 4\}$.
2. Generate a group of 400 4-bit encodings $\mathbf{e}_{1,0-15} = \{\mathbf{e}_{1,j}^{(x,y)} | 0 \leq x \leq 4, 0 \leq y \leq 4, 0 \leq j \leq 15\}$.
3. Compute $\mathbf{e}_{1,0-15}(\mathbf{MB}_1(\mathbf{F}(\text{pad}(K)||0^c)))$, and release it to the client.

5 White-Box Implementations of Basic Operations of KMAC

In this section, we describe our white-box implementations of the three basic operations $(X \lll \alpha) \oplus (Y \lll \beta)$, $X \oplus Y \oplus RC_i$ and $(\neg X)\&Y$, where X and Y are respectively protected in their white-box forms $\mathbf{e}_{0-15}^X(\mathbf{MB}^X(X))$ and $\mathbf{e}_{0-15}^Y(\mathbf{MB}^Y(Y))$, with $\mathbf{MB}^X$ and $\mathbf{MB}^Y$ being 64×64-bit mixing bijections, and $\mathbf{e}_{0-15}^X$ and $\mathbf{e}_{0-15}^Y$ being two groups of sixteen 4-bit encodings. In particular, we do not need to make a white-box implementation of the $\lll$ operation.

5.1 White-Box Implementation of $(X \lll \alpha) \oplus (Y \lll \beta)$

The outputs of the XOR and rotation operations are uniformly distributed (under all possible inputs), and thus we use a general mixing bijection to protect them. Besides, matrix multiplication operation is distributive over XOR, and the rotation operation is right-distributive over XOR, more specifically, suppose

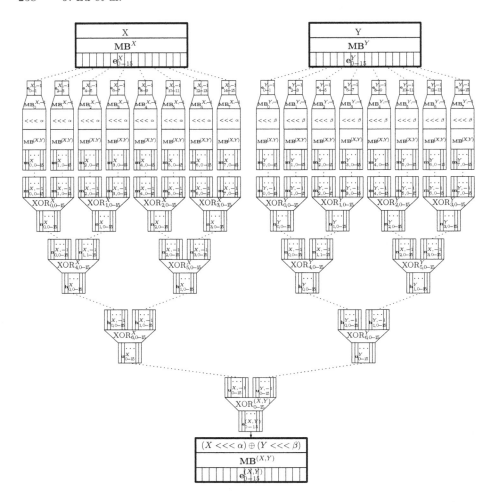

Fig. 3. White-box implementation of $(X \lll \alpha) \oplus (Y \lll \beta)$ in 8-bit tables

$X = X_0 \oplus X_1 \oplus \cdots \oplus X_7$ (with $X_0, X_1, \cdots, X_7$ being 32-bit variables), then $X \lll \alpha = (X_0 \lll \alpha) \oplus (X_1 \lll \alpha) \oplus \cdots \oplus (X_7 \lll \alpha)$.

Illustrated in Fig. 3, our white-box implementation of $(X \lll \alpha) \oplus (Y \lll \beta)$ consists of the following three layers at a high level:

- The first layer is made up of sixteen 8×64-bit tables. For the part processing $\mathbf{e}_{0-15}^X(\mathbf{MB}^X(X))$, each 8×64-bit table is generated by applying sequentially the inverses $\mathbf{e}_{2j-(2j+1)}^{X,-1}$ of the two 4-bit encodings $\mathbf{e}_{2j-(2j+1)}^X$, the corresponding 64×8-bit part $\mathbf{MB}_j^{X,-1}$ of the inverse $\mathbf{MB}^{X,-1}$ of the mixing bijection $\mathbf{MB}^X$, the $\lll \alpha$ operation, a general 64×64-bit mixing bijection $\mathbf{MB}^{(X,Y)}$ used to protect the result $X \oplus Y$, and a layer of sixteen 4-bit

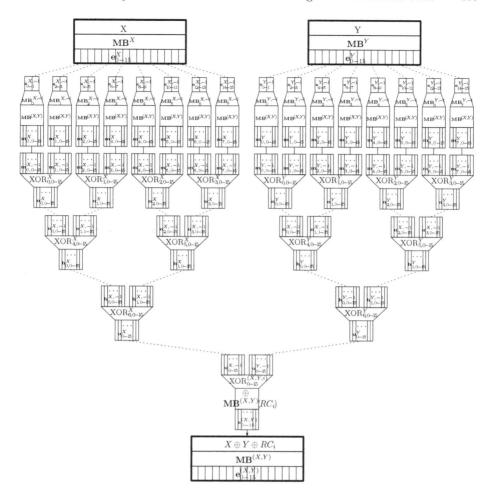

Fig. 4. White-box implementation of $X \oplus Y \oplus RC_i$ in 8-bit tables

encodings $\mathbf{m}^X_{j,0-15}$, where $\mathbf{MB}^{X,-1} = (\mathbf{MB}^{X,-1}_0, \mathbf{MB}^{X,-1}_1, \cdots, \mathbf{MB}^{X,-1}_7)$, and $j = 0, 1, \cdots, 7$. Similarly for the part processing $\mathbf{e}^Y_{0-15}(\mathbf{MB}^Y(Y))$, where we apply the $\lll \beta$ operation instead of the $\lll \alpha$ operation.

- The second layer is made up of 224 8×4-bit tables $\mathrm{XOR}^X_{j,l}$ and $\mathrm{XOR}^Y_{j,l}$. The final output of the $\mathrm{XOR}^X_{j,l}$ tables is X protected by the mixing bijection $\mathbf{MB}^{(X,Y)}$ and a layer of sixteen 4-bit encodings $\mathbf{u}^X_{0-15}$; and the final output of the $\mathrm{XOR}^Y_{j,l}$ tables is Y protected by the mixing bijection $\mathbf{MB}^{(X,Y)}$ and a layer of sixteen 4-bit encodings $\mathbf{u}^Y_{0-15}$, where $j = 0, 1, \cdots, 6, l = 0, 1, \cdots, 15$. (To generate each $\mathrm{XOR}^X_{j,l}$ or $\mathrm{XOR}^Y_{j,l}$, we apply the inverse of the corresponding

4-bit encoding from the previous operation for either 4-bit input, and apply a 4-bit encoding to protect the 4-bit output of the XOR operation.)

– The last (i.e. third) layer is made up of sixteen 8×4-bit tables $XOR_l^{(X,Y)}$, with the result $X \oplus Y$ being protected finally by the mixing bijection $\mathbf{MB}^{(X,Y)}$ and a layer of sixteen 4-bit encodings $\mathbf{e}_{0-15}^{(X,Y)}$, where $l = 0, 1, \cdots, 15$.

The $\lll \alpha$ (or β) operation is null when α (respectively, β) is 0. The white-box $(X \lll \alpha) \oplus (Y \lll \beta)$ implementation becomes white-box $X \oplus Y$ implementation when $\alpha = \beta = 0$, and becomes white-box $X \oplus (Y \lll \beta)$ implementation when $\alpha = 0$. Note that as mentioned in Sect. 4.1 there exist only the cases $X \oplus (Y \lll 1)$ and $(X \oplus Y) \lll (\frac{(t+1) \cdot (t+2)}{2} \mod 64)$ in KMAC, which correspond to Eq. (2) and the combinations of Eq. (3) with Step 3 of θ.

5.2   White-Box Implementation of $X \oplus Y \oplus RC_i$

Illustrated in Fig. 4, our white-box implementation of $X \oplus Y \oplus RC_i$ is obtained by slightly modifying the above white-box $(X \lll \alpha) \oplus (Y \lll \beta)$ implementation:

– Remove the $\lll \alpha$ and $\lll \beta$ operations in the first layer.
– For each of the sixteen 8×4-bit $XOR_l^{(X,Y)}$ tables in the last (i.e., third) layer of the white-box $X \oplus Y$ implementation, we apply the XOR operation with the corresponding 4-bit part of $\mathbf{MB}^{(X,Y)}(RC_i)$ immediately before applying the layer of sixteen 4-bit encodings $\mathbf{e}_{0-15}^{(X,Y)}$.

Note that each of the 24 rounds has a different set of the sixteen 16×8-bit tables $XOR_{0-15}^{(X,Y)}$ tables, which cannot be reused in the iterative process of the white-box KMAC implementation.

5.3   White-Box Implementation of $(\neg X)\&Y$

The outputs of the AND operation are not uniformly distributed, with the most frequent being zero, which remains zero if multiplying with a linear mixing bijection, and thus we use an affine mixing bijection to protect them with additional security. The NOT operation is not distributive over XOR, that is, $\neg X \neq (\neg X_0) \oplus (\neg X_1) \oplus \cdots \oplus (\neg X_7)$, where $X = X_0 \oplus X_1 \oplus \cdots \oplus X_7$. Matrix multiplication operation is not distributive over AND. Thus, white-box implementation of $(\neg X)\&Y$ cannot similarly adopt the above white-box $(X \lll \alpha) \oplus (Y \lll \beta)$ implementation.

Illustrated in Fig. 5, our white-box implementation of $(\neg X)\&Y$ consists of the following four layers at a high level:

– The first layer is made up of sixteen 8×64-bit tables. For the part processing $\mathbf{e}_{0-15}^X(\mathbf{MB}^X(X))$, each 8×64-bit table is generated by applying sequentially the inverses $\mathbf{e}_{2j-(2j+1)}^{X,-1}$ of the two 4-bit encodings $\mathbf{e}_{2j-(2j+1)}^X$, the corresponding 64×8-bit part $\mathbf{MB}_j^{X,-1}$ of the inverse $\mathbf{MB}^{X,-1}$ of the mixing bijection

$\mathbf{MB}^X$, a 64×64-bit mixing bijection $\mathbf{DB}^X$ and a layer of sixteen 4-bit encodings $\mathbf{m}_{j,0-15}^X$, where $\mathbf{DB}^X$ is of the form

$$
\begin{pmatrix}
\mathbf{DB}_0^X & 0 & 0 & 0 & 0 & 0 & 0 & 0 \\
0 & \mathbf{DB}_1^X & 0 & 0 & 0 & 0 & 0 & 0 \\
0 & 0 & \mathbf{DB}_2^X & 0 & 0 & 0 & 0 & 0 \\
0 & 0 & 0 & \mathbf{DB}_3^X & 0 & 0 & 0 & 0 \\
0 & 0 & 0 & 0 & \mathbf{DB}_4^X & 0 & 0 & 0 \\
0 & 0 & 0 & 0 & 0 & \mathbf{DB}_5^X & 0 & 0 \\
0 & 0 & 0 & 0 & 0 & 0 & \mathbf{DB}_6^X & 0 \\
0 & 0 & 0 & 0 & 0 & 0 & 0 & \mathbf{DB}_7^X
\end{pmatrix},
$$

with $\mathbf{DB}_j^X$ being an invertible (general) 8×8-bit matrix, $\mathbf{MB}^{X,-1} = (\mathbf{MB}_0^{X,-1}, \mathbf{MB}_1^{X,-1}, \cdots, \mathbf{MB}_7^{X,-1})$, and $j = 0, 1, \cdots, 7$. Similarly for the part processing $\mathbf{e}_{0-15}^Y(\mathbf{MB}^Y(Y))$.

- The second layer is made up of 224 8×4-bit tables $\mathrm{XOR}_{j,l}^X$ and $\mathrm{XOR}_{j,l}^Y$. The final output of the $\mathrm{XOR}_{j,l}^X$ tables is X protected by the mixing bijection $\mathbf{DB}^X$ and a layer of sixteen 4-bit encodings $\mathbf{u}_{0-15}^X$; and the final output of the $\mathrm{XOR}_{j,l}^Y$ tables is Y protected by the mixing bijection $\mathbf{DB}^Y$ and a layer of sixteen 4-bit encodings $\mathbf{u}_{0-15}^Y$, where $j = 0, 1, \cdots, 6, l = 0, 1, \cdots, 15$.

- The third layer is made up of eight 16×64-bit tables $\mathrm{AND}_l^{(X,Y)}$, each of which is generated by applying sequentially the inverses of the two corresponding 4-bit encodings from the second layer, the inverse $\mathbf{DB}_l^{X,-1}$ (or $\mathbf{DB}_l^{Y,-1}$, respectively) of the corresponding 8×8-bit part $\mathbf{DB}_l^X$ (or $\mathbf{DB}_l^Y$, respectively) of the mixing bijection $\mathbf{DB}^X$ (or $\mathbf{DB}^Y$, respectively) for either 8-bit input, the bitwise complement ($\neg$) operation only for the 8-bit input from X, the AND value of the two resulting 8-bit values, the corresponding 64×8-bit part $\mathbf{AB}_l^{(X,Y)}$ out of an affine mixing bijection $\mathbf{AB}^{(X,Y)}$ used to protect the result $(\neg X)\&Y$, and a layer of sixteen 4-bit encodings $\mathbf{v}_{l,0-15}^{(X,Y)}$, where $\mathbf{AB}^{(X,Y)}(\cdot) = (\mathbf{AB}_0^{(X,Y)}, \mathbf{AB}_1^{(X,Y)}, \cdots, \mathbf{AB}_7^{(X,Y)})(\cdot) = \mathbf{MB}^{(X,Y)}(\cdot) \oplus \mathbf{b} = (\mathbf{MB}_0^{(X,Y)}, \mathbf{MB}_1^{(X,Y)}, \cdots, \mathbf{MB}_7^{(X,Y)})(\cdot) \oplus \mathbf{b}$, and $\mathbf{AB}_l^{(X,Y)}(\cdot) = \mathbf{MB}_l^{(X,Y)}(\cdot) \oplus \mathbf{b}_l$, with $\mathbf{MB}^{(X,Y)}$ being an invertible (general) 64×64-bit matrix and $\mathbf{b}_l$ and $\mathbf{b} = \sum_{l=0}^7 \mathbf{b}_l$ being 64-bit constants ($l = 0, 1, \cdots, 7$).

- The last (i.e. fourth) layer is made up of 112 8×4-bit tables $\mathrm{XOR}_{j,l}^{(X,Y)}$, with the result $(\neg X)\&Y$ being protected finally by the affine mixing bijection $\mathbf{AB}^{(X,Y)}$ and a layer of sixteen 4-bit encodings $\mathbf{e}_{0-15}^{(X,Y)}$, where $j = 0, 1, \cdots, 6, l = 0, 1, \cdots, 15$.

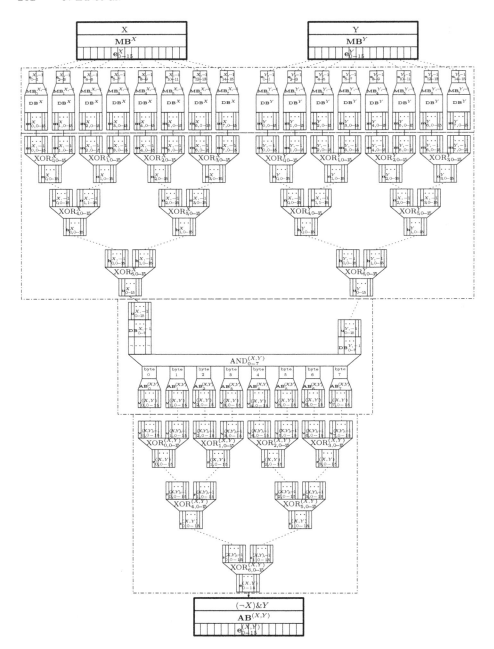

Fig. 5. White-box implementation of $(\neg X)\&Y$ in 8-bit and 16-bit tables

6 An Efficient White-Box KMAC Implementation

In this section, we first build white-box implementations of the components of the KMAC round function with the basic white-box operations of Sect. 5, and finally present an efficient white-box implementation of KMAC. Figure 6 illustrates a high-level overview of the white-box KMAC implementation.

6.1 White-Box Implementation of Steps 1 and 2 of θ

Illustrated in Fig. 6, white-box implementation of Step 1 of θ can be composed with $5 \times 4 = 20$ applications of the white-box $X \oplus Y$ implementation, and white-box implementation of Step 2 of θ can be composed with 5 applications of the white-box $X \oplus (Y \lll 1)$ implementation.

6.2 White-Box Implementation of $(\theta : \text{Step } 3) \circ \rho \circ \pi$

Illustrated in Fig. 6, white-box implementation of $(\theta : \text{Step } 3) \circ \rho \circ \pi$ can be composed with 1 application of the white-box $X \oplus Y$ implementation and 24 applications of the white-box $(X \lll (\frac{(t+1)\times(t+2)}{2} \mod 64)) \oplus (Y \lll (\frac{(t+1)\times(t+2)}{2} \mod 64))$ implementation.

6.3 White-Box Implementation of $\chi \circ \iota$

Illustrated in Fig. 6, white-box implementation of $\chi \circ \iota$ can be composed with 25 applications of the white-box $(\neg X)\&Y$ implementation, 24 applications of the white-box $X \oplus Y$ implementation and 1 application of the white-box $X \oplus Y \oplus RC_i$ implementation. As mentioned earlier, the set of the sixteen 8×4-bit tables $\text{XOR}_{0-15}^{(X,Y)}$ tables in the white-box $X \oplus Y \oplus RC_i$ implementation of Fig. 4 is different from round to round.

6.4 White-Box KMAC

As a result, a white-box implementation of the state transformation function $\mathbf{F}$ of KMAC can be readily built from the above white-box implementation of the round function, as shown in Fig. 6. All the white-box operations except the 8×4-bit tables $\text{XOR}_{0-15}^{X,Y,i}$ tables of the white-box $X \oplus Y \oplus RC_i$ implementation of Fig. 4 can be reused in the iterative process of the 24 rounds.

The starting $A^{(x,y)}$ for the white-box KMAC lies in the input message XOR part of Fig. 6, whose inputs are $\mathbf{e}_{1,0-15}(\mathbf{MB}_1(\mathbf{F}(\text{pad}(K)\|0^c)))$ and $\mathbf{e}_{0,0-15}(\mathbf{MB}_0(M_l))$. Since $r = 1088$, there are 17 applications of the white-box $X \oplus Y$ implementation in the XOR with a message block in the absorbing phase. At last, after receiving $\mathbf{e}_{1,0-15}(\mathbf{MB}_1(\mathbf{F}(\text{pad}(K)\|0^c)))$ and $\mathbf{e}_{0,0-15}(\mathbf{MB}_0(M_l))$ from the server ($l = 0, 1, \cdots$), the client can run the white-box KMAC implementation to produce a protected digest, while there is no input message operation in the squeezing phase.

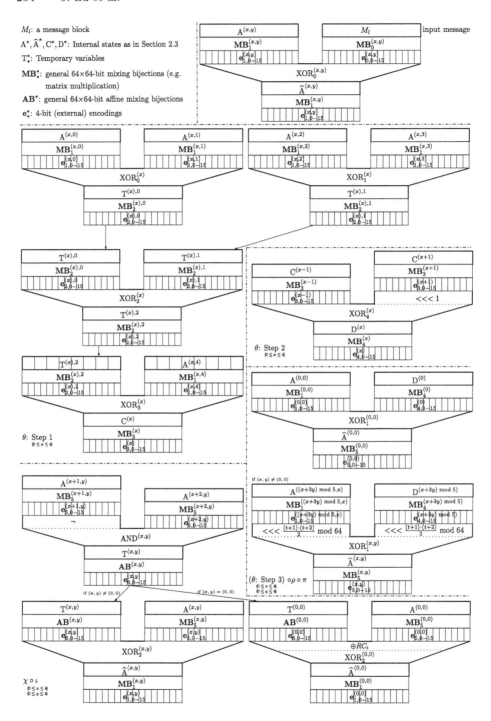

Fig. 6. An overview of the white-box KMAC implementation

Note that this white-box KMAC implementation also works when the user key is updated, that is, the same set of white-box tables can be reused for different user keys, as long as the server releases the corresponding protected form of the new key to the client. Thus, the server does not need to generate another set of white-box tables every time a user key is updated, which reduces computational and communication complexity. Of course, it is better to limit the maximum number of keys used under a set of white-box tables, to avoid a security loss in this situation.

7   Security Analysis

By [21,33], the number of invertible 64×64-bit matrices is $\prod_{i=0}^{63}(2^{64}-2^i) \approx 2^{4095}$. The number of 4-bit encodings is $16! \approx 2^{44.25}$. Thus, the white-box tables have a sufficiently large white-box diversity [11] and white-box ambiguity [11] against exhaustive search attacks over the used mixing bijections and encodings.

Our white-box KMAC implementation only involves bitwise XOR, rotation, NOT and AND operations. The outputs of the XOR, rotation and NOT operations are uniformly distributed. Thus, it is impossible to attack the white-box $X \oplus Y$ and $(X \lll \alpha) \oplus Y$ implementations.

However, the outputs of the AND operation are not uniformly distributed. In the basic case of 8-bit AND operation as in our white-box $(\neg X)\&Y$ implementation of Sect. 5.3, the outputs can be divided into nine groups by frequency, which consist of outputs with a Hamming weight from 0 to 8, respectively; the nine groups contain respectively $\binom{8}{0} = 1$, $\binom{8}{1} = 8$, $\binom{8}{2} = 28$, $\binom{8}{3} = 56$, $\binom{8}{4} = 70$, $\binom{8}{5} = 56$, $\binom{8}{6} = 28$, $\binom{8}{7} = 8$ and $\binom{8}{8} = 1$ values, and a simple analysis shows that each value in the nine groups takes place 6561, 2187, 729, 243, 81, 27, 9, 3 and 1 times, respectively. Thus, the nine groups have respectively a total frequency of $1 \times \frac{6561}{2^{16}} \approx 2^{-3.32}$, $8 \times \frac{2187}{2^{16}} \approx 2^{-1.91}$, $28 \times \frac{729}{2^{16}} \approx 2^{-3.68}$, $56 \times \frac{243}{2^{16}} \approx 2^{-2.27}$, $70 \times \frac{81}{2^{16}} \approx 2^{-3.53}$, $56 \times \frac{27}{2^{16}} \approx 2^{-5.44}$, $28 \times \frac{9}{2^{16}} \approx 2^{-10.02}$, $8 \times \frac{3}{2^{16}} \approx 2^{-11.42}$ and $1 \times \frac{1}{2^{16}} = 2^{-16}$. For each white-box $\mathrm{AND}_l^{(X,Y)}$ table, since 0 is the most frequent output with 6561 times and 255 is the least frequent output with only 1 time, the two cases can be easily distinguished; and the other seven groups can also be easily distinguished, but there is no way to further distinguish the specific values in each of the seven groups. The (1600-bit) **F** state immediately after the AND operations is made up of the outputs of $5 \times 5 \times 8 = 200$ $\mathrm{AND}_l^{(X,Y)}$ tables, so it is expected that there is a probability of $(2^{-3.32})^{200} = 2^{-664}$ to have an original full state of 1600 zeros, and it is dramatically smaller for any other specific output; at a group level, the second group produces the largest probability of $(2^{-1.91})^{200} = 2^{-382}$ to have an original full state, but it produces $8^{200} = 2^{600}$ indistinguishable possible values in this case. Therefore, it is not possible to recover the full 1600-bit **F** state, not to mention recovering the previous 1600-bit state and the initial state of the protected key described in Sect. 4.3. (This is somewhat similar to that the preimage security of the sponge construction is still secure while r bits are output in each round in black-box domain.) On the other hand, we next consider the security of recovering the white-box protection operations for either input in each $\text{AND}_l^{(X,Y)}$ table. Since the two output cases of 0 and 255 can be easily distinguished, one can deduce the cases of 0 and 255 for either input operand by the fact that the AND output of 0 with any value is always zero and the AND outputs of 255 with all 256 values are different one another, and one may divide the inputs into several groups by the output groups, however, it is not possible to further distinguish the specific values in each input group. The white-box protection is only a layer of two 4-bit encodings for the input 0 and is a layer of 8-bit mixing bijection and a layer of two 4-bit encodings for every other nonzero input; considering that the white-box protected outputs for the two cases of 0 and 255 are known from above, the layers of mixing bijection and two 4-bit encodings produce at least a diversity of $\prod_{i=0}^{7}(2^8 - 2^i) \times (14!)^2 \approx 2^{144.89}$ for either input operand, still large enough.

KMAC does not involve algebraic operations like the MixColumns operation of the AES block cipher. Thus, such algebraic white-box attacks like BGE attacks [6, 18] do not apply in the white-box KMAC implementation.

In summary, although the AND operation is not friendly in white-box domain, our white-box KMAC implementation should be sufficiently practically secure against key extraction and code lifting attacks.

8 Performance Evaluation

There are various lengths of messages, and here we evaluate the basic case with only one 1088-bit message block.

8.1 Storage and Time Complexity

The white-box $X \oplus Y$ implementation from Fig. 3 has $16 + 15 \times 16 = 256$ look-up tables, and requires $16 \cdot 2^8 \cdot 64 + 15 \cdot 16 \cdot 2^8 \cdot 4 = 31 \cdot 2^{14}$ bits of storage. Same for the $X \oplus (Y \lll 1)$ implementation from Fig. 3, the $(X \lll (\frac{(t+1)\cdot(t+2)}{2} \bmod 64)) \oplus (Y \lll (\frac{(t+1)\cdot(t+2)}{2} \bmod 64))$ implementation from Fig. 3 and the $X \oplus Y \oplus RC_i$ implementation of Fig. 4.

The white-box $(\neg X)\&Y$ implementation of Fig. 5 has $16 + 224 + 8 + 112 = 360$ look-up tables, and $16 \cdot 2^8 \cdot 64 + 224 \cdot 2^8 \cdot 4 + 8 \cdot 2^{16} \cdot 64 + 112 \cdot 2^8 \cdot 4 = 2085 \cdot 2^{14}$ bits of storage.

In total, the white-box implementation of one round has $20 + 1 + 24 = 45$ applications of the white-box $X \oplus Y$ implementation, 5 applications of the white-box $X \oplus (Y \lll 1)$ implementation, 24 applications of the white-box $(X \lll (\frac{(t+1)\cdot(t+2)}{2} \bmod 64)) \oplus (Y \lll (\frac{(t+1)\cdot(t+2)}{2} \bmod 64))$ implementation, 1 application of the white-box $X \oplus Y \oplus RC_i$ implementation and 25 applications of the white-box $(\neg X)\&Y$ implementation.

The white-box $X \oplus Y \oplus RC_i$ implementation in each of the 23 rounds after the first round has 16 8×4-bit XOR tables different from the white-box $X \oplus Y \oplus RC_0$ implementation of the first round.

The input message part has a total of 17 applications of the white-box $X \oplus Y$ implementation. The complexity for the remaining parts are negligible.

Therefore, the white-box KMAC implementation has a total of about $(45 + 5 + 24 + 1) \times 256 + 25 \times 360 + 23 \times 16 + 17 \times 256 = 32920$ look-up tables with a storage complexity of about $(45 + 5 + 24 + 1) \cdot 31 \cdot 2^{14} + 25 \cdot 2085 \cdot 2^{14} + 23 \times 16 \cdot 2^8 \cdot 4 + 17 \cdot 31 \cdot 2^{14} \approx 107.7$ MB. That is, a time complexity of 32920 table look-up operations, (without considering the table sizes).

Note that the storage complexity is independent with message and has nothing to do with message length, as long as message blocks are processed one by one when there are more than one blocks. The storage complexity is dominated by the white-box $(\neg X)\&Y$ tables, particularly the 16×64-bit tables $\text{AND}_l^{(X,Y)}$ tables, and it can be reduced greatly by using 8×64-bit tables $\text{AND}_*^{(X,Y)}$ tables at the expense of a possibly reduced security and a slightly larger number of table look-ups.

8.2   Performance Test

We have implemented the above white-box KMAC implementation, and have tested its performance on a DELL Precision T5610 workstation with Intel Xeon E5-2650 v2 Processor (2.6 GHz, 16 GB memory) and 64-bit Ubuntu 16.04 LTS operation system. We used the **F** function KeccakF1600_ StatePermute() of the Keccak-readable-and-compact.c file from Keccak Code Package (released by Keccak Team) as a benchmark for testing. Performing 100 key-message pairs as a unit, the (plain) **F** function of Keccak Team has a running time of about 0.004 ms (per key-message pair) on average, and the white-box KMAC implementation has a running time of about 1.5 ms, about 375 times slower than the plain **F** function, which is acceptable.

9   Implementation Variants

There are variants with different trade-offs between security and performance. For example, we can use different dimension sizes of mixing bijections, encodings and white-box tables. We can only protect part of a (1600-bit) internal state, leaving the remaining part unprotected.

We can use an unrolled manner to process the 24 rounds of the state transformation function and use an iterative manner to process the squeezing phase that reuses the white-box operations of the 24-th round of the state transformation function, which has a total of about $[(45 + 5 + 24 + 1) \times 256 + 25 \times 360] \times 24 + 17 \times 256 = 681152$ look-up tables with a storage complexity of about $[(45 + 5 + 24 + 1) \times 31 \cdot 2^{14} + 25 \times 2085 \cdot 2^{14}] \times 24 + 17 \times 31 \cdot 2^{14} \approx 2.5$ GB.

10   Concluding Remarks

We have described efficient white-box KMAC implementations with strong resistance against both key extraction and code lifting attacks, which can still work with an updated user key. Our implementation methods can be similarly used to develop white-box implementations for other cryptographic algorithms like variants and extensions (e.g., the duplex construction [5]) of the sponge construction.

Generally speaking, white-box cryptography is more friendly to KMAC than to block ciphers in the sense that it is not compulsory to regenerate a new set of white-box tables when updating a key and it may reach the desired full security against key extraction attacks by releasing the protected form of the hash result on the key as a starting point.

References

1. Banik, S., Bogdanov, A., Isobe, T., Jepsen, M.B.: Analysis of software countermeasures for whitebox encryption. IACR Trans. Symmetric Cryptol. **2017**(1), 307–328 (2017)
2. Bellare, M., Canetti, R., Krawczyk, H.: Keying hash functions for message authentication. In: Koblitz, N. (ed.) CRYPTO 1996. LNCS, vol. 1109, pp. 1–15. Springer, Heidelberg (1996). https://doi.org/10.1007/3-540-68697-5_1
3. Bertoni, G., Daemen, J., Peeters, M., Van Assche, G.: Sponge functions. In: ECRYPT Hash Workshop 2007 (2007)
4. Bertoni, G., Daemen, J., Peeters, M., Van Assche, G.: The Keccak SHA-3 submission. SHA-3 Submission (2011)
5. Bertoni, G., Daemen, J., Peeters, M., Van Assche, G.: Duplexing the sponge: single-pass authenticated encryption and other applications. In: Miri, A., Vaudenay, S. (eds.) SAC 2011. LNCS, vol. 7118, pp. 320–337. Springer, Heidelberg (2012). https://doi.org/10.1007/978-3-642-28496-0_19
6. Billet, O., Gilbert, H., Ech-Chatbi, C.: Cryptanalysis of a white box AES implementation. In: Handschuh, H., Hasan, M.A. (eds.) SAC 2004. LNCS, vol. 3357, pp. 227–240. Springer, Heidelberg (2004). https://doi.org/10.1007/978-3-540-30564-4_16
7. Biryukov, A., Bouillaguet, C., Khovratovich, D.: Cryptographic schemes based on the ASASA structure: black-box, white-box, and public-key. In: Sarkar, P., Iwata, T. (eds.) ASIACRYPT 2014. LNCS, vol. 8873, pp. 63–84. Springer, Heidelberg (2014)
8. Bogdanov, A., Isobe, T.: White-box cryptography revised: space-hard ciphers. In: ACM CCS 2015, pp. 1058–1069. ACM (2015)
9. Bogdanov, A., Isobe, T., Tischhauser, E.: Towards practical whitebox cryptography: optimzing efficiency and space hardness. In: Cheon, J.H., Takagi, T. (eds.) ASIACRYPT 2016. LNCS, vol. 10031, pp. 126–158. Springer, Heidelberg (2016). https://doi.org/10.1007/978-3-662-53887-6_5
10. Bos, J.W., Hubain, C., Michiels, W., Teuwen, P.: Differential computation analysis: hiding your white-box designs is not enough. In: Gierlichs, B., Poschmann, A.Y. (eds.) CHES 2016. LNCS, vol. 9813, pp. 215–236. Springer, Heidelberg (2016). https://doi.org/10.1007/978-3-662-53140-2_11
11. Chow, S., Eisen, P., Johnson, H., Van Oorschot, P.C.: White-box cryptography and an AES implementation. In: Nyberg, K., Heys, H. (eds.) SAC 2002. LNCS, vol. 2595, pp. 250–270. Springer, Heidelberg (2003). https://doi.org/10.1007/3-540-36492-7_17

12. Chow, S., Eisen, P., Johnson, H., Van Oorschot, P.C.: A white-box DES implementation for DRM applications. In: Feigenbaum, J. (ed.) DRM 2002. LNCS, vol. 2696, pp. 1–15. Springer, Heidelberg (2003). https://doi.org/10.1007/978-3-540-44993-5_1

13. Damgård, I.B.: A design principle for hash functions. In: Brassard, G. (ed.) CRYPTO 1989. LNCS, vol. 435, pp. 416–427. Springer, New York (1990). https://doi.org/10.1007/0-387-34805-0_39

14. Fouque, P.-A., Karpman, P., Kirchner, P., Minaud, B.: Efficient and provable white-box primitives. In: Cheon, J.H., Takagi, T. (eds.) ASIACRYPT 2016. LNCS, vol. 10031, pp. 159–188. Springer, Heidelberg (2016). https://doi.org/10.1007/978-3-662-53887-6_6

15. GitHub Website: HMAC-SHA256 Whitebox. Posted online on 12 April 2017. https://github.com/aguinet/hmac_sha256_whitebox

16. Goubin, L., Masereel, J.-M., Quisquater, M.: Cryptanalysis of white box DES implementations. In: Adams, C., Miri, A., Wiener, M. (eds.) SAC 2007. LNCS, vol. 4876, pp. 278–295. Springer, Heidelberg (2007). https://doi.org/10.1007/978-3-540-77360-3_18

17. Kolegov, D., Oleksov, N., Broslavsky, O.: White-box HMAC: make your cryptography secure to white-box attacks, Moscow, Russia, 17–18 May 2016. Video posted online on 20 May 2016. https://www.youtube.com/watch?v=FAiz0_bWaac

18. Lepoint, T., Rivain, M., De Mulder, Y., Roelse, P., Preneel, B.: Two attacks on a white-box AES implementation. In: Lange, T., Lauter, K., Lisoněk, P. (eds.) SAC 2013. LNCS, vol. 8282, pp. 265–285. Springer, Heidelberg (2014). https://doi.org/10.1007/978-3-662-43414-7_14

19. Marián Čečunda: Whitebox cryptography implementation proposals of RSA and HMAC algorithms. Master thesis, Masaryk University, Czech Republic (2014)

20. Merkle, R.C.: Secrecy, authentication, and public key systems. Ph.D. thesis, Stanford University, USA (1979)

21. Muir, J.A.: A tutorial on white-box AES. In: Kranakis, E. (ed.) Advances in Network Analysis and its Applications. Mathematics in Industry, vol. 18, pp. 209–229. Springer, Heidelberg (2013). https://doi.org/10.1007/978-3-642-30904-5_9

22. National Bureau of Standards (NBS): Data Encryption Standard (DES), FIPS-46 (1977)

23. National Institute of Standards and Technology (NIST): Advanced Encryption Standard (AES), FIPS-197 (2001)

24. National Institute of Standards and Technology (NIST): Secure Hash Standard, FIPS-180-1 (1995)

25. National Institute of Standards and Technology (NIST): Specifications for the SECURE HASH STANDARD, FIPS-180-2 (2001)

26. National Institute of Standards and Technology (NIST): SHA-3 Standard: Permutation-Based Hash and Extendable-Output Functions, FIPS-202 (2015)

27. National Institute of Standards and Technology (NIST): SHA-3 Derived Functions: cSHAKE, KMAC, TupleHash and ParallelHash, NIST Special Publication 800–185 (2016)

28. The Internet Engineering Task Force (IETF): The MD5 message-digest algorithm. Request for Comments 1321 (1992)

29. Wang, X., Yu, H.: How to break MD5 and other hash functions. In: Cramer, R. (ed.) EUROCRYPT 2005. LNCS, vol. 3494, pp. 19–35. Springer, Heidelberg (2005). https://doi.org/10.1007/11426639_2

30. Wang, X., Yin, Y.L., Yu, H.: Finding collisions in the Full SHA-1. In: Shoup, V. (ed.) CRYPTO 2005. LNCS, vol. 3621, pp. 17–36. Springer, Heidelberg (2005). https://doi.org/10.1007/11535218_2
31. Wood, G.: Ethereum: A Secure Decentralised Generalised Transaction Ledger. EIP-150 Revision (2017). https://ethereum.github.io/yellowpaper/paper.pdf
32. Wyseur, B., Michiels, W., Gorissen, P., Preneel, B.: Cryptanalysis of white-box DES implementations with arbitrary external encodings. In: Adams, C., Miri, A., Wiener, M. (eds.) SAC 2007. LNCS, vol. 4876, pp. 264–277. Springer, Heidelberg (2007). https://doi.org/10.1007/978-3-540-77360-3_17
33. Xiao, Y., Lai, X.: A secure implementation of white-box AES. In: Proceedings of Second International Conference on Computer Science and its Applications, pp. 1–6. IEEE (2009)

Cryptography II

Improving Signature Schemes with Tight Security Reductions

Tiong-Sik Ng[1]([⊠])[iD], Syh-Yuan Tan[2][iD], and Ji-Jian Chin[3][iD]

[1] Multimedia University, Melaka, Malaysia
`ng.tiong.sik@gmail.com`
[2] Newcastle University, Newcastle upon Tyne, UK
`syh-yuan.tan@newcastle.ac.uk`
[3] Multimedia University, Cyberjaya, Malaysia
`jjchin@mmu.edu.my`

Abstract. In 2003, Katz and Wang proposed the claw-free trapdoor full domain hash (CFT-FDH) which achieves a tight security for FDH signature schemes using the bit selector technique. However, it is noted that the CFT-FDH is not backward compatible with its original FDH counterpart, since the selected bit is hashed with the message, modifying the structure of the original signature. In this paper, we take a step further to propose a general framework that is able to achieve backward compatibility while maintaining the tight reduction of FDH signatures using the properties of trapdoor samplable relations and also Katz-Wang's bit selector technique.

Keywords: Digital signatures · Tight security · Full domain hash · General framework

1 Introduction

After the formalization of provable security by Goldwasser and Micali in 1984 [25], it is said that a cryptographic scheme is secure if mathematical arguments can be used to prove its security. Though a scheme may be proven to be secure, the scheme may not achieve a tight security reduction. As a result, a longer key length is required to compensate for the security loss. Therefore, if the probability of breaking a cryptographic scheme is equivalent to the probability of breaking a mathematical hard problem the scheme is based on, it can be said that the scheme has achieved a tight security reduction.

As an example, the security of the RSA-FDH [14] is expressed as $\varepsilon_{FDH} = (q_s + q_h + 1)\varepsilon_{RSA}$, where ε_{FDH} is the probability of breaking the RSA-FDH, while q_s and q_h represent the sign queries and hash queries a forger can make respectively, and ε_{RSA} is the probability of breaking the RSA [40] problem. By allowing $q_s = 2^{30}$ and $q_h = 2^{60}$ for a 128-bit security, the actual security of the RSA FDH is only 68-bit: $(2^{60})2^{-128} = 2^{-68}$. Since the security reduction is not tight, a longer public key length ($|\mathbb{N}| + |e|$) of 15360 bits is needed for the

© Springer Nature Switzerland AG 2019
S.-H. Heng and J. Lopez (Eds.): ISPEC 2019, LNCS 11879, pp. 273–292, 2019.
https://doi.org/10.1007/978-3-030-34339-2_15

RSA-FDH instead of the originally intended 6144 bits, to achieve the security level of 128 bits.

With that, many new schemes and security reduction techniques have been proposed or improved on to achieve a tight security confidence in security proofs. Techniques particularly revolved around the practical usage of a scheme, since a longer key length would result in extra memory and power consumption.

One particularly significant work is Katz-Wang's [31] framework that tightens the security of FDH signature schemes using the bit selector technique, also known as the Claw-Free Trapdoor FDH (CFT-FDH). In this paper, we improve Katz-Wang's CFT-FDH, which will be further elaborated in the contributions section later on.

1.1   FDH Signatures

Full Domain Hash (FDH) signature schemes are defined with doubly enhanced trapdoor permutations [28]. An example FDH signature scheme would be the RSA-FDH signature scheme that was formalized by Bellare and Rogaway [14]. The signature scheme was designed such that the message is first hashed before being signed with the secret key. However, the scheme was not tightly secure, i.e., the probability of breaking the scheme is not closely related to the probability of breaking the underlying hard problem. Therefore, Coron [17] revisited the security of the RSA-FDH, and managed to tighten the security of the RSA-FDH by removing the factor of q_h.

In the very same work where the RSA-FDH was proposed, Bellare and Rogaway [14] then designed the RSA-PSS scheme. With the generation of a random salt, the tightness of the RSA-PSS is said to be closely related to the RSA problem, where $\varepsilon_{PSS} = \varepsilon_{RSA}$. Some time later, Coron [18] proposed a variant of RSA-PSS, namely, the Probabilistic Full Domain Hash (RSA-PFDH) signature and proved its security with tight reduction by combining the techniques of the RSA-PSS and RSA-FDH. Besides that, Coron stated that 30 bits is the optimal length for the generated random salt in both RSA-PFDH and RSA-PSS, and increasing the number of bits would not increase the security tightness of the scheme.

In 2003, Katz and Wang proposed a framework that tightens the security of FDH type signatures by applying some modifications. By hashing the message with a randomly generated salt, it is said that the FDH signature schemes are tightly secure with the loss of just one bit in the security reduction. Besides that, the randomly generated salt need not be as long as 30 bits as in the RSA-PFDH, as just one bit is necessary to achieve the tightness. The bit selector method by Katz and Wang was applied on the BLS signature [10], an FDH signature which is said to be short in length since it uses properties of Elliptic Curve Cryptography (ECC) which features pairing, by Bellare et al. in [11]. It is shown that Bellare et al.'s BLS variant is able to achieve a tight security reduction similar to Katz-Wang's framework. The instantiations of Katz-Wang's methods on FDH type signatures are roughly described by Katz in [28]. However, since the way of hashing in the CFT-FDH scheme is not the same as that of its original counterpart, the former is not backward compatible to the latter.

In a recent work by Guo et al. [23], a scheme that is similar to a framework to tighten the security of schemes was proposed. The security reduction was particularly focused on but not limited to just the BLS. In their proposed scheme, Guo et al. used the technique of hashing the message with a signed message. In addition to that, the hash-and-sign process was done for a total of three blocks, similar to the structure of a block-chain. Guo et al. came up with a security reduction that results in a loss of at most $2q_h^{\frac{1}{2}}$ for the applicable schemes. However, it is admitted that the scheme is lacking in efficiency in comparison to the original BLS signature considering the number of blocks for the signature. It is noted that the scheme is not backward compatible as well as each block of the signature has a rather similar structure to Katz-Wang's CFT-FDH.

1.2   Our Contributions

In this paper, we propose a general framework to tighten the security of FDH signature schemes. We would like to highlight that the tightened signature schemes are backward compatible to their original scheme, solving the issue of Katz and Wang's Claw-Free Trapdoor FDH (CFT-FDH) [31] signature scheme. By backward compatibility, it means that the signature from the original non-tight schemes can be verified using the verification algorithm of our proposed framework. We will further elaborate the backward compatibility of our framework in a later section.

In 2009, Coron [19] proposed a tightly secure IBE scheme which is backward compatible to the original Boneh-Franklin IBE scheme, thanks to the extra public key element as well as an extra salt in the user secret key. Our proposed technique also ties the selector bit to an additional public key element instead of hashing it together with the message, similar to Coron's method. We then generalize the whole process with the help of Bellare et al.'s samplable trapdoor relations [12]. Although our improvement increases the public key size and slightly slow down the signing process, it does not need to modify the structure of existing signatures to enjoy the tight security benefits provided as in Katz and Wang's CFT-FDH. In fact, it is an acceptable sacrifice to be made to achieve backward compatibility.

In a nutshell, our framework can be viewed as the combination of the tight reduction techniques from Katz and Wang's CFT-FDH and Coron's IBE scheme [19] plus the generalization of Bellare et al.'s samplable trapdoor relations. Integrating these two techniques, we propose a framework for FDH signatures with backward compatibility property. Besides that, we also generalize the hard problems for the captured schemes using the trapdoor samplable relations. As a proof of concept for our framework, we apply our framework on the RSA-FDH.

1.3   Organization

We structure our paper according to the following the organization. We begin by stating the formal definitions of a digital signature and then review its security model in Sect. 2. Then, we proceed to describe our framework for tightly secure FDH signature schemes and the corresponding security proof in Sect. 3. Subsequently, we give two instantiations of the framework in Sect. 4. In Sect. 5, we discuss the potential application to other cryptosystems and the advantage against Katz-Wang's CFT-FDH. The conclusion is provided in Sect. 6.

2   Definitions

Here, we present the basic definitions of a digital signature and its security model. We also present the definitions of related mathematical assumptions that are used throughout this paper.

We denote $\{0,1\}^*$ as the set of bit strings. Let $a \xleftarrow{R} S$ denote a uniformly and randomly element a chosen from a finite set of S. Finally, $\mathbb{Z}_p$ denotes a set consisting of positive integers modulo with a large prime number p.

Definition 1. *A digital signature can be viewed as a scheme composed of three polynomial-time algorithms:* **Key Generation** *($\mathcal{KG}$),* **Sign** *($\mathcal{SN}$), and* **Verify** *($\mathcal{VR}$). The algorithms are described as follows:*

1. **Key Generation** *($\mathcal{KG}$) (1^k): In this algorithm, given a security parameter input of 1^k, a public and secret key pair (pk, sk) is generated. It is noted that pk is safe to be distributed openly, whilst the user keeps sk as a secret.*
2. **Sign** *($\mathcal{SN}$) (m, sk): Given sk and a message m as input, a signature denoted as σ is generated by the user.*
3. **Verify** *($\mathcal{VR}$) (m, σ, pk): Given pk and σ, a verifier ensures that σ is truly generated by the user, where the algorithm returns "1" if the signature is authentic; and "0" otherwise.*

2.1   Security Notions

We base our security model on the *strong existential unforgeability under chosen message attacks (seuf-cma)* security notion. Therefore, we define the security model of a digital signature as game between an Adversary $\mathcal{A}$ and a Simulator $\mathcal{S}$:

1. **Setup.** During the Setup phase, a Simulator $\mathcal{S}$ who wants to compute a solution for the hard problem generates and then sends the public parameters to Adversary $\mathcal{A}$, who wants to forge the signature.
2. **Hash Query.** In this phase, $\mathcal{A}$ is given the power to make multiple hash queries for message m. It receives obtain $H(m)$ as a response.
3. **Sign Query.** In this phase, $\mathcal{A}$ is given the power to make multiple signature queries for message m to acquire σ. $\mathcal{S}$ then computes and responds with σ to $\mathcal{A}$.

4. **Forgery.** Once $\mathcal{A}$ has completed the training phase, $\mathcal{A}$ would forge a message-signature pair, (m^*, σ^*). If (m^*, σ^*) is a valid message-signature pair and the pair is not a product of the sign query, then the forgery is considered successful.

Definition 2. *Based on the definition by Huang et al. [27], a digital signature scheme is $(t_{sig}, q_h, q_s, \varepsilon_{sig})$-secure against strong existential forgery under adaptive chosen message attacks (seuf-cma) for a given adversary $\mathcal{A}$ running with time of t, successfully forges a signature for a given message that was not the signature returned during q_s, i.e.*

$$\left| \Pr[\text{Ver}(pk, m, \sigma^*) = 1 : (m^*, \sigma^*) \leftarrow \mathcal{A}^{\mathcal{O}_{sk(\cdot)}}(pk); (m^*, \sigma^*) \notin \mathcal{Q}] \right| \leq \varepsilon_{sig}.$$

for $\mathcal{Q} = (m_i, \sigma_i)$ where m_i represents the i-th query for the signature which corresponds to signature σ_i, where $\mathcal{A}$ is allowed to make sign queries to the signing oracle $\mathcal{O}_{sk(\cdot)}$ for n times and can make hash queries and signing queries of not more than q_h and q_s respectively.

2.2 Computational Problems

In this work, we follow the definition of the CDH problem from Bao et al.'s work [4] as follows:

Definition 3. *Computational Diffie-Hellman (CDH) Problem. It is said that a polynomial-time algorithm $\mathcal{S}$ $(t_{CDH}, \varepsilon_{CDH})$-solves the CDH problem for $\mathcal{S}$ running for a time of at most t_{CDH} and furthermore:*

$$\left| \Pr[a, b \leftarrow \mathbb{Z}_q^* : \mathcal{S}(g, g^a, g^b) = g^{ab}] \right| \geq \varepsilon_{CDH}$$

We assume the CDH problem to be $(t_{CDH}, \varepsilon_{CDH})$-hard in $\mathbb{G}$ if

$$\Pr[\mathcal{S} \text{ solves CDH}] \leq \varepsilon_{CDH}$$

for any $\mathcal{S}$ that runs in time t_{CDH}.

In this work, we follow the definition of the co-CDH problem[1] from Bellare et al.'s work [11] as follows:

Definition 4. *Computational co-Diffie-Hellman (co-CDH) Problem. It is said that a polynomial-time algorithm $\mathcal{S}$ $(t_{co-CDH}, \varepsilon_{co-CDH})$-solves the co-CDH problem for $\mathcal{S}$ running for a time of at most t_{co-CDH} and furthermore:*

$$\left| \Pr[a, b \leftarrow \mathbb{Z}_q^* : \mathcal{S}(g_1, g_1{}^a, g_1{}^b, g_2{}^a) = g_1{}^{ab}] \right| \geq \varepsilon_{co-CDH}$$

We assume the co-CDH problem to be $(t_{co-CDH}, \varepsilon_{co-CDH})$-hard in $\mathbb{G}_1$ and $\mathbb{G}_2$ if

$$\Pr[\mathcal{S} \text{ solves co} - \text{CDH}] \leq \varepsilon_{co-CDH}$$

for any $\mathcal{S}$ that runs in time t_{co-CDH}.

---

[1] It is worth mentioning that the co-CDH problem is a Type-3 Pairing counterpart to the CDH problem which is based on the Type-1 Pairing [11].

In this work, we follow the definition of the DBDH problem from Coron's work [19] as follows:

Definition 5. *Decisional Bilinear Diffie-Hellman (DBDH) Problem. Let β be a binary coin and let $z = e(g,g)^{abc}$ if $\beta = 1$; else let z be a random element if otherwise. Given (g, g^a, g^b, g^c, z), output a guess β' of β. It is said that a polynomial-time algorithm $\mathcal{S}$ $(t_{DBDH}, \varepsilon_{DBDH})$-solves the DBDH problem for $\mathcal{S}$ running for a time of at most t_{DBDH} and furthermore:*

$$\left| \Pr[\beta' = \beta] - \frac{1}{2} \right| \geq \varepsilon_{DBDH}$$

We assume the DBDH problem to be $(t_{DBDH}, \varepsilon_{DBDH})$-hard in $\mathbb{G}_1$ and $\mathbb{G}_2$ if

$$\Pr[\mathcal{S} \text{ solves DBDH}] \leq \varepsilon_{DBDH}$$

for any $\mathcal{S}$ that runs in time t_{DBDH}.

In this work, we adopt the definition of the co-DBDH problem[2] as a Type-3 Pairing counterpart to the DBDH problem by combining the co-CDH and the DBDH problems as follows:

Definition 6. *Decisional Bilinear co-Diffie-Hellman (co-DBDH) Problem. Let β be a binary coin and let $z = e(g_1, g_2)^{abc}$ if $\beta = 1$; else let z be a random element if otherwise. Given $(g_1, g_2, g_1{}^a, g_1{}^b, g_2{}^a, g_2{}^c, z)$, output a guess β' of β. It is said that a polynomial-time algorithm $\mathcal{S}$ $(t_{co-DBDH}, \varepsilon_{co-DBDH})$-solves the co-DBDH problem for $\mathcal{S}$ running for a time of at most $t_{co-DBDH}$ and furthermore:*

$$\left| \Pr[\beta' = \beta] - \frac{1}{2} \right| \geq \varepsilon_{co-DBDH}$$

We assume the co-DBDH problem to be $(t_{co-DBDH}, \varepsilon_{co-DBDH})$-hard in $\mathbb{G}_1$ and $\mathbb{G}_2$ if

$$\Pr[\mathcal{S} \text{ solves co} - \text{DBDH}] \leq \varepsilon_{co-DBDH}$$

for any $\mathcal{S}$ that runs in time $t_{co-DBDH}$.

In this work, we follow the definition of the RSA problem from Cramer and Shoup's work [20] as follows:

Definition 7. *RSA Problem. It is said that a polynomial-time algorithm $\mathcal{S}$ $(t_{RSA}, \varepsilon_{RSA})$-solves the RSA problem for $\mathcal{S}$ running for a time of at most t_{RSA} and furthermore:*

$$|\Pr[d \leftarrow \mathbb{Z}_N : \mathcal{S}(N, e) = d]| \geq \varepsilon_{RSA}$$

---

[2] We denote this hard problem as the co-DBDH problem as the Type-3 Pairing version of the DBDH problem, to distinguish between the DBDH problem which is based on the Type-1 Pairing. It is noted that in a work by Vercauteren [41], the co-DBDH problem itself is denoted as the DBDH problem, which covers the specification of both Type-1 and Type-3 pairings.

We assume the RSA problem to be (t, ε)-hard in $\phi(N)$ if

$$\Pr[\mathcal{S} \text{ solves RSA}] \leq \varepsilon_{RSA}$$

for any $\mathcal{S}$ that runs in time t_{RSA}.

In this work, we follow the definition of the strong-RSA problem from Cramer and Shoup's work [20] as follows:

Definition 8. *Strong-RSA Problem. It is said that a polynomial-time algorithm $\mathcal{S}$ $(t_{SRSA}, \varepsilon_{SRSA})$-solves the strong-RSA problem for $\mathcal{S}$ running for a time of at most t_{SRSA} and furthermore:*

$$|\Pr[w, d \leftarrow \mathbb{Z}_N : \mathcal{S}(N, e, w^e) = w]| \geq \varepsilon_{SRSA}$$

We assume the strong-RSA problem to be $(t_{SRSA}, \varepsilon_{SRSA})$-hard in $\phi(N)$ if

$$\Pr[\mathcal{S} \text{ solves strong} - \text{RSA}] \leq \varepsilon_{SRSA}$$

for any $\mathcal{S}$ that runs in time t_{SRSA}.

2.3 Pseudorandom Bit Generator

We adopt the definition of the pseudorandom bit generator from Katz et al.'s work [34] as follows:

Definition 9. *A pseudorandom bit generator is defined as a computable function that is efficient. When F^1 and F^2, an output of a generated and a truly random sequence of a similar length respectively are presented to a distinguishing algorithm $\mathcal{S}$, $\mathcal{S}$ is unable to correctly differentiate the function used with a probability of more than $1/2$, i.e.*

$$\left| |\Pr_{g \xleftarrow{R} F^2} [\mathcal{S}^g = 1] - \Pr_{g \xleftarrow{R} F^1} [\mathcal{S}^g = 1]| - \frac{1}{2} \right| \leq \varepsilon$$

where the probabilities are defined over the choices g and also the coin tosses $\mathcal{C}$ for a non-negligible ε.

2.4 Trapdoor Samplable Relations

We adopt the definition of the Trapdoor Samplable Relations from Bellare et al.'s work [12] as follows.

Definition 10. *A relation is defined as a finite set of ordered pairs. The range of a relation $\mathbf{R}$, the set of images of x, and the set of inverses of y, are defined as:*

$$Rng(\mathbf{R}) = \{y : \exists x \text{ such that} (x, y) \in \mathbf{R}\}$$
$$\mathbf{R}(x) = \{y : (x, y) \in \mathbf{R}\}$$
$$\mathbf{R}^{-1}(y) = \{x : (x, y) \in \mathbf{R}\}$$

A family of trapdoor samplable relation (TDG, Smp, Inv) possesses the following properties:

1. Efficient Generation : *Given an input* 1^k *where* $k \in \mathbb{N}$ *is the security parameter,* TDG *would output the description* $\langle \mathbf{R} \rangle$ *of a relation* $\mathbf{R}$ *alongside the trapdoor information* td.
2. Samplability : *Given an input* $\langle \mathbf{R} \rangle$, *the output of the algorithm* Smp *would be uniformly distributed over* $\mathbf{R}$.
3. Inversion : *Given the inputs of a relation description* $\langle \mathbf{R} \rangle$, *the corresponding trapdoor* td, *and an element* $y \in Rng(\mathbf{R})$, *a randomized algorithm* Inv *would output a random element* $\mathbf{R}^{-1}(y)$.
4. Regularity : *For every relation* $\mathbf{R}$ *in the family, there exists an integer* d *such that* $|\mathbf{R}^{-1}(y)| = d$ *for all* $y \in Rng(\mathbf{R})$.

The family of relations is defined as:

$$\{\mathbf{R} : \exists k, \text{td such that } (\langle \mathbf{R} \rangle, \text{td}) \in [\text{TDG}(1^k)]\}$$

A family of trapdoor samplable relations is a result of a family of one-way permutations. For every member f *of the family of one-way permutations, there corresponds the relation* $\mathbf{R}$ *consisting of the set of pairs* $(x, f(x))$ *for* x *in the domain of the function* f.

3   The Tight Security Framework

In this section, we propose a framework which can capture the FDH signature schemes alongside a full security proof. Similar to Katz-Wang's CFT-FDH [31], we use the bit selector technique as well, though we follow Coron's technique [19] instead of modifying the hash value. We also make use of the trapdoor samplable relations proposed by Bellare et al. [12] to generalize our framework and the security proof.

3.1   Generic Form of Captured FDH Signatures

Before proposing our framework, we first demonstrate the generic form of FDH signatures using the trapdoor samplable relations defined in Sect. 2.4 as follows:

1. **Key Generation** ($\mathcal{KG}$): Run $\text{TDG}(1^k)$ to obtain the relation description $\langle \mathbf{R} \rangle$ and the trapdoor information td. Then, select a full domain hash function $H : \{0,1\}^* \rightarrow Rng(\mathbf{R})$. Return the public keys $\{\langle \mathbf{R} \rangle, H\}$ and the secret key td.
2. **Sign** ($\mathcal{SN}$): Given a message $m \in \{0,1\}^*$ and trapdoor td as input, run $\text{Inv}(\langle \mathbf{R} \rangle, \text{td}, H(m))$ to return the signature $\sigma = \mathbf{R}^{-1}(H(m))$.
3. **Verify** ($\mathcal{VR}$): The verification for the signature σ of a message m can be done by evaluating the correctness of $\mathbf{R}(\sigma) = H(m)$.

3.2   The Proposed Framework

We now propose the general framework that tightens the security of FDH signatures using properties of the trapdoor samplable relations. The security tightening process is done with the help of an extra Smp algorithm and an extra bit r.

1. **Key Generation** ($\mathcal{KG}$): Run $\mathsf{TDG}(1^k)$ to obtain relation description $\langle \mathbf{R} \rangle$ and trapdoor information td. Then, run $\mathsf{Smp}(\langle \mathbf{R} \rangle)$ to obtain $(x, y) \in \langle \mathbf{R} \rangle$ as well as select a full domain hash function $H : \{0, 1\}^* \to \mathrm{Rng}(\mathbf{R})$. Return the public keys $\{(\langle \mathbf{R} \rangle, y), H\}$ and the secret keys (td, x).
2. **Sign** ($\mathcal{SN}$): Given a message $m \in \{0, 1\}^*$ and trapdoor td as input, choose a random bit[3] $r \overset{R}{\leftarrow} PRBG(m, \mathsf{td})$ and run $\mathsf{Inv}((\langle \mathbf{R} \rangle, y), \mathsf{td}, H(m), r)$ to return the signature $\sigma = (\delta, r) = (\mathbf{R}^{-1}(H(m) \cdot y^r), r) = (\mathbf{R}^{-1}(H(m)) \cdot x^r, r)$.
3. **Verify** ($\mathcal{VR}$): The verification for the signature σ of a message m can be done by evaluating the correctness of $\mathbf{R}(\delta) = H(m) \cdot y^r$.

The proposed framework is different from the original signature schemes in the sense that a "randomisation" of a one bit r is added to the signature. However, since r is chosen whenever a signature is generated, the signature is deterministic for a given message.

3.3   Backward Compatibility

Based on the framework defined in Sect. 3.2, the non-tight signatures that were previously generated can be verified using the verification algorithm of our framework without having to modify the structure of current signatures. It can be noticed that by setting the value of $r = 0$, the signature would be returned as $\sigma = (\delta, 0) = (\mathbf{R}^{-1}(H(m)), 0)$, which is actually the value from the original scheme. Therefore, in order to perform an upgrade from previously generated signatures, the user would just have to set the value of r into 0.

On the other hand, new signatures has to perform the Smp algorithm first in order to generate the new parameters. Moreover, the new signatures has to be generated based on our framework to achieve a tight security reduction. The parameters that were previously generated may be kept and used for the new signatures, depending on the user, though the key distribution for the PKG has to follow the framework.

3.4   Security Proof

In this section, we proceed to describe the full security proof to the framework described in Sect. 3.2.

---

[3] The signer may enclose the bit r alongside σ to avoid confusion during verification where two different signatures for a message (i.e. $r \in \{0, 1\}$) may exist at once, as stated in [31].

Theorem 1. *The signature scheme above is* $(t_{sig}, q_h, q_s, \varepsilon_{sig})$*-seuf-cma secure if the one-wayness of the trapdoor permutations is* $(t_{owtd}, \varepsilon_{owtd})$*-secure, where:*

$$\varepsilon_{sig} = 2\varepsilon_{owtd}$$
$$t_{sig} = \mathcal{O}(t_{owtd})$$

Proof. Assuming that there exists a $(t_{sig}, q_h, q_s, \varepsilon_{sig})$-adversary $\mathcal{A}$ running in time of at most t_{sig} making at most q_h hash queries and at most q_s signing queries against the signature scheme. We construct a Simulator $\mathcal{S}$ that wants to break the one-wayness of the trapdoor permutations with an advantage of at least ε_{owtd} while interacting with $\mathcal{A}$ that wants to forge the signature.

Setup. $\mathcal{S}$ runs $\mathsf{TDG}(1^k)$ and receives the challenge $(\langle \mathbf{R} \rangle, y)$. It is noted that $\mathcal{S}$ does not know the value of td.

Hash Query. When $\mathcal{A}$ submits a fresh query[4] $H(m)$ for a message m, $\mathcal{S}$ runs $\mathsf{Smp}(\langle \mathbf{R} \rangle)$ to obtain $(\tilde{x}, \tilde{y})$. $\mathcal{S}$ first generates a random value $y_1 \xleftarrow{R} \mathrm{Rng}(\mathbf{R})$. $\mathcal{S}$ then generates a random bit $\tilde{r} \xleftarrow{R} PRBG(m, y_1)$ and then proceeds to store $\{m, \tilde{x}, \tilde{y}, \tilde{r}\}$ in a hash list H_{list}. $\mathcal{S}$ returns $H(m) = \tilde{y} \cdot y^{-\tilde{r}}$ to $\mathcal{A}$ as a reply to the hash query. If m was queried before, $\mathcal{S}$ searches from H_{list} and returns the same value $H(m) = \tilde{y} \cdot y^{-\tilde{r}}$.

Sign Query. When $\mathcal{A}$ submits a signing query for a message m, we assume that the hash query has already been made. If not, $\mathcal{S}$ goes ahead and makes the hash query. In either case, $\mathcal{S}$ can recover $\{\tilde{x}, \tilde{y}, \tilde{r}\}$ from H_{list} and return $\sigma = (\delta = \tilde{x}, \tilde{r})$. This signature for the message m is valid as:

$$\delta = \mathbf{R}^{-1}(H(m) \cdot y^{\tilde{r}}) = \mathbf{R}^{-1}(\tilde{y} \cdot y^{-\tilde{r}} \cdot y^{\tilde{r}}) = \mathbf{R}^{-1}(\tilde{y}) = \tilde{x}$$

Forgery. Without a loss of generality, we assume that the message m^* in the forgery $(m^*, \sigma^* = (\delta^*, r^*))$ produced by $\mathcal{A}$ has already been queried to the hash oracle; else, $\mathcal{S}$ then proceeds to issue a hash query for m^*. We differentiate the forgery produced by $\mathcal{A}$ into 2 cases:

Case 1: Suppose $\mathcal{A}$ produces a valid signature and message $(m^*, \sigma^* = (\delta^*, r^*))$ pair where the signature of m^* was never queried before, $\mathcal{S}$ aborts if $r^* = \tilde{r}$; else if $r^* \neq \tilde{r}$, $\mathcal{S}$ solves the one-wayness problem of the trapdoor permutations with the help of (m^*, σ^*).

Case 2: Suppose $\mathcal{A}$ produces a valid signature and message $(m^*, \sigma^* = (\delta^*, r^*))$ pair where σ^* is not the response returned by $\mathcal{S}$ during the signing query, $\mathcal{S}$ solves the one-wayness problem of the trapdoor permutations with the help of (m^*, σ^*).

We recall that $\mathcal{A}$ is an adversary in the *seuf-cma* security notion. Therefore, we take both *Case 1* and *Case 2* into consideration. In both cases, we define the

---

[4] Different from Katz-Wang's work in [31], $\mathcal{A}$ is not able to query for the value of r considering it is not a portion of the hash input.

one-wayness problem of the trapdoor permutations that $\mathcal{S}$ wants to solve as the following:

$$\text{Given } (\langle \mathbf{R} \rangle, y), \text{ find } (x = \mathbf{R}^{-1}(y)).$$

$\mathcal{S}$ solves the one-wayness problem of trapdoor permutations by finding x as follows:

$$\begin{pmatrix} \delta^* \\ \tilde{x} \end{pmatrix} = \begin{pmatrix} \mathbf{R}^{-1}(H(m) \cdot y^{r^*}) \\ \tilde{x} \end{pmatrix} = \begin{pmatrix} \mathbf{R}^{-1}(H(m)) \cdot x^{r^*} \\ \tilde{x} \end{pmatrix} = \begin{pmatrix} \mathbf{R}^{-1}(\tilde{y} \cdot y^{-\tilde{r}}) \cdot x^{r^*} \\ \tilde{x} \end{pmatrix}$$

$$= \begin{pmatrix} (\tilde{x} \cdot x^{-\tilde{r}}) \cdot x^{r^*} \\ \tilde{x} \end{pmatrix} = \begin{pmatrix} x^{-\tilde{r}+r^*} \end{pmatrix}$$

In the case where $\tilde{r} = 0$ and $r^* = 1$, $x = \begin{pmatrix} \delta^* \\ \tilde{x} \end{pmatrix}$.

In the case where $\tilde{r} = 1$ and $r^* = 0$, $x = \begin{pmatrix} \delta^* \\ \tilde{x} \end{pmatrix}^{-1}$.

It is noted that if the values of $\tilde{r} = r^*$, $\mathcal{S}$ is unable to solve the one-way trapdoor permutations, and $\mathcal{S}$ has to abort the simulation. To proceed with the probability calculation, we note the summary of both *Case 1* and *Case 2* in the Table 1.

Table 1. Possible forgeries for σ^*.

Case	σ^*	
	m^*	r^*
1	0	0
	0	1
2	1	0
	1	1

In Table 1, we denote 0 for the value of m^* to signify *Case 1*, where m^* is never queried before, while we denote 1 for the value of m^* to signify *Case 2*, where m^* has been queried during the sign query, but the forgery σ^* is different from the signature produced during the sign query. For both cases, the values of 0 and 1 under the column r^* represents $\tilde{r} \neq r^*$ and $\tilde{r} = r^*$ respectively. Since $r \in \{0, 1\}$, it is obvious that the probability of $\tilde{r} = r^*$ is $\frac{1}{2}$ for each case. By combining both *Case 1* and *Case 2* together, the probability of $\tilde{r} = r^*$ is resulted as $\frac{1}{2}$. The probability of computing a solution for the one-wayness of the trapdoor permutations is then calculated as the following:

$$\Pr[\mathcal{S} \text{ solves one-way trapdoor}] = \Pr[\mathcal{A} \text{ outputs valid } \sigma^* \wedge \mathcal{S} \text{ does not abort}]$$
$$\varepsilon_{owtd} = \Pr[\mathcal{A} \text{ outputs valid } \sigma^*] \wedge \Pr[\mathcal{S} \text{ does not abort}]$$
$$= \Pr[\mathcal{A} \text{ outputs valid } \sigma^*] \wedge \Pr[\tilde{r} \neq r^*]$$
$$= \varepsilon_{sig} \times \frac{1}{2}$$
$$= \frac{1}{2}\varepsilon_{sig}$$

Given the *seuf-cma* security notion, $\mathcal{S}$ is able to carry out the simulation all the way from the setup stage up to the sign queries without aborting. However, there is a $\frac{1}{2}$ probability of aborting if the values of $\tilde{r} = r^*$ during the computation of a solution for the one-way trapdoor permutations. The time $t_{\mathcal{A}}$ taken by the adversary $\mathcal{A}$ to break the scheme is represented by the overall computation time of $\mathcal{S}$ such that $t_{\mathcal{A}} = \mathcal{O}(t_{sig})$. This results in a tight security reduction of only 1-bit loss where $\varepsilon_{sig} = 2\varepsilon_{owtd}$.   □

4   Applying the Framework

We now provide the instantiations to show the application of our proposed framework, as well as the backwards compatibility property of the new schemes. We first present the original schemes using the trapdoor samplable relations, while showing the application of our framework to tighten the security of the signature schemes. We then define the tight version of each respective schemes, and show a brief security proof as well.

Referring to Sect. 3.2, the algorithms TDG and Smp define the setup, $\mathcal{KG}$ of a digital signature, while Inv defines the signing, $\mathcal{SN}$ of a digital signature. We will describe the verification algorithm, $\mathcal{VR}$ for each of the instantiated scheme as well.

In the schemes that we will instantiate later on, we show that the Smp algorithm is derived from the scheme itself, although the parameters generated from the algorithm are not presented in the original scheme. Therefore, the Smp can be viewed as a method to tighten the security of a scheme, while having the properties of backward compatibility.

We would like to point out a notation that we will use later on, the maps to ($\mapsto$) symbol. To begin, the values on the right hand side of the $\mapsto$ character are mapped to the values of the left hand side. As an example, $\langle \mathbf{R} \rangle \mapsto (N, e, z)$ shows that the values (N, e, z) are mapped to the value of $\langle \mathbf{R} \rangle$ of the trapdoor samplable relation.

4.1   Instantiation Using RSA-FDH

The RSA-FDH was proposed in [14], where it was introduced as a "signature" version of the RSA encryption. The RSA-FDH is originally based on the RSA problem [20]. However, by applying the framework, our variant of the RSA-FDH is based on the strong-RSA problem. The trapdoor samplable relation for RSA-FDH [14] is as follows:

Algorithm 1. Trapdoor Samplable Relation for RSA-FDH

$\mathsf{TDG}(1^k)$:

$(N, e), H, d \xleftarrow{R} \mathsf{Kg_{rsa}}(1^k)$, where $ed = 1 \bmod \varphi(N)$ and $H : \{0,1\}^* \rightarrow \mathbb{Z}_N$
Return $(PK = ((N, e), H), SK = d)$

$\mathsf{Smp}(1^k, N, e)$: $(w \in \mathbb{Z}_N, z = w^e)$
Return (w, z)

$\mathsf{Inv}((1^k, N, e), d, H(m))$:
$\sigma \leftarrow (\delta) = (H(m)^d)$,
Return σ

Note: The relation described by $(1^k, N, e)$ is $\mathbf{R} = \{(\sigma, H(m)) \in \mathbb{Z}_N^* \times \mathbb{Z}_N^* | \sigma^e = H(m)\}$. Based on the relation described above, the TDG and the Smp algorithms define the $\mathcal{KG}$ of the RSA-FDH. As the Smp algorithm is not presented in the original scheme, the original signature is generated in terms of $\mathsf{Inv}((1^k, N, e), d, H(m))$. With the new key pair (PK, SK) generated from the Smp algorithm alongside a random bit $r \in \{0,1\}$, we sign a message $m \in \{0,1\}^*$ with the Inv algorithm such that $\mathsf{Inv}(((1^k, N, e), z), d, H(m), r)$ where $\sigma = (\delta, r) = ((H(m) \cdot z^r)^d, r)$, to tighten the security of RSA-FDH whilst retaining the backward compatibility of the scheme.

Following the trapdoor samplable relation, we are ready to define the tight RSA-FDH as follows:

1. **Key Generation** ($\mathcal{KG}$): Generate two primes p, q and compute $N = pq$. Select a prime $e \xleftarrow{R} \mathbb{Z}_{\phi(N)}$ such that $gcd(e, \phi(N)) = 1$ and compute d where $e \cdot d = 1 \bmod \phi(N)$. Next, choose $w \xleftarrow{R} \mathbb{Z}_N$ and calculate $z = w^e$. Lastly, select a hash function $H : \{0,1\}^* \rightarrow \mathbb{Z}_N$. Set $PK = ((N, e, z), H)$ and $SK = (d, w)$.
2. **Sign** ($\mathcal{SN}$): Given a message $m \in \{0,1\}^*$ and SK as input, generate a random bit $r \xleftarrow{R} PRBG(m, d)$ and generate the signature $\sigma = (\delta, r) = ((H(m) \cdot z^r)^d, r)$.
3. **Verify** ($\mathcal{VR}$): The verification for the signature σ of a message m can be done by evaluating $\delta^e \overset{?}{=} H(m) \cdot z^r$. The check equation for the correctness is as follows:

$$\delta^e = ((H(m) \cdot z^r)^d)^e$$
$$= H(m) \cdot z^r$$

Notice that the original RSA-FDH signature $H(m)^d$ only needs to be multiplied with z^{rd}, where the hash value is not modified at all, thus retaining the properties of the original RSA-FDH signature. As the verification of the original RSA-FDH is done by computing $\sigma^e = H(m)$, the new verification algorithm then can be done by multiplying z^r to the right hand side. Therefore, the non-tight RSA-FDH verification can be done with our new verification by initializing the value of z^r to be 1.

Theorem 2. *The proposed RSA-FDH signature scheme above is* $(t_{sig}, q_h,$ $q_s, \varepsilon_{sig})$*-seuf-cma secure if Strong-RSA is* $(t_{SRSA}, \varepsilon_{SRSA})$*-secure, where:*

$$\varepsilon_{sig} = 2\varepsilon_{SRSA}$$
$$t_{sig} = \mathcal{O}(t_{SRSA})$$

Proof. Theorem 1 implies that the proposed RSA-FDH signature scheme has a tight reduction to the trapdoor one-wayness in the Smp property, which is the strong-RSA problem: given $(\langle \mathbf{R} \rangle, y) \mapsto ((N, e), z)$, find $x \mapsto w$.

Concisely, let $H(m) = \tilde{x}^e \cdot z^{-\tilde{r}}$ where $\tilde{x}, \tilde{x}_1 \xleftarrow{R} \mathbb{Z}_N$ and $\tilde{r} \xleftarrow{R} PRBG(m, \tilde{x}_1)$, the forgery produced is $\sigma^* = (\delta^*, r^*) = ((\tilde{x}^e \cdot z^{-\tilde{r}} \cdot z^{r^*})^d, r^*)$. In the case where $r^* = \tilde{r}$, $\mathcal{S}$ aborts the simulation; else $\mathcal{S}$ computes the solution w for the strong-RSA problem as follows:

$$\left(\frac{\delta^*}{\tilde{x}} \right) = \left(\frac{(H(m) \cdot z^{r^*})^d}{\tilde{x}} \right) = \left(\frac{((\tilde{x}^e \cdot z^{-\tilde{r}}) \cdot z^{r^*})^d}{\tilde{x}} \right) = \left(\frac{((\tilde{x}^e \cdot w^{-e\tilde{r}}) \cdot w^{er^*})^d}{\tilde{x}} \right)$$

$$= \left(\frac{(\tilde{x})(w^{(-\tilde{r}+r^*)})}{\tilde{x}} \right) = \left(w^{-\tilde{r}+r^*} \right)$$

In the case where $\tilde{r} = 0$ and $r^* = 1$, $w = \left(\frac{\delta^*}{\tilde{x}} \right)$.

In the case where $\tilde{r} = 1$ and $r^* = 0$, $w = \left(\frac{\delta^*}{\tilde{x}} \right)^{-1}$.   □

4.2   Instantiation Using BLS

The BLS signature scheme [10] was introduced by Boneh et al. as a short signature based on the Computational Diffie-Hellman (CDH) problem. Lacharité [32] proposed the BLS signature using the Type-3 Pairing [39] based on the co-CDH problem. The trapdoor samplable relation for BLS [10] is as follows:

Algorithm 2. Trapdoor Samplable Relation for BLS

$\mathsf{TDG}(1^k)$:

$((\mathbb{G}_1, \mathbb{G}_2, q, g_1, g_2, x_1 = g_1{}^a, y = g_2{}^a), H, a) \xleftarrow{R} \mathsf{Kg}(1^k)$, where $H : \{0,1\}^* \to \mathbb{G}_1$
Return $(PK = ((\mathbb{G}_1, \mathbb{G}_2, q, g_1, g_2, x_1, y), H), SK = a)$

$\mathsf{Smp}(\mathbb{G}_1, \mathbb{G}_2, g_1, g_2, x_1, y)$: $((b \in \mathbb{Z}_q, g_1{}^{ab}), x_2 = g_1{}^b)$
Return $((b, g_1{}^{ab}), x_2)$

$\mathsf{Inv}((g_2, y), a, H(m))$:
$\sigma \leftarrow \delta = H(m)^a$
Return σ

Note: The relation described by $(1^k, \mathbb{G}_1, \mathbb{G}_2, q, g_1, g_2)$ is $\mathbf{R} = \{(\sigma, H(m)) \in \mathbb{G}_1 \times \mathbb{G}_1 | e(H(m), y) = e(\sigma, g_2)\}$. Based on the relation described above, the TDG and the Smp algorithms define the $\mathcal{KG}$ of the BLS. As the Smp algorithm is not presented in the original scheme, the original signature is generated in terms of $\mathsf{Inv}((g_2, y), a, H(m))$. With the new key pair (PK, SK) generated from the Smp algorithm alongside a random bit $r \in \{0, 1\}$, we sign a message $m \in \{0, 1\}^*$ with the Inv algorithm such that $\mathsf{Inv}(((g_2, y), x_2), a, H(m), r)$ where $\sigma = (\delta, r) = ((H(m) \cdot x_2^r)^a, r)$, to tighten the security of BLS whilst retaining the backward compatibility of the scheme.

Following the trapdoor samplable relation, our tight BLS signature scheme turns out to be the same as Ng et al.'s signature scheme [37], thereby providing an additional theoretical explanation for its tight reduction proof.

5   Discussions

5.1   Upgrade to Existing Schemes

Since FDH signature scheme is a popular tool in constructing more complex cryptsystems, the technique from our framework can be applied on these cryptosystems to improve their security and performance. For instance, we briefly explain how to apply our technique in enhancing Coron's BF-IBE [19] scheme whose user secret key is a BLS signature on the user public identity ID. Following the trapdoor samplable relation for BLS in Sect. 4.2, we describe Coron's *IND-ID-CPA*-secure BF-IBE [19] as follows:

1. **Setup**: Generate two random integers $a, b \xleftarrow{R} \mathbb{Z}_q$ and generators $g_1 \in \mathbb{G}_1, g_2 \in \mathbb{G}_2$. Compute the values $x_1 = g_1^a, x_2 = g_1^b, y = g_2^a$. Next, establish the pairing function $e : \mathbb{G}_1 \times \mathbb{G}_2 \to \mathbb{G}_T$. Lastly, select a hash function $H : \{0, 1\}^* \to \mathbb{G}_1$. Set $PK = ((\mathbb{G}_1, \mathbb{G}_2, g_1, g_2, x_1, x_2, y, e), H)$ and $SK = (a, b)$.
2. **Keygen**: Given an identity $ID \in \{0, 1\}^*$ and SK as input, generate a random bit $r \xleftarrow{R} PRBG(ID, a)$ and generate the secret key $d_v = (\delta, r) = ((H(ID) \cdot x_2^r)^a, r)$.
3. **Encryption**: Generate a random integer $w \xleftarrow{R} \mathbb{Z}_q$. The encryption of a message m is given as: $C = (g_2^w, e(x_2, y)^w, m \oplus H_2(e(H_1(ID), y)^w))$.
4. **Decryption**: Given the ciphertext $C = (c_1, c_2, c_3)$ and the secret key $d_v = (\delta, r)$, the message is decrypted as $m = c_3 \oplus H_2(e(\delta, c_1) \cdot c_2^{-r})$ because:

$$
\begin{aligned}
e(H_1(ID), y)^w &= e(H_1(ID), g_2^a)^w = e(H_1(ID)^a, g_2^w) = e(\delta \cdot x_2^{-ar}, g_2^w) \\
&= e(\delta, g_2^w) \cdot e(x_2^{-ar}, g_2^w) = e(\delta, c_1) \cdot e(x_2, g_2^a)^{-wr} \\
&= e(\delta, c_1) \cdot e(x_2, y)^{-wr} = e(\delta, c_1) \cdot c_2^{-r}
\end{aligned}
$$

It can be noticed that there is hardly any difference for the scheme described above in comparison with Coron's BF-IBE, with the exception of the scheme being defined using Type-3 pairing, and we use a single bit r instead of an integer in the group $\mathbb{Z}_q$, as the exponent for the public key x_2.

Theorem 3. *The IBE above is $(t_{ibe}, q_h, q_e, \varepsilon_{ibe})$-IND-ID-CPA secure if co-DBDH is $(t_{co-DBDH}, \varepsilon_{co-DBDH})$-secure, where:*

$$\varepsilon_{ibe} = 4\varepsilon_{co-DBDH}$$
$$t_{ibe} = \mathcal{O}(t_{co-DBDH})$$

Proof. (*Sketch.*) The trapdoor samplable relations for the BLS covers the **Setup** and **Keygen** stages of the IBE in the security proof, where the TDG and the Smp algorithms define the **Setup** stage, while the Inv define the **Keygen** stage. Concisely, let $H(ID) = g_1{}^p \cdot x_2{}^{-\tilde{r}}$, where $p, p_1 \xleftarrow{R} \mathbb{Z}_q$ and $\tilde{r} \xleftarrow{R} PRBG(m, p_1)$, the simulator can answer hash queries for every ID, including the challenge ID. The rest of the proof can be followed in accordance with Coron's BF-IBE security proof except that the challenge ID must have $\tilde{r} = 1$ or the simulator aborts. $\square$

Besides Coron's BF-IBE scheme, our technique is applicable on Agrawal et al.'s lattice IBE scheme [2] that uses Katz and Wang's bit selector technique. Subsequently, our technique is also useful for Boyen and Li's lattice signature [9] scheme which was based on Agrawal et al.'s lattice IBE scheme. Moreover, FDH -based undeniable signature schemes, such as Ogata et al.'s undeniable signature [38] can benefit from our technique as well.

5.2   Comparison with Katz and Wang's Work

In 2003, Katz and Wang [31] managed to tighten the security of FDH signature schemes by hashing a bit with the message. By basing their scheme off the claw-free trapdoor, they proposed a general framework for FDH signature schemes, which was also instantiated in Katz's work [28]. The proposed CFT-FDH scheme was tightly secure with just a loss of 1-bit.

Similar to their work, we proposed a general framework for FDH signature schemes with the help of an extra bit and an extra public key. However, the families of FDH signatures are captured using the trapdoor samplable relations proposed by Bellare et al., different from the claw-free trapdoor used by Katz-Wang. By applying the proposed framework, the captured FDH signature schemes are tightly secure.

Apart from that, different from Katz-Wang's work, the proposed framework can be considered as an upgrade as the original signature is altered with an additional multiplication operation instead of modifying the hash. Therefore, it can be said that the proposed framework covers different ranges of FDH signature schemes, which also solves the backward compatibility problem of Katz-Wang's scheme. We summarize a self-explanatory comparison for the RSA-FDH variants with ours in Table 2.

Table 2. Comparison between the RSA-FDH variants at 128-bit security level

Property	RSA-FDH (Ideal)	RSA-FDH [14]	CFT-FDH [28]	This Work
Hard problem	RSA	RSA	CFT	strong-RSA
Security notion	euf-cma	euf-cma	seuf-cma	seuf-cma
Public key length (bits)	$2\|\mathbb{N}\| = 2 \times 3072 = 6144$	$2\|\mathbb{N}\| = 2 \times 7680 = 15360$	$2\|\mathbb{N}\| = 2 \times 3072 = 6144$	$3\|\mathbb{N}\| = 3 \times 3072 = 9216$
Signature length (bits)	$\|\mathbb{N}\| = 3072$	$\|\mathbb{N}\| = 7680$	$\|\mathbb{N}\| + \|r\| = 3073$	$\|\mathbb{N}\| + \|r\| = 3073$
Security tightness	$\varepsilon_{RSA-FDH} = \varepsilon_{RSA}$	$\varepsilon_{RSA-FDH} = (q_s + q_h + 1)\varepsilon_{RSA}$	$\varepsilon_{RSA-FDH} = 2\varepsilon_{CFT}$	$\varepsilon_{RSA-FDH} = 2\varepsilon_{SRSA}$
Backward compatibility	Original	Original	No	Yes

6   Conclusion

In this paper, we proposed a generalized framework using the trapdoor samplable relations that covers FDH signature schemes which enjoys the benefit of tight security. Furthermore, we have extended the usage of the trapdoor samplable relations to propose a more general security proof as well. Besides that, different from Katz and Wang's CFT-FDH, our framework enjoys backward compatibility as we do not change the way of hashing as in the bit selector technique.

Acknowledgement. The authors would like to thank Thomas Groß for the helpful comments on an earlier version of this paper. The authors would also like to acknowledge the Fundamental Research Grant Scheme (FRGS/1/2019/ICT04/MMU/02/5) by the Ministry of Education of Malaysia in providing financial support for this work.

References

1. Abdalla, M., An, J.H., Bellare, M., Namprempre, C.: From identification to signatures via the fiat-shamir transform: minimizing assumptions for security and forward-security. In: Knudsen, L.R. (ed.) EUROCRYPT 2002. LNCS, vol. 2332, pp. 418–433. Springer, Heidelberg (2002). https://doi.org/10.1007/3-540-46035-7_28

2. Agrawal, S., Boneh, D., Boyen, X.: Efficient lattice (H)IBE in the standard model. In: Gilbert, H. (ed.) EUROCRYPT 2010. LNCS, vol. 6110, pp. 553–572. Springer, Heidelberg (2010). https://doi.org/10.1007/978-3-642-13190-5_28

3. An, J.H., Dodis, Y., Rabin, T.: On the security of joint signature and encryption. In: Knudsen, L.R. (ed.) EUROCRYPT 2002. LNCS, vol. 2332, pp. 83–107. Springer, Heidelberg (2002). https://doi.org/10.1007/3-540-46035-7_6

4. Bao, F., Deng, R.H., Zhu, H.F.: Variations of Diffie-Hellman problem. In: Qing, S., Gollmann, D., Zhou, J. (eds.) ICICS 2003. LNCS, vol. 2836, pp. 301–312. Springer, Heidelberg (2003). https://doi.org/10.1007/978-3-540-39927-8_28

5. Bresson, E., Lakhnech, Y., Mazaré, L., Warinschi, B.: A generalization of DDH with applications to protocol analysis and computational soundness. In: Menezes, A. (ed.) CRYPTO 2007. LNCS, vol. 4622, pp. 482–499. Springer, Heidelberg (2007). https://doi.org/10.1007/978-3-540-74143-5_27

6. Beth, T.: Efficient zero-knowledge identification scheme for smart cards. In: Barstow, D., et al. (eds.) EUROCRYPT 1988. LNCS, vol. 330, pp. 77–84. Springer, Heidelberg (1988). https://doi.org/10.1007/3-540-45961-8_7

7. Boneh, D., Franklin, M.B.: Identity-based encryption from the weil pairing. In: Kilian, J. (ed.) CRYPTO 2001. LNCS, vol. 2139, pp. 213–229. Springer, Heidelberg (2001). https://doi.org/10.1007/3-540-44647-8_13

8. Bellare, M., Fischlin, M., Goldwasser, S., Micali, S.: Identification protocols secure against reset attacks. In: Pfitzmann, B. (ed.) EUROCRYPT 2001. LNCS, vol. 2045, pp. 495–511. Springer, Heidelberg (2001). https://doi.org/10.1007/3-540-44987-6_30

9. Boyen, X., Li, Q.: Towards Tightly Secure Short Signature and IBE. IACR Cryptology ePrint Archive – Report 2016/498, pp. 514–532 (2001)

10. Boneh, D., Lynn, B., Shacham, H.: Short signatures from the weil pairing. In: Boyd, C. (ed.) ASIACRYPT 2001. LNCS, vol. 2248, pp. 514–532. Springer, Heidelberg (2001). https://doi.org/10.1007/3-540-45682-1_30

11. Bellare, M., Namprempre, C., Neven, G.: Unrestricted aggregate signatures. In: Arge, L., Cachin, C., Jurdziński, T., Tarlecki, A. (eds.) ICALP 2007. LNCS, vol. 4596, pp. 411–422. Springer, Heidelberg (2007). https://doi.org/10.1007/978-3-540-73420-8_37

12. Bellare, M., Namprempre, C., Neven, G.: Security proofs for identity-based identification and signature schemes. J. Cryptol. **22**(1), 1–61 (2009)

13. Bellare, M., Rogaway, P.: Random oracles are practical: a paradigm for designing efficient protocols. In: Proceedings of the 1st ACM Conference on Computer and Communications Security – ACM CCS 1993, pp. 62–73. ACM (1993)

14. Bellare, M., Rogaway, P.: The exact security of digital signatures-how to sign with RSA and rabin. In: Maurer, U. (ed.) EUROCRYPT 1996. LNCS, vol. 1070, pp. 399–416. Springer, Heidelberg (1996). https://doi.org/10.1007/3-540-68339-9_34

15. Choon, J.C., Hee Cheon, J.: An identity-based signature from gap Diffie-Hellman groups. In: Desmedt, Y.G. (ed.) PKC 2003. LNCS, vol. 2567, pp. 18–30. Springer, Heidelberg (2003). https://doi.org/10.1007/3-540-36288-6_2

16. Chaum, D.: Zero-knowledge undeniable signatures (extended abstract). In: Damgård, I.B. (ed.) EUROCRYPT 1990. LNCS, vol. 473, pp. 458–464. Springer, Heidelberg (1991). https://doi.org/10.1007/3-540-46877-3_41

17. Coron, J.-S.: On the exact security of full domain hash. In: Bellare, M. (ed.) CRYPTO 2000. LNCS, vol. 1880, pp. 229–235. Springer, Heidelberg (2000). https://doi.org/10.1007/3-540-44598-6_14

18. Coron, J.-S.: Optimal security proofs for PSS and other signature schemes. In: Knudsen, L.R. (ed.) EUROCRYPT 2002. LNCS, vol. 2332, pp. 272–287. Springer, Heidelberg (2002). https://doi.org/10.1007/3-540-46035-7_18

19. Coron, J.S.: A variant of Boneh-Franklin IBE with a tight reduction in the random oracle model. Des. Codes Crypt. **50**(1), 115–133 (2009)

20. Cramer, R., Shoup, V.: Signature schemes based on the strong RSA assumption. ACM Trans. Inf. Syst. Secur. (TISSEC) **3**(3), 161–185 (2000)

21. Kerry, C.F., Director, C.R.: FIPS PUB 186–4 federal information processing standards publication digital signature standard (DSS). FIPS Publication (2013)

22. ElGamal, T.: A public key cryptosystem and a signature scheme based on discrete logarithms. In: Blakley, G.R., Chaum, D. (eds.) CRYPTO 1984. LNCS, vol. 196, pp. 10–18. Springer, Heidelberg (1985). https://doi.org/10.1007/3-540-39568-7_2

23. Guo, F., Chen, R., Susilo, W., Lai, J., Yang, G., Mu, Y.: Optimal security reductions for unique signatures: bypassing impossibilities with a counterexample. In: Katz, J., Shacham, H. (eds.) CRYPTO 2017. LNCS, vol. 10402, pp. 517–547. Springer, Cham (2017). https://doi.org/10.1007/978-3-319-63715-0_18

24. Goh, E.-J., Jarecki, S.: A signature scheme as secure as the Diffie-Hellman problem. In: Biham, E. (ed.) EUROCRYPT 2003. LNCS, vol. 2656, pp. 401–415. Springer, Heidelberg (2003). https://doi.org/10.1007/3-540-39200-9_25

25. Goldwasser, S., Micali, S.: Probabilistic encryption. J. Comput. Syst. Sci. **28**(2), 270–299 (1984)

26. Guillou, L.C., Quisquater, J.-J.: A practical zero-knowledge protocol fitted to security microprocessor minimizing both transmission and memory. In: Barstow, D., et al. (eds.) EUROCRYPT 1988. LNCS, vol. 330, pp. 123–128. Springer, Heidelberg (1988). https://doi.org/10.1007/3-540-45961-8_11

27. Huang, J., Huang, Q., Pan, C.: A black-box construction of strongly unforgeable signature schemes in the bounded leakage model. In: Chen, L., Han, J. (eds.) ProvSec 2016. LNCS, vol. 10005, pp. 320–339. Springer, Cham (2016). https://doi.org/10.1007/978-3-319-47422-9_19

28. Katz, J.: Full-domain hash (and related) signature schemes. In: Katz, J. (ed.) Digital Signatures, pp. 143–153. Springer, Boston (2010). https://doi.org/10.1007/978-0-387-27712-7_7

29. Koblitz, N., Menezes, A.J.: The random oracle model: a twenty-year retrospective. Des. Codes Crypt. **77**(2–3), 587–610 (2015)

30. Kiltz, E., Masny, D., Pan, J.: Optimal security proofs for signatures from identification schemes. In: Robshaw, M., Katz, J. (eds.) CRYPTO 2016. LNCS, vol. 9815, pp. 33–61. Springer, Heidelberg (2016). https://doi.org/10.1007/978-3-662-53008-5_2

31. Katz, J., Wang, N.: Efficiency improvements for signature schemes with tight security reductions. In: ACM CCS 2003, pp. 155–164 (2003)

32. Lacharité, M.S.: Security of BLS and BGLS signatures in a multi-user setting. In: Advances in Cryptology 2016, vol. 2 – ARCTICCRYPT 2016, pp. 244–261 (2016)

33. Lynn, B.: On the implementation of pairing-based cryptosystems. Doctoral dissertation, Stanford University (2007)

34. Katz, J., Menezes, A., Van Oorschot, P., Vanstone, S.: Handbook of Applied Cryptography. CRC Press, Boca Raton (1996)

35. Morita, H., Schuldt, J.C.N., Matsuda, T., Hanaoka, G., Iwata, T.: On the security of the schnorr signature scheme and DSA against related-key attacks. In: Kwon, S., Yun, A. (eds.) ICISC 2015. LNCS, vol. 9558, pp. 20–35. Springer, Cham (2016). https://doi.org/10.1007/978-3-319-30840-1_2

36. Barker, E., Barker, W., Burr, W., Polk, W., Smid, M.: Recommendation for key management-part 1: general (revised). NIST Special Publication (2006)

37. Ng, T.-S., Tan, S.-Y., Chin, J.-J.: A variant of BLS signature scheme with tight security reduction. In: Hu, J., Khalil, I., Tari, Z., Wen, S. (eds.) MONAMI 2017. LNICST, vol. 235, pp. 150–163. Springer, Cham (2018). https://doi.org/10.1007/978-3-319-90775-8_13

38. Ogata, W., Kurosawa, K., Heng, S.-H.: The security of the FDH variant of chaum's undeniable signature scheme. In: Vaudenay, S. (ed.) PKC 2005. LNCS, vol. 3386, pp. 328–345. Springer, Heidelberg (2005). https://doi.org/10.1007/978-3-540-30580-4_23

39. Pereira, G.C., Simplício, M.A., Naehrig, M., Barreto, P.S.: A family of implementation-friendly BN elliptic curves. J. Syst. Softw. **84**(8), 1319–1326 (2011)
40. Rivest, R.L., Shamir, A., Adleman, L.: A method for obtaining digital signatures and public-key cryptosystems. Commun. ACM **21**(2), 120–126 (1978)
41. Vercauteren, F.: Final report on main computational assumptions in cryptography. European Network of Excellence in Cryptography II (2013)

Improved Digital Signatures Based on Elliptic Curve Endomorphism Rings

Xiu Xu[3,4,5]([⊠]), Chris Leonardi[1], Anzo Teh[1], David Jao[1,2], Kunpeng Wang[3,4,5], Wei Yu[3,4,5], and Reza Azarderakhsh[6]

[1] Department of Combinatorics and Optimization,
University of Waterloo, Waterloo, Canada
[2] evolutionQ, Inc., Waterloo, ON, Canada
[3] State Key Laboratory of Information Security, Institute of Information
Engineering, Chinese Academy of Sciences, Beijing, China
xuxiu2017@gmail.com
[4] Data Assurance and Communications Security Research Center, Beijing, China
[5] School of Cyber Security, University of Chinese Academy of Sciences,
Beijing, China
[6] Florida Atlantic University, Boca Raton, USA

Abstract. In AsiaCrypt 2017, Galbraith-Petit-Silva proposed a digital signature scheme based on the problem of computing the endomorphism ring of a supersingular elliptic curve. This problem is more standard than that of the De Feo-Jao-Plût SIDH scheme, since it lacks the auxiliary points which lead to the adaptive active attack of Galbraith-Petit-Shani-Ti. The GPS signature scheme applies the Fiat-Shamir or Unruh transformation to the raw identification protocol obtained from the endomorphism ring problem, and makes use of the Kohel-Lauter-Petit-Tignol quaternion isogeny path algorithm to find a new ideal. However, the GPS signature scheme is not very practical. In this paper, we take a first step towards quantifying the efficiency of the GPS signature scheme. We propose some improvements in the underlying algorithms for the GPS scheme, along with a new method which trades off key size for signature size to decrease the signature size from around 11 kB to 1 kB at the 128-bit security level by using multi-bit challenges. We also provide a concrete implementation of the GPS signature scheme using Sage and CoCalc.

Keywords: Post-quantum · Digital signature · Supersingular isogeny · Endomorphism ring

1 Introduction

Supersingular isogeny cryptosystems have emerged as a promising post-quantum system with the introduction of the Supersingular Isogeny Diffie-Hellman scheme of Jao and De Feo [12]. Although SIDH is believed to resist attacks from quantum computers, it relies on a variation of the standard isogeny-finding hard problem

© Springer Nature Switzerland AG 2019
S.-H. Heng and J. Lopez (Eds.): ISPEC 2019, LNCS 11879, pp. 293–309, 2019.
https://doi.org/10.1007/978-3-030-34339-2_16

of Charles et al. [3] which involves sending auxiliary point information that enables an adaptive active attack [9], which can recover a static secret key bit by bit over many protocol runs. By contrast, the problem of computing the endomorphism ring of a supersingular curve is known to be equivalent to the standard isogeny-finding problem on supersingular isogeny graphs [7].

In the realm of digital signatures, a signature scheme based on the SIDH problem can be obtained by applying the either Fiat-Shamir or Unruh transformation to the zero-knowledge proof of identity proposed in [8]. Such a scheme was proposed by Galbraith et al. [10] and Yoo et al. [20] independently. In addition, [10] also proposes a second signature scheme which requires only the hardness of computing endomorphism rings of a supersingular elliptic curve, which we call the GPS scheme after the authors of [10]. Although [10] provides concrete parameter sizes and key lengths for the 128-bit security level, as well as asymptotic runtime estimates, no concrete implementation results are reported, and we are not aware of any available published implementation of the GPS scheme for real parameter sets of cryptographic size.

Our Contributions

1. We provide the first published description of a concrete implementation of the GPS scheme in Sage, albeit for parameter sizes which fall short of cryptographic size. Our efforts indicate that the main bottleneck in GPS is likely to be the process of translation from the new ideal generated by the Kohel et al. algorithm [14] to a new isogeny, which involves constructing torsion points over large extension fields at a relatively great cost.

2. We propose a new strategy for computing the aforementioned new isogeny by taking advantage of the fact that all supersingular curves can be defined over $\mathbb{F}_{p^2}$, in order to renormalize the codomain of each component isogeny in the chain, which helps control the growth of the extension field degree. Our new isogeny chain is structured as follows:

$$E_0/\mathbb{F}_{p^2} \xrightarrow[\langle P_1 \rangle]{\phi_1} E_1'/\mathbb{F}_{p^{d_1}} \xrightarrow{f_1} E_1/\mathbb{F}_{p^2} \xrightarrow[\langle f_1 \cdot \phi_1(P_2) \rangle]{\phi_2} E_2'/\mathbb{F}_{p^{d_2}} \xrightarrow{f_2} E_2/\mathbb{F}_{p^2} \to \dots$$

3. We propose an optimization of GPS using multi-bit challenges at the expense of large public keys, based on a new assumption involving the forking lemma. This answers an open problem that was posed in [6] concerning how to obtain a similar tradeoff between public key size and signature size as in SeaSign for the SIDH setting. Our variant is secure under the random oracle model, and reduces GPS signature sizes to 1 kB, close to that of SeaSign. The time cost is reduced as well, since we run $\lambda/\log s$ parallel computations instead of λ, where $\log s$ is the challenge size in bits and λ is the security parameter. Our construction uses a modified quaternion isogeny path algorithm whose starting point can be any maximal order (not only the special order $\mathcal{O}_0$), which is of independent interest.

4. We also consider some improvements in the algorithms for translating between isogeny and ideal, including point halving, fast discrete logarithm and Minkowski basis computation.

Related Work. Stolbunov [17] and Couveignes [5] presented initial versions of identification protocols and sketches of a signature scheme based on isogenies. They did not give a secure solution for how to represent the ideal $\mathfrak{b}_k\mathfrak{a}^{-1}$ in the case where the value of the challenge bit is $b_k = 1$, without leaking the private key. SeaSign [6] utilizes the idea of rejection sampling in exactly the way proposed by Lyubashevsky [15] to solve this problem. In addition, [6] sketches an approach to use multi-bit challenges, trading off challenge size for public key size. Large public keys can be easily stored in some settings, such as software signing and license checks, so this tradeoff is worthwhile in some cases.

Outline. The rest of this paper is organised as follows. Section 2 gives basic notation for isogenies and endomorphism rings, related assumptions, and the description of the identification scheme. Section 3 describes the new signature scheme we propose, with multiple challenge bits, and explains its efficiency and security. Section 4 describes our implementation of the original algorithms in the GPS signature scheme. Finally Sect. 5 presents our conclusions.

2   Preliminaries

2.1   Isogeny and Endomorphism Ring

An isogeny is a rational map from one curve E_0 to another curve E_1, mapping the infinite point of E_0 to the infinite point of E_1. An isogeny is group homomorphism, and (if separable) uniquely determined up to isomorphism by its kernel. An endomorphism is an isogeny from an elliptic curve to itself. The endomorphisms of an elliptic curve form a ring under pointwise addition and composition. For a non-constant separable isogeny, its degree is exactly the order of its kernel subgroup. Every isogeny $\phi\colon E_0 \to E_1$ has a dual isogeny $\hat{\phi}\colon E_1 \to E_0$ such that $\hat{\phi}\phi = [\deg \phi]$. From a computational point of view, the general method to compute an isogeny is to use Vélu's formulas [19].

 Over a finite field, an ordinary elliptic curve E_0 is one whose endomorphism ring $\mathrm{End}(E_0)$ is isomorphic to an order in an imaginary quadratic field $\mathbb{Q}(\pi)$, and a supersingular elliptic curve is one whose endomorphism ring is isomorphic to a maximal order in the quaternion algebra $B_{p,\infty}$ ramified at p and ∞. Such an algebra can be represented as $B_{p,\infty} = \mathbb{Q}\langle i,j\rangle$ with $i^2 = -1, j^2 = -p, k = ij = -ji$. Every supersingular elliptic curve is isomorphic to a curve defined over $\mathbb{F}_{p^2}$ for some p. Conjugation, reduced trace, reduced norm, and the bilinear form associated to the reduced norm are defined as follows:

1. $\alpha = a + bi + cj + dk \to \bar{\alpha} = a - bi - cj - dk$, where $a, b, c, d \in \mathbb{Q}$.
2. $\mathrm{Trd}(\alpha) = \alpha + \bar{\alpha} = 2a$.
3. $\mathrm{Nrd}(\alpha) = \alpha\bar{\alpha} = a^2 + b^2 + pc^2 + pd^2$.
4. $\langle x, y\rangle = \mathrm{Nrd}(x + y) - \mathrm{Nrd}(x) - \mathrm{Nrd}(y)$.

 An ideal I in $B_{p,\infty}$ is a $\mathbb{Z}$-lattice of rank 4 and an order $\mathcal{O}$ is not only an ideal but also a ring. The left order of an ideal I is defined as $\mathcal{O}(I) = \{h \in B_{p,\infty} \mid hI \subset I\}$, and I is called a left $\mathcal{O}$-ideal. If I is a left $\mathcal{O}$-ideal, then $I\bar{I} = N\mathcal{O}$ and

$I = \mathcal{O}N + \mathcal{O}\alpha$ where N is the norm of the ideal and $N \mid \mathrm{Nrd}(\alpha)$. We say two left $\mathcal{O}$-ideals I_1 and I_2 are in the same equivalence class if $I_1 = I_2 q$ for some $q \in B_{p,\infty}^*$. Two orders $\mathcal{O}_1$ and $\mathcal{O}_2$ are of the same order type if $\alpha \mathcal{O}_1 \alpha^{-1} = \mathcal{O}_2$ for $\alpha \in B_{p,\infty}^*$.

The Deuring correspondence states that there is a bijection from j-invariants of supersingular curves to maximal orders in the quaternion algebra $B_{p,\infty}$. For the supersingular curve $E_0 : y^2 = x^3 + x$ over $\mathbb{F}_{p^2}$ where $p \equiv 3 \pmod 4$, the endomorphism ring of E_0 is isomorphic to the maximal order $\mathcal{O}_0 = \langle 1, i, \frac{1+k}{2}, \frac{i+j}{2} \rangle$, and there is an isomorphism of quaternion algebras $\theta : B_{p,\infty} \to \mathrm{End}(E_0) \otimes \mathbb{Q}$ sending $(1, i, j, k)$ to $(1, \phi, \pi, \pi\phi)$ where π is the Frobenius endomorphism mapping (x, y) to (x^p, y^p) and $\phi : (x, y) \to (-x, iy)$.

If we have an isogeny $\phi : E \to E'$ over $\mathbb{F}_{p^2}$ of degree n, then we can construct a left $\mathrm{End}(E)$-ideal $I = \mathrm{Hom}(E', E)\phi$ of norm n. Conversely, in order to construct an isogeny from a left $\mathrm{End}(E)$-ideal I, we define $E[I] = \bigcap_{\alpha \in I} \ker(\alpha)$. Then there is an associated isogeny $\phi_I : E \to E/E[I]$. If $(n, p) = 1$, then $E[I] = \{P \in E(\mathbb{F}_{p^2}) : \alpha(P) = \infty$ for all $\alpha \in I\}$.

2.2   Hard Problems

For more information on hard problems related to isogenies, see [7,10,11].

Problem 1. *Given two supersingular curves E, E' defined over $\mathbb{F}_{p^2}$, find an isogeny $\phi : E \to E'$.*

This problem is the most general problem related to finding isogenies. The fastest known algorithm for finding isogenies between supersingular curves in general takes $O(\sqrt{p} \log^2 p)$ [3]. It can be viewed as a graph navigation problem on a Ramanujan graph.

In SIDH, we choose a prime of the form $p = \ell_A^{e_A} \ell_B^{e_B} \cdot f \pm 1$ where ℓ_A and ℓ_B are small primes and f is a cofactor. We fix a supersingular elliptic curve E defined over $\mathbb{F}_{p^2}$. Furthermore, $E[\ell_A^{e_A}] = \mathbb{Z}/\ell_A^{e_A}\mathbb{Z} \oplus \mathbb{Z}/\ell_A^{e_A}\mathbb{Z} = \langle P_A, Q_A \rangle$, $E[\ell_B^{e_B}] = \mathbb{Z}/\ell_B^{e_B}\mathbb{Z} \oplus \mathbb{Z}/\ell_B^{e_B}\mathbb{Z} = \langle P_B, Q_B \rangle$.

Problem 2. *Let $\phi_A : E \to E_A$ be an isogeny with its kernel $\langle R_A \rangle$ where R_A is a point of order $\ell_A^{e_A}$. Given $E_A, \phi_A(P_B), \phi_A(Q_B)$, find a generator of $\langle R_A \rangle$.*

This is the computational supersingular isogeny (CSSI) problem upon which SIDH relies [8]. It can be reduced to a claw finding problem. Its classical and quantum complexities are $\mathcal{O}(p^{1/4})$ and $\mathcal{O}(p^{1/6})$, respectively. Recently, the van Oorschot-Wiener (vOW) golden collision finding algorithm [1,4] was argued to be the most efficient quantum algorithm for CSSI.

Problem 3. *Given a supersingular curve E defined over $\mathbb{F}_{p^2}$, determine the endomorphism ring of E.*

For some special curves, the endomorphism rings are easy to compute, but for an arbitrary supersingular curve, finding its endomorphism ring is hard. The best quantum algorithm still runs in exponential complexity [13]. Problems 1 and 3 are known to be equivalent [7,10].

2.3 Identification Protocol Based on Endomorphism Ring

We briefly describe the Galbraith-Petit-Silva [10] identification protocol.

1. The public key is (E_0, E_1), and the private key is an isogeny $\phi \colon E_0 \to E_1$.
2. The prover chooses a random walk of degree L from E_1 in the graph, arriving at a curve E_2 with $\psi \colon E_1 \to E_2$. The prover sends E_2 to the verifier.
3. The verifier randomly chooses a challenge bit b and sends b to the prover.
4. If $b = 0$, the prover answers ψ. If $b = 1$, the prover publishes a new isogeny $\eta \colon E_0 \to E_2$, where $\eta \neq \psi\phi$.
5. The verifier accepts the proof if the answer is indeed an isogeny between E_1 and E_2 or between E_0 and E_2.

The GPS signature scheme uses four key algorithms in the process of computing a new path η: loading the isogeny chains, translating from an isogeny to an quaternion ideal, finding a new path (using the quaternion isogeny path algorithm) and translating from the new ideal back to an isogeny. The reason that a new path η is published instead of the original isogeny $\psi\phi$ is that publishing $\psi\phi$ might reveal information about the secret ϕ. In order to produce a new path to avoid the leakage of the secret key, the quaternion isogeny path algorithm [14] is used.

Definition 1. *A signature Π=(KeyGen, Sign, Verify) is said to be existentially unforgeable under adaptive chosen-message attacks if for all probabilistic polynomial time adversaries $\mathcal{A}$ with access to the oracle $\mathcal{O}$,*

$$\left| \Pr \left[\begin{array}{c} (\mathrm{PK}, \mathrm{SK}) \leftarrow \mathsf{KeyGen}(1^\lambda); \sigma_i \leftarrow \mathcal{O}(\mathrm{m_i}) \text{ for } 1 \leq \mathrm{i} \leq \mathrm{k}; \\ (m, \sigma) \leftarrow \mathcal{A}(\mathrm{PK}, \mathrm{m_i}, \sigma_i) : \\ \mathsf{Verify}(m, \sigma) = 1 \text{ and } m \neq m_i \end{array} \right] \right| \leq \mathrm{negl}(\lambda).$$

Theorem 1 ([10]). *If the identification is non-trival and recoverable, then the signature derived from this identification using the Fiat-Shamir transform is secure against chosen-message attacks in the random oracle model.*

2.4 Quaternion Isogeny Path Algorithm

The quaternion isogeny path algorithm from Kohel et al. [14] plays an important role in finding a new ideal that corresponds to another isogeny path between two curves. [10] used the power-smooth version of the quaternion ℓ-isogeny algorithm to compute another path from E_0 to E_2 in the quaternion algebra. The new path is independent of E_1 and corresponds to an ideal J.

We recall the quaternion isogeny path algorithm briefly, adopting the notations in [10]. The inputs are a special maximal order $\mathcal{O}_0$ in the quaternion algebra $B_{p,\infty}$ and a corresponding left $\mathcal{O}_0$ ideal I given by a $\mathbb{Z}$-basis of elements in $\mathcal{O}_0$. This is equivalent to inputting two maximal orders $\mathcal{O}_0$ and $\mathcal{O}_1$, as the right order $\mathcal{O}_1$ of I is the set $\{h \in B_{p,\infty} \mid Ih \subset I\}$. The algorithm aims to find a new ideal J such that $J = Iq$ for some $q \in B_{p,\infty}^*$. Here are the main steps of the process:

1. Find I' such that I' has a prime norm N and $I' = Iq$.
2. Choose $\alpha \in I'$ such that $\gcd(\mathrm{Nrd}(\alpha), N^2) = N$, so that $I' = \mathcal{O}_0 N + \mathcal{O}_0 \alpha$.
3. Set a bound $s = \frac{7}{2} \log p$, and odd integers $S_1 > p \log p$ and $S_2 > p^3 \log p$.
4. Find $a, b, c, d \in \mathbb{Z}$ such that $N S_1 = a^2 + b^2 + p(c^2 + d^2)$. Then set $\beta_1 = a + bi + cj + dk$ of norm $N S_1$.
5. Find $\beta_2 \in \mathbb{Z} j + \mathbb{Z} k$ such that $\beta_1 \beta_2 = \alpha \bmod N\mathcal{O}_1$, and set $\beta_2 = Cj + Dk$.
6. Find β_2' of norm S_2 such that $\beta_2' - \lambda\beta \in N\mathcal{O}_0$ for some $\lambda \in \mathbb{Z}$.
7. Return $J = I' \beta_1 \beta_2' / N$.

We see that the norm of the new ideal J is $S = \frac{\mathrm{Nrd}(I')\mathrm{Nrd}(\beta_1\beta_2')}{N^2} = S_1 S_2$ with $\log S \approx \frac{7}{2} \log p$, and an improvement in [16] reduces its norm to $\frac{5}{2} \log p$. The large norm of the new ideal is the root of the difficulty in implementing GPS signatures. We remark that implementing the quaternion isogeny path algorithm is of independent interest separating from the GPS signature scheme—it breaks the quaternion order analog of the CGL hash function [3], and also can be used to compute the j-invariant corresponding to a quaternion order. We also note here that the quaternion isogeny path algorithm in [10] is just suitable for the case that the input quaternion order is $\mathcal{O}_0$. However, we believe that it will also work for any other input quaternion after a little modification to the step 4 of the above algorithm which is also of independent interest. So in the following, we still call it the quaternion isogeny path algorithm even the input is not the special order $\mathcal{O}_0$.

3   Digital Signature Based on Endomorphism Ring

3.1   Modified Identification Protocol

We propose a modified identification protocol based on that of Sect. 2.3, using multi-bit challenges.

Phase 1 (done once)

Perform random walks ϕ_i from E_0 to $E_{A,i}$, where $i \in \{0, 1, ..., s - 1\}$.

Phase 2 (repeated $t = \frac{\lambda}{\log s}$ times)

1. The prover sends the verifier a random walk w from E_0 to some curve E_B.
2. The verifier responds with $b \in \{0, 1, ..., s - 1\}$.
3. The prover computes a dual isogeny $\hat{\phi}_b$ and with the quaternion isogeny path algorithm, produces a path w_b' between $E_{A,b}$ and E_B. The prover sends w_b' to the verifier.
4. The verifier accepts the proof if the answer is really an isogeny from $E_{A,b}$ to E_B.

Fig. 1. The multiple bit version of the identification protocol.

We give a brief analysis of the properties of the above protocol. It is obvious that this identification is non-trivial and recoverable.

Completeness. Just follow the procedure in Fig. 1 and the verifier accepts the proof.

Soundness. Suppose we are given transcripts $(\text{CMT}, c, d, \text{RSP}_1, \text{RSP}_2)$, where $\text{CMT} = E_B$. For two different challenges c and d, we can compute two isogenies $w'_c : E_{A,c} \to E_B$ and $w'_d : E_{A,d} \to E_B$. Then we can obtain an isogeny $\hat{w'_d} w'_c$ from $E_{A,c}$ to $E_{A,d}$, which is a solution to Problem 4 that we propose in the following section.

Zero-knowledge. This simulator is almost identical as the one for the classical graph isomorphism. If the verifier is dishonest, we can remove these rounds from the simulator transcript. The distributions of the transcript $(\text{CMT}, c, \text{RSP})$ are indistinguishable from the real one. The data revealed in step 3 is an isogeny produced by the quaternion isogeny path algorithm and this algorithm leaks no information about the input isogeny.

3.2 Proposed Digital Signature Scheme

In [10] it is proved that that any 2-special sound identification scheme can be transformed into a non-trivial scheme by running t sessions in parallel, where $t \geq \lambda/c$ with security parameter λ and challenge bit length c. Hence, one of the main reasons that this kind of signature scheme is of low efficiency is that the signature has to run t times. Using the multi-bit challenge approach, the resulting signatures gain higher efficiency and a smaller size. Algorithms 1, 2, and 3 present the resulting signature scheme using the Fiat-Shamir transform in the classical case.

Public Parameters. A security parameter λ and a prime p of the form $4 \cdot \ell_1 \cdots \ell_n - 1$ where ℓ_i is a small prime. The prime p satisfies $p \equiv 3 \mod 4$. Small fixed parameters B, S_1, S_2, where $B = 2(1 + \epsilon) \log p$, $\epsilon > 0$, $S_k = \prod_i \ell_{k,i}^{e_{k,i}}$, $\ell_{k,i}^{e_{k,i}} < B$, $\gcd(S_1, S_2) = 1$ and $\prod_i \left(\frac{2\sqrt{\ell_{k,i}}}{\ell_{k,i}+1} \right)^{e_{k,i}} < (p^{1+\epsilon})^{-1}$. A supersingular curve $E_0/\mathbb{F}_{p^2} : y^2 = x^3 + x$, and a cryptographic hash function H with at least λ bits of output. Suppose that the length of the challenge is $\log s$, i.e. $t = \lambda/\log s$.

Algorithm 1. KeyGen(λ)

1: Perform s random isogeny walks ϕ_m of degree S_1 from E_0 to curves $E_{A,m}$ with j-invariant $j_{A,m}$, where $m \in \{0, 1, ..., s-1\}$.
2: Compute the ideal $I_{A,m}$ corresponding to each isogeny.
3: Compute $\mathcal{O}_{A,m} = \text{End}(E_{A,m})$.
4: $pk \leftarrow (j_{A,0}, j_{A,1}, .., j_{A,s-1})$.
5: $sk \leftarrow (I_{A,0}, I_{A,1}, ..., I_{A,s-1})$ or $(\mathcal{O}_{A,0}, \mathcal{O}_{A,1}, ..., \mathcal{O}_{A,s-1})$.
6: **return** (pk, sk).

Since we set the challenge bit to be $\log s$, we compute s isogenies during the generation of the public and secret keys. This key generation procedure can be performed in advance. Although the public and secret keys can be generated

---

Algorithm 2. Sign(sk, m)

1: **for** $i = 1$ to t **do**
2:    Perform a random isogeny walk w_i of degree S_2 from E_0 to $E_{B,i}$ with j-invariant $j_{B,i}$, and compute the corresponding ideal $I_{B,i}$.
3:    Compute the hash value $h = H(m, j_{B,1}, j_{B,2}, .., j_{B,t})$ and set $h \leftarrow b_1||b_2||...||b_t$, where $b_i \in \{0, 1, ..., s - 1\}$.
4: **end for**
5: **for** $i = 1$ to t **do**
6:    Compute the dual isogeny $\hat{\phi}_{b_i}$ and the corresponding ideal I_{A,b_i}^{-1}.
7:    On input $I_{A,b_i}^{-1} I_{B,i}$ and $\mathcal{O}_{A,b_i}$, perform the modified quaternion isogeny path algorithm to produce a new ideal J_i between $\mathcal{O}_{A,b_i}$ and $\mathcal{O}_{B,i}$. Then translate J_i to an isogeny w_i' between j_{A,b_i} and $j_{B,i}$.
8:    Set $z_i \leftarrow w_i'$.
9: **end for**
10: The signature is $\sigma = (h, z_1, z_2, ..., z_t)$.

Algorithm 3. Verify(pk, m, σ)

---

for $i = 1$ to t **do**
    Use z_i to compute the image curve $j_{B,i}$ from j_{A,b_i}.
end for
Then compute $h' \leftarrow H(m, j_{B,1}, j_{B,2}, ..., j_{B,t})$.
if $h' = h$ **then**
    return 1.
end if

---

offline, the number s cannot be too large, or else large storage will be needed. An illustration of how to generate the key pairs is presented in Fig. 2. The path can be represented by the isogeny between two j-invariants of curves or the ideal connecting two endomorphism rings. By taking $B = 2(1 + \epsilon) \log p$, we can guarantee that the output of random walks is uniformly distributed as proved in [10].

During the Sign step, the commitments of our scheme are different from those in [10]. We perform the isogeny from j_0 to j_B but not from j_A to j_B. As the number of j_A's is s, there would be $s \cdot t$ isogenies to be computed which costs too much. So we use instead the path from j_0 to j_B. In this case additional dual isogenies and the inverse of ideals have to be computed, but it is not hard to do that. As for the z_i's, since an isogeny can be determined by its kernel point and the Montgomery curve has a special structure in $\mathbb{P}_1$, each z_i can be set as the x-coordinate of R_i where ker $w_i' = \langle R_i \rangle$. For the i-th round, we clarify in Fig. 3 how to find a new path J_i.

Efficiency. We provide a rough estimate for the parameters and efficiency for our version of the signature scheme. For classical security, we choose $\log p = 2\lambda$. For λ bits of security, we set $t = \lambda / \log s$. The uniform distribution of random walk output requires that the output walk has length $2(1 + \varepsilon) \log p \approx 4\lambda$ in GPS signatures, and the public keys are 6λ bits. Hence, in our multi-bit signature, if

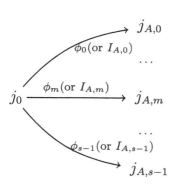

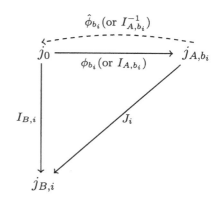

Fig. 2. Illustration of KeyGen.

Fig. 3. Find one new path for the i-th parallel round.

s isogeny walks are computed, then the size of the private key and public key increases by a factor of s. The average size of our signature is $\lambda + \frac{\lambda}{\log s}(2(1 + \varepsilon)\log p) \approx \frac{4}{\log s}\lambda^2$. We mention that the verification of GPS signature and ours both have a cost about $\mathcal{O}(\lambda^4)$ bit operations, but not $\mathcal{O}(\lambda^6)$ bit operations as stated in [10]. We only require $\lambda/\log s$ calls to the four key algorithms in the GPS scheme, which reduces the overall cost by a factor of $\log s$. An asymptotic comparison between GPS signatures and ours is listed in Table 1, and a concrete comparison in Table 2 using $\log s = 8$. By contrast, the shorter signature version of Seasign [6] uses $\log s = 16$. If we also take $\log s = 16$, the signature size will be halved, but the size of private and public key will be quite large.

Table 1. Comparison about Galbraith-Petit-Silva endomorphism ring signature [10] with ours in key size and cost. "$\log s$" is the challenge bit and it is a positive integer.

Scheme	Private key	Public key	Signature size	Sign cost	Verify cost
GPS17 [10]	4λ	6λ	$\frac{11}{2}\lambda^2$	$\mathcal{O}(\lambda^6)$	$\mathcal{O}(\lambda^4)$
Ours	$4s\lambda$	$4s\lambda$	$\frac{4}{\log s}\lambda^2$	$\mathcal{O}(\lambda^6)$	$\mathcal{O}(\lambda^4)$

Security. Recall that the signature is accepted if and only if for every step, the prover can find a path that leads to a curve with the correct j-invariant. To ensure that the scheme is secure, the probability of each potential j must be nearly uniformly likely to be the j-invariant of the resulting curve. The random walk theorem proven in [10] states that for every j-invariant $\tilde{j}$ we have

$$|Pr[j = \tilde{j}] - \frac{1}{N_p}| \le \prod_{i=1}^{r}\left(\frac{2\sqrt{\ell_i}}{\ell_i + 1}\right)^{e_i},$$

Table 2. A concrete efficiency comparison at the security level of 128 bits and we choose our challenge bit $\log s = 8$. These sizes are all counted in bytes. We list the performance of the shorter signature version of SeaSign [6].

Scheme	Private key	Public key	Signature size
GPS17 [10]	64	96	11264
SeaSign [6]	16	$4032 \cdot 10^3$	944
Ours	16384	16384	1024

where N_p is the number of all supersingular j-invariants over $\mathbb{F}_{p^2}$. In order to make the isogeny path random, the right-hand term of the above formula should be smaller than $(p^{1+\epsilon})^{-1}$ for any positive ϵ. We guarantee this in our parameters by using $B = 2(1 + \epsilon) \log p$.

The single-bit version of the GPS signature scheme has been proved to be secure in the random oracle model under a chosen message attack in Theorem 10 of [10], if Problem 1 is computationally hard. For the multi-bit version, the signature derived from the non-trivial canonical recoverable identification still works. But we can also consider the security reduction from another perspective. We treat this signature with multi-bit challenges as a kind of multi-signature, but in the case that the only one signer has multiple public keys signing one message. This idea is inspired by the smaller signature version of SeaSign.

We recall the forking lemma from Bellare and Neven [2].

Lemma 1. *Fix an integer $q \geq 1$. Let A be a randomized algorithm that takes input $h_1, \ldots, h_q \in \{0,1\}^t$ and outputs (J, σ) where J is an integer $1 \leq J \leq q$ with probability γ. The forking algorithm proceeds as follows: $h_1, \ldots, h_q$ are chosen randomly in $\{0,1\}^t$. $A(h_1, \ldots, h_q)$ outputs (J, σ) with $J \geq 1$. Then randomly choose $h'_J, \ldots, h'_q \in \{0,1\}^t$. $A(h_1, \ldots, h_{J-1}, h'_J, \ldots, h'_q)$ outputs (J', σ'). Then the probability that $J = J'$ and $h'_J \neq h_J$ is larger than $\gamma(\frac{\gamma}{q} - \frac{1}{2^t})$.*

Note that by the forking lemma, there are two signatures for some $b_k \neq b'_k$. Hence we can get two paths J'_k and J_k to j_{B_k} from j_{A,b'_k} and j_{A,b_k}, respectively. So $(J'_k)^{-1}J_k$ is the path from j_{A,b_k} to j_{A,b'_k}. Therefore, we propose a new assumption for our multi-bit signature scheme.

Problem 4. *Given $\{j_{A,0}, \ldots, j_{A,s-1}\}$, produced by performing s random isogeny walks of degree ℓ^e from E_0 with j-invariant j_0, compute an ideal I corresponding to an isogeny $E_{A,m} \to E_{A,m'}$ with j-invariants $j_{A,m}$ and $j_{A,m'}$ for $m \neq m'$.*

This problem can be easily reduced to Problem 3. If Problem 3 is solved, then we can compute the endomorphism rings $\mathcal{O}_{A,m}$ and $\mathcal{O}_{A,m'}$ corresponding to $j_{A,m}$ and $j_{A,m'}$, respectively. Then we compute an ideal I which is a left $\mathcal{O}_{A,m}$-ideal and its right order is isomorphic to $\mathcal{O}_{A,m'}$ for $m \neq m'$. The quaternion isogeny path algorithm will now work to find an isogeny path between curves $E_{A,m}$ and $E_{A,m'}$. The main reduction is given in Algorithm 9 in [7].

Theorem 2. *If Problem 4 is computationally hard, then our multi-bit challenge signatures are existentially unforgeable under chosen-message attacks in the random oracle model.*

Proof (sketch). Suppose there is a probabilistic polynomial time adversary $\mathcal{A}$ against the signature. Then the public key is known to $\mathcal{A}$, and $\mathcal{A}$ can query the hash function H and the signing oracle $\mathcal{O}_{sign}$. Suppose the adversary $\mathcal{A}$ can make at most q hash oracle queries and n signing oracle queries. In order to simulate the random oracles, $\mathcal{A}$ should maintain the hash list L_H and the signature list L_{sign} corresponding to the queries and answers of the H-oracle and $\mathcal{O}_{sign}$.

Querying H-oracle with $(m, j_1, \ldots, j_t)$: If there exists $(m, j_1, \ldots, j_t, h) \in L_H$ then return h. Otherwise, $\mathcal{A}$ randomly chooses h, returns h and records $(m, j_1, \ldots, j_t, h)$ in L_H.

Querying $\mathcal{O}_{sign}$ with message m: The simulator chooses random bit-string $b_1, \ldots, b_t \in \{0, 1, \ldots, s - 1\}$. For $i = 1, \ldots, t$, the simulator computes a random isogeny walk z_i from E_0 to $E_{B,i}$. We update the hash list that $H(m, j_{B,1}, \ldots, j_{B,t}) = b_1 \ldots b_t$, unless the random oralce has already been defined on this input in which case the simulation fails. Then return and record $(b_1 \ldots b_t, z_1, \ldots, z_t)$ in the list L_{sign}. This simulation fails at a negligible probability according to the above random walk theorem. Hence, the output is a valid signature and is indistinguishable from the real signature.

We consider the case that when the adversary replays the same tape, one of the hash queries is answered with a different binary string. With non-negligible probability $\mathcal{A}$ outputs a forgery $(b'_1 \ldots b'_t, z'_1, \ldots, z'_t)$ for the same message m and the same $(m, j_{B,1}, \ldots, j_{B,t})$ to H with a output $b'_1 \ldots b'_t$. Without loss of generality, we assume that $b_k \neq b'_k$. Then the isogeny paths z_k from $\mathcal{O}_{A,k}$ to $\mathcal{O}_{B,k}$ and z'_k from $\mathcal{O}_{A,k'}$ to $\mathcal{O}_{B,k'}$ with $\mathcal{O}_{B,k} = \mathcal{O}_{B,k'}$ are such that $(z'_k)^{-1} z_k$ is a solution to Problem 4. □

4   Analysis and Implementation of Galbraith-Petit-Silva Signature

Parameters. We first choose an odd and power-smooth number $n = \prod_{i=1}^{r} \ell_i$ such that $p = 4n - 1$ is a prime. These ℓ_i are selected as distinct odd primes; a straightforward way is to choose n as the product of the first few primes. For example, we take $n = 3 \times 5 \times 7$ and then $p = 419$ is prime. Table 3 shows the primes that we adopt, where the notion $[a, b]$ means all primes in the range $[a, b]$ and $[a, b] + [c]$ means all primes $[a, b]$ along with c. The global curve E_0 is chosen as $y^2 = x^3 + x$ over $\mathbb{F}_{p^2}$ with the initial j-invariant 1728 and the endomorphism ring $\mathcal{O}_0 = \langle 1, i, \frac{i+j}{2}, \frac{1+k}{2} \rangle$.

There are four main algorithms involved in the signature scheme, including loading isogenies, translating the isogeny to the ideal, finding a new ideal, and translating the new ideal to the isogeny. The loading isogenies algorithm inherits the strategy of SIDH to run in a sequential manner. To be precise, suppose that the degree of an isogeny is $\prod_{i=1}^{r} \ell_i^{e_i}$; then we split it into e_i successive ℓ_i-isogenies for every i.

Table 3. The choice of the global parameters.

n	Notation	$\log_2 p$
$3 \times 5 \times 7$	$[3, 10]$	8.711
$3 \times 5 \times \cdots \times 19$	$[3,20]$	24.210
$3 \times 5 \times \cdots \times 43 \times 97$	$[3, 43] + [97]$	61.138
$3 \times 5 \times \cdots \times 113$	$[3, 113]$	155.469
$3 \times 5 \times \cdots \times 373 \times 587$	$[3, 373] + [587]$	510.668

Minkowski Basis Computation. Up to dimension four basis, Minkowski is arguably optimal compared to all other known reductions, since it can reach all the so-called successive minima. Given a basis $\{v_1, v_2, \ldots, v_n\}$, v_i must have a norm smaller or equal to $v_i + \sum_{j=1, j \neq i}^n a_j v_j$ for any combinations of integers a_j in the Minkowski-reduced basis. In the quaternion algebra setting, we focus on the $n = 4$ case. We set $i = 1$ for illustration purposes here. Denote by v_{ij} the j-th coordinate of the vector v_i. We have

$$||v_1 + a_2 v_2 + a_3 v_3 + a_4 v_4|| = \sum_{j=1}^4 s_j (v_{1j} + a_2 v_{2j} + a_3 v_{3j} + a_4 v_{4j})^2$$

where $s_1 = s_2 = 1$ and $s_3 = s_4 = p$. In the quaternion algebra, the inner product of two elements $v_1 + v_2 i + v_3 j + v_4 k$ and $w_1 + w_2 i + w_3 j + w_4 k$ is $v_1 w_1 + v_2 w_2 + p v_3 w_3 + p v_4 w_4$. Then for each $k = 2, 3, 4$ we have

$$\frac{d}{da_k} ||v_1 + a_2 v_2 + a_3 v_3 + a_4 v_4|| = \sum_{j=1}^4 2 v_{kj} s_j (v_{1j} + a_2 v_{2j} + a_3 v_{3j} + a_4 v_{4j})$$

$$= 2(\boldsymbol{v_k} \cdot \boldsymbol{v_1} + a_2 \boldsymbol{v_k} \cdot \boldsymbol{v_2} + a_3 \boldsymbol{v_k} \cdot \boldsymbol{v_3} + a_4 \boldsymbol{v_k} \cdot \boldsymbol{v_4}).$$

When a_2, a_3, a_4 are the numbers that give the minimal possible norm, we have

$$\begin{pmatrix} \boldsymbol{v_2} \cdot \boldsymbol{v_1} \\ \boldsymbol{v_3} \cdot \boldsymbol{v_1} \\ \boldsymbol{v_4} \cdot \boldsymbol{v_1} \end{pmatrix} + a_2 \begin{pmatrix} \boldsymbol{v_2} \cdot \boldsymbol{v_2} \\ \boldsymbol{v_3} \cdot \boldsymbol{v_2} \\ \boldsymbol{v_4} \cdot \boldsymbol{v_2} \end{pmatrix} + a_3 \begin{pmatrix} \boldsymbol{v_2} \cdot \boldsymbol{v_3} \\ \boldsymbol{v_3} \cdot \boldsymbol{v_3} \\ \boldsymbol{v_4} \cdot \boldsymbol{v_3} \end{pmatrix} + a_4 \begin{pmatrix} \boldsymbol{v_2} \cdot \boldsymbol{v_4} \\ \boldsymbol{v_3} \cdot \boldsymbol{v_4} \\ \boldsymbol{v_4} \cdot \boldsymbol{v_4} \end{pmatrix} = \begin{pmatrix} 0 \\ 0 \\ 0 \end{pmatrix}.$$

This can be solved as

$$\begin{pmatrix} a_2 \\ a_3 \\ a_4 \end{pmatrix} = - \begin{pmatrix} \boldsymbol{v_2} \cdot \boldsymbol{v_2} & \boldsymbol{v_2} \cdot \boldsymbol{v_3} & \boldsymbol{v_2} \cdot \boldsymbol{v_4} \\ \boldsymbol{v_3} \cdot \boldsymbol{v_2} & \boldsymbol{v_3} \cdot \boldsymbol{v_3} & \boldsymbol{v_3} \cdot \boldsymbol{v_4} \\ \boldsymbol{v_4} \cdot \boldsymbol{v_2} & \boldsymbol{v_4} \cdot \boldsymbol{v_3} & \boldsymbol{v_4} \cdot \boldsymbol{v_4} \end{pmatrix}^{-1} \begin{pmatrix} \boldsymbol{v_2} \cdot \boldsymbol{v_1} \\ \boldsymbol{v_3} \cdot \boldsymbol{v_1} \\ \boldsymbol{v_4} \cdot \boldsymbol{v_1} \end{pmatrix}.$$

The resulting a_2, a_3, a_4 might not be integers and we can replace them by the nearest integers. After finding the optimal $v_1 + a_2 v_2 + a_3 v_3 + a_4 v_4$, we replace v_1 with this expression and repeat this procedure for all $i = 1, 2, 3, 4$. This Minkowski method manages to bring N down to $p^{0.5+o(1)}$ in the finding new path algorithm.

Improvements for Isogeny-to-Ideal. First we recall the runtime analysis of this algorithm given by Galbraith-Petit-Silva. This algorithm finds a point Q_i of order $\ell_i^{e_i}$ that generates the kernel of ϕ_i by considering the kernel polynomial ψ_i of the $\ell_i^{e_i}$-isogeny which takes a total of $\ell_i^{e_i}$ steps. The next step is to find $\alpha_i \in I$ satisfying $\alpha_i Q_i = \infty$, where I is the ideal generated in the previous step. The algorithm identifies the basis $\beta_1, \beta_2, \beta_3, \beta_4$ of I and tries a random solution to $\alpha = \omega\beta_1 + x\beta_2 + y\beta_3 + z\beta_4$ by setting ω, x, y randomly to see if there is a z satisfying this condition. The new ideal is the set as $I_{i-1}\ell_i^{e_i} + \mathcal{O}_0\alpha_i$. This involves an average of $\ell_i^{e_i}$ tries to find the suitable α and computing αQ_i takes $\mathcal{O}(\log^2 p)$ bit operations.

Next, the algorithm needs to perform point halving due to the fact that the coefficient of elements in the associated ideal can be non-integer, with denominator at most 2. Nevertheless, the original algorithm chooses points that have odd order N. For each a we have $\frac{a}{2} \equiv a(\frac{N+1}{2}) \mod N$ and so for each point P of order N we have $\frac{a}{2}P \equiv a(\frac{N+1}{2})P$. Thus we save the cost of point halving.

The main improvement comes from the step of finding ω, x, y, z satisfying $(\omega\beta_1 + x\beta_2 + y\beta_3 + z\beta_4)Q_i = \infty$. We can break down the $\ell_i^{e_i}$ tries into solving a modular ℓ_i equivalence for e_i times. When at step j, we want $\alpha(\ell_i^{e_i})Q_i = \infty$, or in other words $\omega(\ell_i^{e_i-j})P_1 + x(\ell_i^{e_i-j})P_2 + y(\ell_i^{e_i-j})P_3 + z(\ell_i^{e_i-j})P_4 = \infty$, where $P_i = \beta_i Q_i$ for $i = \{1, 2, 3, 4\}$. The procedure goes as follows at each step j:

1. Set $S = \omega(\ell_i^{e_i-j})P_1 + x(\ell_i^{e_i-j})P_2 + y(\ell_i^{e_i-j})P_3 + z(\ell_i^{e_i-j})P_4$. Notice that S has order either 1 or ℓ_i. This is true if $j = 1$, and for $j > 1$ it follows from the loop invariant that we had $\omega(\ell_i^{e_i-j+1})P_1 + x(\ell_i^{e_i-j+1})P_2 + y(\ell_i^{e_i-j+1})P_3 + z(\ell_i^{e_i-j+1})P_4 = \infty$ from the previous step.
2. Choose ω', x', y' randomly from $\{0, 1, \ldots, \ell_i\}$. In the case of $j = 1$, care must be taken so that not all ω', x', y' are divisible by ℓ_i.
3. Consider the point $T = S + \omega'(\ell_i^{e_i-1})P_1 + x'(\ell_i^{e_i-1})P_2 + y'(\ell_i^{e_i-1})P_3$, and see whether T and $(\ell_i^{e_i-1}P_4)$ are linearly dependent in the ℓ_i torsion space. If so, solve for $T + z'(\ell_i^{e_i-1})P_4 = \infty$. Otherwise, repeat the loop.
4. Now that $S + \omega'(\ell_i^{e_i-1})P_1 + x'(\ell_i^{e_i-1})P_2 + y'(\ell_i^{e_i-1})P_3 + z'(\ell_i^{e_i-1})P_4 = \infty$, we update $\omega = \omega + \omega'(\ell_i^{j-1}), x = x + x'(\ell_i^{j-1}), y = y + y'(\ell_i^{j-1}), z = z + z'(\ell_i^{j-1})$. This update gives $\omega(\ell_i^{e_i-j})P_1 + x(\ell_i^{e_i-j})P_2 + y(\ell_i^{e_i-j})P_3 + z(\ell_i^{e_i-j})P_4 = \infty$.

Improvements for Ideal-to-Isogeny. If we just translate the original ideal with a small norm, but not the newly-generated ideal from the quaternion isogeny path algorithm, Algorithm 2 in [10] can work out the correct isogeny path. But if we want to translate the new ideal with a large norm, we have to modify some steps. For example, if we take the prime $p = 4 \cdot 3 \cdot 5 \cdot 7 - 1$, we can produce a new ideal with norm $3^2 \cdot 5^2 \cdot 7^2 \cdot 11^2 \cdot 13^2 \cdot 17 \cdot 19 \cdot 23$. If we then want to translate this new ideal back to an isogeny, we first have to compute bases for the $3^2, \ldots, 23$ torsion. However, all of these torsion points are no longer defined on $\mathbb{F}_{p^2}$, but over large extension fields.

We discuss the details and complexities of the ideal-to-isogeny algorithm that involves constructing torsion subgroups and their associated finite field extensions. Recall that the ideal J returned by the quaternion isogeny path algorithm has a norm of S which may be divisible by prime powers. Write the norm of ideal J as $n = \prod_{i=1}^{r} \ell_i^{e_i}$. In order to construct the isogeny ϕ corresponding to J, we must construct a point P_i for each prime power dividing n. Then a generator of the kernel of ϕ is the point $\sum_{i=1}^{r} P_i \in E_0(\overline{\mathbb{F}})$. The required torsion subgroups fall into two main types:

1. $\ell_i^{e_i} \mid p + 1$,
2. $\ell_i^{e_i} \nmid p + 1$.

For the type 1, torsion subgroups will exist in $E_0(\mathbb{F}_{p^2})$. For the other type of prime powers we will need to work over some extension field $\mathbb{F}_{p^d}$ for $d \in \mathbb{N}$. We now examine how to determine d explicitly in this type. Fix $\ell^e = \ell_i^{e_i}$ for simplicity. The x-coordinates of the ℓ^e-torsion points are the roots of the division polynomial $\psi_{\ell^e}(x)$. While this polynomial has degree $\frac{\ell^{2e}-1}{2}$ for odd ℓ and is guaranteed to split over an extension of that degree, the minimal extension we are required to work over may be smaller. We determine the extension degree d as follows: factor $\psi_{\ell^e}(x)$ over $\mathbb{F}_p$ and set d_0 to be the lowest common multiple (LCM) of the degrees of each factor.

For the type 2, we still have two cases to discuss. One case can be $d = 2d_0$ if $\ell^{2e} \mid \#E_0(\mathbb{F}_{p^{2d_0}})$. This is due to the fact that the y-coordinates are required to solve $y^2 = x^3 + x$ and therefore should be defined over a quadratic extension of the field containing x. For the other case, we set $d = 4d_0$ through experimental observation.

Once the extension d is determined for $E_0[\ell^e]$, we turn to solving for the kernel point $P \in E_0[\ell^e]$. The procedure is to find a basis for $E_0[\ell^e]$, and then solve for P (see [10, §4.4]).

The final step is to determine the isogeny with kernel $\langle \sum_{i=1}^{r} P_i \rangle \subset E_0(\overline{\mathbb{F}}_p)$. Suppose each point P_i is defined over an extension of degree d_i, $1 \leq i \leq r$. If we naively add all the points P_i together then we would end up in an extension of degree $\mathrm{LCM}\{d_i : 1 \leq i \leq r\}$. Instead we propose a new method which only requires arithmetic in an extension of degree $\max\{d_i : 1 \leq i \leq r\}$, using the fact that all supersingular elliptic curves have j-invariants in $\mathbb{F}_{p^2}$.

For each $1 \leq i \leq r$:

1. construct the isogeny $\phi_i : E_{i-1} \to E_i'$ with kernel $\langle P_i \rangle$,
2. compute the j-invariant $j_i = j(E_i')$,
3. construct the elliptic curve E_i with j-invariant j_i and coefficients in $\mathbb{F}_{p^2}$,
4. construct the isomorphism $f_i : E_i' \to E_i$,
5. set $P_{i+1} \leftarrow f_i(\phi_i(P_{(i+1)}))$.

Performance. We implemented the main algorithms from the GPS signature scheme using Sage [18] and ran it on the cloud platform CoCalc for demonstrative purposes. We choose five values of n that make p prime. The results are listed in Table 4. It should be pointed out that translation from the new ideal to an isogeny is not included in this table, as we were not able to run it to completion.

When we attempt to implement translation from the new ideal to an isogeny, we have to generate these new large torsion points. First, we find the smallest extension fields containing these points. For example, when $p = 4 \cdot 3 \cdot 5 \cdot 7 - 1$, the new ideal produced by the quaternion isogeny path algorithm has a norm of $3^2 \cdot 5^2 \cdot 7^2 \cdot 11^2 \cdot 13^2 \cdot 17 \cdot 19 \cdot 23$. All these torsion points are not so large, except for the 13^2-torsion point. The smallest extension field containing the 13^2-torsion points is $\mathbb{F}_{p^{156}}$, too big for Sage to manage in this computation, despite the fact that these torsion points can be precomputed in advance. We emphasize that the security level of this p is only 8.711 bits, which is obviously well short of cryptographic size. When we set $p = 4 \cdot 3 \cdot 5 \cdot 7 \cdot 11 \cdot 13 \cdot 17 - 1$, the new ideal norm will be $3^2 \cdot 5^2 \cdot 7^2 \cdot 11^2 \cdot 13^2 \cdot 17^2 \cdot 19^2 \cdot 23^2 \cdot 29 \cdot 31 \cdot 37 \cdot 41 \cdot 43 \cdot 53 \cdot 59$. The largest extension in this case is determined by the 23^2-torsion points. We tested it using Magma and found that the smallest extension degree needs to be $\mathbb{F}_{p^{1012}}$ in this case, which will be very expensive (Table 5).

Table 4. The performance of these main algorithms in Galbraith-Petit-Silva signature [10]. "LI" represents loading the isogeny chains. "Is-to-Id" means translation from an isogeny to an ideal. "Id-to-Is" means translation from an ideal to an isogeny and this ideal is not the newly-generated one by the quaternion isogeny path algorithm, but just the ideal after "Is-to-Id". "New-Path" means the quaternion isogeny path algorithm. These times are listed in seconds.

n	$\log_2 p$	LI	Is-to-Id	Id-to-Is	New-path
$[3, 10]$	8.711	0.100	0.0734	0.064	0.109
$[3, 20]$	24.210	0.217	0.2146	0.366	0.190
$[3, 43] + [97]$	61.138	1.000	1.356	0.883	0.492
$[3, 113]$	155.469	6.356	9.442	6.989	2.297
$[3, 373] + [587]$	510.668	174.917	126.520	173.020	45.270

Table 5. Torsion generation in translation from the new ideal to an isogeny. This is the case of $p = 4 \cdot 3 \cdot 5 \cdot 7 - 1$. "$i$-th torsion" means the order of the torsion point we compute. "Extension field" means the smallest field that the torsion point is defined over. "Time" is counted by seconds.

i-th torsion	Extension field	Time
3^2	$\mathbb{F}_{p^{12}}$	0.1452
5^2	$\mathbb{F}_{p^{20}}$	0.2517
7^2	$\mathbb{F}_{p^{28}}$	0.4287
11^2	$\mathbb{F}_{p^{88}}$	1.5817
13^2	$\mathbb{F}_{p^{156}}$	125.6406
17	$\mathbb{F}_{p^{32}}$	0.4609
19	$\mathbb{F}_{p^4}$	0.0584
23	$\mathbb{F}_{p^{44}}$	1.5015
29	$\mathbb{F}_{p^{28}}$	0.3422

5   Conclusion

Our efforts to implement GPS signatures indicate that the scheme is impractical for parameters of cryptographic size. Translation from the new ideal to a new isogeny is not as easy as indicated in the Ideal-to-Isogeny algorithm in [10]. Particular care needs to be taken to control the explosion of extension field degree in the computation of the torsion points. In addition, we also propose a variant signature scheme with multi-bit challenges that has smaller signature sizes and lower computational cost, at the expense of a large public key, but even ignoring the extra costs of our modified quaternion isogeny path algorithm, the scheme is still impractical even with these improvements unless all the necessary torsion points are precomputed in advance. Further efforts are still needed to make signatures based on endomorphism ring more viable at useful parameter sizes.

Acknowledgments. The authors would like to thank the anonymous reviewers for their detailed reviews and helpful comments. This work is supported by the National Natural Science Foundation of China (No. 61872442, No. 61502487) and the National Cryptography Development Fund (No. MMJJ20180216), as well as NSERC, CryptoWorks21, Public Works and Government Services Canada, Canada First Research Excellence Fund, and the Royal Bank of Canada. Furthermore, Xiu Xu acknowledges the scholarship provided by the China Scholarship Council.

References

1. Adj, G., Cervantes-Vázquez, D., Chi-Domínguez, J.J., Menezes, A., Rodríguez-Henríquez, F.: On the cost of computing isogenies between supersingular elliptic curves. In: Cid, C., Jacobson Jr., M. (eds.) SAC 2018. LNCS, vol. 11349. Springer, Cham (2019). https://doi.org/10.1007/978-3-030-10970-7_15
2. Bellare, M., Neven, G.: Multi-signatures in the plain public-key model and a general forking lemma. In: Proceedings of the 13th ACM Conference on Computer and Communications Security, CCS 2006, New York, NY, USA, pp. 390–399. ACM (2006)
3. Charles, D.X., Lauter, K.E., Goren, E.Z.: Cryptographic hash functions from expander graphs. J. Cryptology **22**(1), 93–113 (2009)
4. Costello, C., Longa, P., Naehrig, M., Renes, J., Virdia, F.: Improved classical cryptanalysis of the computational supersingular isogeny problem. Cryptology ePrint Archive, Report 2019/298 (2019). https://eprint.iacr.org/2019/298
5. Couveignes, J.-M.: Hard homogeneous spaces. Cryptology ePrint Archive, Report 2006/291 (2006). https://eprint.iacr.org/2006/291
6. De Feo, L., Galbraith, S.D.: SeaSign: compact isogeny signatures from class group actions. In: Ishai, Y., Rijmen, V. (eds.) EUROCRYPT 2019. LNCS, vol. 11478, pp. 759–789. Springer, Cham (2019). https://doi.org/10.1007/978-3-030-17659-4_26
7. Eisenträger, K., Hallgren, S., Lauter, K., Morrison, T., Petit, C.: Supersingular isogeny graphs and endomorphism rings: reductions and solutions. In: Nielsen, J.B., Rijmen, V. (eds.) EUROCRYPT 2018. LNCS, vol. 10822, pp. 329–368. Springer, Cham (2018). https://doi.org/10.1007/978-3-319-78372-7_11

8. De Feo, L., Jao, D., Plût, J.: Towards quantum-resistant cryptosystems from super-singular elliptic curve isogenies. J. Math. Cryptology **8**(3), 209–247 (2014)

9. Galbraith, S.D., Petit, C., Shani, B., Ti, Y.B.: On the security of supersingu-lar isogeny cryptosystems. In: Cheon, J.H., Takagi, T. (eds.) ASIACRYPT 2016. LNCS, vol. 10031, pp. 63–91. Springer, Heidelberg (2016). https://doi.org/10.1007/978-3-662-53887-6_3

10. Galbraith, S.D., Petit, C., Silva, J.: Identification protocols and signature schemes based on supersingular isogeny problems. In: Takagi, T., Peyrin, T. (eds.) ASI-ACRYPT 2017. LNCS, vol. 10624, pp. 3–33. Springer, Cham (2017). https://doi.org/10.1007/978-3-319-70694-8_1

11. Galbraith, S.D., Vercauteren, F.: Computational problems in supersingular elliptic curve isogenies. Quantum Inf. Process. **17**(10), 265 (2018)

12. Jao, D., De Feo, L.: Towards quantum-resistant cryptosystems from supersingular elliptic curve isogenies. In: Yang, B.-Y. (ed.) PQCrypto 2011. LNCS, vol. 7071, pp. 19–34. Springer, Heidelberg (2011). https://doi.org/10.1007/978-3-642-25405-5_2

13. Kohel, D.: Endomorphism rings of elliptic curves over finite fields. Ph.D. thesis, University of California, Berkeley, (1996)

14. Kohel, D., Lauter, K.E., Petit, C., Tignol, J.-P.: On the quaternion ℓ-isogeny path problem. LMS J. Comput. Math. **17**(A), 418–432 (2014)

15. Lyubashevsky, V.: Fiat-Shamir with aborts: applications to lattice and factoring-based signatures. In: Matsui, M. (ed.) ASIACRYPT 2009. LNCS, vol. 5912, pp. 598–616. Springer, Heidelberg (2009). https://doi.org/10.1007/978-3-642-10366-7_35

16. Petit, C., Smith, S.: An improvement to the quaternion analogue of the l-isogeny path problem. In: Proceedings of MATHCRYPT 2018 (2018)

17. Stolbunov, A.: Cryptographic schemes based on isogenies. Ph.D. thesis, Norwegian University of Science and Technology (2012)

18. The Sage Developers. SageMath, the Sage Mathematics Software System (Version 8.5) (2019). https://www.sagemath.org

19. Vélu, J.: Isogénies entre courbes elliptiques. C. R. Acad. Sci. Paris Sér. A-B **273**, A238–A241 (1971)

20. Yoo, Y., Azarderakhsh, R., Jalali, A., Jao, D., Soukharev, V.: A post-quantum digital signature scheme based on supersingular isogenies. In: Kiayias, A. (ed.) FC 2017. LNCS, vol. 10322, pp. 163–181. Springer, Cham (2017). https://doi.org/10.1007/978-3-319-70972-7_9

Identity-Based Signature Scheme Secure in Ephemeral Setup and Leakage Scenarios

Łukasz Krzywiecki[✉], Marta Słowik, and Michał Szala

Department of Computer Science,
Faculty of Fundamental Problems of Technology,
Wrocław University of Science and Technology, Wrocław, Poland
{lukasz.krzywiecki,marta.slowik}@pwr.edu.pl

Abstract. We propose the identity-based signature (IBS) scheme resilient to ephemerals leakage and setup. The scheme is applicable to scenarios, where signers can not trust thoroughly the signing devices, and doubts about the fairness of randomness the hardware and the operating system generate are justified. Our construction is based on the lightweight IBS by Galindo and Garcia. We present a formal security model for IBS in which all values coming from randomness source in signing procedure are leaked or set by adversary. We argue that the original scheme is vulnerable to universal forgery in our security model. We give details on our modified construction and provide a formal security proof in Random Oracle Model, claiming that even such a strong adversary cannot forge a signature in our scheme.

Keywords: Identity-based signature · Ephemeral secret setting · Ephemeral secret leakage · Untrusted device

1 Introduction

Regular digital signature schemes, as well as many other authentication methods, are often based on public key infrastructure (PKI) that may be cumbersome to implement in real life. In everyday scenarios, a person that interacts with IT system, uses a unique information, linked to its identity, such as e-mail address or domain nickname, that is usually publicly available and verifiable by others. A first identity-based signature scheme (IBS), that gets rid of the need for expensive PKI, and uses such values instead, was proposed by Shamir [24]. The only requirement is that there exists a trusted third party, that extracts private keys from verified public data, and distributes them for users in a secure manner. Then, verifying parties may check signature genuineness using public identifiers,

This research was partially supported by Wroclaw University of Science and Technology grant 049U/0044/19.

S.-H. Heng and J. Lopez (Eds.): ISPEC 2019, LNCS 11879, pp. 310–324, 2019.
https://doi.org/10.1007/978-3-030-34339-2_17

without communicating with public key databases and other third party services, or sharing some information with signing party beforehand. With all that mentioned, IBS schemes may be used in many areas of modern technology. There are many IBS solution for different scenarios, e.g.: for Wireless Sensor Networks by Wei, Zhang, Huang, Zhang [27], for Vehicular Communication by Zhang, Yang, Wang [30], or as IEEE P1363 standard for public key cryptography [1], analyzed in white-box model in [31]. IBS schemes are also considered for biometric systems, e.g.: by Yang, Hu, Zhang in [29] or by Burnet, Byrne, Dowling, Duffy in [5].

Untrusted Signing Device. The signers, as the end users of the deployed scheme, usually do not have the thorough control over the signing devices. Especially the hardware production phase, and the implementation of the installed OS are beyond the users control. On the other hand the secret keys of users, put inside the device during profiling, and later used in the scheme, are only conditionally secure assuming the underlying hardware and software implementation is fair, and the randomness used to mask the secret keys does not leak, nor is set maliciously via a hidden side channel. The problem for potential ephemeral leakage from untrusted devices is important, and analyzed already for other cryptographic schemes, including e.g. Authenticated Key Exchange (AKE) protocols [12,14,17,19,20,26], Identification Schemes (IS), [13,15,16], or credential systems [18].

Motivation and Problem Statement. In signing algorithm, run on the user's device, random numbers called ephemerals are generated. The ephemeral values are used in computation together with secret key material, and a digital signature over specified message is produced as a result. However, we consider potential threats that may emerge when the secrecy of ephemerals and fairness of randomness source appear.

1. What would happen if mentioned ephemeral values leaked?
2. Would the scheme be secure after the leakage?
3. If not, how to modify the scheme to achieve resistance against such threat?

Such a leakage may happen in many scenarios. The reasons may be design or implementation flaws such as imprecise specification, usage of non-secure (pseudo) random number generator or coding errors. Another possible cause is a fault at hardware level that affects values produced or obtained from randomness source. The examples provided above are accidental but a leakage may occur on purpose, for instance, when a malicious agent is capable of tampering with a signing device or a piece of hardware which is used as randomness source at some production stage. In our model, we assume leakage or setting of the entire ephemeral, i.e. all bits of random number are known or chosen by the adversary.

Contribution. Our contribution is following:

1. We introduce a new, stronger security model for IBS in which ephemeral values may be either leaked in all bits or set by the adversary.
2. We show that the Galindo-Garcia scheme [9] is not secure in our model.
3. We propose a modification of Galindo-Garcia scheme that makes it secure in our security model.
4. We formally prove the security of our modified scheme in our proposed model.
5. We provide comparisons (in number of operations) of the base scheme and our modifications. We also present execution time of signing and verifying procedures for both schemes.

Previous Work. Given paper is based on publication by Galindo and Garcia [9]. The modification is based according to the paper of Krzywiecki [13]. The concept of identity-based signature was proposed by Shamir [24]. The description of Schnorr Signatures can be found in one of Schnorr's papers [23]. Their construction varies for example they can be based on quadratic residues like in the paper by Chai, Cao, Dong [7]. Based on elliptic curves there are papers by Han, Wang, Liu [10], or by Lin, Wu, Zhang, Hwang [21]. Others are used together with the ring structure like the paper by Ki, Hwang, Lee [11], or the paper by Deng, Zeng [8].

The ephemeral leakage problem was raised and analyzed by Canetti et al. [6] and also by Alwen, Dodis, Wichs [3]. A similar concept of *subversion resilience* for digital signatures was introduced [4], and later extended in [22].

A problem of leakage resilience for IBS schemes has been previously considered by Wu, Tseng, Huang in [28] and by Tseng, Tsai, Huang in [25]. In case of the former, the leakage model does not allow adversary to obtain all bits originating from random number generator. However the scheme is vulnerable to universal forgery, when analyzed in our stronger proposed model, cf. Appendix A for more details. The model from [25] allows adversary to learn entire value of random number. However, it seems to be weaker than our model, as adversarial randomness injection is not considered. The scheme presented there appears to be secure in our model, but it requires more operations for both signature and verification. Thus, our scheme is more efficient. For comparison, we briefly list the number of operations of [25] in Table 3.

Paper Organization. Presented paper is divided into 7 sections. In Sect. 2 we present the notation used in the paper and provide necessary definitions. In Sect. 3 we recall the definition of IBS scheme and related security game. We also recall Galindo-Garcia scheme details. In Sect. 4 we present the new security model and show the vulnerability of the Galindo-Garcia scheme in this model. In Sect. 5 we propose a modification of the scheme and the proof of security. In Sect. 6 we provide an analysis of efficiency of our modification. Section 7 concludes the paper.

2 Preliminaries

In this paper we use notation similar to the one that can be found in [3] and [13]. Let X be a finite set. We use notation $x_1, \ldots, x_n \leftarrow_\$ X$ to specify that each x_i is selected uniformly at random from X. Let λ be a security parameter. We denote negligible values as ϵ. A function $\mathcal{H} : \{0,1\}^* \to \mathbb{A}$ is a secure hashing function that transforms any binary string into an element of $\mathbb{A}$.

Bilinear Map: Let $\mathbb{G}_1$, $\mathbb{G}_2$, $\mathbb{G}_T$ be groups with generators g_1, g_2, g_T respectively. Let $q = |\langle g_1 \rangle| = |\langle g_2 \rangle| = |\langle g_T \rangle|$. Let $\hat{e} : \mathbb{G}_1 \times \mathbb{G}_2 \to \mathbb{G}_T$ be a pairing function with the following properties:

1. *Bilinearity*: $\forall (a, b \in \mathbb{Z}_q, g_1 \in \mathbb{G}_1, g_2 \in \mathbb{G}_2)$: $\hat{e}(g_1^a, g_2^b) = \hat{e}(g_1, g_2)^{ab}$
2. *Computability*: Computing $\hat{e}$ is efficient
3. *Non-degeneracy*: $\exists (g_1 \in \mathbb{G}_1, g_2 \in \mathbb{G}_2) : \hat{e}(g_1, g_2) \neq 1$

If $\mathbb{G}_1 = \mathbb{G}_2$, pairing is symmetric. In such a case, we drop lower indices for both group and generator in notation.

Function $Gen(1^\lambda)$ returns a tuple $(\mathbb{G}, g, q)$ such that $\mathbb{G}$ is a group of prime order q and g is its generator. Function $Gen_{BP}(1^\lambda)$ returns a symmetric bilinear mapping tuple: $(\mathbb{G}, \mathbb{G}_T, g, g_T, q, \hat{e} : \mathbb{G} \times \mathbb{G} \to \mathbb{G}_T)$.

Gap Computational Diffie-Hellman: Let $\mathcal{O}_{dh}$ denote an oracle for decisional Diffie-Hellman problem, i.e. given a tuple (g, g^x, g^y, g^z), where g is a generator of cyclic group $\mathbb{G}$ of order q and $g^x, g^y, g^z \in \mathbb{G}$ are random, it outputs 1 if $z = xy$ and 0 otherwise. Having access to $\mathcal{O}_{dh}$, given a tuple (g, g^x, g^y), compute g^{xy}.

Gap Computational Diffie-Hellman is denoted as GDH. We assume that it is hard in groups that we use throughout this paper, i.e. the probability that any PPT algorithm solves the problem is negligible.

3 Identity Based Signature Scheme

Let us recall the model and the security game for IBS from the original paper.

Definition 1 (Identity Based Signature Scheme). *Identity Based Signature scheme consists of four algorithms (*ParGen, KeyExtract, Sign, Verify*), where:*

- ParGen: *is a parameter generation algorithm that takes the security parameter λ as input and outputs master public key* mpk *containing parameters available for all system users and master secret key* msk.
- KeyExtract: *is a key extraction algorithm that given* msk, mpk *and user's identifier* id *as input, returns a user's secret key* sk$_{id}$.
- Sign: *is a signing algorithm that given* mpk, sk$_{id}$ *and a message m as input, outputs a signature σ over the message m on behalf of user with identity* id.
- Verify: *is a verification algorithm that given* σ, mpk, id *and m, outputs*

- accept *or* 1 *if* σ *is a valid signature over* m *for given user* id,
- reject *or* 0 *otherwise.*

Definition 2 (Correctness). *The IBS scheme is correct iff for any* id, sk_{id}:

$$Pr[\text{Verify}(\text{Sign}(mpk, sk_{id}, m), mpk, id, m) = 1 \mid$$
$$sk_{id} \leftarrow \text{KeyExtract}(mpk, msk, id)] = 1$$

Definition 3 (Security). *The security game is defined as follows:*

- *System parameters are obtained from generation algorithm* $(mpk, msk) \leftarrow$ ParGen(λ).
- *A forger* $\mathcal{F}$ *is initiated with* mpk. *It is also given an access to two oracles: a key extraction oracle* $\mathcal{O}_{\mathcal{E}}$ *that given some* id *returns a corresponding secret key (*$\mathcal{F}$ *can query it only once per* id*), and a signing oracle* $\mathcal{O}_S$ *that given* id *and* m, *produces a valid signature* σ *such that* Verify$(\sigma, mpk, id, m) = 1$.
- *After performing polynomially bounded number of oracle queries,* $\mathcal{F}$ *outputs a tuple* (id^*, m^*, σ^*) *such that* $\mathcal{O}_{\mathcal{E}}$ *has not been queried for* id^* *and* $\mathcal{O}_S$ *has not been queried for* (m^*, id^*).

The IBS scheme is secure if

$$Pr[\mathcal{F}^{\mathcal{O}_{\mathcal{E}}, \mathcal{O}_S}(mpk) \rightarrow (id^*, m^*, \sigma^*) \wedge \text{Verify}(\sigma^*, mpk, id^*, m^*) = 1] < \epsilon$$

3.1 Lightweight IBS Scheme

Let us briefly recall the scheme from [9] in Fig. 1.

ParGen(λ):	KeyExtract(mpk, msk, id):
$(\mathbb{G}, g, q) \leftarrow Gen(1^\lambda)$	$r \leftarrow_\$ \mathbb{Z}_q$
$\mathcal{H}_1 : \{0,1\}^* \rightarrow \mathbb{Z}_q$	$y = r + z \cdot \mathcal{H}_2(g^r, id)$
$\mathcal{H}_2 : \{0,1\}^* \rightarrow \mathbb{Z}_q$	$sk_{id} = (y, g^r)$
$z \leftarrow_\$ \mathbb{Z}_q,\ Z = g^z$	
$(mpk, msk) = ((\mathbb{G}, g, q, \mathcal{H}_1, \mathcal{H}_2, Z), z)$	
IDSign(mpk, sk_{id}, m):	Verify(σ, mpk, id, m):
$a \leftarrow_\$ \mathbb{Z}_q$	$g^b \overset{?}{=} g^a (g^r Z^{\mathcal{H}_2(g^r, id)})^{\mathcal{H}_1(id, g^a, m)}$
$b = a + y \cdot \mathcal{H}_1(id, g^a, m)$	
$\sigma = (g^a, b, g^r)$	

Fig. 1. Galindo-Garcia scheme overview

4   New Stronger Security Model for IBS

To address the scenario with ephemeral leakage/injection we propose a new, stronger security model for IBS schemes, based on models introduced in [13,15]. In this model a malicious forger $\mathcal{F}$ has the ability to inject ephemeral secrets to the Sign procedure.

Definition 4. *Let* IBS = (ParGen, KeyExtract, Sign, Verify) *be an IBS scheme. We define security experiment* $\mathrm{Exp}_{\mathsf{IBS}}^{\mathrm{CEF},\lambda,\ell}$:

Init : (mpk, msk) ← ParGen(λ).

IDGen Oracle : *The oracle* $\mathcal{O}_{\mathsf{IDGen}}$ *accepts identifiers* id. *It registers* id, *and the vector of values* Data *bound to this* id. *For the* i-*th component of* Data, *a notation* Data(id, i) *is used.*[1]

IDRev Oracle : *The oracle* $\mathcal{O}_{\mathsf{IDRev}}$ *accepts identifier* id, *and index* i. *It outputs only* Data(id, i).

IDSign Oracle : *The oracle* $\mathcal{O}_{\mathsf{IDSign}}^{\bar{a}}$ *accepts an identifier* id, *a messages* m_i, *ephemerals* $\bar{a}_i$, *and outputs corresponding valid signatures* σ_i *generated with the* $\bar{a}_i$, *i.e.* $\mathcal{O}_{\mathsf{IDSign}}^{\bar{a}_i}(\mathsf{id}, m_i) \to \sigma_i$, *s.t.* Verify($\sigma_i$, mpk, id, m_i) = 1. *The oracle models the device in which the signatures are generated via the algorithm* Sign, *with injected ephemerals controlled externally by the adversary:* $\sigma \leftarrow \mathsf{Sign}^{\bar{a}}(m)$.

Adversary : *Let the adversary* $\mathcal{A}^{\mathcal{O}_{\mathsf{IDGen}},\mathcal{O}_{\mathsf{IDRev}},\mathcal{O}_{\mathsf{IDSign}}^{\bar{a}}}(\mathsf{mpk})$, *be a malicious algorithm initialized with the public key* mpk, *having access to the oracles* $\mathcal{O}_{\mathsf{IDGen}}$, $\mathcal{O}_{\mathsf{IDRev}}$, *and the signing oracle* $\mathcal{O}_{\mathsf{IDSign}}^{\bar{r}}$. *It issues a number* ℓ *of queries to oracles. Let* $I = \{\mathsf{id}_i, g^{r_i}\}_1^\ell$ $A = \{\bar{a}_i\}_1^\ell$, $\mathcal{M} = \{m_i\}_1^\ell$, *and* $\mathcal{L} = \{\sigma_i\}_1^\ell$ *denote respectively the set of identifiers, the set of the ephemerals, the set of the messages, and the corresponding signatures the oracles process.*

Forgery Type I : *The adversary generates a tuple:*

$(m^*, \sigma^*, \mathsf{id}) \leftarrow \mathcal{A}_{\mathrm{I}}^{\mathcal{O}_{\mathsf{IDGen}},\mathcal{O}_{\mathsf{IDRev}},\mathcal{O}_{\mathsf{IDSign}}^{\bar{a}}}(\mathsf{mpk})$ *for an* id *previously queried to* $\mathcal{O}_{\mathsf{IDRev}}$ *or* $\mathcal{O}_{\mathsf{IDSign}}^{\bar{a}}$ *oracles. The case in which the adversary queries* $\mathcal{O}_{\mathsf{IDRev}}$ *for all* Data *entries for a particular user is excluded because it means that it obtained* $\mathsf{sk}_{\mathsf{id}}$. *If a signature contains elements of* Data, *also the case in which the adversary obtains these data from* $\mathcal{O}_{\mathsf{IDSign}}$ *and the remaining data from* $\mathcal{O}_{\mathsf{IDRev}}$ *is excluded.*

Forgery Type II : *The adversary generates a tuple:*

$(m^*, \sigma^*, \mathsf{id}) \leftarrow \mathcal{A}_{\mathrm{II}}^{\mathcal{O}_{\mathsf{IDGen}},\mathcal{O}_{\mathsf{IDRev}},\mathcal{O}_{\mathsf{IDSign}}^{\bar{a}}}(\mathsf{mpk})$ *for a new* id *that has been never queried to* $\mathcal{O}_{\mathsf{IDRev}}$ *or* $\mathcal{O}_{\mathsf{IDSign}}^{\bar{a}}$ *oracles.*

We say that the signature scheme is secure if for each forgery type the probability that the adversary produces a valid signature is negligible.

Theorem 1. *Galindo-Garcia IBS Scheme (presented in Fig. 1) is not secure in Ephemeral Leakage Model.*

---

[1] In case of Galindo-Garcia scheme, Data consists of two elements: Data(id, 1) = y, Data(id, 2) = g^r.

Proof. After system is initialized, forger $\mathcal{F}$ selects $\bar{a} \leftarrow_\$ \mathbb{Z}_q$ and queries $\mathcal{O}^{\bar{a}}_{\mathsf{IDSign}}$ for an arbitrary message m and attacked $\mathtt{id}$. Then, it receives a valid signature tuple $\sigma = (g^{\bar{a}}, b, g^r)$. Having this knowledge, it is capable of calculating y of $\mathsf{sk}_{\mathtt{id}}$. $\mathcal{F}$ transforms the equation in Sign: $b = \bar{a} + y \cdot \mathcal{H}_1(\mathtt{id}, g^{\bar{a}}, m)$ into $y = \frac{b - \bar{a}}{\mathcal{H}_1(\mathtt{id}, g^{\bar{a}}, m)}$. Since it knows all the values in the right side of equation, it can compute y. Thus, at the end forger ends up with a complete $\mathsf{sk}_{\mathtt{id}}(y, g^r)$, and from now on can create signatures of arbitrary messages on behalf of unaware signer, simply running Sign procedure with calculated secret key.   □

5   Proposed Modification of IBS Scheme

Our scheme addresses the issues with malicious ephemerals setting. To achieve this goal, we utilize bilinear pairings in verification procedure.

Original Scheme [9]	**Modified Scheme**
ParGen(λ): $(\mathbb{G}, g, q) \leftarrow Gen(1^\lambda)$ $\mathcal{H}_1 : \{0,1\}^* \to \mathbb{Z}_q$ $\mathcal{H}_2 : \{0,1\}^* \to \mathbb{Z}_q$ $z \leftarrow_\$ \mathbb{Z}_q,\ Z = g^z$ $(\mathsf{mpk}, \mathsf{msk}) = ((\mathbb{G}, g, q, \mathcal{H}_1, \mathcal{H}_2, Z), z)$	ParGen(λ): $(\mathbb{G}, \mathbb{G}_T, g, g_T, q, \hat{e}) \leftarrow Gen_{BP}(1^\lambda)$ $\mathcal{H}_1 : \{0,1\}^* \to \mathbb{Z}_q$ $\mathcal{H}_2 : \{0,1\}^* \to \mathbb{Z}_q$ $\mathcal{H}_g : \{0,1\}^* \to \mathbb{G}$ $z \leftarrow_\$ \mathbb{Z}_q,\ Z = g^z$ $(\mathsf{mpk}, \mathsf{msk}) = ((\mathbb{G}, \mathbb{G}_T, g, g_T, q, \hat{e}$ $\qquad\qquad\qquad \mathcal{H}_1, \mathcal{H}_2, \mathcal{H}_g, Z), z)$
KeyExtract ($\mathsf{mpk}, \mathsf{msk}, \mathtt{id}$): $r \leftarrow_\$ \mathbb{Z}_q$ $y = r + z \cdot \mathcal{H}_2(g^r, \mathtt{id})$ $\mathsf{sk}_{\mathtt{id}} = (y, g^r)$	KeyExtract is the same.
Sign($\mathsf{mpk}, \mathsf{sk}_{\mathtt{id}}, m$) $a \leftarrow_\$ \mathbb{Z}_q$ $b = a + y \cdot \mathcal{H}_1(\mathtt{id}, g^a, m)$ $\sigma = (g^a, b, g^r)$	Sign($\mathsf{mpk}, \mathsf{sk}_{\mathtt{id}}, m$) $a \leftarrow_\$ \mathbb{Z}_q$ $\hat{g} = \mathcal{H}_g(m, g^r, \mathtt{id})$ $b = a + y \cdot \mathcal{H}_1(\mathtt{id}, \hat{g}^a, m)$ $\hat{g}^b = \hat{g}^{a + y\mathcal{H}_1(\mathtt{id}, \hat{g}^a, m)}$ $\sigma = (\hat{g}^a, \hat{g}^b, g^r)$
Verify($\sigma, \mathsf{mpk}, \mathtt{id}, m$) Check if $g^b \stackrel{?}{=} g^a (g^r Z^{\mathcal{H}_2(g^r, \mathtt{id})})^{\mathcal{H}_1(\mathtt{id}, g^a, m)}$	Verify($\sigma, \mathsf{mpk}, \mathtt{id}, m$) Compute $\hat{g} = \mathcal{H}_g(m, g^r, \mathtt{id})$. Check if $\hat{e}(\hat{g}^b/\hat{g}^a, g) \stackrel{?}{=} \hat{e}(\hat{g}, (g^r Z^{\mathcal{H}_2(g^r, \mathtt{id})})^{\mathcal{H}_1(\mathtt{id}, \hat{g}^a, m)})$

Fig. 2. Galindo-Garcia scheme is on the left. Our modified scheme is on the right.

The modified scheme is presented in the right-hand side of Fig. 2. The original scheme [9], recalled already in Sect. 3.1, is repeated in the left-hand side for comparison.

5.1 Correctness of the Scheme

Theorem 2. *Our modified scheme as presented on the right-hand side of Fig. 2 is correct.*

Proof. Let $w = \mathcal{H}_2(g^r, \texttt{id})$, $u = \mathcal{H}_1(\texttt{id}, \hat{g}^a, m)$.
  Thus $b = a + y \cdot u$,
  and $y = r + zw$,
  Therefore:

$$\hat{e}(\hat{g}^b/\hat{g}^a, g) = \hat{e}(\hat{g}^{b-a}, g) = \hat{e}(\hat{g}, g^{b-a}) = \hat{e}(\hat{g}, (g^r g^{zw})^u)$$
$$= \hat{e}(\hat{g}, (g^r g^{z\mathcal{H}_2(g^r, \texttt{id})})^{\mathcal{H}_1(\texttt{id}, \hat{g}^a, m)})$$

□

5.2 Security Analysis

Theorem 3. *Let* IBS *denote the modified Identity-Based Signature Scheme (as in the right-hand side of Fig. 2).* IBS *is secure against* **Forgery Type I** *(in the sense of Definition 4).*

Proof (Sketch of the Proof)

Case 1: A forgery has been made for an id s.t. $\mathcal{O}_{\mathsf{IDRev}}(\texttt{id}, 0)$ has been queried. Suppose there is an adversary $\mathcal{F}$ that creates a valid signature in this case. Then, it can be used to create a forgery of Schnorr signature. Let $Z = g^z$ be a public key in Schnorr signature scheme. Initialize $\mathcal{F}$ with $\texttt{mpk} = Z$. When an adversary queries to $\mathcal{O}_{\mathsf{IDRev}}(\texttt{id}, 0)$, the oracle selects $y \leftarrow_\$ \mathbb{Z}_q$ and returns y to an adversary. If $\mathcal{F}$ manages to produce a valid forgery $(\texttt{id}, m, \sigma = (\hat{g}^a, \hat{g}^b, g^r))$, output $(\texttt{id}, (y, g^r))$ as a Schnorr signature forgery $\sigma^* = (y, g^r)$ over a message $m^* = \texttt{id}$ for the public key Z.

Case 2: In the second scenario, a forgery has been made for an id s.t. either $\mathcal{O}_{\mathsf{IDRev}}(\texttt{id}, 1)$ or $\mathcal{O}_{\mathsf{IDSign}}(\texttt{id}, \cdot)$ has been queried.
  Let (g, g^α, g^β) be an instance of **GDH** problem. We setup the system s.t. $\texttt{mpk} = Z = g^\alpha$. We provide the adversary the access to $\mathcal{O}_{\mathsf{IDGen}}$, and $\mathcal{O}_{\mathsf{IDSign}}$ oracles.
  Serving IDGen Oracle : We allow ℓ_1 fresh inputs to the $\mathcal{O}_{\mathsf{IDGen}}$ oracle. We choose the random index $j \leftarrow_\$ \{1, \ldots, \ell_1\}$, which denotes the j-th invocation of $\mathcal{O}_{\mathsf{IDGen}}$, for which we assume the forgery will happen.
  – On i-th $(i \neq j)$ invocation of $\mathcal{O}_{\mathsf{IDGen}}$ with a fresh id, we choose $y, h \leftarrow_\$ \mathbb{Z}_q$. We compute $R = g^r = g^y/Z^h$. We register in the ROM table for $\mathcal{H}_2$ the value h as an answer from $\mathcal{H}_2(g^r, \texttt{id})$, as well as values (y, g^r) as **Data** bound to id.
  – On j-th invocation of $\mathcal{O}_{\mathsf{IDGen}}$ with a fresh id we choose $r, h \leftarrow_\$ \mathbb{Z}_q$. We compute $R = g^r$. We register in the ROM table for $\mathcal{H}_2$ the value h as answer from $\mathcal{H}_2(g^r, \texttt{id})$, as well as values $(\bot, g^r)$ as **Data** bound to id. We record the value r for those tuples.

Serving IDRev Oracle $\mathcal{O}_{\mathsf{IDRev}}(\mathsf{id}, \mathsf{idx})$: On inputting a fresh id, we first use
$\mathcal{O}_{\mathsf{IDGen}}(\mathsf{id})$ oracle to register the new id. We locate the id in ROM table for
$\mathcal{H}_2$, and return the values $y = \mathsf{Data}(\mathsf{id}, 1)$, $g^r = \mathsf{Data}(\mathsf{id}, 2)$ bound to id,
respectively for $\mathsf{idx} = 1$ and $\mathsf{idx} = 2$ as the output.

Serving IDSign Oracle $\mathcal{O}_{\mathsf{IDSign}}^{\bar{a}}(\mathsf{id}, m)$: On inputting a fresh id, we first use
$\mathcal{O}_{\mathsf{IDGen}}(\mathsf{id})$ oracle to register the new id.

- On id related to i-th $(i \neq j)$ fresh invocation of $\mathcal{O}_{\mathsf{IDGen}}$ we locate (y, g^r),
  and use the values to produce a positively verifiable signature σ. We
  return the σ as the output.
- On id related to j-th fresh invocation of $\mathcal{O}_{\mathsf{IDGen}}$ we locate $(\perp, g^r)$. We
  use injected $\bar{a}$, generate $k \leftarrow_\$ \mathbb{Z}_q$. We set $h = \mathcal{H}_2(g^r, \mathsf{id})$. We register
  the value $\hat{g} = \mathcal{H}_g(m, g^r, \mathsf{id}) = g^k$ in the ROM table for $\mathcal{H}_g$. We set
  $c = \mathcal{H}_1(\mathsf{id}, \hat{g}^{\bar{a}}, m)$. We compute

$$\hat{g}^b = \hat{g}^{\bar{a}} \cdot \hat{g}^{yc} = g^{k\bar{a}} \cdot g^{(r+zh)kc} = g^{k\bar{a}} \cdot g^{rkc} \cdot Z^{kch}$$

At the end we return $\sigma = (\hat{g}^{\bar{a}}, \hat{g}^b, g^r)$.

Serving $\mathcal{O}_{\mathcal{H}_g}$ **Oracle** : We allow ℓ_2 fresh inputs to the $\mathcal{O}_{\mathcal{H}_g}$ oracle. We choose
the random index $j \leftarrow_\$ \{1, \ldots, \ell_2\}$, which denotes the j invocation of $\mathcal{O}_{\mathcal{H}_g}$,
for which we assume the forgery will happen.

- On i-th, $(i \neq j)$, fresh input m, g^r, id, we compute $k \leftarrow_\$ \mathbb{Z}_q$, register the
  value $\hat{g} = \mathcal{H}_g(m, g^r, \mathsf{id}) = g^k$ in the ROM table for $\mathcal{H}_g$. We return the $\hat{g}$
  as the output.
- On j-th, fresh input m, g^r, id, we set $\hat{g} = (g^\beta)$ and register that value in
  the ROM table for $\mathcal{H}_g$. We return the $\hat{g}$ as the output.

Processing the Forgery : Suppose there exists $\mathcal{F}_{\mathsf{I}}^{\mathcal{O}_{\mathsf{IDGen}}, \mathcal{O}_{\mathsf{IDRev}}, \mathcal{O}_{\mathsf{IDSign}}^{\bar{a}}}$ forging
successfully (m, σ, id) with non-negligible probability, s.t. the outputted id
was queried in jth issue to the $\mathcal{O}_{\mathsf{IDGen}}$, or $\mathcal{O}_{\mathsf{IDSign}}$ oracles, and registered with
g^r, for known and recorded r, in ROM for $\mathcal{H}_2$, i.e. $h = \mathcal{H}_2(g^r, \mathsf{id})$. Therefore
we have:

$$\hat{g}^b = \hat{g}^a \cdot \hat{g}^{yc}$$

Thus we have:

$$\hat{g}^b/\hat{g}^a = \hat{g}^{yc}$$
$$(\hat{g}^b/\hat{g}^a)^{1/c} = \hat{g}^y = \hat{g}^{(r+zh)} = \hat{g}^r \cdot (\hat{g}^z)^h = (g^\beta)^r \cdot ((g^\beta)^z)^h$$
$$\left(\frac{((\hat{g}^b/\hat{g}^a)^{1/c})}{(g^\beta)^r}\right)^{1/h} = \hat{g}^z = Z^\beta = g^{\alpha\beta}$$

□

Theorem 4. *Let* IBS *denote the modified Identity-Based Signature Scheme (as
in the right-hand side of Fig. 2).* IBS *is secure against* **Forgery Type II** *(in the
sense of Definition 4).*

Proof (Sketch of the Proof). Let (g, g^α, g^β) be an instance of GDH problem. We setup the system s.t. $\texttt{mpk} = Z = g^\alpha$. We provide the adversary the access to $\mathcal{O}_{\mathsf{IDGen}}$, and $\mathcal{O}_{\mathsf{IDSign}}$ oracles.

$\texttt{Serving IDGen Oracle}$: On inputting a fresh $\texttt{id}$ we choose $y, h \leftarrow_\$ \mathbb{Z}_q$. We compute $R = g^r = g^y/Z^{h_2}$. We register in the ROM table for $\mathcal{H}_2$ the value h_2 as answer from $\mathcal{H}_2(g^r, \texttt{id})$, as well as values (y, g^r) bound to $\texttt{id}$.

$\texttt{Serving IDRev Oracle}$: On inputting a fresh $\texttt{id}$, we first use $\mathcal{O}_{\mathsf{IDGen}}(\texttt{id})$ oracle to register the new $\texttt{id}$. We locate the $\texttt{id}$ in ROM table for $\mathcal{H}_2$ and return the values (y, g^r) bound to $\texttt{id}$ as the output.

$\texttt{Serving IDSign Oracle}\mathcal{O}_{\mathsf{IDSign}}^{\tilde{a}}(\texttt{id}, m)$: On input a fresh $\texttt{id}$ we first use $\mathcal{O}_{\mathsf{IDGen}}(\texttt{id})$ oracle to register the new $\texttt{id}$. We locate the $\texttt{id}$ in ROM table for $\mathcal{H}_2$ and use the values (y, g^r) bound to that $\texttt{id}$ to produce the positively verifiable signature σ. We return the σ as the output.

$\texttt{Serving }\mathcal{O}_{\mathcal{H}_g}\texttt{ Oracle}$: On a fresh input we generate a mask $d \leftarrow_\$ \mathbb{Z}_q$, compute $\hat{g} = (g^\beta)^d$, register that value in the ROM table for $\hat{g} = \mathcal{H}_g(m, g^r, \texttt{id}) = (g^\beta)^d$. We return the $\hat{g}$ as the output.

$\texttt{Processing the Forgery}$:

Suppose there exists $\mathcal{F}_{\mathrm{II}}^{\mathcal{O}_{\mathsf{IDGen}}, \mathcal{O}_{\mathsf{IDRev}}, \mathcal{O}_{\mathsf{IDSign}}^{\tilde{a}}}$ forging successfully $(m, \sigma, \texttt{id})$ with non-negligible probability, s.t. the outputted $\texttt{id}$ was not queried to the $\mathcal{O}_{\mathsf{IDGen}}$, $\mathcal{O}_{\mathsf{IDSign}}$ oracles. Thus by the *Forking Lemma* on $\mathcal{H}_2$, we get two tuples, namely: $(m, \hat{g}^{a_1}, \hat{g}^{b_1}, g^r, \texttt{id}, c_1, h_1)$, $(m, \hat{g}^{a_2}, \hat{g}^{b_2}, g^r, \texttt{id}, c_2, h_2)$, with two different hash values $h_1 = \mathcal{H}_2(g^r, \texttt{id})$ and $h_2 = \mathcal{H}_2(g^r, \texttt{id})$ respectively for the first and the second run. Let us denote $c_1 = \mathcal{H}_1(\texttt{id}, \hat{g}^{a_1}, m)$, and $c_2 = \mathcal{H}_1(\texttt{id}, \hat{g}^{a_2}, m)$, for whatever a_1, a_2 was used in those runs. Therefore we have:

$$\hat{g}^{b_1}/\hat{g}^{a_1} = (g^\beta)^{dc_1(r+zh_1)}$$

$$\hat{g}^{b_2}/\hat{g}^{a_2} = (g^\beta)^{dc_2(r+zh_2)}$$

Thus we have $(\hat{g}^{b_1}/\hat{g}^{a_1})^{(1/dc_1)}/(\hat{g}^{b_2}/\hat{g}^{a_2})^{(1/dc_2)} = (g^\beta)^{z(h_1-h_2)}$. Therefore

$$\left((\hat{g}^{b_1}/\hat{g}^{a_1})^{(1/dc_1)}/(\hat{g}^{b_2}/\hat{g}^{a_2})^{(1/dc_2)}\right)^{(1/(h_1-h_2))} = (g^\beta)^z = Z^\beta = g^{\alpha\beta}.$$

$\square$

6   Implementation and Performance

In this section we approach the complexity for both base and modified scheme. We measure execution times on $\texttt{SS512}$ curve. Our proof of concept implementations was prepared in $\texttt{Python}$ with $\texttt{CryptoCharm}$ library [2].

Table 1. Number of operations in base scheme

Operation	Amount
Sign	
G: Add	–
G: Mul	1
Verify	
G: Add	2
G: Mul	3

Table 2. Number of operations in modified scheme

Operation	Amount
Sign	
G: Add	–
G: Mul	2
G: H1	1
Verify	
G: Add	2
G: Mul	2
G: H1	1
pairing	2

Table 3. Number of operations in [25]

Operation	Amount
Sign	
$\mathbb{G}_1$: Add	1
$\mathbb{G}_1$: Mul	2
$\mathbb{G}_2$: Mul	1
$\mathbb{G}_2$: H2	1
Verify	
$\mathbb{G}_1$: Add	1
$\mathbb{G}_2$: Add	1
$\mathbb{G}_1$: Mul	2
$\mathbb{G}_2$: Mul	–
$\mathbb{G}_2$: H2	2
pairing	3

6.1   Number of Operations

We present the amount of time expensive operations for both base and modified scheme: addition in $\mathbb{G}$, scalar multiplication in $\mathbb{G}$, hash into group $\mathbb{G}$, and pairing operation. We denote the operations as Add, Mul, H1 respectively. We present number of operations for base scheme in Table 1 and for modified scheme in Table 2. For the sake of comparison, we also provide operations metrics for [25] in Table 3, proving that our scheme is more efficient.

6.2   Execution Time Measurements

We present the execution time measurements for base and modified scheme implemented on SS512 curve. We measured the execution time of Sign and Verify procedures as well as the execution time of operations mentioned in the previous section. The measurement was conducted on Ubuntu 18.04 running on Intel i5 2.50 GHz. We performed 100 attempts for each operation. The results of measurements for base and modified schemes are presented in Tables 4 and 5 respectively. As it can be seen from both tables, the modified scheme is approximately five times slower than the base scheme. However, the increase of computation cost is expected and is a price to pay when resilience to stronger adversary is required.

Table 4. Execution times for base scheme implemented on SS512 curve

Operation	Time [ms]
Sign	
$\mathbb{G}$: Mul	1.5060
$\mathbb{G}$: Add	–
Verify	
$\mathbb{G}$: Add	0.00822
$\mathbb{G}$: Mul	4.51431
Sign & Verify ≈ 6.02853 ms	

Table 5. Execution times for modified scheme implemented on SS512 curve

Operation	Time [ms]
Sign	
$\mathbb{G}$: Mul	3.107
$\mathbb{G}$: Add	–
$\mathbb{G}$: H1	7.066
Verify	
$\mathbb{G}$: Add	0.008852
$\mathbb{G}$: Mul	2.9626
$\mathbb{G}$: H1	7.1953
$\mathbb{G}$: Pairing	5.537
Sign & Verify ≈ 25.876752 ms	

7 Conclusion

In this paper we presented a modification of a signature scheme from [9]. We proposed an IBS model in which an adversary can inject ephemeral values used in the signing procedure. We showed that Galindo-Garcia scheme is not secure in said model and we have formally proven that our modification is.

A   Vulnerability of Leakage-Resilient IBS by Wu et al. in Our Model

We briefly present the protocols from [28]. The scheme is based on the idea that the secret keys are replaced with new values after each usage to prevent adversary from using leaked data accumulated in multiple protocol runs to recreate the secret. However, we show that the scheme is vulnerable to universal forgery in our security model where random values in signing procedure are leaked in full. Only one genuine signature is needed for forgery in our model.

- **ParGen:** Given a security parameter λ, generate type-1 bilinear pairing parameters: $(G, G_T, g \in G, p = |\langle g \rangle|, \hat{e} : G \times G \rightarrow G_T)$. Then:
  1. Select x, α at random from $\mathbb{Z}_p^*$ and g_2 at random from G. Compute system original key $X = g_2^x$ and $X_T = \hat{e}(g^x, g_2)$.
  2. The system current private key is $(S_{0,1}, S_{0,2}) = (g_2^\alpha, X \cdot g_2^{-\alpha})$.
  3. Select ui_0, ui_1, mi_0, mi_1 at random from $\mathbb{Z}_p^*$, compute $U_0 = g^{ui_0}, U_1 = g^{ui_1}, M_0 = g^{mi_0}, M_1 = g^{mi_1}$.
  4. Public parameters are $PP = (G, G_T, g, g_2, p, \hat{e}, X_T, U_0, U_1, M_0, M_1)$.
- **KeyExtract**(ID), where ID is user's identifier:
  1. Pick a, γ at random from $\mathbb{Z}_p^*$.
  2. $S_{i,1} = S_{i-1,1} \cdot g_2^a$.
  3. $TI_E = S_{i,1} \cdot (U_0 \cdot U_1^{ID})^\gamma$.
  4. $QID_{ID} = g^\gamma$.
  5. $S_{i,2} = S_{i-1,2} \cdot g_2^{-a}$.
  6. $SID_{ID} = S_{i,2} \cdot TI_E$.
  7. Output $DID' = (SID_{ID}, QID_{ID})$.
  8. Upon receiving secret keys, a user selects random β and computes $DID = (DID_{0,1} = g_2^\beta, DID_{0,2} = SID_{ID} \cdot g_2^{-\beta}, QID_{ID})$. DID is from now on the user's key.
- **Sign**(m_j)
  1. Select b, η at random from $\mathbb{Z}_p^*$.
  2. $DID_{j,1} = DID_{j-1,1} \cdot g_2^b$.
  3. $TI_S = DID_{j,1} \cdot (M_0 \cdot M_1^{m_j})^\eta$.
  4. $\sigma_2 = g^\eta$.
  5. $DID_{j,2} = DID_{j-1,2} \cdot g_2^{-b}$.
  6. $\sigma_1 = DID_{j,2} \cdot TI_S$.
  7. Output signature: $(\sigma_1, \sigma_2, QID_{ID})$.
- **Verify**: Accept signature iff

$$\hat{e}(g, \sigma_1) = X_T \cdot \hat{e}(\sigma_2, M_0 \cdot M_1^m) \cdot \hat{e}(QID_{ID}, U_0 \cdot U_1^{ID}).$$

In the description above, we can notice that $DID_{j,1} \cdot DID_{j,2}$ is constant in terms of j because $g_2^b \cdot g_2^{-b} = 1$. Also note that $\sigma_1 = DID_{j,2} \cdot DID_{j,1} \cdot (M_0 \cdot M_1^{m_j})^\eta$. We can launch the following attack on the scheme:

1. Query for one signature on arbitrary message m and obtain $(\sigma_1, \sigma_2, QID_{ID})$. From ephemeral values leakage, also obtain random values used in **Sign**, i.e. b, η.
2. Knowing random value η, public values M_0, M_1 and signed message m, compute $E = (M_0 \cdot M_1^m)^\eta$.
3. Compute $F(= DID_{j,2} \cdot DID_{j,1}) = \sigma_1 \cdot E^{-1}$.
4. From now on, you can select any message m' and any random value η', and forge the signature of m':

$$(\sigma_1 = F \cdot (M_0 \cdot M_1^{m'})^{\eta'}, \sigma_2 = g^{\eta'}, QID_{ID}).$$

References

1. IEEE P1363.3/D9, May 2013: IEEE Standard for Identity-Based Cryptographic Techniques Using Pairings. IEEE (2013)
2. Akinyele, J.A., et al.: Charm: a framework for rapidly prototyping cryptosystems. J. Cryptogr. Eng. **3**(2), 111–128 (2013)
3. Alwen, J., Dodis, Y., Wichs, D.: Leakage-resilient public-key cryptography in the bounded-retrieval model. In: Halevi, S. (ed.) CRYPTO 2009. LNCS, vol. 5677, pp. 36–54. Springer, Heidelberg (2009). https://doi.org/10.1007/978-3-642-03356-8_3
4. Ateniese, G., Magri, B., Venturi, D.: Subversion-resilient signature schemes. In: Proceedings of the 22nd ACM SIGSAC Conference on Computer and Communications Security, Denver, CO, USA, 12–16 October 2015, pp. 364–375 (2015)
5. Burnett, A., Byrne, F., Dowling, T., Duffy, A.: A biometric identity based signature scheme. Int. J. Netw. Secur. **5**(3), 317–326 (2007)
6. Canetti, R., Goldreich, O., Goldwasser, S., Micali, S.: Resettable zero-knowledge (extended abstract). In: Yao, F.F., Luks, E.M. (eds.) Proceedings of the Thirty-Second Annual ACM Symposium on Theory of Computing, Portland, OR, USA, 21–23 May 2000, pp. 235–244. ACM (2000)
7. Chai, Z., Cao, Z., Dong, X.: Identity-based signature scheme based on quadratic residues. Sci. China Ser. F: Inf. Sci. **50**(3), 373–380 (2007)
8. Deng, L., Zeng, J.: Two new identity-based threshold ring signature schemes. Theor. Comput. Sci. **535**, 38–45 (2014)
9. Galindo, D., Garcia, F.D.: A Schnorr-like lightweight identity-based signature scheme. In: Preneel, B. (ed.) AFRICACRYPT 2009. LNCS, vol. 5580, pp. 135–148. Springer, Heidelberg (2009). https://doi.org/10.1007/978-3-642-02384-2_9
10. Han, S., Wang, J., Liu, W.: An efficient identity-based group signature scheme over elliptic curves. In: Freire, M.M., Chemouil, P., Lorenz, P., Gravey, A. (eds.) ECUMN 2004. LNCS, vol. 3262, pp. 417–429. Springer, Heidelberg (2004). https://doi.org/10.1007/978-3-540-30197-4_42
11. Ki, J.H., Hwang, J.Y., Lee, D.H.: Identity-based ring signature schemes for multiple domains. TIIS **6**(10), 2692–2707 (2012)
12. Kim, M., Fujioka, A., Ustaoglu, B.: Strongly secure authenticated key exchange without NAXOS' approach under computational Diffie-Hellman assumption. IEICE Trans. **95-A**(1), 29–39 (2012)
13. Krzywiecki, Ł.: Schnorr-like identification scheme resistant to malicious subliminal setting of ephemeral secret. In: Bica, I., Reyhanitabar, R. (eds.) SECITC 2016. LNCS, vol. 10006, pp. 137–148. Springer, Cham (2016). https://doi.org/10.1007/978-3-319-47238-6_10
14. Krzywiecki, Ł., Kluczniak, K., Kozieł, P., Panwar, N.: Privacy-oriented dependency via deniable SIGMA protocol. Comput. Secur. **79**, 53–67 (2018)
15. Krzywiecki, Ł., Kutyłowski, M.: Security of Okamoto identification scheme: a defense against ephemeral key leakage and setup. In: Proceedings of the Fifth ACM International Workshop on Security in Cloud Computing, SCC@AsiaCCS 2017, Abu Dhabi, United Arab Emirates, 2 April 2017, pp. 43–50 (2017)
16. Krzywiecki, Ł., Słowik, M.: Strongly deniable identification schemes immune to prover's and verifier's ephemeral leakage. In: Farshim, P., Simion, E. (eds.) SecITC 2017. LNCS, vol. 10543, pp. 115–128. Springer, Cham (2017). https://doi.org/10.1007/978-3-319-69284-5_9
17. Krzywiecki, Ł., Wlisłocki, T.: Deniable key establishment resistance against eKCI attacks. Secur. Commun. Netw. **2017**, 7810352:1–7810352:13 (2017)

18. Krzywiecki, Ł., Wszoła, M., Kutyłowski, M.: Brief announcement: anonymous credentials secure to ephemeral leakage. In: Dolev, S., Lodha, S. (eds.) CSCML 2017. LNCS, vol. 10332, pp. 96–98. Springer, Cham (2017). https://doi.org/10.1007/978-3-319-60080-2_7
19. LaMacchia, B., Lauter, K., Mityagin, A.: Stronger security of authenticated key exchange. In: Susilo, W., Liu, J.K., Mu, Y. (eds.) ProvSec 2007. LNCS, vol. 4784, pp. 1–16. Springer, Heidelberg (2007). https://doi.org/10.1007/978-3-540-75670-5_1
20. Lee, J., Park, J.H.: Authenticated key exchange secure under the computational Diffie-Hellman assumption. Cryptology ePrint Archive, Report 2008/344 (2008)
21. Lin, C.-Y., Wu, T.-C., Zhang, F., Hwang, J.-J.: New identity-based society oriented signature schemes from pairings on elliptic curves. Appl. Math. Comput. **160**(1), 245–260 (2005)
22. Russell, A., Tang, Q., Yung, M., Zhou, H.-S.: Cliptography: clipping the power of kleptographic attacks. IACR Cryptology ePrint Archive, 2015/695 (2015)
23. Schnorr, C.-P.: Efficient signature generation by smart cards. J. Cryptol. **4**(3), 161–174 (1991)
24. Shamir, A.: Identity-based cryptosystems and signature schemes. In: Blakley, G.R., Chaum, D. (eds.) CRYPTO 1984. LNCS, vol. 196, pp. 47–53. Springer, Heidelberg (1985). https://doi.org/10.1007/3-540-39568-7_5
25. Tseng, Y.-M., Tsai, T.-T., Huang, S.-S.: Leakage-free ID-based signature. Comput. J. **58**(4), 750–757 (2015)
26. Ustaoglu, B.: Obtaining a secure and efficient key agreement protocol from (H)MQV and NAXOS. Cryptology ePrint Archive, Report 2007/123 (2007)
27. Wei, L., Zhang, L., Huang, D., Zhang, K.: Efficient and provably secure identity-based multi-signature schemes for data aggregation in marine wireless sensor networks. In: Fortino, G., et al. (eds.) 14th IEEE International Conference on Networking, Sensing and Control, ICNSC 2017, Calabria, Italy, 16–18 May 2017, pp. 593–598. IEEE (2017)
28. Wu, J.-D., Tseng, Y.-M., Huang, S.-S.: Leakage-resilient ID-based signature scheme in the generic bilinear group model. Secur. Commun. Netw. **9**(17), 3987–4001 (2016)
29. Yang, Y., Hu, Y., Zhang, L.: An efficient biometric identity based signature scheme. TIIS **7**(8), 2010–2026 (2013)
30. Zhang, Y., Yang, L., Wang, S.: An efficient identity-based signature scheme for vehicular communications. In: 11th International Conference on Computational Intelligence and Security, CIS 2015, Shenzhen, China, 19–20 December 2015, pp. 326–330. IEEE Computer Society (2015)
31. Zhang, Y., He, D., Huang, X., Wang, D., Choo, K.-K.R.: White-box implementation of the identity-based signature scheme in the IEEE P1363 standard for public key cryptography. IACR Cryptology ePrint Archive, 2018/814 (2018)

Recovering Internal States of Grain-v1

Deepak Kumar Dalai and Santu Pal[(⊠)]

National Institute of Science Education and Research, HBNI,
Bhubaneswar 752050, India
{deeepak,santu.pal}@niser.ac.in

Abstract. In this paper, we analyze the non-linear part of the output function h of Grain-v1 and use a guess and determine strategy to recover 33 state bits from 33 consecutive keystream bits of Grain-v1 by fixing 45 bits and guessing 82 bits. This reduces the conditional sampling resistance of Grain-v1, which is best till now. We apply the Time-Memory-Data Trade-Off (TMDTO) attack on Grain-v1 with this conditional sampling resistance to get a trade-off curve which improves the preprocessing time complexity and online time complexity with improved memory.

Keywords: Cryptanalysis · Grain-v1 · Guess and determine attack · Time-Memory-Data Trade-Off (TMDTO) Attack

1 Introduction

Grain-v1 is one of three selected stream ciphers for hardware category in eSTREAM [1,11]. It is a bit-oriented NFSR based stream cipher with an 80 bit nonlinear feedback shift register(NFSR), an 80 bit linear feedback shift register (LFSR) and a nonlinear filter function of 5 variables. For the simplicity in structure and efficiency in hardware implementation, it is a popular stream cipher among cryptanalysts. Since its inception, the cryptanalysts are analyzing the cipher by exploiting different kinds of techniques. The Time-Memory-Data Trade-Off (TMDTO) attack [2,3,10] is one of the highly used techniques to analyze Grain-v1. In this work, we analyze Grain-v1 using guess and determine attack and the TMDTO attack. In both the attacks, the attacker finds a state value of the cipher at a particular clock/round and hence can generate the keystream by clocking forward and possibly, the key by backward clockings if the state is invertible.

The main idea of guess and determine attack is to determine a portion of state bits by using some known keystream bits and guessing the remaining portion of state bits. Using the idea of BSW-sampling [3,4], a special cipher states can be generated and enumerated efficiently from which some subsequent keystream bits with fixed string are generated. If a state of n bits can be recovered by guessing $n - l$ bits with knowledge of some initial keystream bits, the sampling resistance of the cipher is defined to be $R = 2^{-l}$. The sampling resistance of

© Springer Nature Switzerland AG 2019
S.-H. Heng and J. Lopez (Eds.): ISPEC 2019, LNCS 11879, pp. 325–337, 2019.
https://doi.org/10.1007/978-3-030-34339-2_18

Grain-v1 is at most 2^{-18} [5]. The sampling resistant can be extended by using guess and determine strategy with some restriction on state bits. Such type of sampling resistance is considered as conditional sampling resistance. So by fixing some state bits, one can extend sampling resistance of Grain-v1 by $2^{-l}, l > 18$. So one can recover the state bits by guessing some state bits and fixed values of some initial keystream bits by using guess and determine strategy. In the case of BSW sampling, one should take the first few fixed keystream bits, since it is very difficult to force a large number of keystream bits to have a specific value. So one can use TMDTO attack with BSW sampling to recover the state bits of Grain-v1. Although the TMDTO attack incepted during the second half of 90's [2–4,10], the relatively new stream cipher Grain-v1 is being analysed extensively by the attack in recent days [5,7,8,14–16,18]. Several other popular works on TMDTO attack on stream ciphers [9,13,17] are available in the literature of cryptanalysis.

The TMDTO attack is implemented in two phases: preprocessing (or, offline) phase and real time (or, online) phase. During the preprocessing phase, the attacker generates one or more large tables of states of the cipher in a particular order from the structure of the cryptosystem. During the real time phase, having some keystream data, the attackers aim is to find the actual state generating the known keystream. As the preprocessing phase is performed offline, the attacker is allowed for a longer time than the real time phase. As the name of the attack suggests that the amount of computation time (T), Memory (M) and Data (D) are balanced by satisfying a set of equalities and inequalities. As a result, the attacker performs better than the exhaustive search attack by trading off the available resources. A brief idea of TMDTO attack is presented in Sect. 2.1. The interested readers can read the papers [3,6,7] for a detailed study about the attack.

1.1 Previous Contributions

For the first time, in 2008, Bjørstad [5] mounted a TMDTO attack on Grain-v1, using BSW sampling to recover the state. Showing that Grain-v1 has low sampling resistance, he could reduce the time T and memory M by increasing data D. In 2012, Mihaljević et al. [15] used the normality of order two of the non-linear functions of Grain-v1 for BSW sampling to recover 18 state bits where 18 consecutive key-stream bits are set as zero. It needed to fix 54 state bits and to guess 88 state bits and then BS TMDTO [3] with single table look-up in pre-processing phase is used to recover the state bits. In 2015, Jiao et al. [14] recovered 28 state bits from 28 consecutive key-stream bits by using normality order of the nonlinear function of Grain-v1. They fixed 51 state bits and guessed 81 state bits to reduce the sampling resistant from 2^{-18} to 2^{-28}. Then they used TMDTO attack to recover state bits. The TMDTO curve was $TMD = 2^r N$, where r is the number of fixed bits. In 2017, Mihaljević et al. [16] used the same strategy to recover 24 and 31 state bits from the same number of consecutive key-stream bits in two different instants respectively. It is needed to fix 6 and 31 state bits and guess 130 and 97 state bits respectively. Then BS TMDTO is implemented over the reduced space to recover state bits. The latest, this year,

Siddhanti et al. [18] proposed TMDTO attack by recovering 32 state bits, fixing none state bits and guessing 96 state bits with 36 known consecutive keystream bits. The comparison of T, M and D of the mentioned attacks is presented in Table 7.

1.2 Our Contribution

We reduced the sampling resistant of Grain-v1 by careful analysis of the structure of its non-linear function with some condition on state bits. Four different observations on the non-linear function in Grain-v1 are used for our purpose. We have followed the strategy implemented by Jiao et al. [14] and Mihalijevic et al. [16]. Implementing guess and determine attack we could recover the whole state by guessing 82 state bits, fixing 45 state bits and recovering rest 33 state bits from first 33 keystream bits. Further, we apply different TMDTO techniques to find the best suiting one.

1.3 Organization of Paper

We have already outlined our research objectives. Rest of the paper is organized as follows. Section 2 introduces the TMDTO attack and the structure of the stream cipher Grain-v1. Section 3 contains our contribution, which is divided into three subsections. Subsect. 3.1 presents some conditions on the inputs of the non-linear function h of Grain-v1 to get simpler functions. In Subsect. 3.2, guess and determine strategy is discussed to recover the state bits of Grain-v1 by fixing and guessing some state bits. Further in Subsect. 3.3, the TMDTO attack is implemented to recover the state bits. In the last section, we conclude the paper with future work.

2 Preliminary

In this section, we describe the TMDTO attack on stream ciphers and the design structure of the stream cipher Grain-v1.

2.1 TMDTO Attacks on Stream Ciphers

As described in [3], the following five parameters are related in any TMDTO attack.

- N: the size of the search space of the state.
- P: the time required for the preprocessing phase.
- M: the amount of memory requirement for the attack.
- T: the time required for the real time phase of the attack.
- D: the amount of real time data required for the attack.

The Time-Memory Trade-Off (TMTO) attack was introduced by Hellman on block cipher [12] to invert the vectorial Boolean function used in the cipher. This attack combines the exhaustive state value search and table lookup method for trading off the time T and memory M and provides a general technique to invert one-way function. Its trade-off equations are obtained as $TM^2 = N^2$ and $P = N$ where N is the number of possible states. Since the keystream bits are independent of the plain text in the case of stream ciphers, Babbage [2] and Golić [10] took advantage of keystream bits (i.e., data D) to involve in the trade-off to further reduce the time and memory costs. The attack is known as BG-TMDTO and the trade-off equations are $TM = N, P = M$ and $T = D$. In this technique, a single $m \times t$ table was proposed to cover the whole space of states, which actually will not cover as there will be a large amount repetition of states due to the collisions. To avoid the large collisions, t tables of size $m \times t$ (each one is generated from different functions) which satisfies $mt^2 = N$ to cover all state space except a few. Later Biryukov and Shamir [3] extended BG-TMDTO attack to stream cipher by utilizing multiple data points which is known as BS-TMDTO. The number of tables reduced to $\frac{t}{D}$, if D data is available. As a result, the obtained trade-off equations are $TM^2D^2 = N^2$ and $P = N/D$ with a restriction $1 \leq D^2 \leq T$.

To exploit BSW sampling with the BS-TMDTO attack, it is needed to fix first k bits of keystream. Hence, the available data is reduced to $\frac{D}{2^k}$ for the TMDTO. This generic technique is proposed in [4] and the attack was deployed on the stream cipher A5/1. In case of BSW sampling, if the sampling resistance of a stream cipher is R $(0 < R < 1)$, then both ultimate state space size N and data D are reduced by NR and $DR(> 1)$ respectively for the attack. Hence, the trade-off curve is the same as $TM^2D^2 = N^2$, but the range of $T > D^2$ is wider by $T > (RD)^2$ and the number of disk operations is reduced from t to tR.

2.2 Description of Grain-v1

Grain-v1 [11] is a hardware based stream cipher consisting of an 80-bit NFSR, an 80-bit LFSR and a nonlinear filter function h of 5 variables, where $b_i, s_i, 0 \leq i \leq 79$ are the state bits of the NFSR and LFSR respectively. The state update functions of LFSR and NFSR are presented in Eqs. 1 and 2 respectively.

$$s_{t+80} = s_{t+62} + s_{t+51} + s_{t+38} + s_{t+23} + s_{t+13} + s_t, \text{ for } t \geq 0. \tag{1}$$

$$
\begin{aligned}
b_{t+80} = {} & s_t + b_{t+62} + b_{t+60} + b_{t+52} + b_{t+45} + b_{t+37} + b_{t+33} \\
& + b_{t+28} + b_{t+21} + b_{t+14} + b_{t+9} + b_t + b_{t+63}b_{t+60} + \\
& b_{t+37}b_{t+33} + b_{t+15}b_{t+9} + b_{t+60}b_{t+52}b_{t+45} + b_{t+33}b_{t+28}b_{t+21} + \\
& b_{t+63}b_{t+45}b_{t+28}b_{t+9} + b_{t+60}b_{t+52}b_{t+37}b_{t+33} + b_{t+63}b_{t+60}b_{t+21} \\
& b_{t+15} + b_{t+63}b_{t+60}b_{t+52}b_{t+45}b_{t+37} + b_{t+33}b_{t+28}b_{t+21}b_{t+15}b_{t+9} \\
& + b_{t+52}b_{t+45}b_{t+37}b_{t+33}b_{t+28}b_{t+21}, \text{ for } t \geq 0. \tag{2}
\end{aligned}
$$

The algebraic normal form of the nonlinear filter function h is given by

$$h(s_{t+3}, s_{t+25}, s_{t+46}, s_{t+64}, b_{t+63}) = s_{t+25} + b_{t+63} + s_{t+3}s_{t+64} + s_{t+46}s_{t+64} +$$
$$s_{t+64}b_{t+63} + s_{t+3}s_{t+25}s_{t+46} + s_{t+3}s_{t+46}s_{t+64} + s_{t+3}s_{t+46}b_{t+63} +$$
$$s_{t+25}s_{t+46}b_{t+63} + s_{t+46}s_{t+64}b_{t+63}. \tag{3}$$

The keystream bit z_t of the cipher is calculated by combining the output of the nonlinear filter function and some state bits of the NFSR. The algebraic expression of the keystream bit at t-th round is

$$z_t = b_{t+1} + b_{t+2} + b_{t+4} + b_{t+10} + b_{t+31} + b_{t+43} + b_{t+56}$$
$$+ h(s_{t+3}, s_{t+25}, s_{t+46}, s_{t+64}, b_{t+63}), \text{ for } t \geq 0. \tag{4}$$

There are two phases, key scheduling and pseudorandom bit generation, in Grain-v1 algorithm which follows the Key Scheduling Algorithm (KSA) and Pseudorandom Generation Algorithm (PRGA) respectively. After running 160 rounds of KSA the cipher starts the pseudorandom bit generation phase, where the cipher produces keystream bits as output.

3   State Recovery of Grain-v1

This section contains the main contribution of the paper to recover the internal state of Grain-v1 at a particular clock. A study on the subfunctions (i.e., fixing some variables of the function) of the nonlinear function h is presented in the following subsection. The study is useful for the state recovery of Grain-v1.

3.1   Analysis of the Non-linear Filter Function

The nonlinear function h (Eq. 3) is a 3 degree polynomial on 5 variables. The algebraic normal form (ANF) of h contains only 8 nonlinear terms. The sparseness of nonlinear terms in the ANF helps to find the affine or constant subfunctions by fixing a few variables. It is observed that all 3-degree monomials and one 2-degree monomial contain the variable bit s_{t+46}. Therefore, fixing $s_{t+46} = 0$, h can be made a quadratic function with 2 nonlinear terms. In addition to this fixing, if we fix $s_{t+64} = 0$ or 1, we will have a linear function independent of the variable s_{t+3} or, b_{t+63} respectively. Moreover, exploiting the normality order of h (i.e., 2), we can have a constant function by fixing 3 variables. We listed the observations on the ANF of h as follows.

Observations:

1. $h(s_{t+3}, s_{t+25}, 0, s_{t+64}, b_{t+63}) = s_{t+25} + b_{t+63} + s_{t+3}s_{t+64} + s_{t+64}b_{t+63}$;
    1.1. $h(s_{t+3}, s_{t+25}, 0, 1, b_{t+63}) = s_{t+3} + s_{t+25}$;
        1.1.1. $h(s_{t+3}, 1, 0, 1, b_{t+63}) = 1 + s_{t+3}$;
    1.2. $h(s_{t+3}, s_{t+25}, 0, 0, b_{t+63}) = s_{t+25} + b_{t+63}$;
2. $h(1, 0, s_{t+46}, 1, b_{t+63}) = 1$;

3. $h(s_{t+3}, 0, s_{t+46}, 0, 0) = 0$;
4. $h(s_{t+3}, 0, 1, s_{t+64}, b_{t+63}) = s_{t+64} + b_{t+63} + s_{t+3}b_{t+63}$.
   4.1. $h(1, 0, 1, s_{t+64}, b_{t+63}) = s_{t+64}$.

By fixing some state bits, we use these observations to extract relations (mostly linear) among the state bits. These relations help to recover some state bits by guessing rest of state bits. We use the relations in observation in Item 1 for $17-20$ rounds, in Item 1.1. for 3, 4, 11 rounds, in Item 1.1.1. for $5-10$ rounds, in Item 1.2. for $0-2, 16$ rounds, in Item 2 for $12-14$ rounds, in Item 3 for 15 round, in Item 4 for $21-26$ rounds and in Item 4.1. for $27-32$ rounds of Grain-v1. Table 1 lists the observations of the relations of state bits in terms of the subfunctions of h in the order of round. The state bits in brackets are previously fixed with the same value and the bits in bold letters are having position greater than 79, which can be expressed in terms of recurrence as defined in Eqs. 1 and 2.

Table 1. Relations of state bits in Grain-v1 as the subfunctions of h

Round (t)	Observation	Fixed bit	h function
$0-2$	1.2	$s_{t+46} = 0, s_{t+64} = 0$	$s_{t+25} + b_{t+63}$
$3-4$	1.1	$s_{t+46} = 0, s_{t+64} = 1$	$s_{t+3} + s_{t+25}$
$5-10$	1.1.1	$s_{t+25} = 1, s_{t+46} = 0, s_{t+64} = 1$	$1 + s_{t+3}$
11	1.1	$s_{t+46} = 0, s_{t+64} = 1$	$s_{t+3} + s_{t+25}$
$12-14$	2	$s_{t+3} = 1, s_{t+25} = 0, s_{t+64} = 1$	1
15	3	$s_{t+25} = 0, s_{t+64} = 0, b_{t+63} = 0$	0
16	1.2	$s_{t+46} = 0, \mathbf{s_{t+64}} = 0$	$s_{t+25} + b_{t+63}$
17	1	$s_{t+46} = 0$	$s_{t+25} + \mathbf{b_{t+63}} + s_{t+3}\mathbf{s_{t+64}} + \mathbf{s_{t+64}}\mathbf{b_{t+63}}$
$18-20$	1	$(s_{t+46} = 0)$	$s_{t+25} + \mathbf{b_{t+63}} + s_{t+3}\mathbf{s_{t+64}} + \mathbf{s_{t+64}}\mathbf{b_{t+63}}$
$21-26$	4	$(s_{t+25} = 0, s_{t+46} = 1)$	$\mathbf{s_{t+64}} + \mathbf{b_{t+63}} + s_{t+3}\mathbf{b_{t+63}}$
$27-32$	4.1	$(s_{t+3} = 1, s_{t+25} = 0, s_{t+46} = 1)$	$\mathbf{s_{t+64}}$

3.2 Guess and Determine Strategy

Exploiting the relations among the state bits presented in Table 1, the guess and determine strategy is used to recover 33 state bits from the first 33 keystream bits of Grain-v1. Having 33 known keystream bits $(z_t, 0 \le t \le 32)$, appropriately replacing the h function in Eq. 4 by the equation presented in the Table 1, we will have a system of 33 equations. For this process, 45 state bits (presented in 3rd column in Table 1) need to be fixed. If the system of equations is linearly independent, it is possible to recover 33 state bits by guessing the rest (i.e., $160 - (45 + 33) = 82$) of the state bits.

Since some equations are nonlinear and some state bits are represented by nonlinear recurrence relations, it is not obvious to choose appropriate recovery bits and guessing bits. As the gap between the terms b_{t+10} and b_{t+31} in Eq. 4 is maximum and the terms are involved linearly, we consider those bits as recovery bits. The recovery process of the state bits is presented below. The detailed order of evaluation and evaluation process is presented in Tables 4 and 5.

R1. For $0 \le t \le 2$, (i.e., for first 3 rounds), we use the observation (Item 1.2.) for h to get a linear equation on state bits for z_t by fixing two state bits as mentioned in Table 1. Here, each linear equation contains 9 terms as $b_{t+1} + b_{t+2} + b_{t+4} + b_{t+10} + b_{t+31} + b_{t+43} + b_{t+56} + s_{t+25} + b_{t+63} = z_t$ for $0 \le t \le 2$. Now, we can recover three state bits $b_{t+10}, 0 \le t \le 2$ by guessing remaining state bits in the equations.

R2. For $t = 3, 4, 11$, the observation (Item 1.1.) for h is used to get a linear equation on state bits for z_t by fixing two state bits as mentioned in Table 1. Here, each linear equation contains 9 terms as $b_{t+1} + b_{t+2} + b_{t+4} + b_{t+10} + b_{t+31} + b_{t+43} + b_{t+56} + s_{t+3} + s_{t+25} = z_t$ for $t = 3, 4, 11$. Similarly, three state bits $b_{t+10}, t = 3, 4, 11$ are recovered by guessing remaining state bits in the equations.

R3. For $5 \le t \le 10$, the observation (Item 1.1.1.) for h is used to get a linear equation on state bits for z_t by fixing three state bits as mentioned in Table 1. Here, each linear equation contains 8 terms as $b_{t+1} + b_{t+2} + b_{t+4} + b_{t+10} + b_{t+31} + b_{t+43} + b_{t+56} + s_{t+3} + 1 = z_t$ for $5 \le t \le 10$. Here, Six state bits $b_{t+10}, 5 \le t \le 10$ are recovered by guessing remaining state bits in the equations.

R4. For $12 \le t \le 14$, the observation (Item 2) for h is used to get a linear equation on state bits for z_t by fixing three state bits as mentioned in Table 1. Here, each linear equation contains 7 terms as $b_{t+1} + b_{t+2} + b_{t+4} + b_{t+10} + b_{t+31} + b_{t+43} + b_{t+56} + 1 = z_t$ for $12 \le t \le 14$. Here, three state bits $b_{t+10}, 12 \le t \le 14$ are recovered by guessing remaining state bits in the equations.

R5. For $t = 15$, the observation (Item 3) for h is used to get a linear equation on state bits for z_t by fixing three state bits as mentioned in Table 1. The linear equation contains 7 terms as $b_{t+1} + b_{t+2} + b_{t+4} + b_{t+10} + b_{t+31} + b_{t+43} + b_{t+56} = z_t$ for $t = 15$. Here, the state bit $b_{t+10}, t = 15$ is recovered by guessing remaining state bits in the equation.

It can be observed that for $t \ge 16$, at least one term in fixed bits or in h function (written in the bold letter in Table 1) which is expressed as a linear or nonlinear combination of other state bits. For example, at $t = 16$, we need to fix $s_{t+16} = s_{80} = s_0 + s_{13} + s_{23} + s_{38} + s_{51} + s_{62} = 0$ (see Eq. 1). Therefore, the involved bits need to be considered for fixing or guessing bits. Tables 2 and 3 contain the involved bits in the linear update state relations and the nonlinear update state relations respectively.

Table 2. The state bits involved to calculate the linear feedback bits

Feedback bits	State bits used	Feedback bits	State bits used
s_{80}	$s_0, s_{13}, s_{23}, s_{38}, s_{51}, s_{62}$	s_{81}	$s_1, s_{14}, s_{24}, s_{39}, s_{52}, s_{63}$
s_{82}	$s_2, s_{15}, s_{25}, s_{40}, s_{53}, s_{64}$	s_{83}	$s_3, s_{16}, s_{26}, s_{41}, s_{54}, s_{65}$
s_{84}	$s_4, s_{17}, s_{27}, s_{42}, s_{55}, s_{66}$	s_{85}	$s_5, s_{18}, s_{28}, s_{43}, s_{56}, s_{67}$
s_{86}	$s_6, s_{19}, s_{29}, s_{44}, s_{57}, s_{68}$	s_{87}	$s_7, s_{20}, s_{30}, s_{45}, s_{58}, s_{69}$
s_{88}	$s_8, s_{21}, s_{31}, s_{46}, s_{59}, s_{70}$	s_{89}	$s_9, s_{22}, s_{32}, s_{47}, s_{60}, s_{71}$
s_{90}	$s_{10}, s_{23}, s_{33}, s_{48}, s_{61}, s_{72}$	s_{91}	$s_{11}, s_{24}, s_{34}, s_{49}, s_{62}, s_{73}$
s_{92}	$s_{12}, s_{25}, s_{35}, s_{50}, s_{63}, s_{74}$	s_{93}	$s_{13}, s_{26}, s_{36}, s_{51}, s_{64}, s_{75}$
s_{94}	$s_{14}, s_{27}, s_{37}, s_{52}, s_{65}, s_{76}$	s_{95}	$s_{15}, s_{28}, s_{38}, s_{53}, s_{66}, s_{77}$
s_{96}	$s_{16}, s_{29}, s_{39}, s_{54}, s_{67}, s_{78}$	s_{97}	$s_{17}, s_{30}, s_{40}, s_{55}, s_{68}, s_{79}$

R6. For $t = 16$, the observation (Item 1.2.) for h is used to get a linear equation on state bits for z_t by fixing two state bits $s_{62} = 0$ and $s_0 = s_{13} + s_{23} + s_{38} + s_{51} + s_{62}$ as mentioned in Table 1. The linear equation contains 9 terms as $b_{t+1} + b_{t+2} + b_{t+4} + b_{t+10} + b_{t+31} + b_{t+43} + b_{t+56} + s_{t+25} + b_{t+63} = z_t$ for $t = 16$. Here, the state bit $b_{t+63}, t = 16$ is recovered by guessing remaining state bits in the equation.

From this step onward, the non-linear state update relations are involved for some terms available in the h function.

Table 3. The state bits involved to calculate the non-linear feedback bits

Feedback bits	State bits used	Feedback bits	State bits used
b_{80}	$b_0, b_9, b_{14}, b_{15}, b_{21}, b_{28}, b_{33},$ $b_{37}, b_{45}, b_{52}, b_{60}, b_{62}, b_{63}, s_0$	b_{81}	$b_1, b_{10}, b_{15}, b_{16}, b_{22}, b_{29}, b_{34},$ $b_{38}, b_{46}, b_{53}, b_{61}, b_{63}, b_{64}, s_1$
b_{82}	$b_2, b_{11}, b_{16}, b_{17}, b_{23}, b_{30}, b_{35},$ $b_{39}, b_{47}, b_{54}, b_{62}, b_{64}, b_{65}, s_2$	b_{83}	$b_3, b_{12}, b_{17}, b_{18}, b_{24}, b_{31}, b_{36},$ $b_{40}, b_{48}, b_{55}, b_{63}, b_{65}, b_{66}, s_3$
b_{84}	$b_4, b_{13}, b_{18}, b_{19}, b_{25}, b_{32}, b_{38},$ $b_{41}, b_{49}, b_{56}, b_{64}, b_{66}, b_{67}, s_4$	b_{85}	$b_5, b_{14}, b_{19}, b_{20}, b_{26}, b_{33}, b_{39},$ $b_{42}, b_{50}, b_{57}, b_{65}, b_{67}, b_{68}, s_5$
b_{86}	$b_6, b_{15}, b_{20}, b_{21}, b_{27}, b_{34}, b_{40}$ $, b_{43}, b_{51}, b_{58}, b_{66}, b_{68}, b_{69}, s_6$	b_{87}	$b_7, b_{16}, b_{21}, b_{22}, b_{28}, b_{35}, b_{41},$ $b_{44}, b_{52}, b_{59}, b_{67}, b_{69}, b_{70}, s_7$
b_{88}	$b_8, b_{17}, b_{22}, b_{23}, b_{29}, b_{36}, b_{42},$ $b_{45}, b_{53}, b_{60}, b_{68}, b_{70}, b_{71}, s_8$	b_{89}	$b_9, b_{18}, b_{23}, b_{24}, b_{30}, b_{37}, b_{43},$ $b_{46}, b_{54}, b_{61}, b_{69}, b_{71}, b_{72}, s_9$

R7. For $27 \leq t \leq 32$, the observation (Item 4.1.) for h is used to get equations on state bits for z_t by fixing three state bits as mentioned in Table 1 which are already fixed in previous steps. Most of the state bits involved in the equations are already guessed or fixed in earlier steps. In this step, six state bits $b_{28}, b_{29}, b_{30}, b_{73}, b_{74}, b_{75}$ can be recovered by guessing two bits s_{24} for $t = 27$ and b_{27} for $t = 30$. We brought these rounds before some previous rounds (for $17 \leq t \leq 26$), because the recovered bits b_{73}, b_{74}, b_{75} are used for the equations in the rounds $t = 17, 18, 19$ respectively.

Further, in this step, we recover bits from the equations of the rounds in the order of $t = 29, 28, 27, 30, 31, 32$ (see Tables 4 and 5). b_{30}, b_{29}, b_{28} are recovered in this order, because b_{30} and b_{29} are required for the recovery of b_{29} and b_{28} respectively and b_{28} is required for the recovery of b_{74}.

R8. For $17 \leq t \leq 20$, the observation (Item 1) for h is used to get non-linear equations on state bits for z_t by fixing a state bit $s_{t+46} = 0$ as mentioned in Table 1. However, $s_{t+46} = 0$ for $18 \leq t \leq 20$ is already fixed in step R1. From the equation and update relations, the state bit $s_{t+25}, 17 \leq t \leq 20$ can be recovered by guessing the remaining state bits in the equation.

R9. For $21 \leq t \leq 26$, from the non-linear equation of h observations (Item 1), six state bits $s_{18} - s_{19}$ and $s_{58} - s_{61}$ are recovered as the linear bits in the respective equations. In this step the b_{77}, b_{78} bits are guessed for $t = 21, 22$ respectively.

From the above process, we recover 33 state bits from known 33 consecutive keystream bits. To recover the whole internal state, we need to fix 45 state bits (out of which 44 bits as a constant value and one bit as a linear equation of state bits) and guessing rest 82 bits. For this purpose, we exploited 33 equations. The detailed process of recovery of bits with the fixed, recovered and guessed bits are presented in Tables 4 and 5. The rows of the Table is presented in order of recovery. The terms in brackets are previously assigned (i.e., fixed or, guessed or, recovered).

In comparison with the previous works, we can recover 33 state bits by fixing 45 state bits and guessing rest 82 bits. In earlier results, it is possible to recover $18, 28, 31, 32$ bits fixing $54, 51, 32, 0$ state bits and guessing rest of state bits respectively. Hence, our result improves the conditional sampling resistance to 2^{-33}. The comparison is presented in Table 6.

3.3   TMDTO Attack

In this section, we have exploited the TMDTO attack technique to recover the state bits by using the above results to recover state bits. Here we consider two TMDTO attacks, by Jiao et al. [14] and by Mihalijevic et al. [16] as the later TMDTO curve is the modified version of the TMDTO curve followed by Bjørstad [5] and Mihaljević et al. [15].

The TMDTO parameters by the attack by Jiao et al. [14] are as following.

- Data requirement (D): 2^{s+s^*};
- Pre-processing time complexity (P): 2^{n-s-s^*};
- Online time complexity (T): $t2^s$;
- Memory requirement: (M): $m = \frac{2^{n-s-s^*}}{t}$;

where n is the number of state bits, s is the number of fixed bits, s^* is the number of recovered bits, m is the number of rows in the state storing matrix and t is the number of columns of the matrix such that $m \times t = 2^{n-s-s^*}$.

Table 4. Recovery of state bits

Round (t)	Constrains	Key bits (z_t)	Recovery equation	Guessed bits	Recovered bit
0	$s_{46} = 0, s_{64} = 0$	z_0	$b_{10} = z_0 + b_1 + b_2 + b_4 + b_{31} +$ $b_{43} + b_{56} + s_{25} + b_{63}$	$b_1, b_2, b_4, b_{31}, b_{43},$ b_{56}, s_{25}, b_{63}	b_{10}
1	$s_{47} = 0, s_{65} = 0$	z_1	$b_{11} = z_1 + b_2 + b_3 + b_5 + b_{32} +$ $b_{44} + b_{57} + s_{26} + b_{64}$	$(b_2), b_3, b_5, b_{32}, b_{44},$ b_{57}, s_{26}, b_{64}	b_{11}
2	$s_{48} = 0, s_{66} = 0$	z_2	$b_{12} = z_2 + b_3 + b_4 + b_6 + b_{33} +$ $b_{45} + b_{58} + s_{27} + b_{65}$	$(b_3, b_4), b_6, b_{33}, b_{45},$ b_{58}, s_{27}, b_{65}	b_{12}
3	$s_{49} = 0, s_{67} = 1$	z_3	$b_{13} = z_3 + b_4 + b_5 + b_7 + b_{34} +$ $b_{46} + b_{59} + s_6 + s_{28}$	$(b_4, b_5), b_7, b_{34},$ $b_{46}, b_{59}, s_6, s_{28}$	b_{13}
4	$s_{50} = 0, s_{68} = 1$	z_4	$b_{14} = z_4 + b_5 + b_6 + b_8 + b_{35} +$ $b_{47} + b_{60} + s_7 + s_{29}$	$(b_5, b_6), b_8, b_{35},$ $b_{47}, b_{60}, s_7, s_{29}$	b_{14}
5	$s_{51} = 0, s_{69} = 1,$ $s_{30} = 1$	z_5	$b_{15} = z_5 + b_6 + b_7 + b_9 + b_{36} +$ $b_{48} + b_{61} + s_8 + 1$	$(b_6, b_7), b_9,$ $b_{36}, b_{48}, b_{61}, s_8$	b_{15}
6	$s_{52} = 0, s_{70} = 1,$ $s_{31} = 1$	z_6	$b_{16} = z_6 + b_7 + b_8 + b_{10} + b_{37} +$ $b_{49} + b_{62} + s_9 + 1$	$(b_7, b_8, b_{10}), b_{37},$ b_{49}, b_{62}, s_9	b_{16}
7	$s_{53} = 0, s_{71} = 1,$ $s_{32} = 1$	z_7	$b_{17} = z_7 + b_8 + b_9 + b_{11} + b_{38} +$ $b_{50} + b_{63} + s_{10} + 1$	$(b_8, b_9, b_{11}), b_{38},$ $b_{50}, (b_{63}), s_{10}$	b_{17}
8	$s_{54} = 0, s_{72} = 1,$ $s_{33} = 1$	z_8	$b_{18} = z_8 + b_9 + b_{10} + b_{12} +$	$(b_9, b_{10}, b_{12}), b_{39},$ $b_{51}, (b_{64}), s_{11}$	b_{18}
9	$s_{55} = 0, s_{73} = 1,$ $s_{34} = 1$	z_9	$b_{19} = z_9 + b_{10} + b_{11} + b_{13} +$ $b_{40} + b_{52} + b_{65} + s_{12} + 1$	$(b_{10}, b_{11}, b_{13}), b_{40},$ $b_{52}, (b_{65}), s_{12}$	b_{19}
10	$s_{56} = 0, s_{74} = 1,$ $s_{35} = 1$	z_{10}	$b_{20} = z_{10} + b_{11} + b_{12} + b_{14} +$ $b_{41} + b_{53} + b_{66} + s_{13} + 1$	$(b_{11}, b_{12}, b_{14}), b_{41},$ b_{53}, b_{66}, s_{13}	b_{20}
11	$s_{57} = 0, s_{75} = 1$	z_{11}	$b_{21} = z_{11} + b_{12} + b_{13} + b_{15} +$ $b_{42} + b_{54} + b_{67} + s_{14} + s_{36}$	$(b_{12}, b_{13}, b_{15}), b_{42},$ $b_{54}, b_{67}, s_{14}, s_{36}$	b_{21}
12	$s_{15} = 1, s_{76} = 1,$ $s_{37} = 0$	z_{12}	$b_{22} = z_{12} + b_{13} + b_{14} + b_{16} +$ $b_{43} + b_{55} + b_{68} + 1$	$(b_{13}, b_{14}, b_{16},$ $b_{43}), b_{55}, b_{68}$	b_{22}
13	$s_{16} = 1, s_{77} = 1,$ $s_{38} = 0$	z_{13}	$b_{23} = z_{13} + b_{14} + b_{15} + b_{17} +$ $b_{44} + b_{56} + b_{69} + 1$	$(b_{14}, b_{15}, b_{17},$ $b_{44}, b_{56}), b_{69}$	b_{23}
14	$s_{17} = 1, s_{78} = 1,$ $s_{39} = 0$	z_{14}	$b_{24} = z_{14} + b_{15} + b_{16} + b_{18} +$ $b_{45} + b_{57} + b_{70} + 1$	$(b_{15}, b_{16}, b_{18},$ $b_{45}, b_{57}), b_{70}$	b_{24}
15	$b_{78} = 0, s_{79} = 0,$ $s_{40} = 0$	z_{15}	$b_{25} = z_{15} + b_{16} + b_{17} + b_{19} +$ $b_{46} + b_{58} + b_{71}$	$(b_{16}, b_{17}, b_{19},$ $b_{46}, b_{58}), b_{71}$	b_{25}
16	$s_{62} = 0, s_0 = s_{13} +$ $s_{38} + s_{23} + s_{51}$	z_{16}	$b_{79} = z_{16} + b_{17} + b_{18} + b_{20} +$ $b_{26} + b_{47} + b_{59} + b_{72} + s_{41}$	$(b_{17}, b_{18}, b_{20}, b_{47},$ $b_{59}, s_{13}, s_{38}, s_{51}),$ $b_{26}, b_{72}, s_{23}, s_{41}$	b_{79}
29	$(s_{75} = 1, s_{54} = 0,$ $s_{32} = 1)$	z_{29}	$b_{30} = z_{29} + b_{31} + b_{33} + b_{39} +$ $b_{60} + b_{72} + b_{85} + s_{93}$	$(b_{31}, b_{33}, b_{60},$ $b_{72}, b_{39})$	b_{30}

Now we will fit our case $s = 45, s^* = 33$ and $n = 160$ with this curve as following.

- Data requirement (D): $2^{45+33} = 2^{78}$;
- Pre-processing time complexity (P): $2^{160-45-33^*} = 2^{82}$;
- Online time complexity (T): $t2^{45}$;
- Memory requirement: (M): $m = \frac{2^{82}}{t}$;

If we take the number of columns in the stored matrix $t = 2^{16}$, then the required memory is $M = 2^{82-16} = 2^{66}$ and the online time complexity is $T = 2^{45+16} = 2^{61}$. The TMDTO curve is $TMD = 2^{61} . 2^{66} . 2^{78} = 2^{45} . 2^{160} = 2^s N$. So, we have seen that the required data is reduced by half and the memory requirement is reduced by 2^{-5}, compared to their attack [8].

Table 5. Recovery of state bits continued

Round (t)	Constrains	Key bits (z_t)	Recovery equation	Guessed bits	Recovered bit
28	$(s_{74}=1, s_{53}=0, s_{31}=1), s_{63}=0$	z_{28}	$b_{29}=z_{28}+b_{30}+b_{32}+b_{38}+b_{59}+b_{71}+b_{84}+s_{92}$	$(b_{30},b_{32},b_{59}, b_{71},b_{38})$	b_{29}
27	$(s_{73}=1, s_{52}=0, s_{30}=1)$	z_{27}	$b_{28}=z_{27}+b_{29}+b_{31}+b_{37}+b_{58}+b_{70}+b_{83}+s_{91}$	$(b_{29},b_{31},b_{58}, b_{70},b_{37}),s_{24}$	b_{28}
30	$(s_{76}=1, s_{55}=0, s_{33}=1)$	z_{30}	$b_{73}=z_{30}+b_{31}+b_{32}+b_{34}+b_{40}+b_{61}+b_{86}+s_{94}$	$(b_{31},b_{32},b_{34},b_{61}, b_{40}),b_{27}$	b_{73}
17	$(s_{63}=0)$	z_{17}	$s_{42}=z_{17}+b_{18}+b_{19}+b_{21}+b_{48}+b_{60}+b_{27}+b_{73}+h(s_{20},s_{81},b_{80})$	$(b_{18},b_{19},b_{21},b_{48}, b_{60},b_{73}),s_1,s_{20},(b_{28})$	s_{42}
31	$(s_{77}=1, s_{56}=0, s_{34}=1)$	z_{31}	$b_{74}=z_{31}+b_{32}+b_{33}+b_{35}+b_{41}+b_{62}+b_{87}+s_{95}$	$(b_{32},b_{33},b_{35},b_{62}, b_{41},b_{28})$	b_{74}
18	$(s_{64}=0)$	z_{18}	$s_{43}=z_{18}+b_{19}+b_{20}+b_{22}+b_{28}+b_{49}+b_{61}+b_{74}+h(s_{21},s_{82},b_{81})$	$(b_{19},b_{20},b_{22},b_{49}, b_{61},b_{74}),s_2,s_{21},(b_{29})$	s_{43}
32	$(s_{78}=1, s_{57}=0, s_{35}=1)$	z_{32}	$b_{75}=z_{32}+b_{33}+b_{34}+b_{36}+b_{42}+b_{63}+b_{88}+s_{96}$	$(b_{33},b_{34},b_{36},b_{63}, b_{42},b_{29})$	b_{75}
19	$(s_{65}=0)$	z_{19}	$s_{44}=z_{19}+b_{20}+b_{21}+b_{23}+b_{29}+b_{50}+b_{62}+b_{75}+h(s_{22},s_{83},b_{82})$	$(b_{20},b_{21},b_{23},b_{50}, b_{62},b_{75}),s_3,s_{22},(b_{30})$	s_{44}
20	$(s_{66}=0)$	z_{20}	$s_{45}=z_{20}+b_{21}+b_{22}+b_{24}+b_{30}+b_{51}+b_{63}+b_{76}+h(s_{23},s_{84},b_{83})$	$(b_{21},b_{22},b_{24},b_{51}, b_{63}),b_{76},s_4,(s_{42})$	s_{45}
21	$(s_{67}=1, s_{46}=0)$	z_{21}	$s_{56}=z_{21}+b_{22}+b_{23}+b_{25}+b_{31}+b_{52}+b_{64}+b_{77}+h(s_{85},b_{84})$	$(b_{22},b_{23},b_{25},b_{52},b_{64}, b_{31}),b_{77},s_5,(s_{43})$	s_{18}
22	$(s_{68}=1, s_{47}=0)$	z_{22}	$s_{57}=z_{22}+b_{23}+b_{24}+b_{26}+b_{32}+b_{53}+b_{65}+b_{78}+h(s_{86},b_{85})$	$(b_{23},b_{24},b_{26},b_{53},b_{65}, b_{32},s_{44}),b_{78}$	s_{19}
23	$(s_{69}=1, s_{48}=0)$	z_{23}	$s_{58}=z_{23}+b_{24}+b_{25}+b_{27}+b_{33}+b_{54}+b_{66}+b_{79}+h(s_{87},b_{86})$	$(b_{24},b_{25},b_{27},b_{54},b_{66}, b_{33},b_{79},s_{45})$	s_{58}
24	$(s_{70}=1, s_{49}=0)$	z_{24}	$s_{59}=z_{24}+b_{25}+b_{26}+b_{28}+b_{34}+b_{55}+b_{67}+b_{80}+h(s_{88},b_{87})$	$(b_{25},b_{26},b_{28},b_{55}, b_{67},b_{34},b_{28})$	s_{59}
25	$(s_{71}=1, s_{50}=0)$	z_{25}	$s_{60}=z_{25}+b_{26}+b_{27}+b_{29}+b_{35}+b_{56}+b_{68}+b_{81}+h(s_{89},b_{88})$	$(b_{26},b_{27},b_{29}, b_{56},b_{68},b_{35},b_{29})$	s_{60}
26	$(s_{72}=1, s_{51}=0)$	z_{26}	$s_{61}=z_{26}+b_{27}+b_{28}+b_{30}+b_{36}+b_{57}+b_{69}+b_{82}+h(s_{90},b_{89})$	$(b_{27},b_{28},b_{30},b_{57}, b_{69},b_{36},b_{30})$	s_{61}

Table 6. Comparison of our result with previous results

References	Fixed bits	Recovered bits	Required keystream bits	Guessed bits
Björstad [5]	0	21	21	139
Mihaljević et al. [15]	54	18	18	88
Jiao et al. [14]	51	28	28	81
Mihaljević et al. [16]	32	31	31	97
Siddhanti et al. [18]	0	32	36	96
Our work	45	33	33	82

Then Mihaljević et al. [16] used the BS-TMDTO attack as follows. In this method, the number of fixed bits s and the number of recovered bits s^* reduce the total space $N = 2^n$ to $N' = 2^{n-s-s^*}$. The number of stored $m \times t$ table is t such that $mt^2 = N'$. The used BS trade-off curve is $T'M'^2D'^2 = N'^2$ such that $T' \geq D'^2$, where $T' = t^2$ and $M' = mt$. The probability of n bits having s fixed bits and s^* recovered bits is $p = 2^{-(s+s^*)}$ and the probability of occurring the given keystream with first s bits are fixed is $p' = 2^{-s}$. The total time complexity is $T = p'^{-1}T'$ and required total data is $D = p^{-1}D'$.

In our case, we have $s = 45, s^* = 33$ and then $N^{'} = 2^{82}$. If we take $t = 2^{12}$, then $T^{'} = 2^{24}$. Now by considering $D^{'} = 2^{0}$, we need memory $M^{'} = 2^{70}$ by TMDTO curve. The pre-processing complexity $P^{'} = \frac{N^{'}}{D^{'}} = 2^{82}$. The probabilities $p = 2^{-78}$ and $p^{'} = 2^{-45}$. Then total data is $D = p^{-1}D^{'} = 2^{78}$ and the total time is $T = p^{'-1}T^{'} = 2^{69}$.

For our case, the TMDTO curve followed by Jiao et al. [14] gives the best result. Now we compare our result with the previous results in the following Table 7.

Table 7. Comparison of our result with previous results

References	Time (T)	Memory (M)	Keystream (D)	Pre-processing (P)
Bjørstad [5]	2^{70}	2^{69}	2^{56}	2^{104}
Mihaljević et al. [15]	2^{54}	2^{88}	2^{61}	2^{88}
Jiao et al. [14]	2^{61}	2^{71}	2^{79}	2^{81}
Mihaljević et al. [16]	2^{58}	2^{71}	2^{76}	2^{84}
	2^{70}	2^{71}	2^{70}	2^{90}
Siddhanti et al. [18]	$2^{68.06}$	2^{64}	2^{64}	2^{96}
Our work	2^{61}	2^{66}	2^{78}	2^{82}

4 Conclusion and Future Work

We have shown that the conditional sampling resistant of Grain-v1 can be reduced to 2^{-33} by fixing 45 bits and guessing 82 bits. Then we get the best TMDTO curve using this result as a sampling resistance, especially in the cases of the parameters pre-processing time P, online time T and memory M. Our future work will focus to reduce the sampling resistant of Grain-v1 which can further give a better result for TMDTO attack.

References

1. eSTREAM: Stream cipher project for ECRYPT (2005). http://www.ecrypt.eu. org/stream/
2. Babbage, S.: A space/time tradeoff in exhaustive search attacks on stream ciphers. In: European Convention on Security and Detection, no. 408. IEE Conference Publication (1995)
3. Biryukov, A., Shamir, A.: Cryptanalytic Time/memory/data tradeoffs for stream ciphers. In: Okamoto, T. (ed.) ASIACRYPT 2000. LNCS, vol. 1976, pp. 1–13. Springer, Heidelberg (2000). https://doi.org/10.1007/3-540-44448-3_1
4. Biryukov, A., Shamir, A., Wagner, D.: Real time cryptanalysis of A5/1 on a PC. In: Goos, G., Hartmanis, J., van Leeuwen, J., Schneier, B. (eds.) FSE 2000. LNCS, vol. 1978, pp. 1–18. Springer, Heidelberg (2001). https://doi.org/10.1007/3-540-44706-7_1
5. Bjørstad, T.E.: Cryptanalysis of grain using time/memory/data tradeoffs (2008). http://www.ecrypt.eu.org/stream

6. van den Broek, F., Poll, E.: A comparison of time-memory trade-off attacks on stream ciphers. In: Youssef, A., Nitaj, A., Hassanien, A.E. (eds.) AFRICACRYPT 2013. LNCS, vol. 7918, pp. 406–423. Springer, Heidelberg (2013). https://doi.org/10.1007/978-3-642-38553-7_24

7. Ding, L., Jin, C., Guan, J., Qi, C.: New treatment of the BSW sampling and its applications to stream ciphers. In: Pointcheval, D., Vergnaud, D. (eds.) AFRICACRYPT 2014. LNCS, vol. 8469, pp. 136–146. Springer, Cham (2014). https://doi.org/10.1007/978-3-319-06734-6_9

8. Ding, L., Jin, C., Guan, J., Zhang, S., Li, J., Wang, H., Zhao, W.: New state recovery attacks on the Grain-v1 stream cipher. China Commun. 13(11), 180–188 (2016)

9. Dunkelman, O., Nathan, K.: Treatment of the initial value in time-memory-data tradeoff attacks on stream ciphers. Inf. Process. Lett. 107(5), 133–137 (2008)

10. Golić, J.D.: Cryptanalysis of alleged A5 stream cipher. In: Fumy, W. (ed.) EUROCRYPT 1997. LNCS, vol. 1233, pp. 239–255. Springer, Heidelberg (1997). https://doi.org/10.1007/3-540-69053-0_17

11. Hell, M., Johansson, T., Meier, W.: Grain: a stream cipher for constrained environments. Int. J. Wirel. Mob. Comput. 2(1), 86–93 (2007)

12. Hellman, M.: A cryptanalytic time-memory trade-off. IEEE Trans. Inf. Theory 26(4), 401–406 (1980)

13. Hong, J., Sarkar, P.: New applications of time memory data tradeoffs. In: Roy, B. (ed.) ASIACRYPT 2005. LNCS, vol. 3788, pp. 353–372. Springer, Heidelberg (2005). https://doi.org/10.1007/11593447_19

14. Jiao, L., Zhang, B., Wang, M.: Two generic methods of analyzing stream ciphers. In: Lopez, J., Mitchell, C.J. (eds.) ISC 2015. LNCS, vol. 9290, pp. 379–396. Springer, Cham (2015). https://doi.org/10.1007/978-3-319-23318-5_21

15. Mihaljević, M., Gangopadhyay, S., Paul, G., Imai, H.: Internal state recovery of Grain-v1 employing normality order of the filter function. IET Inf. Secur. 6(2), 55–64 (2012)

16. Mihaljević, M., Sinha, N., Gangopadhyay, S., Maitra, S., Paul, G., Matsuura, K.: An improved cryptanalysis of lightweight stream cipher Grain-v1. In: Cryptacus: Workshop and MC Meeting (2017)

17. Oechslin, P.: Making a faster cryptanalytic time-memory trade-off. In: Boneh, D. (ed.) CRYPTO 2003. LNCS, vol. 2729, pp. 617–630. Springer, Heidelberg (2003). https://doi.org/10.1007/978-3-540-45146-4_36

18. Siddhanti, A.A., Maitra, S., Sinha, N.: Certain observations on ACORN v3 and Grain-v1-implications towards TMDTO attacks. J. Hardw. Syst. Secur. 3(1), 64–77 (2019)

Data and User Privacy

GDPR-Compliant Reputation System Based on Self-certifying Domain Signatures

Mirosław Kutyłowski[1(✉)], Jakub Lemiesz[1(✉)], Marta Słowik[1], Marcin Słowik[1], Kamil Kluczniak[2], and Maciej Gebala[1]

[1] Department of Computer Science, Faculty of Fundamental Problems of Technology, Wrocław University of Science and Technology, Wrocław, Poland
{miroslaw.kutylowski,jakub.lemiesz}@pwr.edu.pl
[2] CISPA Helmholtz Center for Information Security, Saarbrücken, Germany

Abstract. Creating a distributed reputation system compliant with the GDPR Regulation faces a number of problems. Each record should be protected regarding its integrity and origin, while the record's author should remain anonymous, as long as there is no justified legal reason to reveal his real identity. Thereby, the standard digital signatures cannot be applied to secure the records.

In this paper we propose a Privacy Aware Distributed Reputation Evaluation system, where each subject of evaluation holds its recommendation record. By application of a novel technique of domain signatures we are able to guarantee that (a) integrity of each entry is strongly protected; in particular, the evaluation subject cannot modify it, (b) the author of each entry is anonymous, however all entries of the same author on the same subject appear under the same pseudonym (so the Sybil attacks are repelled), (c) the entries corresponding to the same author but for different evaluation subjects are unlinkable, (d) only registered users can create valid entries, (e) the real identity of the author of an entry can be revealed by relevant authorities by running a multiparty protocol, (f) for each entry one can create a pseudorandom key in a deterministic way.

The first five features correspond directly to the requirements of the GDPR Regulation. In particular, they guard against profiling the users based on the entries created by them.

In order to facilitate practical applications we propose to maintain a pseudorandom sample of all entries concerning a given evaluation subject. We show how to guarantee that the sample is fairly chosen despite the fact that the sample is kept by the evaluation subject. We present a few strategies enabling to mimic some important probability distributions for choosing the sample.

This research has been supported by Polish National Science Centre grant OPUS, number 2014/15/B/ST6/02837 and later by grant 049U/0044/19 at Wrocław University of Science and Technology.

S.-H. Heng and J. Lopez (Eds.): ISPEC 2019, LNCS 11879, pp. 341–361, 2019.
https://doi.org/10.1007/978-3-030-34339-2_19

Keywords: Reputation system · Privacy · Anonymity · Pseudonym ·
Domain signature · LRSW · Certificate · GDPR · Probabilistic
counter · Random sample

1   Introduction

1.1   Importance of Reputation Systems

Reputation systems play a fundamental role in the business and social life. This
concerns formal systems offered as services and backed by data processing IT
systems as well as informal systems existing as a social phenomenon. The practical impact of reputation systems is comparable with the role of the existing
legal and law enforcement systems – in many cases the threat of losing face is
enough to prevent a dishonest behavior. An efficient and fair reputation system
may prevent misconduct as effectively as implementing the rules of the civil and
criminal law. In some areas it is the only source of trust – the criminal law is
concentrated on the most extreme cases and cannot deal with, say, poor quality
of services of a craftsman.

Today many commercial systems offer opinions of the former customers about
the services and goods offered. On the other hand, there are forums created independently and enabling to post comments on the services and goods and ranking
them. In all these traditional solutions (see e.g. [16]) the opinions and scores created by evaluators are passed to a central server where they are moderated,
stored and aggregated. The aggregation method is almost always computing the
average score in the scale defined by the system. Such methods are somewhat
biased: evaluators with extreme opinions (including the evaluators working for
the competitors or hired by the party being evaluated) may significantly change
the score and the overall picture. A common technique is also a Sybil attack –
inserting many biased opinions under different names by a single person.

The problem becomes even more acute in the democratic societies, where
informal reputation systems are frequently under attack of specialized agencies
hired to disseminate fake news, unfair opinions, etc. for the benefit of malicious
parties attempting to influence democratic elections.

The importance of reputation systems rapidly increases with the number
of purely digital interactions. The amount of uncertainty increases due to the
fact that the partnerships are created in the virtual world, frequently without
any data verification in the real world. Moreover, the cyber sphere becomes a
dominant source of information, while in most cases the data themselves are not
subject to independent verification.

1.2   Basic Principles of Reputation Systems

Any reputation framework is based on the records on the past behavior of the
evaluated party. Taking into account these records we make a prediction on
the future behavior assuming that the past data provides a good basis for such
conclusions. There are two important points here:

1. We commonly believe that even if the behavior of the evaluated party may change, there should be some observable trend that shows what might be the likely behavior in the future.
2. In social interactions we do not take into account a complete history of our potential partners, but we concern some fairly small sample from the past. This also concerns human generated opinions available online: a reader is not likely to read more than, say, 10 different opinions and scroll more than a few screens. Consequently, presenting a list of all opinions may distort the evaluation outcome: the users are likely to take into consideration only a few most recent reports.

1.3   Basic Threats of Reputation Systems

Trustworthiness of a reputation system depends very much on its resilience to manipulation aimed to either increase or decrease the score in an unfair way. Let us name a few situations:

deleting entries: An attacker removes the opinions that do not match his expectations (this does not concern the situation when deletions follow explicitly from the scheme – e.g. removing obsolete entries),

modifying entries: An attacker manipulates opinions entered by other participants,

flooding and Sybil attacks: In order to conceal the opinions entered by other participants, the attacker floods the system with a large number of biased opinions preferably under many different names (Sybil attack),

aggregation: The amount of data stored or viewed by the participants might be limited so an aggregation process might be inevitable. However, an aggregation process without reliable monitoring may easily lead to distortion of the outcome.

Note that flooding and Sybil attacks become now a standard practice for instance in the social media before political elections.

An effective way to prevent unauthorized modifications and Sybil attacks would be to require to authenticate each entry posted in the system with a digital signature of its author. In this case the final recipient of a reputation record would be able verify the entries himself, without relaying on the parties running the system. However, this approach creates fundamental privacy protection problems. Each signed record reveals some small but non-negligible information about its author. If the opinions are created systematically, then these chunks of information aggregate resulting in a strongly authenticated profile of the author. On the other hand, today most of the evaluators prefer to remain anonymous, so it is unlikely that they would contribute to reputation systems under their own name. Consequently, the reputation systems would be biased – the only opinions available would be the ones originating from extroverted participants that are not particularly concerned about their privacy.

1.4   GDPR, Legal Risks and Obligations

From the legal point of view a reputation system falls into the scope of the European General Data Protection Regulation (GDPR) [21] as a *profiling system*, if any target of evaluation is an identifiable physical person. In this case, strict rules concerning personal data protection must be respected by the party running the profiling system. The GDPR applies regardless of the location of the profiling system, as long as it concerns activities occurring in the European Union.

Moreover, even if the targets of evaluation are not physical persons but, say, some material products, the rules of the GDPR may apply. This happens, if any data concerning an identifiable person appear in the system. This concerns in particular the data of the authors of the opinions. As long as one can identify their real identity – and this is the case when digital signatures are used for authenticating opinions' origin and integrity – the rules of GDPR do apply.

The GDPR regulation formulates many principles for processing personal data. Many of them lead to substantial technical and organizational problems for the party deploying the reputation system. Failure to comply with these rules may result in very high administrative fines imposed on the GDPR violators. Moreover, the recent trends indicate that the European authorities may not hesitate to impose such fines even on the most powerful global corporations.

Let us mention a few important issues resulting from the GDPR in the context of a reputation system:

the right-to-be-forgotten: The right to request erasure of own personal data has been recognized as one of the fundamental human rights. This concerns in particular the right to destroy own recommendations or at least their link to the author. With authentication via digital signatures invalidation of the cryptographic proof is impossible (even through revoking a certificate), unless special cryptographic techniques are used [13]). The real problem is dissemination of these opinions: it is hard to enforce erasure of all copies once a system is a global one and the access to it is not strictly limited.

Even more problematic is the case when the evaluation subject is concerned. There is a long discussion, also within the European Union, on what is the demarcation line between the private sphere (for which the data protection rules apply) and the professional or public sphere (where the rights of the data subject are overridden by other rights). A good example is the case of opinions on a physician's practice: to what extent a physician has the right to request for removal of negative opinions about his medical services?

accountability and privacy-by-design: The major difference between the situation in the past and the current situation is that a system processing personal data must by-design apply sufficient safeguards preventing unlawful data processing. The safeguards might be both organizational and technical, as well as proportional to the existing risks. At first glance, it seems that the situation is advantageous for a party running a reputation system. However, in fact it means that this party is obliged to create a risk assessment and is responsible for any failure to address realistic threats. Last not least, the party running the reputation system must be able to *demonstrate* that the system is compliant with the data protection rules. This goes beyond purely technical *provable security*, as we have to deal with the system in a social, economic and political context. This context might be hard to guess in the case of global systems due to profound cultural differences.

information for the data subject: The GDPR regulation imposes strict rules concerning an obligation to provide certain informations to the data subjects as well as collect their consents. This might be annoying to the users of the reputation systems and risky to the party running the system due to possible mistakes in fulfilling these obligations.

In the situation described, it seems that the most pragmatic strategy is to avoid any unnecessary processing of personal data. Consequently, it would be desirable to replace data authentication with standard digital signatures by some equivalent mechanism not involving personal data.

1.5   Architecture of Reputation Systems

The reputation systems can be classified in the following way:

single dataset, centralized database: The system is run by a single party responsible for data correctness and privacy protection,

single dataset, P2P database: While there is a single dataset, physically it is stored in a distributed way by a number of independent protocol participants exchanging data in a kind of a P2P protocol,

fully distributed: Each evaluation subject holds itself a record of opinions obtained from other users.

The first approach seems to be the most popular in the current commercial systems. The last one is dominant in the traditional business and professional relationships for providing credentials to potential partners.

A fully centralized system might be believed as the simplest solution from the technical point of view. However, authenticating the entries is a serious problem. If the records are not authenticated by their authors, then the party running the system can arbitrarily manipulate the evaluation result. On the other hand, strong authentication creates substantial privacy protection issues.

In a distributed trust system (including such prominent cases as the Bitcoin mechanism for validating transactions) there is no central server and information is appended to the common dataset. Similar systems have been proposed e.g. in [20,23]. In those systems each peer has to maintain its own opinion about all other peers. The opinion is based on peer's own experience as well as on opinions collected over the time from other peers. This approach allows to avoid many of the problems of the centralized system, however, in a dynamic environment it may lead to problems with the information flow. Namely, the survey paper [16] by Jøsang et al. states that: *"In a distributed environment, each partici-pant is responsible for collecting and combining ratings from other participants. Because of the distributed environment, it is often impossible or too costly to obtain ratings resulting from all interactions with a given agent"*. In particular, such an architecture seems to be unsuited for the case when a decision has to be made on-the-spot, e.g. in opportunistic networks. Other problematic aspects of distributed reputation systems are connected with the flooding of the network with a large number of event notifications and storing all gathered information in each node. Last not least, implementing procedures of data erasure based on the right-to-be-forgotten rule might be a technical nightmare.

In this paper we follow the fully distributed approach presented in [18], where each peer stores and carries only its own scores (received from other participants) and presents them upon request. The protocol should guarantee that if a peer modifies or hides its scores, then in all likelihood their misbehavior will be detected.

1.6   Paper Contribution

We propose a generic approach based on pseudonymous signatures for authentication and protection of the entries in the reputation system. A specially tailored signature scheme enables to achieve the following properties:

- each record is authenticated with a pseudonymous signature, so any manipulation of the signed data will be detected unless a new signature is created,
- each pseudonymous signature includes a pseudonym of the signer, the pseudonym is unique for a pair (the signer, the evaluation subject) and the signer cannot create a different valid pseudonym for a given evaluation subject,
- it is infeasible to determine whether two different pseudonyms and signatures concerning different evaluation subjects correspond to the same signer,
- in special circumstances (e.g. law enforcement) it is possible to link a pseudonym with the real identity of the signer, thereby fulfilling a GDPR requirement [21].

Moreover, the signature scheme yields pseudorandom values that are unique in a given situation and verifiable. This enables to design a distributed reputation system where

- the records with the opinions are stored directly by the evaluation subject,
- the number of stored records is fixed, the records to be stored are chosen based on pseudorandom deterministic process which is verifiable,
- in a fairly flexible way the protocol parameters enable to determine the probability distribution of the above pseudorandom choice. E.g., one can choose a record to be stored "uniformly at random" from the set of all records; or to concentrate on the recent records. The construction is based on probabilistic counters.

In our opinion, the combination of pseudonymous signatures and probabilistic counters is a pragmatic design strategy that may have many other practical applications. What is more, this approach might turn out to be very convenient for the designers facing conflicting technical requirements of the GDPR regulation.

2   Pseudonymous Signature

Below we recall the concept of a pseudonymous signatures (in the literature also known as domain signatures). Some details – the way in which the domains are created – are adjusted to our particular needs:

- The actors of a pseudonymous signature scheme are: the Issuer and the signers. Additionally, any party may verify a signature.
- There are domains. In this paper we focused on the case where for each evaluated entity there is a domain corresponding to this entity.
- Each signer obtains (or registers) a single secret key from the Issuer to be used as a signing key for all domains.
- Using its secret, a signer can derive its pseudonym for a given domain. The pseudonym is unique – the signer cannot derive two valid pseudonyms for the same domain.
- With its secret key, a signer can derive a signature corresponding to any of its domain specific pseudonyms. Verification of the signature requires the signature, the domain name, the signer's pseudonym in this domain and the signed data. Neither the real identity of the signer nor any other implicit identifier (such as a single public key) is required.
- Seclusiveness: a pseudonymous signature yields a proof that it has been created by a party enrolled to the system by the Issuer.
- Unlinkability: despite the fact that a user holds a single signing key, its signatures and pseudonyms in different domains are not linkable. A strict cryptographic formulation of this property is that it is infeasible for an external observer to distinguish between the following cases:
  1. the pseudonyms and the signing keys are created according to the scheme,
  2. for each domain a participant gets a different key chosen at random from the pool of valid keys; this key is used to create the domain specific pseudonym and signatures.

Apart from the above properties, a pseudonymous signature scheme should satisfy the standard properties like *unforgeability*.

Examples of Pseudonymous Signature Schemes. Prominent examples of signature schemes involving privacy protection are Direct Anonymous Attestation (DAA) [3], Enhanced Privacy ID (EPID) [2,4] and Domain-Specific Pseudonymous Signatures (DSPS) [1]. DAA and EPID schemes are designed for attesting that computation has been done inside a trusted execution environment, Trusted Platform Module [12] and Intel Software Guard [14], respectively. The attestation does not reveal the signer, but proves that the signer belongs to the group managed by the Issuer. There is a high level of privacy protection: no identity information except for the group membership is proved. The domain concept is not explicitly supported by DAA and EPID. On the other hand, DSPS schemes are designed mainly for authentication using the German personal identity documents. Here, the domain is a leading concept. In the meantime, the above schemes already became industrial standards [5,12,15].

Domain Certificate System (DCS) [19] follows a slightly different philosophy than the regular pseudonymous signature schemes. Essentially, the user obtains a pre-certificate in a form of an LRSW signature under his blinded secret key and on-the-fly may generate domain-specific certificates for standard signature and identification schemes (such as Schnorr, DSA or ElGamal).

The main conceptual difference, which distinguishes DSPS signature scheme from DAA and EPID, is that a domain is represented by a domain public key $D \in \mathbb{G}$ where $\mathbb{G}$ is a cyclic group of a prime order p. Additionally, D has to be authenticated by a trusted party. Then, the basic approach for deriving a pseudonym corresponding to a domain public key D is to compute $nym = D^x$, where $x \in \mathbb{Z}_p$ is a users' secret key. Therefore, two pseudonyms D_1^x and D_2^x for $D_1, D_2 \in \mathbb{G}$ and $D_1 \neq D_2$ are indistinguishable from random elements under the DDH assumption. (The actual construction of a pseudonym in the DSPS scheme [5] is a bit more complex).

DCS does not impose any direct requirement on the form of domain public keys D and even allow scenarios, where there is more than one component, as long as the pseudonym is a tuple (possibly one element) of products of domain public keys raised to private keys. This includes the simplest case of $nym = D^x$, but also more complex ones such as $nym = (D_1^{x_1} D_2^{x_2}, D_3^{x_3})$.

In the case of DSPS it is easy to deanonymize a pseudonym, if $y = \log_g(D)$ for a group generator $g \in \mathbb{G}$ is known. Namely, for a pseudonym $nym = D^x$ one can compute $nym^{1/y}$ and the result $(D^x)^{1/y} = g^{yx/y} = g^x$ is independent of the domain. The value g^x is the main public key of the user holding the private key x and it can be retained by the Issuer for deanonymization purposes. If needed, the domain public key D may be computed as $g^{y_1 \cdot y_2 \cdots y_k}$ in a distributed manner such that the ith authority determines y_i at random. In this case all authorities have to cooperate in order to deanonymize a user. For the DAA and EPID schemes instead of deanonymization procedure the signer has to prove that it does not appear on a blacklist.

The main problem for a DSPS scheme is that if secret keys leak from two or more different devices, then it is easy to compute the Issuer's secret key and create new identities. For the case of the proposed reputation system this would mean necessity of tamper-proof devices, where tamper reseliance must be unconditional including the most powerful parties. For DAA and EPID schemes this problem does not occur, however their functionalities do not correspond to our needs.

The deanonymization technique from DSPS may be applied when selecting D for DCS as well. Additionally, if D is to be selected as for DAA or EPID, another deanonymization technique may be applied, such as the one designed for revocation of the group signatures by Camenisch and Lysyanskaya [6]. Another simple solution would be to encrypt a generic deanonymization token g^x for the deanonymization authority using ElGamal encryption, prove its correctness and include this proof in a certificate.

Domain Certificate System [19]. Although DSPS scheme is the most lightweight one of the presented schemes, it suffers from the fact that it must be implemented on tamper-proof devices. For real-life reputation systems this is an unlikely scenario. We rather have to assume that the users are holding standard devices where the secret keys are only software protected. For these reasons we recommend using DCS instantiated with Schnorr signatures for maximum flexibility. Below we describe more design details.

Setup: The Issuer chooses a bilinear pairing friendly setup, including groups $\mathbb{G}_1, \mathbb{G}_2$ and $\mathbb{G}_T$ of a prime order p and a pairing function e. The setup should be of type 2 or 3, so that there is no efficiently computable homomorphism from $\mathbb{G}_1$ to $\mathbb{G}_2$. Additionally, two group generators are designated: $g_1 \in \mathbb{G}_1$ and $g_2 \in \mathbb{G}_2$.

Subsequently, the Issuer chooses private keys $x, y, z \in \mathbb{Z}_p$ and computes the public keys for the User Registration procedure: $X_1 = g_1^x$, $Y_1 = g_1^y$, $Z_1 = g_1^z$ and the public keys for the Verification procedure: $X_2 = g_2^x$, $Y_2 = g_2^y$, $Z_2 = g_2^z$.

User Registration: This procedure allows an authenticated user to obtain a *master certificate* for his private key. A user i generates his secret key sk_i and computes the corresponding main public key $pk_i = g_1^{sk_i}$. Subsequently, he generates a randomizing factor f and computes a commitment $F = Z_1^f$.

Then the user i approaches the Issuer and after authenticating himself presents his public key pk_i and the commitment F. Then he proves the knowledge of the secret values as follows: First the user commits to random values r_1, r_2 by sending $T = g_1^{r_1} Z_1^{r_2}$ to the Issuer. Then the Issuer responds with a randomly chosen challenge c. The user replies with $s_1 = r_1 - c \cdot sk_i \bmod p$ and $s_2 = r_2 - c \cdot f \bmod p$. The Issuer verifies the responses by checking whether $(pk_i \cdot F)^c \cdot g_1^{s_1} \cdot Z_1^{s_2} = T$.

Finally, the Issuer generates the master certificate in the form of an LRSW signature. Namely, he selects a random value $\alpha \in \mathbb{Z}_p$ and computes the tuple

$$\sigma = (g_1^\alpha, g_1^{z\alpha}, g_1^{y\alpha}, g_1^{zy\alpha}, g_1^{x\alpha}(pk_i \cdot F)^{xy\alpha}).$$

The Issuer registers the public key pk_i for possible future deanonymization and sends the User the master certificate σ.

The user must remember the secret key sk_i, the randomizing factor f and the master certificate σ.

CreateDomain: This procedure creates the domain public key of a domain j. The procedure takes as input the public parameters and outputs $D_j = g^{d_j}$, for a random d_j. This procedure may be executed by multiple parties, so that $D = g^{\prod_k d_k}$ and the kth party knows only d_k. This would allow to deanonymize a user only when all parties cooperate. Additionally, we may require that D_j is certified by the Issuer, or another trusted party and a user will be able to verify the certificate before computing and presenting a pseudonymous signature for this domain.

Domain Certificate generation: This procedure creates a pseudonym and a domain certificate for the User i and a domain public key $D_j \in \mathbb{G}_1$. When approaching domain j for the first time, the User must determine his pseudonym and prepare a proof of its correctness in a form of a domain specific certificate.

Recall the User holds the secret key sk_i, the randomizing factor f and the master certificate $\sigma = (A_0, A_1, B_0, B_1, C)$. The pseudonym is extraced simply as $nym = D_j^{sk_i}$.

The certificate σ must be re-randomized to ensure unlinkability. For this purpose the User selects at random the factors $r, r' \in \mathbb{Z}_p$. The new certificate is created by computing

$$(\widetilde{A_0}, \widetilde{A_1}, \widetilde{B_0}, \widetilde{B_1}, \widetilde{C}) = (A_0^r, A_1^r, B_0^r, B_1^r, C^{rr'})$$

and a non-interactive proof that the original signature would verify correctly. To create such a proof, the User creates a commitment using three more random values, $k_0, k_1, k_2 \in \mathbb{Z}_p$, by computing $T_C = \widetilde{A_0}^{k_0} \cdot \widetilde{B_0}^{k_1} \cdot \widetilde{B_1}^{k_2}$. The user also commits to the pseudonym by computing $T_D = D_j^{sk_i \cdot k_0 - k_1}$. A challenge is obtained by computing a hash over the commitments, the randomized certificate and the pseudonym

$$c = H(T_C, T_D, \widetilde{A_0}, \widetilde{A_1}, \widetilde{B_0}, \widetilde{B_1}, \widetilde{C}, nym) \tag{1}$$

The proof is finalized by computing

$$s_0 = k_0 - c \cdot r' \bmod p, \quad s_1 = k_1 - c \cdot r' \cdot sk_i \bmod p, \quad s_2 = k_2 - c \cdot r' \cdot f \bmod p.$$

Finally, the domain certificate equals

$$(T_C, T_D, \widetilde{A_0}, \widetilde{A_1}, \widetilde{B_0}, \widetilde{B_1}, \widetilde{C}, nym, s_0, s_1, s_2).$$

Domain Certificate verification: This procedure should be executed once by a Verifier aiming to entrust a pseudonym nym.

To verify correctness of the certificate $(T_C, T_D, \widetilde{A_0}, \widetilde{A_1}, \widetilde{B_0}, \widetilde{B_1}, \widetilde{C}, nym, s_0, s_1, s_2)$, the Verifier first recomputes the challenge value c according to Eq. (1). Next, he verifies if the blinded LRSW signature is valid, by checking whether

$$e(\widetilde{C}^c, g_2) = e(T_C/(\widetilde{A_0}^{s_0} \cdot \widetilde{B_0}^{s_1} \cdot \widetilde{B_1}^{s_2}), X_2), \quad e(\widetilde{A_0}, Z_2) = e(\widetilde{A_1}, g_2),$$
$$e(\widetilde{A_0}, Y_2) = e(\widetilde{B_0}, g_2), \quad \text{and} \quad e(\widetilde{A_1}, Y_2) = e(\widetilde{B_1}, g_2).$$

Finally, the Verifier checks that the commited pseudonym matches the signature by checking whether $nym = (T_D D_j^{s_1})^{1/s_0}$.

Signature creation: Since the system is instantiated with Schnorr signatures, an obvious choice it to use the standard Schnorr signature scheme. For a message m and a domain public key $D_j \in \mathbb{G}_1$, the signature is computed by selecting a random $k \in \mathbb{Z}_p$, committing to it by $T = D_j^k$, computing challenge $c = H(T, m)$ and response $s = k - c \cdot sk_i \bmod p$. The signature itself is a pair of (s, c).

Signature verification: To verify correctness of a signature, if the pseudonym *nym* is trusted, a simple verification of the Schnorr signature is sufficient. The Verifier simply computes $T = nym^c \cdot D_j^s$ and verifies if the hash value matches $c = H(T, m)$.

For the sake of our reputation system we need also a pseudorandom number related to a tuple (evaluation author, evaluation subject, additional parameters). This can be computed as a hash value $H(nym_D, D, \text{additional parameters})$, where D is the public key of the evaluation subject, nym_D is the pseudonym of the evaluation author for the domain D.

3   Reputation Systems Based on Probabilistic Counters

In this section we present three different systems for distributed reputation systems based on probabilistic counters. We use for them the name **P**rivacy **A**ware **D**istributed **R**eputation **E**valuation, or PADRE for short.

3.1   PADRE-1

In PADRE-1, each evaluated party holds two one-dimensional tables: $\mathcal{N}$ for the negative scores and $\mathcal{P}$ for the positive scores. Each table has size k, where k is a system parameter. It is a constant, however k has direct influence on quality of the approximation of the number of positive and negative scores.

Entering a Score. When a participant A provides a service to another participant B, then a new entry for either $\mathcal{N}$ or $\mathcal{P}$ of A is prepared by B. The following data are created:

- a pseudonym $nym_{A,B}$ of B with respect to the domain of A,
- a pseudonymous signature s of participant B concerning:
  - $nym_{A,B}$,
  - the score $b \in \{0, 1\}$,
  - the time t of signature creation,
- an index $i = H(nym_{A,B})$, where cryptographic hash function H takes values in the set $\{0, 1, \ldots, k - 1\}$.

Then the entry $(nym_{A,B}, t, b, s)$ is written on position i into $\mathcal{N}$ (if the score is negative), or into $\mathcal{P}$ (if the score is positive).

The parameter b can be skipped as it follows from the context, while for verification of s the right value can be guessed. Optionally, the entry may also contain a text T, which is either a detailed opinion (of a fixed length) written by B or a hash (serving also as a link) to the opinion written by B.

Enforcing to Store a Score. Presumably, there is a subprocedure that ensures that A will actually store the entry obtained from B in one of their tables. It may be realized by the following additional steps:

starting interaction: A sends to B a commitment to store an entry received from B,
finalizing interaction: A returns to B the tables $\mathcal{N}$ and $\mathcal{P}$ with the entry from B and signed by A with the (regular) digital signature of A.

In this case, if say the table $\mathcal{N}$ emerges where the entry from B is missing, then the following situations may occur:

1. the relevant position contains an entry with a later date – in this situation there is no irregularity, as newer entries overwrite the old ones,
2. the relevant position is empty or contains an entry older than created by B – in this case the signed table presented at the step finalizing the interaction between A and B as well as the current state of the tables of A is a strong cryptographic proof of misconduct of A.

Verification of integrity of $\mathcal{N}$ and $\mathcal{P}$. A user obtaining the tables $\mathcal{N}$ and $\mathcal{P}$ may check their integrity by verifying that

– for each entry of the table verification of pseudonymous signature yields the positive result (the standard verification process of pseudonymous signature),
– each entry is written into the appropriate position $i = H(nym_{A,B})$ of the table.

Interpretation of the tables $\mathcal{N}$ and $\mathcal{P}$. Finally, a user of a reputation system has to determine the reputation score based on the entries from $\mathcal{N}$ and $\mathcal{P}$. The score can be based on an estimate for the number of positive and negative opinions and derived from the contents of the tables $\mathcal{N}$ and $\mathcal{P}$. In fact, both $\mathcal{N}$ and $\mathcal{P}$ can be treated as probabilistic counters. In one round we do the following:

– choose time difference Δ,
– create copies $\mathcal{N}_\Delta$ and $\mathcal{P}_\Delta$ of tables $\mathcal{N}$ and $\mathcal{P}$, by removing from them all entries older than Δ,
– apply the estimator described below in Sect. 3.2 for the number of negative and positive votes in the time interval $[T_0 - \Delta, T_0]$, where T_0 is the current time.

The whole procedure can be repeated for different values Δ. For instance, Δ might be 1 week, 1 month, 1 year, etc.

Note that this is quite important not only to see the average opinions, but also their evolution in time. Indeed, many cases of fraud start with a phase of building a good reputation followed by a short phase of cheating the business partners. In our system, even if the scores are aggregated in two tables of a fixed size, the recent scores get some preference and we get almost a complete list of scores from the recent transactions. Nevertheless, some old entries persist to exist (unlike in the case of FIFO queues) due to the Coupon Collector phenomenon.

3.2   Estimator for PADRE-1

To estimate the number of scores in a given time period we can use a classic probabilistic counter (see e.g. [22]) based on the *balls and bins model*. Namely, assume that we put at random n balls in k bins, and let X_n be the random variable denoting the number of bins that are left empty. It is has been proved in [22] that

$$\hat{n} = -k \ln (X_n/k) \tag{2}$$

is almost unbiased and well concentrated estimator of the parameter n. Namely, for the ratio $r := n/k$ we have

$$\frac{\mathbb{E}\,[\hat{n}]}{n} \sim 1 + \frac{e^r - r + 1}{2n},$$

and

$$\mathbb{SE}\,[\hat{n}] \sim \frac{\lambda(r)}{\sqrt{k}}, \quad \text{where} \quad \lambda(r) := (e^r - r - 1)^{1/2}\, r^{-1},$$

where $\mathbb{E}\,[X]$ stands for the expected value and $\mathbb{SE}\,[X]$ stands for the standard error of the random variable X. From the above it can be deduced that the smaller the ratio r, the higher concentration of the estimator.

Based on the above facts we can derive, for example, an estimator of the number of positive scores Y_Δ in time period $[T_0 - \Delta, T_0]$, where T_0 is the current time. Namely, we can calculate the number V_Δ of positions that have a time-stamp $t \in [T_0 - \Delta, T_0]$, and if $V_\Delta < k$ we can use estimator of the form:

$$\hat{Y}_\Delta = -k \ln \frac{k - V_\Delta}{k}.$$

PADRE-1 Versus FIFO Policy. At this point one would like to compare PADRE-1 with a simple FIFO policy for storing the records. FIFO has the advantage over PADRE-1 that the numbers concerning the number of most recent entries are exact, while for PADRE-1 we are talking about estimates only. Of course, once in the considered period the number of entries is higher than the size of the table where they go to, then the FIFO policy fails to provide valuable data. In case of PADRE-1 we trade sharpness of numbers for a longer time horizon. This is motivated by two reasons. The first is that the number of interactions of the evaluated party is itself a random variable and as well as the opinions depend on some random decisions. So it does not make sense to put too much effort to keep precision of the numbers. Second, for small values of Δ the estimator given in (2) is quite precise. On the other hand, it provides a valuable information long after the number of records inserted exceeds the table size k. Indeed, note that when we enter k records at random into a table of size k, then due overwriting the same positions the expected number of unaffected positions is about k/e. So still there is plenty room for the older records.

3.3 PADRE-2

The strategy to insert scores into all positions of a table with the same probability presented in PADRE-1 is just one of many available options. For instance, one can create a counter where probability to write into a position i strongly decreases with i. In this way we get a few most recent entries at the beginning. As on each trial we have a small chance to write into a position with a high i, these places in the table are normally occupied by older entries. Such a counter has better potential for counting a large number of entries, however the recent history is not that visible.

Below we present a construction that is focused on choosing a sample of k opinions uniformly at random over the whole past history. At the same time we keep track on the overall number of generated records.

3.4 Construction of PADRE-2

As for PADRE-1, $\mathcal{N}$ and $\mathcal{P}$ are tables of a fixed size k. The entries in the table are similar as in Sect. 3.1, however there are substantially different rules concerning inserting them.

Entering a Score. Assume that a reputation record written by a participant B about a participant A has to be entered. The following data are prepared:

- a pseudonym $nym_{A,B}$ of B with respect to domain A,
- a pseudonymous signature s of participant B concerning:
  - $nym_{A,B}$,
  - score $b \in \{0,1\}$,
- a hash value $h = H(nym_{A,B}, s)$, where H is a cryptographic hash function and $h \in [0,1)$.

Then the following entry is prepared for storing in $\mathcal{N}$ (if the score is negative), or in $\mathcal{P}$ (if the score is positive):

$$E = (nym_{A,B}, h, b, s).$$

As for PADRE-1 there is an option of inserting a field T with an evaluation text. The rules for storing an entry E are the following.

1. If there are less than k entries in the table, then store E in an empty place.
2. If there already k entries in the table:
   (a) if value of h in entry E is higher than the second component of each stored entry, then E is dropped,
   (b) otherwise, E replaces an entry with the highest second component.

Note that according to this strategy the reputation record of a user A contains k entries (or less at the beginning of the process) with the smallest hash values h.

Note that the value h depends on the signature s that is not known for A beforehand. It is necessary, since for $h = H(nym_{A,B})$ the party A knowing already $nym_{A,B}$ would also know in advance if the new record obtained from B is going to be retained in its reputation tables. In such a case the reputation system would fail to serve its purpose.

Time Uniformness. Using the value $h = H(nym_{A,B}, s)$ for the decision to store or drop a record leads to the following properties:

– The final contents of the tables do not depend on the order of incoming records – we always store the records with the lowest k values of the second component of E. Of course, the intermediate contents depends on the order of incoming records.
– For a good hash function we may assume that the values are evenly distributed over the interval $[0, 1)$.

3.5 Estimator for PADRE-2

Order Statistics of the Uniform Distribution. Let $U_1, U_2, \ldots, U_n$ be a sequence of random variables. If the realization of those random variables is arranged in increasing order and written as

$$U_{1:n}, U_{2:n}, \ldots, U_{n:n},$$

then the random variable $U_{k:n}$ is called the kth order statistic.

Further, we assume that variables $U_1, U_2, \ldots, U_n$ are independent and uniformly distributed on the interval $(0, 1)$. Then it can be shown that the random variable $U_{k:n}$ has a distribution belonging to the well known Beta distribution family (cf. [10])

$$U_{k:n} \sim Beta(k, n + 1 - k). \tag{3}$$

Cardinality Estimation. Order statistics are quite useful for cardinality estimation, see e.g. [7,8,11]. In distributed environments we can use for example Partial Counting [8].

Let $\mathcal{M}$ stand for the table $\mathcal{P}$ or $\mathcal{N}$. For the cardinality estimation the only component of an entry considered is the hash value $h \in [0, 1)$. So for the sake of readability let us assume that $\mathcal{M}$ will store only these hash values and that $\mathcal{M}$ is initialized with ones. The estimator is presented below as Algorithm 1.

Algorithm 1. Estimator for PADRE-2

1: **if** $\exists_{1 \leq i \leq k} \mathcal{M}[i] = 1$ **then**
2:     **return** $\hat{n} \leftarrow |\{i : \mathcal{M}[i] \neq 1\}|$
3: **else**
4:     $U_{k:n} \leftarrow \max\{\mathcal{M}[1], \ldots, \mathcal{M}[k]\}$
5:     **return** $\hat{n} \leftarrow (k-1)/U_{k:n}$
6: **end if**

Note that if an unknown cardinality n is smaller than the value of k, then Algorithm 1 will return the exact value of n with a very high probability (only hash collisions result in an inaccurate result). In other cases we estimate the number of elements n by

$$\hat{n} = \frac{k - 1}{U_{k:n}}. \tag{4}$$

The above formula is intuitively clear, as we consider observations from the uniform distribution over $[0, 1)$ and we might expect that $U_{k:n} \approx \frac{k}{n}$. Fortunately, apart from this argumentation there is the following strict mathematical result:

Theorem 1. ([9]). *Let* $3 \le k < n$. *Then the random variable* $\hat{n}$ *defined by Eq. (4) is a strictly unbiased estimator of the number* n *(i.e.* $\mathbb{E}[\hat{n}] = n$*) with the variance*

$$\mathbb{V}\mathrm{ar}[\hat{n}] = \frac{n(n - k + 1)}{k - 2}. \tag{5}$$

Reputation Score. Let us assume that there was n positive and m negative scores in total, we hash them and sample k and l scores respectively, according to the above procedure. Note that we need not to have $k = l$, the proportion between them may depend on cultural and social issues. Then we can estimate the number of positive ($\hat{Y}$) and negative ($\hat{N}$) scores as

$$\hat{Y} = \frac{k-1}{Y_{k:n}} \quad \text{and} \quad \hat{N} = \frac{l-1}{N_{l:m}}.$$

To obtain an easily interpretable single-number summary we could define a reputation score $\hat{R}$ for example as

$$\hat{R} = \frac{\hat{Y}}{\hat{Y} + \hat{N}}.$$

Note that (by the delta method) we can show that

$$\mathbb{V}\mathrm{ar}\left[\hat{R}\right] \approx \frac{(mn)^2}{(m+n)^4} \left(\frac{1}{k-2} + \frac{1}{l-2} \right),$$

which indicates that the variance of such estimator decreases as sample sizes k and l increase but it is finite as long as those sizes are at least 3.

3.6 PADRE-3

The last scheme is based on the sequential reservoir sampling [17]. We assume that each protocol participant needs to keep a sample of k records stored in k bins (one record per bin). The following properties are fulfilled:

1. for each bin the choice of the record to be stored is independent from the choices for other bins,
2. given a bin i, there is a dedicated family of probability distributions $P_{i,n}$ over all n so far received records. Namely, after receiving n records the record stored in the bin i is chosen according to the probability distribution $P_{i,n}$.

The distributions need not to be the same for each bin, we can choose them independently. Remarkably, the second property holds after each step n of the process, even if the only operation allowed is to replace the record in the bin by a new record (the past records are not stored apart from the records in the bins).

There is a very wide range of distributions that may be used, they are specified in the way described below, however the most important feature is that there are possibilities to specify them so that, say, recent records or old records are preferred in a way that is under our control.

From now on we focus on a single bin. Let $w(s_i)$ be the weight assigned to the ith obtained record and $W_j = \sum_{i=1}^{j} w(s_i)$ be the sum of weights for the first j records. Upon arrival of the nth record the owner of the bin makes a decision whether to store it in the bin "with probability" $\frac{w(n)}{W_n}$. Of course, the choice has to be deterministic, so the record has to be stored in the bin if

$$h_n < \frac{w(n)}{W_n},$$

where h_n is the parameter h from the nth record. The records are constructed analogously as for Sect. 3.4, and the parameters h may be treated as a number in the interval $[0, 1)$. Due to the properties of the hash function, we may treat the numbers h as chosen uniformly at random from $[0, 1)$. Namely, for a record issued for A by B, which is the ith record created for A, with the signature s, and aimed for bin l, we set

$$h = H(nym_{A,B}, s, l, i)$$

where, as before, H is a cryptographic hash function.

The most important and remarkable property of sequential reservoir sampling is the following. Assume that n records were obtained in total. Then the probability that the considered bin contains the ith record is

$$\frac{w(i)}{W_n}. \tag{6}$$

This is obvious for the nth record, however this is true also for any earlier record (see [17]).

Choice of the Weight Functions. It is straightforward to express many distribution preferences by the weight function $w(s_i)$. For example by setting $w(s_i) = 1$ we get a uniform distribution, as according to (6), $\frac{w(i)}{W_n} = \frac{1}{n}$.

By setting $w(i) = 2^i$ we get a geometric distribution with the preference to the most recent scores. Namely, the probability that the record i is stored when n records have been presented in total is approximately 2^{i-n-1}.

4   Experimental Results

Now we present the experimental comparison of three proposed aggregation schemes: PADRE-1, PADRE-2 and PADRE-3. For PADRE-3 we test two selected weight functions.

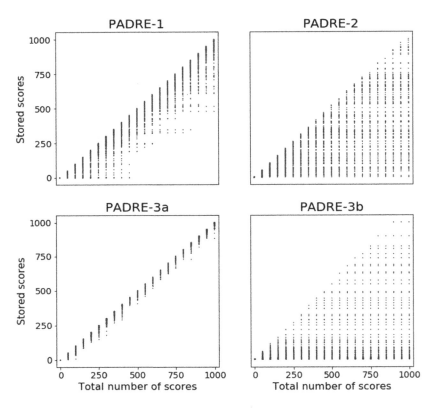

Fig. 1. Experimental comparison of different PADRE schemes. Charts present the content of different schemes in time as new scores are encountered. The total number of scores received to a given time is placed on the horizontal axis. Indexes of stored scores are placed on the vertical axis. In each scheme a maximal number of scores to keep at any given time is 100.

In Fig. 1 we present experimental comparison of three proposed aggregation schemes. For each scheme we set the maximal number of scores to keep as $m = 100$ and we show how the content of schemes changes in time as we collect $n = 1000$ scores. For the readability of charts we plot only the content after every 50 steps.

For PADRE-1, which is based on balls and bins model, we can see that the content reflects rather recent history. There are also some isolated cases of slightly older scores related to Coupon Collector phenomenon.

For PADRE-2, which is based on order statistics, we can confirm that at each step the content reflects a uniform sample from the whole history.

In plot titled PADRE-3a we show the results for scheme PADRE-3 with the weight function $w(i) = c^i$, where $c = 1.05$. As the weight function grows rapidly the content of the scheme at each step reflects very recent history. If we would increase the value of c the concentration on the latest history would be even higher.

In plot titled PADRE-3b we show the results for scheme PADRE-3 with the weight function $w(i) = 1/(i + 1)$. As the weight function decreases the content of the scheme is more concentrated on older scores.

In each plots we see a strong relationship between neighboring columns. Such an effect occurs for any system where only a one new record may be inserted at a time and where a record once forgotten cannot be recovered anymore.

Conclusions and Future Work

As we have shown, application of pseudonymous signature scheme enables to create strongly authenticated reputation records. Thereby we create a framework in which one can process reputation data without the fear of violating personal data protection rules.

An important point for improving the scheme for practical deployments would be designing signature schemes that would be based on standard groups.

For practical reasons (e.g. scalability), it is rather impractical to keep all reputation records. Therefore, we have to adopt some fair method of deleting data, however without enabling manipulations aiming to influence the resulting overall reputation score. Three schemes are presented explicitly in the paper. However, definitely there are many other possibilities. An important point is that pseudorandomness resulting from domain pseudonyms enables to mimic any probabilistic sampling scheme in a verifiable way.

References

1. Bender, J., Dagdelen, Ö., Fischlin, M., Kügler, D.: Domain-specific pseudonymous signatures for the German identity card. In: Gollmann, D., Freiling, F.C. (eds.) ISC 2012. LNCS, vol. 7483, pp. 104–119. Springer, Heidelberg (2012). https://doi. org/10.1007/978-3-642-33383-5_7
2. Brickell, E., Li, J.: Enhanced privacy ID from bilinear pairing for hardware authentication and attestation. In: 2010 IEEE 2nd International Conference on Social Computing, pp. 768–775, August 2010
3. Brickell, E., Camenisch, J., Chen, L.: Direct anonymous attestation. In: Proceedings of the 11th ACM Conference on Computer and Communications Security, pp. 132–145. ACM (2004)
4. Brickell, E., Li, J.: Enhanced privacy ID: a direct anonymous attestation scheme with enhanced revocation capabilities. Cryptology ePrint Archive, Report 2007/194 (2007)

5. BSI: Technical guideline TR-03110 v2.21 - advanced security mechanisms for machine readable travel documents and eIDAS token (2016). https://www.bsi. bund.de/EN/Publications/TechnicalGuidelines/TR03110/BSITR03110.html
6. Camenisch, J., Lysyanskaya, A.: Signature schemes and anonymous credentials from bilinear maps. In: Franklin, M. (ed.) CRYPTO 2004. LNCS, vol. 3152, pp. 56–72. Springer, Heidelberg (2004). https://doi.org/10.1007/978-3-540-28628-8_4
7. Chassaing, P., Gerin, L.: Efficient estimation of the cardinality of large data sets. In: 4th Colloquium on Mathematics and Computer Science, DMTCS Proceedings, pp. 419–422 (2006)
8. Cichoń, J., Lemiesz, J., Szpankowski, W., Zawada, M.: Two-phase cardinality estimation protocols for sensor networks with provable precision. In: Proceedings of IEEE Wireless Communications and Networking Conference, WCNC 2012, Paris, France. IEEE, April 2012
9. Cichoń, J., Lemiesz, J., Zawada, M.: On cardinality estimation protocols for wireless sensor networks. In: Frey, H., Li, X., Ruehrup, S. (eds.) ADHOC-NOW 2011. LNCS, vol. 6811, pp. 322–331. Springer, Heidelberg (2011). https://doi.org/10. 1007/978-3-642-22450-8_25
10. David, H., Nagaraja, H.: Order Statistics. Wiley Series in Probability and Mathematical Statistics. Wiley, Hoboken (2003)
11. Giroire, F.: Order statistics and estimating cardinalities of massive data sets. Discrete Appl. Math. **157**(2), 406–427 (2009)
12. Group, T.C.: Main Specification version 2.0 (2016). https://trustedcomputing group.org/tpm-main-specification/
13. Hanzlik, L., Kutyłowski, M., Yung, M.: Hard invalidation of electronic signatures. In: Lopez, J., Wu, Y. (eds.) ISPEC 2015. LNCS, vol. 9065, pp. 421–436. Springer, Cham (2015). https://doi.org/10.1007/978-3-319-17533-1_29
14. Intel: Intel Software Guard Extensions (Intel SGX). https://software.intel.com/ en-us/sgx
15. ISO/EIC: 20008-1:2013, anonymous digital signatures - part 1: General (2013). https://www.iso.org/standard/57018.html
16. Jøsang, A., Ismail, R., Boyd, C.: A survey of trust and reputation systems for online service provision. Decis. Support Syst. **43**(2), 618–644 (2007)
17. Kolonko, M., Wäsch, D.: Sequential reservoir sampling with a nonuniform distribution. ACM Trans. Math. Softw. **32**(2), 257–273 (2006)
18. Liau, C.Y., Zhou, X., Bressan, S., Tan, K.-L.: Efficient distributed reputation scheme for peer-to-peer systems. In: Chung, C.-W., Kim, C.-K., Kim, W., Ling, T.-W., Song, K.-H. (eds.) HSI 2003. LNCS, vol. 2713, pp. 54–63. Springer, Heidelberg (2003). https://doi.org/10.1007/3-540-45036-X_6
19. Slowik, M., Wszola, M.: An efficient verification of CL-LRSW signatures and a pseudonym certificate system. In: Proceedings of the 4th ACM International Workshop on ASIA Public-Key Cryptography, APKC 2017, New York, NY, USA, pp. 13–23. ACM (2017)
20. Teacy, W.T.L., Patel, J., Jennings, N.R., Luck, M., Systems, M.: Coping with inaccurate reputation sources: experimental analysis of a probabilistic trust model. In: Proceedings of the 4th International Joint Conference on Autonomous Agents and Multiagent Systems, AAMAS 2005, pp. 997–1004. ACM Press (2005)
21. The European Parliament and the Council of the European Union: Regulation (EU) 2016/679 of the European Parliament and of the Council of 27 April 2016 on the protection of natural persons with regard to the processing of personal data and on the free movement of such data, and repealing Directive 95/46/ec (General Data Protection Regulation). Official Journal of the European Union **119**(1) (2016)

22. Whang, K.Y., Vander-Zanden, B.T., Taylor, H.M.: A linear-time probabilistic counting algorithm for database applications. ACM Trans. Database Syst. **15**(2), 208–229 (1990)
23. Zhou, R., Hwang, K.: PowerTrust: a robust and scalable reputation system for trusted peer-to-peer computing. IEEE Trans. Parallel Distrib. Syst. **18**(4), 460–473 (2007)

Defining a New Composite Cybersecurity Rating Scheme for SMEs in the U.K.

Andrew Rae and Asma Patel$^{(\boxtimes)}$ (iD)

School of Computing and Digital Technologies, Staffordshire University,
Stoke-on-Trent, UK
r021335f@student.staffs.ac.uk, asma.patel@staffs.ac.uk

Abstract. The 5.7 million small to medium enterprises (SMEs) in the U.K. play a vital role in the national economy, contributing 51% of the private sector. However, the cyber threats for SMEs are increasing with four in ten of businesses experiencing a cyber attack in the last twelve months. One significant treatment of this growing concern is in the implementation of long-established information security standards and best-practices. Yet, most SMEs are not undergoing the certification process, even though the current threats are now widely published by the government. In this paper, we look at the disconnect of cyber threats faced by SMEs considering their current security postures and perceptions. We also identify the influencing factors needed to improve security behaviours and engagements with information security best-practices. We then propose a new foundational composite cybersecurity rating scheme, which is aimed at SMEs in the U.K., but it also has the potential to be scaled internationally. The focus of our scheme is to ascertain and measure the security behaviours, perceptions and risk propensity of each SME, as well as their technical systems. To that end, we define our 5×5 matrices based scheme by combining the measurements ascertained from the behavioural as well as technical audits. The preliminary evaluation results demonstrate that this approach provides a higher level of insight, engagement and accuracy as to an SME's individual security posture.

Keywords: Cybersecurity · Data security · Information security · Cyber Essentials · ISO 27001 · SMEs · Security behaviours · Risk propensity

1 Introduction

In 2018, a survey done by the U.K. government revealed that four in ten U.K. businesses suffered a cyber-attack within the last twelve months, with the average cost for an SME of £1,570 per attack [13]. However, another survey [9] on the security of small businesses showed that less than a quarter of small businesses cited cybersecurity as one of their top concerns. There appears to be a disconnect in what SMEs, particularly smaller businesses, perceive as top risks when asked. This contradictory situation is in a time when, in May 2018, the U.K. put into

© Springer Nature Switzerland AG 2019
S.-H. Heng and J. Lopez (Eds.): ISPEC 2019, LNCS 11879, pp. 362–380, 2019.
https://doi.org/10.1007/978-3-030-34339-2_20

force the new data protection regulation [20]. This regulation now places the onus and legal requirements on businesses to not only protect their data, but to also proactively notify the Information Commissioner's Office of any breaches or face serious financial consequences such as fines of up to 4% global turnover or €20 million.

Running in parallel with this concern is the increasing requirement within the public sector to engage SMEs and push businesses into achieving a recognised cyber or information standard before being allowed into the procurement process. The U.K. government has gone further and set a 2022 target of achieving 33% procurement of all their contracts undertaken by SMEs [8]. As this aim of the government moves forward, it produces opportunities, but it also presents significant challenges. The perception and current security postures of SMEs, especially around data and information security risks, are critical challenges. Consequently, these challenges contribute to the lack of SMEs' engagement to existing standards. Cyber Essentials [26] and ISO 27001 [21] are the two prime examples that provide the key criterion for working with the government; however, the take up of these standards is still very low since the release of Cyber Essentials in June 2014 and [21] last major update in 2015. As the U.K. government's own Minister for Digital and Culture admitted [17], just over 0.1% of the 5.7 million SMEs in the U.K. have undertaken Cyber Essentials even though that was particularly designed to help facilitate and encourage smaller businesses to achieve a recognised standard.

This paper proposes a new robust and consumer-friendly cyber rating scheme. This scheme provides better-personalised security insights of the persons reasonable for a business and how their behaviours, awareness and risk propensity impact on these insights. Following are the core principles which defines the new composite cybersecurity rating scheme:

– To provide a preliminary outline of a robust consumer-friendly cyber rating scheme which considers the technical requirements, as well as the behavioural insights of SMEs, through a new composite rating threshold-based model.
– To devise a scheme which has the capability of promoting and incentivising secure behaviours as well as helping encourage progression into recognised information security standards.
– Enable higher levels of protection and increase informed decision-making opportunities for consumers and organisations within a supply chain.

Rest of the paper is organised as follows. Section 2 illustrates the related work. Section 3 outlines the proposed model design and Sect. 4 demonstrates the initial evaluations using expert interviews and two quantitative surveys. Section 5 concludes and presents future research workstreams.

2   Related Work

This section discusses the related work in the key research areas that also highlight the need of defining a new scheme.

2.1   SME Security Behaviours and Perceptions

When looking at the literature concerning U.K. SME security behaviours and perceptions, the options are quite limited. In [18], authors identified some attitudinal changes needed within SMEs to increase the uptake in existing security standards. The big hypothesis put forward is that SMEs choose not to spend on information security as they believe the risks are acceptable and, therefore, do not see the benefits of investing in this area. This suggests that SMEs need clear, short-term and measurable benefits or incentives to better embrace cyber and data security. Another study [16] identified that perception is a major factor which has become engrained in the small business culture to prevent a firm fully understanding the risks and costly mistakes made by uninformed employees. It also highlights the perception of information assurance as a field of concern and concedes that some form of financial assistance and cyber insurance products do have some impact. However, it can be argued that this study do not cover national and more widespread impacts to facilitate the culture change needed.

Another factor outlined to try drive more secure behaviours is with the use of industry products. This leads to another assertion around current behaviours within SMEs relating to market failure. It is argued that the market did help drive the development of products such as cyber insurance, but as discussed in [34], less than 2% of all businesses in the U.K. in 2016 had taken up that insurance option due to the complexity of the offerings of insurance companies.

Although SMEs are aware of the law, they disconnect to the reality of the threats, how relevant they are for their business and, also, cannot justify the effort to reward ratio in implementing a more secure posture. Therefore, it is logical to suggest that without the basics such as enforceable legislative or financial drivers in place, there is an apathy shown towards standards and investments into cybersecurity by smaller businesses when cost control is such a major challenge. There are several factors that need to be analysed to understand the behaviours of SMEs around cyber or information security. In [5], authors suggest the focus of research has been too centred around a single behavioural trait; namely policy compliance. This is further narrowed as the outcome variable is set to the 'intention to comply with the information security policy'. This approach lacks several other factors such as organisational security maturity and legislative obligations and the questionable perception that SMEs fully understand the legal implications or requirements.

2.2   Attitudes and Awareness to Cyber or Information Security standards

In [18], authors suggest that smaller companies would not undertake the larger established standards such as ISO 27001. And it indicated attitudes and awareness related challenges including lack of internal expertise or understanding the risks of not having such a system in place; the cost to implement and manage the standard; the complexity of implementing the standard; SMEs perceived ISO27001 suitable for only larger organisations. Similarly, authors in [1] specify that, "...cost and lack of awareness of the standard contents act as a main barrier for adopting the standard ISO 27001". A study [18] was published only a year after the scheme had been officially released. However, the follow-up study [19] was two years after Cyber Essentials had been released, but this still showed a low take up of the scheme. It showed that out of a total of 1688 Cyber Essentials and CE Plus certifications, 540, 777, 352 and 19 certificates were issued by CREST, IASME, QMGS and APMG certification bodies, respectively.

A recent survey [33] highlights that, overall, only 9% of UK businesses were aware of the Cyber Essentials scheme. This percentage increased in another survey [32] which showed 21% of UK businesses were aware of Information Security Management 27001. It disclosed that around 70% of U.K. SMEs are not aware of the recognised certifications in cyber or information security.

2.3   Comparable Behaviours and Approaches from Other Industries

This section looks at other industries that have implemented assurance schemes and how they have successfully influenced behaviours within SMEs. A comparable area that has come from reviewing related work shows the areas of health and environmental activities as one to further investigate [3]. One example is [6] who argues that health psychology has connected relevance to cybersecurity psychology as health behaviours are similarly sensitive to that of information security.

In the U.K., the Food Standards Agency has successfully implemented a local authority mandated scheme called the Food Hygiene Rating Scheme (FHRS) [14]. The FHRS rating system is measured on the standards of food hygiene found at a business following an inspection. This then allows consumers to make an informed decision on whether to eat at that business based on the assessed hygiene standards, measured from 1 – worst to 5 – the best. This mandated scheme has proved to be a driver to encourage businesses not performing well to do better and those that are achieving high scores, to use that as a marketing tool to attract customers. Consumers are used to seeing number ratings or star-based scores for areas like hotel ratings, business reviews, and food hygiene as they provide an instant and understandable reference point to help enable a consumer's buying decision. When looking at how to drive-up standards in SMEs, FHRS provides additional insight as reported by BBC News [4], who showed a significant rise in Welsh businesses aiming and achieving the top 5 rating, which was up from 45% to just under 61% in 2015. It also reported that the "ratio of firms rated satisfactory or better (scores 3 to 5) rose from 86.9% to 94.4%, while the number of outlets with a zero-rating halved from 134 to 61, around one in 500".

Treating cybersecurity like the government treats infectious diseases is a must, and it is widely accepted that individuals are responsible to make life choices to improve their own well-being, though we also often engage in some degree of risky behaviour [28]. FHRS aims to reduce the incidence of food borne illness and the associated costs to the economy. A similar objective can be argued for cybersecurity, where the aim is to reduce the incidences of data breaches and cybercrimes and the associated costs and disruption to the economy, business, and the public. Hence, the need of aligning the merits of cybersecurity with an established scheme such as FHRS.

2.4 Information Availability and Its Dispersion to SMEs

A key challenge identified was around how SMEs find security-related information and the impact the dispersion of information has had on the SMEs security posture [2, 34, 35]. These studies highlight the confusing landscape that the vast array of online channels offer when searching for information. The key question is how to deliver consistency as the content is not regulated? It is not clear how an SME would judge whether the source is trustworthy, or that the guidance given is relevant for them. SMEs are confused about what information to go with due to the sheer volume of available data and, often, do not know where to begin. The study [34] showed that only 7% of businesses consulted government websites and the UK government's survey showed only 2%. It argues that for the sake of publicity, concerned news or media reports tend to focus on high-profile data breach cases even if similar attacks happen against SMEs. That may lead to the misguided assumption that SMEs are not at risk. Hence, the UK government's attempts at priming or a warning SMEs do not influence the degree of information disclosure [22].

The European Union Agency for Network and Information Security (ENISA) organisation did provide a contribution to this topic around an effective way to share information through the utilisation of the U.K.'s Cybersecurity Information Sharing Partnership (CISP) [12]. This would position CISP as a trusted exchange partner for business to seek guidance on cyber threats and data security issues. ENISA [12] does state, "...such an initiative requires high levels of trust that maybe difficult to achieve amongst large groups of participants". That seems to be a fair assessment of SMEs sharing their information, which raises the question as to whether using anything associated to the government would be deemed suspicious by SMEs as trust in the U.K. government has broadly remained unchanged since 2017 at 36% [11].

2.5 Drivers to Help Deliver Increases in Positive Security Behaviours

Authors in [30] suggest that management can increase compliance in the domain of information security, by using the social bond theory and the involvement theory as encourages sharing of knowledge and collaboration. Several useful areas were rationalised around how to engage and develop behavioural changes more effectively [5]. One area put forward was the use of vignettes to highlight behaviours as it helps remove the need to admit to personal information but still gain insight into the person's behavioural traits. In addition, individuals are influenced by subconscious cues and this 'priming' through visualisation is an important element needed for behavioural change. A further driver raised for consideration is around incentivisation the U.K. government introduced a now defunct scheme of £5,000 innovation vouchers for SMEs back in 2013 [15]. These vouchers could be used to improve information security aspects but even though the actual number of vouchers taken up is unclear, the take up was at a level the government saw as not being effective. Therefore, three years later from its introduction they were ceased. This outcome partly supports that market failure is a major factor in the low adoption of standards. The five drivers were compliance with laws and regulations, protection of brand and reputation, physical cost of a breach, market pressure for a recognised standard, and stock market price [18,25].

Several barriers can be extrapolated from the literature that the U.K. SMEs need to face when trying to achieve positive cybersecurity postures [2,7,23,27]. These barriers include: lack of time or financial resource; lack of understanding the risks or threats; lack of incentives to undertake standards or change behaviours; lack of pressure for cyber security within their supply chain or via consumers; lack of compliance drivers; lack of trust in experts or quality of information (including a single source); lack of expertise within the business; and unclear or confusing legislation requirements. These studies also highlight potential opportunities to overcome these barriers that include: protecting cashflow; focusing IT expenditure to deliver the most impact and best ROI; cleansing customer databases for higher engagement and response rates; reducing applicable costs such as cyber insurance or IT financing; better understanding the risks and potential threats for the business; opening new market or business opportunities to support business growth; and developing a competitive advantage. Although any SME will have different weighting ratios of importance against their identified risk factors, the following key research gaps were identified in achieving positive cybersecurity postures for the UK SMEs:

- The perceived benefits for implementing security standards are outlined. But these benefits did not appear to be a compelling solution to help encourage and facilitate U.K. SMEs to take up those standards outside of it being a requirement for a public sector contract.
- Behavioural models are discussed, but a clearly defined incentive-based model that understands the motivational influences for U.K. SMEs to engage in more secure behaviours was missing.
- Several points are raised around needing a nationally mandated model but seemed to just use existing standards even though the market had shown a relatively low take up to date. Therefore, a foundational solution is required that could be mandated, but it must also demonstrate a relevant value proposition to an SME to be deemed as highly advantageous.
- Further work is needed to ascertain how cybersecurity information is obtained and the perceived complexity of it, including the potential impact. The literature also suggest a gap of a single-source trusted information point that is not government controlled.
- There was a lack of a solution that could address informed decision making by consumers around cyber or data security that also could be used by industry as a benchmark.

– Comparable behaviours in other industries are discussed, but no actual solution is suggested to make effective use of that behavioural approach.

These identified gaps also facilitate the identification of the external and internal influencing factors and their likely collective outcomes when looking at safer behaviours and developing a more secure organisational culture. Since the current standards do not capture and help form the behavioural basis, it has provided the necessary insights to develop a new model.

3   Proposed Rating System

This section presents the proposed cyber rating scheme.

3.1   System Evaluation Method

The literature highlights limitations of the current cybersecurity standards such as theory choices to influence positive security behaviours, encouraging factors for standards adoption, the ineffectiveness of standards, approach aligned with a comparable industry and standards, perceptions and awareness of SMEs. After analysing these limitations, we defined six hypotheses (H) to influence and refine the development of the new cybersecurity-based rating scheme for SMEs:

H1. Incentive theories will influence security behaviours more effectively compared to rational choice theories.
H2. Widespread adoption of a cybersecurity standard requires mandated local authority compliance.
H3. Cybersecurity needs to be more aligned with environmental health in its appreciation and delivery process.
H4. Businesses lack awareness and perception of relevance or value with current cybersecurity standards.
H5. Perceived complexity in cybersecurity perpetuates inactivity and a higher risk acceptance due to the scale of the issue and the diversity of information available.
H6. Giving people rational security information does not guarantee positive behaviour change.

Below are the evaluation methods defined to test the validity of the six noted hypotheses (Sect. 3.1) and the feasibility of a new scheme:

(a) Quantitative and qualitative surveys - To provide a data collection method from a question set around technical and behavioural concerns associated with cyber and data security. Also, to gather feedback and positions from areas SMEs experienced or perceived.
(b) Expert interviews - Through unstructured interviews with industry and academic experts generate qualitative data and gain a deeper understanding of their views and their expert feedback against the submitted hypotheses.

Table 1. Mapping the new scheme sections to the five sections in Cyber Essentials.

Sr. no	New scheme technical sections	Cyber Essential control sections
1	Protecting your network	Firewalls and internet gateways
2	Ensuring your systems are securely configured	Secure configuration
3	Controlling who accesses your systems	Access control
4	Protecting against malware	Malware protection
5	Keeping your systems up-to-date	Patch management

3.2 Proposed Rating Method

The relatively low take up of existing standards, primarily focus on technical and management systems when undertaking audits. It is also true to highlight the growing threats to SMEs [24], yet there is a lack of awareness or even the implementation of security measures. As only 49% of businesses not having implemented the government's five basic technical controls from Cyber Essentials; hence, this approach is not working [13]. **H6** states providing information, regardless of how rational the arguments, is not enough to positively change behaviours. It also supports the view that rational choice theories are not enough to bring the change; there may be an opportunity for a better incentivised approach to deliver success (**H1**).

A key part of the proposed approach is in the measuring of an SMEs security posture and being able to generate a single-digit (1 to 5) rating to illustrate the cyber competence and data security effectiveness of that business. To achieve this rating, the paper proposes utilising two distinct audit areas to generate a composite rating. The two proposed areas are the SME's security behaviours and their technical systems. The aim being to understand both the technical systems in place to provide mitigation against the various cyber threats as well as understand and, where needed, influence the SMEs behaviours in how those systems are utilised, managed and improved.

One half of the rating function will focus on the technical aspects and for ease of progression will be aligned with Cyber Essentials. The technical audit will cover five sections similar to Cyber Essentials, with Table 1 illustrating how the new scheme's technical audit sections would map across to Cyber Essential's current five sections. The other half of the rating function focuses on behaviours and risk propensity of an SME. From the literature review and industry analysis (i.e., expert reviews as described in Sect. 4.2), the first iteration of a new quadrant behavioural model has been developed to illustrate what influences may affect an SME's security posture and then allow for levels of weighting to be applied depending on the ratings scored during the audit process.

Figure 1 shows the assembled new model, named the 'Fan of Influence', derived from the combined analysis of peer research, internal testing, and expert interviews. The four distinct segments deriving from Fig. 1 include:

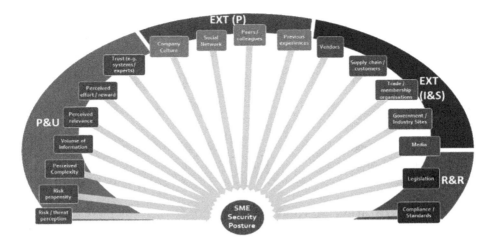

Fig. 1. Proposed behavioural influencing model for an SME's security posture.

(a) Perception and Understanding [P&U] segment relates to decision influencing coming from how the respondent views and perceives the relevance, threat, risk, and trust of information available. It also covers awareness and how the respondent views the effort to reward ratio.

(b) External (Personal) [EXT (P)] segment relates to external decision influencing coming from within the respondent(s) peer (social or work) network and from past experiences.

(c) External (Inform and Service) [EXT (I&S)] segment relates to external decision influencing coming from entities or organisations that the respondent may interface with during normal business operations. This could be areas which have a greater influence on the respondent(s) business operations such as the supply chain or the vendors they use.

(d) Regulation and Requirements [R&R] segment relates to fixed decision making which are typically a requirement (be it legally or as a standard) that the respondent must follow. There is usually little to no influence the business themselves could have on these factors.

This behavioural influencing model concept allows each of the four segments (and/or segment piece) to be weighted depending on the business and the threat requirements generated through dynamic means, such as intelligence-based decision making [10]. The ability for this model to incorporate individualistic influencing factors and recognise the context of an SME's security decision making, helps improve the opportunity of better SME engagement. It also develops positive security behavioural change through SME owners understanding the relevant value proposition to their business and the potential benefits of implementing such measures aligned to the current and changing threat landscape. This level of granularity and behavioural analysis provides a distinctly different approach to existing security standards. It is envisaged that the proposed behavioural model would utilise a top-to-bottom approach when dealing with cybersecurity improvements and issues as SMEs are typically owner-led that is the vital source for delivering an organisation-wide culture of security. The challenges to information security best practices and corporate culture come from at least three factors: level of threat perceived; location; and lack of cooperation and communication between management and staff. Recent research has shown that positive information security culture encourages security-vigilant behaviour of employees and therefore can help to avoid human-related security breaches [7].

3.3   Defining the Rating Matrices

The proposed scheme would use a composite rating based upon two layers of assessments, namely, the behavioural and technical audit scores. The result will deliver a single-digit score aiming to be easily understood by consumers and businesses alike.

In terms of the scoring matrices themselves, we propose the use of a recognised 5×5 approach [29, 31]. Typically, the size of a matrix tends to be a personal choice and aligned to many aspects, such as what is used by the industry? or what customers require to use? The 5×5 size of the chosen matrices will provide enough granularity when defining priorities for secure behaviours and identifying consequences of threats and maps well for the proposed composite rating and its associated thresholds needed to define a single-digit visible rating. This size of matrix is also compatible with the recognised standards of Cyber Essentials, ISO 27001/05, and IEC 31010.

The first layer required to generate the composite rating is based on results from the audit around an SME's behaviours and risk propensity. This scoring focusses on aspects of insecure behaviours which would impact on the business and its customers. It is envisaged that the first layer of scoring (see Fig. 2) measures the likelihood of insecure behaviours against the consequences to the business, with the highest score demonstrating the most insecure behaviour posture. This rating will be used with the technical audit score to produce the nal composite score.

To deliver an actionable plan from the first layer findings, an additional phase within the behaviour layer is required. This phase will utilise the behavioural models outlined in Sect. 3.2 to identify priorities which have the maximum opportunity to influence secure behavioural change in that SME. This phase scoring is based on the premise that just identifying insecure behaviours is not enough and identification of actions is also required. Regular undertaking of this approach will ensure continual improvement as it will assist with the definition of priorities through the individually identified influencing factors for each business and ensure costs and outcomes are aligned to that business' objectives. Any identified action implemented or not could then influence the scoring following a review of the first phase. Both Figs. 2 and 3 use the proposed scoring matrix dimension, and each provides a key as to how the numbers are interpreted in terms of priorities for action or in measuring the impact of insecure behaviours. The score

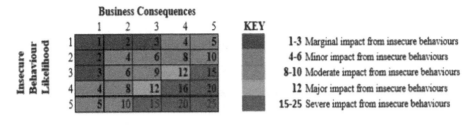

Fig. 2. Phase 1 of behavioural scoring matrix around an SME's security posture.

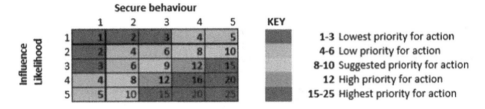

Fig. 3. Phase 2 of behavioural scoring matrix around an SME's security posture.

from Fig. 3 is not currently used in the composite score as it is designed to be remedial only.

The second layer to be scored is around the technical and systems side of a business. For this, the information is gathered using a modified audit from the Cyber Essentials standard. That then enables the promotion of the five baseline controls needed for business and streamlines the progression to achieve Cyber Essentials certification. The proposed 5 × 5 matrix is based on two measures: threat likelihood and business consequences. Much like a traditional risk assessment of impact and likelihood, this structure allows for any easier way to understand the risks for a business and therefore, its customers. That is a vital piece of knowledge when looking to design a rational and comprehensive cyber rating. Figure 4 shows the proposed scoring matrix and provides a key as to how the numbers are interpreted in terms of business consequences. The score generated from this matrix and the summation from the results from Fig. 2 provides the final composite rating (see Sect. 3.4).

3.4 Composite Scoring

A key foundation to the need of this composite rating is that the current standards are lacking understanding of SME's behaviour and risk propensity. Part of the implementation of this scheme is to develop fresh approaches which achieve perception change around cybersecurity and deliver safer behaviours by understanding and influencing behaviours through personalised motivating factors.

This is achieved through a rating mechanism utilised successfully in other compliance-led industries, like food hygiene, which enables informed decision

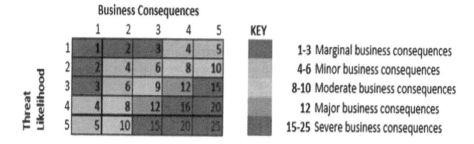

Fig. 4. Proposed 5×5 scoring matrix around an SME's technical risk and threat vulnerability.

KEY	Threshold	Rating Description	Rating	Min %	Max %
	2-17	Excellent	5	80%	100%
	18-24	Good	4	64%	74%
	25-31	Satisfactory	3	50%	62%
	32-37	Above Basic	2	36%	48%
	40-50	Basic	1	4%	34%

Fig. 5. Proposed composite table to derive the new scheme's final security rating.

making and addresses current market failures in encouraging a greater standard take-up and more secure behaviours. Therefore, to achieve this, the process is to take the results from both matrices shown in Fig. 2 and 4 and generate the final score from a summation of those two matrices. Figure 5 shows the thresholds and its associated rating. The threshold can be refined based on further research, but with the use of a 5×5 for the two scoring models it allows for most of the results to fit within 'Satisfactory' ratings and below and provide a higher threshold for 'Good' and 'Excellent' ratings. This is seen as desirable as businesses should be at a high level in both of the audited layers to demonstrate secure behaviours as well as secure systems as a business must have at least one '5' rating to achieve a 'Good' or above. It also means businesses have to score at least 50% in total to be deemed 'Satisfactory'. The min and max percentage ranges in Fig. 5 show the range of scores that would be achieved in that rating's banding.

The threshold for the scoring follows the model of the previously discussed FHRS rating in Sect. 2.3 as that has been proven both successfully implemented and managed regionally.

Once a composite rating is calculated from Fig. 5, it then leads to the visible rating seen by consumers and businesses. To further align it with successful models, such as FHRS, the proposed scheme will use a simplified and recognised scoring approach of 1 to 5 stars with a simple rating explanation included (columns three and four of Fig. 5). A rating of zero is not included as that would

Table 2. Profiles of experts.

Expert reference	Background	Expertise and experience
Expert 1	Academia and research	Noted and published professor in cybersecurity with vast research experience in human-centred security and behaviours towards business (especially SME sizes) and cyber and data security
Expert 2	Financial and legal industry	Head of innovation within a large, blue-chip service organisation specialising in offering financial and legal products for business. Oversees innovation projects such as one with machine learning based on behaviours
Expert 3	Local government	Information Governance Manager for a large district council. Oversees multi-agency information sharing to ensure processing is compliant with data protection legislation. Remit also includes awareness of governance and training through the boroughs and local enterprises around many cyber and data centric subjects
Expert 4	Local government	Information Governance Manager for a city council. Many years of experience in all areas of governance and information assurance, including working with local authority business development teams to help local businesses grow. Also, has long experience with data security regulations and supply chain procurement processes within the local authority
Expert 5	Banking industry	Lead manager in digital engagement for a major international bank. Their role focuses on businesses with turnovers up to £6 million and is tasked to help provide guidance and raise awareness in cyber and information security. Proven experience in training and event presenting with an expertise in cyber fraud

mean the business is unrated and failed the audit. This approach is to immediately provide consumers and other businesses the ability to make informed decisions as these ratings would be visually displayed at the entrance, near the payment area and online.

4   Evaluation

This section presents the initial scheme testing and evaluation strategy. Following the defined system evaluation methods (described in Sect. 3.1), the testing will be done over two distinct methods: (a) quantitative surveys with at least one qualitative question and (b) expert non-structured interviews. These evaluation methods are designed for preliminary evaluation of the scheme, but the results do provide evidence around its feasibility and applicability and help form a foundation for further extensive testing and research.

4.1   Surveys

There were two surveys completed: a technical and a behavioural survey with the same 15 respondents and with 10 questions in each questionnaire to collect both quantitative and qualitative data. The sample size is too small to be representative of the SME population. However, the conducted surveys do provide indicative conclusions and useful insights to support the initial evaluation of the new scheme.

The results from the technical controls and systems survey are given below:

- Nearly 9 in 10 businesses (87%) stated they had one or more firewalls protecting their network. However, 54% of those businesses stated that they do not regularly review their firewall rules.
- A third of all surveyed businesses admitted that they do use the same password across multiple accounts, with 80% of all surveyed micro businesses stating that they did this.
- 8 out 10 surveyed businesses stated that they change their passwords every quarter or twice a year, with only around 1 in 10 (13%) stating their change passwords monthly or less.
- 6 out of 10 surveyed businesses stated that they did have a user account creating process, but 80% of micro and 33% of small-sized businesses said they did not.
- The majority (53%) of surveyed businesses indicated that they did not have anti-virus or malware protection for every Internet-enabled device, which included 83% of all small-sized businesses. From those that did have malware protection, businesses regularly scanned for viruses daily/weekly or monthly.
- 60% of all surveyed businesses did state that they ensured at 'most times' they had the latest updates on installed software.
- Over 7 in 10 businesses (73%) stated that they did not perform regular vulnerability scans on their owned networks, with only medium-sized businesses stating that they did.

The results from the behavioural and risk propensity survey are given below:

- A third of surveyed businesses did not consider cyber threats or data loss a significant risk to them.

- Most businesses felt that GDPR was relevant to their business (60% stated fairly or very relevant responses). However, most businesses (80%) found the new data protection regulations fairly or very difficult to understand.
- Almost equal amount of businesses was aware of Cyber Essentials and ISO 27001 (53% to 47% were not aware of them) with 100% of Accommodation and food services businesses and 66% of Professional, scientific, and technical businesses not being aware of Cyber Essentials.
- The majority of businesses (66%), especially the Education businesses surveyed, would speak to friends or colleagues when wanting help on a cybersecurity issue.
- Most businesses (73%) found understanding information on cybersecurity to be either fairly or very difficult to understand, especially from the small-sized businesses surveyed.
- A third of businesses felt like there was not enough information about cybersecurity available to them, but 40% of businesses stated that there was either slightly too much or overall, too much information available.
- Trust in the information available was reasonable with 47% trusting most of the information with 53% trusting some of it.
- The most stated theme when looking at what cybersecurity areas the surveyed businesses needed help with was around compliance and auditing. The two main technical responses were around network security & threat analysis and incident handling. The other key theme raised was around better training, guidance and awareness.

Table 3. Summary of experts supportive of the hypotheses from Sect. 3.1

Hypotheses		Supported by
H1	Incentive theories will influence security behaviours more effectively compared to rational choice theories	Experts 1, 2
H2	Widespread adoption of a cyber security standard requires mandated local authority compliance	Experts 3, 4
H3	Cybersecurity needs to be more aligned with environmental health in its appreciation and delivery to business	Experts 2
H4	Businesses lack awareness and perception of relevance or value with current cyber security standards	Experts 1, 2, 3, 4, 5
H5	Perceived complexity in cyber security perpetuates inactivity and a higher risk acceptance due to the scale of the issue and the diversity of information available	Experts 2, 3, 4, 5
H6	Giving people rational security information does not guarantee positive behaviour change	Experts 1, 2, 5

4.2   Expert Interviews

The experts selected for unstructured interviews fitted across the following three profiles: commercial or industry, academia, and local government. These profiles helped to give a broad understanding of the various aspects associated with the proposed scheme. Table 2 lists the profiles of the five experts engaged with for this paper.

During expert interviews, the initial discussions were on the expert's experience and thoughts around a new foundational scheme in cybersecurity for SMEs. In addition, the six hypotheses from Sect. 3.2 were discussed. Table 3 lists the six hypotheses and, the experts who supported each of these statements.

5   Conclusion and Future Work

To sum up, there is a perception of complexity around cyber and data security, especially with the new data protection regulations, and a big area that is needed is behavioural change. The U.K. government wants more SMEs involved in their supply chain but there is little evidence to suggest that there will be enough secure and well managed SMEs in terms of cybersecurity that could help achieve that aim. To that extent, the movement away from purely rational choice-based theories and information dispersion needs to be looked in-depth as this paper has suggested. The proposed system helps gain a personalised understanding of the risk propensity and influences on secure behaviours for each business, rather than just what secure technical systems and policies are in place. Further work is needed to generate larger levels of evidence, but it demonstrated there are core reasons around why SMEs are not embracing the merits of robust cybersecurity standards and best-practices more widely, such as Cyber Essentials which was specifically developed to engage U.K. SMEs. Awareness of such standards and the perceived relevance and risk propensity are major factors for the current market failures. To make this scheme a success, these factors would need to be addressed. This could be achieved by following the FHRS model of enforcing such a programme at regional level through local government authorities mandating any businesses handling personal data as an example. Then, the composite approach involving understanding and measuring behaviours and influencing factors to ensure that SMEs are engaged through relevant, personalised measurements and actionable plans which generate value-based outcomes and develop positive security behavioural change. The immediate future work includes:

- Undertake larger survey base to test and refine the two-layer audit model for robust testing of the 'Fan of Influence' model and the six hypotheses. Develop the required audits against the two-layered scoring models and then map the answers to suitable scoring within the matrices.
- Develop a new model for the weighting ratio required for the proposed scheme as a 50/50 ratio would not be reflective of industry needs. The new weighting model could utilise intelligence-based decision making from data generated by accredited national security surveys and other such industry accepted sources.

Attack types could then be sub-divided into behavioural-based (or the 'human error' factor) and technically-based to facilitate a dynamic annual weighting to be applied to the composite rating process which would focus the weighting ratio on the current threat landscape each year and not rely on the knowledge of the persons undertaking their risk assessments within the current security frameworks.

– Further develop the incentivised benefits and drivers, including investigating a mandated supply chain process which could be mirrored within the public sector at a regional level.
– Extend the mapping exercises of the new scheme against ISO 27001 and Cyber Essentials to see what percentage of each standard have been undertaken and, therefore, provide a visual guidance to a business in how much more work is required to meet other standards to further encourage take-up.
– Include analysis on other non-U.K. standards, such as NIST-800 and the Cybersecurity Framework to identify if anything of value could be learned which helps facilitate this model being utilised in other countries.
– Carry out a detailed quantitative pilot study within chosen regional locations and with approximately 20–30 active business. Using sectors, such as retail, would provide responses from both consumers and businesses on their perceptions of the new scheme. Also, having a visible cybersecurity rating may allow for measurements in areas like commercial advantage and consumer confidence which help develop the value proposition of the scheme.

References

1. Alqatawna, J.: The challenge of implementing information security standards in small and medium e-business enterprises. J. Softw. Eng. Appl. **7**(10), 883–890 (2014)
2. Bada, M., Sasse, A.M., Nurse, J.R.: Cyber security awareness campaigns: why do they fail to change behaviour? arXiv preprint arXiv:1901.02672 (2019)
3. Barton, K.A., et al.: Information system security commitment: a study of external influences on senior management. Comput. Secur. **59**, 9–25 (2016)
4. BBC News: Food hygiene ratings scheme in wales 'a big success' (2015). https://www.bbc.co.uk/news/uk-wales-politics-34943449
5. Blythe, J.: Cyber security in the workplace: understanding and promoting behaviour change. Proc. CHItaly Dr. Consort. **1065**, 92–101 (2013)
6. Blythe, J.M., Coventry, L., Little, L.: Unpacking security policy compliance: the motivators and barriers of employees' security behaviors. In: Eleventh Symposium On Usable Privacy and Security, pp. 103–122 (2015)
7. Connolly, L., Lang, M.: Information systems security: the role of cultural aspects in organizational settings (2013)
8. Crown Commercial Service - GOV.UK: The SME spend target must go on (2018). https://www.gov.uk/government/news/the-sme-spend-target-must-go-on
9. Cyberaware.gov.uk: Small business reputation and the cyber risk- cyber streetwise and KPMG. Technical report, Cyber Streetwise and KPMG (2015)
10. Dilek, S., Çakır, H., Aydın, M.: Applications of artificial intelligence techniques to combating cyber crimes: a review. arXiv preprint arXiv:1502.03552 (2015)

11. Edelman: Trust barometer 2018 - UK findings (2018). https://www.edelman.co. uk/magazine/posts/edelman-trust-barometer-2018/
12. ENISA: Cyber security information sharing: an overview of regulatory and non-regulatory approaches (2015). https://www.enisa.europa.eu/
13. Finnerty, K., et al.: Cyber security breaches survey 2018 (2018). https://www.gov. uk/government/statistics/cyber-security-breaches-survey-2018
14. Food Standards Agency - FHRS: Food hygiene rating scheme (2019). https://www. food.gov.uk/safety-hygiene/food-hygiene-rating-scheme
15. Gov.uk: Innovate UK widens the appeal of £5,000 vouchers for small firms to seek expert advice (2014). https://www.gov.uk/government/news/innovation-vouchers-for-all
16. Gundu, T., Flowerday, S.: Ignorance to awareness: towards an information security awareness process. SAIEE Afr. Res. J. **104**(2), 69–79 (2013)
17. Matt Hancock's cyber security speech at the institute of directors conference, March 2017. https://www.gov.uk/government/speeches/matt-hancocks-cyber-security-speech-at-the-institute-of-directors-conference
18. Henson, R., Garfield, J.: What attitude changes are needed to cause smes to take a strategic approach to information security? Athens J. Bus. Econ. **2**(3), 303–318 (2016)
19. Henson, R., Garfield, J.: SMEs attitudes to "information assurance" and consequences for the digital single market. In: Athens: ATINER'S Conference Paper Series, No: SME2016-2278, pp. 1–19. Athens Institute for Education and Research (2017)
20. ICO: Guide to the general data protection regulation (GDPR), April 2019. https://ico.org.uk/for-organisations/guide-to-data-protection/guide-to-the-general-data-protection-regulation-gdpr/
21. ISO: ISO/IEC 27000 family, April 2019. https://www.iso.org/isoiec-27001-information-security.html
22. Junger, M., Montoya, L., Overink, F.J.: Priming and warnings are not effective to prevent social engineering attacks. Comput. Hum. Behav. **66**, 75–87 (2017)
23. Kabanda, S., Tanner, M., Kent, C.: Exploring sme cybersecurity practices in developing countries. J. Organ. Comput. Electron. Commer. **28**(3), 269–282 (2018)
24. Kurpjuhn, T.: The SME security challenge. Comput. Fraud Secur. **2015**(3), 5–7 (2015)
25. McIlwraith, A.: Information Security and Employee Behaviour: How to Reduce Risk Through Employee Education, Training and Awareness. Routledge, New York (2016)
26. NCSC (National Cyber Security Centre): Cyber essentials: the SME spend target must go on, April 2019. https://www.cyberessentials.ncsc.gov.uk/
27. Osborn, E., Simpson, A.: On small-scale IT users' system architectures and cyber security: a UK case study. Comput. Secur. **70**, 27–50 (2017)
28. Renaud, K., et al.: Is the responsibilization of the cyber security risk reasonable and judicious? Comput. Secur. **78**, 198–211 (2018)
29. Ristić, D.: A tool for risk assessment. Saf. Eng. **3**(7), 2017 (2013)
30. Safa, N.S., Von Solms, R., Furnell, S.: Information security policy compliance model in organizations. Comput. Secur. **56**, 70–82 (2016)
31. Shuttle, M.: Project risk manager: risk matrix sizing: does size really matter? (2017). https://www.project-risk-manager.com/blog/risk-matrix-sizing/
32. Statista: U.K. businesses' awareness of ISO 27001 in 2017 (2017). https://www.statista.com/statistics/586556/iso-27001-awareness-by-united-kingdom-uk-businesses/

33. Statista: U.K. businesses' that are aware of the cyber essentials scheme in 2018 (2018). https://www.statista.com/statistics/586565/cyber-essentials-scheme-awareness-by-united-kingdom-uk-businesses/
34. Topping, C.: The role of awareness in adoption of government cyber security initiatives: a study of SMEs in the UK (2017)
35. Tsohou, A., Karyda, M., Kokolakis, S., Kiountouzis, E.: Managing the introduction of information security awareness programmes in organisations. Eur. J. Inf. Syst. **24**(1), 38–58 (2015)

Privacy Preserving Approach in Dynamic Social Network Data Publishing

Kamalkumar Macwan$^{(\boxtimes)}$ and Sankita Patel

Sardar Vallabhbhai National Institute of Technology, Surat, Gujarat, India
kamal.macwan@yahoo.com, sankitapatel@gmail.com

Abstract. In recent years, social networks have gained special attention to share information and to maintain a relationship with other people. As the data produced from such platforms are being analyzed, the privacy preservation methods must be applied before making the data publicly available. The anonymization techniques consider one-time releases and do not re-publish the dynamic social network data. The relationship between individuals changes with time so it may breach user privacy in dynamic social networks. In this paper, we propose an anonymization approach to preserve the user identity from all the published time-series dataset of a social network.

Multiple instances of the social network may allow the adversary to identify the user by joining the information together. The existing anonymization methods for a single instance of a social network are not enough to preserve user privacy across multiple instances. Moreover, it requires all instances together for the social graph anonymization process. We proposed a method that anonymizes the current instance of the social graph and publishes it as soon as the instance is available. The proposed anonymization technique modifies the current social graph irrespective of further instances. The average relative error calculates the deviation in query results for different privacy levels. The experimental results highlight that the proposed approach generates fewer dummy nodes.

Keywords: Social network data publishing · Privacy · k-anonymity · Time-series social dataset

1 Introduction

Recently, the social network platforms have gained the attention of people worldwide. People post, share and update their views freely on such platforms. The huge data generated on social networks are utilized in various fields. This useful information can be helpful for research, market analysis, product popularity, prediction, etc. Although it provides so much useful information, it raises the issue regarding user's privacy whose data is present in that dataset. Stronger anonymization techniques [1,2] alter the original graph structure in fine ways to

© Springer Nature Switzerland AG 2019
S.-H. Heng and J. Lopez (Eds.): ISPEC 2019, LNCS 11879, pp. 381–398, 2019.
https://doi.org/10.1007/978-3-030-34339-2_21

provide privacy. The updated social graph structure has a deviation from the original one. So, it leads to a decrease in the utility of social dataset.

A single instance of social network dataset represented as a graph fails to reveal the dynamic nature of social network data. So, instead of publishing a static network, releasing multiple instances of the same social network make the datasets richer for analysis. Ensuring user privacy while maintaining the usefulness of the released dataset is more challenging in the dynamic social network dataset. It is observed that anonymizing each version of the network independently can leak information by comparing all the published instances [3].

The anonymization concept can also apply to dynamic social networks. The attacker having background knowledge can identify the hidden information of users having unique attributes. It is not easy to breach the privacy of those users who possess the same kind of attributes. So, if there are multiple users or user-pairs having the same kind of changes in their attributes in successive instances of the published social dataset then an attacker is unable to reveal the hidden information with full confidence.

1.1 Single Graph Anonymization

A simple solution to protect user privacy in published social network dataset is to replace the identities of users by anonymous character. As the attacker may reveal the private hidden information from the published dataset, this solution is not enough [1,4]. The existing anonymization techniques provide privacy against various background knowledge attacks [5,6]. These techniques are categorized into two types: nodes with attributes [4,7] and without attributes [2,3,8].

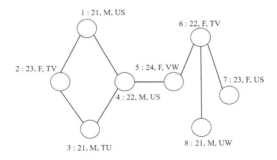

Fig. 1. Published social network graph G

We consider social network graph $G = (V, E, L)$, where nodes V represents users, edges E represents interaction among the users and labels L is used to describe a specific user. Figure 1 shows the published social network graph G. The node is associated with a label and each label has <age, gender, location> attributes to describe the user.

To achieve k-anonymity in the published dataset [7], a class-label represented as $l(v)$ is replaced with the original label of a node v, satisfying that the original label of v must be contained in $l(v)$. So, the class-label is generated by including actual labels of different k nodes. The nodes presented in one class carry the same class label. So, the attacker has a probability of $\frac{1}{k}$ to guess the correct label of a node. For the given social graph G in Fig. 1, the nodes are divided into different classes. The produced 2-anonymized graph G' is shown in Fig. 2. Here, the nodes are classified into four different classes including $A = \{1, 8\}$, $B = \{2, 5\}$, $C = \{3, 6\}$ and $D = \{4, 7\}$. Different algorithms highlight constraints for node classification to achieve a better-anonymized result. A simple greedy approach to partition the nodes into classes is considered in [7]. The utility of the anonymized graph is improved by considering the attributes of the nodes for sorting operations. So, similar nodes can be merged into one class to achieve more utility.

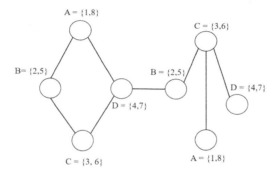

Fig. 2. Anonymized social network graph G' at $k = 2$

1.2   Privacy Breach Across Multiple Releases

For the given two instances of the social network graph, the anonymization approach can be applied to the individual graph. The classification process for nodes produces different class-labels for the same node in different instances.

For example, two instances of a social graph, G and G_1 is shown in Figs. 1 and 3(a) respectively. G_1 is the incremental version of G, where edges $<4, 9>$, $<7, 10>$ are added. The 2-anonymized graph for the same is represented in Figs. 2 and 3(b) respectively. As these two graphs are published at two different timestamps, more information can be extracted for analysis. An attacker can use these two graphs for comparative analysis and reveal sensitive information from it. If we focus on the node $v = \{4\}$ in G and G_1, the attached class-labels are $\{4, 7\}$ and $\{4, 10\}$ respectively. Since it is assumed that the evolution of the graph is incremental, the true identity of that node is revealed.

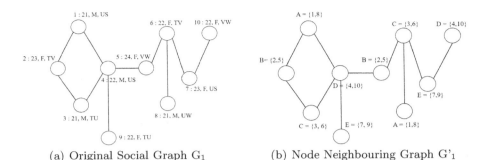

(a) Original Social Graph G_1 (b) Node Neighbouring Graph G'_1

Fig. 3. Published social network graph

1.3 Problem Definition

We consider a privacy problem on different instances (time-series) of social network graph. The time-series of a social network graph is represented as $g = <G_0, G_1, ..., G_t>$. A social network graph at time t is denoted as $G_t = <V_t, E_t, L_t>$ where V_t is a set of nodes representing users at time t, E_t is the set of edges representing interaction among the users and L_t, set of labels, describe a specific user with different attributes. Here, we assume that g is incremental, i.e. $V_{t-1} \subseteq V_t, E_{t-1} \subseteq E_t$ and $L_{t-1} \subseteq L_t$.

We want to publish the anonymized graphs where each of its released version should satisfy the below condition:

- An attacker who does not have any background knowledge about the original graph can figure out the participation of user u in edge e with a probability at most equal to $\frac{1}{k}$.
- An attacker who does not have any background knowledge about the original graph can guess the interaction among any two users u and v with a probability at most equal to $\frac{1}{k}$.

1.4 Motivation

Previous work on graph anonymization focused on publishing a single graph instance. As analysis from the dynamic social network has gained a high demand in the market, there should be an efficient anonymization approach to maintain privacy while providing more information in the published dataset. The previous study focuses on anonymizing a social network graph at different timestamps. In order to achieve k-anonymity, a common class-label is assigned to at least k nodes at timestamp t. Now, the same anonymization operation generates different class-labels at timestamp $t+1$. As per the class-label generation method, the original label of the node appears in every class-label assigned to that node. Thus, by comparing different class-labels assigned at different instances, the actual label of a node may be revealed. The previous work [9] applies anonymization on different instances of a time-series social graph in reverse order. It needs all instances together for the anonymization process. So, the immediate publishing of the current instance is not possible. It fails to incorporate the change in the successive release of the social graph to achieve anonymization.

1.5 Challenges

The main challenge is to design a constraint for node selection to make a group of them, by considering the effect of modification in further graph instances to maintain the privacy with multiple releases. The label attached to the node may be different at the different timestamp. So, it violates user privacy. Without knowing how the network will grow, it is difficult to do proper anonymization early on. Moreover, the anonymized graph should be useful to obtain accurate answers to queries.

1.6 Contribution

In this proposed work, we investigate the problem of maintaining user identity while publishing multiple instances of the same social network dataset. Our focus is to maintain the privacy of newly added nodes in successive instances of the graph. The two anonymization approaches are mentioned: firstly, the basic anonymization algorithm applicable to the initial release of the social graph. Secondly, the anonymization methods to incorporate the newly added nodes in a new instance of the graph. So, our proposed approach anonymizes sequential graphs to satisfy the privacy objective.

1.7 Organization

In this paper, it is focused on preserving user privacy in dynamic social network data publishing. First, Sect. 2 presents an overview of the existing work on user identity preservation approaches in dynamic social network data publishing. Section 3 contains the preliminaries and different safety constraints to avoid attacks. The graph clustering approach and proposed anonymization approach are also discussed in this section. Section 4 contains an experimental analysis of the proposed approach. Finally, this paper concludes the contributions of this work and highlights several possible directions for future research in Sect. 5.

2 Related Work

The anonymization approach is extended to the social network dataset after it was introduced to the tabular data [10]. The anonymization approaches are divided into two parts [5]: (1) Graph modification approach (2) Clustering-based approach. The graph modification approach adds/removes nodes and edges so that the same structure or properties of nodes and edges appear multiple times. This helps to defeat attacks that try to link to the known structure in the published graph [4,11]. The anonymization operations may be performed on degree of the nodes [2] or neighborhood [8] or edge weights [12]. It requires to make a lot of modification before publishing the graph. Clustering-based approaches convert the nodes and edges into super-node which reflects the graph properties of the sub-graph. The privacy of the social network dataset is categorized as node-privacy and edge-privacy. The anonymization methods for node-privacy focuses on node re-identification [8] and disclosure of node attributes [13]. Some of the existing privacy preservation work in the field of a dynamic social network are listed here.

2.1 Preserving User Identity in Multiple Release

The privacy issues in sequential data publishing are first considered for relational databases. Wang and Fung [14] proposed a method to sequentially release the dataset. They consider quasi-identifier attributes to anonymize the data based on the previous release of dataset, so the confidence to infer attribute can be restricted. Xiao and Tao [15] proposed m-variance approach to infer the confidence by adding fake tuples. Then, the privacy preservation approach for multiple instances of the same social network dataset is also investigated. Zou [3] suggested that their proposed graph modification method can be extended for dynamic social datasets too. It is suggested to add more dummy edges to mirror the newly arriving edges in k places around the graph. But, that brings high deviations in graph topological properties. Tai [16] suggested a new privacy model named dynamic k^w-SDA, to provide the privacy of node and multi-community identities in sequential publications. But, they only considered the label of communities.

Wang [17] proposed an approach for preventing attacks in a static network by considering one-hop neighbors as background knowledge. However, it is not applicable for publishing a dynamic social network dataset. Bhagat [18] proposed an anonymization method to protect the association of labels between directly connected nodes. But, it fails to provide the identity protection of those nodes. Wang [19] covered the degree attack model to a dynamic dataset with the possibility of privacy leakage in sequential releases but did not build models for privacy protection. The perturbation method is also being used to achieve anonymization in social graphs. Liu [20] uses the randomization method to protect the edge weights of the social network. Liu [21] also proposes the GA algorithm to achieve k-possible anonymity. As the different labels for the same node or edge may reveal the actual identity of it, the perturbation method for a dynamic dataset is not effective. Anonymizing each instance of the dynamic social graph separately fails to preserve the privacy of the published dataset. So, the node v should contain identical label in all the published instances of the graph. The anonymization steps should incorporate with the time-series class safety condition to meet the privacy requirement. The existing approaches for dynamic social datasets fail to meet the privacy requirement for multiple instances of the social dataset. To divide the nodes into different classes for labeling is considered as an important task for further instances also.

3   The Proposed Work

A node with a unique label in a social graph can be easily mapped to a victim with the help of background knowledge. Our work aims to achieve k-anonymity for a labeled graph such that there should be at least k nodes having the same label. The label is generally the set of quasi-identifiers (i.e. age, current city, the former company, etc.) that could identify a user.

We consider a social network $G_t = (V_t, E_t, L_t, \tau)$ as a simple, undirected graph which contains no multiple edges, where the nodes set V_t represent individual users at time t, the edge set E_t represent the connection between nodes(individuals) at time t, label set L_t contains attributes attached to nodes and a function $\tau : V_t \Rightarrow L_t$ assigns each node a label. A label contains unique attribute to describe user and a set of properties(such as birthdate, gender, location). Let $G = <G_0, G_1, \ldots, G_t>$ be the sequence of graphs representing the same social network for timestamps $t = 0, 1, \ldots, t$ respectively.

3.1   Class Safety Condition (CSC)

The existing approach for single graph anonymization described in Sect. 2 has some limitations. The different labels attached to the same node across multiple instances of the graph may reveal its identity. So, dividing the nodes randomly into different classes cannot provide privacy. It is also observed that the connecting edges between two classes should be very few. As shown in Fig. 4, the dense link between these two classes reveals that users 2 and 3 have the same friends including users 1 and 4. Such information leads to identity disclosure risk. The existing work for privacy preservation in dynamic social datasets considers the time-series class safety constraint to preserve the sensitive attributes [7].

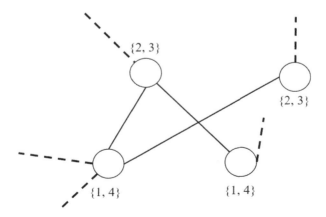

Fig. 4. Dense links between two classes for $k = 2$

Definition 1. *(Time-Series Class Safety Conditions). The distribution of nodes from set V into different classes satisfy the Time-series class safety condition if any node $v \in V_t$ and any class $C \subset V_t$ follow:*

1. *$\forall v \in V_t$ and $w \in V_{t'}$: if $v \in C \wedge w \in C \Rightarrow t = t'$.*
2. *$\forall (v, w) \in E_t$; if $v \in C_v \wedge w \in C_w \Rightarrow C_v \neq C_w$.*
3. *$\forall C_a$ and $C_b \subset V_t$, n_e is the number of edges between C_a and $C_b \Rightarrow n_e \leq k$.*

The first constraint states that the nodes included in one class should appear in the same instance of the graph. The second indicates that the connected nodes should not be part of the same class. The third condition limits the number of interactions between any pairs of classes in each instance of the published graph.

3.2   Graph Clustering

The graph clustering step divides the nodes into different groups based on node connectivity. The node connectivity helps to group closer nodes(few intermediate nodes) to form one cluster. It is useful to find out densely connected groups in a large graph. The existing graph clustering approaches [22–24] target on graph structure to have strong connection in each partition. Graph clustering measures node closeness based on connectivity and structure similarity. It reflects locally homogenous edge distribution among nodes of the network, with a high density of edges within a cluster and low density of edges between nodes from different clusters.

In our work [25], rather than using an already existing clustering algorithm, we build a separate algorithm. The proposed clustering approach helps to assign newly inserted nodes to an existing cluster based on their connectivity. Our goal for graph clustering is to partition the entire graph into different clusters. Then, we can choose one node from each cluster to assign a class and then assign a label accordingly. In node connectivity based graph clustering approach, a node having a higher degree can be useful for cluster formation. Based on this assumption, Algorithm 1 summarizes the clustering approach proposed in [25].

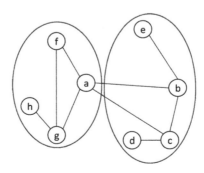

Fig. 5. Clustering of original social network G

In our approach, we want each class to have at least k different nodes. These k nodes should be far away (more intermediate nodes) from each other to satisfy the class safety conditions. The entire social graph should be divided into k different clusters. So, one node can be selected from each cluster to have a class of size k nodes. The cluster formation starts by assigning first k number of nodes having a higher degree as cluster-agent and inserted in respective cluster set. The nodes having 1 or 2° will be directly assigned to the cluster. The other nodes will be assigned to cluster based on their highest connectivity to that cluster. Figure 5 shows the cluster formation after applying Algorithm 1 to social network G.

Algorithm 1. Clustering Algorithm

calculate degree[node];
initialize C_1, C_2, C_3,....,C_n clusters
for each 1-neighborhood of cluster C_i **do**
    if degree[v] == 1 or 2 **then**
      add node v to cluster C_i
    end if
end for
for each 1-neighborhood of cluster C_i **do**
    if (edges between C_i and v) > (degree(v)/2)) **then**
      add node v to C_i;
    end if
end for
for each unvisited node v **do**
    add v to maximum connectivity cluster C_i
end for

Here, the number of clusters can also be extended beyond the anonymization parameter k. It gives more options to choose nodes for creating a class. So, depending on the dataset size, one can vary the number of clusters based on the requirement.

3.3 The Anonymizing Method

Our approach to anonymize a time-series of social network graphs is described in this section. It is divided into two parts: the anonymization for the initial instance and further instances. We consider a sequence of time-series social network graphs $g = <G_0, G_1, \ldots, G_t>$, an anonymization parameter k, and an attribute priority list $list_{attr}$. Algorithm 2 states the steps to anonymize the first instance of the time-series social graph.

The anonymization algorithm contains the clustering approach (Algorithm 1) as a pre-processing step. It divides all nodes into different clusters. It helps to create different classes of nodes to assign a class-label. Sorting of nodes according to $list_{attr}$ arrange the nodes with similar attributes nearby. For each unassigned

---

Algorithm 2. Anonymization for Initial Graph

Apply clustering algorithm to divide all the nodes
V_{list} = Sorted nodes of G_0 according to $list_{\text{attr}}$
Group C[] = ϕ
for each $v \in V_{\text{list}}$ **do**
    flag= false
    for each $c \in$ C[] **do**
        if cluster(v) $\cap$ cluster[C[c]]=ϕ and $size$(C[c]) $< k$ and C[c]$\bigcup v$ does not violate
        CSC **then**
            C[c] = C[c] $\bigcup v$
            flag = true
        end if
    end for
    if flag = false **then**
        create a new group in C[]
        C[size(c)+1] = v
    end if
end for
for each group c of C **do**
    if size(C[c]) $< k$ **then**
        add k - size[C[c]] nodes to C[c]
        assign label similar to the group nodes
    end if
end for

---

node $v \in V_{\text{list}}$, we sequentially find other $k - 1$ nearest nodes from each cluster other than its own cluster. Moreover, the selected nodes must satisfy class safety conditions. At last, we insert dummy nodes to the classes having less than k nodes. Set V_{dummy} contains a list of all inserted dummy nodes. We assign the attributes for each $v \in V_{\text{dummy}}$ as attributes of any node of the class which it belongs. For example, suppose class C = $\{4, 6\}$ and k = 3, user 4 and 6 are with attribute $\{16, M, PR\}$ and $\{17, F, KS\}$. Then, we add a dummy node user 15 with attributes either $\{16, M, PR\}$ or $\{17, F, KS\}$.

These dummy nodes are included in a social network by connecting them to original nodes. The edge set E_g that includes all such new inserted edges is defined as, $E_g = <V_g, V_o>$, where $V_g \in V_{\text{dummy}}$ and $V_o \in V$. The nodes V_g and V_o should be in different classes and should have a minimum connection between their classes. Thus, it satisfies the CSC too.

The Anonymizing Method for Time-Series Social Network Graphs. After the initial anonymization step, the social graph is divided into different clusters. Moreover, the nodes also contain class-label. The new nodes inserted into successive sequential graph will be assigned to one cluster based on their connectivity. So, in each instance of the released graph, our main goal is to identify the newly inserted nodes and to anonymize it. The anonymization steps listed here should be performed for graph instance $G_1, G_2, \ldots, G_t$.

Step 1: Identify the new inserted nodes and edges. This can be done by just simply comparing the new graph with the old one.

Step 2: If the number of inserted nodes is greater than k, make a separate class for them and assign a label.

Step 3: The classes having a number of inserted nodes smaller than k, can be merged under the class safety condition or add dummy nodes and assign a label.

3.4   Example of the Proposed Approach

In this section, we illustrate the working of the proposed method on social graph. The initial graph is shown in Fig. 6(a). The attributes <age, gender, location> of the users are shown in Table 1. The initial step is to divide the nodes into different clusters ($\geqslant k$). The given social graph in Fig. 6(a) is divided into two clusters $C_1 = \{1, 2, 3, 4\}$ and $C_2 = \{5, 6, 7, 8\}$ by considering $k = 2$. Let's assume that priority list for attribute is <age, location, gender>. Table 2 represents all sorted nodes of G_0 according to $list_{attr} = $<age, location, gender>. Now, following the further steps, the nodes are divided into four different classes A = $\{1, 5\}$, B = $\{2, 6\}$, C = $\{4, 7\}$ and D = $\{3, 8\}$. So, we accordingly assign label to each node as shown in Fig. 6(b).

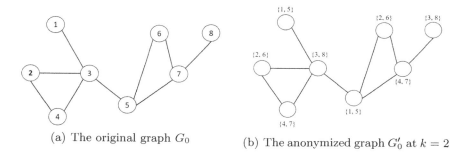

(a) The original graph G_0 (b) The anonymized graph G'_0 at $k = 2$

Fig. 6. Original and published social network graph at $t = 0$

Let's assume that the second instance of graph G, released at $t = 1$, G_1 is shown in Fig. 7(a). Users 9, 10 and 11 are added with attributes <24, M, AS>, <25, F, US> and <29, M, PR> respectively. From the Figs. 6(a) and 7(a), it is clear that edges <1, 9>, <5, 11> and <7, 10> are inserted into the new graph G_1. As the number of inserted nodes is more than the value of k, we can create a new separate class for them. The class has three nodes (three labels) can also be assigned. Here, we add one dummy node 12 to keep the class size 2. So, the anonymized graph G'_1 contains two more classes E = $\{9, 10\}$ and F = $\{11, 12\}$. The attributes of node 11 can be assigned to dummy node 12 too. Figure 7(b) represents the anonymized graph G'_1 for the instance G_1.

Table 1. Attributes of the users <age, gender, location>

1	<23, M, PR>
2	<24, F, US>
3	<26, F, US>
4	<26, M, JK>
5	<21, M, JK>
6	<22, F, US>
7	<26, F, PR>
8	<28, M, PR>

Table 2. Sorted attributes of the users, $list_{attr}$ = <age, location, gender>

5	<21, M, JK>
6	<22, F, US>
1	<23, M, PR>
2	<24, F, US>
4	<26, M, JK>
7	<26, F, PR>
3	<26, F, US>
8	<28, M, PR>

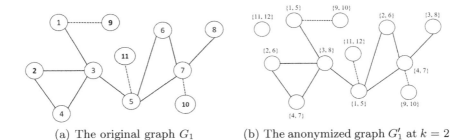

(a) The original graph G_1 (b) The anonymized graph G_1' at $k = 2$

Fig. 7. Original and published social network graph at t = 1

3.5   Analysis

The conditions for ensuring the privacy objectives of our method on dynamic social network data publishing are mentioned in Sect. 3.1. Our proposed approach ensures those conditions to be fulfilled:

- The first condition ($\forall v \epsilon V_t$ and $w \epsilon V_{t'}$: if $v \epsilon C \wedge w \epsilon C \Rightarrow t = t'$) ensures that nodes in same class arrives at the same time in each anonymized graph. In our proposed approach, the node selection procedure for class formation considers the newly added nodes only. So, there is no combination of nodes which are from different instances of the graph.

- The second condition $(\forall \ (v, w) \ \epsilon \ E_t;$ if $v \epsilon C_v \wedge w \ \epsilon \ C_w \Rightarrow C_v \neq C_w)$ constraints that two end nodes should not exist in a class. Our node selection step selects nodes from different clusters only. So, nodes within class are far apart from each other in social graph. The anonymized graph contains two different labels for the connected nodes.
- As the node selection step considers the nodes from k different clusters, the third condition $(\forall \ C_a$ and $C_b \subset V_t, n_e$ is the number of edges between C_a and $C_b \Rightarrow n_e \leq k)$ also satisfies.

The data utility is also an important issue as far as publishing social network dataset for analysis is concerned. The proposed approach inserts dummy nodes to the classes with a size smaller than k. The analysis part on the published dataset contains aggregation queries. The utility of the published social dataset is measured by calculating *average relative error* [7,8,26] as given in Eq. 1, where d and d' are the results of querying on the original graphs and the anonymized graph respectively.

$$Average\,relative\,error = \frac{|d - d'|}{|d|} \qquad (1)$$

We have considered an incremental scenario of the social graph. As the third party can access all the previously published datasets, removing the deleted nodes from the currently published dataset violate user privacy. Moreover, our proposed anonymization approach considers the newly added nodes and it does not change the labels of the old nodes. Keeping the same label for the nodes in all the published instances preserves the privacy of nodes.

In our approach, we focus on anonymizing node labels. So, the node structure remains the same in an anonymized social graph. To overcome the user identity disclosure attack based on node degree information, k-degree anonymization [25] could be performed as a pre-processing step. Likewise, based on the privacy model, the corresponding anonymization method should be performed first and then applying our proposed approach can preserve the user identity against structural and label based attacks.

4   Experimental Evaluation

The utility of the anonymized social network dataset is an important measurement to check the effectiveness of the anonymization approach. The algorithm is implemented in python and performed on a PC with the Intel Core 2 Qusad CPU, 3.20 GHz machine with 4 GB main memory running Windows 10 OS. The utility is measured using average relative error, defined in Sect. 3.5.

4.1   Dataset

We conduct our experiments on Facebook-like Social Network [27] dataset. This network is originated from an online community for students at the University of California, Irvine. The dataset includes the users that sent or received at least one message. Based on the messages, the edges are set among the users. It contains 1899 nodes and 15,684 edges. This dataset was collected between April 2004 and October 2004.

As the dataset includes a timestamp of the respective connection, we have divided it into different graphs according to month wise. Table 3 represents the distribution of the nodes in different groups. Since the datasets have no label, we have assigned a label to each node with the use of the Adult dataset [28]. We generated the labels containing three attributes: age (17–65), gender (male/female) and education (15 qualifications) for each node.

Table 3. The social network dataset

t	Timestamp	Nodes	Edges	Inserted nodes	Inserted edges
0	April"04	668	1749	668	1749
1	May"04	1596	11275	928	9526
2	June"04	1767	13287	171	2012
3	July"04	1801	13999	34	712
4	August"04	1838	14516	37	517
5	September"04	1888	14879	50	363
6	October"04	1899	15069	11	190

4.2   Experiment Results

To evaluate the utility of the time-series anonymized social dataset, we have conducted aggregation queries on it. Here, we have used two kinds of queries: single-hop queries and two-hops queries. The single-hop queries are like: "How many Bachelors are connected to Masters?" It shows the interaction between one user with a specific attribute and another one with another attribute. Two-hop queries observe the attributes of three users. For example, "How many Some-College users connected to Bachelors, who are also connected to Masters?"

We performed different queries on unsorted data and two sorted data, **AEG** : $list_{attr}$ = <Age, Education, Gender> and **EAG** : $list_{attr}$ = <Education, Age, Gender>. The experimental results for the 1-hop query and 2-hop query are shown in Figs. 8 and 9. As the k indicates the number of nodes combined in one class, it leads to assign more labels to each node. So, the average relative rate increases as the value of k is increased. The 2-hop queries involved interaction among 3 nodes whereas 1-hop queries need only 2 nodes. Figures 8 and 9 show

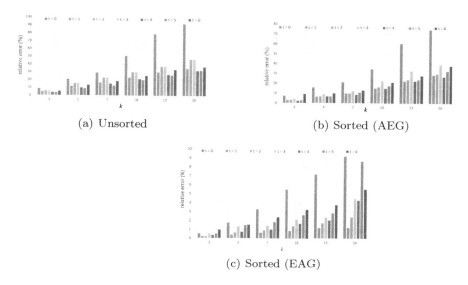

(a) Unsorted   (b) Sorted (AEG)

(c) Sorted (EAG)

Fig. 8. The average relative errors (1-hop query)

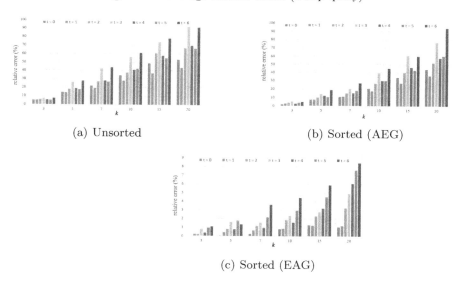

(a) Unsorted   (b) Sorted (AEG)

(c) Sorted (EAG)

Fig. 9. The average relative errors (2-hop query)

that the results obtain for 1-hop queries is better than 2-hop queries in terms of average relative error.

Figures 8(a) and 9(a) represent that unsorted data have the higher error rate compared to the sorted dataset. For our experiment, we considered the attribute 'education' for the queries and applied the queries on both sorted datasets. As

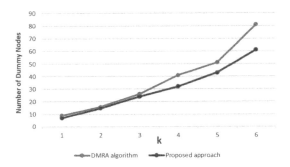

Fig. 10. Comparison with existing algorithm

can be seen, the sorted dataset based on **EAG** (Figs. 8(c) and 9(c)) achieves lower average relative error rate compared to **AEG** (Figs. 8(b) and 9(b)).

Our graph clustering approach provides a platform to select k nodes to make a new class for labeling. So, there will be few classes of size less than k nodes. It requires to add fewer dummy nodes compared to that in the existing approach. We have compared our experimental results with the existing DMRA algorithm. Figure 10 shows that our proposed approach generates fewer dummy nodes compared to the DMRA algorithm [9], which results in a comparatively less average relative error. Moreover, as our proposed approach consider the class safety conditions and select nodes from k different clusters, the attached label to each node will be valid for further instances also.

5   Conclusion

In this paper, we tackled the problem of preserving privacy for time-series social graph publishing. The existing anonymization approach for each instance of the published graph does not guarantee user privacy. To achieve privacy in all instances of the graph, the time series class safety condition should be retained. The anonymization approach works separately for the initial instance of the graph and further instances of the graph. Our analysis of the proposed approach with example justifies that it fulfills the conditions for preserving user privacy. The experimental results show that the proposed approach generates fewer dummy nodes and thus ensure more utility in the published dataset. Our proposed anonymization approach can be extended for node/edge deletion scenarios for a dynamic graph.

References

1. Hay, M., Miklau, G., Jensen, D., Towsley, D., Li, C.: Resisting structural re-identification in anonymized social networks. VLDB J. Int. J. Very Large Data Bases **19**(6), 797–823 (2010)

2. Liu, K., Terzi, E.: Towards identity anonymization on graphs. In: Proceedings of the 2008 ACM SIGMOD International Conference on Management of Data, pp. 93–106. ACM (2008)
3. Zou, L., Chen, L., Özsu, M.T.: K-automorphism: a general framework for privacy preserving network publication. Proc. VLDB Endow. **2**(1), 946–957 (2009)
4. Backstrom, L., Dwork, C., Kleinberg, J.: Wherefore art thou R3579X? Anonymized social networks, hidden patterns, and structural steganography. In: Proceedings of the 16th International Conference on World Wide Web, pp. 181–190. ACM (2007)
5. Zhou, B., Pei, J., Luk, W.: A brief survey on anonymization techniques for privacy preserving publishing of social network data. ACM SIGKDD Explor. Newsl. **10**(2), 12–22 (2008)
6. Wu, X., Ying, X., Liu, K., Chen, L.: A survey of privacy-preservation of graphs and social networks. In: Aggarwal, C., Wang, H. (eds.) Managing and Mining Graph Data. ADBS, vol. 40, pp. 421–453. Springer, Boston (2010). https://doi.org/10.1007/978-1-4419-6045-0_14
7. Bhagat, S., Cormode, G., Krishnamurthy, B., Srivastava, D.: Class-based graph anonymization for social network data. Proc. VLDB Endow. **2**(1), 766–777 (2009)
8. Zhou, B., Pei, J.: Preserving privacy in social networks against neighborhood attacks. In: 2008 IEEE 24th International Conference on Data Engineering, ICDE 2008, pp. 506–515. IEEE (2008)
9. Wang, C.-J.L., Wang, E.T., Chen, A.L.P.: Anonymization for multiple released social network graphs. In: Pei, J., Tseng, V.S., Cao, L., Motoda, H., Xu, G. (eds.) PAKDD 2013. LNCS (LNAI), vol. 7819, pp. 99–110. Springer, Heidelberg (2013). https://doi.org/10.1007/978-3-642-37456-2_9
10. Sweeney, L.: k-anonymity: a model for protecting privacy. Int. J. Uncertain. Fuzziness Knowl.-Based Syst. **10**(05), 557–570 (2002)
11. Narayanan, A., Shmatikov, V.: De-anonymizing social networks. In: 2009 30th IEEE Symposium on Security and Privacy, pp. 173–187. IEEE (2009)
12. Macwan, K.R., Patel, S.J.: Mutual friend attack prevention in social network data publishing. In: Ali, S.S., Danger, J.-L., Eisenbarth, T. (eds.) SPACE 2017. LNCS, vol. 10662, pp. 210–225. Springer, Cham (2017). https://doi.org/10.1007/978-3-319-71501-8_12
13. Song, Y., Karras, P., Xiao, Q., Bressan, S.: Sensitive label privacy protection on social network data. In: Ailamaki, A., Bowers, S. (eds.) SSDBM 2012. LNCS, vol. 7338, pp. 562–571. Springer, Heidelberg (2012). https://doi.org/10.1007/978-3-642-31235-9_37
14. Wang, K., Fung, B.: Anonymizing sequential releases. In: Proceedings of the 12th ACM SIGKDD International Conference on Knowledge Discovery and Data Mining, pp. 414–423. ACM (2006)
15. Xiao, X., Tao, Y.: M-invariance: towards privacy preserving re-publication of dynamic datasets. In: Proceedings of the 2007 ACM SIGMOD International Conference on Management of Data, pp. 689–700. ACM (2007)
16. Tai, C.-H., Tseng, P.-J., Philip, S.Y., Chen, M.-S.: Identity protection in sequential releases of dynamic networks. IEEE Trans. Knowl. Data Eng. **26**(3), 635–651 (2014)
17. Wang, Y., Qiu, F., Wu, F., Chen, G.: Resisting label-neighborhood attacks in outsourced social networks. In: 2014 IEEE International Performance Computing and Communications Conference (IPCCC), pp. 1–8. IEEE (2014)
18. Bhagat, S., Cormode, G., Srivastava, D., Krishnamurthy, B.: Prediction promotes privacy in dynamic social networks. In: WOSN (2010)

19. Medforth, N., Wang, K.: Privacy risk in graph stream publishing for social network data. In: 2011 IEEE 11th International Conference on Data Mining (ICDM), pp. 437–446. IEEE (2011)
20. Liu, L., Wang, J., Liu, J., Zhang, J.: Privacy preserving in social networks against sensitive edge disclosure. Technical Report CMIDA-HiPSCCS 006–08, Department of Computer Science, University of Kentucky, KY (2008)
21. Liu, X., Yang, X.: A generalization based approach for anonymizing weighted social network graphs. In: Wang, H., Li, S., Oyama, S., Hu, X., Qian, T. (eds.) WAIM 2011. LNCS, vol. 6897, pp. 118–130. Springer, Heidelberg (2011). https://doi.org/10.1007/978-3-642-23535-1_12
22. Shi, J., Malik, J.: Normalized cuts and image segmentation. IEEE Trans. Pattern Anal. Mach. Intell. **22**(8), 888–905 (2000)
23. Newman, M.E., Girvan, M.: Finding and evaluating community structure in networks. Phys. Rev. E **69**(2), 026113 (2004)
24. Tian, Y., Hankins, R.A., Patel, J.M.: Efficient aggregation for graph summarization. In: Proceedings of the 2008 ACM SIGMOD International Conference on Management of Data, pp. 567–580. ACM (2008)
25. Macwan, K.R., Patel, S.J.: k-degree anonymity model for social network data publishing. Adv. Electr. Comput. Eng. **17**(4), 117–124 (2017)
26. Yuan, M., Chen, L., Yu, P.S.: Personalized privacy protection in social networks. Proc. VLDB Endow. **4**(2), 141–150 (2010)
27. Opsahl, T., Panzarasa, P.: Clustering in weighted networks. Soc. Netw. **31**(2), 155–163 (2009)
28. Dheeru, D., Karra Taniskidou, E.: UCI machine learning repository (2017). http://archive.ics.uci.edu/ml

Short Paper I

Using Freivalds' Algorithm to Accelerate Lattice-Based Signature Verifications

Arnaud Sipasseuth[(✉)], Thomas Plantard, and Willy Susilo

Institute of Cybersecurity and Cryptology, School of Computing and Information Technology, University of Wollongong, Wollongong, Australia
{as447,thomaspl,wsusilo}@uow.edu.au

Abstract. We present a novel computational technique to check whether a matrix-vector product is correct with a relatively high probability. While the idea could be related to verifiable delegated computations, most of the literature in this line of work focuses on provably secure functional aspects and do not provide clear computational techniques to verify whether a product $xA = y$ is correct where x, A and y are not given nor computed by the party which requires validity checking: this is typically the case for some cryptographic lattice-based signature schemes. This paper focuses on the computational aspects and the improvement on both speed and memory when implementing such a verifier, and use a practical example: the Diagonal Reduction Signature (DRS) scheme as it was one of the candidates in the recent National Institute of Standards and Technology Post-Quantum Cryptography Standardization Calls for Proposals competition. We show that in the case of DRS, we can gain a factor of 20 in verification speed.

Keywords: Diagonal Reduction Signature · Post-Quantum Cryptography · Lattice-based signatures · NIST · Delegated computation verification · Lattice-based cryptography

1 Introduction

Post-Quantum cryptography is currently being widely researched. Quantum computing is improving and it is not clear how long it would take for most currently used cryptographic primitives to be finally broken by quantum algorithms such as Shor's algorithm [25] or Grover's algorithm [13]. This has forced the National Institute of Standards and Technology (NIST) to call for a standardization of post-quantum primitives in the hope of having the readiness of the standarized algorithm when quantum computers arrive [19]. Nevertheless, research in cryptology still continues outside of the NIST standardization process. One such important result is the work of Gama, Izabachene, Nguyen and Xie [11] which proves that the reduction from average cases to worst cases problems on q-ary lattices, demonstrated by Ajtai [1] and Regev [23], can be extended to most random lattices. Therefore one is not required to rely exclusively on q-ary lattices when building a cryptosystem, unlike all lattice-based candidates

© Springer Nature Switzerland AG 2019
S.-H. Heng and J. Lopez (Eds.): ISPEC 2019, LNCS 11879, pp. 401–412, 2019.
https://doi.org/10.1007/978-3-030-34339-2_22

in the second round of the NIST process. However, q-ary lattices can obtain a Hermite Normal Form (HNF) as a basis for almost free, which allows very fast verification whether a random vector belongs to the lattice generated by the said basis, on top of significantly reducing key sizes [17]. Most lattice-based schemes rely on finding a vector of a lattice with specific properties, mostly being short. For non q-ary lattice schemes, obtaining a HNF is often costly. While computing a HNF can be done in polynomial time [20], the actual time used in practice to compute cryptographically secure HNF basis is too long for most applications. We propose in this paper a method to alleviate this issue, using a variant of Freivalds' algorithm [10] to verify the validity of matrix product. While the core ideas are also applicable to q-ary lattices and other HNF basis to some extent, we deem its impact not significant enough to expand on it, and rather we present an application to one of the schemes submitted to the NIST which did not rely on q-ary lattices, the Diagonal Reduction Signature scheme (DRS) [21]. DRS did not use a HNF as a public key: the authors of DRS used an alternative to generate public keys and used another way to verify if a vector belonged to a lattice. Our work provides an alternative to verify lattice signatures if the need arises, showing an interesting trade-off between pre-computation time for signature verification time and memory storage. In this work, we show that by adopting our approach to the proposed DRS parameters [27], we gain a factor of 20 on the verification speed. We also provide another approach on an attack specifically to our modification as the security of our public key remains unchanged. *The rest of this paper is organized as follows.* We will first recall some basic lattice definitions, Freivalds' algorithm and then briefly reintroduce DRS mostly focusing on its verification part. We will proceed with the presentation of our new technique and its results using simple non-optimized implementations, followed by comments on its security and concluding this work by raising open questions.

2   Background

2.1   Lattice Basics

We call an integer lattice when a finitely generated subgroup of $\mathbb{Z}^n$. A basis of the lattice is a basis as a $\mathbb{Z} - module$. In our work we only consider full-rank integer lattices, i.e such that any basis B of a lattice $\mathcal{L}$ (we note $\mathcal{L} = \mathcal{L}(B)$) is full rank.

We call the max norm l_∞ norm: $\forall x \in \mathbb{Z}^n, \|x\|_\infty = \max_{i \in [1,n]} |x_i|$.

A valid signature in the DRS scheme solve an instance of $\mathbf{GDD}_\gamma$ (γ-Guaranteed Distance Decoding): given a lattice $\mathcal{L}$, $x \in \mathbb{Z}^n$ and a bound $\gamma \in \mathbb{Z}$, find $v \in \mathcal{L}$ such that $\|x - v\| \leq \gamma$.

2.2   Freivalds' Algorithm

Freivalds' algorithm (Algorithm 1) for verifying matrix products [10] is one of the first probabilistic algorithms to be introduced to show the efficiency and practicality of non-deterministic programs to solve decision problems over deterministic ones. Freivalds' technique had a major impact on several research fields and is still an active research topic to this date [8,9]. The decision problem solved by Freivalds is the following: given A, B, C, three $n \times n$ matrices over an arbitrary ring $\mathcal{R}$, *can we verify that $A \times B = C$ with a faster method than recomputing $A \times B$*? Freivalds brought a probabilistic solution, which rely on a simple statement: *to check $A \times B = C$, we check instead $A \times (B \times v) = C \times v$ where v is a randomly sampled vector,* and then it follows that the more we run this test, the more we decrease the probability of obtaining a false-positive. This leads to Freivalds' Algorithm 1 which is *perfectly complete*: it will always output **TRUE** whenever $A \times B = C$ is correct. It is also *sound*: the probability of outputting **TRUE** for $A \times B \neq C$ is negligible (as much as we want). The gain in efficiency compared to a deterministic method is quite impactful as this shifts the arithmetical computations from a matrix-matrix product to a matrix-vector multiplication. We are not recalling the proof on the original error probability bound in [10] but we will later give a much tighter upper bound which will be more adapted to our case.

Algorithm 1. Freivalds' algorithm

Require: $A, B, C \in \mathcal{R}^{n \times n}$, $f \in \mathbb{N}$ a failure probability
Ensure: Check the validity of $A \times B = C$ with a chance of false-positive under 2^{-f}
1: $i \leftarrow 0$
2: **while** $i < f$ **do**
3:     $v \leftarrow$ Randomly taken in $\{-1, 1\}^n$
4:     $x \leftarrow Cv,\ y \leftarrow Bv,\ y \leftarrow Ay$
5:     **if** $x \neq y$ **then return FALSE**   ▷ check validity
6:     $i \leftarrow i + 1$
7: **return TRUE**

2.3 DRS and Its Verification Algorithm

DRS is one of the five lattice-based signature schemes that have been proposed to the NIST PQC competition [19]. The original idea behind DRS stemmed from when Plantard, Susilo and Win [22] suggested to use a diagonal dominant matrix to reduce large message vectors to short signatures within a known hypercube as a countermeasure against parallelogram detection attacks [18]. The security of the scheme has been shown to be reduced by a machine learning method [28] and since then it has been modified to resist against this attack at the cost of a slower secret key generation [27]. We will briefly describe both keys, the signature and the verification, the latter being the only part affected by this work. The secret diagonal dominant matrix (as defined in [7]) S_{key} is generated using the work in [27]). The public key P_{key} is generated by the multiplication of $P_{key} = S_{key} \times U$ with U unimodular and randomly taken such that $\|P_{key}\|_\infty < 2^{63}$. The signature algorithm makes use of the structure of S_{key} to output (h, s)

to solve the **GDD**$_D$ problem on m with $hP_{key} = m - s$ and $\|m - s\|_\infty < D$. The verification algorithm, Algorithm 2, checks two points: the first ensuring that the vector s is indeed short enough, and the second ensuring that $m - s$ is indeed a vector of the lattice. *This is where DRS differs from other lattice-based cryptographic schemes even from the original concept from* [22]: *DRS does not use a HNF.* Our understanding is that the computation time of a HNF was deemed too large to be suggested for practical uses, and thus the authors of DRS opted for another solution which impacted the verification algorithm as they could no longer use HNF to check $m - s \in \mathcal{L}$. Another important point about DRS is their choice to fit every computation within 64-bits to ensure that computation of $h \times P_{key}$ does not overflow without the use of multiprecision integers. The principle of this algorithm can be compared to a verification per block: we successively deal with parts of the input, where each part taken h' of h is chosen such that $t = \|h'P_{key}\|_\infty < 2^{63}$ and remove t from $m - s$ until t and h' reach 0 exactly at the same time. While this algorithm could be interesting to improve on its own, we suggest an alternative instance of the scheme where this verification method can be completely discarded.

Algorithm 2. DRS Verify

Require:
    The message $m \in \mathbb{Z}^n$, the public key P_{key} both stored by Alice
    The signature (s, h) given by Bob
Ensure:
    The boolean value ($(hP_{key} = m - s)$ AND $(\|w\|_\infty < D)$)
1: **if** $\|w\|_\infty > D$ **then return FALSE**   ▷ Test for max norm first
2: $q \leftarrow h$, $t \leftarrow v - w$ ▷ Loop Initialization
3: **while** $q \neq 0 \wedge t \neq 0$ **do**
4:     $r \leftarrow q \mod \|P_{key}\|_\infty$, $t \leftarrow rP_{key} - t$
5:     **if** $t \neq 0 \mod \|P_{key}\|_\infty$ **then return FALSE**   ▷ Check correctness
6:     $t \leftarrow t/\|P_{key}\|_\infty$, $q \leftarrow (q - r)/\|P_{key}\|_\infty$
7:     **if** $(t = 0) \veebar (q = 0)$ **then return FALSE**   ▷ Check correctness
8: **return TRUE**

---

3   Modifying Freivalds' Technique for Lattice-Based Signature Verification

3.1   The First Core Idea: Modification of Freivalds' Algorithm

In this work, we modify Freivalds' technique to obtain a faster probabilistic verification algorithm. The vector pairs (k, m) to check are not given by the person who needs the verification but by the signatory, and so is P_{key}. In the case where one public key is re-used over multiple message-signature exchanges, the equality $hP_{key} = m - s = v$ must stand true for all vector triplets (h, s, m) provided. In that case, we can introduce a random vector $x^\top$ and $X = P_{key} \times x^\top$ such that $(h \times X = v \times x^\top)$ which reduce a matrix-vector multiplication check to the comparison of two scalar products (vector-vector multiplications). A difference with the original Frivalds' algorithm is that we don't use $x \in \{-1,1\}^n$ but rather, we will choose a prime p such that $x \in \mathbb{F}_p^n$ is taken randomly, and project the whole equation over the field $\mathbb{F}_p$. *For sufficiently many vectors x, X and primes p, let's say k primes and k vectors x, our new validity condition is then $(h \times X_i = v \times x_i^\top \mod p_i)_{i \in [1,k]}$.* Note that projecting Freivalds' algorithm over a finite field was proposed in [15] for a non-cryptographic purpose, however to the best of our knowledge there is no work that modify the algorithm in the manner we just described. The choice to use multiple different moduli will be expanded in Sect. 4. Let us compute the probability of failure of our verification algorithm. First of all, the algorithm is *perfectly complete*, i.e it will never output a false negative. The last thing to check is then the probability of a false positive. In that regard, rather than thinking of probability of a false positive, let us first compute the proportion of positive results over all possibilities given a prime p. Let us enumerate all possibilities. If v is fixed, then $v * x^\top = a_p$ mod p is also fixed. So the proportion of couples (h, m) giving a positive result is the probability of $\sum_{i=1}^n h[i]X[i] = a_p$ mod p. Without losing generality, if we choose and index j such that $X[j]$ is non-zero (X being obviously chosen non-zero) and fix every other coefficient h_i such that $b_p = a_p(\sum_{i \neq j} h[i]X[i])^{-1}$ mod p, we obtain the result of a positive output with the same proportion as verifying $h[i] = c_p$ mod p which is $1/p$ for a given prime p. As this reasoning is sound for any $v = m - s$ and in any triplet (h, m, s), we determine the quantity of false positives being the difference between the amount of positive outcomes and the amount of valid positive outcomes, which set a proportion of false positives of being strictly under $1/p$ (and by extension its probability over all possible samples). If we repeat this process over k different vectors, the false positive probability lowers to below p^{-k}. Generally speaking, if we try the test once per couple prime/vectors over k primes $\{p_i, x_i\}_{i \in [1,k]}$, then *the probability of obtaining a false positive becomes lower than $\prod_{i=1}^k p_i^{-1}$.* This is a tighter upper bound over Freivalds' initial upper bound, although our work only concerns our very specific case and does not apply to the general scope of Freivalds' technique.

3.2   The Second Core Idea: Changing the Verifier

With our previous idea in mind, we need to explain what we aim to modify in the previous DRS scheme. First let us briefly recall how the sender/verifier Alice and the signatory Bob acts in 5 steps:

1. Bob generates a pair of keys $\{P_{key}, S_{key}\}$.
2. Bob keeps the secret key S_{key}, and sends the public key P_{key} to Alice.
3. Alice sends a random vector m with "large" norm $\|m\|_\infty$ to Bob.
4. Bob uses S_{key} to send the signature $\{h, s\}$ to Alice.
5. Alice verifies that $\|s\|_\infty$ is "low" and $hP_{key} = v = m - s$.

While we can consider the verification process to be entrusted to a third-party like a certification authority, here we restrict ourselves on exclusively modifying the computation of the verification which is step 5, and inserting a precomputation which can be placed after or during step 2. *One important point to stress on is that Alice does not need to communicate to Bob she is using a precomputation.* The whole process is oblivious to Bob and his role does not change at all compared with the existing DRS process. Hence, it seems natural for us to assume Alice will keep her computations secret as there is no apparent benefit in revealing them.

Precomputation. The precomputation construct the samples required to apply our modified Freivalds' test and can be described in two halves as follows:

- Generate a family of tuples $(p_i, x_i)_{i \in [1,k]}$
- Compute $T = (p_i, x_i, X_i)_{i \in [1,k]}$ where $X_i = P_{key} x_i \mod p_i$ given P_{key}

The first half of the precomputation do not requires input from Bob as the dimension is supposed to be public, therefore those can even be precomputed before Bob generating his keys in step 1. The choice of random generators for primes and vectors are important for security and efficiency considerations, however those are not the main point of the paper. As far as our experimental results are concerned, we just used the basic random function "**rand()**" of the library "**stdlib.h**" in C with the classical modulo operator % to generate our vectors, and our primes are randomly taken in a set we will discuss in the security section of this paper, using the MAGMA software [6] to pick primes and write them into a header file used by our code before the compilation. Its computation time is negligeable compared to the second part of the precomputation which involves matrix-vectors modular multiplications.

In the second half of the precomputation, Alice does not need to store P_{key} at the end, and furthermore she does not even need to store the whole public key while computing X_i. Since for each row j of P_{key} Alice can independently compute $P_{key}[j] * x_i = X_i[j] \mod p_i$, Alice can discard every row of P_{key} where the corresponding computation is finished and choose to only receive a certain amount of rows at a time, which would reduce the amount of internal memory required for the whole precomputation (and allow for further parallelism). The cost of the second half of the precomputation is the main cost of the whole precomputation process.

New Verification Method. The new verification method will apply our modification on Freivalds' algorithm using our precomputation step. Alice, at step 5, previously discarded the public key P_{key} and kept some small footprint in the form of a secret list T of triplets and sent a random message m. As she received in step 4 the signature (k, s) from Bob, her verification process is now described by Algorithm 3. This new verification algorithm is more compact than the original one and also simpler to understand. The only remaining point to deal with is to choose how large h and the primes p_i need to be. We will discuss that in the next section when discussing security.

Algorithm 3. New Verification

Require:

a list of triplets $T = (p_i, x_i, X_i)_{i \in [1,k]}$ and a message m from Alice

a signature (h, s) from Bob

a public bound D on the signature norm

Ensure:

a boolean R stating whether (h, s) is a valid signature for m and P_{key}

R is a false-positive with probability strictly less than $\prod_{i=1}^{k} p^{-1}$

1: $R \leftarrow \{\|s\|_\infty < D\}$ ▷ Verifies the max norm of the signature

2: **for** $i \in [1, k]$ **do**

3:      $R \leftarrow R \wedge \{hx_i = (m - s)x_i \mod p_i\}$ ▷ Verifies modular equalities

4: **return** R

4 Security Considerations

While the previous attacks on the old DRS are well-understood heuristics relying either on machine learning [28] or pure lattice reduction as with most other lattice-based schemes (being signature-based or decryption-based), *our modification does not thwart previous attacks nor does it reinforce them and thus rely on the same security assumptions.* However, this is only when considering the only secret was the diagonal dominant matrix S_{key}. Here, we introduce a new secret, which is the list of triplets T generated by Alice. Thus, new attacks venues can be considered which, to the best of our knowledge, were also not considered in others lattice schemes submitted to the NIST. We will consider them in this section. We briefly present the two avenues we found and explain our reasoning on why only the second can be considered, and tackle this issue. Note that our reasoning discard all attack venues that can affect the old DRS independently of our new method, as this would be out of this paper' scope, and we stress it is hard to construct a security proof when an attack aside from exhaustive search cannot be constructed.

4.1 Attack Models

A Malicious Bob. One attack is to try to guess the triplets generated by Alice, as malicious Bob, by sending carefully crafted keys and signatures. While it is definitively an interesting idea, as long as Alice generates a different triplet for each public key (using a hash of P_{key} as a seed for example) and only answers *True* or *False* in the verification, we do not see any gain malicious Bob could have over a honest Bob.

A Honest Bob, and a "Fake Bob" Eve. To the best of our knowledge, the only other attack venue is having a honest Bob, who is giving good signatures, and Eve, who has no knowledge of the secret key S_{key}, wanting to sign as well as Bob but could not in the existing DRS scheme. Let us suppose Eve knows that

Alice is using our technique for signature verification, although assuming she has no knowledge of the triplets T and knows as much as Alice concerning Bob. Can Eve make Alice believe Eve is Bob? To this purpose, we assume Eve has to generate a false-positive from Alice's verification algorithm. As Alice can make the primes p_i and their quantity k as large as she wants, it seems unreasonable to assume Eve can randomly fall into the $\prod_{i=1}^{k} p_i^{-1}$ false-positive probability. Eve cannot resort either to a lattice-reduction technique on an easier lattice stemming from T if she has no knowledge of T. Furthermore, building a false-positive for the modified Freivalds' test is not enough: one has to guarantee the vector-signature s is short enough. It is then possible that the number of false-positives drastically decreases, which reinforces the security of our modification however counting the number of false-positives within a bound seems non-trivial. Therefore, we believe that for Eve to be successful she must at least recover T fully. *It is unclear if the knowledge of the primes p_i is enough for Eve to recover the associated vectors x_i. While this is a very obvious overexaggeration on Eve's attack capabilities, we will assume for a simpler analysis that guessing exactly all p_i is sufficient to trigger a false-positive on Alice's side.* We will now explain how to alleviate this (potential) issue.

4.2   How to Choose the Primes

In order to dissuade Eve from trying to guess the correct set of primes $T_p = (p_i)_{i \in [1,k]}$, we have to make sure the number of possibilities is large enough. In that regard, *we are considering two objectives: one is to reduce the complexity of arithmetical operations used during the verification algorithm, and the other is to match a chosen level of security.* Which naturally brings us to a natural question: is it easier to trigger a random false-positive, i.e to try our luck with an attacker's success of $\prod_{i=1}^{k} p_i^{-1}$, or to guess T_p? As we will observe later, the set of combinations T_p is picked from is actually far below $\prod_{i=1}^{k} p_i$. We also choose primes to obtain efficient arithmetic. To deal with the second objective, we will just fix the level of security to match the same level of security the original DRS algorithm was aiming to achieve with lattices of dimension $\{1108, 1372, 1779\}$: the NIST security levels $\{3, 4, 5\}$ which is basically requiring $\{128, 192, 256\}$ bits of security. To reach that number, let us present how we determine the number of combinations available when choosing primes of a certain amount of bits. Suppose we have a set S of primes, and pick k primes from it which gives $\binom{S}{k}$ combinations to choose from. We now have to determine both S and k. To give an idea of the numbers required, we give Table 1 and refer to a table available online [26] referencing the number of primes. While taking low-bits primes to minimize the amount of modular reductions allows for more efficient arithmetic (see "lazy reductions" in Seiler's work for NewHope [24]), we will very soon show that we have to combine multiple sets of large sizes of primes to achieve a reasonable amount of security. DRS fitted every computation within 64-bits for both speed and convenience, and ideally we should follow that philosophy. Our final choices are:

3 : 128-bits security: $k = 6$ with S the set of 28-bits primes
4 : 192-bits security: $k = 9$ with S the set of 27 and 28-bits primes
5 : 256-bits security: $k = 12$ with S the set of 24 to 28-bits primes

Table 1. Size of set S necessary to achieve $\binom{S}{k} > 2^b$

b \ k	5	6	7	8	9	10
128	132,496,421	7,910,346	1,080,111	-	-	-
192	-	-	610,573,333	63,155,327	10,957,838	2,727,426

b \ k	11	12	13
256	49,751,158	13,974,454	4,801,557

5   Implementation Results

5.1   Time Results on a Basic Implementation

To make a fair comparison, we first give the time given by the original algorithm (setup, sign and verify). Time is given as an average in milliseconds and computations were done using a Intel(R) Xeon(R) Gold 6128 CPU @ 3.40 GHz processor using a non-optimized C implementation and re-using the code provided by the DRS submitters on their website (see Table 2). We then showcase the base case where we do not take account of the number of combinations and use just enough 32-bit integers to reach the product size needed, and compare them with our choices with smaller primes (28-bits or less) in a larger amount to reach the combination size needed (see Table 3). Note that the generation of primes is not included, as we used MAGMA [6] to pick primes and write them into a header file used by our code before the compilation. Picking primes, however did not take any significant amount of time (almost always lower than 10 ms), and we used an external software to select them. Following this, we do not think reporting the time taken for the prime generation is very relevant, as the literature also points out it is on a much lower scale than a matrix-vector multiplication (for our sizes, see [16] and subsequent work on either heuristic or deterministic algorithms). We observe that the precomputation is heavier than the generation of the keys. Which is expected as we are dealing with multiple modular matrix-vectors multiplications, whereas the original DRS setup only had to deal with randomized vectors additions. The number of signatures generated per key to break even in time (*including precomputation*) compared with the old DRS is reached for 256-bits of security with 319 signatures (28-bits case) and 211 (32-bits case).

Table 2. Average time (in ms) for the existing DRS scheme

Security \ Phase	Setup	Signature	Verification
128	67.5	1.495	0.89
192	102	2.46	1.68
256	162.9	3.82	3.50

Table 3. Average time (in ms) for the precomputation/verification algorithms

Phase \ Security	128	192	256
Precompute (32-bits)	100.16	223.9	646.69
Verify (32-bits)	0.1328	0.2515	0.4297
Precompute (28-bits)	153.21	363.1	1005.1
Verify (28-bits)	0.1048	0.2006	0.3429

5.2   Memory Storage

As we mentioned previously, Alice does not need to store Pk in our alternative scheme. Memory-wise, this showcases an obvious advantage for the verifier to require only a quasi-linear amount of memory in function of the dimension rather than a quadratic amount (i.e full public key). Here in all 3 cases we store k prime integers of 28-bits, plus $2*k$ vectors of dimension n containing 28-bits integers, thus the memory taken in bytes is $\lceil 28(k + 2kn)/8 \rceil$ (see Table 4). Another potential worry in term of memory in our modified scheme is that the prime number generation might be taking a lot of memory for the verifier. However, after decades of research on prime number generation we do not believe this is the case [14].

Table 4. Memory storage in bytes for P_{key} and its footprint T

Security	128	192	256
P_k the public key	7,672,900	11,764,900	19,780,257
p_i, x_i, X_i	46,557	86,468	149,478

6   Conclusion

In this paper we introduced a modification of Freivalds' algorithm to introduce a faster verification method to DRS. By introducing a precomputation step that is in the same order of magnitude as the setup in time, we gain a factor of almost 20 for the verification part while also heavily reducing its memory cost. This process is done while not modifying any information given by the signatory. Furthermore, more research should greatly improve this new work. **First**, we assumed almost "paranoiac" security requirements, thus a deeper analysis should improve efficiency. **Second**, we can make use of Residue Number Systems: stemming from [12] with several applications [2–5], finding large arithmetically efficient random groups is exactly what we need. **Third**, generalizing to all lattices and HNF keys. It needs the extra vector h, but any party can compute h in polynomial time with no security loss.

References

1. Ajtai, M., Dwork, C.: A public-key cryptosystem with worst-case/average-case equivalence. In: STOC 1997, pp. 284–293. ACM (1997)
2. Bajard, J.C., Eynard, J., Merkiche, N.: Multi-fault attack detection for RNS cryptographic architecture. IEEE 23rd Symposium on Computer Arithmetic, July 2016
3. Bajard, J.C., Imbert, L.: A full RNS implementation of RSA. IEEE Trans. Comput. **53**(6), 769–774 (2004)
4. Bajard, J.-C., Eynard, J., Hasan, M.A., Zucca, V.: A full RNS variant of FV like somewhat homomorphic encryption schemes. In: Avanzi, R., Heys, H. (eds.) SAC 2016. LNCS, vol. 10532, pp. 423–442. Springer, Cham (2017). https://doi.org/10.1007/978-3-319-69453-5_23
5. Bajard, J.C., Plantard, T.: RNS bases and conversions. In: Optical Science and Technology, the SPIE 49th Annual Meeting, pp. 60–69 (2004)
6. Bosma, W., Cannon, J., Playoust, C.: The Magma algebra system I: the user language. J. Symbolic Comput. **24**(3–4), 235–265 (1997)
7. Brualdi, R.A., Ryser, H.J.: Combinatorial Matrix Theory, vol. 39. Cambridge University Press, Cambridge (1991)
8. Dumas, J.-G.: Proof-of-work certificates that can be efficiently computed in the cloud (*Invited Talk*). In: Gerdt, V.P., Koepf, W., Seiler, W.M., Vorozhtsov, E.V. (eds.) CASC 2018. LNCS, vol. 11077, pp. 1–17. Springer, Cham (2018). https://doi.org/10.1007/978-3-319-99639-4_1
9. Dumas, J.-G., Zucca, V.: Prover efficient public verification of dense or sparse/structured matrix-vector multiplication. In: Pieprzyk, J., Suriadi, S. (eds.) ACISP 2017. LNCS, vol. 10343, pp. 115–134. Springer, Cham (2017). https://doi.org/10.1007/978-3-319-59870-3_7
10. Freivalds, R.: Fast probabilistic algorithms. In: Bečvář, J. (ed.) MFCS 1979. LNCS, vol. 74, pp. 57–69. Springer, Heidelberg (1979). https://doi.org/10.1007/3-540-09526-8_5
11. Gama, N., Izabachène, M., Nguyen, P.Q., Xie, X.: Structural lattice reduction: generalized worst-case to average-case reductions and homomorphic cryptosystems. In: Fischlin, M., Coron, J.-S. (eds.) EUROCRYPT 2016. LNCS, vol. 9666, pp. 528–558. Springer, Heidelberg (2016). https://doi.org/10.1007/978-3-662-49896-5_19
12. Garner, H.L.: The residue number system. In: Papers Presented at the March 3-5, 1959, Western Joint Computer Conference, pp. 146–153. ACM (1959)
13. Grover, L.K.: A fast quantum mechanical algorithm for database search. arXiv preprint: quant-ph/9605043 (1996)
14. Joye, M., Paillier, P.: Fast generation of prime numbers on portable devices: an update. In: Goubin, L., Matsui, M. (eds.) CHES 2006. LNCS, vol. 4249, pp. 160–173. Springer, Heidelberg (2006). https://doi.org/10.1007/11894063_13

15. Kimbrel, T., Sinha, R.K.: A probabilistic algorithm for verifying matrix products using o(n2) time and log2(n) + o(1) random bits. Inf. Process. Lett. **45**(2), 107–110 (1993)
16. Maurer, U.M.: Fast generation of prime numbers and secure public-key cryptographic parameters. J. Cryptology **8**(3), 123–155 (1995)
17. Micciancio, D.: Improving lattice based cryptosystems using the Hermite normal form. In: Silverman, J.H. (ed.) CaLC 2001. LNCS, vol. 2146, pp. 126–145. Springer, Heidelberg (2001). https://doi.org/10.1007/3-540-44670-2_11
18. Nguyen, P.Q., Regev, O.: Learning a parallelepiped: cryptanalysis of GGH and NTRU signatures. J. Cryptology **22**(2), 139–160 (2009)
19. NIST: Post-quantum cryptography standardization (2018). https://csrc.nist.gov/Projects/Post-Quantum-Cryptography
20. Pernet, C., Stein, W.: Fast computation of Hermite normal forms of random integer matrices. J. Number Theory **130**(7), 1675–1683 (2010)
21. Plantard, T., Sipasseuth, A., Dumondelle, C., Susilo, W.: DRS: diagonal dominant reduction for lattice-based signature. In: PQC Standardization Conference, Round 1 Submissions (2018). https://csrc.nist.gov/CSRC/media/Projects/Post-Quantum-Cryptography/documents/round-1/submissions/DRS.zip
22. Plantard, T., Susilo, W., Win, K.T.: A digital signature scheme based on CVP_∞. In: Cramer, R. (ed.) PKC 2008. LNCS, vol. 4939, pp. 288–307. Springer, Heidelberg (2008). https://doi.org/10.1007/978-3-540-78440-1_17
23. Regev, O.: New lattice-based cryptographic constructions. J. ACM (JACM) **51**(6), 899–942 (2004)
24. Seiler, G.: Faster AVX2 optimized NTT multiplication for ring-LWE lattice cryptography. Cryptology ePrint Archive, Report 2018/039 (2018)
25. Shor, P.W.: Polynomial-time algorithms for prime factorization and discrete logarithms on a quantum computer. SIAM J. Comput. **26**(5), 1484–1509 (1997)
26. e Silva, T.O.: Tables of values of pi(x) and of pi2(x) (2018). http://sweet.ua.pt/tos/primes.html
27. Sipasseuth, A., Plantard, T., Susilo, W.: Improving the security of the DRS scheme with uniformly chosen random noise. In: Jang-Jaccard, J., Guo, F. (eds.) ACISP 2019. LNCS, vol. 11547, pp. 119–137. Springer, Cham (2019). https://doi.org/10.1007/978-3-030-21548-4_7
28. Yu, Y., Ducas, L.: Learning strikes again: the case of the DRS signature scheme. In: Peyrin, T., Galbraith, S. (eds.) ASIACRYPT 2018. LNCS, vol. 11273, pp. 525–543. Springer, Cham (2018). https://doi.org/10.1007/978-3-030-03329-3_18

Group-Based Key Exchange Protocol Based on Complete Decomposition Search Problem

Chang Seng Sin[✉] and Huey Voon Chen

Department of Mathematical and Actuarial Sciences,
Lee Kong Chian Faculty of Engineering and Science,
Universiti Tunku Abdul Rahman,
Bandar Sungai Long, 43000 Kajang, Selangor, Malaysia
Jaybao@1utar.my

Abstract. Let G be a finite non-abelian group. Let $A_1, \cdots, A_k$ be non-empty subsets of G, where $k \geq 2$ is an integer such that $A_i \cap A_j = \emptyset$ for integers $i, j = 1, \cdots, k$ $(i \neq j)$. We say that $(A_1, \cdots, A_k)$ is a complete decomposition of G if the product of subsets $A_{i_1} \cdots A_{i_k} = \{a_{i_1} \ldots a_{i_k} | a_{i_j} \in A_{i_j}; j = 1, \cdots, k\}$ coincides with G where the A_{i_j} are all distinct and $\{A_{i_1}, \cdots, A_{i_k}\} = \{A_1, \cdots, A_k\}$. The complete decomposition search problem in G is defined as recovering $B \subseteq G$ from given A and G such that $AB = G$. The aim of this paper is twofold. The first aim is to propose the complete decomposition search problem in G. The other objective is to provide a key exchange protocol based on the complete decomposition search problem using generalized quaternion group Q_{2^n} as the platform group for integer $n \geq 3$. In addition, we show some constructions of complete decomposition of generalized quaternion group Q_{2^n}. Further, we propose an algorithm that can solve computational complete decomposition search problem and show that the algorithm takes exponential time to break the scheme.

Keywords: Group-based key exchange protocol · Complete decomposition search problem · Nonabelian group

1 Introduction

A lot of study regarding group factorization theory of abelian group written additively had been conducted over the years. The study of group factorization was first initiated by Hajos in year 1938 [13]. He successfully solved a geometry problem that raised by Minkowski by using group theoretical equivalent [14]. This scenario attracted the attention of studying the factorization of a finite abelian group into not necessary subgroup factors [15]. Many type of algebraic structures were derived from group factorization. One of the algebraic structure is exhaustion number as defined in [6]. In [8], they investigated the exhaustion number of dihedral group of order $2p$, where p is an odd prime. Another type

© Springer Nature Switzerland AG 2019
S.-H. Heng and J. Lopez (Eds.): ISPEC 2019, LNCS 11879, pp. 413–422, 2019.
https://doi.org/10.1007/978-3-030-34339-2_23

of analogous of group factorization, namely complete decomposition is defined as follows: Let G be a finite non-abelian group. Let $A_1, \cdots, A_k$ be non-empty subsets of G, where $k \geq 2$ is an integer such that $A_i \cap A_j = \emptyset$ for integers $i, j = 1, \cdots, k$ $(i \neq j)$. We say that $(A_1, \cdots, A_k)$ is a complete decomposition of G if the product of subsets $A_{i_1} \cdots A_{i_k} = \{a_{i_1} ... a_{i_k} | a_{i_j} \in A_{i_j}; j = 1, \cdots, k\}$ coincides with G where the A_{i_j} are all distinct and $\{A_{i_1}, \cdots, A_{i_k}\} = \{A_1, \cdots, A_k\}$. The investigation of complete decomposition of some finites groups can be found in [5].

Computational hardness assumptions are essential elements in cryptography. They are building blocks of a cryptographic primitive. Generally, computer scientist relates the hardness of a new problem to a well-known hardness assumption by reduction. Researchers reviewed the proposed hardness problem continuously over the years [4,11,24,25]. There are many hardness problems proposed in the past, such as integer factorization problem, Rivest-Shamir-Adleman (RSA) problem, discrete logarithm problem, knapsack problem etc. In this paper, we proposed some group-based hardness problem. One of the well known group-based hardness problem proposed is the Conjugacy Search Problem (CSP) [20]. The similarity of our proposed hardness problem and CSP is the utilization of non-commutative properties of the underlying group.

Diffie and Hellman [9] first developed the idea of asymmetric key exchange protocol. The security of Diffie-Hellman key exchange protocol depended on the hardness of the discrete logarithm problem (DLP). Two years later, Rivest, Shamir and Aldeman applied the hardness of integer factorization problem (IFP) to propose an encryption scheme which known as RSA encryption scheme [17]. However, Shor [18] proposed an algorithm that can feasibly solve many conventional number theory based problem. Therefore, the security of public-key cryptosystems that relied on some well-studied hardness problem such as DLP and IFP become questionable. Thus, researchers start looking into code-based, lattice-based, hash-based and group-based cryptographic primitives that suspected to remain secure under post-quantum attack [3].

Numerous studies regarding group-based cryptography had been conducted over the years [10]. The idea of constructing some cryptographic primitives based on the non-commutative group has been discussed in [19]. There are some constructions of cryptographic primitives based on the braid group by applying the conjugacy search problem (CSP) [1,7,16]. Baba et al. [2] constructed a relevant analogy from the integer factorization problem to the factorization problem over non-abelian groups. Gu and Zheng proposed several conjugated problems related to the factorization problem over non-abelian groups and showed three constructions of cryptographic primitives based on these conjugacy systems [12]. The idea that using the complexity of infinite non-abelian groups in cryptography was first proposed by Wagner and Magyarik [23]. They devised a public-key protocol based on unsolvability of the word problem in 1985. Search problems are the most suggested protocols and they are variants of decision problems of group theory. They are suitable for the general paradigm of a public key protocol. Some of the key exchange protocols related to non-commutative groups were proposed in [21,22].

Our Contribution. The main contribution of this paper is to propose a new hardness problem called Complete Decomposition Search Problem (CDSP). We construct a key exchange protocol based on CDSP. We choose generalized quaternion group Q_{2^n} as our platform group. We also provide some constructions of complete decomposition of Q_{2^n} to show that the CDSP can be practically applied. Besides, we compare the performance of our scheme with the Diffie-Hellman key exchange protocol. Finally, we present some simple security analysis of the proposed scheme.

2   Some Constructions of Complete Decomposition of Q_{2^n}

The generalized quaternion group Q_{2^n} is a finite non-abelian group with group presentation $\langle x, y | x^{2^{n-1}} = 1, y^2 = x^{2^{n-2}}, yx = x^{2^{n-1}-1}y \rangle$ for integer $n \geq 3$. In this section, we first introduce some of the multiplication rules for the elements in the generalized quaternion group Q_{2^n}. Then, we provide a construction of complete decomposition of Q_{2^n}.

Lemma 1. *Let i, n be some integers such that $1 \leq i \leq 2^{n-1} - 1$ and $n \geq 3$. Then the following properties holds:*

(i) $x^i y = yx^{2^{n-1}-i}$;
(ii) $\langle x \rangle yx^i = \langle x \rangle y$.

Proof. Note that $\langle x \rangle = \{1, x, x^2, \ldots, x^{2^{n-1}-1}\}$ and $\langle x \rangle y = \{y, xy, \ldots, x^{2^{n-1}-1}y\}$. By employing induction on i, the basic step $xy = yx^{2^{n-1}-1}$ for $i = 1$ holds. Assume that it is true when $i = k$ for some positive integers k, then $x^k y = yx^{2^{n-1}-k}$. Now, we show that the case $i = k + 1$ is true. For $i = k + 1$, we have $x^{k+1}y = x^k xy = x^k yx^{2^{n-1}-1} = yx^{2^{n-1}-k}x^{2^{n-1}-1} = yx^{2^{n-1}}x^{2^{n-1}-(k+1)}$. Since $x^{2^{n-1}} = 1$, it follows that $yx^{2^{n-1}}x^{2^{n-1}-(k+1)} = yx^{2^{n-1}-(k+1)}$ as required. For part (ii), we see that $\langle x \rangle yx^i = \{1, x, \ldots, x^{2^{n-1}-1}\}x^{2^{n-1}-i}y = \{x^{2^{n-1}-i}y, x^{2^{n-1}}y, \ldots, x^{2^n-i-1}y\}$. Since $|\{x^{2^{n-1}-i}y, x^{2^{n-1}}y, \ldots, x^{2^n-i-1}y\}| = 2^{n-1}$, it follows that $\{x^{2^{n-1}-i}y, x^{2^{n-1}}y, \ldots, x^{2^n-i-1}y\} = \langle x \rangle y$.

2.1   Construction of Complete Decomposition of Q_{2^n}

Let A, B be the subsets of Q_{2^n}. To show that the complete decomposition of generalized quaternion group Q_{2^n} is not trivial, we first show an example where (A, B) is not a complete decomposition of Q_{2^n}.

Example 1. Let $A = \{1, x, \ldots, x^{2^{n-1}-1}\}$ and $B = \{y, xy, \ldots, x^{2^{n-1}-1}y\}$ be the subsets of Q_{2^n}. Clearly, $A = \langle x \rangle \subseteq Q_{2^n}$ and $B = \langle x \rangle y \subseteq Q_{2^n}$. Since $AB \subseteq \langle x \rangle y$, it follows that (A, B) is not a complete decomposition of Q_{2^n}.

Next, we provide a construction of complete decomposition of generalized quaternion group Q_{2^n} for integer $n \geq 4$. For practical reason, the selection of subsets A and B are restricted to the condition where $A \cup B \subsetneq Q_{2^n}$.

Proposition 1. Let $A = \{1, x, x^2, \ldots, x^{2^{n-1}-3}\} \cup \{x^{2^{n-1}-2}y, x^{2^{n-1}-1}y\}$ and $B_i = (\{y, xy, \ldots, x^{2^{n-1}-3}y\} \cup \{x^{2^{n-1}-2}, x^{2^{n-1}-1}\}) \setminus \{xy, x^3y, \ldots, x^iy\}$ be the subsets of Q_{2^n}, where $i \in \{1, 3, \ldots, 2^{n-1} - 5\}$, $|A| = 2^{n-1}$ and $2^{n-2} + 2 \le |B_i| \le 2^{n-1} - 1$. Then (A, B_i) is a complete decomposition of Q_{2^n} for integer $n \ge 4$.

Proof. To show that (A, B_i) is a complete decomposition, we first consider the case when $i = 2^{n-1} - 5$. We have $B_{2^{n-1}-5} = \{y, x^2y, \ldots, x^{2^{n-1}-6}y, x^{2^{n-1}-4}y\} \cup \{x^{2^{n-1}-3}y\} \cup \{x^{2^{n-1}-2}, x^{2^{n-1}-1}\}$ with size $2^{n-2} + 2$. We compute the product of sets $\{1, x, x^2, \ldots, x^{2^{n-1}-3}\} \subseteq A$ and $\{y, x^2y, \ldots, x^{2^{n-1}-4}y\} \subseteq B_{2^{n-1}-5}$ as follows:

$$\{1, x, x^2, \ldots, x^{2^{n-1}-3}\}\{y, x^2y, x^{2^{n-1}-4}y\}$$
$$= \langle x \rangle y.$$

Then, we compute the product of sets $\{x^{2^{n-1}-2}y, x^{2^{n-1}-1}y\} \subseteq A$ and $\{y, x^2y, \ldots, x^{2^{n-1}-4}y\} \subseteq B_{2^{n-1}-5}$ as follows:

$$L_1 = \{x^{2^{n-1}-2}y, x^{2^{n-1}-1}y\}\{y, x^2y, \ldots, x^{2^{n-1}-4}y\}$$
$$= \{x^{2^{n-1}+2^{n-2}+2}, x^{2^{n-1}+2^{n-2}+3}, \ldots, x^{2^{n-1}+2^{n-2}+2^{n-1}-1}\}$$

where $|L_1| = 2^{n-1} - 2$. Then, we compute the product of sets $\{x^{2^{n-1}-2}y, x^{2^{n-1}-1}y\} \subseteq A$ and $\{x^{2^{n-1}-3}y\} \subseteq B_{2^{n-1}-5}$ as follows:

$$L_2 = \{x^{2^{n-1}-2}y, x^{2^{n-1}-1}y\}\{x^{2^{n-1}-3}y\} = \{x^{2^{n-1}+2^{n-2}+1}, x^{2^{n-1}+2^{n-2}+2}\}.$$

Observe that $L_1 \cup L_2 = \{x^{2^{n-1}+2^{n-2}+1}, x^{2^{n-1}+2^{n-2}+2}, \ldots, x^{2^{n-1}+2^{n-2}+2^{n-1}-1}\}$ with the size $|L_1 \cup L_2| = 2^{n-1} - 1$. We notice that $\langle x \rangle \setminus (L_1 \cup L_2) = \{x^{2^{n-1}+2^{n-2}+2^{n-1}}\}$. Next, we compute the product of sets $\{1, x, \ldots, x^{2^{n-1}-3}\} \subseteq A$ and $\{x^{2^{n-1}-2}, x^{2^{n-1}-1}\} \subseteq B_{2^{n-1}-5}$ as follows:

$$L_3 = \{1, x, \ldots, x^{2^{n-1}-3}\}\{x^{2^{n-1}-2}, x^{2^{n-1}-1}\}$$
$$= \{x^{2^{n-1}-2}, x^{2^{n-1}-1}, \ldots, x^{2^{n-1}+2^{n-1}-4}\}$$

where $|L_3| = 2^{n-1} - 1$. From here, we see that $\langle x \rangle \setminus L_3 = \{x^{2^{n-1}+2^{n-1}-3}\}$. To show that $(L_1 \cup L_2 \cup L_3) = \langle x \rangle y$, we need to show that $x^{2^{n-1}+2^{n-2}+2^{n-1}} \ne x^{2^{n-1}+2^{n-1}-3}$. Clearly $2^{n-1}+2^{n-2}+2^{n-1} \ne 2^{n-1}+2^{n-1}-3$ for any integer $n \ge 4$ which implies $x^{2^{n-1}+2^{n-2}+2^{n-1}} \ne x^{2^{n-1}+2^{n-1}-3}$. Thus, $(L_1 \cup L_2 \cup L_3) = \langle x \rangle y$. Therefore, we say that $(A, B_{2^{n-1}-5})$ is a complete decomposition of Q_{2^n}. Since $B_{2^{n-1}-5} \subseteq B_{2^{n-1}-7} \subseteq \cdots \subseteq B_1$ and $(A, B_{2^{n-1}-5})$ is a complete decomposition of Q_{2^n}, it follows that (A, B_i) is a complete decomposition of Q_{2^n} for $n \ge 4$ and $i \in \{1, 3, \ldots, 2^{n-1} - 5\}$.

3   Application on Cryptography

In this section, we first propose two problems, namely Decisional Complete Decomposition Search Problem and Computational Complete Decomposition Search Problem for arbitrary finite nonabelian group G. We provide a key exchange protocol based on the hardness problem proposed. Finally, we analyze the performance and security of the proposed scheme.

3.1   Complete Decomposition Search Problem (CDSP)

We define two problems as follows:

Decisional Complete Decomposition Search Problem (DCDSP): Let G be a finite non-abelian group. Given A, B and G. Determine whether B satisfies $AB = G$, where $A, B \subseteq G$ and $A \cap B = \emptyset$.

Computational Complete Decomposition Search Problem (CCDSP): Let G be a finite non-abelian group. Given A and G. Find B such that $AB = G$, where $A, B \subseteq G$ and $A \cap B = \emptyset$.

In this paper, we choose our platform group G as generalized quaternion group Q_{2^n}. We construct an algorithm to solve CCDSP in Q_{2^n} below for integer $n \geq 4$. Since $A \cap B = \emptyset$ and $|Q_{2^n}| = 2^n$, it follows that the total combination of subsets B given $|A|$ is $\binom{2^n - |A|}{|B|}$. Let $\{B_j | j = 1, 2, \ldots, \binom{2^n - |A|}{|B|}\}$ represents all the possible subsets of B. The algorithm computes the products $AB_1, AB_2, \ldots, AB_{\binom{2^n - |A|}{|B|}}$ and return B_j if $AB_j = G$ for integer $1 \leq j \leq \binom{2^n - |A|}{|B|}$.

Algorithm 1. Solve CCDSP in Q_{2^n}

- **Input**: $A, |B|, n$.
- **Output**: All possible subsets of B_j for $j = 1, 2, \ldots, \binom{2^n - |A|}{|B|}$.
- For each possible subset $B_j \subseteq Q_{2^n}$, where $1 \leq j \leq \binom{2^n - |A|}{|B|}$, compute $AB_j = D$.
- If $D = G$, then return a solution B_j.
- Return (no solution exists).

3.2   Our Proposed Scheme

Let $A, B \subseteq Q_{2^n}$. In this section, we propose a key exchange protocol based on the computational complete decomposition search problem (CCDSP) in Q_{2^n} between Alice and Bob. Suppose Alice holds a shared key B and wants to share with Bob. They can proceed as follows:

1. **Preparation Step** A and Q_{2^n} are selected and published, where $AB = Q_{2^n}$. Two subsets $A_1, A_2 \subseteq \langle x \rangle$ are selected and kept secretly. Alice chooses $a \in A$ and two distinct elements $b_1, b_2 \in A_1$ secretly. Bob chooses $c \in Q_{2^n}$ and two distinct elements $d_1, d_2 \in A_2$ secretly.
2. **Sharing private key** a
   (a) Alice computes $b_1 a b_2$.
   (b) Bob computes $d_1 b_1 a b_2 d_2$.
   (c) Alice computes $b_1^{-1} b_1 d_1 a d_2 b_2 b_2^{-1}$.
   (d) Bob computes $d_1^{-1} d_1 a d_2 d_2^{-1} = a$.
3. **Sharing private key** c
   (a) Bob computes $d_1 c d_2$.
   (b) Alice computes $b_1 d_1 c d_2 b_2$.
   (c) Bob computes $d_1^{-1} d_1 b_1 c b_2 d_2 d_2^{-1} = b_1 c b_2$.
   (d) Alices computes $b_1^{-1} b_1 c b_2 b_2^{-1} = c$.
4. **Exchange shared key** B
   (a) Alice and Bob compute $ac = b$.
   (b) Alice computes $E = Bb$.
   (c) Bob computes $x = (ac)^{-1} = c^{-1} a^{-1}$.
   (d) Bob computes $Ex = Bbx = Bacc^{-1}a^{-1} = B$.

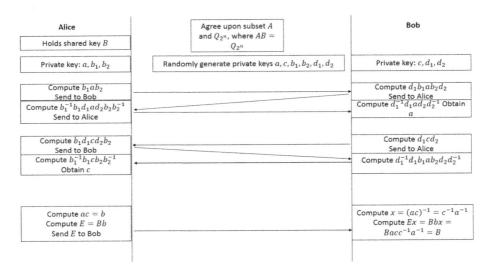

Fig. 1. Proposed key exchange protocol

3.3   Performance Analysis

For our proposed scheme which constructed using finite non-abelian generalized quaternion group, the steps involved are expected to be longer compare to other group-based key exchange protocol which constructed based on the abelian group. From Fig. 1, we see that sharing private key a and c between Alice and Bob involved 8 mathematical computation in total. For the step involving calculating the shared key B, there is a total of 4 mathematical computations required. The computations involved in our proposed scheme are mainly on multiplication between the group elements, which can be done easily due to the well-studied structure of the generalized quaternion group Q_{2^n}.

Comparing with Diffie-Hellman Key Exchange Protocol in Term of Performance. Now, we compare the performance of our proposed scheme with the pioneer of the key exchange protocol, which is Diffie-Hellman key exchange protocol. The parameters used in Diffie-Hellman key exchange protocol are a prime numbers p and q (generator of p). For computation wise, Diffie-Hellman key exchange protocol involved of 4 steps. Besides, only one communication required between Alice and Bob to obtain the shared key. Clearly our proposed scheme takes more steps in term of computation and communication compare to Diffie-Hellman key exchange protocol, however Diffie-Hellman Problem (DHP) might become vulnerable under the post-quantum attack.

3.4   Security of the Scheme

In Sect. 2.1, we show a construction of (A, B) is a complete decomposition of generalized quaternion group Q_{2^n}, where $|A| = 2^{n-1}$ and $2^{n-1} - 2 \leq |B| \leq 2^{n-1} - 1$ for integer $n \geq 4$. We first discuss the security of the scheme by using Algorithm 1 proposed in Sect. 3.1 and consider the case where $|A| = 2^{n-1}$ and $|B| = 2^{n-1} - 2$.

Theorem 1. *Let A, B be the subsets of Q_{2^n}, where $|A| = 2^{n-1}$ and $|B| = 2^{n-1} - 2$ for $n \geq 4$. Adversary takes at least exponential time E to solve Computational Complete Decomposition Search Problem using subsets A, B in Algorithm 1.*

Proof. Note that $|B| = \frac{|Q_{2^n}|}{|A|}$, $A \cap B = \emptyset$ and $|Q_{2^n}| = 2^n$. Since $A \cap B = \emptyset$, we can exclude the elements in subset A and hence left with the remaining $2^n - |A|$ elements. To search for subset B, one will try for different subset B_i, where the choice of elements for B_i comes from $2^n - |A|$ remaining elements. Thus, the worst case for one to obtain such subset B require $\binom{2^n - |A|}{|B|}$ attempts. Next, we show that Algorithm 1 need at least exponential time E to break our scheme. We compare the value between $\binom{2^n - |A|}{|B|}$ and 2^n as follows:

$$\binom{2^n - |A|}{|B|} = \binom{2^{n-1}}{2^{n-1} - 2}$$

$$= \frac{2^{n-1}!}{2!(2^{n-1} - 2)!}$$

$$= \frac{1 \cdot 2 \cdots 2^{n-1}}{2(1 \cdot 2 \cdots (2^{n-1} - 2))}$$

$$=\frac{(2^{n-1}-1)2^{n-1}}{2}$$
$$=(2^{n-1}-1)2^{n-2}$$
$$=2^{2n-3}-2^{n-2}\geq 2^n$$

Clearly, $(2^{n-1}-1)2^{n-2}\geq 2^n$ for $n\geq 4$. Since $\binom{2^n-|A|}{|B|}\geq 2^n$ for $n\geq 4$, it follows that Adversary takes at least exponential time E to break our scheme using Algorithm 1.

Next, we discuss the security of the scheme by assuming that adversary knows some of the private information related to the scheme. Firstly, suppose adversary knows $A_1\subseteq \langle x\rangle$, where $|A_1|=t$. Then, adversary can guess two distinct elements $b_1,b_2\in A_1$ correctly with the probability $Pr(Adv\ guess\ b_1,b_2)=\frac{1}{t}(\frac{1}{t-1})$. From here, adversary is able to compute a from b_1ab_2 by using b_1,b_2. However, adversary has no information about $c\in Q_{2^n}$. Secondly, suppose adversary knows $A_2\subseteq \langle x\rangle$, where $|A_2|=u$. Then, the probability of adversary guesses two distinct elements $d_1,d_2\in A_2$ correctly is $Pr(Adv\ guess\ d_1,d_2)=\frac{1}{u}(\frac{1}{u-1})$. By using d_1 and d_2, adversary can compute c from d_1cd_2. However, the information about a remains unknown to adversary. Finally, suppose that adversary knows $A_1,A_2\subseteq \langle x\rangle$, then adversary is able to compute a,c with the probability $Pr(Adv\ guess\ b_1,b_2,d_1,d_2)=\frac{1}{t}(\frac{1}{t-1})+\frac{1}{u}(\frac{1}{u-1})$. Adversary can use a,c to compute $c^{-1}a^{-1}$ then followed by shared key B. To summarize this, adversary is not able to compute the shared key B if he knows either A_1 or A_2 but not both. If adversary knows A_1,A_2, where $|A_1|=t,|A_2|=u$, then the probability of adversary computes shared key B correctly is $\frac{1}{t}(\frac{1}{t-1})+\frac{1}{u}(\frac{1}{u-1})$. Thus, if t and u are large integers, then $\lim_{t\to\infty}\frac{1}{t}=\lim_{t\to\infty}\frac{1}{t-1}=\lim_{u\to\infty}\frac{1}{u}=\lim_{u\to\infty}\frac{1}{u-1}=0$. Hence, the probability of adversary to compute shared key B correctly is negligible and the scheme is secured. We summarize the results in the following Table 1.

Table 1. Security of the scheme with the assumption that the adversary knows some information

Information that adversary knows	Can adversary computes a correctly from the given information?	Can adversary computes c correctly from the given information?	Can adversary computes shared key B correctly from the given information?
A_1 with size t	Yes, with the probability of $\frac{1}{t}(\frac{1}{t-1})$	No	No
A_2 with size u	No	Yes, with the probability of $\frac{1}{u}(\frac{1}{u-1})$	No
A_1 and A_2	Yes, with the probability of $\frac{1}{t}(\frac{1}{t-1})$	Yes, with the probability of $\frac{1}{u}(\frac{1}{u-1})$	Yes, with the probability of $\frac{1}{t}(\frac{1}{t-1})+\frac{1}{u}(\frac{1}{u-1})$

3.5   Open Questions

For future research direction, researchers should analyze which assumptions can be reduced from Complete Decomposition Search Problem as proposed in this paper. We believe that there exists a relation between CDSP and Subset Sum Problem which known to be NP-hard. However, we are not able to provide any formal proof for this statement here. For the implementation of the proposed scheme in a real work scenario, one can investigate on the value of security parameter, for instance the size of subsets A and B to be used so that it provides the same security level like 2048 bit or 4098 bit Diffie Hellman key exchange. Besides, formal security proof or generic model of the proposed scheme should be considered.

Acknowledgments. The project was funded by the Fundamental Research Grant Scheme (FRGS), project number FRGS/1/2017/STG06/UTAR/02/3.

References

1. Anshel, I., Anshel, M., Goldfeld, D.: An algebraic method for public-key cryptography. Math. Res. Lett. **6**, 287–291 (2001)
2. Baba, S., Kotyada, S., Teja, R.: A non-abelian factorization problem and an associated cryptosystem. Cryptology Eprint Archive Report 2011/048 (2011)
3. Bernstein, D.J., Lange, T.: Post-quantum cryptography dealing with the fallout of physics success. IACR Cryptology Eprint Archive/2017/314 (2017)
4. Boudot, F.: On improving integer factorization and discrete logarithm computation using partial triangulation. Cryptology Eprint Archive Report 2017/758 (2017)
5. Chin, A.Y.M., Chen, H.V.: Complete decompositions of finite abelian groups. AAECC **30**, 263–274 (2018)
6. Chin, A.Y.M.: Exhaustion numbers of maximal sum-free sets of certain cyclic groups. Matematika **15**(1), 57–63 (2009)
7. Dehornoy, P.: Braid-based cryptography. Contemp. Math. **360**, 5–33 (2004)
8. Wong, C.K.D., Wong, K.W., Yap, W.S.: Exhaustion 2-subsets in dihedral groups of order $2p$. Asian Eur. J. Math. World Sci. Publ. Co. **11**(3), 1–13 (2018)
9. Diffie, W., Hellman, M.E.: New direction in cryptography. IEEE Trans. Inf. Theory **22**(6), 644–654 (1976)
10. Fine, B., Habeeb, M., Kahrobaei, D., Rosenberger, G.: Aspects of nonabelian group based cryptography: a survey and open problems. JP J. Algebra Number Theorie Appl. **21**, 1–40 (2011)
11. Goldwasser, S., Kalai, Y.T.: Cryptographic Assumptions: A Position Paper. TCC, pp. 505–522 (2015)
12. Gu, L., Zheng, S.: Conjugacy systems based on nonabelian factorization problems and their applications in cryptography. J. Appl. Math. **52**(2), 1–9 (2014)
13. Hajos, G.: Covering multidimensional spaces by cube lattices. Mat. Fiz. Lapok **45**, 171–190 (1938)
14. Hajos, G.: Uber Einfache und Mehrfache Bedeckung des n-dimensionalen Raumes Mit Einem Urfelgitter. Math. Zeit. **47**, 427–467 (1942)
15. Hajos, G.: Sur la Factorisation des Groupes Abeliens. Casopis Pes. Mat. Fys. **74**, 157–162 (1949)

16. Ko, K.H., Lee, S.J., Cheon, J.H., Han, J.W., Kang, J., Park, C.: New public-key cryptosystem using braid groups. In: Bellare, M. (ed.) CRYPTO 2000. LNCS, vol. 1880, pp. 166–183. Springer, Heidelberg (2000). https://doi.org/10.1007/3-540-44598-6_10

17. Rivest, R.L., Shamir, A., Adleman, L.: A method for obtaining digital signatures and public-key cryptosystems. Commun. ACM **21**(2), 120–126 (1978)

18. Shor, P.W.: Polynomial-time algorithm for prime factorization and discrete logarithms on quantum computer. SIAM J. Comput. **26**(5), 1484–1509 (1997)

19. Shpilrain, V., Ushakov, A.: Thompson's group and public key cryptography. In: 3rd International Conference on Applied Cryptography and Network Security, ACNS 2005, pp. 151–163 (2005)

20. Shpilrain, V., Ushakov, A.: The conjugacy search problem in public key cryptography: unnecessary and insufficient. Appl. Algebra Eng. Commun. Comput. **17**, 285–289 (2006)

21. Ustimenko, V., Klisowski, M.: On noncommutative cryptography and homomorphism of stable cubical multivariate transformation groups of infinite dimensional affine spaces. Cryptology Eprint Archive Report 2019/593 (2019)

22. Ustimenko, V.: On inverse protocol of post quantum cryptography based on pairs of noncommutative multivariate platforms used in tandem. Cryptology Eprint Archive Report 2019/897 (2019)

23. Blakley, G.R., Chaum, D. (eds.): CRYPTO 1984. LNCS, vol. 196. Springer, Heidelberg (1985). https://doi.org/10.1007/3-540-39568-7

24. Yana, K., Yulia, K.: Merkle-Hellman knapsack cryptosystem in undergraduate computer science curriculum. FECS, pp. 123–128 (2010)

25. Zhu, H.: Survey of computational assumptions used in cryptography broken or not by shor's algorithm. Master in Science, Mc Gill University Montreal (2001)

Development Activities, Tools and Techniques of Secure Microservices Compositions

Peter Nkomo and Marijke Coetzee[(✉)] [iD]

University of Johannesburg, Johannesburg, South Africa
ptnkomo@gmail.com, marijkec@uj.ac.za

Abstract. The decomposition of an application into independent microservices increases the attack surface, and makes it difficult to monitor each microservice in order to secure and control their network traffic. The adoption of microservices, together with new trends in software development that aim to quickly deliver software in short software development iterations often leaves software engineers with little time to give attention to the security of such applications. Consequently, it is not uncommon for many software development teams to release software without performing full-scale security testing. Although various tools and techniques are available to assist software engineers with the development of secure microservices throughout their life cycle, there is limited guidance on how these tools and techniques can be integrated into the software engineer's daily software development tasks. The aim of this paper is to identify and review tools and techniques that software engineers can use as part of security-focused activities incorporated into the software development process, so that security is given early attention during the development of microservices.

Keywords: Security · Microservices · Secure development activities

1 Introduction

A new architectural style called the microservices architecture has gained considerable attention to simplify and quicken the development of software applications [1, 2]. Microservices communicate using point-to-point exchanges of message by means of lightweight mechanisms over the hypertext transfer protocol or by listening to events within their operating environment [3] and are ideally developed within fast software release cycles [4, 5]. The microservices architectural style leans towards Agile practices [6] that aims to shorten software development cycles and is a natural fit to DevOps that aims to integrate software development and the maintenance of software releases through the use automation [7, 8]. Many Agile teams tend to release software without performing full-scale security testing [9, 10] as limited guidance is available on how current security tools and techniques can be integrated into daily software development tasks. The main research question addressed by this paper is - *what security-focused tools and techniques can software engineers integrate in the software development process so that security becomes part of the daily software development tasks?* This research question is addressed by identifying secure development activities and performing a systematic review of relevant techniques and security-focused tools.

© Springer Nature Switzerland AG 2019
S.-H. Heng and J. Lopez (Eds.): ISPEC 2019, LNCS 11879, pp. 423–433, 2019.
https://doi.org/10.1007/978-3-030-34339-2_24

Knowledge gained from this systematic review can assist software engineers to adopt appropriate real-world security-focused tools and techniques to create a coordinated security strategy to cultivate a security-conscious culture in a software development team. Such a security-conscious culture can ensure the development of secure and resilient microservices [11].

This paper is organised as follows; Sect. 2 identifies a set of security-focused development activities that support the development of a secure microservices composition. Section 3 describes how to effectively incorporate tools and techniques into the five secure development activities to improve security of microservices compositions. A conclusion follows in Sect. 4.

2   Secure Development Activities of a Microservices Composition

A set of secure microservices software development activities are now identified by understanding the security challenges of microservices compositions from the perspective of a potential attacker. Possible threats are identified here by reviewing the microservices architecture using an imaginary on-demand PickMeUp taxi application shown in Fig. 1, similar to Uber and supporting the most common features of such applications [1]. Several potential entry points that can pose potential security threats exist as listed next.

- *The application programming interface (API) gateway and the microservices API.* The attacker may perform various types of injection attacks on the APIs.
- *The service registry.* The attacker may control the service registry to ensure disrupt the process on microservices discoverying each other.
- *Message broker.* The attacker may gain access to messages exchanged by microservices or to bring the message broker down so that the composition cease to function.
- *Container or virtual machine.* The attacker may gain control of the runtime environment and shut down the microservices composition.

A threat exists typically when an entry point into the system provides access to an asset [14]. The security threats derived from the four entry points listed previously are (1) insecure application programming interfaces; (2) unauthorized access; (3) insecure microservice discovery; (4) insecure runtime infrastructure; and (5) insecure message broker.

These five security threats provide a basis to elicit security-focused software development activities, that software engineers can adopt to develop secure microservices. Five security-focused activities were elicited by previous research, referred to as the *secure development activities* of a microservices composition [15]:

1. *Document security requirements of microservices compositions.*
2. *Adopt secure programming best practices.*

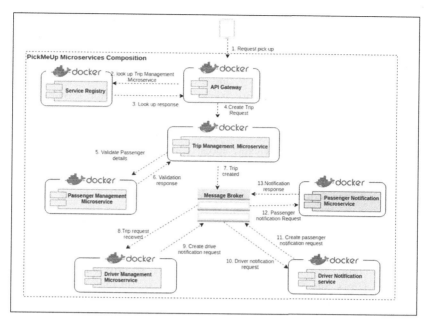

Fig. 1. PickMeUp application

3. *Validate security requirements and secure programming best practices.*
4. *Secure configuration of runtime infrastructure.*
5. *Coninously monitor the behaviour of components of the microservices composition.*

The next section aims to understand how to effectively incorporate tools and techniques into five secure development activities.

3   Tools and Techniques of Secure Development Activities

As the microservices architecture can be considered a relatively new area of research [16] this paper adopts a systematic mapping research approach [17] used for research in software engineering [18]. In each case, research questions are formulated to direct the research.

3.1   Document Security Requirements of Microservices Compositions

- *Q1 - What types of security policies are required to document protection measures for a microservices composition comprehensively?*
- *Q2 - What should be considered when designing security policies for a microservices composition?*

Types of Security Policies (Q1). Six types of security policies are identified namely a *data protection policy* [20], an *access control policy, a microservice technology-*

specific policy that focuses on mitigating weaknesses in libraries as they may contain vulnerabilities [10], a *network security policy* to control access to components and to specify how logical addresses managed for containers or virtual machines. *Microservices composition security policies* combines the policy that protects message exchanges and an access control policy, and finally the *virtual machine and container security policies* that mitigate security weakness on the runtime environments, as containers can also be a source of vulnerabilities [21].

Designing Security Policies in a Microservices Composition (Q2). Components in a microservices composition may delegate access control decisions to other components because not every component can directly ask the end-user for authentication details [22]. The security policy should determine protection mechanisms to enable a *trust relationship* between collaborating components and should support *hierarchical security policy domains* [23].

3.2   Adopt Secure Programming Best Practices

Microservices compositions are not immune to known security attacks such as SQL injections and Cross Site Scripting (XSS) [24]. To assist in understanding how best practices can be adopted in developing safe microservices the following research questions are formulated.

- *Q3 - Which secure programming practices can assist engineers to avoid known security flaws when developing microservices?*
- *Q4 - How can engineers adopt secure programming practices without affecting the rate of microservices releases?*

Taxonomy of Secure Programming Best Practices (Q3). The Microsoft Secure Development Lifecycle [25] defines four security principles that this research uses as basis to reason about secure microservices composition.

Secure-by-design. Various best practices should be incorporated into the initial architectural design of microservices compositions [25]. The following best practices can ensure microservices composition that is secure-by-design:

- *Keeping design of microservices simple.* Complex designs increase the likelihood of errors being made in implementation, configuration [27].
- *Ensuring input validation on microservices API.* All input data from untrusted data sources must be validated to eliminates injection attacks.
- *Giving attention to source code compiler warnings.* The highest source code compiler warning level should be used. Compiler warnings should be eliminated by modifying the source code [28].
- *Sanitizing data sent between components in a microservices composition.* Sanitization involves cleaning or filtering microservices input data by checking for invalid UTF-8 encoding, removing line breaks, tabs and extra white space and stripping octets in the input. Sanitizing data helps prevents cross-site scripting attacks.

Secure-by-default. Microservices compositions can be developed in a manner that makes them inherently safe when engineers adopt the following best practices:

- *Adhering to the principle of least privilege.* Code should have the least set of permission required to perform a task [29]. Access to directories, databases tables, and any other resources that are not required by a component to complete a task at hand should be prohibited.
- *Practicing defense-in-depth.* Software engineers can manage security risks in a microservices composition by using multiple defense strategies [30].
- *Denying access by default.* A protection scheme should be in place defining conditions when access is only permitted [31].

Secure-by-deployment. The deployment process of a microservices composition can provide a path that an attacker can exploit to make harmful changes and deploy the changes into production environments or even perform a denial of service attack and should be protected [32].

Secure-by-communication. Secure-by-communication requires that software development teams respond promptly to reports of security weaknesses and communicate information about security updates. To this end, engineers need to keep abreast with new security weaknesses and have access to the latest security information.

Enforcing Secure Programming Practices (Q4). Proposed methods to enforce secure programming practices provide a practice-oriented effort to incorporate secure programming practices in the development of secure microservices compositions. In addition, software engineers may be required to change their perception about security. The benefits of adopting secure programming best practices may be realized when security testing is treated as an essential step in the microservices development process. To this end, the next section discusses how security testing can be incorporated into the development process as an essential activity.

3.3   Validate Security Requirements and Secure Programming Best Practices

Security testing generally validates the correct implementation of specified security requirements and identifies unintended vulnerabilities [33, 34]. In a fast-paced development environment, it makes sense to automate the validation process. The following two questions are formulated to assist understand security testing for microservices.

- *Q5 - What attributes should a security-focused tool possess to seamlessly integrate into a fast-paced microservices development environment?*
- *Q6 - Can existing security testing tools be used to automate security testing in microservices?*

Required Attributes of Security Testing Tools (Q5). The effective use of a tool for automated security testing in microservices depends on how seamlessly the tools integrate into the microservices development process. In fast-paced development environments a tool with the following attributes is likely to seamlessly integrate into the development process:

- *Easy to integrate* [35]. A security testing tools should be easy to integrate into a software engineers's IDE.
- *Easy to use* [36]. An ideal testing tool should not require software engineers to have advanced security knowledge.
- *Natural results interpretation* [37]. Software engineers should be able to understand reported security flaws without much effort, and if possible, the tool should provide guidance on how to address identified weaknesses.
- *Extensive language support and portability.* Tools should not limit software engineers to a particular programming language or development platforms.
- *Extensibility.* The tool should allow engineers to add new capability when new security weaknesses are reported.

Various security testing tools are readily available that can be used for security testing in microservices composition [38]. The challenge for software engineers is to identify which tools to integrate into software development process. The next section gives available tools and briefly describes their suitability for automation.

Security Testing Tools (Q6). Software engineers do not fully exploited the capabilities provided by tools [39]. A general ignorance of security testing in many development teams is reported [40]. Two types of security testing are *static security testing* that checks the source code, design documents to find errors, code flaws, and potentially malicious code when the code is not being executed. *Dynamic security testing* validates the runtime behavior of security mechanisms in an application when source code is being executed or the application is running.

Popular, readily available, and non-proprietary tools are GauntIt [38], SonarQube [41], and FindSecurityBugs [38]. Tools such as SonarQube, GauntIt, and FindSecurityBugs can easily be integrated into software engineers' IDEs and other build tools. These tools are easy to use and extensible. SonarQube seems is more suitable because it supports many languages and frameworks, provides both static and dynamic testing, and is easy to use and allow other tools such as FindSecurityBugs to be integrated to it. The next section reviews the activity of securing the runtime infrastructure.

3.4   Secure Configuration of Runtime Infrastructure

Most types of attacks on microservices ultimately target the runtime environments where data is stored, and the microservices run. The first step towards ensuring a secure runtime environment is to formalize a secure configuration baseline of both hardware and software components, and then later validate the configuration when microservices are deployed [42]. The following questions are formulated to assist in reviewing the suitability of available tools.

- *Q7 - What capabilities makes a tool suitable for creating secure runtime environments as part of the microservices development process?*
- *Q8 - Can the widely used configuration management tools be easily used to create secure microservices runtime environment?*

Tool Capabilities for Secure Configurations (Q7). Essential capabilities that a tool should poss are support for different security requirements where each component has its own security configuration that defines the security concerns of the component. Security configuration files should be treated similar to software source code so that any changes on the configuration files are tracked. Any changes to configurations should be tested first to ensure configurations are not a source of vulnerabilities. Dependency between security configuration files may become unavoidable. These dependencies should preferably be expressed the same way as software source code dependencies for easier maintenance. Security configuration files should be written in languages that are close to natural language to make it easy for the engineers with less security knowledge to be able to maintain.

Review of Tools for Secure Configurations (Q8). Tools that are common in the industry for configuration management are Chef [43], Puppet [44], Ansible [45]. The available configuration management tools are primarily similar in functionality, and software engineers of microservices should be able to use any tool of their choice. In a development team that has no previous experience with any tool, choosing an ideal tool may be hard.

The next section identifies mechanisms to ensure that engineers are always aware of the behavior of the components of a microservices composition at all times.

3.5 Continuously Monitor Components of the Microservices Composition

Distributed tracing of communication between components and access to each component's log files are vital to understanding attacks. It is essential to identify the features of each component at design time that are necessary and sufficient to describe and understand the component's runtime security behavior. These features can then be used to determine how any changes affect the overall status and health of the microservices composition.

- *Q9 - What is required to monitor distributed microservices effectively?*
- *Q10 - Can available tools assist gain better visibility of microservices and the runtime environment to ensure continuous security?*

Requirements for Security Monitoring (Q9). It is essential for tools that are candidates for monitoring tool to be *customizable* as different components require different security monitoring metrics; *complete* to provide a comprehensive view of the all components of the microservices composition and the runtime infrastructure; *scalable* as the number of components in a microservices composition increase as new business functionality is automated; and *portable* as components in a microservices composition are portable artefacts deployable on different platforms.

The next section identifies and review existing tools that can assist gain better visibility of microservices composition at runtime.

Review of Existing Monitoring Tools (Q10). The general observation is that existing monitoring tools can be classified as *proprietary tools* that belong *to*

Infrastructure provider or third-party organizations and *free or open-source tools* that are freely available.

The most common monitoring tools are CloudWatch [46], CloudMonix [47], Dynatrace[48], Zabbix [49], Prometheus[50], and AppDynamics [51]. A review of currently available monitoring tools, both open source and proprietary, shows that these tools can adequately monitor microservices, containers and virtual machines and are production-ready. The monitoring tools provide proper logging of all relevant and essential information required by engineers to understand the state of the microservice at any time.

4   Conclusion

The goal of creating secure microservices compositions can be achieved when a set of secure development activities that focus on the security aspects of a composition is integrated both early and throughout the development process. Microservices compositions can be developed in a manner that makes them inherently secure when engineers exploit new opportunities that security testing tools bring into the microservices development environment. Conducting security testing early in the development process allow security weaknesses to be identified. Identified security weaknesses can be addressed early in the software development process. Code-driven, configuration management tools, should also be adapted to provide standardized, secure configurations of the runtime environments using commonly tested templates. Microservices compositions can be made more secure by using mechanisms to detect any anomalies at runtime which can compromise security.

The next step as future research work is to develop a practice-oriented framework to assist software engineers in fast-paced teams in developing secure microservices compositions. The framework will provide guidance to software engineers on how to incorporate the five secure development activities discussed in this paper and the various tools and techniques into their daily software development tasks.

References

1. Pahl, C., Jamshidi, P.: Microservices: A Systematic Mapping Study. In: CLOSER (1), pp. 137–146 (2016)
2. Newman, S.: Building Microservices: Designing Fine-Grained Systems. O'Reilly Media Inc., Newton (2015)
3. Dragoni, N., et al.: Microservices: yesterday, today, and tomorrow. Present and Ulterior Software Engineering, pp. 195–216. Springer, Cham (2017). https://doi.org/10.1007/978-3-319-67425-4_12
4. Nadareishvili, I., Mitra, R., McLarty, M., Amundsen, M.: Microservice Architecture: Aligning Principles, Practices, and Culture. O'Reilly Media Inc, Newton (2016)
5. Bossert, O.: A two-speed architecture for the digital enterprise. In: El-Sheikh, E., Zimmermann, A., Jain, Lakhmi C. (eds.) Emerging Trends in the Evolution of Service-Oriented and Enterprise Architectures. ISRL, vol. 111, pp. 139–150. Springer, Cham (2016). https://doi.org/10.1007/978-3-319-40564-3_8

6. Schmidt, C.: Agile Software Development. Springer, Cham (2016). https://doi.org/10.1007/978-3-319-26057-0
7. Ravichandran, A., Taylor, K., Waterhouse, P.: DevOps foundations. In: DevOps for Digital Leaders, pp. 27–47. Apress (2016)
8. Oyetoyan, T.D., Cruzes, D.S., Jaatun, M.G.: An empirical study on the relationship between software security skills, usage and training needs in agile settings. In: 2016 11th International Conference on Availability, Reliability and Security (ARES), pp. 548–555. IEEE (2016)
9. Heinrich, R., et al.: Performance engineering for microservices: research challenges and directions. In: Proceedings of the 8th ACM/SPEC on International Conference on Performance Engineering Companion, pp. 223–226. ACM (2017)
10. Veracode (2017)
11. AlHogail, A.: Design and validation of information security culture framework. Comput. Human Behav. **49**, 567–575 (2015)
12. Cramer, J., Krueger, A.B.: Disruptive change in the taxi business: The case of Uber. Am. Econ. Rev. **106**(5), 177–182 (2016)
13. Merkel, D.: Docker: lightweight linux containers for consistent development and deployment. Linux J. **2014**(239), 2 (2014)
14. Kissel, R.: Glossary of key information security terms. NIST Interagency Reports NIST IR, 7298(3) (2013)
15. Nkomo, P., Coetzee, M.: Software development activities for secure microservices. In: Misra, S., et al. (eds.) ICCSA 2019. LNCS, vol. 11623, pp. 573–585. Springer, Cham (2019). https://doi.org/10.1007/978-3-030-24308-1_46
16. Di Francesco, P., Malavolta, I., Lago, P.: Research on architecting microservices: trends, focus, and potential for industrial adoption. In: 2017 IEEE International Conference on Software Architecture (ICSA), pp. 21–30. IEEE (2017)
17. Petersen, K., Feldt, R., Mujtaba, S., Mattsson, M.: Systematic mapping studies in software engineering. In: EASE, vol. 8, pp. 68–77 (2008)
18. Kitchenham, B., Charters, S.: guidelines for performing systematic literature reviews in software engineering. Technical Report EBSE 2007- 001, Keele University and Durham University Joint Report (2007)
19. ISO I.: 7498-2. information processing systems open systems interconnection basic reference model-part 2: Security architecture. ISO Geneva, Switzerland (1989)
20. Satoh, F., Tokuda, T.: Security policy composition for composite web services. IEEE Trans. Serv. Comput. **4**(4), 314–327 (2011)
21. Gummaraju, J., Desikan, T., Turner, Y.: Over 30% of official images in docker hub contain high priority security vulnerabilities, pp. 1–6 (2015). https://banyanops.com
22. Nacer, H., Djebari, N., Slimani, H., Aissani, D.: A distributed authentication model for composite Web services. Comput. Secur. **70**, 144–178 (2017)
23. Dell'Amico, M., Serme, G., Idrees, M.S., De Oliveira, A.S., Roudier, Y.: Hipolds: a hierarchical security policy language for distributed systems. Inf. Secur. Tech. Rep. **17**(3), 81–92 (2013)
24. Ahmadvand, M., Ibrahim, A.: Requirements reconciliation for scalable and secure microservice (de) composition. In: IEEE International on Requirements Engineering Conference Workshops (REW), pp. 68–73. IEEE (2016)
25. Howard, M., Lipner, S.: The Security Development Lifecycle (SDL): A Process for Developing Demonstrably More Secure Software. Microsoft Press (2006)
26. Kadam, S.P., Joshi, S.: Secure by design approach to improve the security of object-oriented software. In: 2015 2nd International Conference on Computing for Sustainable Global Development (INDIACom), pp. 24–30. IEEE (2015)

27. Sahu, D.R., Tomar, D.S.: Analysis of web application code vulnerabilities using secure coding standards. Arab. J. Sci. Eng. **42**(2), 885–895 (2017)
28. White, G.K.: Secure coding practices, tools, and processes (No. LLNL-CONF-671591). Lawrence Livermore National Laboratory (LLNL), Livermore, CA (2015)
29. Neumann, P.G.: Fundamental trustworthiness principles. New Solutions for Cybersecurity (2018)
30. Gkioulos, V., Wolthusen, S.D.: Security requirements for the deployment of services across tactical SOA. In: Rak, J., Bay, J., Kotenko, I., Popyack, L., Skormin, V., Szczypiorski, K. (eds.) MMM-ACNS 2017. LNCS, vol. 10446, pp. 115–127. Springer, Cham (2017). https://doi.org/10.1007/978-3-319-65127-9_10
31. Bertolino, A., Busch, M., Daoudagh, S., Lonetti, F., Marchetti, E.: A toolchain for designing and testing access control policies. In: Heisel, M., Joosen, W., Lopez, J., Martinelli, F. (eds.) Engineering Secure Future Internet Services and Systems. LNCS, vol. 8431, pp. 266–286. Springer, Cham (2014). https://doi.org/10.1007/978-3-319-07452-8_11
32. Bass, L., Weber, I., Zhu, L.: DevOps: A Software Architect's Perspective. Addison-Wesley Professional, Boston (2015)
33. Paul, M.: Official (ISC) 2 Guide to the CSSLP. CRC Press, Boca Raton (2016)
34. Tian-yang, G., Yin-Sheng, S., You-yuan, F.: Research on software security testing. World Acad. Sci. Eng. Technol. **21**(70), 647–651 (2010)
35. Kaur, H.: Automating Static Code Analysis for Risk Assessment and Quality Assurance of Medical Record Software (2017)
36. Le Ru, Y., Aron, M., Gerval, J.-P., Napoleon, T.: Tests generation oriented web-based automatic assessment of programming assignments. In: Uskov, Vladimir L., Howlett, Robert J., Jain, Lakhmi C. (eds.) Smart Education and Smart e-Learning. SIST, vol. 41, pp. 117–127. Springer, Cham (2015). https://doi.org/10.1007/978-3-319-19875-0_11
37. de Andrade Gomes, P.H., Garcia, R.E., Spadon, G., Eler, D.M., Olivete, C., Correia, R.C.M.: Teaching software quality via source code inspection tool. In: 2017 IEEE Frontiers in Education Conference (FIE), pp. 1–8. IEEE (2017)
38. Kuusela, J.: Security testing in continuous integration processes (2017)
39. Peischl, B., Felderer, M., Beer, A.: Testing security requirements with non-experts: approaches and empirical investigations. In: 2016 IEEE International Conference on Software Quality, Reliability and Security (QRS), pp. 254–261. IEEE (2016)
40. Cruzes, D.S., Felderer, M., Oyetoyan, T.D., Gander, M., Pekaric, I.: How is security testing done in agile teams? A cross-case analysis of four software teams. In: Baumeister, H., Lichter, H., Riebisch, M. (eds.) XP 2017. LNBIP, vol. 283, pp. 201–216. Springer, Cham (2017). https://doi.org/10.1007/978-3-319-57633-6_13
41. Campbell, G., Papapetrou, P.P.: SonarQube in Action. Manning Publications Co., New York (2013)
42. Hochstein, L., Moser, R.: Ansible: Up and Running: Automating Configuration Management and Deployment the Easy Way. O'Reilly Media Inc., Newton (2017)
43. Taylor, M., Vargo, S.: Learning Chef: A Guide to Configuration Management and Automation. O'Reilly Media Inc., Newton (2014)
44. Loope, J.: Managing Infrastructure with Puppet: Configuration Management at Scale. O'Reilly Media Inc., Newton (2011)
45. Hall, D.: Ansible configuration management. Packt Publishing Ltd., Birmingham (2013)
46. CloudWatch: Amazon cloudwatch (2014)
47. Cloudmonix: CloudMonix (2018). http://www.cloudmonix.com/. Accessed 9 May 2018

48. Willnecker, F., Brunnert, A., Gottesheim, W., Krcmar, H.: Using dynatrace monitoring data for generating performance models of java ee applications. In: Proceedings of the 6th ACM/SPEC International Conference on Performance Engineering, pp. 103–104. ACM (2015)
49. Zabbix, S.I.A.: Zabbix. The Enterprise-class Monitoring Solution for Everyone (2014)
50. AppDynamics, A.I.P.: AppDynamics Pro Documentation

Generating Phishing Emails
Using Graph Database

Nasim Maleki[✉] and Ali A. Ghorbani

Canadian Institute for Cybersecurity, Faculty of Computer Science,
University of New Brunswick, 46 Dineen Drive, Fredericton, NB, Canada
{nmaleki,aghorbani}@unb.ca

Abstract. We need Phishing Awareness Tools to train employees because existing anti-phishing filters are not 100% capable of detecting phishing attacks, especially zero-day attacks. Current awareness tools can make phishing campaigns targeting the employees, but they contain an only limited number of predefined email templates. In this work, we designed a framework and built a tool generating new phishing emails automatically from a graph database perspective. Then, we conducted a three-round experiment. We sent the automatically-generated emails to some uninformed members of our community. On average, 72.85% of victims opened the emails, the click-through rate was 54.05% among who opened the emails, and all recipients who completed the survey stated that the content of emails was meaningful. In this experiment, we also showed which parts of the email are more luring and what the result might be if emails are carefully-crafted or from a person of authority.

Keywords: Phishing email · Phishing Awareness Tool · Generating phishing email

1 Introduction

Downs et al. [5] has divided computer security attacks into three categories: physical attacks, syntactic attacks, and semantic attacks. Semantic attacks target people's vulnerability, not the machines'. Hence, Phishing Attack belongs to the semantic attack type and mostly happens in the form of email fraud.

Researchers and industry have proposed many detection methods to filter incoming phishing emails although they are not 100% accurate. As a result, if an anti-phishing tool cannot filter a phishing email and it arrives right at the recipient's inbox, the recipient should verify that the email is real or fake. We require a Security Awareness Tool to train employees of companies to be aware of phishing characteristics. Phishing awareness tools send simulated phishing attacks toward employees to assess their awareness level. However, current tools only contain a limited number of email templates to make the campaigns. We have designed and developed a framework to generate contents of phishing email attacks automatically.

© Springer Nature Switzerland AG 2019
S.-H. Heng and J. Lopez (Eds.): ISPEC 2019, LNCS 11879, pp. 434–449, 2019.
https://doi.org/10.1007/978-3-030-34339-2_25

To this end, we analyze phishing emails, their topics, and the types of companies that phishing emails are impersonating such as payment, shipping, etc. After analyzing hundreds of phishing emails from the APWG dataset and also getting inspiration from Palka et al. [11], we dissect phishing emails into the meaningful fragments such as Problem, Solution, Link Indicator, etc. So each phishing email's body is semantically broken apart to a number of meaningful parts then tagged and finally stored in a Neo4j graph database as a knowledge base. Based on algorithms in Sect. 4 data fragments or nodes with a higher weight would be selected to generate a new email.

We sent the automatically-generated emails to some members of our community in three unannounced tests with different topics and severity. On average, 72.85% of victims opened the emails, the click-through rate was 54.05% among who opened the emails, and all recipients who read the generated emails and completed the survey stated that the contents were meaningful.

Our contributions in this study are:

- We created a knowledge base including the data segments of 300 phishing attacks from the APWG Dataset [1]. They have semantic tags and weights based on the number of incoming/outgoing edges. See Sects. 4.1 and 4.1 for details.
- Built a web application tool to generate new meaningful phishing contents automatically. See Sect. 4.
- Our tool can return the generated email to the knowledge base for increasing the weight of its data segments. High-weighted nodes are probable to be chosen again, but data segments with the lowest weight are gradually removed from the knowledge base. See Sect. 4.1.
- Conducted three practical experiments on uninformed members of our community to show generated emails are meaningful.
- We also have shown that spear phishing attacks have different severities. For example, the spear phishing impersonating a person of authority made more people fall into the trap. The tests show which parts of the email are more luring and what the result will be if emails are carefully-crafted. Refer to Sects. 5 and 6 for details.

In the rest of the paper, Sect. 2 is dedicated to the related works and comparison with existing tools. We analyzed phishing emails in Sects. 3 and 7 has been devoted to the conclusion.

2   Related Works

2.1   Phishing Email Generation

Generating phishing attacks is a novel idea to test anti-phishing tools for recognizing their flaws and weak points. This framework [11] works as a Fuzzer to find the weak points of anti-phishing tools. This method creates phishing emails dynamically and semantically consistent throughout the email using generative grammars. At first, the language had 30 rules with assigned weights. The weights are dynamically changing. For instance, if a rule can bypass the filters, its weight would increase and vice versa. Based on the experiment, the click-through rate is 9% in their framework, and in the manual model, the success rate is 8.5% showing the power of their method compared to the manual one. Palka et al. [12] have improved [11] by adding N-Gram Analysis to the previous framework. Their original idea was avoiding repetition in e-mails for exercises using n-grams, and the same approach works for intelligent fuzzing. Also, it recognizes which parts of the rules (emails have different elements in their content like greeting, signature, resolve, problem, etc.) can cause filtering. After four rounds of testing over the production environment and trained environment, their generator was able to bypass all detection filters and get all 100 e-mails into the inbox. [12] made an effort to generate phishing email, however, they only considered 30 rules in Context-free grammar. Each rule is a sentence, so making different types of phishing email using only 30 rules is not possible. Hence, we still face the issue of generating meaningful phishing emails with various topics automatically on a larger scale and in our proposed framework, we tried to overcome this issue.

2.2 Phishing Awareness Training and Tools

There is plenty of research that has been done in phishing awareness training. [4] conducted some phishing tests to assess the failure/success level regarding different criteria such as phishing attack type, class of students(victims), and exercise version. In [6], the authors analyzed previous phishing emails from 2008 to 2017 to show different principles of persuasion in luring victims. Through content analysis, together with the sample characterization in terms of visual elements and targeted content they revealed that principles of persuasion in phishing emails were 'Authority', 'Strong Effect', 'Integrity' and 'Reciprocation'.

Six available open source or free products exist in the market to simulate phishing attacks based on some fixed and predesigned email templates. These tools Gophish [7], Phishing Frenzy [13], King Phisher [8], SpeedPhish Framework [18], Social-Engineer Toolkit (SET)[17], SpearPhisherBETA [3] and two commercial tools such as Phishsim [16] and Lucy [9] mostly help in technical parts such as sending over SMTP server, campaign management, scheduling, giving statistical reports, etc. For instance, Social Engineering Toolkit [17] helps to conduct spear phishing attacks by email spoofing or name spoofing. These tools have a lack of phishing email scenarios, and they only have a limited number of email samples. In our framework, we try to fill this gap by generating new phishing emails for various phishing scenarios automatically (Table 1).

3   Generating Phishing Email

Phishing emails basically impersonate a company with an expected topic from that company, for instance, a phishing email from the Paypal company with the *To update the account information in a limited amount of time* topic. Our main purpose is to generate new phishing email content *automatically* if the user specifies a topic, a victim company, and an attack type.

The idea is to generate variable parts of the email and inject them into the fixed segments of the email. First and foremost, we analyze email structure to know what parts of an email are variable and should be generated automatically. Variable parts will change if the attack type, the company type, and the topic change.

3.1   Phishing Email Structure

We inspect header, body, and attachments of emails with phishing perspective in the following parts.

Email Body

Content. We analyzed many phishing emails. They generally derive from the following meaningful fragments: Subject, Greeting, Problem, Solution, Signature, Apology, and Note. In a phishing attack after greeting, the usual behavior is that first phishers start describing a **problem** such as "Someone is trying to get

Table 1. Comparison table

Phishing awareness tools	Automatically generating phishing email contents	Reporting	Campaign management and scheduling	Email sender module	Cross platform
Gophish [7]	No	Yes	Yes	Yes	Yes (Web App)
Phishing Frenzy [13]	No	Yes	Yes	Yes	No (Linux-based)
King Phisher [8]	No	Yes	Yes	Yes	No (Linux-based)
SpeedPhish Framework [18]	No	No	No	Yes	No (Console Application-Linux)
Social Engineer Toolkit (SET) [17]	No	No	No	Yes	No (Console Application-Linux)
SpearPhisher BETA [3]	No	No	No	Yes	No (Windows-based)
SecurityIQ PhishSim [16]	No	Yes	Yes	Yes	Yes
LUCY [9]	No	Yes	Yes	Yes	No (Debian-based)
Our Tool	**Yes**	Yes	Yes	Yes (Integrated with existing tools)	Yes (Web App)

access to your account, so we suspended it.". Then they provide a **solution** to resolve the problem, e.g., "To get access your account, click the link and confirm your information.". Finally, there is a link indicator, e.g., "Click Here!". There are also other data fragments such as **Greeting**, **Signature**, **Apology**, and **Note** (The note contains extra information about the companies at the bottom of the email.).

Fig. 1. Information Fragments in a phishing email

Links. Phishing emails typically contain a URL which is directing users to a fake website, or the URL is a drive-by-download link compel people to download a file.

Logo and Email Template. Each company has a specific email template or email appearance. This template can be an HTML page which is also containing the logo of the company. These are the fixed graphical parts that we already make them for any existing company in the framework (Fig. 1).

Attachment. The attachment itself is not a variable object in our process of generating the email. However, if an email has an attachment, the tool should create sentences indicating there is an attachment.

Header. We analyze the header to conduct phishing experiments. To bypass the phishing filters, we have to manipulate some fields in the header such as From, Return-path, and Sender. These headers are standard headers based on RFC822 [15], RFC1036 [14]. Besides that, for impersonation, we may do name spoofing or email spoofing to pretend that the email is coming from a genuine person or company.

3.2   Analysis of Attack Type, Company Type, and Topic

Each phishing email impersonates a company and has a specific topic and attack type. These three features play the input roles to generate new phishing email in the framework. For instance, if an attack type is through a link, it is necessary to have statements such as "clicking on the links." Otherwise, it requires other indicators regarding the attack type. Requiring company type, company name, and the topic has similar reasons which we describe in the following subsections.

Company Type. Phishing attacks with the same or similar industry type mostly have similar ideas to fool people. Hence, considering "Company Type" as an entity in our framework helps to generate related content. According to the APWG report in [2], there are about eight organization types affected by the phishing attack. The most targeted organizations are Payment, Webmail, and Financial Institutions.

Topics/Battery. Phishing emails have different topics, but they follow similar scenarios that targeted companies mostly use in their emails. For example, people receive lots of phishing attacks impersonating PayPal company every day. Phishers use the subjects which are common in the emails sent from PayPal company to its customers. During the data gathering phase, few topics have been gathered and assigned to each company. For instance, Facebook has some general topics such as Notification Email, Security Problem, Changing Password, Account Updating, etc. General topics are like a semantic tag helping to find the best match for other fragments of the email such as subject, problem, and solution.

Attack Type. Phishing attacks may contain a hyperlink pointing to a fake website. The other ways to give credentials away are through Reply to the email or Data entry via an embedded form in the body of the email. Moreover, Drive-by Download is a method forcing victims to download a malicious file. The last type is through an email attachment which is mostly occurring in spear phishing emails with an infectious file such as invoices in PDF formats.

1-Link 2-Data entry 3-Reply 4-Drive-by download 5-File attachment

4 Algorithms, Design and Implementation

4.1 System Overview

As shown in Fig. 2, the proposed tool has five main modules forming a cycle. The first step is Email-Fragmentation. After analyzing the phishing email dataset, all data fragments of 300 emails from 20 companies are stored in the knowledge base. The second step is to generate phishing emails, based on the constructed knowledge base. With specifying company name, attack type, and selected topic, the framework calculates the nodes' weights regarding the score function. After selecting the nodes with the highest weight, they are combined and put into the fixed parts of the email which are already defined.

Any generated email can be added to the knowledge base again as a new phishing email. However, it can be revised by the administrator if it has any semantic or syntactic errors in the content. Besides, for generating new emails based on newer data, the old and depreciated data are deleted from the database. As a result, self-adaptation is an essential feature of this tool helping knowledge base keep data fresh through removing old data and maintaining important fragments at the top of the list.

Fig. 2. System overview

Email Fragmentation. "Anti-phishing Working Group (APWG) is the international coalition unifying the global response to cybercrime across industry, government and law-enforcement sectors and NGO communities." [2]. It provides a real and organized data resource for occurring phishing emails. For our purpose, we analyzed more than one thousand phishing emails which occurred during 2017–2018 and extracted the unique phishing email samples manually. Finally, we obtained 300 phishing emails of 20 companies from 10 different company types with various unique topics and contents. Data fragments of each email are inserted as a node into the knowledge base with a tag name, i.e., if it is a problem fragment, it is stored as a problem node. For instance, in Fig. 3, the value of the problem node is "we have sent you this email because we have strong reason your account has been compromised." After inserting the node itself, the relations with other nodes such as topic, organization, and attack type nodes are made. Here this phishing attack belongs to the Amazon company, the attack type is through a link, and the general topic is "Limiting account access".

Knowledge Base Design. All extracted fragments of data are inserted into a knowledge base. The knowledge base is a NoSQL graph database which is a Directed Acyclic Graph to store data. NoSQL databases provide many-to-many relations, tree-like structure, many nullable fields, etc. If we meet such conditions, it is better to use NoSQL Database Models [19].

In this framework, the relationships between data fragments or nodes matter more than the individual nodes themselves. Hence, we need a database model in which data relationships are stored as a first-class entity. Also in comparison to relational databases, for highly-connected data, we require graph traversal or multiple expensive joins and search string queries. Vicknair et al. [19] has proved that graph databases do perform much better in these cases. As a result, we come up with a graph database perspective.

One of the most popular frameworks for implementing graph database is NEO4J [10], and its query language is Cypher. In Fig. 3, each email with its data

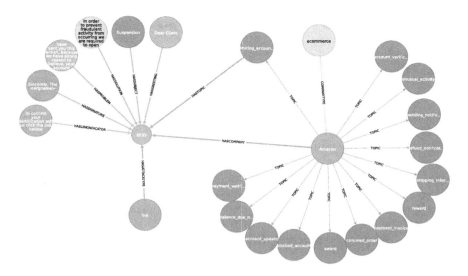

Fig. 3. Data fragments of a sample email in a graph database schema

fragments is inserted into the knowledge base. It also includes the relationships between attack type node which is "link" here, company and topic nodes. Also, each company connects to all its potential topic nodes and its company type node. An important point here is that there are no two nodes with the same value, i.e., while adding a new data fragment, no node is created if the data fragment exists. Instead, we make a relationship with the existing node containing the data fragment.

Generation Algorithms. First, we need to know which company this email belongs to, what the topic and the type of attack are. These are the inputs of our framework. Then, the framework should query the knowledge base and find the most related data fragments (signature, greeting, problem, solution, etc.) to the inputs. After that, we put all the selected fragments together to generate a new email.

The basic idea to select data fragments is based on a score function. The higher the computed score for a node, the more probable it is to be selected. For instance, there may be 1000 signatures in the knowledge base, but only one of which is suitable to be a signature of the new phishing email.

Generating Signature and Greeting Data Fragments. Each company usually has its specific signature and greeting style. So for selecting the best signature/greeting data fragment among all existing ones, we use "Company Name" and "Company Type" for computing the score of all signatures/greetings. Signature statements are selected based on the Algorithm 1. We have provided the pseudo code for finding *Signature* here which can be used for finding *Greeting* as well. The naive idea is that the most frequent data fragment in emails is the winner.

In Algorithm 1, lines 3 and 4 are used to find the nodes with the company's name and type. The lines 5 to 15 traverse all signatures nodes. In each iteration, it has a current signature. Then, line 7 counts the number of emails connected to the current signature node, and the company node. For instance, to find a suitable signature for the Amazon company, we count the emails connected to both Amazon company and the current signature node in each iteration. After that, line 8 counts the number of emails connected to the current signature and only connected to the company type node, i.e., in Amazon example, we count the emails used the current signature and belong to E-commerce company type, but do not belong to the Amazon company. For computing the score, each of C_1 and C_2 has a weight. These weights are not static and can be changed during evolving of the knowledge base. Finally from lines 13 to 16, if the score is higher than the maximum score, we will keep the signature. Otherwise, we discard it.

Algorithm 1. Algorithm to find the best Signature

Require: Knowledge base(KB), CompanyName, CompanyType
Ensure: Returns Signature
1: $node_{highestScore} \leftarrow Null$
2: $Maxscore \leftarrow 0$
3: $CN \leftarrow Node(CompanyName)$
4: $CT \leftarrow Node(CompanyType)$
5: **while** Traverse all signature nodes in KB **do**
6:    $SN \leftarrow SignatureNode$
7:    $C1 \leftarrow Count$(Email Nodes connected to SN and CN)
8:    $C2 \leftarrow Count$(Email Nodes connected to SN and CT(indirectly) and not connected to CN)
9:    $Score_{SN} \leftarrow weight_1 \times C1 + weight_2 \times C2 + \dfrac{1}{usageScore_{SN}}$
10:    **if** $Score_{SN} \geq Maxscore$ **then**
11:       $Maxscore \leftarrow Score_{SN}$
12:       $node_{highestScore} \leftarrow SN$
13:    **end if**
14: **end while**
15: **return** $node_{highestScore}$

Generating Subject, Problem, and Solution Data Fragments. For finding the best choice for the problem, solution, and the subject, the basic idea is similar to the previous part. Besides "Company" and "Company Type" the other parameter is "Topic" which helps to select a more related problem, solution, and subject. So in Algorithm 2, line 6 only traverses the nodes connected to the intended topic. In addition to line 8 and 9 existed in Algorithm 1, we add line 10 to Algorithm 2 to consider the count of emails only has the intended topic with a different company name and company type. We have provided the pseudo code for finding the best subject here. However, it works for finding the best solution and problem data fragments as well. After the fragments generated, because proper names like company names or people's name had been replaced by a general tag like <name> during the insertion step, system administrators are supposed to manipulate these parts based on their preferences.

Algorithm 2. Algorithm to find the best Subject

Require: KB, Topic, CompanyName, CompanyType
Ensure: Returns the best choice Subject
1: $node_{highestScore} \leftarrow Null$
2: $Maxscore \leftarrow 0$
3: $CN \leftarrow Node(CompanyName)$
4: $CT \leftarrow Node(CompanyType)$
5: $T \leftarrow Node(Topic)$
6: **while** Traverse all subject nodes connected to T node in KB **do**
7:   $SN \leftarrow SubjectNode$
8:   $C1 \leftarrow Count$(Email Nodes connected to SN and CN)
9:   $C2 \leftarrow Count$(Email Nodes connected to SN and CT(indirectly) and not connected to CN)
10: $C3 \leftarrow Count$(Email Nodes connected to a different CT, and a different CN)
11: $Score_{SN} \leftarrow weight_1 \times c1 + weight_2 \times c2 + weight_3 \times c3 + \dfrac{1}{usageScore_{SN}}$
12: **if** $Score_{SN} \geq Maxscore$ **then**
13:     $Maxscore \leftarrow Score_{SN}$
14:     $node_{highestScore} \leftarrow SN$
15: **end if**
16: **end while**
17: **return** $node_{highestScore}$

Self-adaptation and Back to Knowledge Base. The administrator can edit or refine the newly generated email. The system is like a cycle into which all generated email can be entered again. We can add all fragments of the new email into the knowledge base, especially once it is successful in bypassing the filters and trapping the victims.

Because the data fragment already exists in the database, only an edge goes to the existing node containing that fragment. As a result, the degree of the node is getting higher, and it becomes more critical and more likely to be chosen in the future again. However, we assign a usage score to each node that every time a data fragment is generated, it will increase. Usage score helps to avoid starving, and it allows the other suitable and newer fragments to be selected. After a while, we can remove the data with the lowest weights. Hence, the usage score not only keeps the knowledge base fresh, but it also keeps its size small and efficient.

(a) Needed Fields to Generate a New Email   (b) A sample of generated email

Fig. 4. Dashboard pages

Phishing Web Application. We have implemented a web application tool for our framework. It has an insertion page for entering phishing attacks to the knowledge base. The generation page as shown in Fig. 4a gets the attack type, company, company type, and the topic as inputs. Then it can generate the phishing email shown in Fig. 4b. The generated email has been put in a text area which is editable by the admin. The email can be revised and returned to the system again.

5   Experiment Setup

The purpose of our idea in this work is to generate contents of phishing emails in awareness tools automatically. We have designed a three-round experiment to evaluate the effect of the contents on our targets. There are three factors we assessed in these experiments:

1. **Meaningful Content:** Generated contents should be meaningful and concrete. Being concrete means all generated fragments have to make sense when combined in creating a new email.
2. **Opening Rate:** By opening an email, the probability of clicking on the link or downloading the attachment increases. Previously by opening an email, some scripts could have executed. Now email software (webmail or desktop) prevents any Javascript codes from executing. Some email clients no longer load the images by default or can be configured to do so.
3. **Click Through Rate:** It shows the rate of clicking on the link/attachment in phishing emails. Once people click on the link in an email, they will be directed to a survey page shown in Fig. 5a. They are asked to answer some questions such as whether email contents were meaningful or not.

These experiments were part of the awareness program in the institute which allowed us to send emails to our members to identify the readiness to deal with the phishing contents. In all rounds, the targets were not aware of the experiments. The duration between the experiments was roughly a month, so people were less potential to be biased. And results show that they still have got manipulated by the emails in each round. The number of targets increased after round 1 to achieve a more reliable result.

To deal with the stress level of the targets, first, the phishing topics were chosen such that to be less stressful, e.g., Sharing a file. Second, the victims immediately got informed of the experiment on the landing page. Also, all retrieved information was kept anonymously.

5.1   Experiment Design - First Round

We carried out an experiment with ten members of our research team. The generated email in Fig. 5b had the following characteristics:

1. **Email Spoofing:** The email was coming from a Google drive of a **person of authority** sharing a file, and the domain of the sender's email address was google.com.

(a) Landing page which is a survey in the experiments.   (b) Generated Phishing Email

Fig. 5. Experiment pages

2. **Spear phishing:** In spear phishing, attackers mostly apply social engineering to be more successful in attacking. So we added the recipient's name and the file name into the email to be more convincing.
3. **Script:** A hidden image was added to track the sent emails. However, this is not promising if the users configure their email client not to open the image automatically. So all statistics about opening the emails is probably more than what has been reported. Moreover, also once a link was clicked, it sent a request to our server, so we were able to gather who clicked on the link.
   - **Email is opened or not?**
     <img src="http://domain.com/image?email=..." style="visibility:hidden">
   - **Link is clicked or not?**
     <a href="http://domain.com/index?email=...">

To spoof the email addresses on Google domain, we used a third party service[1] that could relay emails successfully toward the account holders' inboxes without being spammed.

5.2   Experiment Design - Second and Third Round

In the second and third rounds, our first goal is to assess previous criteria with more victims and new phishing attack scenarios. So we targeted 35 people who are all experts or familiar with security.

Spear phishing inherently targets specific groups of people. However, it can possess a different severity level. As a second goal, we conducted a two-round experiment with different severities. Unlike the previous experiment, using third-party services for email spoofing failed. Spoofing email address of the specific owners was very challenging. We had to find a vulnerability and exploit it to pass the filters and arrive in the inbox without being spammed.

The severe spear phishing specifications (round 2):

---

[1] https://emkei.cz/.

1. We applied email address spoofing attack and impersonated a **person of authority** (Director).
2. The content was an invitation email to an event.
3. Used the attachment attack type. It can be an infectious file in a real attack.
4. Inserted a hidden image into the email to track whether it was opened or not.

Less severe spear phishing specifications (round 3):

1. We applied email address spoofing attack and impersonated a **less important sender** which was the *university gym*.
2. The content was a general announcement to all.
3. Embedded a fake obfuscated link into the email.
4. Inserted a hidden image into the email to track whether it was opened or not.

6   Results

6.1   First Round

The result of the first experiment has been shown in the following Fig. 6 and Table 2 showing the answers of the victims. 9 out of 10 people have opened the email. All people confirmed the content was meaningful to them. 6 out of 9 people who opened the email clicked on the link. 2 out of 3 people detected the phishing email stated that they could detect by noticing to the URL. From those people who could not detect the phishing email, 2 of them claimed that the header was fooling. One person stated the content was deceptive. The others did not mention any reasons. The 10th person had got the email but ignored it with no reason. In this round after the experiment, we asked all targeted people to complete the survey, so people who could detect the phishing email and did not click on the link also stated the reason for detection in the survey.

6.2   Second Round

For sending the emails, we used SMTP2Go[2] as a reputable service to avoid spamming. It also can report that all sent emails were delivered successfully. In the second experiment which was more severe, as shown in the Fig. 6, 3 out of 35 people ignored the email, and 13 victims out of 32 people who opened the email also opened the attachment (40.62%). Because we cannot track opening of attachments, what we have reported in this paper is based on those people who completed our survey. 13 people completed the survey and indicated that they opened the attachment. It is plausible that the number of people who opened the attachment might have been more than 13. These 13 people stated in the survey Table 3 that the content of the email was meaningful to them. In the survey Table 3, five people chose "sender name" as a deceptive part, 3 of them mentioned "sender email address", 3 of them chose the content/subject, and 2 of them did not mention any reasons. So totally, 8 out of 13 people have fallen

---

[2] https://www.smtp2go.com/.

Table 2. First experiment survey

Did you detect it?	Meaningful content	Deceptive part	Reason of detecion
Yes	Yes	–	Content
Yes	Yes	–	URL
Yes	Yes	–	URL
No	Yes	Unknown	–
No	Yes	Header	–
No	Yes	Unknown	–
No	Yes	Content	–
No	Yes	Header	–
No	Yes	Unknown	–

Table 3. Second experiment survey

Meaningful content	Deceptive part
Yes	Sender name
Yes	Content/subject
Yes	Sender email address
Yes	Content/subject
Yes	Sender name
Yes	Sender email address
Yes	Sender email address
Yes	Sender name
Yes	Sender name
Yes	Unknwon
Yes	Sender name
Yes	Unknown
Yes	Content/subject

into the trap because of the sender's name and email address. In this and the next round, we did not ask all targeted people to complete the survey after the experiment. What is reported is based on the responses of who fell into the trap and completed the survey. So the third column which is the reason for detection has been remained empty and deleted from Table 3.

6.3 Third Round

In comparison with the second round, the third round was less intense. It included the content with a more general topic, and also emails came from a person of less authority. As shown in Fig. 6, 13 out of 35 people opened the email, and 8 victims out of 13 people who opened the email also clicked on the link (61.53%). Only 2 people completed the survey and stated that the content of the email was meaningful. One of them explained that the reason for being fooled was his curiosity about the content, and the other person did not mention any reason.

6.4 Discussion

Around 40% to 60% of people fell into the attack when they received the spear phishing. In the second experiment, because the spear phishing was more severe and coming from a person of authority, only three people ignored it. While in the third experiment with less intensity 23 people had ignored the email. Hence we can conclude that once more people open the email, the probability of click-through rate would increase.

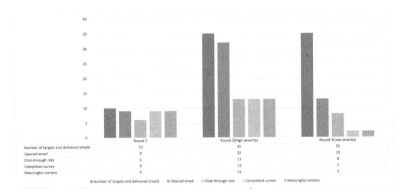

Fig. 6. Comparison of three experiments

In the second experiment, 8 out of 13 people who completed the survey have stated that the reason for not detecting was the spoofed sender name and the spoofed email address. In the third experiment, from 8 people who completed the survey, only one person stated that the reason for opening the link was his curiosity about the email's subject. The others did not mention any reason for opening the email/clicking on the link. In the first round with fewer people, 90% opened the email, and 60% of people were fooled by the email. Again in the second experiment with more victims but the same severity, 91.42% opened the email, and around 37% could not recognize the email is coming from an untrusted source. The results of both experiments which were severe spear phishing are similar, especially in attracting people to open the emails. About 90% of people in both experiments opened the email.

In these three rounds on average, 72.85% of victims had opened the emails, the click-through rate was 54.05% among who opened the emails, and all people who completed the survey stated that the content was meaningful.

7   Conclusion

In this paper, to empower the Phishing Awareness Tools, we built a system to generate automatically meaningful phishing emails based on the different topics, company types and the attack types using a graph database. We analyzed hundreds of the latest phishing emails in APWG dataset. Finally, we inserted 300 emails' data fragments (from 20 different companies with different topics) into the knowledge base. In this tool, we can return the generated email to the knowledge base for increasing the weight of its data fragments. High-weighted nodes are probable to be chosen again, but data segments with the lowest weights are gradually removed from the knowledge base. After generating phishing emails, we conducted three rounds of phishing campaigns to uninformed members of the institute. We assessed these factors: being meaningful content, click-through rate, and the opened by recipient percentage. On average, 72.85% of victims had opened the emails, the click-through rate was 54.05% among who opened the emails, and all people who completed the survey stated that the content was meaningful. For future work, we can expand our email generation to be more intelligent by applying dynamic approaches such as machine learning algorithms.

Acknowledgement. The authors generously acknowledge the funding from the Atlantic Canada Opportunity Agency (ACOA) through the Atlantic Innovation Fund (AIF) and through grant from the National Science and Engineering Research Council of Canada (NSERC) to Dr. Ghorbani.

References

1. apwg: Apwg report. https://www.antiphishing.org/resources/apwg-reports/. Accessed 01 April 2019
2. APWG: Apwg report q4 (2017). https://docs.apwg.org//reports/apwg_trends_report_q4_2017.pdf. Accessed 01 April 2019
3. Beta, S.: Spearphisher beta. https://www.trustedsec.com/2013/09/introducing-spearphisher-simple-phishing-email-generation-tool/. Accessed 01 April 2019
4. Dodge Jr., R.C., Carver, C., Ferguson, A.J.: Phishing for user security awareness. Comput. Secur. **26**(1), 73–80 (2007)
5. Downs, J.S., Holbrook, M.B., Cranor, L.F.: Decision strategies and susceptibility to phishing. In: Proceedings of the Second Symposium on Usable Privacy and Security, pp. 79–90. ACM (2006)
6. Ferreira, A., Teles, S.: Persuasion: how phishing emails can influence users and bypass security measures. Int. J. Hum Comput Stud. **125**, 19–31 (2019)
7. Gophish: Gophish. https://getgophish.com/. Accessed 01 April 2019
8. kingphisher: Knuth: computers and typesetting. https://king-phisher.readthdocs.io/en/latest/. Accessed 01 April 2019
9. LUCY: Lucy. https://www.lucysecurity.com/en/. Accessed 01 April 2019
10. neo4j: Why graph databases? https://neo4j.com/why-graph-databases/. Accessed 01 April 2019
11. Palka, S., McCoy, D.: Dynamic phishing content using generative grammars. In: 2015 IEEE Eighth International Conference on Software Testing, Verification and Validation Workshops (ICSTW), pp. 1–8. IEEE (2015)
12. Palka, S., McCoy, D.: Fuzzing e-mail filters with generative grammars and n-gram analysis. In: WOOT (2015)
13. phishingfrenzy: phishingfrenzy. https://www.phishingfrenzy.com/. Accessed 01 April 2019
14. RFC: Rfc1036. https://tools.ietf.org/html/rfc1036. Accessed 01 April 2019
15. RFC: Rfc822. https://tools.ietf.org/html/rfc822. Accessed 01 April 2019
16. SecurityIQ: Securityiq phishsim. https://www.infosecinstitute.com/securityiq/phishing/. Accessed 01 April 2019
17. (SET), S.E.T.: Social-engineer toolkit (set). https://www.trustedsec.com/2013/09/introducing-spearphisher-simple-phishing-email-generation-tool/. Accessed 01 April 2019
18. SPF: Speedphish framework (spf). https://github.com/tatanus/SPF. Accessed 01 April 2019
19. Vicknair, C., Macias, M., Zhao, Z., Nan, X., Chen, Y., Wilkins, D.: A comparison of a graph database and a relational database: a data provenance perspective. In: Proceedings of the 48th Annual Southeast Regional Conference, p. 42. ACM (2010)

Short Paper II

Evaluating Intrusion Sensitivity Allocation with Support Vector Machine for Collaborative Intrusion Detection

Wenjuan Li[1], Weizhi Meng[2(✉)], and Lam For Kwok[1]

[1] Department of Computer Science,
City University of Hong Kong, Hong Kong, China
[2] Department of Applied Mathematics and Computer Science,
Technical University of Denmark, Lyngby, Denmark
weme@dtu.dk

Abstract. The aim of collaborative intrusion detection networks (CIDNs) is to provide better detection performance over a single IDS, through allowing IDS nodes to exchange data or information with each other. Nevertheless, CIDNs may be vulnerable to insider attacks, and there is a great need for deploying appropriate trust management schemes to protect CIDNs in practice. In this work, we advocate the effectiveness of intrusion sensitivity-based trust management model and describe an engineering way to automatically allocate the sensitivity values by using a support vector machine (SVM) classifier. To explore the allocation performance, we compare our classifier with several traditional supervised algorithms in the evaluation. We further investigate the performance of our enhanced trust management scheme in a real network environment under adversarial scenarios, and the experimental results indicate that our approach can be more effective in detecting insider attacks as compared with similar approaches.

Keywords: Collaborative intrusion detection · Intrusion sensitivity · Supervised learning · Trust management · Insider threat

1 Introduction

To protect various computer or network assets, intrusion detection systems (IDSs) are one of the most commonly adopted solutions in practice [19]. As intrusions are becoming more complicated, collaborative intrusion detection networks (CIDNs) are proposed to enhance the detection performance of a single IDS [22,23]. A CIDN allows various IDS nodes to exchange data and learn with each other.

However, CIDNs may be vulnerable to insider attacks due to the distributed architecture, in which an intruder can control an internal node within the network. For instance, if an attack successfully hijack one internal node, then more attacks can be launched via this compromised node. Insider threat can greatly

© Springer Nature Switzerland AG 2019
S.-H. Heng and J. Lopez (Eds.): ISPEC 2019, LNCS 11879, pp. 453–463, 2019.
https://doi.org/10.1007/978-3-030-34339-2_26

degrade the security of collaborative systems and networks. Therefore, it is very important to design appropriate trust management schemes to help safeguard CIDNs.

Motivations. In real scenarios, it is found that IDS nodes may have different detection capability regarding one particular attack. This may be caused by different configuration and settings, i.e., one node has more detection rules than the other. In the previous work [8], the authors defined a term called *intrusion sensitivity* to describe the capability of identifying specific attacks. The use of *intrusion sensitivity* is expected to enhance the detection performance by highlighting the impact of expert nodes. To the best of our knowledge, there are few studies focusing on exploring the influence of intrusion sensitivity in practice. In [10], their results indicated that the application of intrusion sensitivity can provide more efficient detection of pollution attacks. However, how to assign the sensitivity values in an automatic way still remains a challenging issue.

Contributions. Previous work [11] showed that using supervised learning algorithms is a good way to help intelligently allocate the sensitivity values, while it requires at least 60 labeled alarms to achieve good accuracy. Motivated by this observation, in this article, we target on this challenge and enhance the intrusion sensitivity-based trust management scheme by leveraging a support vector machine (SVM) classifier to reduce the required labeled alarms for allocating sensitivity values. Further, we provide an engineering way of allocating the sensitivity based on SVM in a real scenario. The contributions can be summarized as follows.

- We improve the intrusion sensitivity-based trust management scheme in [11] by using a support vector machine (SVM) classifier to allocate sensitivity values. Our experimental results indicate that our approach can reduce the required number of labeled alarms, as compared with several traditional algorithms like decision tree and KNN.
- We introduce an engineering way of implementing both the allocation of sensitivity values and the derivation of satisfaction level for the received feedback for CIDNs. In practice, expert knowledge is very helpful and important to ensure the quality of allocation.
- We collaborate with an IT organization and evaluate the performance of our enhanced trust management scheme in a real network environment under adversarial scenarios, like newcomer and betrayal attack. Our experimental results indicate that our approach can achieve better performance in identifying untruthful insider nodes as compared with similar approaches.

The reminder of this article is structured as follows. We review related studies on distributed and collaborative intrusion detection in Sect. 2. Section 3 introduces the basic architecture of intrusion sensitivity-based trust management scheme for CIDNs, and presents an engineering way of allocating sensitivity values using the SVM classifier. In Sect. 4, we present and analyze evaluation results. Section 5 concludes our work.

2   Related Work

Distributed or collaborative intrusion detection schemes are usually vulnerable to insider attacks (or internal attacks). To construct an effective trust management scheme is a necessary and important solution. For this purpose, some trust management models have been designed in the literature. An Overlay IDS was proposed by Duma *et al.* [3], aiming to defend distributed intrusion detection against insider attacks. The major limitation is that it could not be effective in detecting malicious nodes that have good reputation before in a fast manner. This is because all nodes have the same impact regardless of the behavior changes.

Fung *et al.* [4] then introduced a kind of challenge-based CIDN, which the reputation was measured by identifying the satisfaction levels between the received feedback and the expected answers. They also enhanced the detection using a forgetting factor, which highlights the recent behavior of a node. Then, Dirichlet-based trust model [5] was proposed to help improve the trust evaluation and the balance between detection and false rates. Several other related studies on collaborative intrusion detection can be referred to [2, 6, 7, 14, 16, 20, 22].

Discussion. CIDNs have been gradually adopted by many organizations, but it is very important to protect the security of these mechanisms against insider threat. Most existing research provided many approaches to improve the detection like [6], whereas they did not consider different detection capability of IDS nodes in practice.

In the previous work [8], the authors firstly defined a notion of *intrusion sensitivity* by noticing the different levels of detection sensitivity among IDS nodes. This term aims to help enhance the trust computation and alarm aggregation by highlighting the influence of expert nodes, those who have stronger detection accuracy regarding certain attacks. However, allocating the value manually is time-consuming and error-prone with the increasing size of nodes. How to automatically allocate the values remains a challenging issue.

For this issue, relevant work [11] had shown that supervised learning can help allocate sensitivity values in an automatic way. Motivated by this observation, in this work, we target on this issue and enhance the intrusion sensitivity-based trust management model by using an SVM classifier. This classifier can achieve the same accuracy by reducing the required labeled alarms. We also provide an engineering way of implementing the value allocation and investigate the performance in a real network environment. Our experimental results demonstrate that our approach can help defend CIDNs against insider attacks more effectively than similar approaches.

3   Intrusion Sensitivity-Based Trust Management Model for CIDNs

This section introduces the basic architecture of CIDNs like components and interaction, and then describe how to use the SVM classifier to allocate sensitivity values for IDS nodes.

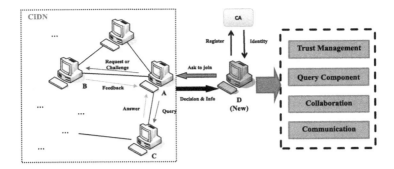

Fig. 1. The CIDN architecture including exchanged messages and major components.

3.1 CIDN Architecture

Figure 1 depicts the architecture of CIDNs like exchanged messages and major components, i.e., *trust management component, query component, collaboration component* and *communication component*.

Node Registration. Such kind of CIDN allows each node selecting its partner nodes based on its own rules or policies, and recording them in a list. If a node wants to join, the first step is to obtain an identity from a certificate authority (CA). As shown in Fig. 1, a new node D should deliver a joining request to CIDN nodes, say node A. Based on the predefined policies, node A can make a decision whether to accept node D or not.

Trust Management Component. The main task of this component is to manage trust computation. In this work, we adopted the feedback-based trust (or challenge-based trust) [4], in which the reputation is measured by identifying the satisfaction level regarding the received feedback.

Collaboration Component. This component handles the communication among different nodes. There are three types of messages can be used in a challenge-based CIDN, such as *normal requests, challenges* and *feedback*. More details can refer to previous work [11].

Query Component. This component is used to measure the intrusion sensitivity of other nodes. A query containing a set of alarms can be sent to the target node. Based on the feedback, it can decide the sensitivity level accordingly.

Communication Component. This component mainly handles the connection with other nodes, i.e., building and maintaining a P2P connection among IDS nodes.

3.2 Trust Computation and Evaluation

To measure the reputation of an IDS node, a *challenge* can be sent to the target node periodically via a random generation process (i.e., the time of sending is random). To facilitate the comparison with similar approaches, in this work, we adopt and update the trust computation based on relevant studies [4,11], as below.

$$T_{value}^{i,j} = w_s \frac{\sum_{k=0}^{n} F_k^j \lambda^{tk}}{\sum_{k=0}^{n} \lambda^{tk}} \qquad (1)$$

where $F_k^j \in [0,1]$ represents the satisfaction level for the received feedback k, n means the total amount of received feedback, λ represents a *forgetting factor* that highlights more weight to the recent response and behavior, w_s is a *significant value*, which can be varied based on the total amount of received feedback. That is, if the number of received feedback is smaller than a value m, then $w_s = \frac{\sum_{k=0}^{n} \lambda^{tk}}{m}$; otherwise we set w_s to 1.

Then, we adopt the following weighted majority approach to derive the reputation of a node j.

$$T_j = \frac{\sum_{T \geq r} T_{value}^{i,j} D_i^j I_s^i}{\sum_{T \geq r} T_{value}^{i,j} D_i^j} \qquad (2)$$

where $T_{value}^{i,j} (\in [0,1])$ means the reputation level of node i according to node j, $D_i^j (\in [0,1])$ indicates the relationship between these two nodes and the in-between hops, r represents a threshold to filter those nodes whose reputation is smaller than the threshold, $I_s^i (\in [0,1])$ indicates the value of intrusion sensitivity of node i.

3.3   Intrusion Sensitivity Allocation in an Engineering Way

Traditionally, research studies often measure the detection capability among various nodes using a normal distribution, but it cannot reflect the real-world applications [4,5]. We advocate that *intrusion sensitivity* provides a metric to evaluate the detection capability of an IDS node in practice.

In the above CIDN architecture, sensitivity values can be derived by sending *queries* to other nodes. However, as human efforts are error-prone and expensive, it is still a big challenge on how to allocate the values in an intelligent and automatic way [8].

Focused on this challenge, in this work, we advocate the use of supervised learning to help allocate the values based on expert knowledge in [11], while we propose to use a multi-class support vector machine (SVM) classifier [12] to enhance the allocation performance. The merits of using such classifier are shown below [1]:

– SVM provides flexibility in selecting the form of the threshold, which does not need to be linear and even not require the same functional form for each data item. This is because its function can operate locally and be non-parametric.
– SVM is robust especially for a small amount of data items. There is no assumption needed about the functional form of the transformation, i.e., human expertise judgement beforehand is not needed.

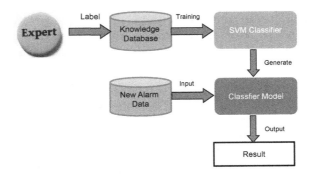

Fig. 2. The allocation of sensitivity values using SVM classifier in an engineering way.

- SVM can provide a unique and robust solution, i.e., a good out-of-sample generalization. In other words, SVM can be still robust even under biased training samples as long as selecting an appropriate generalization grade.

Similar to the previous studies [11], in this work, we also invited three security experts (with more than six years' experience) from the participating organizations (in our evaluation) to help label some alarm items. Figure 2 shows how to allocate the sensitivity values using the SVM classifier and expert knowledge in an engineering way.

4   Evaluation

4.1   Classifier Performance

In this part, we compare the performance of SVM with three commonly used supervised classifiers in allocating the values of intrusion sensitivity, including k-nearest neighbors (KNN), back-propagation neural networks (BPNN) and decision tree (DT).

- *KNN.* This is a kind of instance-based learning, which can classify new instances based on the similarity to the known items. The detailed steps can refer to the previous work [11].
- *BPNN.* This classifier is a kind of supervised classifier that can minimize the error by adjusting the weight values via the process of back propagation. We use the typical BPNN developed in [15], which has three layers like input, output and hidden layer.
- *DT.* This is a popular classifier that can generate a model to predict the label of an item by using a tree-like structure. In the comparison, we employ the algorithm developed in [24].

In this comparison, similar to [11], we investigate different alarm numbers in training like 30, 40, 50 and 60 alarms. We define *intrusion sensitivity* (I_s^i) to be

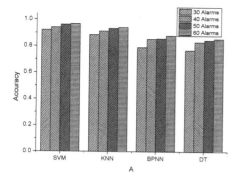

Fig. 3. The classification accuracy among different classifiers.

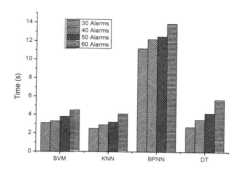

Fig. 4. The time consumption among different classifiers.

ten levels such as expert (1.0), excellent (0.9), very high (0.8), high (0.7), good (0.6), neural (0.5), not good (0.4), low (0.3), very low (0.2), and bad (0.1). In the evaluation, we mainly considered Snort, which is an open-source signature-based IDS [18,21]. Its alarm has three priority levels: high, medium and low.

In particular, we collected 300 labeled alarms that were labeled by security experts. In the phase of training, each classifier was trained with a set of labeled alarms. The process is similar to [11], we trained the classifier with 60 alarms (randomly selected from the database) for labeling 30 new alarms, while we trained the classifier with 120 alarms (randomly selected from the database) for labeling 60 new alarms. We repeated this experiment for ten times (via cross-validation) to avoid some bias. Figures 3 and 4 shows the classification accuracy and time consumption, respectively. The main observations are discussed below:

- *Classification accuracy.* It is found that SVM could reach better classification accuracy than other three classifiers, i.e., it can achieve an accuracy rate of 0.941, 0.961, and 0.966 for 40, 50, and 60 alarms, respectively. In the comparison, our SVM classifier can achieve the same accuracy by reducing the required labeled alarms in the training phase, i.e., SVM can achieve the accuracy of above 0.96 for 50 alarms, while KNN [11] requires 60 alarms for reaching the same accuracy.
- *Time consumption.* Intuitively, inputting more alarms would require more time consumption in both training and classification. It is visible that KNN could normally reach the smallest time consumption among all classifiers, whereas the time consumption of SVM is very close to KNN. There is no significant difference between KNN and SVM.

Our results demonstrate that SVM can achieve the best detection accuracy among all classifiers, and can make a good balance between accuracy and time consumption. It is worth noting that SVM can help reduce the required number of labeled alarms as compared with the results in previous work [11].

Table 1. Some parameter settings in the evaluation.

Parameters	Value	Description
μ_1	15/day	Arrival rate for challenges
μ_2	5/day	Arrival rate for queries
λ	0.9	Forgetting factor
r	0.8	Trust threshold
$T_{dir,initial}$	0.5	Trust value for newcomers
m	10	Lower limit of received feedback
$k1$	5	Satisfaction levels
$k2$	10	Intrusion sensitivity levels

4.2 Evaluation in a Practical Environment

It is found that most existing trust management models have not been studied in a real network. In this part, we therefore aim to evaluate our enhanced trust management scheme in a practical CIDN environment by collaborating with an IT organization.

There are up to 71 nodes in this CIDN environment, and our trust management model was implemented with the help of security administrators from the participating organization due to privacy concerns. In this evaluation, we mainly consider two typical insider attacks like newcomer attack and betrayal attacks, as compared with the performance of DSOM trust model [3] and challenge-based trust model [4]. These two are the most relevant approaches to our work. We adopted the same satisfaction mapping method in [11].

To facilitate the comparison, similar to [11], we adopt that each *challenge* is comprised of 5 alarms ($c = 5$) and each *query* contains 50 alarms ($q = 50$). Some parameters are summarized in Table 1.

Defending Against Newcomer Attack and Betrayal Attack. The type of attack (also called re-entry attack) indicates a situation where a malicious node tries to register as a new user to erase its bad record. By contrast, betrayal attack is a major type of insider attacks, in which a trusted node (with high reputation) turns into a malicious node, i.e., behaving harmfully to the network. In this part, we investigate the performance of our trust management model against both newcomer and betrayal attack.

In practice, cyber-criminals often launch a newcomer attack to leverage the reputation, and then conduct a betrayal attack when the node obtains high reputation. After the trust values become stable in the network, we randomly selected 5 nodes in collaboration with security administrators, to conduct a betrayal attack from the 51st day, by sending malicious packets and false alarm rankings. The results of nodes' reputation under different trust models are shown in Fig. 5 and Fig. 6, respectively. We discuss the main observations as below.

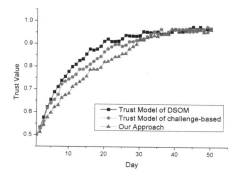
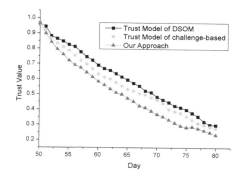

Fig. 5. The trust value of newcomers under different trust models.

Fig. 6. The trust value of malicious nodes under betrayal attack.

- In our network settings, new nodes can become trusted only by increasing its trust values above the threshold of 0.8 (see Table 1); otherwise, it cannot affect the trust evaluation and alarm aggregation process. According to Fig. 5, it is found that the nodes under DSOM and challenge-based trust model could increase their reputation faster than our approach, i.e., our approach requires 4 days and 8 days more in comparison with challenge-based and DSOM model, respectively. This indicates that our approach is relatively less vulnerable to newcomer attack.
- Under betrayal attack, when a node becomes malicious, Fig. 6 shows the trust values under different trust models. It is visible that challenge-based trust model could outperform DSOM model by decreasing the trust value of malicious nodes faster. This is because challenge-based approach employed a forgetting factor. In comparison, our approach could reduce malicious nodes' reputation faster than the other two approaches. This is mainly because our approach applies intrusion sensitivity to emphasize the impact of expert nodes.

Overall, the results demonstrate that our trust management scheme can outperform the other two similar approaches by decreasing the trust values of malicious nodes faster. The main reason is that our approach applies *intrusion sensitivity* to highlight the impact of expert nodes. In this case, our approach is more sensitive to malicious behavior and more robust against insider attacks like betrayal attack. Our observation is also confirmed by the security administrators from the participating organization after repeating the experiments five times.

5   Conclusion

In this work, we advocate the effectiveness of sensitivity-based trust management model and develop an engineering way to automatically allocate the sensitivity values by using a support vector machine (SVM) classifier. In the evaluation, we compare the SVM classifier with three typical supervised classifiers in value allocation, and found that SVM can provide better accuracy and make a better balance between accuracy and time consumption than other classifiers. We further investigate our trust management model in a real network environment by collaborating with an IT organization. Our results demonstrate that our model can reach better detection performance than similar approaches under both newcomer and betrayal attack, by reducing the trust values of malicious nodes faster.

Acknowledgments. This work was partially supported by National Natural Science Foundation of China (No. 61802077).

References

1. Auria, L., Moro, R.A.: Support vector machines (SVM) as a technique for solvency analysis. DIW Berlin Discussion Paper no. 811 (2008)
2. Bao, F., Chen, I.R., Chang, M., Cho, J.H.: Hierarchical trust management for wireless sensor networks and its applications to trust-based routing and intrusion detection. IEEE Trans. Netw. Serv. Manage. **9**(2), 169–183 (2012)
3. Duma, C., Karresand, M., Shahmehri, N., Caronni, G.: A trust-aware, P2P-based overlay for intrusion detection. In: Proceedings of DEXA Workshop, pp. 692–697 (2006)
4. Fung, C.J., Baysal, O., Zhang, J., Aib, I., Boutaba, R.: Trust management for host-based collaborative intrusion detection. In: De Turck, F., Kellerer, W., Kormentzas, G. (eds.) DSOM 2008. LNCS, vol. 5273, pp. 109–122. Springer, Heidelberg (2008). https://doi.org/10.1007/978-3-540-87353-2_9
5. Fung, C.J., Zhang, J., Aib, I., Boutaba, R.: Robust and scalable trust management for collaborative intrusion detection. In: Proceedings of IM, pp. 33–40 (2009)
6. Li, J., Li, R., Kato, J.: Future trust management framework for mobile ad hoc networks. IEEE Commun. Mag. **46**(2), 108–114 (2008)
7. Liu, X., Zhu, P., Zhang, Y., Chen, K.: A collaborative intrusion detection mechanism against false data injection attack in advanced metering infrastructure. IEEE Trans. Smart Grid **6**(5), 2435–2443 (2015)
8. Li, W., Meng, W., Kwok, L.F.: Enhancing trust evaluation using intrusion sensitivity in collaborative intrusion detection networks: feasibility and challenges. In: Proceedings of the 9th International Conference on Computational Intelligence and Security (CIS), pp. 518–522 (2013)
9. Li, W., Meng, W., Kwok, L.-F., Ip, H.H.S.: PMFA: toward passive message fingerprint attacks on challenge-based collaborative intrusion detection networks. In: Chen, J., Piuri, V., Su, C., Yung, M. (eds.) NSS 2016. LNCS, vol. 9955, pp. 433–449. Springer, Cham (2016). https://doi.org/10.1007/978-3-319-46298-1_28
10. Li, W., Meng, W.: Enhancing collaborative intrusion detection networks using intrusion sensitivity in detecting pollution attacks. Inf. Comput. Secur. **24**(3), 265–276 (2016)
11. Li, W., Meng, W., Kwok, L.F., Ip, H.H.S.: Enhancing collaborative intrusion detection networks against insider attacks using supervised intrusion sensitivity-based trust management model. J. Netw. Comput. Appl. **77**, 135–145 (2017)

12. LIBSVM Tools: Multi-label classification. https://www.csie.ntu.edu.tw/~cjlin/libsvmtools/multilabel/
13. Meng, Y., Kwok, L.F.: Adaptive false alarm filter using machine learning in intrusion detection. In: Wang, Y., Li, T. (eds.) Practical Applications of Intelligent Systems. AINSC, vol. 124. Springer, Berlin (2011). https://doi.org/10.1007/978-3-642-25658-5_68
14. Meng, Y., Li, W., Kwok, L.: Evaluation of detecting malicious nodes using bayesian model in wireless intrusion detection. In: Lopez, J., Huang, X., Sandhu, R. (eds.) NSS 2013. LNCS, vol. 7873, pp. 40–53. Springer, Heidelberg (2013). https://doi.org/10.1007/978-3-642-38631-2_4
15. Paola, J.D., Schowengerdt, R.A.: A detailed comparison of backpropagation neural network and maximum-likelihood classifiers for urban land use classification. IEEE Trans. Geosci. Remote Sens. **33**(4), 981–996 (1995)
16. Qin, Z., Jia, Z., Chen, X.: Fuzzy dynamic programming based trusted routing decision in mobile ad hoc networks. In: Proceedings of the 5th IEEE International Symposium on Embedded Computing (SEC), pp. 180–185 (2008)
17. Resnick, P., Kuwabara, K., Zeckhauser, R., Friedman, E.: Reputation systems. Commun. ACM **43**(12), 45–48 (2000)
18. Roesch, M.: Snort: lightweight intrusion detection for networks. In: Proceedings of Usenix Lisa Conference, pp. 229–238 (1999)
19. Scarfone, K., Mell, P.: Guide to intrusion detection and prevention systems (IDPS). NIST Special Publication 800–94, Feburary 2007
20. Shamshirband, S., Anuar, N.B., Kiah, M.L.M., Patel, A.: An appraisal and design of a multi-agent system based cooperative wireless intrusion detection computational intelligence technique. Eng. Appl. Artif. Intell. **26**(9), 2105–2127 (2013)
21. Snort, Homepage. http://www.snort.org/
22. Vasilomanolakis, E., Karuppayah, S., Muhlhauser, M., Fischer, M.: Taxonomy and survey of collaborative intrusion detection. ACM Comput. Surv. **47**(4), 55 (2015)
23. Wu, Y.S., Foo, B., Mei, Y., Bagchi, S.: Collaborative intrusion detection system (CIDS): a framework for accurate and efficient IDS. In: Proceedings of ACSAC, pp. 234–244 (2003)
24. Yuan, Y., Shaw, M.J.: Induction of fuzzy decision trees. Fuzzy Sets Syst. **69**(2), 125–139 (1995)

The (Persistent) Threat of Weak Passwords: Implementation of a Semi-automatic Password-Cracking Algorithm

Chris Pelchen[✉], David Jaeger, Feng Cheng, and Christoph Meinel

Hasso Plattner Institute for Digital Engineering gGmbH, Potsdam, Germany
{chris.pelchen,david.jaeger,feng.cheng,christoph.meinel}@hpi.de

Abstract. Password-based authentication remains the main method of user authentication in computer systems. In case of a leak of the user database, the obfuscated storage of passwords is the last remaining protection of credentials. The strength of a password determines how hard it is to crack a password hash for uncovering the plain text password. Internet users often ignore recommended password guidelines and choose weak passwords that are easy to guess. In addition, service providers do not warn users that their chosen passwords are not secure enough. In this work we present a semi-automatic password cracking algorithm that orders and executes user-chosen password cracking attacks based on their efficiency. With our new approach, we are able to accelerate the cracking of password hashes and to demonstrate that weak passwords are still a serious security risk. The intention of this work is to point out that the usage of weak passwords holds great dangers for both the user and the service provider.

1 Introduction

Cybercriminals take a special interest in obtaining user's credentials, since those credentials gives them access to digital identities. User passwords are usually stored in a hashed form, although the majority of (breached) online services uses weak and fast hash methods. To reveal the password that is obfuscated behind the stored hash, so-called hash cracking attacks are performed. The efficiency of those attacks demonstrate, how predictable passwords chosen by users are. A high crack rate can disclose that people still choose weak and easy to guess passwords for protecting their accounts.

This paper describes a semi-automatic password cracking algorithm which automatically orders and executes user-defined cracking attacks by their efficiency. Section 2 takes a deeper look into password storage, different kinds of hash functions and additional methods for improving the security against cracking attacks. Furthermore, we analyze leaked plain text passwords to investigate how users choose their passwords. In Sect. 3 we explain the implementation and

© Springer Nature Switzerland AG 2019
S.-H. Heng and J. Lopez (Eds.): ISPEC 2019, LNCS 11879, pp. 464–475, 2019.
https://doi.org/10.1007/978-3-030-34339-2_27

working principle of our semi-automatic password cracking algorithm and we describe how to define efficient attack lists. Section 4 compares the efficiency of semi-automatic password cracking against traditional password cracking. Finally, we conclude our work in Sect. 5.

2   Background and Previous Work

2.1   Password Storing

In the course of creating an account for any kind of online service, users are usually asked to specify a password. This password is later used to authenticate the user during the login process. Therefore, passwords have to be stored persistently in a database. According to the National Institute of Standards and Technology, service providers which have to verify memorized secrets should store those secrets in a form that is resistant to offline attacks [2]. To fulfill this requirement, service providers usually use cryptographic hash functions to obfuscate the plain text passwords.

Additionally, so-called *salts* can be used to increase the security of stored passwords. A general requirement for any cryptographic hash function is that the same input value constantly results in the same output value. This leads to the problem that for users with the same password, the same hash value is stored. This means, if a hacker is able to crack the hash for one user, all other users with the same password are also exposed. Salts are used to solve this problem. Those are random strings which are concatenated with the entered password of a user before a hash method is applied. A salt is generated dynamically for every new password. Therefore, a salt value is always stored in the database together with the password hash.

Based on 3093 data breaches we collected, we were able to analyze which types of cryptographic hash functions are most commonly used by service providers. 21% of all platforms that were affected by a data breach stored the passwords in plain text. This means that the attacker had direct access to all credentials immediately after the data was stolen. About 40% of all websites used weak hash methods for password storing. 32% of all affected services used hash methods in combination with salts and only 7% used strong hash methods.

2.2   Password Cracking

The terms "password cracking" and "hash cracking" are synonyms for "password recovery". Since all cryptographic hash functions are by definition one-way functions, the only way to recover a password from its hashed form is to guess a possible password, use then the same hash algorithm that generated the targeted hash value, and compare the hashes to each other. If they are identical, the plain text password was found and the hash was "cracked". Therefore, the efficiency of password cracking is influenced by the choice of possible passwords candidates for that guessing.

The tool called "hashcat" is a popular open-source password recovery tool initially developed by Jens "atom" Steube. This program supports nearly 250 different hashing algorithms and allows to perform 5 different attack types. The current version is 5.1.0. and is released under MIT license. Hashcat is available for Windows, MacOS and Linux systems.

2.3 Password Analysis

For getting a basic understanding of how users choose and generate their passwords, a reasonable first step is to analyze already leaked plain text passwords. Therefore, we created a word list of all plain text passwords from all publicly accessible leaks we collected. This word list contains about 604 million distinct passwords. For a general analysis of these passwords, we have used the "Password Analysis And Cracking Kit".[1]

Distribution of Password Lengths. 78% of all passwords include between 6 and 11 characters. Passwords with 8 characters are most frequently selected (29%). This is also consistent with NIST's password selection guidelines, which state that memorized secrets should contain at least 8 characters [2]. Knowledge about most commonly used password lengths helps to perform efficient length-based password cracking attacks, like brute-force attacks or hashcat's PRINCE attacks.

Distribution of Character Classes. Almost 50% of all passwords represent a combination of lowercase letters and numbers. 20% of all passwords consist solely of lowercase letters and 11% are a simple combination of numbers. 6% of all passwords are made up of a combination of uppercase letters, lowercase letters and numbers. Knowledge about the most frequently used character classes leads to more efficient brute-force attacks and mask attacks. Especially in combination with knowledge about most commonly used password lengths.

Frequently Used Password Masks. Besides frequently used password lengths and character classes, it is also reasonable to take a look at commonly used password masks. A password mask defines the concrete structure of a password. 12% of all passwords can be categorized as a sequence of 8 lowercase letters. 7% of all passwords consist only of numbers and have a length between 8 and 11 characters. This information can be used to perform efficient mask attacks.

3   Semi-automatic Password Cracking

A major problem of hash cracking is that at some point every hash cracking attack will be inefficient and the crack rate decreases. The reason for this is that shorter and less complex passwords are tested first. At this point, the user has to stop the current attack to start a different attack on the targeted hashes in

---

[1] Password analysis and cracking kit (Version 0.0.4) - https://github.com/iphelix/pack (accessed 1 April 2019).

order to keep the crack rate consistently high. Therefore, we developed a semi-automatic password cracking algorithm. The basic idea is to specify a work list of multiple cracking attacks, which should be applied on a targeted hash list. Our algorithm then executes the attacks in order of their efficiency and only as long as they are efficient enough. When the crack rate of an attack drops down, the attack will be stopped or paused and a more efficient attack will be started or restarted. In that way, our algorithm dynamically switches between the attacks to ensure the best possible crack rate of all attacks.

In the following section, we will explain the implementation and the working principle of our algorithm. We also explain how and why the working principle differs for slow hash function and fast hash functions.

3.1   Implementation

Basically, our system include a Java application and an extended version of hashcat. The Java application is used to process the user defined work lists, to start, stop, pause and restore attacks with hashcat and to monitor the cracking processes. Furthermore, the application generates log files for subsequent attack evaluation. To enable communication between our Java application and hashcat, we extended hashcat with a network thread by modifying hashcat's source code. This thread allows us to send control commands to hashcat and to receive status messages from hashcat. All messages are sent as UDP packets.

Since our algorithm starts all attacks with hashcat automatically, all properties and attack settings need to be defined in advance. The properties file contains information about paths to executable files, global hashcat parameters, the port number for network communication, user-defined character sets, the chunk size for hash lists and whether it is an attack on slow or fast hashes. It is also possible to set a maximum runtime to stop the entire process after a certain time. Additionally, you can set a maximum idling runtime for all attacks. This value determines how long an attack may run unsuccessfully before it is stopped and marked as completed. It is also possible to set a certain threshold for this idling runtime, e.g. less than 20 cracked hashes per minute is defined as idling. Another important parameter defines the monitor interval. This value determines how long every stage has to be processed before the crack rate is compared with the threshold.

A work list includes a work list name and a set of stages. Each stage represents a concrete hash cracking attack. Depending on the attack mode, further parameters can or need to be set. For dictionary attacks and PRINCE attacks, a rule set can be added. For dictionary attacks, combinator attacks, hybrid attacks and mask attacks, a work size or a work fraction can be set. This values influence the workload that hashcat loads into the memory and that needs to be processed before the next checkpoint is reached.

Hashcat provides a functionality for stopping and restoring cracking attacks, called "Checkpoint". By sending a specific command, hashcat creates a restore file after processing the current workload. This restore file can be used to continue the process on the same or a different machine at a later date. The crucial factor for the efficiency of this method is the time required to process the current workload. The more modifiers used for the attack, such as rules, salts and multiple hash rounds, the longer the processing will take. The size of the workload depends on the used hardware and is usually automatically defined by hashcat. To be able to modify this workload size to reduce processing time, we extended the source code of hashcat. A too small workload can lead to the problem that the full capacity of the available hardware is not fully utilized. Therefore, it is necessary to have knowledge about the hardware capacities for defining reasonable workload sizes.

Our Java application monitors the cracking processes and observes thresholds and other values. In order to allow subsequent analyses, a log file is written for every processed work list.

3.2   Working Principle

In this section we will describe how our semi-automatic algorithm works and how we handle slow and fast hash methods differently.

The general working principle differs for slow hash functions and fast hash functions. The reason for this is the usability of the checkpoint function provided by hashcat. The main problem is the time needed to process this workload. For fast hash functions like MD5 or SHA-1, every password candidate just needs to be hashed once for the comparison against all targeted hashes, since those algorithms do not use salts or pepper in order to improve the security of the passwords. The workload is then processed quite fast and the next checkpoint is reached soon. With slow hash functions using salts or pepper, each password candidate needs to be concatenated with each salt or pepper, before the hash function is applied. Therefore, it takes much more time to process the current workload and to reach the next checkpoint. Therefore, it makes no sense to switch frequently between attacks when using slow functions.

Semi-automatic Password Cracking on Fast Hashes. During the first crack round, each stage of the work list is evaluated with regard to its efficiency. Therefore, all stages are executed sequentially in the order in which they are defined in the work list. The execution time for each stage is equal to the predefined monitor time. All cracked hashes are removed from the hash list and the next attacks are applied on the remaining hashes. After the monitor time runs out, the checkpoint command is sent and the execution stops when the current workload is processed. It is also possible that the stage already finishes during this monitor interval. In this case, the stage is marked as finished. The Java application stores the last measured crack rate for each unfinished stage.

When the first round is completed, the finished stages are removed from the work list. The last measured crack rates of the remaining unfinished stages are used to calculate a threshold. This threshold is calculated by dividing the second best crack rate from crack round 1 by 4. The calculated threshold represents the minimal crack rate for the next round. If an attack's crack rate drops below this value during the next round, the attack is paused using the checkpoint function.

It is very important to calculate reasonable threshold values, since too high thresholds lead to frequent changes of stages while too small thresholds lead to idling attacks. The calculation method mentioned provided the best results in our tests.

The achieved crack rates of all unfinished stages are compared to the calculated threshold. All stages with a smaller crack rate are put on a waiting list and will not be further processed in the next crack round. Stages with a crack rate larger than the calculated threshold are included in the work list for the second crack round. When all attacks have been assigned to a list, the attacks in the work list for the next round are sorted in descending order according to their crack rates.

The second crack round starts with restoring the first and so far most efficient stage. The defined monitor interval is the minimal runtime for each stage, as long as the attack does not finished during that time frame. After the monitor time runs out, the crack rate is continuously compared with the threshold. While the crack rate is higher than the threshold, the attack is further processed. When the crack rate goes down and drops below the threshold, the checkpoint command is sent and the attack pauses after processing the current workload. The crack rate is further monitored until the attack pauses. When the first stage pauses successfully, the second stage is restored and processed, until the crack rate drops below the threshold. Then the third stage is processed, then the fourth, and so on. When all stages are processed, the second crack round finishes. Then, all unfinished stages from the last round and all stages from the waiting list are put together. Afterwards, a new threshold is calculated and all stages with a higher crack rate are put on the work list for the third crack round and ordered by their cracking rates. According to this scheme, all attacks are processed until they are either completely terminated, until they are inefficient for too long, until the maximum runtime is reached, or until all hashes are cracked.

Semi-automatic Password Cracking on Slow Hashes. Also for slow hash algorithms, the first round is used to evaluate the efficiency of each stage in the work list. Therefore, all stages are executed sequentially in the specified order. The execution time corresponds to the predefined monitor interval. When this time period runs out, the attacks are completely stopped, because waiting for the next checkpoint could take too long. This means that in the second crack round all attacks are started from the beginning.

In contrast to the procedure for fast hash functions, the cracked hashes are not removed from the targeted hash list during the first crack round. This has the disadvantage that there is no cracking progress during the first round. On the other hand, all attacks are then applied against the full hash list and as a result we get the actual number of cracked passwords, that can be achieved by each stage during the monitor time. This provides a better overview of the efficiency of the individual attacks. Since the guess rate for slow hash functions is much lower, it is very important to know which attacks are the most promising.

After the first round finishes, all stages are reordered according to their efficiency. Another difference to the procedure for fast hashes is that the absolute number of cracked hashes is used to reorder the attacks, not the relative crack rate. Since slow hash methods usually do not reach high crack rates like fast hash methods, it is reasonable to compare the stages using the absolute number of cracked hashes achieved. Attacks with the highest number of cracked hashes will be executed first in the next round and attacks with smaller number will be processed afterwards.

In contrast to the procedure for fast hash functions, no threshold is calculated for the second crack round. The main threshold is the value defined for idling runtime in the properties file. This threshold determines the minimal crack rate up to which the attacks are executed. Therefore, the user can influence the runtime for each stage by modifying the threshold for idling runtime. With a lower threshold, the attacks are processed longer, even at low crack rates, so that in the end more hashes should be cracked. Therefore, a threshold value of 0 means, that all stages are processed to the end. A higher threshold results in a consistently high crack rate and an earlier termination of attacks. This means that less hashes are cracked overall, since the attacks are not executed to the end, but more hashes can be cracked in a shorter time compared to a lower threshold.

The second crack round starts with the processing of the first stage in the reordered work list. The attack is processed until the crack rate drops below the threshold and stays below it for the defined maximum idling time, or until the attack finishes. Then the next attack is executed.

The entire process ends when the last stage of round 2 is completed or stopped.

3.3 Defining Efficient Work Lists for Password Cracking

The efficiency of our semi-automatic algorithm mainly relies on the work list used and the attacks it includes. The right choice of attacks is very important. In traditional password cracking, also the order of attacks plays an important role. Since the order in which the attacks are processed is automatically determined by our algorithm, we do not need to take care of this. For our approach, we need to ensure that the selected attacks cover all possible password structures. The results of the analysis of existing user passwords can be used to find out, which password structures and lengths are commonly used.

Attack Complexity. In general, it is important to consider the complexity of the individual attacks when creating a work list. Each attack can be characterized by it's key space. The larger the key space, the more possible passwords are covered, but the longer it takes to finish the attack. Typically attacks with a larger key space have a lower crack rate than attacks with a smaller key space. In order to achieve a high crack rate as well as a high number of cracked hashes, the work list should include both attacks with a smaller key space and attacks with a larger key space. Based on the speed of the hash function and used hardware, the estimated runtime for each attack can be calculated. As an example, the professional hash cracker Jeremi Gosney build a cluster of 8 Nvidia GTX 1080

GPUs and he was able to calculate 307 billion MD5 hashes per second. With such a high performance setup, it is even possible to finish a Combinator Attack with a key space of more than 143 trillion password candidates in less than 7 min. Using the same setup, but the slow hash function bcrypt, it is possible to calculate 105,000 hashes per second. Therefore, it would take more than 43 years to finish this attack.

Defining Efficient Work Lists for Attacks on Fast Hashes. The main characteristic of our semi-automatic algorithm for fast hash methods is switching between attacks to ensure the highest possible crack rate. To achieve this, a compromise between frequent switching and letting attacks proceed is necessary. Every change costs time in which no progress is made. There are two main reasons for frequent changes. On the one hand, there is the threshold calculated for every crack round. If this value decreases only slightly between two rounds, the attacks are processed only for a short time before their crack rates fall below the new threshold again and the attacks are paused. On the other hand, attacks with a too small key space finish too fast and lead to frequent changes. This can be handled by choosing attacks with an appropriate key space. A good example of this problem is attacking passwords with a shorter length. Testing all passwords with a length of 6 can be done by defining multiple mask attacks for different password formats, e.g. only lowercase, only digits or uppercase letters with two digits at the end. Since the guess rate for fast hash functions is quite high and the key space is quite small, all of these attacks will finish after a very short runtime. A better option to test all passwords with a length of 6 is to define a mask attack that allows any character class for any position in the password string. The resulting key space can be processed in an acceptable time frame and frequent switching is avoided. Our work list for attacks on fast hashes contains 17 different attacks selected based on the results of our password analysis. Some of the included attacks have a short runtime and some attacks take a while to finish. The order in which the attacks are executed is dynamically determined by our semi-automated algorithm. For shorter passwords, we have chosen mask attacks with all character classes. For passwords with a length between 7 and 11, we have chosen mask attacks with numbers only and with combinations of lowercase letters and numbers. Furthermore, we have added a dictionary attack with a list of the 50 million most used passwords in combination with a rule set of 52,000 rules. For handling longer, but still insecure passwords, we have added 2 PRINCE attacks with a list of the 10,000 most used passwords. A PRINCE attack builds chains of combined words taken from the word list. For our work list, we have chosen PRINCE attacks for chains of 9 and 10 characters.

Defining Efficient Work Lists for Attacks on Slow Hashes. As already mentioned in Sect. 3.2, hashcat's Checkpoint function is not efficient enough using slow hash functions, since reaching checkpoints can take too much time. Therefore, two crack rounds are performed. The first round determines the attack order and in the second round all attacks are executed sequentially. Using slow hash methods, it is very important to consider the key space of chosen attacks. If the key space is too large, the crack rate will be to low. Therefore, it is reasonable to choose attacks with both smaller and larger key spaces. Attacks with a smaller key space can reduce the number of targeted hashes before more complex attacks are applied. A good example of this is attacking longer passwords. This can be done in two ways. One possibility is a mask attack to try out all different character combinations for a given password length. With shorter passwords, such an attack ends in a manageable time frame because the resulting key space is comparatively small. With longer passwords, the key space of a mask attack can be so large that it would take several months to test all possible passwords. Therefore, it makes sense to use other attack forms first. Users often use a combination of multiple words in order to create long and memorable passwords - so-called passphrases. Efficient techniques to reproduce such passwords are Combinator Attacks and PRINCE attacks. Those attacks concatenate multiple words in order to generate password candidates. Dictionaries or lists of popular passwords can be used as an input for those attacks. The key space of these attack types is not as high as the key space of mask attacks, but they help to reduce the amount of hashes in the target list to speed up subsequent, more complex attacks. Our work list for attacks on slow hash functions includes 21 attacks selected based on the analysis of leaked plain text passwords. Compared to our work list for fast hash functions, most attacks have a smaller key space. Additionally, we selected more attacks using lists of frequently used passwords. For shorter passwords with a length upto 4 characters, we have chosen mask attacks with all character classes. For passwords with a length between 5 and 10, we have added mask attacks with numbers only and lowercase letters only. Since password with a length of 7 and 8 consisting of lowercase letters and numbers are quite common, we added 2 respective mask attacks to the list. Furthermore, we added 1 dictionary attack with a list of the 10 million most used passwords in combination with set of 64 rules. The remaining 4 attacks are PRINCE attacks. We have added 2 PRINCE attacks with a list of the 10.000 most used passwords for generating chains with a length of 7 and 8 characters, and 2 PRINCE attacks with a list of the 5.000 most used passwords for building word chains with a length of 10 and 11 characters.

Preparation of Data Sets for Testing Semi-automatic Password Cracking. After implementing our semi-automatic password cracking algorithm and defining individual work lists for fast and slow hashes, we tested our approach with different types of hashes. Therefore, we built hash lists of distinct password hashes from verified data breaches. We build lists of MD5 hashes, SHA-1 hashes and vBulletin hashes. For each hash method, we selected 5 different data breaches from services using that hash method and exported all password hashes and if necessary salts. The MD5 hash list includes 304.2 million hashes from badoo.com, youku.com, last.fm, 17.media and gamigo.com. The SHA-1 hash list consists of 122.2 million hashes from linkedin.com, xsplit.com, elance.com, thefaveapp.com and forum.avast.com. The vBulletin hash lists comprises 111.9 million hashes from imesh.com, gfan.com, hiapk.com, tgbus.com and r2games.com (2017).

As a next step, we created subsets from these hash lists, since our hardware setup is not able to handle the complete lists. We randomly selected 10 million hashes from the MD5 list and the SHA-1 list as well as 5 million hashes and corresponding salts from the vBulletin list.

4   Evaluation

To compare our semi-automatic approach with normal password cracking, we implemented an option for deactivating the semi-automatic functionality, called "normal mode". When attacking fast hashes in normal mode, all attacks are executed sequentially based on the order in the work list. When attacking slow hashes in normal mode, the first crack round, in which no cracking progress is made, is used to order the attacks according to their efficiency, as in semi-automatic mode. But in the second crack round, all attacks are executed until they terminate.

Our hardware setup includes an Intel®Core™i5-4430 processor with 3,0 GHz and 2 AMD Radeon™R9 290X graphic cards.

Semi-Automatic Password Cracking on Fast Hashes. For each cracking mode, semi-automatic and normal, we set a maximum runtime of 50 min or 3,000 s. The monitoring interval was set to 90 s for semi-automatic cracking. First, we applied both crack modes to the list of 10 million MD5 hashes. Figure 1 (a) show the progression of the number of cracked hashes in relation to the required time. The first crack round, which is used to evaluate the efficiency of each stage, ended after 1,036 s. At this point, our semi-automatic approach was able to crack 6,612,616 hashes. The threshold for the second round was automatically set to 52,605 cracked hashes per minute. Round two finished after a total runtime of 1,565 s. Round 3 got a threshold of 9,854 cracked hashes per minute and finished after a total runtime of 2,786 s. At this point, 7,496,567 hashes were cracked. Round 4 started with a threshold of 793 cracked hashes per minute. After 3,000 s, the process stopped, because the maximum runtime was reached. With our semi-automatic approach, we were able to crack 7,652,288 hashes.

Due to switching between attacks to keep the crack rate constantly high, the number of cracked hashes increases much faster using our semi-automatic mode than the normal mode. Using the normal mode, 6,044,623 hashes were cracked after 3000 s. At this point, stage 10 was reached.

After testing our approach with MD5 hashes, we did the same experiments with the list of SHA-1 hashes. Figure 1 (b) illustrates the curves for the number of cracked hashes in relation to the required time for our semi-automatic approach and normal password cracking. Just as in the first test, the semi-automatic approach keeps the crack rate constantly high and the number of cracked hashes increases significantly faster than in normal mode. When the maximum runtime of 3,000 expired, a total of 6,549,225 hashes were cracked with our semi-automatic approach and 3,735,448 hashes in normal mode.

After finishing the first tests with a maximum runtime of 3,000 s, we tried both experiments with unlimited runtime. For both hash lists the result was the same: With increasing runtime the number of cracked hashes for the normal and semi-automatic cracking mode gradually adjusts.

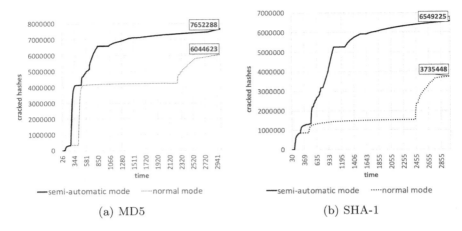

(a) MD5   (b) SHA-1

Fig. 1. Semi-automatic and normal password cracking on MD5 and SHA-1 hashes

Semi-automatic Password Cracking on Slow Hashes. Due to the slower calculation speed of slow hash functions, we increased the maximum runtime to 36,000 s or 10 h. The first crack round, which is used to order the attacks by their efficiency and in which no cracking progress is made, is included in this maximum runtime.

While testing the semi-automatic mode, we noticed that the settings for the idle threshold and the maximum idle time have a huge influence on the cracking process. A lower idle threshold leads to long-running attacks, even if the crack rate is low. A longer maximum idle runtime also leads to long-running attacks, since the crack rates increases from time to time, exceeding the idle threshold for a short time and thus resetting the maximum idle runtime.

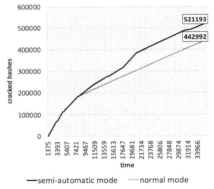

Fig. 2. Semi-automatic and normal password cracking on vBulletin hashes

For our hardware setup and a maximum runtime of 10 h, we achieved the best results by setting the idle threshold to 80 cracked hashes per minute and a maximum idle runtime of 2 min. With those settings, our semi-automatic approach was able to crack 521,193 hashes within the maximum runtime. The normal cracking mode was able to crack 442,992 hashes within the same time frame. Figure 2 shows the curves for the number of cracked hashes for both modes.

5   Conclusion

With our semi-automatic password cracking approach, we are able to speed up password cracking, especially in the early stages. A lack of knowledge about password regulations is compensated by automatically determining the most efficient cracking attacks with our algorithm. With the help of multiple setting options, the algorithm can be significantly influenced. A higher idle threshold and a shorter idle runtime result in a consistently high cracking rate and enable fast cracking success. But since the attacks are not fully executed, not all password candidates are tested. Using a lower idle threshold and a longer idle runtime, the attacks are executed over a longer period of time, even with a lower crack rate. Furthermore, it is possible to generate various work lists with different sets of password cracking attacks. For our test work lists we chose attacks based on the analysis of leaked plain text passwords.

The results show that hashes of weak and too short passwords can be cracked very quickly. Service providers should therefore use proper password policies and reject passwords that are considered weak. Passwords should be highly complex and contain both lowercase and uppercase letters, as well as numbers and special characters. Furthermore, passwords should be sufficiently long. The National Institute of Standards and Technology states that memorized secrets require a minimum length of 8 characters [2]. Especially when fast and insecure hash methods are used to store passwords, this length is not sufficient. From our point of view, the password should be at least 12 characters long. Service providers should also check whether the selected user password already occurs in a public leak. Attackers can use lists of such leaked passwords for a dictionary attack. The leak notification service "Have I Been Pwned?" provides a functionality to check a password against more than 550 million leaked passwords[2]. In order to help users choosing secure passwords, service providers should use techniques like Password Strength Meters. Researchers have investigated what properties a strength meter needs to fulfill and how good existing solutions are [1].

References

[1] Golla, M., Dürmuth, M.: On the accuracy of password strength meters. In: Proceedings of the 2018 ACM SIGSAC Conference on Computer and Communications Security. CCS 2018, pp. 1567–1582. ACM, New York (2018). https://doi.org/10.1145/3243734.3243769
[2] National Institue of Standards and Techonology: Digital Identity Guidelines - Authentication and Lifecycle Management (NIST Special Publication 800–63B) (5 2018)

---

[2] https://haveibeenpwned.com/Passwords, (accessed 1 April 2019).

A Novel and Comprehensive Evaluation Methodology for SIEM

Mahdieh Safarzadeh$^{(\boxtimes)}$, Hossein Gharaee, and Amir Hossein Panahi

Iran Telecommunication Research Center, Tehran, Iran
{m.safarzadeh,gharaee,panahi}@itrc.ac.ir

Abstract. Many SIEM products have been produced. However, there is no comprehensive methodology to evaluate them. We present a novel and comprehensive three-dimensional methodology to evaluate SIEM products. We consider a SIEM product as a set of dimensions, namely capability, architectural component, and common feature, then subdivide each dimension-according to its definition-into sub-dimensions. Afterward, we develop multiple criteria for evaluating each sub-dimension. The dimensions can have a different impact and importance on SIEM product, to determine the magnitude of the impact and importance of each dimension we use a factor called the impact factor. We also consider some impact factors for the impact and importance of each sub-dimension and each criterion. Since there are different methods, algorithms, and standards for developing the criteria, so we provide maturity levels for each criterion. The results of the evaluations show that this methodology can evaluate the criteria coverage, completeness and correctness of criteria, and determine the superiority of criteria in the SIEM products as well.

Keywords: Security information and event management · SIEM evaluation methodology · SIEM evaluation · SIEM maturity · SIEM capabilities

1 Introduction

Cybersecurity threats regardless of size and type of organizations, have significantly increased [1,2]. To protect and defend against such threats, each organization must have the ability to detect and respond to threats. For this purpose, organizations use a variety of security and monitoring tools at various levels, such as application-level, operating system-level, network-level, and host-level, and get benefits from contextual data that is obtained through penetration testing, or by referring to news bulletins and standards that provide best practices. These tools include Network Intrusion Detection System (NIDS), Host Intrusion Detection System (HIDS), and vulnerability scanner. Each of these tools stores security alerts and logs locally. In this way, a large number of security alerts and logs store separately in different tools locally. Because of the large volume and

© Springer Nature Switzerland AG 2019
S.-H. Heng and J. Lopez (Eds.): ISPEC 2019, LNCS 11879, pp. 476–488, 2019.
https://doi.org/10.1007/978-3-030-34339-2_28

dispersion of the security alerts and logs, it is impossible to verify, reduce, and correlate them with each other and with the contextual data by security experts. In this way, security experts cannot achieve a comprehensive view of the network security state. For this reason, using these security systems and checking security alerts and logs locally, is not enough solely. As mentioned in [3], one of the reasons that lead to weakness in defense is the lack of proper security systems. One of the good tools recommended in [3] for use in the security event management process is security information and event management (SIEM) product. The SIEM product collects security alerts, logs, and contextual data centrally, and helps to resolve or reduce the challenges that have already been mentioned.

Security experts in selecting a SIEM product in accordance with the requirements of their organization, manufacturers to develop, and manufacture the SIEM products and evaluators to evaluate SIEM products, confront with some challenges. Some examples of these challenges are mentioned in the following:

- What are the capabilities of the SIEM product? And each of these capabilities is at which level of maturity?
- What is the security state of the SIEM product?
- If the manufacturers want to produce a SIEM product, which capabilities should they consider?

In this paper, we address these challenges by proposing a novel and comprehensive methodology that evaluates the SIEM product from three complementary perspectives. We consider a SIEM product as a set of dimensions, namely capability, architectural component, and common feature, then subdivide each dimension into sub-dimensions, and for evaluating each sub-dimension, we develop multiple criteria. We present a formula for calculating the SIEM product maturity. Because the dimensions can have a different impact and importance on SIEM product evaluation to consider the magnitude of the impact and importance of each dimension, we use a factor called the impact factor. We also consider some impact factors for the impact and importance of each sub-dimension and each criterion. Since there are different methods, algorithms, and standards for designing and developing the criteria, and these methods, algorithms, and standards are superior to each other, so we provide maturity levels for each criterion proportional to the scope of the criterion and based on methods, algorithms, and standards that are provided for designing and developing it.

The rest of the paper is organized as follows. In Sect. 2, we review existing security evaluation methodologies, especially SIEM security evaluation. It is necessary to define SIEM and its capabilities to introduce the SIEM evaluation methodology, which is described in Sect. 3. Our novel and comprehensive methodology is presented in Sect. 4. The tests carried out to evaluate the methodology and results are presented in Sect. 5. Section 6 presents the conclusion.

2   Related Work

In this section, we review researches that perform in security evaluation. Institutions and laboratories such as Gartner and NSS Labs carry out security evaluation, and security standards such as Common Criteria are provided. However, Gartner is the only one who has provided a method to evaluate the SIEM product. Gartner considers a set of common core capabilities for SIEM technology [4]. It has determined the impact of each of these common core capabilities on different use cases of SIEM. Then it evaluates SIEM based on these core capabilities and their impacts. Gartner has considered functional capabilities to evaluate SIEM products. These are useful capabilities, but it does not evaluate the SIEM security-relevant capabilities like cryptography and auditing. In [4] calculation formula is not specified exactly, but based on what is published, it does not consider the maturity level of each capability in its calculation. If two SIEM products offer a capability, but one of them implemented it more safely or efficiently, Gartner does not consider it. The NSS Labs laboratory and Common Criteria standard has not provided a SIEM-specific evaluation methodology. However, we examined the methodologies presented by them for similar products to present our methodology. NSS Labs evaluates security effectiveness, performance stability and reliability, and total cost of ownership and value for each product [5]. Each of these four categories is divided into smaller sub-categories. In terms of performance, stability, and reliability, it evaluates the product well. Like Gartner, this laboratory does not check the security-relevant capabilities like cryptography and auditing and does not consider the maturity of each criterion in its assessment. Common Criteria specify individual security functions [6], which may be provided by a product in eleven classes. These security functions are common in software or appliances. security functions in the classes are well organized. Common Criteria does not consider class or classes for the product's core capabilities. Like Gartner and NSS Labs, it does not consider the maturity of the criteria involved in each class in its evaluation. Igor and Elena [7] present a technique for countermeasure selection in SIEM systems. The developed technique is based on the suggested complex of security metrics. Key features of the suggested technique are the application of the attack and service dependencies graphs, the introduced model of the countermeasure and the suggested metrics of the countermeasure effectiveness, cost, and collateral damage. Kavita and Hemant [8] discuss some of the important critical capabilities for any product and vendors for the SIEM product. Rafal and Michal [9] propose an approach to the evaluation of open source SIEM for situation awareness platform in the smart grid environment. They present two criteria groups: primary and secondary, primary evaluation criteria were identified based on the analysis of desirable features of SIEM systems and secondary were derived from well-known software engineering non-functional requirements. The first group contains essential requirements and facilities, whereas all nonessential attributes are included in the secondary drivers group. They do not evaluate the SIEM security-relevant capabilities like cryptography and auditing and does not consider class or classes for the product's core capabilities. Its evaluation criteria are limited.

3 Security Information and Event Management (SIEM) System

Different approaches can be taken to address or reduce the challenges mentioned earlier. (see Sect. 1 for more information). One of these approaches is using SIEM.

Definition 1 (SIEM). *Security information and event management system to manage security information and events, collects a wide variety of real-time and non-real time security alerts, event logs and contextual data, stores them for short-term and long-term storage. It performs several functions through the real-time and historical analysis that assist in the aggregation of similar events, analysis and correlate multiple event logs belong to the same attack scenario. SIEM can support security incident investigation and regulatory compliance using historical analysis of collected data.*

SIEM is a set of components that can communicate with each other, as shown in Fig. 1, a SIEM collects a wide variety of security alerts, logs and contextual data using various protocols from various security systems and tools which are used in the cybersecurity defense layers. The SIEM stores them in a live repository after normalizing collected data, then using the rich and diverse knowledge repositories, performs analysis on the collected data. Some of these analyses include categorization, verification, filtering, data mining, prioritization, data

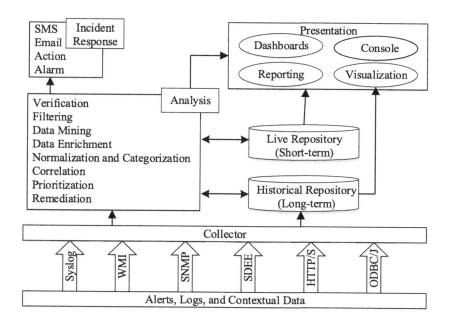

Fig. 1. SIEM architectural components.

enrichment, and correlation. During the analysis, the attack scenarios extract from the original raw security alerts, logs, and contextual data. Also, a copy of collected raw data is stored in a historical repository for digital investigation and historical analysis. In this way, advanced persistent attacks may also be detected. In response to discovered attack scenarios, SIEM may create a meta-alert. It can even send SMS or email or run a script or program to neutralize the attack effect or stop it. Eventually, it can generate a variety of reports and visualize network security status on the dashboards. SIEM definition and architecture have been extracted from the study of several SIEM products [10–12].

4   Methodology for SIEM

We examined a SIEM system from different and complementary perspectives to develop a comprehensive methodology for evaluating a SIEM product. SIEM, as a product is developed to provide a multitude of capabilities that are needed for security monitoring and analysis, as a system may comprise of some architectural components connected [13–15], as shown in Fig. 1, and as software or appliance it has common features with other software or appliances. However, as a whole, we can evaluate a SIEM from three perspectives, capability, architectural component, and common feature.

So our evaluation methodology is a three-dimensional methodology. We consider a SIEM system as a set of dimensions, namely capability, architectural component, and common feature. We subdivide each dimension according to its definition into sub-dimensions. Table 1 shows these dimensions and lists all types of sub-dimensions that each dimension contains. Afterward, we developed multiple criteria for evaluating each sub-dimension. For lack of space, we cannot list all of the criteria. Here we give an example. For example, correlation and analysis is a sub-dimension for capability dimension we developed multiple criteria for it, such as cross-correlation, single-stage attack correlation, multi-stage attack correlation, distributed attack correlation, zero-day attack detection, and anomaly detection.

Because each dimension, sub-dimension, and criterion can have a different impact and importance on SIEM product evaluation, to determine the magnitude of the impact and importance of each dimension, each sub-dimension, and each criterion, we use a factor called the impact factor. In this evaluation, we determined the impact factors based on the main mission of the SIEM product, as stated in the SIEM definition and our studies in SIEM products. These values can be customized as needed. Since there are different methods, algorithms, and standards for designing and developing the criteria, and these methods, algorithms, and standards are superior to each other, so we provide maturity levels for each criterion proportional to the scope of the criterion and based on methods, algorithms, and standards that are provided for designing and developing it. For example, cross-correlation is a criterion of correlation and analysis sub-dimension. We built maturity levels for it based on different methods that extracted from our studies of several SIEM product. These maturity

Table 1. SIEM capabilities, architectural components, and common features.

DI_1: Capability	β_{DI_1}	DI_2: Architectural component	β_{DI_2}	DI_3: Common feature	β_{DI_3}
Security alerts, logs, and context data collection and normalization	10	Sensor	8	Identification and authentication	7
Collected data retention	5	Collector	14	Cryptography	8
Efficient indexing and searching	5	Database (Short-term repository)	11	Auditing	12
Threat intelligence	9	Analysis	25	Compression	3
Correlation and analysis	30	Logger (long-term repository)	15	User data protection	7
Incident investigation and forensic	13	Incident response	11	Security management	6
Incident response	8	Console, dashboard	16	Protection of the product	7
Representation and visualization	11	–	–	Trusted path/ channels	7
Regulatory compliance	9	–	–	Resource utilization	5
–	–	–	–	Product access	5
–	–	–	–	Deployment and support simplicity	6
–	–	–	–	Scalable architecture and flexible deployment	6
–	–	–	–	Installation, configuration and maintenance	5
–	–	–	–	Information Flow control and access control	7
–	–	–	–	Support and training	6
–	–	–	–	Product and manufacturer	3

levels are shown in Table 2. At the lowest level, there is no correlation, and at the highest level (level 4), the SIEM system cross-correlate heterogeneous and diverse security alerts and logs for single-stage attack with the unknown pattern. The maturity levels for data collection and normalization criteria are shown in Table 2, too. For other criteria, these levels of maturity have also been developed, but for brevity, we do not provide them here. Each maturity level has a score called maturity score; the fourth column of Table 2 shows this score. We design a set of test cases to evaluate each criterion and determine its maturity level. After running test cases that each criterion includes, corresponds to the maturity level of each criterion, the numerical value as the maturity score is assigned to it. We set the maturity score equal to the maturity level number. Table 3 shows the number of sub-dimension, criteria, and test cases for each dimension.

Formally, we model each SIEM system S by a finite set of dimensions $S = \{DI_1, DI_2, \ldots, DI_m\}$ that hereon we have three dimensions, namely capability, architectural component, and common feature. More formally, for any given SIEM system S, we write $DI_i(s)$ to denote its associated dimension. Moreover, each $DI_i(s)$ is a finite set of sub-dimensions $DI = \{SubDI_1, SubDI_2, \ldots, SubDI_n\}$. For any given dimension DI_i we write $SubDI_j(DI_i)$, to denote its associated sub-dimensions. Finally, we model each sub-dimension by a finite set of criteria $SubDI_k = \{Crit_1, Crit_2, \ldots, Crit_o\}$ for any given $SubDI_k$, we write $Crit_k(SubDI_j)$ to denote its associated criterion. We calculate the maturity of the SIEM system using the Eq. 1 as the final score (FS):

$$FS = \sum_{i=1}^{m}\sum_{j=1}^{n}\sum_{k=1}^{o} \alpha_i \beta_j \gamma_k \frac{Crit_k}{Ideal_k} \tag{1}$$

Let α, β, and γ be the impact factors of dimension, sub-dimension, and criterion, respectively. We assign criterion K maturity score and maximum maturity score to $Crit_k$ and $Ideal_k$ respectively. We consider dimensions impact factors (α_i) between 0 and 1. These are 0.5, 0.3, and 0.2 for capability, architectural component, and common feature respectively. We consider the sub-dimensions impact factors (β_j) that are provided in Table 1, and criteria impact factors (γ_k) between 0% and 100%. $Crit_k$ is a number between 0 and maximum maturity score.

5   Experiments and Discussion

In this section, we first demonstrate how the methodology is used to evaluate the SIEM product. Then, we compare it with other techniques available in the literature. We chose three products to evaluate the proposed methodology. The first product is the ArcSight ESM because it is one of the best SIEM products, the second one is AlienVault OSSIM, because it is free and available, and the third one is E-SIEM that is developed in our country.

Table 2. Cross-correlation and data collection and normalization maturity levels.

Maturity levels	Criterion name		
	$Crit_i$: Cross-correlation	$Crit_j$: Data collection and normalization	Maturity score
Level 0	No cross-correlation	No logs, security alerts, and contextual data are collected	0
Level 1	Cross-correlation of heterogeneous and diverse security alerts for single-stage attacks with a well-known pattern	Collect and display logs and security alerts from specific tools and protocols	1
Level 2	Cross-correlation of heterogeneous and diverse security alerts from specific tools for single-stage attacks with a well-known pattern	Collect, display, and use of logs and security alerts from specific tools and protocols	2
Level 3	Cross-correlation of heterogeneous and diverse security alerts from specific tools for single-stage attacks with unknown pattern	Collect, display, and use of logs and security alerts from specific tools and protocols with the option of adding plugins to receive data from new tools and protocols	3
Level 4	Cross-correlation of heterogeneous and diverse security alerts for single-stage attack with unknown pattern	Collect, display, and use of logs and security alerts of more tools and protocols with the option of adding plugins to receive data from new tools and protocols	4
Level 5	–	Collect, display, and use of logs and security alerts of more tools and protocols with the option of adding plugins to receive data from new tools and protocols receive contextual data	5

Table 2. (*continued*)

Maturity levels	Criterion name		Maturity score
	$Crit_i$: Cross-correlation	$Crit_j$: Data collection and normalization	
Level 6	–	Collect, display, and use of logs security alerts, and contextual data of more tools and protocols, with the option of automatically add plugins for receive data from new tools and protocols	6
Level 7	–	Collect, display, and use of logs security alerts, and contextual data from All types of known tools and protocols, with the option of automatically add plugins for receive data from new tools and protocols	7

5.1 Evaluation Lab

We deployed all SIEM architectural components in network infrastructure to evaluate the SIEM product's criteria. We added four assets in network infrastructure; each of them had several services and some number of vulnerabilities and weaknesses. We used DARPA [16] and KDD Cup [17] datasets to generate security alerts. Since these datasets did not generate the logs and some security alerts, we launched several attacks on the assets. We also generated contextual data using Nessus vulnerability scanner and Nmap network and host discovery tool. Two NIDSes and one firewall monitor the network traffic to detect attacks against the assets. Four HIDSes monitors the activities and events occurring on four assets.

Table 3. Number of criteria and test cases for each dimension.

Dimension name	Number of sub-dimension	Number of criteria	Number of test cases
Capability	9	125	259
Architectural component	7	94	202
Common feature	16	172	286

Table 4. Selected criteria for methodology evaluation.

#	Criteria	α	β	γ	ArcSight	OSSIM	E-SIEM	Ideal
1	Event Per Second Rate	0.5	10%	14%	3	4	4	6
2	Cross-Correlation	0.5	30%	9%	3	2	2	4
3	Historical Analysis	0.5	30%	12%	3	0	2	6
4	Integration with other systems	0.5	8%	7%	1	0	3	4
5	User Authentication	0.2	7%	18%	4	2	2	6
6	Encryption Operation	0.2	8%	15%	4	3	3	7

5.2 Evaluation Results

To evaluate our methodology, we selected 20 criteria from a set of developed criteria and run test cases related to the criteria. For brevity, some of these criteria are presented in Table 4. They are chosen from all dimensions and various sub-dimensions. Table 5 shows the obtained results. The results are multiplied by 100 for normalization. The first column shows SIEM evaluated products and an ideal hypothetical SIEM product. The second, third, and fourth columns show obtained values for capability, architectural component, and common feature dimensions for each product and the fifth column shows the final score for each product. From the table, we observe ArcSight totally is better than the other two products. But in terms of dimension, ArcSight is better than the other two products in capability and common feature criteria, and OSSIM is better than the other two products in architectural component criteria. Figure 2 shows the assessed criteria based on their maturity. Also, in addition to the final score and score obtained for each dimension, as shown in Table 5, using this methodology, it is also possible to compare the products based on the maturity levels of their criteria.

Table 5. Obtained results in experiments.

Tool	Capability	Architectural component	Common feature	FS
ArcSight	3.92	1.36	0.91	6.19
OSSIM	2.76	1.61	0.72	5.09
E-SIEM	3.46	1.6	0.83	5.89
Ideal	7.78	2.88	1.64	12.3

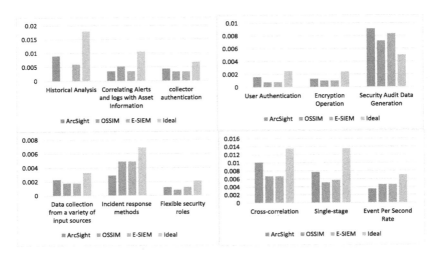

Fig. 2. Compare SIEMs based on maturity levels of their criteria.

5.3 Comparison

Because of the similarity of our methodology and [4–6] we decide to compare our methodology with them. These studies did not present their evaluation results; then, we make a qualitative comparison between our methodology and them. Gartner has considered functional capabilities to evaluate SIEM products; then it does not evaluate the second and third dimensions criteria of our methodology. NSS Labs does not evaluate second and third dimensions criteria; it evaluates some criteria from the first dimension. Common Criteria has considered common features only and does not evaluate the first and second dimensions criteria of our methodology. By executing test cases when evaluating the criteria, we found that while the three SIEM products provided a criterion, the provided criterion have different maturities. By using the impact factors and the maturity levels determined for the criteria and using them in calculating the score of a SIEM product, this methodology can correctly rank the SIEM products based on criteria maturity levels as shown in Fig. 2. We score the maturity of criteria based on methods, algorithms, and standards is developed for designing and implementing them. ArcSight ESM for cross-correlation criteria had the most mature level than the other two SIEM products. Therefore, the proposed methodology can test the SIEM product well and compare it with other SIEM products to select the required SIEM product. These methodologies did not consider any impact factors for dimension and sub-dimension or maturity level for criteria in their evaluations. Thus, they cannot determine the superiority of the products towards each other by expressing the details of superiority such as superiority in a specific dimension, some specific sub-dimensions, or some criteria.

6   Conclusions

In this paper, we proposed a novel and comprehensive methodology that evaluates the SIEM product from three complementary perspectives. In this methodology, we divided the SIEM product into a set of dimensions, namely capability, architectural component, and common feature. We subdivided each dimension according to its definition into sub-dimensions, then developed multiple criteria for evaluating each sub-dimension and designed a set of test cases to evaluate each criterion and determine its maturity level. We presented a formula for calculating the maturity of the SIEM product. Because the dimensions can have a different impact and importance on SIEM product evaluation, to consider the magnitude of the impact and importance of each dimension, we used a factor called the impact factor. We also considered some impact factors for the impact and importance of each sub-dimension and each criterion. Since there are different methods, algorithms, and standards for designing and developing the criteria, and these methods, algorithms, and standards are superior to each other, so we provided maturity levels for each criterion proportional to the scope of the criterion and based on methods, algorithms, and standards that are provided for designing and developing it.

The methodology has been able to show the superiority of products totally and for any dimension and their sub-dimensions. Also, the methodology was able to determine the excellence of products in terms of their criteria maturity. It provides the ability for security experts in selecting a SIEM product in accordance with the requirements of their organization, for manufacturers to develop and manufacture a SIEM product and for evaluators to assess a SIEM product.

References

1. Verizon. https://enterprise.verizon.com/resources/reports/2019-data-breach-investigations-report.pdf. Accessed 7 June 2019
2. Symantec. https://www.symantec.com/content/dam/symantec/docs/reports/istr-24-2019-en.pdf. Accessed 7 June 2019
3. Sans. https://www.sans.org/reading-room/whitepapers/ICS/paper/35502
4. Mark, N., Kelly, M.K.: Critical Capabilities for Security Information and Event, May 2013. Accessed 7 June 2019
5. NSS Labs: NGIPS Test Methodology V4.0. https://research.nsslabs.com/library/network-security/next-generation-intrusion-prevention-system/
6. Common Criteria. https://www.commoncriteriaportal.org/files/ccfiles/CCPART2V3.1R3%20-%20marked%20changes.pdf
7. Igor, k., Elena, D.: Countermeasure selection in SIEM systems based on the integrated complex of security metrics. In: 23rd Euromicro International Conference on Parallel, Distributed, and Network-Based Processing, pp. 567–574. IEEE, Turku(2015)
8. Kavita, A., Hemant, M.: A study on critical capabilities for security information and event management. Int. J. Sci. Res. (IJSR) **4**(7), 1893–1896 (2015)
9. Leszczyna, R., Wróbel, M.R.: Evaluation of open source SIEM for situation awareness platform in the smart grid environment. In: World Conference on Factory Communication Systems (WFCS), pp. 1–4. IEEE, Palma de Mallorca (2015)

10. Sandeep, B., Pratyusa, K.M., Loai, Z.: The operational role of security information and event management systems. IEEE Secur. Priv. **12**(5), 35–41 (2014)
11. Cesario, D.S., Alessia, G., Ilaria, M., Marco, V.: A novel security information and event management system for enhancing cyber security in a hydroelectric dam. Int. J. Crit. Infrastruct. Protect. **13**(5), 39–51 (2016)
12. Filip, H., Josef, H., Sona, N., Stanislav, Z., Ondrej, M.: The deployment of security information and event management in cloud infrastructure. In: 25th International Conference Radioelektronika (RADIOELEKTRONIKA), pp. 399–404. IEEE, Pardubice (2015)
13. David, R.M., Shon, H., Allen, H., Stephen, V., Chris, B.: Security Information and Event Management (SIEM) Implementation, 1st edn. McGraw-Hill Education, New York (2011)
14. David, N.: Designing and Building A Security Operations Center, 1st edn. Syngress, Massachusetts (2015)
15. Joseph, M., Gary, M., Nadhem, A.: Security Operations Center: Building, Operating, and Maintaining your SOC. Cisco Press, Indiana (2016)
16. MIT Lincoln Lab. http://www.ll.mit.edu/IST/ideval/data/2000/2000_data_index. html. Accessed 7 June 2019
17. KDDCup. http://kdd.ics.uci.edu/databases/kddcup99/kddcup99.html

Author Index